Routledge Handbook
of Public Diplomacy

D0781208

"Snow, Taylor, and a distinguished group of scholars have produced the definitive sourcebook on one of the most important subjects of our time. This collection offers a highly readable and comprehensive look at how the U.S. has veered off course in the battle for the hearts and minds of much of the world. This is a must-read for students and scholars, and should be placed in the hands of the policymakers who inherit the challenge of restoring the public image and credibility of this wayward superpower."
—Lance Bennett, Professor of Political Science & Ruddick C. Lawrence Professor of Communication, Director, Center for Communication and Civic Engagement, University of Washington

"Since 9/11, public diplomacy has emerged as a critical, but little understood, component of foreign policy. This Handbook explains what it is, what it isn't, who does it well, and who doesn't. In short, it is essential to understanding how countries present themselves to the world."
—Ambassador Cunthia P. Schneider, PhH, Distinguished Fellow in the Practice of Diplomacy, Georgetwon University, Senior Non Resident Fellow, Brookings Institution

"Snow and Taylor's *Routledge Handbook of Public Diplomacy* offers valuable and timely advice about China as it struggles to tell its story of Tibet and the 2008 Beijing Olympics. The editors take a global perspective to address the public diplomacy issue in a well-admired effort to build a global dialogue between the East and the West."
—Li Xiguang, Dean, International Center for Communication Studies, Tsinghua University Vice-Chairman, Journalism Education Committee of Chinese Ministry of Education

The *Routledge Handbook of Public Diplomacy* provides a comprehensive overview of public diplomacy, national image, and perception management, from the efforts to foster pro-West sentiment during the Cold War to the post-9/11 campaign to "win the hearts and minds" of the Muslim world. Editors Nancy Snow and Philip M. Taylor present materials on public diplomacy trends in public opinion and cultural diplomacy as well as topical policy issues. The latest research in public relations, credibility, soft power, advertising, and marketing is included and institutional processes and players are identified and analyzed. While the field is dominated by American and British research and developments, the book also includes international research and comparative perspectives from other countries.

Nancy Snow is Associate Professor of Public Diplomacy in the S.I. Newhouse School of Public Communications at Syracuse University. She is Senior Research Fellow in the USC Center on Public Diplomacy.

Philip M. Taylor is Professor of International Communications at the University of Leeds and acknowledged as one of the foremost authorities in propaganda history and public diplomacy.

Routledge Handbook of Public Diplomacy

Edited by
Nancy Snow
Syracuse University

Philip M. Taylor
University of Leeds

Published in association with the USC Center on Public Diplomacy at the Annenberg School based at the University of Southern California

Routledge
Taylor & Francis Group

NEW YORK AND LONDON

First published 2009
by Routledge
270 Madison Avenue, New York NY 10016

Simultaneously published in the UK
by Routledge
2 Park Square, Milton Park, Abingdon, Oxon, OX14 4RN

Routledge is an imprint of the Taylor & Francis Group, an informa business

© 2009 Taylor & Francis

Typeset in Bembo by RefineCatch Limited, Bungay, Suffolk
Printed and bound in the United States of America on acid-free paper by
Edwards Brothers, Inc.

Library of Congress Cataloging in Publication Data
Routledge handbook of public diplomacy / edited by Nancy Snow, Philip M. Taylor.
    p. cm.
  "Published in association with the USC Center on Public Diplomacy at the Annenberg School
based at the University of Southern California."
  Includes bibliographical references and index.
  1. International relations – Handbooks, manuals, etc. 2. Diplomacy – Handbooks, manuals, etc.
I. Snow, Nancy. II. Taylor, Philip M. III. Annenberg School for Communication
(University of Southern California). Center on Public Diplomacy.
  JZ1305.R685 2008
  327.2—dc22

                                                                    2008012605

ISBN10: 0–415–95301–4 (hbk)
ISBN10: 0–415–95302–2 (pbk)
ISBN10: 0–203–89152–X (ebk)

ISBN13: 978–0–415–95301–6 (hbk)
ISBN13: 978–0–415–95302–3 (pbk)
ISBN13: 978–0–203–89152–0 (ebk)

Contents

Preface and Introduction   ix
Notes on Contributors   xiii

Introduction

1   Rethinking Public Diplomacy   3
    Nancy Snow

2   Public Diplomacy and Strategic Communications   12
    Philip M. Taylor

Part 1: The Context of Public Diplomacy

3   Public Diplomacy before Gullion: The Evolution of a Phrase   19
    Nicholas J. Cull

4   Public Diplomacy as Loss of World Authority   24
    Michael Vlahos

5   Public Opinion and Power   39
    Ali S. Wyne

6   Exchange Programs and Public Diplomacy   50
    Giles Scott-Smith

7   Arts Diplomacy: The Neglected Aspect of Cultural Diplomacy   57
    John Brown

Part 2: Public Diplomacy Applications

8 Operationalizing Public Diplomacy
   Matthew C. Armstrong   63

9 Between "Take-offs" and "Crash Landings": Situational Aspects of
   Public Diplomacy
   John Robert Kelley   72

10 Mapping out a Spectrum of Public Diplomacy Initiatives: Information
   and Relational Communication Frameworks
   R.S. Zaharna   86

11 The Nexus of U.S. Public Diplomacy and Citizen Diplomacy
   Sherry Mueller   101

Part 3: Public Diplomacy Management: Image, Influence, and Persuasion

12 Public Diplomacy in International Conflicts: A Social
   Influence Analysis
   Anthony Pratkanis   111

13 Credibility and Public Diplomacy
   Robert H. Gass and John S. Seiter   154

14 The Culture Variable in the Influence Equation
   Kelton Rhoads   166

15 Military Psychological Operations as Public Diplomacy
   Mark Kilbane   187

Part 4: State and Non-State Actors in Public Diplomacy

16 American Business and Its Role in Public Diplomacy
   Keith Reinhard   195

17 The Public Diplomat: A First Person Account
   Peter Kovach   201

18 The Case for Localized Public Diplomacy
   William P. Kiehl   212

19 The Distinction Between Public Affairs and Public Diplomacy
   Ken S. Heller and Liza M. Persson   225

20 Valuing Exchange of Persons in Public Diplomacy
   Nancy Snow   233

Part 5: Global Approaches to Public Diplomacy

21 Four Seasons in One Day: The Crowded House of Public Diplomacy
    in the UK   251
    Ali Fisher

22 German Public Diplomacy: The Dialogue of Cultures   262
    Oliver Zöllner

23 Origin and Development of Japan's Public Diplomacy   270
    Tadashi Ogawa

24 China Talks Back: Public Diplomacy and Soft Power for the Chinese Century   282
    Gary D. Rawnsley

25 Central and Eastern European Public Diplomacy: A Transitional Perspective
    on National Reputation Management   292
    György Szondi

26 Australian Public Diplomacy   314
    Naren Chitty

Part 6: Advancing Public Diplomacy Studies

27 How Globalization Became U.S. Public Diplomacy at the End of the
    Cold War   325
    Joseph Duffey

28 Ethics and Social Issues in Public Diplomacy   334
    Richard Nelson and Foad Izadi

29 Noopolitik: A New Paradigm for Public Diplomacy   352
    David Ronfeldt and John Arquilla

    Select Bibliography   367
    Index   373

Preface and Introduction

Nancy Snow and Philip M. Taylor

Public diplomacy is one of the most salient political communication issues in the 21st century. Its revival arises within the context of the post-September 11, 2001 declaration of war on terrorism largely aimed at radical, anti-American/West Islamic militants and manifested via military interventions in the Muslim majority countries of Afghanistan and Iraq. The United States and the United Kingdom are the two leading nations in the global effort to "win hearts and minds" of indigenous citizen populations in the Greater Middle East. Whereas public diplomacy in the 20th century emerged from two world wars and a balance of power Cold War framework between the communist East and capitalist West, the 21st century trend is a post 9/11 environment dominated by fractal globalization, preemptive military invasion, information and communication technologies that shrink time and distance, and the rise of global non-state actors (terror networks, bloggers) that challenge state-driven policy and discourse on the subject.

The new social groups involved in public diplomacy's articulation and formulation have made the topic of public diplomacy (and its negative, pejorative corollary: propaganda) recognizable and meaningful to a varied and vast arena of publics, even as traditional elites in government and private think tanks continue to dominate media coverage with their reports, hearings, and initiatives to overcome negative (i.e., "Why do they hate us?") or indifferent attitudes. In the United States alone, since 9/11 prominent Washington, D.C.-based organizations inside and outside government have published scores of reports and white papers, formed crisis communication task forces, or promoted new public diplomacy initiatives. However, with the exception of expanded international broadcasting and mass media projects targeting the Middle East and some expansion of exchanges, all have been advisory and shared a common cry for more public diplomacy efforts without laying out a conceptual framework. Within this highly politicized arena of public diplomacy and foreign policy formulation, empirical data and reasoned analysis from academic schools of thought are often overlooked in favor of perfunctory opinion editorials and discourse from a narrowcast of retired generals and diplomats.

The *Routledge Handbook of Public Diplomacy* was first conceived in 2004 as a project to provide a comprehensive overview of public diplomacy and national image and perception management, enabling an understanding of its 21st-century revival to informed members of the public as well as academics and traditional practitioners. The handbook presents materials on public diplomacy trends in public opinion and cultural diplomacy as well as topical policy issues. The latest research in public relations, credibility, social influence tactics, advertising, and marketing is included, and institutional processes and players are identified and analyzed.

We acknowledge that our survey of public diplomacy reflects the dominance of American and British research findings and developments in the field, but we have made great effort to include international research and comparative perspectives from other countries. Thus we have included leading scholars from all over the world. In this first edition by a U.S. and U.K. scholar, we have over 30 contributors, 20 of whom are from North America (Canada and the United States), eight from Europe (five from the United Kingdom, one each from Germany, Hungary, and Sweden), one from Australasia, one from East Asia, and one from the Middle East (Iran). Stated simply, we do not wish for the United States and the United Kingdom to remain the dominant countries in the public diplomacy conversation. Our hope as co-editors across the Great Pond is to work with other scholars and practitioners to make this field we love truly global in its scope. Future editions will reflect this.

The *Routledge Handbook of Public Diplomacy* is designed for a wide audience. We invited recognized authorities in their respective fields to write about hot topics in the field as well as share personal narratives of just what public diplomats do. We had to account for the many state and non-state actors and institutions involved in the making of public diplomacy, which is why we have several chapters from scholars and practitioners who consult with or have worked in the military, foreign affairs departments, as well as nongovernmental organizations. The Introduction to the book includes two chapters from the co-editors. Chapter 1 by Nancy Snow invites the reader to rethink the role of public diplomacy in the 21st century. Chapter 2 by Philip M. Taylor places public diplomacy in the context of strategic communications, namely, the information and ideological wars at play in the long war struggle that has followed the war on terror.

"Part 1: The Context of Public Diplomacy" that includes Chapters 3 through 7 addresses public diplomacy's historical evolution (Cull), as well as specific contextual tie-ins like public opinion formation, exchange programs, and arts diplomacy. "Part 2: Public Diplomacy Applications" includes Chapters 8 through 11, and lays out very specific on-the-ground realities of the field. In Chapter 8, Matt Armstrong argues that public diplomacy wears combat boots, applying its application to the military sphere. In Chapter 9, John Robert Kelley frames public diplomacy as a duel between advisory and advocacy roles of foreign policy practitioners. Zaharna's Chapter 10 provides a theoretical frame for public diplomacy initiatives that emphasize relationship building and information exchange. In Chapter 11, citizen diplomacy leader and expert Sherry Mueller explores the legacy of U.S. public diplomacy in citizen diplomacy.

"Part 3: Public Diplomacy Management: Image, Influence, and Persuasion" broadens the state of the art to other arenas. Anthony Pratkanis provides a detailed, in-depth analysis in Chapter 12 of social influence and its application to public diplomacy in conflict situations. Gass and Seiter (Chapter 13) explain why credibility is a key feature of public diplomacy in national image and reputation. In Chapter 14, Kelton Rhoads challenges the primacy-of-culture perspective that dominates much of our thinking about public diplomacy and calls for a more balanced perspective that takes into account cultural difference but also recognizes and utilizes influence universals. Chapter 15 by Mark Kilbane is a short synopsis of the value of psyops in relationship to public diplomacy.

"Part 4: State and Non-State Actors in Public Diplomacy" includes chapters from business leaders, foreign diplomats, and public affairs/public relations experts. Keith Reinhard (Chapter 16) calls for the business and private sector to be more relevant in public diplomacy making. In Chapter 17, Peter Kovach provides personal vitae on public diplomacy in the field. Chapter 18 by former senior State Department official Bill Kiehl shows how public diplomacy is integral to localized diplomatic engagement and cites specific cases in Finland, the former Czechoslovakia, and Thailand. Snow (Chapter 20) provides a personal account of how her background in exchanges influenced her specialization in public diplomacy.

"Part 5: Global Approaches to Public Diplomacy" takes our dialogue to the global level, with six chapters on its application across Europe and Asia. Understandably, we would like to have covered the globe in this section and our hope is to incorporate more regional and continental perspectives in future editions. The value of Part 5 is that it illustrates how varied public diplomacy is in practice and application. In Chapter 25, György Szondi links public diplomacy in Central and Eastern Europe to national reputation management and public relations, underscoring how such endeavors are recognized as central to public diplomacy in other nations. Finally, "Part 6: Advancing Public Diplomacy Studies" shows how public diplomacy is applicable to globalization studies (Chapter 27), ethics (Chapter 28), and a new paradigm, Noopolitik (Chapter 29), a direct challenge to Realpolitik that so dominated 20th-century thinking.

We expect this volume to be an authoritative text but with wide appeal: from the layperson interested in an introduction to public diplomacy, its definitions, approaches, trends, and institutions, to the graduate student in search of a comprehensive collection of current research, to the advanced practitioner who will find the processes and philosophies of persuasion management to be very useful.

This endeavor has been an ambitious project that required several years of fruition to the level of product. It would very likely have never gotten off ground into flight had it not been for the generous support of outside institutions. In particular, we are very grateful to the Behavioural Dynamics Institute (BDI), which sponsored the Strategic Communication and Public Diplomacy conference September 6–8, 2006 at Cliveden House in the United Kingdom. Nearly half of our contributors to this handbook presented perspectives and papers on the state of public diplomacy at the five-year anniversary of 9/11 and just a little over a year after the London bombings that came to be known as 7/7. The Behavioural Dynamics Institute was founded in 1990 and serves as an academic think tank that specializes in better understanding social influence and persuasion in order to shift attitudes and behavior in political and military campaigns. In short, it is communication for conflict reduction. We hope this volume helps to further our understanding along those lines. We also acknowledge every contributor to this volume, without whom we have no handbook, and whose leadership in public diplomacy made our job as editors much more pleasant. Working with outstanding, hard-working people is always a joy and we thank each one of them for their patience in seeing this project through.

Nancy Snow
Philip M. Taylor
February 2008

Notes on Contributors

Matthew C. Armstrong is an analyst and publisher of http://mountainrunner.us, a blog concentrating on the struggle for the minds and wills of people in the 21st century. Mr Armstrong obtained both his B.A. in International Relations and Master of Public Diplomacy at the University of Southern California (USC) and has done work at the University of Wales, Aberystwyth in the areas of U.S. Intelligence, Contemporary European Security, and the Middle East. He has published papers and book chapters on public diplomacy, the privatization of force, and unmanned warfare. He is frequently invited to present at the U.S. Army War College, National Defense University, and the Foreign Service Institute. He is a fellow of Proteus USA, a think tank based out of the U.S. Army War College's Center for Strategic Leadership, a member of the Senior Information Operations Advisory Council, and a member of the International Institute for Strategic Studies.

John Arquilla is Professor of Defense Analysis at the U.S. Naval Postgraduate School. He holds a PhD in political science from Stanford University. He is best known for his collaborative work with David Ronfeldt, especially *In Athena's Camp* (1997) and *Networks and Netwars* (2001). Dr. Arquilla has also written separately on a range of topics in foreign policy and security affairs, his most recent books being *The Reagan Imprint: Ideas in American Foreign Policy from the Collapse of Communism to the War on Terror* (2006) and *Worst Enemy: The Reluctant Transformation of the American Military* (2008).

John Brown, a Senior Fellow at the Center on Public Diplomacy at the University of Southern California, is a Research Associate at the Institute for the Study of Diplomacy at Georgetown University as well as an Adjunct Professor of Liberal Studies, also at Georgetown. A consultant for the Library of Congress's "Open World" exchange program with the Russian Federation, Brown was a member of the U.S. Foreign Service from 1981 until March 10, 2003 and served in London, Prague, Krakow, Kiev, Belgrade, and Moscow, specializing in press and cultural affairs. Brown received a Ph.D. in Russian History from Princeton University in 1977.

Naren Chitty is Foundation Chair in International Communication and Deputy Dean of the Division of Society, Culture, Media and Philosophy at Macquarie University, Sydney, Australia. He has previously headed the Department of International Communication and the Department of Media. He was a Visiting Professor at the University of Paris III-Sorbonne in 2004 and had previously held visiting appointments at Michigan State University and the American University in Washington D.C. His Ph.D. in International Relations is from the School of International Service of American University. His publications include *Framing South Asian Transformation* (1994); *Mapping Globalisation: International Media and the Crisis of Identity* (2002); *Studies in Terrorism: Media & the Enigma of Terrorism in the 21st Century* (co-edited, 2003); and *Alternative Media: Idealism and Pragmatism* (co-edited, 2007). He has been Editor-in-Chief of the *Journal of International Communication* (JIC) since it was founded in 1994. He is on the editorial boards of *Revista Nau* (Brazil), *Journal of Communication Arts* (Thailand) and the Australian, Canadian, Chinese, Mediterranean, and U.S. editions of *Global Media Journal*. He was Secretary General of the International Association of Media and Communication Research (IAMCR) between 1996 and 2000. He was a senior diplomat in Washington, D.C. during most of the Reagan Administration with a portfolio that included responsibility for public diplomacy.

Nicholas J. Cull is Professor of Public Diplomacy at the University of Southern California, where he directs the Masters Program in Public Diplomacy. He has written widely on issues of propaganda and international information. His works include: *The Cold War and the United States Information Agency: American Propaganda and Public Diplomacy, 1945–1989* (Cambridge University Press, 2008) and a report for the Foreign and Commonwealth Office, Public Diplomacy: Lessons from the Past (2007). Cull took both his B.A. and Ph.D. at the University of Leeds. He also studied at Princeton as a Harkness Fellow of the Commonwealth Fund of New York. From 1992 to 1997 he was lecturer in American History at the University of Birmingham. From 1997 to 2005 he was Professor of American Studies and Director of the Centre for American Studies at University of Leicester. His first book, *Selling War*, published by OUP in 1995, was named by *Choice* magazine as one of the ten best academic books of that year. He is the co-editor (with David Culbert and David Welch) of *Propaganda and Mass Persuasion: A Historical Encyclopedia, 1500–Present* (2003) which was one of *Book List* magazine's reference books of the year, and co-editor with David Carrasco of *Alambrista and the U.S.-Mexico Border: Film, Music, and Stories of Undocumented Immigrants* (University of New Mexico Press, Albuquerque, 2004). He is president of the International Association for Media and History.

Joseph Duffey served as Director of the USIA from 1993 to 1999 under President Bill Clinton. He was Assistant Secretary of State for Educational and Cultural Affairs and Chairman of the National Endowment for the Humanities under Presidents Jimmy Carter and Ronald Reagan and was Chancellor of the University of Massachusetts and President of American University. During the 1970s, he was a member of the faculty at Yale University and a Fellow of the JFK School of Government at Harvard University. Dr. Duffey holds 14 honorary degrees from American colleges and universities and in 1993 was awarded the honorary Doctor of Letter by Ritsemaken University in Japan. In 1980, he was named Commander of the Order of the Crown by the King of Belgium. He has been a member of the Council On Foreign Relations since 1979. A native of West Virginia and a graduate of Marshall University, Duffey received graduate degrees from Yale University, Andover Newton Theological School, and the Hartford Seminary Foundation. He has published widely on themes relating to higher education and social and economic issues.

Ali Fisher is Director of Mappa Mundi Consultants, where he works as a consultant and researcher in cultural relations, public diplomacy and information operations. He was previously director of Counterpoint, the British Council's research think tank, and taught as Lecturer in International Relations at the University of Exeter. Fisher is co-author of *Options for Influence: Global Campaigns of Persuasion in the New Worlds of Public Diplomacy*, and is working on incorporating the strength of "open source" methodology into public diplomacy. Fisher holds a Masters in U.S. Intelligence Services and a Ph.D. in American Studies from the University of Birmingham, where he wrote his doctoral thesis on American cultural operations in the early Cold War.

Robert H. Gass received his Ph.D. from the University of Kansas. He is Professor of Human Communication Studies at California State University, Fullerton. He teaches courses in argumentation, persuasion, compliance gaining, and research methods. Most recently, his research interests have focused on visual persuasion, compliance gaining, and compliance resisting. He has authored over 70 books, book chapters, scholarly journal articles, published conference proceedings, and professional papers. His Allyn and Bacon book with John S. Seiter, *Persuasion, Social Influence, and Compliance Gaining*, is in its third edition.

Ken S. Heller is currently a senior consultant for Booz Allen Hamilton. He retired from the United States Army in 2007 after 21 years, most of which he spent conducting Public Affairs in international theaters for which he was awarded the Legion of Merit. The Ventura, California native's more recent experiences prior to retirement included: Assisting in the evacuation of the American citizens from Lebanon to Cyprus in 2006, which earned him the Public Relations Society of America Silver Anvil award for the United States Naval Forces Central Command; participating in immediate relief efforts after Hurricane Katrina struck New Orleans in 2005 which earned him the PRSA Silver Anvil award for Northern Command; receiving the Bronze Star for accomplishments during Operation Iraqi Freedom in 2003, to include creating and running the Coalition Press Information Center, which directly embedded media members into their tactical units of assignment in Kuwait prior to the war; and working with the 101st Airborne Division under General David Petraeus in the Northern Iraq city of Mosul. While in Mosul, he and his Public Affairs team created the Internal Information publication that won the Department of the Army's Keith L. Ware award for Field Newspaper that year; established two independent Iraqi newspapers; two independent Iraqi radio stations and one independent Iraqi television station garnering the praise of both Petraeus and the Office of Reconstruction and Humanitarian Assistance in helping settle the inital unrest in via direct communication with the population. Heller has also been a primary spokesperson for the North Atlantic Treaty Organization in Hungary and Croatia during Operation Joint Endeavour in 1995 and the United Nations Protection Forces serving in the Republic of Macedonia in 1933.

Foad Izadi is a Doctoral Candidate and Instructor at the Manship School of Mass Communication, Louisiana State University. His dissertation is "U.S. Public Diplomacy and Policy Communications: The Case of Iran." Izadi received his master's (mass communication studies) and bachelor's (economics) degrees from the University of Houston. His research interests include propaganda, public diplomacy, and persuasive communication. In 2006, Izadi completed a research externship at the University of Southern California Center on Public Diplomacy. In 2007, he was competitively selected for participation in the National Doctoral Honors Seminar sponsored by the National Communication Association.

John Robert Kelley is a Postdoctoral Fellow at the Center for International Studies, University of Southern California. He received his PhD from the London School of Economics and Political Science in 2007. His dissertation titled "From Monologue to Dialogue: U.S. Public Diplomacy in the Post-9/11 Era" delves into the recent history of American public diplomacy activities, offers empirically-based tools for interpretating these activities, and advocates new directions in strategy and organization. Prior to this, Dr Kelly served as a Program Officer in the Office of Foreign Missions, U.S. Department of State, and also for several years as an intercultural business consultant to American and Japanese firms. His most recent publications appear in *Orbis*, the *Hague Journal of Diplomacy*, and *Foreign Policy in Focus*.

William P. Kiehl is the President and CEO of PD Worldwide, consultants in international public affairs, higher education management and cross-cultural communications based in Washington, D.C. During a 33-year career in the U.S. Foreign Service Dr. Kiehl served as Principal Deputy Assistant Secretary, Bureau of Educational and Cultural Affairs, Department of State and in numerous public diplomacy positions at home and abroad. Since leaving the diplomatic service he has taught public diplomacy at the Foreign Service Institute and has lectured at a number of colleges and universities at home and abroad. He served as Diplomat-in-Residence at the U.S. Army War College's Center for Strategic Leadership as Senior Fellow of the U.S. Army Peacekeeping Institute. From 2004 to 2007 he was Executive Director of the Public Diplomacy Council, School of Media and Public Affairs, George Washington University, and currently is a member of the Council's Board. He retired from the U.S. Foreign Service with the rank of Minister-Counselor in 2003. He holds a doctorate in Higher Education Management from the University of Pennsylvania. Dr. Kiehl earned an honors degree from the University of Scranton and an M.A. in Foreign Affairs from the University of Virginia. His book, *America's Dialogue with the World*, is in its second edition.

Mark Kilbane is a former Army captain and Commandant's Graduate of the U.S. Army Field Artillery School. He was educated at Western Illinois, the University of London School of Slavonic Studies, the JFK Special Warfare Center, and the Johns Hopkins School of Advanced International Studies. A Washington, D.C.-based writer, Kilbane has published articles on military psychological operations and multinational corporations' relationships to U.S. public diplomacy. He is also a professional actor.

Peter Kovach is a member of the Department of State's Senior Foreign Service and a career public diplomacy specialist. From 2006 to 2008 he was Visiting Professor and Diplomat in Residence in the School of Public Affairs at UCLA, where he applied his long experience building bridges to the Muslim world to counseling on State careers, teaching, writing, and activity in the local interfaith movement. At State, Kovach continued his interagency work coordinating US Government international public information efforts. Kovach has had diplomatic postings in Yemen, Bahrain, Morocco, Jordan, Japan, and Pakistan; in Washington, he has directed the Department's three Foreign Press Centers and the Office of Public Diplomacy for the Bureau of East Asian and Pacific Affairs. Kovach did thesis work on the legal status of the Palestinian citizens of Israel at the Fletcher School of Law and Diplomacy, completed an M.A. at UC Berkeley in Asian Studies and majored in history of religion at Wesleyan University, spending his junior year at Banaras Hindu University. He has taught religion at the University of Massachusetts-Boston, Goddard College, starred in a TV series on Japan's NHK and worked as a photojournalist, a stevedore and as a stonemason.

Sherry Mueller, a leader in the field of citizen diplomacy and international exchange Sherry Mueller is the president of the National Council for International Visitors (NCIV). NCIV is a nonprofit organization comprised of 91 community member organizations that practice and promote excellence in citizen diplomacy. She received her Ph.D. at the Fletcher School of Law and Diplomacy focusing the evaluation of exchange programs. Previously, Sherry worked eighteen years at the Institute of International Education, first as a Program Officer and then as Director of the Professional Exchange Programs. Her new book, co-authored with Mark Overmann, entitled *Working World: Careers in International Education, Exchange and Development* will be available October 2008 published by Georgetown University Press.

Richard Nelson holds a Ph.D. from Florida State University. He is Professor of Mass Communication and Public Affairs at Louisiana State University's Manship School of Mass

Communication in Baton Rouge. He is editor of *Journal of Promotion Management* and *Journal of Website Promotion*. Nelson is professionally accredited by the Public Relations Society of America (PRSA) and is past president of the International Management Development Association (IMDA) and the International Academy of Business Disciplines (IABD), as well as former head of the Public Relations Division of the Association for Education in Journalism and Mass Communication (AEJMC). Nelson's research focuses on public policy, strategic planning, management, and political communications issues. He is the author of more than 75 refereed articles, essays, and reports. His books include *A Chronology and Glossary of Propaganda in the United States* and *Issues Management: Corporate Public Policymaking in an Information Society* (co-authored with Robert L. Heath).

Tadashi Ogawa is a native of Kobe, Japan. He serves as Managing Director of the Japan Foundation Center for Global Partnership. He has worked with the Japan Foundation for over 25 years, in previous positions that include Assistant Director of the Japan Culture Center in Jakarta, Indonesia and Director of the Japan Foundation office in New Delhi, India. He was educated at Waseda University where he now lectures in the Graduate School of Asia-Pacific Studies. His major publications include "Indonesia as a Multi-Ethnic Nation" (1993), "Emergence of Hindu Nationalism" (2000, Asian Pacific Award Special Prize), "Updating India: Superpower of Diversity" (2001), "Fundamentalism: from USA, Middle East to Japan" (2003), "Fundamentalism: Twisted Terror and Salvation" (2007), and a co-authored work, "Public Diplomacy" (2007).

Liza M. Persson, a native of Boras, Sweden, is a certified Behavioral Scientist. She is currently working toward her Master's Degree in Psychology with a focus on Post Traumatic Stress Disorder. She is an avid physical fitness fan embracing a holistic view of health, and an amateur nutritionist. In her spare time, she dabbles in blogging, photography, music, and singing. She also has an intense interest in international politics, history, and communications. With the ability to speak several languages, she loves to engage people at all levels of life while seeking to learn more about their perspectives and our world. She has also served in the Swedish National Defense forces as a medic.

Anthony Pratkanis is Professor of Psychology at the University of California, Santa Cruz, where he studies social psychology and social influence and is a fellow at the University of Southern California Center on Public Diplomacy at the Annenberg School. He is the co-author of the popular classroom textbook, *Age of Propaganda: The Everyday Use and Abuse of Persuasion* (with Elliot Aronson). From 2004 to 2007, he served as Visiting Professor of Information Sciences at the Naval Postgraduate School in Monterrey, CA where he developed many of the ideas in his chapter. He received his Ph.D. in Social Psychology from the Ohio State University.

Gary D. Rawnsley is Professor of Asian International Communications in the Institute of Communications Studies, University of Leeds, United Kingdom. He was previously Senior Lecturer in Politics at the University of Nottingham and then Dean of the University of Nottingham, Ningbo, China. Professor Rawnsley's research interests include information operations, propaganda and information warfare, and public diplomacy, within an Asian (especially Far Eastern) context. He has also published widely on elections campaigns in Taiwan, and the media, the internet and democratization in Taiwan and China. His latest book is a co-edited volume for RoutledgeCurzon, *Global Chinese Cinema: The Culture and Politics of Hero*. Professor Rawnsley is Visiting Professor at Shi Hsin University in Taipei and Adjunct Professor at the University of Technology Sydney (UTS), Australia. He is researching Radio Free Asia and is particularly interested in its impact on China's Harmonious Society and on the construction and projection of America's China policy.

Keith Reinhard is President of Business for Diplomatic Action (BDA), a not-for-profit private sector effort to enlist the U.S. business community in actions aimed at improving the standing of America in the world. Reinhard is also Chairman Emeritus of DDB Worldwide, which ranks among the world's largest and most creative advertising agency networks with 206 offices in 96 countries. He is a member of the Advertising Hall of Fame and was referred to as the advertising industry's soft-spoken visionary by *Advertising Age*, the magazine which in 1999 named him as one of the top 100 industry influentials in advertising history. Reinhard is a past Chairman of the American Association of Advertising Agencies and former Chairman of the Board of Union Theological Seminary in New York. He is a member of the Boards of Sesame Workshop, Jazz at Lincoln Center, Episcopal Charities and the Berlin School of Creative Leadership.

Kelton Rhoads is a psychologist, influence consultant, and Adjunct Professor at both the University of Southern California and the U.S. military's Special Operations School. His area of study is influence, which covers persuasion, compliance, indoctrination, and propaganda. In over 270 presentations to professional audiences regarding influence topics, he has addressed NATO, United Nations staff, the JFK Special Warfare Center & School, congressional staff, and a variety of grassroots organizations. He teaches the influence component of the Psychological Operations Officer's Qualification Course at Ft. Bragg. His clients have included the American Heart Association, the National Restaurant Association, Compaq Computer, Dow Chemical, Institute for Defense Analyses, the US Forest Service, Southwest Airlines, US Chamber of Commerce, and many others. At USC's Annenberg School for Communication, Dr. Rhoads teaches influence-related courses like Persuasion, Campaigns, and Influential Communication in the Marketplace.

David Ronfeldt is a senior political scientist (on leave) in the International Security and Policy Group at RAND. During his 30+ years at RAND, he worked initially on U.S.-Latin American security issues. Lately, he has worked on ideas about information-age modes of conflict (e.g., cyberwar, netwar, swarming) and principles for cooperation (e.g., guarded openness, noopolitik). He is co-author (mainly with John Arquilla) of *In Athena's Camp: Preparing for Conflict in the Information Age* (1997), *The Zapatista Social Netwar in Mexico* (1998), *Countering the New Terrorism* (1998), *The Emergence of Noopolitik: Toward an American Information Strategy* (1999), *Swarming and the Future of Conflict* (2000), and *Networks and Netwar: The Future of Terror, Crime, and Militancy* (2001). Since then, he is working on: (1) a framework of the evolution of societies, based on their capacity to use four major forms of organization (tribes, hierarchies, markets, and networks); and (2) a framework for analyzing people's mindsets and cultural cosmologies in terms of their beliefs about social space, time, and action. His latest writings include *In Search of How Societies Work: Tribes—The First and Forever Form* (2006), and *The Future Prospects for Cyberocracy* (Revisited) (in preparation). His education includes a B.A. in International Relations from Pomona College; M.A. in Latin American Studies from Stanford University; and Ph.D. in Political Science from Stanford University.

Giles Scott-Smith is a senior researcher with the Roosevelt Study Center and lecturer in International Relations at the Roosevelt Academy in Middelburg, the Netherlands. His research covers the role of non-state actors and public diplomacy in the maintenance of inter-state (particularly transatlantic) relations during the Cold War. He is co-editor of the *European Journal of American Studies*. His latest book is *Networks of Empire: The US State Department's Foreign Leader Program in the Netherlands, France, and Britain 1950–70* (Peter Lang, 2008). He has published numerous articles in journals such as *The Hague Journal of Diplomacy, British Journal of Politics and International Relations, Cold War History, Revue Française d'Etudes Américaines, Journal of American Studies, Diplomacy and Statecraft*, and *Intelligence and National Security*.

John S. Seiter is Professor in the Department of Languages, Philosophy, and Speech Communication at Utah State University, where he teaches courses in social influence, interpersonal communication, theories of communication, and intercultural communication. His published research includes articles investigating persuasion in applied contexts, perceptions of deceptive communication, and nonverbal behavior in political debates. He has received eight "Top Paper" awards for research presented at professional conferences, was named his college's Researcher of the Year and his university's Professor of the Year. Together with Robert Gass, he authored the book *Persuasion, Social Influence and Compliance Gaining* and edited the book *Perspectives on Persuasion, Social Influence, and Compliance Gaining*. Seiter earned a Ph.D. from the University of Southern California.

Nancy Snow is Associate Professor of Public Diplomacy in the S.I. Newhouse School of Public Communications at Syracuse University where she teaches in the dual degree Masters Program in Public Diplomacy sponsored by the Newhouse and Maxwell Schools. She was a Visiting Professor and Senior Scholar in Public Diplomacy at the School of Journalism and Communication, Tsinghua University, Beijing, China. Dr. Snow is Senior Research Fellow of the Center on Public Diplomacy at the University of Southern California where she also taught for six years as Adjunct Professor in the Annenberg School for Communication. She is a lifetime member of the Fulbright Association and a Fulbright alumna of the Federal Republic of Germany. During Bill Clinton's first presidential term, she was a Presidential Management Fellow at the U.S. Information Agency and U.S. State Department. Her books include *Propaganda, Inc.: Selling America's Culture to the World*; *Information War: American Propaganda, Free Speech and Opinion Control Since 9/11*; *War, Media and Propaganda: A Global Perspective* (co-edited with Yahya Kamalipour); and *The Arrogance of American Power: What U.S. Leaders are Doing Wrong and Why It's Our Duty to Dissent*. She earned her Ph.D. in International Relations from the School of International Service at American University in Washington, D.C. She received a B.A. in Political Science from Clemson University, South Carolina.

György Szondi is a senior lecturer in Public Relations at Leeds Business School, Leeds Metropolitan University, United Kingdom. His Ph.D. at the University of Salzburg, Austria involves researching the concepts of public relations and public diplomacy for the European Union. His interest and publications include international public relations, public diplomacy, country branding, risk and crisis communication, public relations in Eastern Europe, and PR evaluation. He has been a regular conference speaker and strategic communication trainer throughout Eastern Europe, including Hungary, Poland, Estonia, and Latvia. He designed and led training courses for the Health and Safety Executive in the UK; the National School of Government, UK; the Government of Estonia; the Estonian Ministry of Social Affairs, and for several for-profit organizations. His articles have appeared in *Place Branding and Public Diplomacy*, and the *Journal of Public Affairs*. Szondi worked as a consultant for the international public relations firm Hill and Knowlton in Budapest, Hungary, and in its international headquarters in London. He holds a Bachelor degree in Economics, an M.A. in Public Relations from the University of Stirling, UK, and an M.Sc. in Physics. Besides his native Hungarian, he speaks English, Italian, German, French, Polish, and Estonian.

Philip M. Taylor is Professor of International Communications at the University of Leeds, United Kingdom. He is a Fellow of the Royal Historical Society, Fellow of the Center on Public Diplomacy at the University of Southern California, and Adjunct Professor at the Universiti Teknologi Mara, Shah Alam, Malaysia. His many publications include *War and the Media: Propaganda and Persuasion in the Gulf War*; *Munitions of the Mind: A History of Propaganda from the Ancient World to the Present Day*; *Global Communications, International Affairs and the Media since 1945*; and

British Propaganda in the 20th Century: Selling Democracy. His latest book (co-authored with Paul Moorcraft) is *Shooting the Messenger: The Political Impact of War Reporting*, published by Potomac in 2008.

Michael Vlahos is a Fellow and Principal in the National Security Analysis Department (NSAD) at the John Hopkins University Applied Physics Laboratory. Previously, he headed the Center for the Study of Foreign Affairs at the U.S. State Department and served as the director of the Securities Studies Program at the Johns Hopkins School of Advanced International Studies. Dr Vlahos earned his Ph.D. in history and strategic studies from the Fletcher School of Law and Diplomacy at Tufts University and an A.B. from Yale College. He has authored nine books and monographs, including *Terror's Mask: Insurgency Within Islam*. His latest, appearing this November, will be *Fighting Identity: Sacred War and World Change*.

Ali S. Wyne holds a B.S. in Management and Political Science from the Massachusetts Institute of Technology. He served as Vice President of the Undergraduate Association and Editor-in-Chief of the *MIT International Review*, the Institute's first journal of international affairs.

R.S. Zaharna is Associate Professor of Public Communication at the School of Communication, American University in Washington, D.C. She has written extensively on intercultural and international public communication, and specializes in American and Arab cross-cultural communication. In addition to nearly 20 years of teaching communication, she has advised on communication projects for multinational corporations, non-governmental organizations, diplomatic missions, and international organizations, including the United Nations, the World Bank, and USAID. Since 9/11, she has been invited on numerous occasions by the U.S. Congress to testify on U.S. public diplomacy in the Arab and Islamic world and has addressed diplomatic audiences and military personnel in the United States and Europe on cross-cultural political communication strategies. Dr. Zaharna served as a Fulbright Senior Scholar in the West Bank (1996–1997). She holds an undergraduate degree in Foreign Service from Georgetown University and graduate degrees in Communication from Columbia University.

Oliver Zöllner is Professor of Media Marketing and Research at Stuttgart Media University, Stuttgart, and an honorary professor of media and communication studies at the University of Düsseldorf, Germany. After receiving his M.A. in 1993 and his Ph.D. degree in 1996, both from the University of Bochum, he took up a career as an audience researcher in public-service broadcasting. From 1997 to 2004, Zöllner was Director of the market and media research department of Germany's international broadcaster, Deutsche Welle. This was accompanied by various teaching assignments at the universities of Bochum, Bonn, Dortmund, Dresden, Düsseldorf, Erfurt, Paderborn, and Osnabrück from 1996 to 2006. Zöllner is the author and editor of several books on international communication and research methodology, some of them in English. His research interests include public diplomacy, public relations, international and intercultural communication, quantitative and qualitative research methodology.

Introduction

Rethinking Public Diplomacy

Nancy Snow

Public diplomacy is inevitably linked to power. The work by Joseph Nye is well known in this respect, particularly soft power. Soft power is "based on intangible or indirect influences such as culture, values, and ideology."[1] It is arguably the most referenced term in the public diplomacy lexicon, though its prevalence does not mean that we all agree on its definition and application. The term "soft power" was first coined by Nye in 1990. He wrote that the United States must invest in measures that lead to better ties that bind: ". . . the richest country in the world could afford both better education at home and the international influence that comes from an effective aid and information program abroad. What is needed is increased investment in 'soft power,' the complex machinery of interdependence, rather than in 'hard power'—that is, expensive new weapons systems."[2]

Nye defines power as "the ability to influence the behavior of others to get the outcomes one wants," and argues that there are three primary ways to do that:

1 coerce with threats;
2 induce behavioral change with payments; or
3 attract and co-opt.

The latter is soft power—getting others to appreciate you to the extent that they change their behavior to your liking. Nye argues that the three types of power, when exercised judicially and combined with soft power, lead to "smart power." In other words, soft power is not the same as little old ladies sipping tea; it is often used in conjunction with more forceful and threatening forms of compliance and persuasion. Thus, the term "soft" can be misleading to some scholars and practitioners of public diplomacy who view what we do in almost messianic terms. A benign example of American soft power at work is illustrated in the February 2002 edition of *The New Yorker* magazine. Writer Joe Klein describes an Iranian school teacher whose visceral reaction to the 9/11 attacks was in the person of one famous New York filmmaker whose work the school teacher admired. "You know what I was really worried about? Woody Allen. I didn't want him to die. I love his films."[3]

With respect to Woody Allen, soft power is culture power. No other country in the world can match the superpower cultural reach of the United States. American soft power is our Superman. It's a blessing and a curse. The central nervous system of this cultural soft power exists in the Los Angeles megapolis that includes Hollywood and the Thirty Mile Zone[4] of celebrity branding and image in Southern California and the Madison Avenue advertising and marketing firms of New York City. The world will forever have an ambivalent feeling about the U.S. soft power advantage vis-à-vis popular culture and media. It is cast in the refrain, "We Hate You but Send Us Your Baywatch."[5]

Soft power is a new concept for an old habit. Many countries have preceded the American effort to utilize their culture to national image advantage (e.g., France, Italy, Germany, the U.K.). In fact, the United States is a relative latecomer to utilizing culture for diplomatic purposes. Not until World War I and the founding of the Committee on Public Information, known also as the Creel Committee for its founder George Creel, did the U.S. government centralize an effort to shape its image in the global marketplace of ideas. President Wilson assured the world that America's participation in World War I was to make the world safer for democracy and that his war would end all future wars. We know it didn't turn out as Wilson promised, which leads us to how it is that any country can gain or lose a foothold in soft power advantage.

What gives any country a soft power advantage is measured by several dimensions:

1 when culture and ideas match prevailing global norms;
2 when a nation has greater access to multiple communication channels that can influence how issues are framed in global news media; and
3 when a country's credibility is enhanced by domestic and international behavior.

The U.S. is at a comparative advantage with the first two and at a decisive disadvantage with the last dimension. This may explain why so many of the following chapters suggest a rethinking of public diplomacy for the world's sole superpower. If, as Nye first suggested, the U.S. should think about its interdependent soft power ties, then such new thinking should in turn emphasize synergistic practices such as building long-term mutual understanding and global community values over U.S.-led democratic values. The United States holds no patent on soft power or democratic principles. If we could accept that we have no monopoly ownership of the concepts of democracy, liberty and freedom, then we might more readily acknowledge dialogue and dissent around overseas behavior. So far, it seems, we continue to dig in our heels, particularly in how we view ourselves, which leads to charges of hypocrisy from overseas.

The paradox of American soft power revealed itself in the "Report of the U.S. Advisory Group on Public Diplomacy for the Arab and Muslim World," also known as the Djerejian Report for the former U.S. Ambassador to Syria and Israel, Edward Djerejian, who led the delegation. The 2003 report stated the following:

> Surveys show that Arabs and Muslims admire the universal values for which the United States stands. They admire, as well, our technology, our entrepreneurial zeal, and the achievements of Americans as individuals. We were told many times in our travels to Arab countries that "we like Americans but not what the American government is doing." This distinction is unrealistic, since Americans elect their government and broadly support foreign policy, but the assertion that we like you but don't like your policies offers hope for transformed public diplomacy. Arabs and Muslims, it seems, support our values but believe that our policies do not live up to them. A major project for public diplomacy is to reconcile this contradiction through effective communications and intelligent listening.[6]

Therein lies the rub. U.S. citizens most certainly have a greater tolerance for unpopular foreign policies than those on the receiving end of such policies. But that should not lead us into a false sense of security about the rightness of our foreign policies. Is it possible some five years later after the release of the Djerejian report to reconcile "we like you, not your policies?" What may be needed is a public diplomacy campaign led by the public, not the government. If "it's the policy, stupid" prevails, then allow more open channels of communication between the governmental and nongovernmental players involved in carrying out the day-to-day responsibilities of national image and reputation management. U.S. media should work to build stronger and lasting relationships with international journalists. Interpersonal communication is the most important opportunity to build trust, understanding, and friendship, which is why the Fulbright Program, International Visitors Leadership Program, and arts and writer exchanges have the most promise for winning hearts and minds in the United States.

America's soft power ground zero may still be Hollywood and Madison Avenue, at least in the mediated mind's eye. But a fuller, more balanced picture of America emerges from all those in-between states and cities whose international relations could be strengthened through exchanges like those offered by Rotary International, Sister City International, and the World Affairs Council. The State Department itself often touts these citizen and professional exchanges, along with the Fulbright program, as the best value for the buck in the public diplomacy business.

I spent just two years working inside the U.S. Government's agency responsible for "telling America's story to the world." Every day I wandered through the corridor of our building on C Street in Southwest Washington, D.C., I wondered what America's story was becoming. It was in the early 1990s and the Cold War's demise was still fresh. The United States had a spring in its step with the election of a Baby Boomer Democratic president Bill Clinton, the man from Hope, Arkansas, who as a former Rhodes Scholar symbolized a sense of promise for the country's place in the world. Perhaps America's story would be one of U.S. moral leadership in the world, and for a time it seemed to be heading that way. But quickly that leadership emerged as one driven primarily by economic interest. The passage of the North American Free Trade Agreement became a key public diplomacy campaign inside the halls of the U.S. Information Agency, and for a time our telling became a model of selling, particularly America's know-how and prowess in economics and business.

Some 15 years later it is time to shift focus again. Our new thinking in public diplomacy must involve a motto-shift from USIA's "telling America's story to the world" to "sharing values, hopes, dreams, and common respect" with the world. We need a shift from the Clinton doctrine of economic engagement and enlarging markets and the Bush doctrine of preemptive security and the long war to a new doctrine of global partnership and engagement. Former CBS anchor Walter Cronkite captures the spirit of a nation that seeks lessons from the 20th century that can help set things straight in the 21st:

> The way for this nation to win the hearts and minds of those most offended by our Iraqi invasion and occupation is not through press agentry and advertising. Rather, it is by proving to them that the American spirit—which, with good will and unselfish financing, once helped reinvigorate the world after the great wars of the past century—still exists despite the arrogant and bullying tactics with which we have launched the 21st century.[7]

At the time of this writing, the United States is engaged in a presidential campaign unprecedented in its early slate of candidates for the highest office in the land, but one which quickly winnowed down to a final three, a woman and an African-American Senator on the Democratic side, and a former POW Senator on the Republican side. The candidacy of African-American Senator Barack Obama from Illinois is illustrative of new thinking in American public diplomacy. His biography alone is a lesson in new thinking. As writer Barbara Ehrenreich opined:

> A Kenyan-Kansan with roots in Indonesia and multiracial Hawaii, he seems to be the perfect answer to the bumper sticker that says, "I love you America, but isn't it time to start seeing other people?" As conservative commentator Andrew Sullivan has written, Obama's election could mean the re-branding of America. An anti-war black president with an Arab-sounding name: See, we're not so bad after all, world![8]

5

Obama's Democratic opponent Hillary Clinton has promised to send her husband and two-term president Bill Clinton all over the world doing a repair job on the American image. At least the two leading Democrats have a strong sense of what the Djerejian report warned in 2003:

> We have failed to listen and failed to persuade. We have not taken the time to understand our audience, and we have not bothered to help them understand us. We cannot afford such shortcomings.[9]

Along with new thinking about America's image and policies in the world, we could use a public diplomacy that educates its own public. We already have the Congressional legislation that mandates such international education. The original design of the Fulbright program was:

> to increase mutual understanding between the people of the United States and the people of other countries by means of educational and cultural exchange; to strengthen the ties which unite us with other nations by demonstrating the educational and cultural interests, developments and achievements of the people of the United States and other nations and the contributions being made toward a peaceful and more fruitful life for people throughout the world; to promote international cooperation for educational and cultural advancement; and thus to assist in the development of friendly, sympathetic, and peaceful relations between the United States and other countries of the world.[10]

So far, much of the old thinking about U.S. public diplomacy has focused on the one-way exchange of information about the United States to the rest of the world, a preference for telling. We need more two-way exchanges of information if we believe some of the polls of late that have indicated a woeful lack of intelligence and interest among young Americans about international affairs. A 2006 National Geographic-Roper poll indicated that just over one quarter (28%) of 18-to-24-year-olds consider it "necessary to know where countries in the news are located."[11] This was three years into a war with Iraq that has arguably done more to damage America's standing in the world than anything since the war in Vietnam. The same poll found that six out of ten in the same age group (63%) could not locate Iraq on a Middle East map.[12] If we are to reeducate our young people about why international relations matter, then we must shift our understanding of what diplomacy means.

Traditional diplomacy is government-to-government relations (G2G) and if one were to picture it, it would be a photo op of Secretary of State Condoleezza Rice sitting across the table from the foreign affairs minister in another nation state. Traditional *public* diplomacy has been about governments talking to global publics (G2P), and includes those efforts to inform, influence, and engage those publics in support of national objectives and foreign policies. More recently, public diplomacy involves the way in which both government *and* private individuals and groups influence directly and indirectly those public attitudes and opinions that bear directly on another government's foreign policy decisions (P2P). Why the shift from G2P to P2P? One development is the rise in user-friendly communications technologies that have increased public participation in talking about foreign affairs and the subsequent involvement of public opinion in foreign policy making. Another development is the increase in people-to-people exchanges, both virtual and personal, across national borders. This shift from the diplomatic emphasis to the public emphasis has resulted in the rise of two different philosophies about public diplomacy's utility:

1   those who view public diplomacy as a necessary evil, a mere ancillary tactic that supports conventional public diplomacy and traditional diplomacy efforts; and
2   those who view public diplomacy as a context or milieu for how nations interact with each other, from public affairs officers in the field to the citizen diplomat and student exchangee at the grassroots.

One aim of this handbook is to examine just how contentious or compatible these two views will become.

The rise of communications technology in public diplomacy is neither value neutral nor value positive to traditional public diplomats. Joe Johnson, a retired Foreign Service Office and my former supervisor in the Bureau for Educational and Cultural Affairs at the US Information Agency, tells us that new technology is making the practice of public diplomacy much more complicated, at least inside government corridors: "On balance, technology is making public affairs and public communication harder, not easier. The Internet spreads rumors faster than authorities can set the record straight . . . Using information to control rumors will be a major issue."[13] Thus the new public diplomacy in the new digital age is a challenge for public diplomacy practitioners and public affairs officers (PAOs). This is a cautionary note for efforts to utilize the latest bells and whistles in technology to both monitor and respond to dialogue on the Web.

Traditional public diplomacy tends to take the public for granted, or views public opinion measurement as a necessary evil in foreign policy. There was once a greater emphasis on teaching good citizenship and educating U.S. citizens about their rights and duties in this participatory democracy experiment that we still today promote as a beacon of light for hope and change throughout the world. The halcyon exchange period was in the early 1960s with the advent of the Peace Corps, along with an internationally inspiring civil rights movement, and an enthusiastic sense of international mission and zeal associated with a youthful president and French-speaking wife, both of whom inspired new frontiers in thinking and technology from international outlooks to space travel. The Peace Corps emphasized international service to country, as did the proverbial words of John F. Kennedy in asking not what our country can do for us but in what we ourselves can do for our country. In the last 40 years, however, and certainly since 9/11, the government has not defined much of a role or function for its own public when it comes to public diplomacy. More often than not, citizens have been spectators to the process. The missing public participation in public diplomacy seems to mirror the decline in civic participation.

My research and advocacy are to put the public back into diplomacy. Figure 1.1 emphasizes some of the differences between the public versus diplomacy orientation.

Conventional public diplomacy emphasizes citizens but has at times emphasized citizens in asymmetrical one-way efforts to inform and build a case for a nation's position. An exemplar of this is illustrated in the remarks by President Bush one month after 9/11: "I'm amazed that there is such misunderstanding about what our country is about. We've got to do a better job of *making our case*."[14]

In the immediate aftermath of 9/11, the U.S. Government emphasized a public diplomacy based on some communication theories that have since been challenged. First, communications strategies put in place were crisis-driven and self-preservation oriented, some with very ominous sounding names, and many of which had a very short shelf life. These included Coalition Information Centers (CICs), the White House Office of Global Communications (OGC), and the Office of Strategic Influence (OSI) and Total Information Awareness (TIA) at the Department of Defense. These efforts, some more successful than others, were designed to get out more information and to better coordinate information about the U.S. response to 9/11. They are based on the premise that more information leads to better communication. In other words, "they" hate us because they do not understand us. If "they" just knew more about us—if we made a stronger case for ourselves and our position through increasing information about us— then the better off all would be. "They" would like us more.

The emblem of this approach was the Charlotte Beers' directed Shared Values advertising campaign of 2002. Five two-minute adverts presented as documentaries and supported by the Coalition of Muslims for Understanding and the American People were prepared for airing in

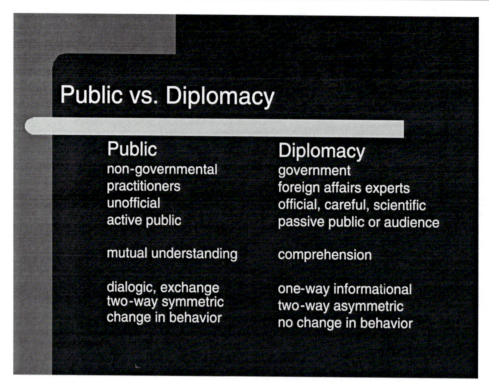

Figure 1.1. Public vs. Diplomacy Orientation

Islamic countries during the Ramadan season. The content of the ads was never in dispute. The problem was that they addressed a communication gap between how Americans view themselves and how others see us. The U.S. position was that 9/11 symbolized a misunderstanding. We were attacked because people did not know who we really were. If we could only show the world that our Muslim American citizens fare well in an open society, then maybe we could work to build bridges with the Middle East, Arab nations, and Islamic believers. What the target audience saw was how well Muslims Americans fared in comparison to how poorly many Muslims fared in U.S.-supported autocratic regimes. The effort to share values ended up showing a harsh contrast between the daily life realities of Muslim people living in the United States and those living under much harsher regimes. Instead of a hoped for message that "our success is your success" it was "our success isn't your success" and here are the images that prove it.

Case making has a long tradition in public diplomacy. In the 21st century it is not enough. Global publics will not allow themselves just to be talked to, but are demanding fuller participation in dialogue and feedback through the help of Web 2.0 communication technologies and new media like Second Life, Facebook, YouTube, and MySpace. These new media offer interactive back-and-forth engagement that was not even fathomable 10 to 15 years ago, much less in the month after 9/11. Even without such technologies, traditional broadcast media, where most of us still get our information about the world, are now around-the-clock and include speculative reporting that includes a lot of instapundits who can judge, fairly or unfairly, a government's case-making strategies in real time. Our media are becoming "I" media and "We" media, so any public diplomacy research must take into account the various publics and diplomacies that are engaging, collaborating, combating, and just bumping into each other. It requires new thinking about what it means to be part of a public, including what it means to be part of that amorphous global public.

In rethinking public diplomacy, old habits are hard to break. Traditional public diplomacy

8

strategies since 9/11 continue to stress more over fewer, faster over slower, and louder over quieter styles of communication. As Seong-Hun Yun points out: "In the United States, the PD problem is conceived as more of a marketing problem that occurs from a lack of enough exposure to messages and hence can be solved through advertising, a vehicle for more exposure."[15] And yet 40 years ago, a U.S. Congressional report, "The Future of U.S. Public Diplomacy," warned the following:

> More communication does not by itself guarantee better communication. In most instances, it merely multiplies the possibilities for misunderstandings and misinterpretation. This happens because bias and distortion continue to play a large role in intergroup communication.[16]

In our rethinking public diplomacy, we will have to confront the two schools of thought that predominate, what have been characterized as the tender-minded versus tough-minded approaches. The tender-minded school is illustrated by P2P and G2P strategies like the International Visitors Leadership Program and the Bureau of Educational and Cultural Affairs (ECA) of the U.S. Department of State, whose stated purpose is to foster mutual understanding between the people of the United States and the people of other countries around the world. The tough-minded school is illustrated by the controversial firm Lincoln Group, whose website slogan, "Insight and Influence. Anywhere, Anytime," stands in sharp contrast to a mutual understanding approach. Signitzer and Coombs state that the tough-minded schools:

> hold that the purpose of public diplomacy is to exert an influence on attitudes of foreign audiences using persuasion and propaganda . . . Objectivity and truth are considered important tools of persuasion but not extolled as virtues in themselves . . . The tender-minded school argues that information and cultural programs must bypass current foreign policy goals to concentrate on the highest long-range national objectives. The goal is to create a climate of mutual understanding . . . Truth and veracity are considered essential, much more than a mere persuasion tactic.[17]

Along with our addressing the two schools within public diplomacy, we will have to forge ahead with greater acknowledgement to the contributions that both intercultural and human communication studies have made to public diplomacy as well as the long-established discipline of public relations. In many op-eds and addresses before Congress, the public relations industry is singled out as the main culprit in why U.S. public diplomacy efforts have failed. For instance, Price Floyd's op-ed, "Public Diplomacy is not PR," makes a distinction between public diplomacy and public relations that is not entirely justified:

> Public diplomacy is more about influencing foreign publics and broadening dialogue between American citizens and institutions and their counterparts abroad than it is about "selling" a particular policy. It is time to admit the failure of disbanding and folding the U.S. Information Agency into the State Department. This agency's successful efforts to promote the U.S. as a counter to communism and the former Soviet Union went a long way toward winning the Cold War. What was formerly an agency that promoted American values and ideals is now just another public relations tool to sell this administration's policies.[18]

Poor public diplomacy sells more than tells. And public diplomacy's roots are in the persuasion industries of PR, marketing, and advertising as well as in the minds of Edward Bernays, Walter Lippmann, Harold Lasswell, and Edward Filene. Yet a cottage industry of indictment continues to single out public relations as the most irresponsible of all the persuasion industries and thus most responsible for the public diplomacy mess we're in, as was noted in a special focus on public diplomacy in the *Foreign Service Journal*:

Public-relations agents burnish the reputations of individuals or businesses, rarely going beyond clichés and superficial explanations. When their clients do well, they tout it. When they behave badly or perform poorly, they make excuses for them.[19]

Even Joseph Duffey, one of our handbook contributors, reported to Congress that public relations and public diplomacy were not close cousins:

Let me just say a word about public diplomacy. It is not public relations. It is not flakking for a Government agency or even flakking for America. It is trying to relate beyond government-to-government relationships the private institutions, the individuals, the long-term contact, the accurate understanding, the full range of perceptions of America to the rest of the world.[20]

The judgment by Duffey that public relations is just flakking for one's clients is out of line with the philosophy put forth by James Grunig that "public relations is the practice of public responsibility."[21] Clearly there is a need to examine public relations and public diplomacy in a comparative context, as many of our global contributors have done. Outside the United States, the public relations industry does not carry such heavy baggage in institutional image and reputation, and is seen as a necessary and valued aspect of national branding.

Rethinking public diplomacy includes measuring the communication context of what we are doing, instead of just information-driven effects and outcomes (e.g., why do they hate us? is too broad and too "us" focused). It includes intercultural communication theory and practice as well as public relations best practices (Personal Influence and Relationship Models). As Seong-Hun Yun concluded in one of the more recent theoretical studies in public diplomacy and public diplomacy based on extensive quantitative research:

Relationships with publics provide the best indicator for the effects of excellence in public relations rather than reputation or image . . . The concept of relationship is associated with publics possessing first-hand experience with the organization or foreign government. In contrast, the concepts of image and reputation are less specific and related to masses with second-hand experience. Thus, a focus of future research should be on the relationships of governments with specific and strategic foreign publics such as congressmen, journalists, and opinion leaders.[22]

Relationships with publics may be our best predictor of actual future behavior. It shifts the focus in public diplomacy from a reactive stance to a proactive stance. Focusing on relationships with publics may also act as a buffer if and when future crises occur. It serves to place public diplomacy in a global context and moves us beyond the U.S.- and UK-centric methods and practices that are all too common in our dialogue and research.

In rethinking public diplomacy we may be heading toward a new 21st-century mindset. As this handbook shows, our public diplomacy philosophies, strategies and tactics are shifting from one-way informational diplomatic objectives to two-way interactive public exchanges; exchange and reciprocity are becoming trust-building measures and we are adding a personal and social dimension (*guanxi*) to other variables of influence and persuasion. Ultimately we may move along a path toward building rapport, commitment, and continuity among global publics, their relationship with governments, corporations, and with each other. Only time—and new leadership—will tell.

Notes

1 http://www.wordspy.com.
2 Joseph S. Nye, Jr., "The misleading metaphor of decline," *The Atlantic Monthly*, March 1990.

3 Joe Klein, "Shadow Land: Who's Winning the Fight for Iran's Future?" *The New Yorker*, February 18, 2002.

4 The "Thirty Mile Zone" is a term used interchangeably with the thirty miles (50 kilometer) studio zone area around the Hollywood television and film industry. It is also the full name origin of the Time Warner company celebrity tabloid news website, TMZ.com. "In the film and TV locations business, contrary to the tenets of astrophysics, there actually is a center of the universe and it's at the corner of La Cienega and Beverly boulevards. Where the Beverly Center meets the Beverly Connection is the dead center of Hollywood's so-called Studio Zone."—Christopher Grove, "Small screen scouts eye underexposed corners," *Variety*, November 25, 2001.

5 The *Guinness Book of World Records* lists *Baywatch* as the most watched TV show in the world of all time. Its audience is estimated to be 1.1 billion viewers. *Baywatch* is a U.S.-based television series about Los Angeles lifeguards. The show ran from 1989 to 2001.

6 Report of the U.S. Advisory Group on Public Diplomacy for the Arab and Muslim World, October 1, 2003, 24, http://www.state.gov/documents/organization/24882.pdf.

7 Walter Cronkite, *The Daily Herald*, October 12, 2003.

8 Barbara Ehrenreich, "Unstoppable Obama," *The Huffington Post*, February 14, 2008.

9 Ibid.

10 Public Law No. 87–256, known interchangeably as The Mutual Educational and Cultural Exchange Act or Fulbright-Hays Act, was signed into law in 1961 by President Kennedy. This Act consolidated U.S. international educational and cultural exchange activities and is still the basic legislative authority for government-sponsored exchange activities. A Bureau of Educational and Cultural Affairs (ECA) inside the State Department oversees the Fulbright and other U.S. government exchange programs, http://exchanges.state.gov.

11 Final Report, National Geographic-Roper Public Affairs, 2006 Geographic Literacy Study, May 2006, 15, http://www.nationalgeographic.com/roper2006/pdf/FINALReport2006GeogLitsurvey.pdf.

12 Ibid., 24.

13 Joe Johnson, "How Does Public Diplomacy Measure Up?" *Foreign Service Journal* 83, no. 10: 44–52, 2006.

14 President George W. Bush remarks, October 11, 2001.

15 Seong-Hun Yun, "Toward Public Relations Theory-Based Study of Public Diplomacy: Testing the Applicability of the Excellence Study," *Journal of Public Relations Research* 18, no. 4 (2006): 287–312.

16 "The Future of U.S. Public Diplomacy," 91st Congress Report No. 91–130, 1968.

17 B.H. Signitzer and T. Coombs, "Public Relations and Public Diplomacy: Conceptual Convergence," *Public Relations Review* 18, no. 2 (1992): 137–147.

18 Price B. Floyd, "Public Diplomacy is Not PR," *Los Angeles Times*, November 17, 2007.

19 Robert J. Callahan, "Neither Madison Avenue nor Hollywood," *Foreign Service Journal* 83, no. 10 (October 2006): 33–38.

20 Joseph Duffey, Senate Foreign Relations Committee, 1995. As cited in Rosaleen Smyth, "Mapping U.S. public diplomacy in the 21st century," *Australian Journal of International Affairs*, 55: 421–444.

21 James E. Grunig, "Public Relations and International Affairs: Effects, Ethics and Responsibility," *Journal of International Affairs*, 47, no. 1, (1993): 138–161.

22 Seong-Hun Yun, "Toward Public Relations Theory-Based Study of Public Diplomacy: Testing the Applicability of the Excellence Study," *Journal of Public Relations Research* 18, no. 4 (2006): 309.

2

Public Diplomacy and Strategic Communications

Philip M. Taylor

Public diplomacy has become the most debated topic in the field of international communications since the cultural imperialism thesis and calls for a new world information order in the 1970s and 1980s. In the United States especially, the debates have focused around the immediate post-9/11 response of "why do they hate us so much?," the alarming subsequent worldwide rise of anti-Americanism, and the long overdue realization that the Global War on Terror needed to be rebranded as a Long War for hearts and minds that can only be won as an "information war" rather than solely by military means. The final point of this trilogy was obvious to those who have studied or practiced public diplomacy for many years and who were particularly alarmed by the closure of the United States Information Agency (USIA) in 1999. That short-sighted step, however, was only part of the problem and may only be partly rectified by the creation of a proposed Centre for Global Engagement.[1] Much more fundamental is the undermining philosophy behind contemporary U.S. public diplomacy, cultivated in part by Joseph Nye's ideas on "soft power" in the 1990s, namely that "to know us is to love us" and that being attractive is sufficient to make others want to be like you.

The 9/11 hijackers knew the West only too well, many of them having been educated to a high level in Europe and having travelled to the United States before that fateful day. They were from the very target audience of traditional public diplomacy—the educated elites that might one day become movers and shakers in their own society. They knew all about western values by watching TV and movies and, far from appearing attractive, they saw how western societies were becoming more tolerant of drugs, divorce, extra-marital relations, and homosexuality. They derided Anglo-American notions about being a force for good in the world and they ignored western military "humanitarian" interventions on behalf of Muslims in Bosnia and Kosovo, instead concentrating upon western "violations" of Islam through supporting Israel in the Middle East, or the sanctions against Iraq, or the sending of "infidel" troops to the holy land of Mecca during Operation Desert Storm. As Al-Qaeda grew in confidence during the 1990s, such accusations largely went unchallenged as the U.S. downplayed its public diplomacy in the afterglow of victory in the Cold War. And, for the first time, terrorism could internationalize itself thanks to the arrival of the World Wide Web.

History may indeed conclude that these were some of the root causes of 9/11. What is already clear is that events since then have made the task of public diplomacy even harder and longer to achieve. Military interventions in Afghanistan and Iraq have reinforced the widespread belief that the West, led by the United States, is engaged in a "clash of civilizations" or a "crusade" against

Islam, and no amount of western denials can shift this perception in the minds of some people. After all, did not President Bush himself initially describe the war on terror as a "crusade?" Around this core message are woven an elaborate sub-set of reinforcing accusations: that 9/11 was a CIA-Mossad conspiracy to provide a pretext for a neoconservative war against Islam, which is why "4000 Jews failed to turn up for work in the World Trade Center;" that the collapse of the Twin Towers was a controlled explosion; that flight 93 was shot down by U.S. planes; and a whole host of other conspiracy theories—many of which originate from within the United States itself.

This is not to underestimate terrorist skill at propaganda. Al-Qaeda have proved particularly adept at opportunistic ploys—exploiting Abu Ghraib and Guantanamo with some skill, and even claiming that Hurricane Katrina was "God's revenge against the city of homosexuals." Their videotapes, websites, CDs, and DVDs target their audiences with a resonance and empathy that are often lacking in western information campaigns directed towards the Islamic world. Of course, they don't have to play by the same rules and they frequently deploy misinformation and disinformation. Their websites have proliferated enormously since 2001 and Al-Qaeda has its own video production unit known as As Sahab ("Clouds"). To give a flavour of one their video-productions, here are some quotes from the narration of the film, *Will of the Martyr*, praising one particular suicide bomber (which they call "martyrdom operations"):

> This Ummah has become subject to the Jews and Christians and has been enslaved by the United Nations Security Council which was created for the security of the *kufr* and its allies. This kufr has put into place a set of international laws against Allah's Shariah. This kufr has contaminated our educational systems with apostasy and heresy. It has trapped our economics in the chains of usury. It has undertaken its program of limiting our population and killed our offspring under the banner of family planning and consequently our sisters and daughters have become barren. And by sheltering under the labels of information technology and culture, it has unleashed a storm of decadence and immorality that has ruined the ethics and character of the young generation and resulted in the death of shame in Muslim societies. And under this very same global structure of kafir, both the theoretical and hands-on training of the thinkers and politicians of the Muslim world started on a basis of atheism, in order to make them capable of upholding Western ideologies and values under a cloak of democracy. With the help of secret conspiracies and clandestine revolutions, these international Tawagheel imposed upon this Ummah of Tawheed, factions and rulers who, instead of prostrating themselves to the Lord of the Ancient House, the Kaaba, prostrate themselves to the Lord of the White House. These apostate leaderships in turn imposed laws of kufr which are in open contradic- tion to our divine Shariah and explicitly ridicule Islamic traditions and our religious rights . . . By using these evil crusader rulers, the pharaoh of our age, America, proceed to personally conquer our lands by establishing military bases throughout the Islamic world. And so today the entire Muslim nation is subject to the tyranny and oppression of this Crusader disbelief . . . To avenge these atrocities of the kuffaar, there rose from the gate of Islam, Sindh, a brilliant star by the name of Hafiz Usman.

The video opens with graphics of a car reversing into an American patrol and exploding. It is skilfully edited with images, *inter alia*, of Israeli troops and their Palestinian "victims" and is overlaid with music and passages from the Koran. This is but one example from a range of "documentaries," news releases, and videotaped speeches, and even features films which Al-Qaeda releases on the internet, including YouTube. Depending on the target audience, As Sahab netcasts CNN-style new bulletins, mimics State Department press releases, and subtitles its state- ments. In other words, it is a much more impressive information campaign than anything yet seen by western governments.

When some observers suggest that the West is losing the information/propaganda war, it is usually because of the levels of anti-Americanism prompted by the latest opinion polls rather than by any sustained analysis of terrorist cyber-propaganda skills. But having said that, Al-Qaeda has not yet achieved its strategic goals which are essentially two-fold: the establishment of an Islamic Caliphate under Shariah law, and the destruction of the U.S. economy. On the other hand, the 2003 invasion of Iraq prompted bin Laden to reconfigure his Caliphate's capital city to Baghdad—thus creating a 9/11 Iraq connection when none had existed before. And the damage caused to the American and world economy by the sub-prime credit crisis from 2007 onwards may well result in another western self-fulfilling prophecy. Too often do western responses, especially with regard to incursions on civil liberties, play into Al-Qaeda's hands. But the real difference between terrorist propaganda and the western approach to information operations, psychological operations, public diplomacy, and public affairs (the four "pillars" of strategic communications) lies in the emphasis given to a long-term approach to achieving their retrospective vision in the information age.

Terrorism and the information age are synonymous. Terrorists would be relegated to the status of anarchists or even common criminals without the information society. By labeling the western response to 9/11 as a Global *War* on Terror or now The Long *War*, it empowered those criminals with the status of "warriors." Terrorists also know that their activity is 10% violence and 90% publicity, whereas the US response in Afghanistan and Iraq is 90% violence and 10% strategic communications. But inverting those figures would still not solve the problem. In the previous ideological conflict fought over a sustained period, it was clear that each side was working to a Grand Strategy. Following the Long Telegram, NSC 68, and other modifying directives, the American vision of how the Cold War would be won focused the activities of the USIA, Radio Free Europe, and all the other "voices" that were broadcast over the Iron Curtain. But, in this Long War of today, what does victory look like? Indeed, how is victory to be defined and what is an acceptable end state? Peace by negotiation? Unconditional surrender? The collapse of jihadist ideology cloaked by a religion?

Al-Qaeda is fighting a long war, and sees itself as having taken up the mantle of the Ummah's centuries-long struggle with the West. For bin Laden, Iraq and Afghanistan are the final battles of a thousand-year crusade against the infidel, an enemy he knows only too well from his time with the mujahedeen in the 1980s when he faced the Godless Russian communists before his Chechyen "brothers" continued the struggle against their capitalist successors. Even now, after a struggle lasting longer than World War II, there is no real western equivalent of a Grand (Information) Strategy. And the fault lies in the nature of contemporary democratic politics.

The way governments do information reflects the way they do democratic politics in the information age. When Harold Wilson famously quipped that a "week is a long time in politics," he recognized that the temporal reality for most modern elected politicians was measured in election cycles. This political short-termism is not necessarily conducive to a national long-term vision. And when Francis Fukiyama described the end of the Cold War as the "end of history," he should really have called it an end of ideology. Democratic politicians since then have moved to the middle or even switched stances completely, which is why so many neo-conservatives are former Democrats, or why Tony Blair's policies would sit quite easily alongside those of Margaret Thatcher. In other words, the objective of modern democratic politicians is to win at the next election rather than serve the nation's long-term interests. This absence of vision has characterized the western response to 9/11 and has impeded its strategic communications efforts against a terrorist network that may be opportunistic but is also driven by a vision of the future that is informed by a carefully crafted image of the past. You would never hear bin Laden respond to a tricky question with the words "Move On."

So the U.S. response to 9/11 was a military one rather than a carefully thought out political long-term vision about how to combat "terror." Although the U.S. reaction was understandable in many respects, European governments with long-standing experience of domestic terrorism had, by contrast, combated terrorism largely with police and intelligence services, not with armies, navies, and air forces. The American President, however, declared "a new kind of war" in which there could be no neutral ground: "You are either with us or against us." People who questioned this military response were either traitors or appeasers—distorting the past in the process. Appeasement in the 1930s was about *negotiating justifiable* grievances, and was abandoned immediately after the Germans invaded the rump of Czechoslovakia, thus incorporating non-Germans into the Third Reich for the first time, in March 1939. So using the appeasement label was as nonsensical as describing the response as a "war"—historically and legally defined as armed conflicts between two or more nation-states. Besides, *negotiating* with terrorists was not supposed be an option for democratic governments (unless you were the British in Northern Ireland!). Had the vision been clearer, had the long-term consequences of the military response been thought through, and had the rhetoric of war not been so polarized, then the job of strategic communications would have been much easier.

But, when a nation goes to war, its warriors are in the driving seat and the job of diplomacy—negotiation—is relegated to the back seat. This gave primacy to military information doctrines and strategies when perhaps public diplomacy should have been made the driver. For although the military are sometimes very good at tactical and operational information and psychological operations, they are less good at the strategic level. Vision that is limited to the area of operations and the commander's mission is not conducive to waging an information war in the global information space, which is what after all Al-Qaeda are doing. Moreover, as the Office of Strategic Influence (OSI) debacle showed in March 2002, certain aspects of information operations doctrine (particularly deception) fit very uneasily with the other pillars of strategic communications, especially public affairs. It needs to be remembered that news of the OSI's existence was leaked to the media from within the Pentagon itself, reflecting considerable philosophical differences about how to conduct an information war, never mind where and how to engage "the enemy."

Similar problems afflicted public diplomacy when Charlotte Beers was appointed Under Secretary for Public Diplomacy and Public Affairs in the State Department from October 2001 to March 2003. Beers was recruited from Madison Avenue and, for a while, many sought solutions in the marketing approach to what was then being called "perception management."[2] But the idea that a diverse nation with complex value systems could be "branded" and then "sold" in the same way as soap powder or (as Colin Powell famously stated) Uncle Ben's Rice reflected more of a business school approach to the problem rather than a diplomatic one. What people in the Muslim world were really not buying was the Bush Doctrine, not the United States of America and its Universalist values.

Once again, we can see a flawed approach to what was then (in 2006–07) renamed strategic communications. The third element of the Bush Doctrine, the selling of democracy, was almost as defective as the "to know us is to love us" approach to public diplomacy. Strategic communications should really be about explaining what kind of people you really are rather than telling "them" to be more like "us." And nearly all communications experts are agreed that the most effective form of communication is face-to-face. But even this can be handled badly if the American face is that of the "ugly American"—and commercial television programme exports like *The Jerry Springer Show*, or Private Lindey England's trophy pictures from Abu Ghraib certainly don't help to explain how Americans can actually be a force for good in the world. Nor did the treatment of Muslim visitors at U.S. airports, nor false reports of the Koran being flushed down the toilet at Guantanamo, nor a whole host of "propaganda own goals."

There are now signs of recognition that western strategic communications needs a clearer vision, that its pillars are in fact more horizontal than vertical, that turf wars between different branches of government only play into the hands of the enemy, and that the principal battle-space in the information war is the internet rather than the mass media. News organizations, by and large, do not broadcast beheading videos. However, the main problem now confronting any public diplomacy emanating from western governmental sources is that of credibility. This is where the issues relating to claims about the Saddam–9/11 connection and weapons of mass destruction have done most harm. They were short-term political justifications for the "regime change" conflict in Iraq, but the long-term damage to Anglo-American credibility is immeasurable. No amount of "Shared Values" campaigns will fix this in the long term. Moreover, the British decision to place public diplomacy emphasis on climate change as a means of bridging the "gulf of misunderstanding" (Tony Blair's phrase) between the West and the Islamic world is also doomed to failure. Now that countries like China and India, but also Muslim countries like Malaysia, are prospering from economic growth, messages that suggest that they forego their new-found wealth by not buying gas-guzzling SUVs when the West has been polluting the atmosphere with them for a century and a half will only be greeted with scepticism. They will sound like a new form of neo-cultural imperialism, of imposing western values and views, and will be seen as yet another example of western hypocrisy and selectivity. Like *Hi* magazine and the Office of Global Communications, they will be counter-productive to the strategic communications effort.

This handbook should provide some fresh ideas about the way forward and hopefully ensure that the practice of public diplomacy does not become bogged down in renewed debates about cultural imperialism.

Notes

1 Defense Science Board Task Force on Strategic Communication, Report on Strategic Communication in the 21st Century, Chair, Vincent Vitto, January, 2008, 1–149.
2 See, e.g., T.C. Helmus, C. Paul, and R.W. Glenn, *Enlisting Madison Avenue: The marketing approach to earning popular support in theatres of operation* (Santa Monica, CA: RAND, 2007).

Part 1

The Context of Public Diplomacy

3

Public Diplomacy before Gullion

The Evolution of a Phrase

Nicholas J. Cull

Every academic discipline has its certainties, and in the small field of public diplomacy studies it is a truth universally acknowledged that the term "public diplomacy" was coined in 1965 by Edmund Gullion, dean of the Fletcher School of Law and Diplomacy at Tufts University and a distinguished retired foreign service officer, when he established an Edward R. Murrow Center of Public Diplomacy. An early Murrow Center brochure provided a convenient summary of Gullion's concept:

> Public diplomacy . . . deals with the influence of public attitudes on the formation and execution of foreign policies. It encompasses dimensions of international relations beyond traditional diplomacy; the cultivation by governments of public opinion in other countries; the interaction of private groups and interests in one country with another; the reporting of foreign affairs and its impact on policy; communication between those whose job is communication, as diplomats and foreign correspondents; and the process of intercultural communications.[1]

This essay will endeavor to look at the forgotten pre-history of this phrase in reportage and diplomatic discourse, a task made possible thanks to the creation of fully text searchable versions of historical newspapers including the *New York Times, Washington Post*, and *Christian Science Monitor*. While this analysis bears out that Gullion was the first to use the phrase in its modern meaning, it also reveals that Gullion's phrase was not so much a new coinage in 1965 as a fresh use of an established phrase. Ironically, this new use of an old term was necessary because the even older term—propaganda, which Gullion confessed he preferred—had accumulated so many negative connotations.[2]

The earliest use of the phrase "public diplomacy" to surface is actually not American at all but in a leader piece from the London *Times* in January 1856. It is used merely as a synonym for civility in a piece criticizing the posturing of President Franklin Pierce. "The statesmen of America must recollect," the *Times* opined, "that, if they have to make, as they conceive, a certain impression upon us, they have also to set an example for their own people, and there are few examples so catching as those of public diplomacy."[3]

The first use quoted by the *New York Times* was in January 1871, in reporting a Congressional debate. Representative Samuel S. Cox (a Democrat from New York, and a former journalist) spoke in high dudgeon against secret intrigue to annex the Republic of Dominica, noting he believed in "open, public diplomacy." It was a use which anticipated the major articulation of the phrase 35 years later in the Great War.[4]

During the Great War the phrase "public diplomacy" was widely used to describe a cluster of new diplomatic practices. These practices ranged from successive German statements on submarine warfare policy, through public declarations of terms for peace, to Woodrow Wilson's idealistic vision—as expressed in the opening point of his "fourteen points" speech of January 8, 1918—of an entire international system founded on "open covenants of peace, openly arrived at." Many writers at the time preferred the phrase "open diplomacy" for this, but "public diplomacy" had its adherents and seems to have been given further currency by reporting French use of the phrase *diplomatie publique*.[5]

The *New York Times* used the phrase on May 9, 1916 in its coverage of the so-called Sussex Pledge, a declaration issued on May 4 by the German government to restrict its submarine warfare. Reviewing U.S. reactions to the pledge the *New York Times* quoted an editorial from that day's *Boston Herald*, which declared: "One of the evils of public diplomacy is the necessity of continued letter-writing, in which the responsible head of each nation must save his face with his own people as well as communicate his purposes to the other side."[6] The observation has its echo today in the problems leaders face now that all their domestic utterances can be heard round the world.

The third use of the phrase "public diplomacy" in the *New York Times* and first use in the *Washington Post* came on December 28, 1917, again quoting an editorial from elsewhere, this time from *Berliner Tageblatt* commenting on the Russo-German peace negotiations at Brest-Litovsk. The paper noted portentously: "nothing can so shake the wall of arms as the new public diplomacy."[7]

On February 11, 1918, President Wilson himself used the phrase in his so-called "Four Principles" speech to Congress, in which he relayed the response of the German Chancellor, Georg von Hertling, to the fourteen points, noting: "He accepts . . . the principle of public diplomacy."[8] Wilson's phrase was adapted from Hertling's original statement to the Reichstag on January 24, 1918 in which he endorsed what he called "*Publizität der diplomatischen Abmachungen*" (rendered "publicity of diplomatic agreements" in the London *Times*).[9] Reports of Wilson's speech occasioned the first use of the term "public diplomacy" in the *Christian Science Monitor*, and the only use of the phrase in the *Los Angeles Times* between 1899 and 1965.[10] In July 1918, the U.S. Senate considered the issue of "public diplomacy" in connection with a bold proposal by Senator William E. Borah (R–Idaho) that its debates over treaties henceforth be public. The proposal was defeated by 50 votes to 23.[11]

The phrase "public diplomacy" endured in its idealistic Wilsonian open covenants' sense throughout the interwar years in the rhetoric of the internationalists like James Shotwell and Clarence Streit, and in similarly inclined editorials in the pages of the *Christian Science Monitor*.[12] In 1928, a *Christian Science Monitor* reporter, J. Roscoe Drummond proclaimed an "era of public diplomacy" in a prize-winning essay, "the press and public diplomacy," which stressed the moral duty of the news media to report international affairs accurately and dispassionately so as to reduce tensions.[13] Its idealism became increasingly remote from the realities of the deteriorating international scene. A correspondent of the London *Times* described the arrival of new British troops in the Saarland in December 1934 with marching bands and abundant good humor towards the locals as "a striking demonstration of public diplomacy" in the face of defiant displays of Nazi banners.[14] In 1936, an Associated Press dispatch from Paris noted that Leftists were applauding the pledge of the new (and short-lived) French premier Albert Sarraut to "use 'public diplomacy' in foreign affairs."[15] The term was seldom used during the Second World War.

The post-war years saw both a reassessment of Wilson and a reemergence of the term public diplomacy. In 1946, the Belgian foreign minister Paul-Henri Spaak spoke enthusiastically of "this age of public diplomacy" during the inaugural session of the United Nations (U.N.) General Assembly in October.[16] In Britain the London *Times* denounced public diplomacy as one of the "catch-phrases and slogans masquerading as principles of foreign policy," and endorsed a call from diplomat and politician Harold Nicolson for a return to private diplomacy.[17]

By the 1950s the usage of the term public diplomacy noticeably shifted towards the realm of international information and propaganda. It was not so much that the term was being used differently but rather that diplomacy was being practiced and understood differently, and key diplomatic events were now recognized as explicit works of public performance. In 1953, Walter Lippmann observed in his widely syndicated column that some diplomats now "might argue that practice of public diplomacy and of propaganda and of psychological warfare had become such a plague" that key Soviet–American talks should be held in private.[18] In a more positive vein, in a speech in the summer of 1958, the UN Secretary General Dag Hammarskjöld declared:

> The value of public diplomacy in the United Nations will depend to a decisive extent on how far the responsible spokesmen find it possible to rise above a narrow tactical approach to the politics of international life, and to speak as men for aspirations and hopes which are those of all mankind.[19]

Observers of the diplomatic scene including Louis Halle, veteran British diplomat Lord Strang, or James Reston of the *New York Times* now used the term public diplomacy to evoke the element of showmanship in the diplomacy of Khrushchev, Kennedy and others.[20] As the *practice* of public diplomacy had come to overlap with propaganda, Gullion needed only to carry the *term* public diplomacy a relatively short distance to relocate it entirely in its new meaning as an alternative for propaganda.

For many years the term had limited traction outside the beltway, its old "open diplomacy" use also remained in circulation in the work of some writers like *Washington Post* diplomatic correspondent, Murrey Marder.[21] The term did not figure in an academic book title until 1972.[22]

The reason that the term public diplomacy took off in 1965 was that there was a real need for such a concept in Washington, DC. A dozen years into its life, the United States Information Agency needed an alternative to the anodyne term information or malignant term propaganda: a fresh turn of phrase upon which it could build new and benign meanings. Gullion's term "public diplomacy" covered every aspect of USIA activity and a number of the cultural and exchange functions jealously guarded by the Department of State. The phrase gave a respectable identity to the USIA career officer, for it was one step removed from the "vulgar" realm of public relations and by its use of the term "diplomacy," explicitly enshrined the USIA alongside the State Department as a legitimate organ of American foreign relations. The term itself became an argument for USIA and against the rump of exchange and cultural work at State. If public diplomacy existed as a variety of diplomacy in the modern world—the argument ran—then surely the United States needed a dedicated agency to conduct this work, and that agency was best structured to control all work in the field. The term paid dividends a decade later. In 1978, USIA was reorganized according to the logic of the new terminology and at last acquired dominion over the entire range of American activity in the information field. The interdependence of the concept of public diplomacy and USIA is suggested by the fact that following the demise of the USIA in 1999, the Murrow Center at Tufts became—and remains—the Murrow Center for International Information and Communications. Yet the phrase had, by 1999, more currency than a single agency or a single country. It was destined to live on.

The Reagan years saw both an increased expenditure on public diplomacy and a widening use of the term in congressional hearings, scholarship, journalism, and among practitioners. The Reagan White House provided an unhelpful challenge to the dominant benign definition when it created its own "Office of Public Diplomacy" to oversee the domestic selling of support to the Contra rebels in Nicaragua. The term hence made an unwelcome appearance at the Iran-Contra hearings.[23]

During the course of the 1990s the term public diplomacy finally entered common use in foreign policy circles overseas. In Britain, for example, the Blair government established a Public Diplomacy Strategy Board. In the years following the attacks of September 11, 2001 it finally entered American public consciousness. In the wake of the Asian tsunami even President George W. Bush used the phrase, though telling an ABC interviewer, "Our public diplomacy efforts aren't . . . aren't very robust and aren't very good compared to the public diplomacy efforts of those who would like to spread hatred and . . . vilify the United States," he went on—with an excruciating lack of tact—to suggest that America's tsunami aid might make a difference to this.[24] The highly publicized appointment and teething troubles of the new Under Secretary of State for Public Diplomacy and Public Affairs, Karen Hughes, gave the final impetus to its currency within the United States, though elsewhere in the world the term could still produce blank looks.

And what lessons can be learned from the 90-year career of the phrase "public diplomacy?" Practitioners and scholars of public diplomacy as presently defined should at least consider that their interlocutors may understand nothing by the term, or still understand the term in its 1856 or 1916 meaning, or may already understand the term in a 2016 sense of which we are not yet aware.

Notes

1 The Murrow Center quote comes from the "what is Public Diplomacy?" page http://fletcher. tufts.edu/murrow/public-diplomacy.html. I am grateful to Prof. Lee McKnight, then director of the Murrow Center, for his account of its origins, given over the phone on March 13, 2001, and to John Brown for his comments on the entire essay.

2 Robert F. Delaney and John S. Gibson, eds., *American Public Diplomacy: The Perspective of Fifty Years* (Medford, MA: The Edward R. Murrow Center of Public Diplomacy, Fletcher School of Law and Diplomacy/Lincoln Filene Center for Citizenship and Public Affairs, 1967), 31. Also cited in John Brown, 'The Anti-Propaganda Tradition in the United States,' *Bulletin Board for Peace*, June 29, 2003, http://www.publicdiplomacy.org/19.htm

3 "The American president with a laudable desire," *Times* (London), January 15, 1856, 6.

4 "Forty-First Congress, Third Session," *New York Times*, January 20, 1871, 2.

5 "L'Allemagne fait lancer par l'Autriche une offre inacceptable de négociations secrètes," *Petit Parisien*, September 16, 1918, 1, which was quoted in translation in a *New York Times* story on September 17, 1918.

6 "An Understanding of the German note," *Boston Herald*, May 9, 1916, 12, cited on p.2.

7 "Forms outline of future peace," *New York Times*, December 28, 1917, 1. This same quotation was the first use of the phrase in the *Washington Post*, ("Berlin Socialist organ calls program too vague," *Washington Post*, December 28, 1917, 4).

8 "President's address to Congress a reply to Hertling's and Czernin's peace terms," *Washington Post*, February 12, 1918, 5.

9 See original text online at http://www.stahlgewitter.com/18_01_24.htm and fully translated in "Enemy on Allied aims," *Times* (London), January 26, 1918, 7.

10 "President finds equivocation in Hertling reply," *Christian Science Monitor*, February 12, 1918, 1. The *Monitor* also ran one of the first academic uses of the term in an essay by the University of Chicago professor Samuel Harper in May 1918. See Samuel Harper, "Russia tending to Public Diplomacy," *Christian Science Monitor*, May 7, 1918, 7.

11 "Public diplomacy opposed in Senate," *Washington Post*, June 11, 1918, 3; "Open treaties beaten," *Washington Post*, June 13, 1918, 2.

12 "New arms treaty arouses interest," *New York Times*, June 19, 1924, 10; "The power of Public Diplomacy," *Christian Science Monitor*, May 12, 1928, 18; "Shotwell reveals world rule plan," *New York Times*, May 19, 1929, 18; "Fathers and sons dine at Columbia," *New York Times*, February 13, 1931, 27; "Press and diplomacy," *Christian Science Monitor*, April 14, 1931, 6; Clarence K. Streit, "Arms debate set for full parley," *New York Times*, May 13, 1933, 2; Clarence K. Streit, "League ends Balkan row . . .," *New York Times*, December 11, 1934, 1, 14.

13 J. Roscoe Drummond, "The Press and Public Diplomacy," *Christian Science Monitor*, September 18, 1928, 20.

14 "Good feeling in Saar," *Times* (London), December 24, 1934, 10.

15 Associated Press, "Sarraut regime gains victory in test ballot," *Washington Post*, February 1, 1936, 4.

16 Arthur G. Altschul, "Addresses by Truman, Impellitteri and Spaak at opening of the UN assembly," October 24, 1946, 2.

17 Leader: "Diplomacy, public and private," *Times* (London), March 14, 1946, 5.

18 Walter Lippmann, "Today and tomorrow: Talking about talking," *Washington Post*, November 19, 1953, 15.

19 Dag Hammarskjöld, "The UN and the major challenges which face the world community," *UN Review*, 4 (June 1958), cited in Richard Hoggart, *An Idea and Its Servants: UNESCO from within*, (London: Oxford University Press, 1978), 190.

20 Louis J. Halle, "The coming test for personal diplomacy," *New York Times Magazine*, August 23, 1959, 7; James Reston, "Kennedy and the American Diplomats," *New York Times*, December 21, 1960, 29; C.L.Sultzberger, "The strategy gap and the two K's," *New York Times*, May 31, 1961, 32; Lord Strang, "Harsh new language in diplomacy," *New York Times Magazine*, April 15, 1962, 14; James Reston, "Mona Lisa approach to diplomacy," *New York Times*, February 11, 1963, 6.

21 For continued "old uses," see Murrey Marder, "Danger of greater war may bring reappraisal in Washington, Moscow," *Washington Post*, January 9, 1966, A1; Murrey Marder, "Nixon dwells on Russia's role," *Washington Post*, March 5, 1969, A11.

22 Glen Fisher, *Public Diplomacy and the Behavioral Sciences* (Bloomington, IN: Indiana University Press, 1972); Gregory Henderson et al., *Public Diplomacy and Political Change: Four case studies: Okinawa, Peru, Czechoslovakia, Guinea* (New York: Praeger, 1973).

23 100th Congress, 1st session, H. Rept. 100–433/S. Rept. 110–216, *Report of the Congressional Committees Investigating the Iran Contra Affair*, November 1987, 34; for summary of these activities see *Public Diplomacy and Covert Propaganda: The declassified record of Ambassador Otto Juan Reich*, edited by Thomas Blanton (Washington, D.C.: National Security Archive briefing book, March 21, 2001, http://www.gwu.edu/~nsarchiv/NSAEBB/NSAEBB40/.

24 David Bazinet, "Bush: Victims thank U.S." *Daily News* (New York), January 14, 2005, 30.

4

Public Diplomacy as Loss of World Authority

Michael Vlahos

In America's Global War on Terrorism, or GWOT, what is called "public diplomacy" represents not the least, but rather a central element of U.S. failure. Arguably, public diplomacy has helped advance a historic loss of American world authority. It did not begin that way. Confidently, the GWOT advanced a revision of that authority, through which the United States' world position would be made permanent and constitutional. Instead, aided by its public diplomacy, it has achieved the opposite. America's recent experience in world revision followed by loss of authority can profit from the public diplomacy of Napoleonic France and early Showa Japan. Their experiences in strategic persuasion have much to tell us today.

"Public diplomacy"—or "propaganda" or "strategic communication"—is essential daily business in regime politics. Yet sometimes it becomes more than normal government grind, because sometimes a great notion moves a regime to equally great enterprise: like war.

Wars require grand strategy—conceptualization at a higher and more acute level than daily business—and successful grand strategy is as dependent on persuasion as it is on money, manpower, or the military.

Hence World War II and the Cold War depended on friendly persuasion just as much as on enforced submission. This truth is embedded in their mythic status. The GWOT boisterously flagged the banderole of both World War II and Cold War, as if to say, "We use the same language, thus our war is both worthy successor and just as sure to succeed. It promises indeed to be equally mythic."

But the GWOT has failed. More than that, the war has undermined the achievements of the two great wars it sought to imitate and extend. World War II and the Cold War revised the world order and made the United States the (informal) world authority.[1] The attempt to make this same authority formal and permanent may result in its permanent loss. In this, public diplomacy must bear the central responsibility.

The GWOT as World Revision

Why did the GWOT undermine American world authority? Moreover, why did the surefire language and arguments of World War II and the Cold War—repackaged for the Great American–Muslim War—fail to persuade? Furthermore, how did GWOT public diplomacy come to actually diminish American authority?

First, the GWOT represented a different model. It was not a national war, a people's war, like World War II and the Cold War (to Vietnam). Moreover while World War II mobilized the "Free World" in collective urgency, the Cold War sought the same mobilization as a less aggressive "protracted conflict." In contrast the GWOT was a more classically imperial enterprise. It was wholly government-owned, and thus risks and rewards were the regime's own. What was asked from the citizenry was passive support and non-interference, as in the President's famous adjuration to the American people to "go about your business."

Its approach to "world commonwealth" partners from World War II and the Cold War was similar. They were expected to support the enterprise, but active participation was not required. This was a practical issue, because the U.S. Government wished to retain total control of the show. Those who chose to participate, however, on U.S. terms, would of course be rewarded as members of the club of "the willing." This too is reminiscent of imperial ventures.

The transformation lay in replacing a commonwealth world order in which American authority was mostly informal with a GWOT-driven, more formal world order. The driver of this transformation was the legal concept of preemption, of preventive war. This differed from previous jurisprudence on war, like just war theory, in that it was not posited as a doctrine to be applied universally. In contrast it was declared as a right of the United States only, which trusted friends and allies would be allowed to share. But we would be the world's "decider."[2]

Certainly the September 11, 2001 attacks made preventive war seem the only possible solution. But the process of implementation was also understood as creating a new world order. For the sake of humanity and world security, the authority to make war, we were told, must be vested in a single, unimpeachably high-minded state, with a "coalition" of other states in support.

Notice that coalition was sought as a desired but not as a necessary condition of authority. If America's old allies came along, their support would make the transformation smooth and painless. It would also create a rhetorical bridge—a comforting apparent continuity—from a world of informal single authority to one of constitutional single authority. But it was not required.

Why shift away from a supremely successful model? Simply, it was argued, a new world of evil vs. civilization made necessary a new imprimatur for American authority. Necessary U.S. actions themselves would extend and solidify its basis. Humanity would be persuaded not only by the necessity for U.S. action—so incontestably sealed by 9/11—but also by the triumphant success of each succeeding U.S. action.[3]

But military interventions and occupations were simply to kick-start a mightier story of world transformation. It was announced that the United States, through Iraq, would "transform the Middle East." But explicitly also, in the President's Second Inaugural Address, he declared that America would also transform the world:

> Our country has accepted obligations that are difficult to fulfill, and would be dishonorable to abandon. Yet because we have acted in the great liberating tradition of this nation, tens of millions have achieved their freedom. And as hope kindles hope, millions more will find it. By our efforts, we have lit a fire as well—a fire in the minds of men. It warms those who feel its power, it burns those who fight its progress, and one day this untamed fire of freedom will reach the darkest corners of our world. . . . So it is the policy of the United States to seek and support the growth of democratic movements and institutions in every nation and culture, with the ultimate goal of ending tyranny in our world.[4]

The act of metamorphosis was inarguable. It was the *force majeure* of historical destiny touched off by the selective use of military force. There was much more to this than simply the "shock and awe" of righteous military takeover but also, just as critically, the unstoppable force of "reconstruction." American sacred narrative—from Civil War radical republicans to Woodrow

Wilson to Marshall and MacArthur—assumed that the enemy would always be uplifted and redeemed.

No one questioned this certainty on the eve of Iraq. We were told: "Just look at Germany and Japan and Korea today!" The force of American virtue in the peace to follow righteous war was, just as surely, pure historical inevitability.

We should appreciate the full task of public diplomacy in this war. It had to sell an audacious vision of world transformation to the American people. This vision went well beyond defeating "terrorism" or reforming Islam, and so public diplomacy needed to go well beyond just reaching out to Muslims. It was centrally about connecting with Americans and selling them on a new world.

On the eve of war *The Atlantic Monthly* admiringly let James Woolsey, a key administration booster, hold forth:

> If you only look forward, you can see how hard it would be to do, [Woolsey said]. Everybody can say, "Oh, *sure*, you're going to democratize the Middle East." But if you look at what we and our allies have done with the three world wars of the twentieth century—two hot, one cold—and what we've done in the interstices, we've already achieved this for two thirds of the world. If you look back at what has happened in less than a century, then getting the Arab world plus Iran moving in the same direction looks a lot less awesome. It's not Americanizing the world. It's Athenizing it. And it is doable.[5]

Here another aspect of GWOT public diplomacy comes into sharp relief. The GWOT pioneered a new kind of public diplomacy, in which "new media" is orchestrated for a domestic persuasion campaign in which the antique, formal information arms of government play only a supporting role. The main body of GWOT public effort was through ostensibly "private" media—talk radio, the Fox News Network, go-to, plugged-in, on-message "commentators" (like Woolsey), and mass network sites like "Lucianne.com" and "FreeRepublic.com."

Yet noisy non-government clamor masked a deep coordination between private media and the White House. Much of this, in the case of talk radio hosts and a bosom commentator fraternity, was informal. Some of it, however, was practically institutionalized. For example, Fox coordinates with the White House every day to make sure its news "talking points" are correctly "on-message."

There is nothing sinister here or even secret—daily message-coordination memos have been leaked and viewed across the web.[6] "However the full extent of White House orchestration was revealed by the *New York Times* in April, 2008. Throughout the course of the war, the administration was able to turn the vast majority of television's military analysts into virtual retainers of the Pentagon, to the point where they were routinely referred to a 'surrogates' and 'force multipliers.'"[7] This late revelation underscores how GWOT public diplomacy was all about persuading the American people—at a new level of sophistication. Their support was the prize. Americans—not Muslims or Euros—were the real transformation target. *Americans had to be sold on the metamorphosis of their own world authority.*

It was a giant story which none of the broadcast media ever owned up to, even after it was exposed in the NYT and other remaining print titans!

Now the failure of GWOT public diplomacy should be clear. Traditional strategic communications—focusing on the enemy and their world—was simply not central to the new grand strategy. Indeed it was suspect for how it had represented and helped sustain a despised "liberal" model of informal world order. Hence established public diplomacy was an adjunct of the main effort. It would be no more than a reseller of core domestic messages: hawking "transformation" and "freedom" and "democracy," *as Americans embraced them,* to Muslims.

Old-style public diplomacy was no more than an ornament of a grand strategy of persuasion at home and *force majeure* abroad. Yet in this new world on the eve of the invasion of Iraq, public diplomacy—however transformed—was still critically important. Thus the subsequent failure of public diplomacy still needs to be examined. Why was the old downgraded? How did both old and new GWOT public diplomacy help unleash catastrophic and unforeseen effects? History, of course, has suggestive answers.

Public Diplomacy and World Revision in History

Napoleonic France and early Showa Japan starkly reveal earlier failures of public diplomacy in grand strategy. Even more suggestively, both bear close resemblance to Bush administration failure in the GWOT. Of course this is not meant in the slightest to suggest any moral equivalence; just as it does not deny the ironies they share.

Napoleon at the end of the 18th century and Japan in the 1930s each sought to decisively revise their world order. Both employed public diplomacy to make the case why this was a good thing, and why established order should accept their revisionist offer. But persuading others was at best a mere helpmate to decision through battle. Their best arguments were saved for their own people. They ignored how hard it might be to revise world order without also having a really good argument for the world. Selling transformation at home was what really mattered.

Hence Napoleon's new order needed to transform revolutionary narrative. The French Revolution had created a new identity for France and the possibility of a new identity for mankind. Napoleon boldly turned the heroic collective man on his head. Through the brushstrokes of David we can see the idea of revolution visibly remake itself: from his *Oath of the Horatii* to the massive *Distribution of the Eagle Standards*.

In the first painting the republican *Horatii*, as brothers and father, embody a fateful and solemn commitment of the people to collective governance. In the *Eagle Standards*, however, Napoleon is both Roman emperor made modern—the ultimate image of universal authority—but also the Revolution's heroic image of Man's will to be God. He accepts the acclamation of the very same people who took the republican oath—France embodied as his army—now taking an oath to his supreme authority. What a transformation of revolutionary vision!

Early Showa Japan also decided, after a sometimes violent domestic debate, to remake the world order in Asia. Perhaps modern Japan had been too successful too soon. After all it had managed to emerge strong and respected out of medieval shadows in an era where all its Asian neighbors had been enslaved by European imperialism. Furthermore in one audacious leap Japan defeated the Russian Empire and emerged the only non-white great power. Quickly taking another step forward, Japan then joined the Allies in 1914 and came out of the Great War era anointed as one of the three world powers. Quite a record for just three generations, especially for those still-living *Genro* (archons-elder statesmen) who had originally brought Nippon out of isolation.

But this fantastic national narrative carried within it the seeds of self-destruction. If Japan had bootstrapped itself to world greatness by the deed, now it was suddenly susceptible to being swept away by the power of the deed. Thus in the 1930s Japanese strategists believed they might go even further, and achieve a world revision, again to be won by the deed: by others submitting to Japanese main force.[8]

Why compare GWOT public diplomacy with the propaganda of Napoleon and early Showa Japan? To begin, all three pursued a similar objective: world order revision. Moreover, their persuasion strategies remarkably shared the same foundation. First, they could not disentangle domestic persuasion from external persuasion—and the domestic effort was always dominant. Second, public diplomacy took a back seat in grand strategies that relied on the power of the deed (battle), with the word as its helpmate. Third, although they all talked a strategic goal of relationship, they all walked a strategy of submission. The failure of this contradiction was in each case abetted by public diplomacy.

The Inner Life of GWOT Public Diplomacy

GWOT public diplomacy can be compared to Napoleonic and Showa propaganda through five tropes that reveal a shared character:

- It was the public diplomacy of military superpower, designed to enhance the power of battle, and its "shock and awe," as the core persuasion strategy.
- The main effort and true "center of gravity" for public diplomacy were the nation, and its people and politics.
- Thus it did not matter that its rhetoric was self-defeating internationally, because only the domestic audience really mattered. This left the world to be persuaded by the deed.
- Rhetoric flowed from a non-reality-based world view. Hence public diplomacy's cynical appropriation of idealism and altruism—in both national ethos and the contemporary spirit of the age—was not seen as ultimately self-defeating.
- Public diplomacy's often-boastful tone reflected a deeply insecure approach to world relationships—with friend, foe, and neutral alike. Submission was preferred over anything approaching an equal relationship.

"Shock and Awe" Authority

Napoleon personally fought 60 battles. They were his canvas and palette, and until the very end he believed that battle was the only real political authority. At the height of his enterprise, who could deny this glittering truth? A single *grande bataille* like Austerlitz after all could bring an entire coalition of enemies to their knees:

> In less than four hours, an army of one hundred thousand men, commanded by the emperors of Russia and Austria, has either been cut to pieces or dispersed. . . . See how, in two months, this third coalition has been beaten and unstrung; peace cannot be far off.[9]

Likewise modern Japanese believed that the entirety of their world status and authority was the creation of *deus ex machina* battle—codified by myth ancient and modern. Napoleon had Austerlitz, and Japan had Tsushima. They were in the early modern sense the prototypes of "shock and awe."

We should remember that the invasion of Iraq was to be, in equal measure, a capstone event in an unfolding narrative mythically marked by great military victories yet to come. The anticipated experience was not simply imitating World War II but, rather, completing its sacred story.

Moreover, so we were told, the U.S. military had become gods of war.[10] The mere demonstration of American power would bring submission and enable "transformation" of the primitive and medieval societies of the Middle East. "Shock and awe" was no military doctrine; rather it was the centerpiece of GWOT public diplomacy.

Believing that transformation lay in battle subtly led to a public diplomacy built around triumphalist battle reporting. Hence, "embedding" journalists during the "Iraq War" was the American equivalent of on-scene battle artists like Gros or Lejeune, whose electric canvases, like our video, was France's eyewitness testament to regime victory and transcendence.[11] Video-embedding the American people with U.S. troops was a vicarious and satisfying participation of the people in their regime's victory. It was the essence of GWOT public diplomacy.

But also like Napoleon, our command of war distorted history and human change. This soon began to show in every video frame. Just as Napoleon clung to the belief of eventual victory by battle alone, so we clung to the hope that we could still achieve World War II-like transformation—as in Germany and Japan—even after years of country-imploding insurgency told us the opposite. We still yearned for the video-venue of the raw fight, as though the firing line on these mean streets was where the war would be won.

In this overheated, inner-directed story, public diplomacy directed at Muslims, and specifically Iraqis, told a different tale. It combined a somnambulist's recitation of World War II propaganda tropes, crudely handled "psyops" (psychological operations) like the Lincoln Group's bribing of local journalists to push out propaganda,[12] and the extreme anti-U.S. counter-narrative of our unconscious creation: Abu Ghraib.

It's All About Your Own

Yet there is no denying that inner-directed domestic public diplomacy works. Early Napoleonic public diplomacy was highly creative. Moreover it was effective not just among the French people, but also across Europe. It was even effective among France's bitterest *ancien régime* enemies. Feudal princes were going down across Germany, new republics rising in Holland and Italy. This brief period, at the very end of the 18th century, represented perhaps the moment when French revolutionary—and world-revising—goals might be achieved.[13]

But then Napoleon went "imperial"—he sought to make French world authority constitutional, with Napoleon holding the orb and scepter. Formal order revision in effect meant not merely the submission but the eventual replacement of the *anciens régimes*. France became a focus of resistance rather than affiliation, not simply for the big powers like Austria and Prussia and Russia, but also small states like Portugal, and notably a debilitating popular insurgency in Spain.

The post-revolutionary French sacred narrative was also inner-directed, at the expense of other European publics. If "France was now the 'torch-bearer' of civilization,"[14] as Stuart Woolf describes, the French Revolution consolidated this appropriation of the role of vector of civilization because of the universality of its political message of "liberty" and "equality." And in the subsequent Napoleonic years the reforms imposed by France on the territories it conquered confirmed the claim to the identification of civilization and French nation. Now, more than ever, the French nation not only incorporated the universal values of civilization but was, in the most literal sense, the carrier of these values to less fortunate peoples.[15]

Naturally this did not make for the most persuasive public diplomacy with others. What gave holy focus to the national effort came across as arrogance and contempt across Europe.[16] Yet the state use of this French "sacred narrative"—including its emphasis on "liberty" and "civilization," its claim to universal authority, and its deep inner-directedness—prefigure the essence of GWOT public diplomacy.

The more beleaguered the French enterprise, the greater the sacrifice demanded of the French people—the more focused propaganda became on persuading the French themselves. One way to do this was to make the war an existential, if still high-minded, struggle: a struggle of us vs. them for the future of French—and thus Western—civilization. As Masséna declared: "Now only the efforts of France can stop Europe from falling back into the barbarism into which her enemies are plunging her."[17]

Another was to appeal to a local sense of existentialism, shoring up the most intimate sinews of the *patrie*. War means we must persevere and make it through as a society. Thus a failing war drives public diplomacy to draw upon essential identity to secure the reserves of national energy needed to finish the job. Napoleon's regime always struggled with resistance to conscription, but us vs. them appeals only undercut whatever shred of persuasive cachet lingered in the outer world.[18] After 2004, like the later French empire, GWOT "home" public diplomacy tried the same dramatic appeal.

Showa propaganda also came to focus on the existential do-or-die—us against them. But it made another existential promise: that through sacrifice national purity would be reified in a sort of collective transcendence. Japan's struggle was inescapably about them. Think of war with the other as a drama of identity politics, and thus a passage leading to national realization. The Showa state operated within a larger cultural context where questions of Western modernity and an idealized Japan dominated. Hence state propaganda could not escape, as Kevin Doak tells us, "the primacy of ethnicity that wartime ethnology so artfully enshrined in public discourse under the multiethnic empire."[19] Issues of American identity crowd our discourse in the GWOT too.

With war as a metaphor for internalized struggle, Japan could not even maintain a pretense of wider altruism toward other Asian peoples. Japanese public diplomacy (even to the "friendly other") was thus never free of the taint of insincerity.[20]

Moreover both Napoleon's and Showa propaganda, through a primary domestic focus, sought to use the war paradigm of existential struggle against the other as a way to solidify the regime. Louise Young describes how this operated during the Manchurian Incident in 1931:

> . . . government propaganda . . . greatly strengthened the view that Japan stood alone and isolated in a hostile world . . . the rhetoric of international embattlement provided a rallying point for political consensus at home about the army's direction of government. . . . The official story wove both images of Chinese aggression and Japanese martyrdom into a constructed narrative of national unity in which "the people" stood together against their enemies in the battlefield and their detractors in the community of nations.[21]

This has been consistently the main public diplomacy strategy of the GWOT. Today we see reflections of both Napoleon's France and early Showa Japan in how we focus our public diplomacy. In *faux* Napoleonic mode our leaders would appear, heroically, in the battle area called Iraq. These appearances carried forward the quintessential element of Napoleon's imperial propaganda: the emperor's dispatches.[22] Thus their heroic appearance in "battle" symbolically showcases our leaders. They are every ounce Napoleon in the fray, personally directing the cause of victory for the nation—for national survival. Hence the fiery rubric: "We fight them over there so that we do not have to fight them here." Leader video-visits must also serve another purpose: to bind themselves to the sacrifice of soldiers: to personally appropriate their loss to further justify the grand enterprise.

Like Showa Japan, we make struggle all about us renewing American virtue and showcasing our national greatness for ancestral approval. They are looking down upon us, and thus the war is about living up to them. It is an exercise in reaffirming identity—and a dangerous exercise at that, because to fail in the GWOT would be to fail as Americans. Charles Royster said this about how Americans saw themselves during their revolution, "To fail as defenders of ideals was to fail as Americans; to succeed was to give the victors, their country, and its liberty the prospect of immortality."[23] This impulse in our ethos, after 2001, became an often-used regime cudgel to enforce domestic support—which worked for a time.

Designed for Self-Defeat

Propaganda that increasingly turns its arsenal of persuasion on its own people suggests a war effort that is losing momentum. Emphasizing "us vs. them" can give the war effort a needed boost, but risks reshaping the message in ways that further alienate audiences to be won over. Of course the immediate enemy is crudely caricatured, but any "us vs. them" message inevitably recasts the whole environment in which the enemy is engaged.

Thus Napoleon's early postrevolutionary propaganda, aimed at the European world, transitioned in his imperial phase to a smaller realm that effectively equated to the borders of the Charlemagnic reich—a correspondence not lost on Napoleon.[24] He succeeded in making Poland and the small states of Germany and Italy a subordinate part of his "us." But a subordinate and dependent "us" was at the mercy of Napoleon's success in wringing submission from the *anciens régimes*. The paradox: to fight the war he needed to elevate the struggle of the French *patrie* against hated enemies, which then separated France from its ring of "allies." What his public diplomacy really needed was to create a united Western European identity that was self-sustaining.[25]

Japan's problem was deeper: it needed its war to reaffirm the worthiness of Japanese identity. Thus the war was driven in a sense by national insecurity. Its public diplomacy was never in a position to effectively persuade others because it needed above all to elevate Japanese identity in contrast to others.[26]

So appeals to "brown people" oppressed by European colonialism were less about liberating "brothers" than making Japanese feel enlightened and benevolent. Hence the images of childlike and primitive peoples yearning for an outstretched Japanese hand were not well received by their target audiences. Moreover in places where Japan had been long engaged, these appeals had a special, twisted irony. For example, one-reelers showing Japanese soldiers gently shepherding Chinese refugee families back to their homes was a vile counterpoint to their ongoing slaughter of the innocents in Nanjing.[27]

Public diplomacy directed at the international community was just as self-defeating. Japan attempted to justify its occupation of Manchuria as a form of self-determination, by creating an allegedly independent "Great Manchu Nation" (*Manchukuo*). But this gambit—bringing in old Qing elites as their puppets—made Japanese ambitions malign: and yet Japan had actually been informally controlling Manchuria for 25 years without a murmur from international opinion!

GWOT public diplomacy took on some of the same self-defeating aspects of both Napoleonic and Showa propaganda. Like Showa persuasion, the U.S. main effort was reaffirming American identity. The surefire narrative was an irresistible good vs. evil, us vs. them story. Domestically driven public diplomacy sought to essentially embed the literary framework of a John Wayne movie into the 24-hour news cycle.

The difficulty this presented in reaching out to Muslims was not necessarily in portraying Takfiris ("terrorists") in the blackest terms; it was rather in how we chose to paint the rest of Islam. Were they simply good, moderate people oppressed by evil rulers? That would have been a powerful argument, save for one inconvenient truth: the oppressors were in general our "friends and allies in the region."

American public diplomacy became self-defeating when it started to openly blame Islam itself for "terrorism." They were all part of a civilization in deep decay. While they might not display the savagery of terrorists, they permitted their world their rise. At best these "good" Muslims were no better than children: letting their world slide into decay, and equally weak to the task of resisting the new savagery within.[28] This trope took on an increasing edge as American's venture in Iraq began visibly failing. Informal public diplomacy (administration-orchestrated) insistently raised the evil "cancer" growing within Islam. Commentators began scolding the very "moderate Muslims" we wished to recruit for their foolishness and pusillanimity. Only we could save them.[29]

Such a message might serve to boost war opinion at home, but it just as surely worked to brand any "moderate Muslims" as collaborators. Moreover it also made the case of the so-called extremists, namely, that the United States seeks the destruction of Islam. The overwhelming majority of Muslims now believes this, not us.[30]

This was the same irreconcilable choice facing Napoleon and Showa leaders after several years of war. How could Japanese public diplomacy seriously advance even the thought that their new world of "Asia for the Asians" believed in equality and altruism, after the Rape of Nanjing? Yet it was a persistent and unashamed trope in late 1930s propaganda. In part this served, however, to reinforce Japanese superiority, and redouble their belief that only they could deliver Asia.

In the same fashion, American rhetoric ignores a US-nurtured framework of tyranny that currently oppresses and holds back Muslim progress and renewal. After all, the US underwrites and sustains a host of despotic regimes, from Egypt to Saudi Arabia to Pakistan. It is easier to ignore this and explain "root causes" in terms of Islam's "failed civilization." U.S.-client kings and U.S. invasion of Muslim lands—is a "cancer."

Hegel's Reality Distortion Field

The power of revolution, which lies at the heart of world order revision, always claims the idealistic and altruistic mantle of "remaking humanity." Such robes are always worth appropriating. Hence Napoleon could seize the original vision of 1789 and make it into a personal apotheosis. Was he not after all leading virtuous French energy against evil Europe's tyrants and Britain's usurious "shopkeepers?"

But to "1789" he added Rome: melding the grand promise of remaking humanity with the historical destiny of the universal. Napoleon's explicit hearkening to Rome at every level of state rhetoric and symbolism—from Emperor to Eagle Standards—was the public diplomacy of ancient universal authority exhumed.[31] He conjured a new revolutionary model built around the history-changing power of his person. Hence Napoleon became the model for Hegel's hero of destiny—"the world-spirit on horseback."[32] It is undoubtedly a grand model, but it has arguably also wreaked havoc on history. The belief that you are the maker of history distorts reality. In the belief is lost not only that necessary sense of personal limits but also of alternative opportunities.

Could Napoleon have revised the world order in favor of French authority? Achieving this would have required a strategy of relationship building in which France nurtured the emergence of truly independent and unified German, Polish, and Italian successor states. These would have been the strategic partners France needed to achieve its goals. But a romantic ideology of the hero and destiny made such a course impossible—because narrative that exalts the hero of necessity requires that the "other" in all forms be highly caricatured. Hence the enemy must be brutish and even sub-human, and even the downtrodden to be redeemed must appear like supplicant children.

The God-hero ideology seeped deeply into French public diplomacy, turning the promised *fraternité* of revolution into a conversation between emperor and his *clientele*. This aspect of French persuasion had an opposite effect, weakening support of French "allies," with the possible exception of the Poles. Early Showa elites, especially in the military, were equally drawn to Hegel—though to history's iron lessons rather than to its hero. World War I had a message for Japan. If Japan were to survive in a world of struggle, it must have the will to take the reins of history into its hands. Ancient belief in the divinity of Japan's course—the State Shinto of Meiji times—only reinforced this.

The United States publicly appropriated the same tropes in its GWOT propaganda. Like Napoleon we officially declared ourselves to be the universal human authority. It may not have been officially Roman (although many "commentators" joyously raised that standard).[33] Yet in clear Greco-Roman terms nonetheless we *were* "civilization" (singular, and it is us). Moreover we officially declared—in terms antiquity would have applauded—that this was a war not *between* civilizations, but *for* civilization (there is only one).

Also, like Napoleon, our struggle reified Hegel, the administration sought to round out the progress of American mission so recently canonized as "The End of History." The president himself had declared that this was "our time in history," and that "the call of history has come to the right country."[34] Inner circles were not afraid to publicly weave together Hegel and Rome:

> The aide said that guys like me were "in what we call the reality-based community," which he defined as people who "believe that solutions emerge from your judicious study of discernible reality." I nodded and murmured something about enlightenment principles and empiricism. He

cut me off. "That's not the way the world really works anymore," he continued. "We're an empire now, and when we act, we create our own reality. And while you're studying that reality—judiciously, as you will—we'll act again, creating other new realities, which you can study too, and that's how things will sort out. We're history's actors . . . and you, all of you, will be left to just study what we do.[35]

However, America is also Hegelian in dark, early Showa hues. America's public diplomacy "community" has become increasingly swept up by the black, unthinkable imagery of defeat, and so driven on by a sort of implicit desperation, so reminiscent of Showa elite discourse. Everywhere commentators have boasted of victory while in the same breath hinting darkly that we would surely lose if we did not "stay the course."[35]

Roman universalism and Hegelian narrative were detrimental to GWOT public diplomacy in two ways. On one hand it presented our friends with a clear declaration that they must buy into our new *über*-vision: where buying in was tantamount to a kind of imperial supplication. On the other hand it declared to the enemy—Muslim—world that any there who joined our cause were really engaged in helping us savor our greater greatness. All our front-talk about helping Muslims was just a loop-back to the endless act of reifying ourselves.

Submission is the Best Relationship

From the beginning, a profound insecurity lay at the heart of GWOT public diplomacy. Although "global" was in its title, its foremost goal was ratifying American sacred narrative. This meant moving humanity toward a millennial outcome ("free peoples will own the future") but the doing was all about us: seizing again, and proving again, our national greatness. The GWOT in this sense was the prisoner of national myth. It needed to show itself constantly worthy, the anointed equal and natural successor to World War II and the Cold War.

Quite unconsciously in the midst of post-9/11 and pre-Iraq boasting, this need represented a deep insecurity that sucked all flexibility and sensitivity towards others out of public diplomacy. Just as the GWOT persuasion campaign was focused primarily on the American electorate, its rhetorical terms were also self-focused. Inflexible mythic standards drove how we allowed ourselves to talk about narrative and "outcome."

This turned out to be a stern historical template. It forced us to put the narrative of defeating evil and uplifting the downtrodden above the realities of conflict and change in the Muslim world. Myth demanded that we approach the world of Islam as though it was long ago Nazi Europe reborn, and this was, above all, a submission story.

"Prove to our satisfaction that you are not a radical"—Daniel Pipes. *"Tariq Ramadan is not a moderate: he is a 'totalitarian' "*—James Woolsey.[37] The documentary *Obsession* whips up its audiences. At one screening there are reactions like: "I think we are on the verge of a third world war," and "We haven't seen anything like this since the Nazis."[38] Here we see the full spectrum public diplomacy of "new media," through which the administration transcended the limits of old-style state propaganda. It is at once, brilliantly, both an authentic "movement" expression and informally orchestrated to regime agenda. Thus commentators like Pipes and Woolsey, and documentaries like *Obsession* work to build almost seamlessly on administration themes of the enemy "other," like "Islamofascism." The public diplomacy of Islamofascism and The Long War helped harness domestic emotion for a Nazi-sequel struggle against the other.

But this mythic vise allowed for liberation only within the (apocalyptic) framework of submission. It was simply inconceivable that what we were offering the Muslim world was anything but "liberation," which they would joyfully embrace. That they might see it instead as submission—and so promising the eventual destruction of Islam itself—was not only unimaginable to Americans, but ideologically or even theologically to be ruled out as impossible.

Napoleon of course began the confusion between liberation and submission. What began with "let freedom reign" became over time a new contract between ruler and subject. The parade of submission politics in Western Europe not only created a fragile web of imperial relationship—it hardened the resistance of already paranoid *anciens régimes* in Eastern and Central Europe. But French public diplomacy only made this situation worse still, because it kept trying to explain submission politics as the politics of liberation and freedom.

Likewise Showa leaders boasted about a "Co-Prosperity Sphere" that would free Asia from colonial domination: "Asia for the Asians." But the visible reality, years (and for Taiwan and Korea, decades) before war with the United States, was of Japanese colonial oppression far crueler than any European administration. Some colonial societies, in the Dutch East Indies particularly, inclined somewhat more to the Showa vision.[39]

But even here, although Japan flirted with creating an independent Indonesia, it failed to take the opportunity. Everywhere Japan failed to seriously consider a commonwealth alternative in which it might act as *primus inter pares*. Even its co-prosperity rhetoric described a "liberated" Asia in starkly paternalistic terms.

This essential redefinition of submission as liberation, so central to Napoleonic and Showa public diplomacy, is also at the heart of U.S. "persuasion."

Conclusion

GWOT public diplomacy, as it has unfolded, has been a supremely self-destructive exercise. What it has wreaked on American world authority, moreover, has been almost entirely self-selected and self-inflicted. In this sense it compares poorly even against the propaganda record of Napoleon and early Showa Japan. The administration after all did not inhabit the straightened situations of France and Japan. Although it too determined to revise world order, the Bush regime entered that enterprise with every possible advantage in its favor. It was not limited to pursuing a propaganda strategy of narcissism, "shock and awe," and submission. It did not need to choose self-defeat.

So why did the Bush administration follow the well-worn, tried-and-true failure path of Napoleonic France and early Showa Japan? Here we return to the shared foundations of Bush, Napoleonic, and Showa grand strategy. First, they could not disentangle domestic persuasion from external persuasion—and the domestic effort was always dominant. Second, public diplomacy took a back seat in grand strategies that relied on the power of the deed (battle), with the word as its adjunct. Third, while pursuing the strategic goal of relationship they all adopted strategies of submission. The failure of the contradiction was in each case abetted by public diplomacy.

A Dominance of Domestic Persuasion

Both Napoleon and Showa leadership shaped their arguments first and always for the French and the Japanese peoples. Then they addressed the world. Inevitably their domestic arguments were the same arguments they offered the world, but what choice did they have? An enterprise of world revision is full of risk and sacrifice: it requires a full national commitment. Moreover, it must offer something of equal value in return—hence the public diplomacy of national–emotional catharsis: a transcendence of national identity. In an age of religious nationalism this has surefire appeal. But in terms of a public diplomacy offering to the enemy and the larger world, it is a set-up for failure.

It is necessarily irresistible, and yet it imposes severe limits on grand strategy. Inner-directed propaganda means strategic realization through *force majeure* and submission, with persuasion of the other at best as helpmate, at worst as clean-up squad. Above all the nation must buy into the proposed world metamorphosis.

Thus the Bush administration made American society the real public diplomacy effort, rather than the world.[40] But in doing so it worked against itself. The only American story sufficiently compelling was the national sacred narrative—which bought three or four years of domestic loyalty to the GWOT. Yet this millennial American story could not unfold without inevitably objectifying the Muslim world as the source of evil, requiring its reconstruction (or in adminis-tration terms, "transformation"). It could not be anything other than *World War II: The Sequel*—if Americans were to keep on buying. But to Muslims this was a codeword for conversion—and the eventual destruction of Islam. Their original suspicion, that America was two-faced and evil, was born out by our public diplomacy.

So it was now up to the power of the deed. Here we sealed our failure. It was the GWOT's essential strategic partners—action and submission—that at last let us down.

A Dominance of Action

Napoleon and Showa leadership believed that battle was dominant, and that public diplomacy, like Herald in *Henry V*, was a mere helpmate. Public diplomacy was not seen an equal key to a world-revising strategy—except for the domestic audience, and of course the families of soldiers. It was felt that world order goals depended first on the authority of the deed, with the word as its adjunct.[41] This seemed a reasonable assumption at the time. From the French and Japanese perspectives they faced discrete enemies whose several discrete armies needed to be defeated. Defeat all the armies, and victory would be theirs. All of the other constituencies in the strategic theater (Europe and East Asia) were weak entities and would presumably comply with the victor's wishes. But still, in their 1942 moment of victory, they could not connect.

Equally the United States could not connect battlefield victory to public diplomacy success. Moreover it had no idea how necessary it was to connect to the "other." For war's neoconserva-tive creators a romantic ideology steeped in visions of "history" and "destiny" described great events that were wholly self-created. The heroic "will" to "change the world" was a vision that naturally inclined toward battle and its seductive promise of high drama and quick decision.

A Dominance of Submission

Thus Napoleon and Showa leaders chose a strategy of submission in a strategic context that above all required relationship. France and Japan did not seek to fight total wars—they knew they could not win in such a struggle. Rather they sought to win over their local world. The enemies they faced were powerful but discrete. They could be defeated one by one. The rest of their worlds—Europe and East Asia—were also full of lesser players, each of which might be success-fully wooed. This argued for a strategy of relationship rather than submission. Even their enemies might eventually be persuaded to accept the revised "world" that France and Japan sought to achieve. That persuasion was the true path to victory. But instead both Napoleon and Showa Japan embarked on strategies of submission. These emphasized war as us vs. them, which trans-lated into a public diplomacy campaign built on the dominant trope of submission. The Bush administration, too, fastened on a strategy of submission early on.

In contrast a grand strategy of relationship represents a very different strategy. Yet it could not be considered because it was politically unwanted. It is often represented still as the "failed policies" of "appeasement" and "neglect" that symbolically connected the GWOT narrative to the 1930s and the run-up to World War II.

Thus it was essential that the GWOT make "a clean break" with prevailing American strategic traditions. For better or worse, public diplomacy had been a shining emblem of a strategy of

American world commonwealth, while what was now desired was constitutional transformation to an American world empire. Prevailing informal world authority was no longer a sufficient end in itself, but rather expected to form the basis for legal legitimization of American world leadership.

This failed for the United States as it had for Napoleon and Japan, because in a non-total war the objective must be in the relationships we make—using all the "tools in our kit"—with enemy and related societies. Moreover, in non-total war our goals as well as means are necessarily limited. Thus a "war of relationship" is in the end all about reshaping the terms of connection. Because the venue for demanding submission from the whole (of a people or a "civilization") is absent, submission by the whole is not a viable option.

Thus it is the task of public diplomacy to send the message that we offer a better deal—*without submission*. This must be the essence of our grand strategic offer, and the essence of what we might call victory.

Public diplomacy continues to represent—like a river smoothing rocks—the substantiation of American world authority through persuasion. Moreover this is how we do things. As Americans, discarding our deep traditions of world authority through persuasion to seek authority instead of through submission risks losing that authority altogether, as the experience of this war so tragically reminds us.

Notes

1 Michael Vlahos, "Losing Mythic Authority," *The National Interest*, May/June 2007.
2 The 2002 National Security Strategy made its world-revising argument this way: "The greater the threat, the greater is the risk of inaction—and the more compelling the case for taking anticipatory action to defend ourselves, even if uncertainty remains as to the time and place of the enemy's attack. To forestall or prevent such hostile acts by our adversaries, the United States will, if necessary, act preemptively. The United States will not use force in all cases to preempt emerging threats, nor should nations use preemption as a pretext for aggression. Yet in an age where the enemies of civilization openly and actively seek the world's most destructive technologies, the United States cannot remain idle while dangers gather." The White House, *The National Security Strategy of the United States of America*, September, 2002, 15. Using both words in the same sentence carefully muddies the key legal distinction between "preempt" and "prevent." Moreover, although the target of preempt/prevent is elsewhere described as "rogue states" and "terrorists," in this passage it is encompassing: "our adversaries." Furthermore the triggering provocation is equally vague: "while dangers gather." Finally, there is not one word on collective decision making or international legitimization.
3 In 2004 it was made official: the U.S. military objective in the GWOT was nothing less than world pacification, or Global Anti-terror Environment (GATE). *The National Military Strategy of the United States of America: A Strategy for Today; A Vision for Tomorrow*, Department of Defense, 2004, iv.
4 George W. Bush, Inaugural Address, January 20, 2005, http://www.whitehouse.gov/news/releases/2005/01/20050120-1.html.
5 James Fallows, "The Fifty-first State?" *The Atlantic Monthly*, November, 2002, http://www.theatlantic.com/doc/200211/fallows. His article is revealing on two counts. First, it shows how unquestioning the Washington elite was about American prospects for reconstructing Iraq. It is not so much that they did not ask questions: they asked the wrong questions. Their entire framework for assessing Iraqi "reconstruction" lay in the literary and mythic terrain of "Germany and Japan." Could it be done as well as the fabled postwar meaning, could we build "good" institutions and police the borders and "de-Nazify," etc.? The actual realities of Iraq bubbling just below the surface in 2002 are entirely missing. Second, the article shows the amazing hold of the "war party," as Fallow politely calls them, over the entire conversation. He gives them unfettered space and the last word, especially to James Woolsey. Fallows has not a word of criticism for Woolsey's amazing millenarianism, but rather, meekly seems to extol it: "Woolsey and his allies might be criticized for lacking a tragic imagination about where war might lead, but at least they recognize that it will lead somewhere. If they are more optimistic in their conclusions than most of the other people I spoke with, they do see that America's involvement in Iraq would be intimate and would be long."

6 For example, "33 internal FOX editorial memos reviewed by MMFA reveal FOX News Channel's inner workings," Media Matters for America, July 14, 2004, http://mediamatters.org/items/200407140002; "The Fox News Memo: Ex-Fox News staffer on The Memo," Poynteronline, October 31, 2003, http://poynter.org/forum/?id=thememo.

7 David Barstow, "Behind TV Analysts, Pentagon's Hidden Hand," *New York Times*, April 20, 2008, http://www.nytimes.com/2008/04/20/washington/20generals.html?_r=2&hp&oref=slogin&oref=login

8 J. Charles Schencking, "The Imperial Japanese Navy and the Constructed Consciousness of a South Seas Destiny, 1872–1921," *Modern Asian Studies* 33, no. 4 (Oct., 1999): 769–796.

9 Napoleon I, *Proclamation after Austerlitz*, 12 Frumaire, An XIV, December 3, 1805.

10 Like this popular paean on our entering Baghdad: "The basic lesson that governments and militaries around the world just learned was this: Don't fight the United States. Period. This stunning war did more to foster peace than a hundred treaties could begin to do. Consider the fear and impotent anger would-be opponents of the United States must feel today? The Iraqi defeat was a defeat for every other military in the world—in a sense, even for our allies, whose forces cannot begin to keep pace with our own." Ralph Peters, "A New Age of Warfare," *New York Post*, April 10, 2003.

11 Susan Locke Siegfried, "Naked History: The Rhetoric of Military Painting in Postrevolutionary France," *The Art Bulletin* 75, no. 2 (Jun., 1993): 235–258.

12 Lynne Duke, "The Word at War," *Washington Post*, March 26, 2006, http://www.washingtonpost.com/wp-dyn/content/article/2006/03/25/AR2006032500983_pf.html.

13 Wayne Hanley, *The Genesis of Napoleonic Propaganda, 1796–1799* (New York: Columbia University Press, 2005).

14 Michael Broers, "Cultural Imperialism in a European Context? Political Culture and Cultural Politics in Napoleonic Italy," *Past and Present* 170 (Feb., 2001): 157.

15 Stuart Woolf, "French Civilization and Ethnicity in the Napoleonic Empire," *Past and Present* 124 (Aug., 1989): 105.

16 Michael Broers, "Cultural Imperialism in a European Context? Political Culture and Cultural Politics in Napoleonic Italy," *Past and Present* 170 (Feb., 2001): 153, 170, 178.

17 Stuart Woolf, "French Civilization and Ethnicity in the Napoleonic Empire," *Past and Present* 124 (Aug., 1989): 106.

18 Albert Boime, "Louis Boilly's Reading of the XIth and XIIth Bulletins of the Grande Armée," *Zeitschrift für Kunstgeschichte*, 54 Bd., H. 3. (1991), 374–387; Isser Woloch, "Napoleonic Conscription: State Power and Civil Society," *Past and Present* 111 (May, 1986): 101–129.

19 Kevin M. Doak, "Building National Identity through Ethnicity: Ethnology in Wartime Japan and After," *Journal of Japanese Studies* 27, no. 1 (2001): 39.

20 John W. Dower, *War Without Mercy: Race and Power in the Pacific War* (New York: Pantheon Books, 1986).

21 Louise Young, *Japan's Total Empire: Manchuria and the Culture of Wartime Imperialism* (Berkeley, CA: University of California Press, 1999), 155.

22 Joseph J. Mathews, "Napoleon's Military Bulletins," *The Journal of Military History* 22, no. 2 (Jun., 1950): 137–144.

23 Charles Royster, *A Revolutionary People at War: The Continental Army and American Character, 1775–1783* (Chapel Hill: University of North Carolina Press, 1979), 3.

24 Michael Broers, "Napoleon, Charlemagne, and Lotharingia: Acculturation and the Boundaries of Napoleonic Europe," *The Historical Journal* 44, no. 1 (Mar., 2001): 135–154.

25 Michael Rowe, "Between Empire and Home Town: Napoleonic Rule on the Rhine, 1799–1814," *The Historical Journal* 42, no. 3 (Sept., 1999): 643–674.

26 Klaus Antoni, "Momotaro (The Peach Boy) and the Spirit of Japan: Concerning the Function of a Fairy Tale in the Japanese Nationalism of the Early Showa Age," *Asian Folklore Studies* 50, no. 1 (1991): 155–188.

27 David Nelson Rowe, "Japanese Propaganda in North China, 1937–1938," *The Public Opinion Quarterly* 3, no. 4 (Oct., 1939): 564–580.

28 Bernhard Lewis legitimated the notion that Islam is a failed civilization in *What Went Wrong: The Clash Between Islam and Modernity in the Middle East* (HarperCollins, 2003). More recent iconic portraits are Tony Blankley's *The West's Last Chance: Will We Win the Clash of Civilizations?* (Regnery, 2005).

29 Michael Hirsh, "Exploring Islam's 'Death Cult'—Muslims must find a way to remove the cancer infecting their religion," *Newsweek*, July 6, 2007, http://www.msnbc.msn.com/id/19636920/site/newsweek/.

30 World Public Opinion/PIPA poll, "Muslims Believe US Seeks to Undermine Islam." April 23, 2007, http://www.worldpublicopinion.org/pipa/articles/home_page/346.php?nid=&id=&pnt=346&lb=hmpg1.

31 John Walker McCoubrey, "Gros' Battle of Eylau and Roman Imperial Art," *The Art Bulletin* 43, no. 2 (Jun., 1961): 135–139.

32 "I saw the Emperor—this soul of the world—go out from the city to survey his reign; it is a truly wonderful sensation to see such an individual, who, concentrating on one point while seated on a horse, stretches over the world and dominates it." Nicolas Broussard, "Napoleon, Hegelian Hero," *Revue du Souvenir Napoleonien* 400, 1995, http://www.napoleon.org/en/reading_room/articles/files/napoleon_hegelian_hero.asp.

33 The warm embrace of Rome spiked before the US invasion of Iraq, as this 2002 report highlights: Emily Eakin, "'It Takes An Empire' Say Several US Thinkers," *New York Times*, April 2, 2002.

34 President Bush's key phrases fit together in fact into a perfect representation of American sacred narrative. Hence this war is nothing less than "the unfolding of a global ideological struggle, our time in history," pitting "progress" and "freedom" against a "mortal danger to all humanity," the "enemy of civilization." Moreover, "the call of history has come to the right country," and "the defense of freedom is worth the sacrifice." Ultimately the "evil ones" will be destroyed, and "this great country will lead the world to safety, security, and peace," a millennial world where "free peoples will own the future." For excerpts from an October 6, 2005 speech: http://www.whitehouse.gov/nes/releases/2005/10/2005/20051006-3.html. Earlier presidential pronouncements cited here are referenced in Michael Vlahos, "Religion and US Grand Strategy," the Globalist.com, June 8, 2003, http://theglobalist.com/StoryId.aspx?StoryId=a3230.

35 Ron Suskind, "Without a Doubt," *New York Times Magazine*, October 14, 2004.

36 This trope is flagged most insistently by the web of GWOT commentators, especially Tony Blankley, Ralph Peters, Victor Davis Hanson, Dennis Prager, Cal Thomas, Mark Steyn, etc.

37 See his test for moderate Muslims, Daniel Pipes "Finding Moderate Muslims: Do you believe in modernity?" *The Jerusalem Post*, November 26, 2003. More recently he has declared that non-violent Islamists are just as evil as Jihadis, Daniel Pipes, "When Conservatives Argue about Islam," *FrontPage-Magazine*, July 6, 2007, http://www.frontpagemagazine.com/Articles/ReadArticle.asp?ID=29067. I asked James Woolsey after a speech in which he declared all Islamists to be "totalitarians" if he really meant *all* Islamists. After all, I said, there is quite a range of Islamist thought, much of it quite moderate. He retreated a bit and admitted it was something of a sliding scale. I followed up and asked if he thought of the celebrated "moderate" Islamist Tariq Ramadan. "He is a totalitarian," Woolsey replied.

38 Jill Kassander, "'Obsession' generates applause, controversy," *JewishLight.com*, July 10, 2007. For other positive responses to the documentary, "Obsession: Radical Islam's War Against the West," see http://www.obsessionthemovie.com/media_online.php.

39 Aiko Kurasawa, "Propaganda Media on Java under the Japanese 1942–1945," *Indonesia* 44 (Oct., 1987): 59–116; Kenichi Goto, "Life and Death of 'Abdul Rachman' (1906–49): One Aspect of Japanese-Indonesian Relationships," *Indonesia* 22 (Oct., 1976): 57–69.

40 A generation before Smith-Mundt was signed into law in 1948, Wilson's war machine pioneered American propaganda. Looking back, its domestic focus seems to prefigure the GWOT persuasion strategy. But it differs in important ways. America emotionally embraced "Great War" with Germany and thus World War I was a collective national experience, however short. In contrast the Bush administration turned a model of electric domestic propaganda to very different ends: namely, reifying the state structure and appropriating sacred rhetoric so that it might "manage" the world as it wished. Neocons transfigured Wilson for a very different cause. In crude terms they celebrated his means but turned them to different ends. The neocon Wilsonian connection was convenient cover: "At any rate, one thing that distinguishes neocons from all other conservatives is their willingness to identify their foreign policy with Woodrow Wilson. They don't much like Wilson himself ('hopelessly naïve,' Max Boot calls him) but they are happy to think of themselves as 'hard Wilsonians' or, in Fukuyama's case, 'realistic Wilsonians.' That is, they agree with his ends but not his means. Most of the neocons reject Wilson's reliance on international law and organizations to keep the peace; they prefer to rely, in hard cases, on the use of force by the U.S., alone or with its allies." (http://www.realclearpolitics.com/articles/2007/07/iraq_and_the_neoconservatives.html).

41 Echoed, surely unconsciously, in Karen Hughes' call for a "diplomacy of deeds." See John Brown, "Karen Hughes and her 'diplomacy of deeds,'" http://www.commondreams.org/archive/2007/04/09/411/.

5

Public Opinion and Power

Ali S. Wyne

So-called "world opinion" is not the unanimous and just consensus that its seekers pretend . . . It is *the irrational and unjust opinion of the world's worst people* . . . The proper response to the anti-American voicers of "world opinion" is to identify them as our ideological and political enemies—and dispense justice accordingly.

Alex Epstein[1]

Unprecedented Hostility

The 2007 Miss Universe Pageant proceeded normally for the most part, with the contestants attempting to outdo one another in a variety of categories. The last round, however, was anything but predictable. As Miss USA began to answer her assigned question, the audience erupted into and sustained its booing. Her remarks were hardly contentious. She discussed her passion for education and adduced her volunteer experience with the Oprah Winfrey Leadership Academy in South Africa. Speaking with Larry King shortly thereafter, the owner of the pageant, Donald Trump, attempted to rationalize the embarrassing spectacle: "They were booing her. It was in Mexico City. They were booing her like I have never seen. And she took it very personally. And I told her, I said they're not booing you, they're booing the policies of our government, unfortunately."

While occurrences of this kind have precedent, the blatancy of this particular one underscores an opposition to American foreign policy that is perhaps more visible and forceful than the United States has ever witnessed. In 2004, Zbigniew Brzezinski asserted that, "In our entire history as a nation, world opinion has never been as hostile toward the United States as it is today."[2]

While it is true that this animus is particularly pronounced in the Arab-Muslim world, it has reached alarming levels even in those countries that America counts as its closest allies. Thus, in 2006, Anthony King, one of the world's preeminent political scientists, observed that, "There has probably never been a time when America was held in such low esteem on this side of the Atlantic."[3] How does this state of affairs impact American foreign policy? Joseph Nye has contributed greatly to the discourse on this question by introducing the notion of "soft power:" A nation wields soft power if it can convince others to support its objectives without having to employ force, economic sanctions, or other coercive instruments of statecraft.[4] Extending his concept, I endeavor to offer a more comprehensive treatment of the question that I posed earlier.

Origins and Characteristics of World Opinion

Detailing the history of innovations in communication technologies could consume volumes, and is unnecessary. Suffice it to say that prior to the 1970s, when globalization began to accelerate the decline in technological costs and barriers to the free flow of capital, these advents largely remained under state auspices. Indeed, while I would be remiss to understate the significance of the telegraph, the radio, and even the television, it would be difficult to argue that any of them substantially empowered the global public to analyze American foreign policy independently and conclusively. Even ARPANET, the progenitor of the Internet, was largely arcane, familiar to only a select group of computer scientists and government officials.

Today, however, the costs that once precluded individuals or nongovernmental organizations from developing their own media have become negligible, largely owing to the emergence of optical fiber communication. Between 1992 and 2002, the cost of storing one gigabyte of information dropped from $1,000 to $2.53.[5] During this same time period, the number of Internet users worldwide grew from approximately 1.14 million to 544 million.[6] By 2014, it is estimated that this figure will rise to over two billion.[7] By any criterion, these trends are remarkable. One can gain some further insight by decomposing this figure so as to determine the evolving geographic makeup of Internet users. In 1998, the United States' share of worldwide users was 48%, while Europe's share was 21%, and Asia's share, excluding Japan, was 9%.[8] By 2007, these figures were, respectively, 19%, 28%, and 36%.[9] The number of Chinese speakers who are using the Internet quintupled between 2000 and 2006, and other languages—for example, Spanish and Arabic—are beginning to make their presence known.[10]

Barring some critical disruptions, this democratization of access is poised to continue, as is the erosion of traditional media: ". . . [T]echnology-driven changes are reshaping international news flows by lowering the economic barriers of entry to publishing and broadcasting and encouraging the proliferation of nontraditional international news sources. The audience—now fragmented and active—is far better able to choose and even shape the news."[11] That is to say, the number of players in the court of global public opinion has risen dramatically, and their demographics and characteristics are much more diverse.

Honesty dictates that I note the limitations of the global communication revolution; it has largely been confined to developed countries. Intuitively, however, this fact is neither surprising nor reasonable cause to dismiss claims that recent communication advents have achieved a striking measure of diffusion. After all, innovations "tend to reflect and fit in with the socioeconomic circumstances of the country or countries in which they originate."[12] Furthermore, given that the Internet has only begun to assume a global character during the last decade, it is premature to dismiss its potential. Indeed, many scholars believe that its geopolitical impact will rival or even surpass that of the printing press.[13]

Witness the impact of YouTube. In May 2007, the Pentagon announced that it would be temporarily cutting off soldiers' access to the immensely popular video-sharing platform, citing bandwidth concerns. The real reason for this stipulation, it is widely believed, is that soldiers were documenting many of the war in Iraq's more unsavory aspects—ranging from their own impoverished conditions to gruesome instances of sectarian violence. Furthermore, candidates for the 2008 presidential election are appealing to voters (and even participating in live discussions) on YouTube. YouTube is, of course, only one of many services that agentive individuals and organizations are using.

Bono, front man for rock group U2, has brought unprecedented attention to the plight of the world's poor by launching endeavors such as DATA and EDUN, and lending support to others, such as the "ONE" campaign. Amnesty International is deploying satellite technology to monitor the ongoing humanitarian crisis in 12 Darfurese villages, thereby "enabling action by private citizens, policy makers and international courts."[14] Unfortunately, though unsurprisingly, the

United States' adversaries have also displayed great technological savvy in attaining their ends. CBS recently ran a chilling broadcast that chronicles Al-Qaeda's exploding presence on the Internet; its "cyberplanning" poses a critical national security challenge.[15] Perhaps most importantly, however, the Internet is allowing the ordinary person to wield critical influence.

In 1997 Jodie Williams won the Nobel Prize by using the Internet to link activists around the world who sought to institute a ban on landmines. Today, people rarely achieve acclaim for such accomplishments, not because their work is any less noble or urgent, but rather, because the novelty of Internet-based activism has largely disappeared. Consider the "green" revolution that is compelling cities, states, nations, and Fortune 500 corporations to engage in more sustainable business practices; and the growing movement to address global warming (because of the publicity that attended to his documentary, "An Inconvenient Truth," Al Gore was able to organize the world's largest concert in history).[16] Both of these phenomena derive not from the work of a remarkable individual, but rather, from the efforts of thousands, if not millions, of Internet activists. While the impact of one blog post here or one video clip there may be negligible, their collective force is undeniable. The "YouTube effect," if it is not yet too premature to speak of such a phenomenon's emergence, promises to be far more powerful than the oft invoked "CNN effect."

A Profile of World Opinion

If world opinion is indeed as powerful as my portrayal suggests, how should the United States respond? Some would argue that nothing should be done. There is certainly some truth to the contention that resentment of a country's foreign policy scales with its power: As the world's most powerful country, the United States is thus bound to inspire great opposition. While it would be foolish to base one's foreign policy entirely on the whims of world opinion, it would be equally, if not more, improvident to trivialize or ignore its impact. Unfortunately, having commanded great influence over American decision-making processes for the past eight years, neoconservatives have succeeded in legitimating this latter posture. In their accounting, because opposition to American foreign policy is inevitable, there is no compelling reason to advocate for alterations to American conduct.

Other scholars have made a yet further unconvincing argument: namely that, no matter the severity or depth of the criticisms that it may issue, the global public is grateful for and wishes to maintain American primacy. The wealth of available polling data yields precisely the opposite conclusion. In 2005, the Program on International Policy Attitudes (PIPA) and GlobeScan surveyed 23 countries on the optimal structure of global governance: 20 of the 23 believed that the European Union's acquiring greater influence than the United States in world affairs would be "mainly positive."[17] That same year, the Pew Global Attitudes Project surveyed 16 countries on numerous issues: Majorities (oftentimes vast) in 15 of them wished to see a military counterforce to the United States.[18] Two years later, these trends persisted. Thus, the Chicago Council on Global Affairs and WorldPublicOpinion.org surveyed 13 countries on China's ascendance: Majorities in all but one believed that it would be "mostly positive" or "equally positive and negative" if China's economy were to become as large as America's.[19] According to the Directors of WatchingAmerica.com, one of the leading monitors of world opinion, only 5% of the current global press about the United States is favorable.[20]

It is convenient, but ultimately fallacious, to ascribe these findings to the Bush Administration. While it has unquestionably exacerbated the chasm between the United States and the global community, current opposition to American power appears to have deeper roots:

... [T]his new global hardening of attitudes amounts to something larger than a thumbs down on the current occupant of the White House. Simply put, the rest of the world both fears and resents the unrivaled power that the United States has amassed since the Cold War ended. In the eyes of others, the U.S. is a worrisome colossus: It is too quick to act unilaterally, it doesn't do a good job of addressing the world's problems, and it widens the global gulf between rich and poor. On matters of international security, the rest of the world has become deeply suspicious of U.S. motives and openly skeptical of its word. People abroad are more likely to believe that the U.S.-led war on terror has been about controlling Mideast oil and dominating the world than they are to take at face value America's stated objectives of self-defense and global democratization.[21]

What is perhaps most disheartening is that the heretofore impenetrable barrier—between opposition to American foreign policy and opposition to the American people—is beginning to dissolve (the import of this phenomenon will become clearer when I discuss anti-Americanism at length below). In his March 2007 testimony before the House of Representatives, Andrew Kohut, President of the Pew Research Center, noted that "it is no longer just the U.S. as a country that is perceived negatively, but increasingly the American people as well, a sign that anti-American opinions are deepening and becoming more entrenched."[22] This trend is especially worrisome when one considers how fractured world opinion is on virtually every issue outside of American foreign policy; it cleaves along political, economic, social, religious, ethnic, and demographic fault lines, among myriad others. A preeminent French researcher and lecturer, Pierre Hassner, lamented that "except in Eastern Europe, Israel, and perhaps India, anti-Americanism provides the only common attitude today in a world otherwise devoid of positive agreement on anything."[23]

World Opinion's Consequences for American Foreign Policy

The current character of world opinion has significant foreign policy consequences. It is instructive to decompose them into three categories: military, economic, and political.

Military

There is a compelling simplicity to the argument that America can ignore world opinion by virtue of its military puissance. The natural rejoinder, however, is yet simpler—what would it accomplish by using overwhelming military force? At a basic level, potential adversaries could inflict considerable damage on its vital interests in the event of their deploying weapons of mass destruction (WMDs). At a more important level, the world's interconnectivity ensures that the use of conventional power is mutually inimical. Consider, for example, the hypothetical scenario in which the United States bombed China. China would be devastated, of course, but so would the United States, considering how greatly American consumption depends on Chinese exports.

This rather implausible example makes a simple point: The boundary between the "national interest" and the "global interest" is increasingly blurry. What are the major foreign policy challenges for the United States? The threats posed by WMD proliferation and terrorism, global warming, the spread of infectious diseases, and increasing inequality among and between countries immediately come to mind. Not surprisingly, these are precisely the global community's chief priorities. It makes little sense for America to corrode its partnerships with the very countries without whose assistance it can make little, if any, progress on these urgent issues. Given the global public's increasing aversion to the accretion and use of conventional military force, spending $500 billion annually on national defense is likely to breed fear of, not respect for, American power.

The enormity of this figure becomes further perplexing when one recognizes that military force's utility is declining—a lesson that the war on terrorism places in sharp relief. In Afghanistan and Iraq, the United States won breathtaking military victories. Both countries, however, have dramatically regressed. Their fate scarcely owes to the deployment of insufficient force—there is a reason why the Bush Administration prominently noted its intention to "shock and awe" the Ba'athists into submission. Rather, Afghanistan and Iraq have devolved because the United States has been unable to secure international support. The American military is woefully unequipped to engage in nation-building, and because the United States has largely alienated world opinion, those countries that would be most useful in this capacity—European countries, in particular—have virtually no presence in either country. Josef Joffe, a prominent conservative author, notes the distinction between military and political objectives: "Very briefly, bombs and bullets do not make an order, and sheer firepower buys political influence only at a hefty discount, if at all. The force that breaks an opponent's capability to fight does not make him a willing democrat. Bombs raze buildings; they do not build nations, and crowbars are useless when a chiseling tool is needed."[24]

Precisely because of the United States' failure to appreciate this distinction, Afghanistan and Iraq are morphing into precisely the fundamentalist states whose emergence neoconservatives hoped to forestall with swift military action.

Economic

World opinion's economic consequences, while subtler, are no less important. Resurgent protectionism, in particular, is of great concern. The collapse of trade negotiations at Doha underscores nationalism's continuing influence on economic policy. With Hugo Chávez and Evo Morales as their figureheads, leaders around the world increasingly frame their opposition to capitalism in patriotic terms. Nationalism has often influenced economic policy, as the interwar period amply demonstrated. However, closer reflection reveals an important difference.

From 1918 to 1939, it was largely nationalism on the part of developed countries that brought globalization to a halt. Today, it is largely nationalism on the part of *developing* countries that challenges globalization's appeal and spread.[25] Nowhere is this phenomenon more apparent than in the Americas, which have witnessed a sweeping revival of socialism. Typically crippled by economic dependency, Latin America and South America are moving toward greater integration and loosening their ties to Washington.

The outcome at Doha appears to be a harbinger of future developments. In June 2007, negotiations between major trade powers collapsed once again. With global trade rounds continuing to stall, countries are increasingly expressing their preferences for bilateral and regional trade agreements. Thus, the members of the Asia-Pacific Economic Cooperation forum, which collectively account for 50% of the world's trade, have already established 21 such pacts (with 17 more under negotiation).[26]

The health of the United States' economy rests, in considerable measure, on the system of multilateral trade governance that emerged in the aftermath of the Second World War. If nationalism and smaller-scale trade partnerships continue to carry the day, globalization may well stagnate. Mindful of the axiom that power confers responsibility, America bears a disproportionate share of the burden for ensuring the global economy's health:

> . . . [A]lthough globalization has passed its peak, it is unlikely to unravel completely. Still, the flaws in multilateral institutions such as the WTO and the growing discontent with globalization will make it harder and harder for politicians to pursue free markets. If the United States, in particular, fails to do more to ensure that the benefits and opportunities of an internationalized economy are spread as widely as possible, there could be an even more potent backlash.[27]

Political

Finally, and most subtly, world opinion has significant political consequences, two of which merit special considderation: It has (1) legitimized alternatives to democratic capitalism and (2) nurtured "soft balancing."

The concept of global democratization gained great currency after the Soviet Union's implosion. In his seminal work, *The End of History*, Francis Fukuyama argued that democracy was the end limit of experimentation with different structures of governance. While his text generated intense controversy, few individuals disputed that collectivist ideologies, and any derivatives thereof, had sustained a great defeat.

Available data certainly support this conclusion. According to Freedom House, there were 91 electoral democracies in the world in 1991, representing 50% of the world's countries at that time. As of 2005, there were 122 electoral democracies in the world, representing 64% of the world's countries.[28] If present trends are indicative, the world's principal power centers will continue to be democratic. However, emerging powers will not be constrained to adopt democratic governance if they wish to wield appreciable influence.

In particular, China's success in sustaining a combination of single-party, authoritarian rule and capitalist economics has buoyed the hopes of authoritarian states. For as long as it can maintain this delicate equilibrium, Beijing appears intent on expanding its economic power without developing democratic institutions. One scholar of China studies observes that "proving that an authoritarian regime can prosper through modernization is exactly what is at stake in the Chinese experiment, which is why dictatorships from Kazakhstan to Iran are keenly watching its progress."[29] While China does not appear to be "exporting" its model of governance, it could derive substantial political clout if other countries begin to emulate it of their own accord. Precisely this phenomenon is occurring.[30] It appears, as well, that world opinion is increasingly skeptical of capitalism's virtues. The former American Ambassador to France, Felix G. Rohatyn, notes the transatlantic divide on this system:

> When President George W. Bush speaks of freedom and democracy, Europeans think of the economic freedom that is fundamental to American capitalism. They are, however, troubled by the social objectives imbedded in American capitalism—by the lack of a solid social safety net, by the speculative aspect of our markets, by the growing inequality created by our large differentials in wealth and by the harsh aspects of extensive deregulation.[31]

A 2006 study of PIPA and GlobeScan reveals that while global support for free markets remains strong, individuals are increasingly calling on governments to regulate corporations.[32] Unbridled capitalism, in their rendition, increases not only inequity but also instability.[33]

As the global public contemplates alternatives to democracy and capitalism, it is resisting the United States' attempt to achieve hegemony. Neoconservatives argue that America's ascendance has thus far failed to inspire countervailing military coalitions. This argument ignores the fact that, unlike those of most dominant powers of the past, the United States' goals are largely not military in nature. If it attempted to, for example, augment its territory through colonization, conquest, or some other aggressive means, it would certainly confront overt resistance.

Other nations are in fact banding together to check American policies, albeit not in military coalitions: "States are beginning to join forces in subtler ways, with the explicit aim of checking U.S. power. Rather than forming an anti-U.S. alliance, countries are 'soft balancing:' coordinating their diplomatic positions to oppose U.S. policy and obtain more influence together."[34]

Examples abound. There are instances of one-time counterbalancing. Thus, in 2002 and 2003, European countries banded together to delay the Bush Administration's attempt at preemptive war in Iraq. Furthermore, Turkey and Saudi Arabia denied American troops the use of their territory.

There are also, perhaps more importantly, instances of sustained counterbalancing. Thus, the Shanghai Cooperation Organization has limited American influence in Central Asia, whose large reserves of natural gas make it a powerful linchpin in the emerging global energy balance. Consider, as well, the crisis in Sudan. In exchange for oil, the Chinese have embarked on lucrative investment projects in the war-torn country. In 2006, Sudan supplied 7% of China's energy needs; in return, China has invested $2 billion in the Merowe hydropower dam project, which, upon opening in 2008, will provide all of Sudan's energy needs.[35] It is difficult for the United States to undermine a regime that is the beneficiary of such enormous largesse. It is difficult, furthermore, for America to dissuade Iran from building its nuclear weapons program because of Sino-Russian influence. Neither China nor Russia is enthusiastic about a nuclear Iran that sits at the heart of an already volatile Middle East. However, they are far more interested in accruing a steady stream of energy dividends than they are in facilitating nonproliferation discussions. We have reached a pretty pass when distinguished political observers say that we have no recourse but to bomb Iran.[36]

My analysis suggests, then, that world opinion challenges not only specific policies of the United States (for example, the war in Iraq), but also the paradigms within which those policies are executed (for example, democratic capitalism).

What is Anti-Americanism?

I discussed opposition to American foreign policy in the last section, but noted at the beginning of this essay that this resistance is starting to spill over into resentment of the American people. This development demands a treatment of anti-Americanism.

Anti-Americanism Defined

As the United States prepared to invade Iraq in March 2003, millions of people around the world protested, a display that was doubly without precedent: Never before had international opposition to a war existed on such a large scale *prior* to its onset. Recognizing global sentiment's newfound power, *The New York Times* famously observed that "the huge anti-war demonstrations around the world this weekend are reminders that there may still be two superpowers on the planet: the United States and world public opinion."[37] While several observers welcomed the outpouring of opposition as a testament to the Information Age's networking capabilities, many others viewed it as a manifestation of resurgent anti-Americanism. This latter set of individuals comprised at least two categories: One believed that the protests were simply aimed at a particular instance of American foreign policy; another argued that the protests manifested a deeply entrenched contempt for American culture.

Distinguishing between these positions would not appear to pose any great challenges. Because, however, each of the two aforementioned categories of individuals ascribed the protests to, or defined them as instances of, anti-Americanism, this task of analysis is made considerably more difficult. Indeed, because opposition to American foreign policy is often conflated with opposition to American culture, it seems futile to aspire towards a definition of the term anti-Americanism. Were its precise denotation but an issue of semantic rigor, I would not be concerned. However, the term's enduring ambiguity has had crucial policy ramifications.

I define anti-Americanism as disdain for American culture, a system of values that combines respect for individual freedoms and pride in the capitalist ethic.[38] These twin pillars have been remarkably stable since the United States' birth. American foreign policy, by contrast, has varied dramatically during that time, encompassing everything along the continuum from isolationism to imperialism. Anti-Americanism is best understood as opposition to the enduring principles of

American society, not to America's conduct in the world, which does not always reflect those principles and, at any rate, is constantly in flux.

Anti-Americanism in Mainstream Scholarship

How does mainstream scholarship define the term? The most respected work, regrettably, has evaded the debate over the term's precise definition by arguing for the existence of multiple anti-Americanisms. The convenience of this argument, as well as its danger, is that it reverses the proper logic: Instead of arguing that the existence of multiple competing definitions should invigorate scholars' search for a single useful operative term, these scholars suggest that this ambiguity repudiates the unitary conception of anti-Americanism.

In their book, *Anti-Americanisms*, Robert Keohane and Peter Katzenstein contend that there are multiple anti-Americanisms. In issuing this argument, however, they volunteer contradictory premises. Although they argue that anti-Americanism would diminish in response to a more multilateral American foreign policy that respects international opinion, they also contend that anti-Americanism is "a psychological tendency to hold negative views of the United States and of American society in general."[39] While the former variant of anti-Americanism, based on American behavior, is likely to be responsive to alterations in American conduct, the latter is nearly pathological. It is difficult, therefore, to ascertain the authors' definition of the term. The subsequent sections of their essay only compound this difficulty.

For example, Keohane and Katzenstein maintain that outside of the Middle East, anti-Americanism largely reflects unfavorable opinion towards American engagement abroad, not an instinctive predilection to blame the United States without having analyzed the factors that are involved in its policy decisions. However, having defined anti-Americanism as if to suggest that it reflects *precisely* this reflexive instinct of condemnation, they discuss four of its forms: intellectual criticism of hypocritical American foreign policy; some democracies' opposition to America's social arrangements; some countries' intense belief that their collective identities and territorial integrity must be preserved at all costs; and the belief that the United States is the "central source of evil."[40] Unless one is convinced that American culture represents the apex of civilized thought, and that American conduct is intrinsically unimpeachable, only the fourth of these forms can easily be construed as irrational.

The reader who is not yet having difficulty in assessing the authors' arguments will likely experience it upon reading their final judgment. Keohane and Katzenstein conclude by arguing that anti-Americanism ultimately reflects American society's polyvalence, as manifest in its (sometimes contradictory) values of hedonism, religiosity, and openness. Neither this assertion nor their earlier definition of anti-Americanism is incorrect. It is unclear, however, why they foist such great attention on a phenomenon that is confined, while deferring a serious treatment of the phenomenon that merits scrutiny. Recall that, as innumerable polls document, while anti-Americanism is quite limited, disdain for American foreign policy is widespread. Given that their own essay offers inconsistent accounts of anti-Americanism, Keohane and Katzenstein are not in a position to assess its true character and influence.

Conflating Two Distinct Phenomena

Accounts like those of Keohane and Katzenstein are beginning to gain currency, providing some intellectual support (wittingly or not) to the conflation that I noted earlier. Because the Bush Administration has made little distinction between opposition to American foreign policy and opposition to American culture, and because it has so often invoked the rhetoric of dichotomies ("you're either with us or against us," for example), the global community has grown more critical of American foreign policy and of the American people for supporting it.

In fact, according to poll after poll, people abroad are increasingly likely to believe that America is using the war on terrorism as a guise to project its power across a wider arc. If this cynicism festers, the Bush Administration will grow deeper in its conviction that anti-American animus, rather than grounded grievances, motivates criticism of its conduct abroad. The extreme limit of these ping-pong exchanges is a scenario in which more aggressive posturing here provokes *actual* anti-Americanism abroad. This suggestion on my part—of a self-fulfilling prophecy—extends to other terms such as "jihad."[41]

The scenario that I have described is not as implausible as some might argue. Indeed, outsiders are beginning to ask themselves, "Does current American foreign policy truly depart from American values, or does it actually reflect them?" Of far greater importance than their answer to this question is the fact that they are even asking it in the first place. Viewing world opinion as an adversary is highly imprudent, as the past eight years vividly affirm. It is more appropriate to regard world opinion as a critical, but malleable, force that is to be engaged actively.

Looking Forward

The purpose of this essay is to introduce a topic that, insofar as I can gather, has scarcely received any attention in mainstream scholarship, let alone the level of attention that it surely merits. There are, admittedly, valuable studies that point in the right direction—in particular, the ones on soft balancing. One of their main limitations, however, is their state-centric framework. Most of the authors who have discussed the concept are of the realist persuasion. Consequently, they fail to appreciate the growing agentive capacity of, for example, individuals and nongovernmental organizations. I do not disagree with their belief that the state will remain the foundational unit of the international order through the foreseeable future, but it is important to note the fluidity of evolving power dynamics.

Indeed, one of the main conclusions at which I have arrived is that the traditional tripartite conception of power—military, economic, and political—is passing into obsolescence. I am calling, then, for scholars to recognize a fourth form of power, one that appreciates world opinion's influence. I would not call it information power, but rather, perceptual power. Perceptions are based not only on information, but also on falsehoods, distortions, our own biases, and herd behavior. Perceptual power is the most important form of power. It is distributed among the greatest number of players; it is the most dynamic, shifting, as it does, on the basis of daily events; and, perhaps most importantly, as seen above, it crucially impacts each of the other three forms of power.

With this thought in mind, it seems fitting to return to Mr. Epstein's quote. I included his observation at the beginning of this essay in the hope that its irony would be self-evident by my conclusion. The ostensible motivation for his posture is pragmatic; it would seem that the United States could accomplish its objectives more efficaciously if it simply pursued its own course. In a theoretical world in which states were completely disconnected from one another, such a prescription would be eminently sensible, no matter the moral issues that it might raise. In a linked and cross-linked world, however, it is nothing short of disastrous.

It is likely that the entrance of a new presidential administration will soften some of the rougher edges of world opinion. However, intense opposition to American power is not going to disappear. Fortunately, the United States only has to fear this fact if it intends to maintain the Bush Administration's unilateralist outlook. It is self-evident that global problems cannot be solved by one country, no matter the power that it commands. Respecting world opinion, ultimately, is to recognize that the United States stands to solidify its centrality in the international order if it engages the global community.

Harry Truman recognized these lessons. After the Second World War, he advanced our national interest by improving the lot of humanity. It was during his tenure that the United States administered the Marshall Plan, helped to form the United Nations, and guided the Nuremberg Trials. As he recognized, America stands to accrue immeasurable benefits from the global community's progress, provided that it does not itself become complacent. It was that simple, but powerful, insight that made the United States the envy of the world; and it is that same lesson that can restore American leadership going forward.

Notes

1 Alex Epstein, "World Opinion Be Damned: America's Attempts to Appease 'World Opinion' Are Depraved and Suicidal," *Capitalism Magazine*, http://www.capmag.com/article.asp?ID=3728 (accessed June 4, 2004).

2 Zbigniew Brzezinski, "Hostility to America Has Never Been So Great," *New Perspectives Quarterly*, Summer 2004, http://www.digitalnpq.org/archive/2004_summer/brzezinksi.html.

3 Anthony King, "Britain falls out of love with America," *The Daily Telegraph*, available at http://www.telegraph.co.uk/news/main.jhtml?xml=/news/2006/07/03/nyank103.xml (April 7, 2006).

4 Joseph S. Nye, Jr., *Soft Power: The Means to Success in World Politics* (New York: Public Affairs, 2004).

5 Michael Malone, "Welcome to the Feedback Universe," *Forbes ASAP*, October 7, 2002, 20.

6 K.G. Coffman and Andrew Odlyzko, "The Size and Growth Rate of the Internet," *First Monday*, October 5, 1998, http://www.firstmonday.org/issues/issue3_10/coffman/index.html.

7 Susan Decker, "Economics and the Internet: The Next Ten Years," presented at SIEPR Associates Meeting, Stanford, CA, December 1, 2004, Slide 4.

8 Ibid, Slide 5.

9 Internet World Stats, "Internet Usage Statistics—The Big Picture," http://www.internetworldstats.com/stats.htm; and "Top 20 Countries With the Highest Number of Internet Users," available at http://www.internetworldstats.com/top20.htm. The figure for Asia includes Japan.

10 Tom O'Neill, "Tower of Babble," *National Geographic*, June 2007.

11 John Maxwell Hamilton and Eric Jenner, "The New Foreign Correspondence," *Foreign Affairs* (September 2003): 132.

12 Jeffrey James, "The Global Information Infrastructure Revisited," *Third World Quarterly* (2001): 814.

13 James A. Dewar, "The Information Age and the Printing Press: Looking Backward to See Ahead," RAND Paper No. 8014, 1998, http://www.rand.org/pubs/papers/2005/P8014.pdf.

14 Amnesty International USA, "Eyes on Darfur," http://www.eyesondarfur.org/about.html.

15 Timothy L. Thomas, "Al-Qaeda and the Internet: The Danger of 'Cyberplanning,'" *Parameters* (Spring 2003).

16 Evan Serpick, "The Concert for Planet Earth," *Rolling Stone*, June 28, 2007, 20.

17 PIPA / GlobeScan, 23 Nation Poll: Who Will Lead the World?, April 6, 2005, http://www.worldpublicopinion.org/pipa/articles/views_on_countriesregions_bt/114.php?nid=&id=&pnt=114&lb=brglm.

18 Pew Global Attitudes Project, "American Character Gets Mixed Reviews: U.S. Image Up Slightly, But Still Negative," June 23, 2005, 30, http://pewglobal.org/reports/pdf/247.pdf.

19 The Chicago Council on Global Affairs, "World Publics Think China Will Catch Up With the US—and That's Okay," May 28, 2007, http://www.thechicagocouncil.org/media_press_room_detail.php?press_release_id=66.

20 Robin Koerner, "About 'WatchingAmerica.com,'" http://www.watchingamerica.com/mediaWA.pdf.

21 Pew Global Attitudes Project, "Global Opinion: The Spread of Anti-Americanism," 2005, 106, http://pewresearch.org/assets/files/trends2005-global.pdf. For even more insightful commentary, see Steven Kull, "It's Lonely at the Top," *Foreign Policy* (July / August 2005): 36–37. He concludes that "People around the world are not only turning away from the United States; they are starting to embrace the leadership of other major powers."

22 Andrew Kohut, Pew Research Center, "America's Image in the World: Findings from the Pew Global Attitudes Project," Testimony before the United States House of Representatives, Washington, D.C., March 14, 2007, http://pewglobal.org/commentary/pdf/1019.pdf.

23 Pierre Hassner, "The Fate of a Century," *The American Interest*, July/August 2007, 37.

24 Josef Joffe, "Power Failure," *The American Interest*, July/August 2007, 53.

25 Interestingly, though, some resistance to globalization is beginning to emerge in its chief beneficiaries, the United States and China. While it is common knowledge that income inequality is soaring in the developing world, less known is that it is also rising quite rapidly in the West. See "A widening gap," *The Economist*, June 21, 2007, http://economist.com/daily/chartgallery/displaystory.cfm?story_id=9358807.

26 Philip Bowring, "When free trade sinks into the 'noodle bowl,'" *International Herald Tribune*, August 16, 2006, http://www.iht.com/articles/2006/08/16/opinion/edbowring.php.

27 Rawi Abdelal and Adam Segal, "Has Globalization Passed Its Peak?" *Foreign Affairs* (January/February 2007): 113.

28 Freedom House, "Freedom in the World 2006: Selected Data from Freedom House's Annual Global Survey of Political Rights and Civil Liberties," October 19, 2005, 5, http://www.freedomhouse.org/uploads/pdf/Charts2006.pdf.

29 Andrew J. Nathan, "Present at the Stagnation: Is China's Development Stalled?" *Foreign Affairs* (July/August 2006): 180.

30 There is a wave of recent scholarship that documents this trend. See, for example, Lucan A. Way, "Authoritarian State Building and the Sources of Regime Competitiveness in the Fourth Wave: The Cases of Belarus, Moldova, Russia, and Ukraine," *World Politics* (January 2005); Bruce Bueno de Mesquita and George W. Downs, "Development and Democracy," *Foreign Affairs* (September / October 2005); Javier Corrales, "Hugo Boss," *Foreign Policy* (January / February 2006); and Azar Gat, "The Return of Authoritarian Great Powers," *Foreign Affairs* (July / August 2007).

31 Felix G. Rohatyn, "Democracy à la carte," *International Herald Tribune*, May 28, 2007, http://www.iht.com/articles/2007/05/28/opinion/edrohatyn.php.

32 PIPA/GlobeScan, "20 Nation Poll Finds Strong Global Consensus: Support for Free Market System, But also More Regulation of Large Companies," January 11, 2006, http://www.worldpublicopinion.org/pipa/articles/btglobalizationtradera/154.php?nid=&id=&pnt=154&lb=btgl.

33 Timothy Garton Ash, "Will capitalism fall victim to its own success?" *Los Angeles Times*, February 22, 2007, A19.

34 Stephen M. Walt, "Taming American Power," *Foreign Affairs*, September/October 2005, http://www.foreignaffairs.org/20050901faessay84509/stephen-m-walt/taming-american-power.html. See also Robert A. Pape, "Soft Balancing Against the United States," *International Security* (Summer 2005); and Andrew Hurrell, "Hegemony, liberalism and global order: what space for would-be great powers?" *International Affairs* (January 2006).

35 Scott Baldauf, "Hu's trip to Sudan tests China-Africa ties," *Christian Science Monitor*, February 2, 2007, http://www.csmonitor.com/2007/0202/p06s01-woaf.html.

36 See, for example, Norman Podhoretz, "The Case for Bombing Iran," *Commentary* (June 2007).

37 Patrick Tyler, "A new power in the streets," *New York Times*, February 17, 2003, A1.

38 There are numerous competing definitions of American culture; all of them agree that freedom and capitalism are two of its pillars and, accordingly, I do not have to fear that my definition will be opposed (at least at a broad level).

39 Peter J. Katzenstein and Robert O. Keohane, "Anti-Americanisms," *Policy Review* (October/November 2006), http://www.hoover.org/publications/policyreview/4823856.html.

40 I find the third form that they list to be especially interesting. Even though those forces that have inspired, and continue to motivate, nationalism around the world are oftentimes quite similar to those that compelled American colonists to free themselves of British dominion, American elites have invariably ascribed them to anti-Americanism. The literature that bears out this assertion is readily available and, accordingly, I will not survey it here.

41 David E. Sanger, "Does Calling It Jihad Make It So?" *New York Times*, August 13, 2006, D1.

6

Exchange Programs and Public Diplomacy

Giles Scott-Smith

Public diplomacy covers an array of different activities, all of which function at various distances from and combinations with the practice of foreign policy and its specific objectives. Among these activities, exchange programs are an interesting case. Whereas most forms of public diplomacy work involve the presentation of image and information, exchanges directly involve the "human factor," where an engagement with the personality and psychology of the participants is central. This chapter will provide an overview of some of the features of exchanges that lend them a special value within the public diplomacy toolbox. Although the inspiration for many of the comments is the U.S. State Department's International Visitor Leadership Program (IVLP), on the whole these are general observations on the practice of exchanges *in toto*.

The International Political Context

The starting point for this analysis is the fact that exchanges, however educational and "apolitical" they may be presented, inescapably operate within the broader political environment of international affairs. The ability of individuals to cross national boundaries has been a matter of major consequence since the arrival of the nation-state, and exchanges are naturally no exception. Even the most politically neutral of exchanges, such as those between high schools, have either political intent behind their creation or are promoted for the purpose of developing cross-border relations that can subsequently lead to political outcomes, such as a reduction in conflict. The best example of the latter here is probably the Franco-German high school exchanges after World War II, which saw upwards of five million students being exchanged by 1997, contributing to the normalization of relations between the two countries. Political outcomes, in other words, can represent a mix of national and general interests, such that it becomes difficult to disentangle strategic communication from "mutual understanding." This is also the case with exchanges run wholly by the private sector, which still operate within a broader political environment (but which are often used by governments exactly to avoid any sense of direct political interference). A good current example are the exchanges being run with Iranians by the U.S. private sector, which successfully involve artists and other non-governmental professional groups, but which are still inevitably heavily burdened by the tension-filled relations between the two countries.[1]

50

The interpersonal nature of the exchange experience, coupled with its inherently private character, have caused this field to be largely written out of the documentation of diplomacy and its conduct in the public realm. What exchanges represent are a form of private international relations, a diffuse interchange of people, ideas, and opinions that are generally so lost in the myriad of global social contacts that their worth is often questioned. Nevertheless, the informal networks established from these relations themselves have major political import. Not for nothing have U.S. ambassadors around the world referred to the IVLP, operational since 1950, as the most valuable tool of public diplomacy at their disposal.[2] As the 1963 study *A Beacon of Hope* stated:

> American Embassies throughout the world have stressed to us, and American leaders have confirmed, the exchange programme's effectiveness in expanding personal contacts and personal outlook, "in setting up a current of contact between the United States and other countries."[3]

Exchanges may be a form of soft power, but a form of power, however diffuse, they remain.

Political Influence

The spectrum of public diplomacy activities stretches from the direct advocacy of specific policies through to the more "noble" pursuits of cultural diplomacy and the use of the arts to gain sympathizers abroad. While exchanges generally fall into the cultural diplomacy category, they are a flexible medium that can be applied in various ways according to the purpose for which they are designed. All social groups can be reached in this way, although the higher in the hierarchy of a profession one aims for, the more prestigious the program has to be, and the likelihood increases that the person will be unable to accept due to work pressure or simply protocol. Exchanges may well be utilized as a form of strategic communication, which refers to the tailoring and directing of information at specific target audiences in order to generate a specific (policy) response.[4] However, this is not without considerable difficulty, or even danger. The offer of an exchange trip for someone directly involved in a policy area of great value to the initiator of the contact will generally be taken as an attempt to gain access to in-house deliberations on that policy, preferably in the short term. This can raise questions as to whether the participant's allegiance is being deliberately influenced. Whether this is deemed acceptable or not will depend on the state of bilateral relations between the two nations.

Nevertheless, if the political environment is favorable, the opportunity is open for using exchanges to acquaint professionals with their policymaking counterparts in order to smooth negotiating processes. This can be a very useful tool when the level of importance of the relations demands constant attention. A good example is the relationship between the United States and the European Union, where European officials were first invited to the U.S. via the State Department's Foreign Leader Program (now the IVLP), and these contacts were subsequently expanded with the arrival of the E.U.'s own Visitor Program in 1974 and various transatlantic training and professional exchange programs that were developed through the 1970s and 1980s.[5]

Risk and Unpredictability

Whatever the goals they are intended to achieve, exchanges are best kept independent from any sense of direct political interference and obligation in order to maintain the integrity of the participants and the credibility of the programmes themselves.[6] Whereas propaganda refers to the deliberate manipulation of information to achieve a desired result, exchanges are (ideally) the most two-way form of public diplomacy, opening up spaces for dialogue and the interchange of alternative viewpoints. "Mutual understanding," the catchphrase for the liberal understanding of cross-border contacts, does mean something here, even in the most politically-orientated programs. Exchanges are at their most effective when they allow the participant to experience openness and honesty in their interaction with the host nation. This openness is optimized if combined with allowances for freedom of choice to enable the construction of a personal itinerary or the satisfaction of individual interests, thereby adding to a sense of empowerment. Inevitably, there is an ever-present risk factor within these kinds of contact. It is impossible to predict exactly how an exchange experience will influence an individual, and the elements of chance and contingency are unavoidable. Exchanges "cannot be easily fine-tuned into a political instrument," and if this is attempted, it is highly likely that the resulting limitations and sense of propaganda that this will project will rebound and undermine the overall impact.[7] The use-value of the exchange for both organizer and participant may not coincide, but that does not mean that the results may be malign, only unpredictable. This goes for all types of exchanges, whether educational, academic, or professional. The process of selecting participants, an essential part of most programs (even those who apply to participate in programs must still be accepted), offers some control over who becomes involved, but this remains a question of judgement based on necessarily incomplete information.

The most notorious case that exemplifies risk is the visit of Seyyed Qutb to the United States in 1948. Qutb, an Egyptian civil servant, went to study the education system in Colorado for the benefit of implementing reforms in his home country. Instead, his disgust at American society and its immoral materialism only furthered his own path towards a pure form of Islamic radicalism, and he subsequently became a major influence within anti-Western fundamentalism. This case highlights how things can seriously go awry, but while the chance of a culture-clash is ever-present, it would be a mistake to use Qutb as a reason to limit exchanges in general. They are hardly an exact science, as even the psywar aficionados of the 1950s were forced to admit.

Cultural Differences

Qutb's case points out how regional and cultural differences have a crucial impact on how exchanges function. In the 1950s, during the early years of the IVLP, it was discovered that the most complaints about the Program were coming from participants from India. The reason was that the U.S. embassy was selecting mainly individuals from the higher castes who expected far more of a VIP treatment than they received, and they did not understand how the U.S. government could run such a Program with so little official protocol (when that was in fact the whole point). The often individual nature of the exchange experience, especially for the longer student exchanges, can also generate problems of negative social isolation for some groups. Risks can be minimized if special attention can be given to this problem by an alert international student advisory/counseling apparatus coordinated through the university system. The issue of "follow-up," i.e. contact between the inviting organization and the participant, can have different connotations for different cultural groups. Whereas some will have no expectations, others may be surprised (and disappointed) if no further contact materializes. It is vital to take into account local perceptions in order to avoid undermining the exchange's purpose.

Uniqueness

Overall, the exchange experience will be valued most because of its uniqueness. The levels of cross-border contact are now so high that it is difficult to appreciate how any particular form of exchange can still offer more, but this is a vital element to making its effects stick. It can take form in many ways. It can be related to the opportunity to gain new knowledge and skills otherwise unavailable locally. This can be combined with absorbing and appreciating a new cultural environment, where first-hand experience will always have a greater effect than second-hand knowledge. For other types of exchange there could be a prestige factor in being invited, which may also involve obtaining access to persons or institutions that would otherwise be either closed off or accessible only via more formal routes. The importance of youth here cannot be over-stated, but this needs to be clarified. Access and prestige can always have some impact, but an exchange will have the greatest impact both if it takes place before the host nation is already familiar for the participant, and if it offers openings and opportunities that the participant can utilize for their own personal and/or professional benefit afterwards. The initial contact, if well managed and well timed, can have a long-lasting effect.

The Opinion Leader

This connects to the important issue of the participant's status after their return home. Here it is ideal if the value of the exchange operation for both organizer and participant can coincide as much as possible. If successful, the experience will contribute towards not just personal know-ledge but also a further encouragement of ambition and, possibly, leadership potential. In the 1940s U.S. communications researchers developed the concept of the "opinion leader" who, based on their recognized knowledge gained from direct experience, could function as key transmitters of information within a given community. Exchanges were first applied to develop this role among participants by the U.S. occupation forces in post-war Germany, as part of the re-education of German society towards democratic principles. Analysis of these programs indicated that the "opinion leader" model did operate as intended, with exchange participants acting (voluntarily) as legitimate and respected sources of opinion and judgement on the United States. Although this example has lost some of its worth due to the saturation of broadcasting from or about the United States, exchange participants can still function as important channels for infor-mation transfer to wider communities (the "multiplier" role) in certain settings. The case of Iran is a prime example, where the relative isolation of much of the population from outside contact enables those who have such experience to gain a more prominent role than they would have otherwise. If the international political environment allowed, exchanges would be an ideal means over the longer term to improve relations between that nation and the West.

The Cultural Broker

Exchanges can function in an important way to create neutral spaces for a form of "cultural brokerage." This generally refers to no more than introducing and linking individuals and institutions working in the same field, and allowing professional inclination to take its course, with unspecified results. Private-sector exchanges with the Soviet Union and Eastern Europe took this approach, looking to break down inter-bloc antagonism through professional inter-change, and with some success.[8] It can also involve the organization of multinational group visits, perhaps based around a specific theme to unite a particular group around a particular goal. Traveling around for days or weeks in a third country will generally contribute to breaking down barriers that would remain intact in other more formal settings, stimulating curiosity, dialogue, and perhaps longer-term contact. This method can then be employed for the deliberate (though perhaps unstated) purpose of removing various individuals from a conflict zone in order to set up, on a low level, a chance at reconciliation within a distant environment. Maximum opportunity must be given for personal contact to break down prejudicial barriers. Once again, selection is crucial in order to ensure only participants with sufficient open-mindedness take part. This is no more than small-scale conflict resolution, and care must be taken not to expect too much once the participants return home, but it is typical of the kind of inter-personal, grass-roots effects that can, if coordinated with determined conflict resolution measures in the "hard policy" field, have a long-lasting effect.

An increasingly important role has been played in this field by what might be called corporate or entrepreneurial cultural diplomacy. The most notorious example is George Soros' Open Society Institute (OSI), which has been promoting the development of civil society and good governance practices across Central Europe and Central Asia since 1993 as part of an explicit strategy of democratization. The Institute runs many fellowship and grant programs to increase professional interchange with the region and encourage leadership potential. Other institutions look to use exchanges to break down cultural barriers within the context of the one-world global market, such as the Atlantic-Pacific Exchange Program (APEP) based in Rotterdam (which began as an effort to improve Dutch-American relations in the mid-1980s) and the Institute for Cultural Diplomacy (ICD) in Berlin. What is most interesting about these operations is that they are not related to any particular national interest. Whereas the OSI is a fully independent actor, the APEP and ICD both function and adapt to the changing needs of their corporate clients over time.

Identity and Orientation

There is quite a body of work on the impact that direct experience of another culture can have on a participant's own psychological outlook.[9] As one astute observer has put it, cross-border contacts can lead to "a subtle but important shift in identity and self-conception," whereby previously fixed political and/or cultural allegiances are not abandoned but become more flexible.[10] Identities are the basis for how interests are defined, and whereas this generally occurs in a routine manner according to the familiar settings we find ourselves in, "sometimes situations are unprecedented in our experience, and in these cases we have to construct their meaning, and thus our interests, by analogy or invent them de novo."[11] One goal of an exchange can be to precisely create that unprecedented experience, thereby dislodging previously fixed notions of identity and interest. For optimum impact, what needs to be created is a wider community or institution that can engage with and encompass the changed outlook of the former participant, so that they can continue to share and develop their new-found perspective. This can mean in the first place involving former grantees in the operation of the program afterwards, particularly in the selection and orientation phase for new candidates. Satisfied former grantees are valuable as the best advertisements available, themselves functioning as "opinion leaders" for a continuing program. An alumni association is also a useful tool, not just to maintain a visible community but also as a "multiplier" organization for the program itself. More broadly, in the professional and academic field this can ideally point towards some form of allegiance to a larger (intellectual) community not limited by the borders of the nation state, thus fomenting a broader conception of national interest itself.

What are the necessary conditions for actors to reinvent their identities? According to social theorist Alexander Wendt, two factors must apply. Firstly, "there must be a reason to think of oneself in novel terms. This would most likely stem from the presence of new social situations that cannot be managed in terms of pre-existing self-conceptions." Secondly, there has to be a pay-off: "The expected cost of intentional role change cannot be greater than its rewards." In other words, if the intention is to guide this process down certain paths, there must be full consideration of the many variables and obstacles involved that need to be overcome to make it successful.[12]

54

Reinforcing Opinions

A subtle variation of the "identity change" approach is the move to use exchange experiences to build on and strengthen already-existing positive sentiments among selected participants, with the goal of thereby strengthening a potential or actual (political) ally for the future. Research into the post-war German programs and other investigations into psychological warfare techniques highlighted the fact that critics will rarely be swayed, but doubters may become believers and supporters will feel empowered. From this perspective, exchanges are a prime means for alliance management, since they can be applied to build up, over the longer term, a community of individuals united around a common cultural affinity that takes positive relations between certain nations more or less for granted. Since 1946 the Fulbright Program has been very successful in developing such an affinity with the United States, firstly via the means of academic exchange itself, and secondly by encouraging the establishment of American Studies in universities around the world. As even arch-Realist Hans Morgenthau recognized, creating and sustaining forms of cultural affinity amongst foreign publics represents a potent form of power:

> The power of a nation, then, depends not only upon the skill of its diplomacy and the strength of its armed forces but also upon the attractiveness for other nations of its political philosophy, political institutions, and political policies. This is true in particular of the United States . . .[13]

Conclusion

It should be apparent that, whatever the particular merits of exchanges, they will only deliver the best results if allowed to function in coordination with foreign policies that promote international cooperation. No public diplomacy campaign will sell bad or unpopular policy, and because of the "human factor" exchanges are particularly vulnerable in an antagonistic political context. Yet in the right circumstances they can achieve significant changes in attitude. In short, this form of public diplomacy won't change the world, but—*pace* the risks exemplified by Qutb—it does contribute towards holding it together.

Notes

1 Negar Azimi, "Hard Realities of Soft Power," *New York Times Magazine*, June 24, 2007, 50–55.
2 *Field Survey of Public Diplomacy Programs*, U.S. Department of State, Washington D.C., 2000.
3 *A Beacon of Hope: The Exchange of Persons Program*, Advisory Commission on International Educational and Cultural Affairs, April 1963, 27–28.
4 See Jarol Manheim, *Strategic Public Diplomacy and American Foreign Policy: The Evolution of Influence* (Oxford: Oxford University Press, 1994).
5 Giles Scott-Smith, "Mending the 'Unhinged Alliance' in the 1970s: Transatlantic Relations, Public Diplomacy, and the Origins of the European Union Visitors Programme," *Diplomacy and Statecraft* 16 (December 2005).
6 On the issue of credibility, see the important work of Sherry Mueller: "The U.S. Department of State's International Visitor Program: A Conceptual Framework for Evaluation" (PhD diss., Fletcher School of Law and Diplomacy, 1977).
7 Lawrence T. Caldwell, "Scholarly Exchanges with Eastern Europe and the Soviet Union," Evaluations of the International Research and Exchanges Board, 1980, Grant No. L79–256, Report No. 012108, archive of the Ford Foundation.
8 The debate on exactly how much such exchanges contributed to the downfall of the Soviet system is still continuing. See Yale Richmond, *Cultural Exchange and the Cold War: Raising the Iron Curtain* (University Park, PA: Pennsylvania State University Press, 2003).
9 See, for instance, Ithiel de Sola Pool, "Effects of Cross-National Contact on National and International

Images," in Herbert Kelman (ed.), *International Behavior: A Social Psychological Analysis* (New York: Holt, Rinehart & Winston, 1965), 106–129.

10 Gail Lapidus, "The Impact of Soviet-American Scholarly Exchanges," Evaluations of the International Research and Exchanges Board, 1980, Grant No. L79–256, Report No. 012108, archive of the Ford Foundation.

11 A. Wendt, "Anarchy is what States make of it: The Social Construction of Power Politics," *International Organization* 46 (Spring 1992): 398.

12 Ibid., 419.

13 Hans Morgenthau, *Politics Among Nations: The Struggle for Power and Peace* (New York: Alfred Knopf, 1985), 169.

7

Arts Diplomacy

The Neglected Aspect of Cultural Diplomacy[1]

John Brown

Why doesn't your embassy sponsor more exhibits and concerts?

France, Germany, Japan, other countries: they organize cultural events—why doesn't the United States do as much as they do?

Doesn't your government have any interest in showing American art abroad?

These are the kind of questions that host country nationals constantly peppered me with during my 20-some years of practicing public diplomacy during the Cold War and its aftermath in Eastern Europe. As this professional experience suggests, a neglected aspect of our cultural diplomacy—at least as our foreign interlocutors see it—has been the poverty, both quantitative and qualitative, of its artistic dimension.

The U.S. government's neglect of (as I call it) arts diplomacy—which can be defined as the use of high art (music, literature, painting) as an instrument of diplomacy—reflects certain long-term traits of the United States: puritanical, democratic, without a national culture. These characteristics do not lead the U.S. (in contrast to countries with more established cultural traditions like France) to seek influence in the world through state-supported artistic presentations abroad—especially given the view of some Americans that the massive entertainment produced by the U.S. private sector, and particularly Hollywood, already "tells America's story" to foreigners.[2] Even during the Cold War, with its near total mobilization of American resources to combat Communism, arts diplomacy was a minor part of the U.S.' overseas activities, despite some memorable events like State Department-sponsored jazz concerts and the establishment of admirable venues for some artistic presentations, the American cultural centers and libraries. It is not surprising, therefore, that today arts diplomacy continues to play second fiddle to other U.S. diplomatic initiatives, public or traditional.

That this situation has not changed (and has in fact deteriorated) in our new century is made clear by the recent report of the Advisory Committee on Cultural Diplomacy, *Cultural Diplomacy: The Linchpin of Public Diplomacy* (2005), in which we learn the following from the committee's fact-finding mission to Muscat, Cairo, and London:

> A theme emerged from a luncheon in Muscat with members of the Omani Fine Arts Society, which we would hear throughout our travels: the need for more exchanges of actors, animators, artists,

directors, writers, state technicians, and Web designers. . . . At the National Cultural Center [in Cairo], a dazzling $60 million complex of theaters, music halls, exhibition spaces, and offices built for the Egyptian people by the Japanese government, we saw the results of cultural diplomacy: 700 performances a year, attended by 300,000 people, each of whom, in some small corner of his or her mind, remembers the benefactors of the space in which they take such pleasure. . . . "You reach the people through art and culture," said an official [from the U.S. Embassy in Cairo]. But our cultural presence in this country no longer exists. The French Cultural Ministry can give you a monthly calendar. We can't do anything, because we don't know when anything will happen.[3]

Another recent critical report on public diplomacy, the Government Accountability Office's (GAO) "U.S. Public Diplomacy: State Department Efforts Lack Certain Communication Elements and Face Persistent Challenges,"[4] underscores (unwittingly, perhaps) the neglect of arts diplomacy by hardly mentioning what activities it encompasses. Indeed, the report is silent about the few new (and low impact) cultural programs that have been undertaken in recent years, such as CultureConnect and the Ambassador's Fund for Cultural Preservation. It does, almost as an afterthought, mention without criticism the "American Corners" established in this new century, which Ambassador Cynthia Schneider (a strong supporter of cultural diplomacy who has written extensively about the subject) describes as "pockets of America placed inside local libraries and cultural institutions [that] offer access to the Internet, plus videos, CDs, and books about the U.S."[5] But while these Corners (cheap substitutes for the cultural centers shut down after the Cold War) can play a valuable educational role on occasion, I know from my own experience as a Cultural Affairs officer in Russia—where the Corners program began—that they often disappointed host country nationals people by their limited, overly modest scale and few available resources, including ones pertaining to high art. Not always directly expressed, but nevertheless often made clear by tactful insinuation, the reaction of many Russians to the Corners was: Is that all America has to offer?

Some foreign-policy professionals would argue that arts diplomacy should not be on our government's radar screen because it is not, in the scheme of things, a priority. Far more significant, they would say, is maintaining a country's hard power while supporting "serious" soft power programs like international broadcasting. I do believe, however, that arts diplomacy is important. Of course, I would never claim that it is a panacea for the low esteem held toward America overseas that has been documented in recent years by poll after poll. Arts diplomacy, I willingly agree, will not suddenly move the needle of global public opinion in favor of the U.S. or its foreign policy in the way gasoline makes a motor move. Foreigners will not instantly begin to drink Diet Coke or eat pounds after pounds of U.S. frozen chicken if they know more American poetry. Nor is it self-evident (Platonic assumptions of well-meaning culture vultures notwithstanding) that art (when "ethically" appropriate for the mind) will necessarily lead to virtue abroad as we Americans see it—for example, to less anti-Americanism in countries that "hate us." How many terrorists will automatically embrace American values after reading *Moby Dick* or listening to Negro spirituals? Very few, if any, is my answer to this question, often posed by those who think the taxpayer-supported promotion of art is a waste of time and resources. Finally, it would be hard to justify government-supported arts diplomacy as a great American tradition (which it was not and still is not) or by its past "triumphs" in the Cold War (which were few and far between).

So I approach the question of justifying the need for arts diplomacy modestly, with the full realization that for many in America it is a superfluous enterprise, and that for the few who do support it, it is (in the words of Frank Ninkovich apropos of public diplomacy as a whole) essentially an "act of faith."[6] I am also aware my justifications may disappoint those who, in their understandable and well-intentioned eagerness to obtain congressional funding for arts diplomacy, make claims about it that are not, in my view, always logically or historically sustainable.

Having said that, three reasons stand out for the U.S. government to engage in arts diplomacy that underscore its importance:

(1) **Arts diplomacy is a response to the desires of overseas publics.** America, for all its faults (and nobody's perfect) continues to fascinate the world. There is a strong desire abroad to know more about our country, even in this age of the Internet and instant communications. Foreign audiences, proud in many cases of their own high culture, expect the U.S. government (not just the American private sector) to expose them to American cultural achievements. Arts diplomacy, when subtly but visibly sponsored by the U.S. government and its embassies abroad, is an answer to this desire: it is a gentle (yet official) gesture showing that we, through our government's promotion of our art, are interested in others, that we want to share our artistic accomplishments with the rest of our small planet. This may sound mushy to some, but as a foreign policy tool, arts diplomacy is certainly is far better for the American image—and certainly cheaper—than bombing Baghdad.

(2) **Arts diplomacy provides a context for American culture.** Arts diplomacy, when not turned into a base propaganda tool, suggests that American culture is of infinite variety. Without necessarily downgrading American popular culture, arts diplomacy demonstrates that it is only one part of that great ongoing experiment, the United States. While it may not have a "message," as information programs do, or "educational goals," as exchanges do,[7] arts diplomacy helps present America as a complex and multidimensional country that cannot be reduced to slogans or simplifications. In a word, it shows that America is human.

(3) **Finally, arts diplomacy provides audiences with unique and memorable experiences.** It is all but impossible to describe the aesthetic experience, which is a highly individual matter. But for many, a work of art is a form of revelation, of illumination. Art creates powerful impressions that are often remembered forever. At the very least, arts diplomacy can make people abroad associate America with the kind of unique moments that make our lives worth living.

Notes

1 The title is adapted from Charles Frankel, *The Neglected Aspect of Foreign Affairs: American Educational and Cultural Policy Abroad* (Washington, D.C.: Brookings Institution, 1966).
2 These thoughts are developed in greater detail in a longer version of this paper that appeared in William P. Kiehl, ed., *America's Dialogue with the World* (Washington, D.C.: Public Diplomacy Council, 2006), 71–90. For Americans and culture, see Alexis de Tocqueville, *Democracy in America* [Henry Reeve Translation, revised and corrected, 1899], Volume II, Section 1, chapter IX, http://xroads.virginia.edu/~HYPER/DETOC/ch1 09.htm.
3 State Department Advisory Committee on Cultural Diplomacy, *Cultural Diplomacy: The Linchpin of Public Diplomacy*, report to the U.S. Department of State, September 2005, 12–13, http://www.publicdiplomacywatch.com/091505Cultural-Diplomacy-Report.pdf.
4 Jess T. Ford, "State Department Efforts Lack Certain Communication Elements and Face Persistent Challenges," testimony before the subcommittee on Science, 109th Congress, 2d sess., May 3, 2006, http://www.gao.gov/new.items/d06707t.pdf.
5 Cynthia Schneider, "Culture Communicates: Diplomacy that Works," Netherlands Institute for International Relations "Clingendael," *Discussion Papers on Diplomacy* 94 (September 2004): 21, http://www.clingendael.nl/publications/2004/20040300_cli_paper_dip_issue94.pdf.
6 Frank Ninkovich, *U.S. Information Policy and Cultural Diplomacy* (New York: Foreign Policy Association, 1966), 58.
7 See John Brown, "The Purposes and Cross-Purposes of American Public Diplomacy," *American Diplomacy* (August 2002), http://www.unc.edu/depts/diplomat/archives_roll/2002_07-09/brown_pubdipl/brown_pubdipl.html.

Part 2

Public Diplomacy Applications

Operationalizing Public Diplomacy

Matthew C. Armstrong

Introduction

American public diplomacy wears combat boots. Over the last two decades, American national security has increasingly relied on the threat of a muscular military intelligence, and technological resources while ignoring more effective, and cheaper, tools of persuasion. The downward spiral of Iraq and Afghanistan, and plummeting public opinions of the United States around the world, suggest the U.S. has decoupled the "big stick" and "speaking softly" of Theodore Roosevelt's time-tested adage without understanding its insight or utility. Fortunately, the value of speaking softly is being rediscovered, albeit by the Defense Department.

In the 21st century, perceptions matter more than facts as "super-empowered" individuals wield technology and manipulate public opinion for their own purposes unburdened by the truth and unchecked by less adroit global powers as they seek support across borders. This chapter looks at the origins and purposes of modern U.S. public diplomacy as a means to engage foreign publics directly, bypassing their governments, in a struggle to support the peace and security of the United States. This diplomacy with publics, which included carrots and sticks similar to traditional diplomacy, was required to fight an unknown enemy that seemed to be everywhere and set on destroying the American way of life.

This chapter begins with a look back at the original purpose and function of public diplomacy born out of the total war period of the early Cold War years. I then describe how public diplomacy transformed from an active and holistic engagement into a passive practice based on emotions as part of a U.S. re-election campaign. This is followed by two sections that form the heart of this chapter. The first is an overview of the importance of information in modern conflict and the second is recommendations to operationalize public diplomacy so that it sits between and informs both strategy and tactics. This chapter concludes with the assertion that this view of public diplomacy must be reinvigorated and made central in Information Age warfare where perceptions trump bullets.

Direct kinetic effects of bullets and bombs are more frequently secondary to their influence on public opinion in 21st-century warfare. An increase in the asymmetry of information operations decreases the fungibility of hard power assets. Information is not a combat multiplier but a strategic equalizer. Dynamic and global Diasporas based on "imagined communities" facilitated by instant communications are subjected to campaigns of strategic influence, as are sympathetic audiences within the U.S. and its allies. "Shock and Awe," for example, targets both the military and civilian psyche through terror, crushing its will to resist. Outside conflict zones, images are broadcast, manipulated, and often framed as a disproportionate and indiscriminate use of force. Meanwhile, within the U.S., Americans, including key decision-makers, who can barely understand the Pentagon's "mil-speak," are fascinated by the "Nintendo Warfare" of disembodied destruction and green screen images.

Modern public diplomacy evolved from the need to counter the communist information offensive played out as a struggle for the minds and wills of friends, foes, and neutrals in the two decades after World War II. As the threat became known and the fear of cancerous subversion occurring everywhere subsided, public diplomacy transformed from a "struggle for the minds and wills of men" to a "winning hearts and minds."

American public diplomacy devolved from a comprehensive effort to both understand and affect the behavior of individuals and groups through engagement and discourse to one of passive "soft power." The soft power approach towards "winning hearts and minds" amounts to a neutered beauty contest relying on cultural exchanges and press releases in the naïve hope that increased knowledge and understanding breed love for the United States. Increasingly, America's public diplomacy efforts look more like domestic political campaigns and correspondingly fail to resonate with foreign audiences.

Modern Information Age conflict requires a fundamental awareness that the struggle to shape perceptions requires the active and complete participation of the whole of government, society, and the military, to connect not just with elites but with other societies as well, just as was done in the early years of the Cold War. This required understanding the attractiveness of the enemy's message, countering it across the board with every element of the government, and drawing in the American public to be inculcated against enemy propaganda.

Today, America's armed forces are all too often "the last three feet" of engagement with publics around the world and very often the face of the U.S. through traditional and new media sources. Former United States Information Agency and broadcaster Edward R. Murrow described the last three feet as the crucial link in international communication, and includes personal experiences, formal and informal media, as well as rumor. Shaping and reinforcing perceptions, often with the encouragement of enemy propaganda, is a task the military is neither trained nor resourced for. These tasks require a greater time horizon than the military's staffing, planning, and bureaucratic structure permit.

Ironically, Americans as a whole are less in touch with their military, while those beyond our borders, especially in today's contested regions, experience America first-hand through our military. Failing to manage perceptions amplifies the mismatch between words and deeds, images and perceptions, allowing the enemy to own the narrative.

The Importance of the "Five-Dollar Word"

In 1952, presidential candidate Dwight D. Eisenhower blasted the sitting President for neglecting the psychological dimension of the Cold War. "Don't be afraid of that term just because it's a five-dollar, five syllable word," Eisenhower said in a San Francisco campaign speech as he promised to make psychological warfare, "the struggle for the minds and wills of men," a central focus of his national security strategy.[1]

The retired general was attacking President Harry S. Truman for ignoring the grass roots, the battleground the enemy was going after. Truman, however, was set on engaging people through the international institutions he was busy promoting, such as the United Nations, NATO, the World Bank, the International Monetary Fund, and even the Marshall Plan. While none of these "looked" like the public diplomacy of today, they were very effective in shaping perceptions. In the struggle for minds and wills, these institutions supported and enhanced the image and impact of the West.

The value of influencing foreign populations directly rose with the rise of the nation-state. Before the nation-state, sovereigns enjoyed greater decision-making autonomy, and attempts to influence foreign populations relied more on changing the opinion of other leaders or tactical psychological tactics such as posting heads on stakes. The United States attempted strategic influence almost immediately after its birth when authorizing privateers to take the fight home to the British to subvert domestic morale and inflict direct financial pain.[2]

In 1946, E.H. Carr described a rise of the "power over opinion" as contemporary war nullified "the distinction between combatant and civilian; and the morale of the civilian population became for the first time a military objective."[3] Decades later, Hans Morganthau, in describing his nine elements of national power, listed two as unstable: national morale and the quality of diplomacy. Their inherent instability comes from the effectiveness of domestic and foreign strategic influence.[4]

The communications and transportation revolution after World War II increased the permeability of borders and the spreading of ideas. The cost of controlling radio and print propaganda became increasingly expensive or outright counterproductive. The better response was to neutralize and inoculate against unfriendly outside influences through direct, active, and aggressive responses.

Fast forward to after the Cold War, and especially after 9/11, and the United States became a one-punch fighter relying on "Shock and Awe" to intimidate global opposition. "Terrorizing the terrorist"[5] was a central tenet of many policy makers, even if it rarely worked and often proved counterproductive by increasing overt and covert support for insurgents and terrorists.

We are nearly six years beyond 9/11, and yet the psychological dimension of Information Age warfare remains largely neglected. Dozens of reports and books have been written on the subject of public diplomacy, many of them toeing the "soft power" line, or the ability to move people by argument or to entice and attract,[6] and others seeking a more muscular approach. Virtually all have dropped public diplomacy's underlying notion of strategic influence, the ability to indirectly control or affect behavior, in favor of strategic communication and an emphasis on controlling the narrative.

However, diplomacy, private or public, is and must be a negotiation involving persuasion, dissuasion, coercion, and rewards. Its purpose is to influence the will of an actor through both anticipating and appropriately affecting the psychological responses of that actor to an event, image, or message. Today's requirement is not better story telling or controlling the narrative, but mastering the discourse.

With insurgencies raging around the planet, shifting borders, and economic, military, and sociological threats everywhere at once, the full impact of perception management, both friendly and unfriendly, must be realized. America increased its strategic influence by engaging in a discourse with both mass audiences and individuals with the goal of exposing the lies and deceit of the enemy. Populations were encouraged to become a participant in the bulwark that rejected the enemy.

In 1948, George Kennan developed a plan for "organized political warfare" to counter the Soviet Union's growing power and influence. To be effective, it required the United States to employ all means possible to achieve its national objective, including overt activities such as political alliances, economic measures, and "white" propaganda, to covert operations such as clandestine support of foreign elements, "black" psychological warfare, to encouraging underground resistance movements in hostile states.[7]

This was not the "diplomacy in public" we know today, but a full-spectrum "diplomacy with publics" that engaged people at all levels and with all means available. Seven years later, Nelson Rockefeller recognized the struggle as "shifting more than ever from the arena of power to the arena of ideas and international persuasion."[8] A then-young Henry Kissinger, stressing the importance of the people, noted the "predominant aspect of the new diplomacy is its psychological dimension."[9]

The early years of the Cold War period, before the first détente, was a period of total war even if armies were not yet engaged in open industrial warfare. With insurgencies around the globe, the Soviet Union taking Eastern Europe, and the perception that China was lost to the Communists, the United States felt threatened to the core. Attempts to prove and dispel the propaganda and realities on both sides included very active information campaigns and "diplomacy of deeds" across economic, political, social, moral, scientific, and military spheres.[10]

This was not a beauty contest to "win" by strutting on the catwalk, or a play for the emotions of the heart. It was a struggle of significance based on trust and achieved by claiming the role of narrator. The goal was to inculcate allies, neutrals, and the home front against enemy subversion by showing the ruinous truth and lies of the enemy's path. It also sought to go "behind the lines" to encourage dissent and political revolt.

However, as it became clear that people behind the Iron Curtain were paying attention, the aggressive nature of what was to become known as public diplomacy softened and the first steps from the "struggle for the minds and wills of men" to "winning hearts and minds" could be seen. During the Kennedy Administration, the geography of the First World and the Second World was largely finalized and the shift from affecting the psychology of people to winning hearts would change the very purpose of public diplomacy.

Even as Edward Gullion settled on the term "public diplomacy" 15 years after Eisenhower's call for "psychological warfare," the world in which it would be used was already morphing as the crisis environment of the early Cold War years waned and the impact of actually mobilizing foreign publics to rise up was felt.[11] Maps were finalized as the cosmic threat of communism settled down and insurgencies around the globe, the aftermath of the massive disruption from World War II, were no longer harbingers of the destabilization of the whole of Western civilization, but it was still acknowledged the U.S. needed to aggressively participate in the arena of international persuasion.

Gullion said he "would have liked to call it 'propaganda'" because "it seemed the nearest thing in the pure interpretation of the word to what we were doing."[12] Public diplomacy's connection to propaganda was not accidental. As Christina Meyer wrote later, "Propaganda grants authority to its makers [and] once a group has the people's ears and eyes, it can manipulate their minds."[13]

The urgency of the struggle waned as the geopolitical situation stabilized and states settled into the First, Second, or other Worlds. The U.S. was now engaged with an enemy it knew and the U.S. knew where that enemy was. No longer focused on populist regime change in Communist states, propaganda and agitation were toned down after it was realized people actually listened, as was the case in Hungary.

American public diplomacy shifted to justification, explanation, and exchange, a far cry from the active and holistic "struggle" of its original purpose. Anything more aggressive was seen as propaganda, and thus "wrong," or worse, something that belonged to the military, and labeled "Psychological Operations," and later, "Information Operations."

By the time of 9/11, the de facto "owner" of foreign engagement outside of cultural exchanges was widely understood to be the Defense Department under former Secretary of Defense Donald Rumsfeld. With discussions, and hesitancy, on "military operations other than war," the Defense Department was often the face of the U.S. through humanitarian aid missions and stability operations. It is noteworthy that after 9/11, Rumsfeld was frequently asked about the need for the United States Information Agency while the Secretaries of State during Rumsfeld's tenure rarely were.

The post-9/11 "Shared Values" campaign showed how far public diplomacy had come from its roots. No longer was there an active fight over the minds and wills, to forcefully engage enemy propaganda at all levels and across all of government. Now, *winning* hearts was the goal and the telling of the story the purpose. Not even attempting to participate in a bilateral conversation, the emphasis was on controlling the narrative, as critics and champions alike adopted the "winning hearts and minds" mantra. Yet few realized this phrase was borrowed from counterinsurgency practices and relied on a stick to back it up, just as few realized the true roots of public diplomacy.

Attempts to resurrect the original intent of public diplomacy were largely met with silence. An attempt to return public diplomacy to its former shape of blurred "traditional distinctions between international and domestic information activities, between public and traditional diplomacy and between cultural diplomacy, marketing and news management"[14] was implicitly rejected in favor of the more selective and passive "soft power."[15] Public diplomacy was now entrenched as little more than brand management. Marginalized further, this contributed to the belief that "like most American journalists, many public diplomatists are political liberals."[16]

Information, Politics, and War

Largely unaware of a global threat already based on a psychological struggle, the U.S. was shocked into the reality with 9/11. No longer will a passive and discordant information policy work. Clausewitz's bifurcation of war and peace where war is an extension of politics[17] is no longer correct: war is politics and every act in war is a political act. Public diplomacy can no longer end at the water's edge with an artificial separation between war and peace, civilian and warrior, or domestic and foreign information campaigns. The struggle for minds and wills has returned to the open battleground over perceptions and support.

Perception management has always been central to success in conflicts throughout history. Thucydides, Sun Tzu, Clausewitz, and virtually every author writing about insurgency and counterinsurgency understood the need to maintain trust and the perception of moral authority in the minds of the population. What these authors did not have to contend with, however, was modern global communications that create and mobilize imagined communities without reference to or restriction by geographic boundaries. Information is the center of gravity, the focal point where a certain centripetal force seems to exist holding everything else together,[18] for friends, foes, and neutrals alike.

Called the "oxygen" of the terrorist by Prime Minister Margaret Thatcher,[19] media is adeptly used by the insurgents for perception management and to replicate the message to a broader audience.[20] Modern insurgent attacks, which use such things as improvised explosive devices, or IEDs, are often designed to elicit the attention of the media and especially the international press, if not simply to create filmable events to broadcast for cut and paste media campaigns in order to generate local and global fear and, at the same time, support for even very small groups. Modern communication technologies act as a force multiplier and equalizer in ways not seen before.

Whereas the public diplomacy practiced by America's Founding Fathers, including pamphlets, privateers sent to the coast of England, and the Declaration of Independence, benefited from the spread of information, its relatively slow transmission speed gave time to frame or rebut. Modern communications, including formal media and YouTube, blogs, email, and text messaging, magnify the potential influence of small insurgent or terrorist groups that might otherwise have remained tactical or regionally strategic. These channels also prevent counterinsurgent tactics like that of the ancient Roman Empire—laying waste to entire towns—or like that of the British response to the Mehdi in the Sudan in 1898. In more recent times, the Zapatista demonstrated the media can reduce the fungibility of the hard power of the counterinsurgents.[21]

Returning to its Roots: Operationalizing Public Diplomacy

In 1999, two Chinese colonels described the future of warfare as one in which all means of power "will be in readiness . . . information will be omnipresent, and the battlefield will be everywhere."[22] In essence, all of the boundaries lying between the war and peace and between military and civilian will become meaningless as modern conflict is de-territorialized and increasingly about ideology and perceptions, with the physical space becoming contested after enough minds are "captured" and their wills turned.

To properly meet the requirement, the perception of public diplomacy must return to a tool that is both strategic and tactical and operating across the government. It must become an "operational art," to borrow the term from the military, to not only guide but actively support ongoing campaigns aimed at accomplishing strategic objectives within a given time and space as well as support perpetual operations. It would contribute to and guide discussions on what assets to deploy as well as monitoring their effectiveness.

All of the country's available resources, including bombs, trade agreements, and cultural exchanges, should be viewed as sliders on an equalizer to be adjusted upward or downward independently of each other and yet synchronized to an end goal. The sliders would shift according to the attributes of the song as well as to the stereo system and the room it is playing in, all with the goal of making the song sound its best. As a metaphor for foreign policy, the sliders would adjust for environmental factors and apply the right frequency of pressure on friend, foe, and neutral to tune them in to America's national security objectives. The success of these actions depends on strategic initiatives to prepare the groundwork and incorporate their success for later missions.

Quaint and misunderstood restrictions, such as the Smith-Mundt Act of 1948, must be reformed to be effective in Information Age conflicts. The intent of the Act was not to curtail the overall information activities of the United States, but to increase its quality and to raise the volume and quality of the current "whisper" of the State's information programs.

However, with time the Act became misconstrued and improperly extended as domestic political winds shifted. The domestic dissemination prohibition ultimately less to do with influencing U.S. audiences as protecting domestic media from competition and concerns over the State Department's loyalties and sympathies. The Act has been improperly extended to cover much of the U.S. government, including the Defence Department, contrary to Congressional intent in 1948 and without understanding the unrelated politics behind later amendments to the Act. This has been done while ignoring the blatant domestic propagandizing tools, ranging from appearances on the Sunday talk show circuit to the role of the President's press secretary.

The Act's primary effect today is to restrict, if artificially, much of the government, often beyond the State Department, from conducting effective message campaigns in a global media environment. It has also been widely over-applied to effectively silence much of the government's potential for responding and neutralizing enemy propaganda, arguably leaving the government with the ability only to make a request that U.S. news networks not broadcast foreign propaganda.[23]

Public diplomacy must be perpetual and holistic to be effective in the modern struggle for minds and wills. It takes time to build the trust necessary to motivate and mobilize an audience, and, once lost, even the benefit of the doubt is hard to come by.

However, the root causes and subsequent responses to events like Abu Ghraib and secret CIA "rendition" flights are too often shaped by U.S. domestic politics. The result is a "diplomacy of deeds" perceived by foreign publics quite different than and distinctly at odds with American values and words and arguably more akin to a "propaganda of deeds" based on violence.

Public diplomacy is a two-way street. If properly architected and managed, it becomes more than a tool of persuasion, but an interrogative through its sociological infrastructure that helps interpret and understand different cultures and Diasporas.

Getting back on course requires a renewed appreciation of Eisenhower's aggressive "five-dollar, five syllable" foundation of public diplomacy. Too many of America's enemies have proven themselves more capable than the U.S. in the psychological struggle for the minds and wills of a regional and global audience. To participate in modern conflict requires accepting an aggressive stance as well as accepting a whole of government approach. Public diplomacy as "psychological warfare . . . is so bound up with the conduct and demeanor of the entire American Government, that you cannot establish a separate department of psychological warriors."[24]

In the early days of Operation Iraqi Freedom in 2003, the common perception in the U.S. military was the "Arab mind" only understood "force, pride, and saving face." U.S. tactics were based on the belief that "with a heavy dose of fear and violence, and a lot of money for projects," it was possible to "convince these people that we are here to help them."[25] Clearly, this was a significant failure of diplomacy with the Iraqi and Arab publics.

The grammar of friend, foe, and undecided is informed by their literature and shaped by culture. One project intended to build confidence and trust in Iraq was for soldiers to give soccer balls to children in the hope of improving our image, an experiment based on the Machiavellian belief of buying loyalty, or as Machiavelli put it, heap "honors on [his advisor], enriching him, placing him in his debt . . . so that he sees that he cannot do better without him." It did not work. The real impact was the emasculation of the fathers with whom the U.S. was trying to build trust and ultimately influence. More effective was giving the soccer balls to the Iraqi Police, who then gave the balls to the fathers to give to their children, indebting the fathers to the police, who were members of the community. This tactic is based on Arab tribal and community culture and suggested by the Arab Machiavelli, Muhammad ibn Zafar al-Siqilli, who understood the different kind of indebtedness in Islamic culture: "Amongst faithful and far-sighted counselors, he is most deserving of attention whose prosperity depends on your own, and whose safety is tied to yours. He who stands in such a position, exerting himself for your interests, will likewise serve and defend himself while fighting for you."[26]

We must take a lesson from Mao and broadcast divisions among the terrorists and their failures to gain support for their cause. Mao observed that "the [people] may be likened to water and the [troops] to the fish who inhabit it." Mao added that "it is only undisciplined troops who make the people their enemies and who, like the fish out of its native element, cannot live."[27] To use Iraq as an example, it should be easy to see the impact of "undisciplined troops," in this case a broad definition of U.S. agents, in losing the struggle for the Iraqi and regional mind and will.

Managing America's image requires understanding the impact of the morale credibility with events like Abu Ghraib. This "arrow in the back of every soldier and Marine" in Iraq was just an example of how America lost whatever symmetrical advantage it had in the information war.[28]

Conclusion

As was the case nearly 50 years ago, the State Department today suffers from "inflexibility," "internal resistance and misunderstanding," and a "lack of enthusiasm and imagination."[29] Public diplomacy can and must contribute to intelligence and operational effectiveness by increasing understanding of the target audience through bilateral conversations and building credibility. Edward R. Murrow's famous plea to be involved "on the take-offs as well as the landings" of policy decision was not so his staff could write better copy, but so the policy and decision makers would be aware of the consequences of the action and adjust accordingly. There is no reason to fear opposition media and lament that, as is often heard in military campaigns in the Middle East, that "Al Jazeera kicked our butts."[30] This short statement exposes the awareness, if unconscious, of the value of information and the inability of the United States to counter or manage it.

NATO spokesman Jamie Shea captured the importance of information and the understanding that success cannot be had if the people do not know who is winning when he said "leaders have to dominate the media and not be dominated by it. Successful conflicts cannot be media driven. Winning the media campaign is just as important as winning the military campaign."[31] However, any successes we have must be exploited and not passively shared. Unless the people think the U.S. is winning, the insurgent narrative will continue to gain traction.

This chapter focused on making public diplomacy relevant today in the minds of decision makers and policy makers by returning to a holistic approach to the struggle using all the tools in America's toolbox. Public diplomacy cannot be done quickly or in crisis mode. Public diplomacy can be proactive and when reactive, it relies on a firm foundation built over time.

Today, we must communicate not only with the individual holding an RPG in the streets of Iraq, but also his family, and the people who facilitated the exchange of money, weapons, and a safe-haven for the attack to take place. Insurgents fight for various reasons, but disaggregation is not convenient for sound bites designed for U.S. domestic consumption. However, disaggregating the enemy is required to properly focus American public opinion, shape the government's posture to the threat, and to manage perceptions of the enemy to lend deny him credibility.

We are not in conflict over hearts and passions, but a psychological struggle over wills and minds. We must stop telling foreign publics what we want our own people to hear. Unless we get our information house in order, the United States will remain virtually unarmed in the battles that shape our future.

Notes

1 Kenneth Alan Osgood, *Total Cold War: Eisenhower's Secret Propaganda Battle at Home and Abroad* (Lawrence: University of Kansas, 2006), 46.

2 Francis R. Stark, *The Abolition of Privateering and the Declaration of Paris* (New York: Columbia University, 1897), 123.

3 Edward Hallett Carr, *The Twenty Years' Crisis, 1919–1939: An Introduction to the Study of International Relations* (London: Macmillan & Co., 1946), 136.

4 Hans J. Morgenthau and Kenneth W. Thompson, *Politics among Nations: The Struggle for Power and Peace*, 6th ed. (New York: Knopf : Distributed by Random House, 1985).

5 Mark Juergensmeyer, *Terror in the Mind of God: The Global Rise of Religious Violence*, 3rd ed., Comparative Studies in Religion and Society (Berkeley: University of California Press, 2003), 237.

6 William A. Rugh, ed., *Engaging the Arab & Islamic Worlds through Public Diplomacy* (Washington, D.C.: Public Diplomacy Council, 2004), xiii.

7 Angel Rabasa et al., *Building Moderate Muslim Networks* (Santa Monica, CA: RAND Corporation, 2007), 11.

8 Kenneth Alan Osgood, *Total Cold War: Eisenhower's Secret Propaganda Battle at Home and Abroad* (Lawrence: University of Kansas, 2006), 46.

9 Ibid., 182.

10 It is sadly ironic that the phrase "diplomacy of deeds," a phrase adopted by Under Secretary of State for Public Diplomacy and Public Affairs Karen Hughes, comes from "propaganda by deed" that used violence to draw attention to, generate publicity for, and inform, educate, and rally the masses behind revolution.

11 For example, the Hungarian Revolution can be seen as a successful combination of covert and overt engagement the U.S. was not prepared to follow up. Realizing this, the U.S. retreated from future similar operations. For more, see Michael Nelson, *War of the Black Heavens: The Battles of Western Broadcasting in the Cold War*, 1st UK ed. (London; Washington: Brassey's, 1997).

12 Richard T. Arndt, *The First Resort of Kings: American Cultural Diplomacy in the Twentieth Century*, 1st ed. (Dulles, VA: Potomac Books, 2005), 480.

13 Christina Meyer, *Underground Voices: Insurgent Propaganda in El Salvador, Nicaragua, and Peru* (Santa Monica, CA: RAND Corporation, 1991).

14 Rhiannon Vickers, "The New Public Diplomacy: Britain and Canada Compared," *British Journal of Politics & International Relations* 6, no. 2 (2004).

15 Joseph S. Nye, *Soft Power: The Means to Success in World Politics*, 1st ed. (New York: Public Affairs, 2004).

16 Carnes Lord, *Losing Hearts and Minds?: Public Diplomacy and Strategic Influence in the Age of Terror* (Westport, CT: Praeger Security International, 2006), 58.

17 Carl von Clausewitz, *On War*, trans. Michael Eliot Howard and Peter Paret (Princeton, NJ: Princeton University Press, 1976), 87.

18 Antulio J. Echevarria, "Clausewitz's Center of Gravity: It's Not What We Thought," *Naval War College Review* LVI, no. 1 (2003).

19 Bruce Hoffman, *Inside Terrorism*, Rev. and expanded ed. (New York: Columbia University Press, 2006), 184.

20 Dorothy Denning in Ibid., 201–02, See also Daniel Kimmage and Kathleen Ridolfo, *Iraqi Insurgent Media: The War of Images and Ideas* (Washington, DC: RFE/RL, 2007).

21 See David F. Ronfeldt and Arroyo Center, *The Zapatista "Social Netwar" in Mexico* (Santa Monica, CA: Rand, 1998).

22 Qiao Liang and Wang Xiangsui, "Unrestricted Warfare" (Beijing, China: PLA Literature and Arts Publishing House, 1999), http://conflictwiki.org/files/unrestricted_warfare.pdf.

23 It is noteworthy that when signing the International Covenant on Civil and Political Rights, the U.S. reserved Article 20 which prohibits propaganda in time of war. See http://www.ohchr.org/english/law/ccpr.htm#art20.

24 *Washington Post*, May 24, 1953 quoted in Kenneth Alan Osgood, *Total Cold War: Eisenhower's Secret Propaganda Battle at Home and Abroad* (Lawrence: University of Kansas, 2006), 76.

25 Filkins Dexter, "Tough New Tactics by U.S. Tighten Grip on Iraq Towns," *New York Times*, 2003.

26 Joseph A. Kechichian, R. Hrair Dekmejian, and Muhammad ibn Abd Allah Ibn Zafar, *The Just Prince: A Manual of Leadership: Including an Authoritative English Translation of the Sulwan Al-Muta* Fi *Udwan Al-Atba by Muhammad Ibn Zafar Al-Siqilli (Consolation for the Ruler During the Hostility of Subjects)* (London: Saqi, 2003), 105.

27 Mao Tse-tung, *On Guerrilla Warfare* (Champaign, IL: University of Illinois Press, 2000), 93.

28 See General Anthony Zinni (ret.) keynote in Johns Hopkins University, *Unrestricted Warfare Symposium 2006*, ed. Ronald R. Luman, Proceedings on Strategy, Analysis, and Technology (Laurel, MD: The Johns Hopkins University Applied Physics Laboratory, 2006).

29 Kenneth Alan Osgood, *Total Cold War: Eisenhower's Secret Propaganda Battle at Home and Abroad* (Lawrence: University of Kansas, 2006), 85.

30 Max Boot, *War Made New: Technology, Warfare, and the Course of History, 1500 to Today* (New York: Gotham Books, 2006), 414.

31 Jamie Shea, "The Kosovo Crisis and the Media: Reflections of a NATO Spokesman" (speech before the Atlantic Council of the United Kingdom, Reform Club, London: 1999).

9

Between "Take-offs" and "Crash Landings"

Situational Aspects of Public Diplomacy

John Robert Kelley

Introduction

It was in a serendipitous moment of frustration that Edward R. Murrow, the legendary American broadcaster and one-time lead figure for American public diplomacy as the director of the United States Information Agency (USIA), uttered a powerful lamentation of his plight in trying to manage the American image and reputation in the aftermath of the failed Bay of Pigs gambit in early 1961. Having learned of the ploy only after it had been launched and sensing the damage control he would soon be undertaking he grumbled, "If they want me in on the crash landings, I'd better damn well be in on the take-offs."[1] In so doing, Murrow had inadvertently sketched the borderlines within which public diplomacy becomes salient in the planning and execution of foreign policy: the "take-offs" represent participation in the genesis and planned articulation of policy, and "crash landings" the attempt to manage policy failures. For the study of public diplomacy, the statement is so serendipitous because it neatly symbolizes two opposing interpretations of the proper role for practitioners, albeit in a very general way. That is, any scholar or practitioner will acknowledge that there is much more to the public diplomacy process than origins and outcomes.

But without reading too much into Murrow's spontaneity, there is something to be said for the perception that public diplomacy is bedeviled by evidence of competing goals. Government-sponsored broadcasters often must strive to maintain their independence from political interference brought forth by the very lawmakers that allocate their funds.[2] Diplomatic emissaries who interface with publics abroad are expected to advocate official policy and at the same time show a willingness to understand when policies are criticized. Information programs frequently address short-term needs while cultural diplomacy requires more time for results to materialize. "Take-offs" and "crash landings," of course, are merely metaphors for framing the dueling advisory and advocacy roles of practitioners in relation to foreign policy formulation and execution.[3] With so many responsibilities at odds with each other, how are practitioners to decide which goal takes precedence?

Public diplomacy is fundamentally a two-part process shared by the substance of foreign policymaking and the message exchange capacity of international communications. In this essay, the case will be made that much of what steers the public diplomacy process depends on the situational aspects surrounding it. Situations pose threats and introduce opportunities that often dictate the movements of international actors. In one sense, they force states to be cautionary in dealing with Macmillan's "events, dear boy, events" as obstacles to political achievement, while from a communications angle a situation also may create an opening to steer mass perception into viewing events with a certain significance that may ultimately benefit policy implementation. Scholars have difficulty arriving at a concise answer to the question of what is public diplomacy. Because contingencies are ever-present: public diplomats may be cultivating an important relationship one day and managing an international crisis the next. The point to be made here is that more may be learned about the empirical pursuit of public diplomacy by examining the nature—the dynamics influencing the selection of certain approaches—beyond its constituent parts.

Public Diplomacy Dimensions

Scholars have long grappled with a concise definition of public diplomacy. Much debate could have been averted had the majority accepted the Fletcher School of Law and Diplomacy's early definition of the term some believe to have been coined in 1965 by its dean, Edmund Gullion.[4] But the Fletcher definition proved to be only the first of a litany of attempts, and even reaching consensus on a clear definition has beguiled both scholars and practitioners for so long that a recent Wilton Park conference concluded that "public diplomacy has entered the lexicon of 21st century diplomacy without clear definition of what it is or how the tools it offers might best be used."[5] For example, no one can dispute the fact that the conduct of public diplomacy includes at its core a communications component, but there remains some confusion over whether this communication takes place in a purely domestic or foreign sphere. While some interpret the former to be the case,[6] others such as Melissen assert that public diplomacy is: "aimed at foreign publics, and strategies for dealing with such publics should be distinguished from the domestic socialization of diplomacy."[7] Another point of contention exists in the role public diplomacy should play within governments; this centers on the question of whether it is purely distinct from, or simply a support mechanism beneath more traditional forms of diplomacy. In the United Kingdom, public diplomacy is regarded as "part of a wider strategy to break down communication barriers both at home and abroad."[8] Other countries, such as Norway and Canada, have been seen to regard public diplomacy as highly as other diplomatic activities.[9] And these representations refer only to state-level actors. Information communications technologies have helped endow private citizens more diplomat-like powers, thus narrowing the gap between members of the public and diplomats. Non-state actors are challenging the pre-existing monopoly of governments on public diplomacy institutions and activities.[10]

However, in light of such debates it is promising to find that the viewpoints of both scholars and practitioners, if not perfect reflections of one another, do share considerable common ground from time to time. A few close observers have been bold enough to distinguish general categories of activity, which usually consist of

1   *Information*: information management and distribution with an emphasis on short-term events or crises;
2   *Influence*: longer-term persuasion campaigns aiming to effect attitudinal change amongst a target population (sometimes referred to as "moving the needle"); and
3   *Engagement*: building relationships, also over the long term, to cultivate trust and mutual understanding between peoples (be they groups, organizations, nations, etc.).

Condiser the three following interpretations. In the first, Nye divides the purposes of public diplomacy into three distinct dimensions ". . . [requiring] different relative proportions of direct government information and long-term cultural relationships":

The first and most immediate dimension is daily communications, which involves explaining the context of domestic and foreign policy decisions . . . The day-to-day dimension must also involve preparation for dealing with crises and countering attacks . . . The second dimension is strategic communication, in which a set of simple themes is developed, much like what occurs in a public campaign . . . The third dimension of public diplomacy is the development of having relationships with key individuals over many years through scholarships, exchanges, training, seminars, conferences, and access to media channels . . . Each of these three dimensions of public diplomacy plays an important role in helping to create an attractive image of a country and this can improve its prospects for obtaining its desired outcomes.[11]

Ambassador Christopher Ross, a career diplomat in the American foreign service, draws a very similar picture to the one described by Nye, distinguished mainly by a reduction from three dimensions to two by virtue of the consolidation of communication activities:

The first is the communication of policy. Whereas the task is ongoing, intensive, and fraught with difficulties, public diplomacy is basically a short-term effort with a simple goal: to articulate U.S. policy clearly in as many media and languages as are necessary to ensure that the message is received . . . As demanding as articulating U.S. policy to foreign publics is, it is only half of public diplomacy's responsibility. The other half is a longer-term effort to develop an overseas understanding and appreciation of U.S. society—the people and values of the United States . . . Success on the information front can be measured. In contrast, gauging the success of exchange programs is more intangible and requires time and patience . . . Throughout the Cold War, public diplomacy efforts ran essentially one way. Programs and activities were pushed out to target audiences. In today's world, the United States is more likely to meet with success if it structures activities in ways that encourage dialogue.[12]

While it is true that Ross operates from his American frame of reference, British scholar Mark Leonard offers a more generalized definition, nevertheless yielding strong resemblances to the preceding ones:

In fact, public diplomacy is about building relationships: understanding the needs of other countries, cultures and peoples; communicating our points of view; correcting misperceptions; looking for areas where we can find common cause . . . One way of conceptualising public diplomacy is as a grid of three rows and columns. On one axis are the spheres on which it is played out: political/military, economic and societal/cultural. In each of these spheres, we can characterize three dimensions of public diplomacy activities: (1) reacting to news events as they occur in a way that tallies with our strategic goals; (2) proactively creating a news agenda through activities and events which are designed to reinforce core messages and influence perceptions; (3) building long-term relationships with populations to win recognition of our values and assets and to learn from theirs. Each of these dimensions operates according to a different timescale.[13]

Reading over these three separate attempts to give shape to public diplomacy, which by no means represent a full spectrum, one finds there to be more agreement than not over its core elements. Figuring prominently on one side is communication, which largely consists of "strategic communications" or messages specially crafted to support policy initiatives by eliciting a desired response from target audiences.[14] On the other, the three authors also mention the need to build relationships with individuals or groups abroad in hopes that the resulting goodwill will enhance a country's image and increase the likelihood that the "desired outcomes" of that country's foreign policies will be met.

One important divergence worth noting here, since it will be explored later, is the notion of the "population" or "public" understood to be the recipient or interlocutor in a typical "relationship." The significance of this grouping is often generalized, as seen in the samples from Ross and Leonard, to the point of ambiguity, thus making it difficult to qualify what exactly constitutes the "public" beyond sometimes amorphous constituencies whose commonalities change depending on context. In contrast, Nye asserts concentrating relationship-building on "key individuals," which begs the question of whether public diplomacy is as "public" as the name implies. Hocking has noted that explaining what is meant by the "public" in clearer terms is a priority for contemporary analysis, as this divide over a seemingly basic assumption simply illustrates.[15]

It is nevertheless important to draw attention to three often overlooked dimensions containing oft-cited sub-traits involving the nature of public diplomacy that shape the views of a large portion of analysts and which are reflected in the samples above. It can be surmised from witnessing the application of public diplomacy approaches during the Cold War that information and influence approaches normally dominate (but not to the point of exclusion) over engagement (John Robert Kelley, "US Public Diplomacy: A Cold War Success Story?" *Hague Journal of Diplomacy* 2 (2007), pp. 53–79). Thus, there appears to be a fluid relationship shared amongst the primary approaches of public diplomacy in a hierarchical sense: although they seem to coexist, one approach assumes dominance over, but not to the exclusion of others. With the following, it is suggested that each set presents two counterpart qualities that are in fact intricately connected and demonstrate more or less intensity in relation to its opposite part depending on situational factors. The first set deals with patterns in communication styles ranging from propagandistic to fully transparent vis-à-vis the goal of conveying messages designed to support policy initiatives. The second involves timeframes—public diplomacy operating on either a short-term or long-term track. Lastly, the third set of parameters address behavior, sometimes shaping campaigns centred on certain themes, and other times shaped by unexpected events or statements. They will be referred to as reactive and proactive communication postures.

Propagandistic and Transparent Communication Styles

Among scholars and practitioners, one of the longest-running debates about public diplomacy involves to what extent it should employ propagandistic techniques to influence foreign public opinion, or more broadly whether propaganda should be related to public diplomacy at all. Some would submit that propaganda and public diplomacy are mutually exclusive styles, as Zaharna does by contrasting the "secrecy, deception and coercion" of the former with the "open public communication" of the latter.[16] To be sure, prevailing norms since the start of the postwar period reinforce negative connotations associated with propaganda, and Cull's etymological history of the term in this book confirms its gradual recession in favor of the more benign "public diplomacy" coming into fashion by 1965.[17] Others like Snow maintain the fading of propaganda in name only and minimize the shift in norms to think of it as interchangeable with public diplomacy.[18] Some American officials have reinforced this notion in their public statements. U.S. Ambassador Richard Holbrooke wrote in 2001, "call it public diplomacy, or public affairs, or psychological warfare, or—if you really want to be blunt—propaganda."[19] A more positive explanation offered up by another American FSO called public diplomacy, "the finest form of propaganda."[20] This owes to the fact that even after years of expansion in government-sponsored communications activities and the accompanying sanitization in terminology, the propagandistic style never disappeared but instead became incorporated into the array of continued U.S. public diplomacy approaches. The Central Intelligence Agency (CIA) funded Radio Free Europe and Radio Liberty in the 1950s and 1960s, and operated covert "disinformation" media projects involving the publishing of books, magazines, and newspapers until these projects were exposed in 1977.[21] Well past the anointed cleansing years of the 1960s, the propagandistic tendencies of public diplomacy occasionally reappeared more publicly as a way to further foreign policy imperatives even in the 1980s to support anti-communist maneuvers in Central America and, in a more recent case in 2002, when the secret Office of Strategic Influence run by the Department of Defense was exposed by the *New York Times* and subsequently disbanded.[22] All of this has occurred notwithstanding the U.S. military's tactical use of its own broadcasting, leaflet-dropping, and other psychological operations.

In fact, influence-related activities that sometimes draw on propagandistic communication seem to have a natural home in the idiom of "strategic" public diplomacy. According to Manheim, strategic public diplomacy is "public diplomacy practiced less as an art than as an applied transnational science of human behavior. It is . . . the practice of propaganda in the earliest sense of the term, but enlightened by half a century of empirical research into human motivation and behavior."[23] This re-conceptualization of public diplomacy to include a "science" of political manipulation in fact reveals not a mutual exclusion between public diplomacy and propaganda, nor perfect substitution of one term for another, but the incorporation of an "enlightened" propagandistic communication style into the public diplomacy domain.

Conversely, there is an alternative technique that does not rest on the disinformation and manipulation associated with propaganda, but rather on the credibility of transparent communication. Adherents to this style may share a revulsion to propaganda (although it arguably helped raise the profile of public diplomacy in the first place) and prefer instead to project trustworthy and credible communications via free and fair media channels. This was a guiding principle first espoused by the late journalist and former USIA Director Edward R. Murrow,[24] reiterated in the findings of a 1975 blue-ribbon panel led by Frank Stanton on the reorganization of U.S. public diplomacy,[25] and has to a large extent governed the style and content of U.S. government-sponsored broadcasting. Moral arguments surrounding "tough-minded" and "tender-minded" factions notwithstanding, many recognize the necessity of transparency in an age when "citizens can see quite graphically the effects of their leaders' foreign policy decision and how diplomats cope with them on the ground."[26] Recognition of this reality has yielded strong assertions from leading diplomats, scholars, and journalists that the credibility of governments must be fiercely protected since the proliferation of information communication technologies has made it easier to expose discrepancies between word and deed.[27]

Short-term and Long-term Timeframes

Public diplomacy characteristically reinforces policies that are impermanent. Therefore, as Nye mentions above, it is often short-term by design. Rosenau has generally described foreign policy action, the very action public diplomacy is called upon to support, as "constantly unfolding" and susceptible to event sequences in the international realm.[28] A typical example of the relationship between events, foreign policy, and public diplomacy can be seen in the way the United States lobbied against Soviet resistance over the NATO-sanctioned deployment of intermediate-range nuclear forces (INF) in Western Europe in 1983 to counter a mid-1970s upgrading of Soviet missiles to the new SS-20, which at that time established relative parity between Western and Soviet nuclear capabilities in Europe. At the onset of the deployment, political tensions between the two superpowers ran high after negotiations to reduce INF in Europe broke down.[29] Publicly, however, the dispute touched off numerous protests by Europeans opposed to any accelerations in the arms race, which the Soviet government was quick to exploit in support of its own position. The United States countered with what Reagan National Security Council (NSC) staffer Carnes Lord called a public diplomacy "effort of unprecedented intensity and degree of coordination throughout the U.S. government."[30] Lord cites a propagandistic arms control and public diplomacy campaign to have been critical for raising European suspicions over Soviet security motives in the region and exposing "the record of Soviet misbehavior under existing arms control regimes."[31] With the European public outcry over American intentions somewhat muted as a result, the deployment proceeded as planned. George Shultz recalled afterwards, "I don't think we could have pulled it off if it hadn't been for a very active program of public diplomacy."[32] (As a preface to the next section it is worth mentioning that the American response to European protestors and Soviet opposition to the buildup constitutes a reactive posture.)

Aside from its propagandistic style, it is important to note that the timeframe of the INF campaign represented an instance of public diplomacy being used to build public support for an immediate dividend. Although one could argue the relevance of the long-running international debate pertaining to nuclear buildups during the Cold War, the INF campaign did not seek to settle larger questions dealing with arms control and disarmament. It can be better characterized as the outgrowth of imperatives laid out in President Reagan's National Security Decision Directive 77, in which he deemed public diplomacy "to generate support for our national security objectives" and therefore ordered the creation of a short-lived "special planning group" (SPG) to operate within the NSC and coordinate interagency strategic communication efforts.[33] Most noted for organizing responses to the INF situation and the Soviet downing of Korean Air Lines Flight 007, the SPG also orchestrated support for the *contras* in Nicaragua. Equally notable may be how swiftly the importance of the SPG declined after such policy imperatives faded.

Echoing earlier statements that public diplomacy is essentially a short-term effort, it seems plausible to suggest that the limited shelf-life of policy initiatives makes it easier for practitioners to pursue simple and immediate goals, and these goals are consequently made simpler yet should practitioners concentrate their focus on a narrow timeframe, thereby eliminating a complex and cumbersome set of long-term concerns. From a planning perspective, short-term initiatives allow easier accounting for available resources, full concentration on situations at hand, and immediate returns from performance assessment. Alternatively, long-term initiatives bring forth greater complexity, in that available human and financial resources are harder to maintain, concentration wanders to other pressing matters, and successes, if any, take longer to materialize and prove with measurable indicators. Nevertheless, long-term initiatives represent a staple in the public diplomacy strategies of many states and organizations, albeit they are almost always subjugated in favor of short-term interests. The language associated with the long term often involves terms like "development," "incubating," and "transformation," and justifiably so since long-term challenges require a sustained commitment to create change. Exchange programs assume an important place in the arsenal of long-term tactics, emphasizing niche areas such as the arts and sciences, and promoting the cultures of sponsoring countries. Seldom known is the fact that the United States and Soviet Union engaged in a long-running cultural exchange program that remained in place for nearly the entire duration of the Cold War. Other prestigious programs include Britain's Rhodes Scholarship and the Japan Exchange and Teaching (JET) Program, both of which provide a unique opportunity for highly-qualified foreign scholars to pursue academic and professional endeavors.

In the promotion of cultural identities, the foreign ministries of France, Germany, and more recently China dedicate globally-operating organizations and centers to extend to foreign populations the heritage of their respective languages, cultures and political values. France's General Directorate for International Cooperation and Development focuses on extending awareness of French culture through the Alliance Française, and Germany utilizes its vast network of Goethe Instituts to actively spread German language and culture in attempts to foster a positive image of German politics and society in nearly 90 countries. The Chinese Ministry of Education opened up its first Confucius Institute in August 2006 to foster interest in Chinese language and culture, and support teachers of the Chinese language overseas. By 2010, the Ministry plans to have 100 such Institutes in operation.[34]

It must not be overlooked that while exchanges over the long term create continued opportunities for personal contact, the media also play an important role in communicating messages that sustain the underlying ideas and values of sponsoring countries. Media outlets can be the differential in the marathon race to deliver information to international audiences, and it is incumbent upon the media to build and maintain their credibility in part to reflect positively on the societies they represent. For state-owned media this means maintaining an appearance of distance from government interests, and some say it is chiefly for this reason the BBC World Service enjoys a larger audience than all U.S. international broadcasting services combined, despite a smaller annual budget.[35] At the same time, the linkages between media outlets and the worldviews they represent are not lost on audiences, and thus the media possess, sometimes unwittingly, the ability to cultivate positive associations for or draw hostility to their sponsoring country. This helps explain the controversy that resulted in Denmark and more broadly within Western societies when in September 2005 a Danish newspaper editor ran cartoons depicting the Prophet Mohammad in a negative light only to invite a firestorm of criticism from Muslim countries.[36] This has caused long-term damage to the Danish image, and it is in the wake of the crisis that the government has decided to prepare for such crises by investing more public diplomacy.

Reactive and Proactive Postures

As with the case of Denmark, sometimes a nation or organization finds itself having to answer to charges that place at risk its reputation with particular populations. To salvage the public trust during a crisis situation, it may employ the tactic of reactive public diplomacy, which can be useful for bypassing layers of media and local political interference and explaining positions directly to publics, and also in allowing for a quick response mechanism to prevent allegations from spinning wildly out of control. Others have termed this notion as "crisis" public diplomacy,[37] or "surge capability"[38]—a temporary recourse distinguishable from the longer-term, "proactive" campaigns intended to steer public opinion into a favorable mood. Reactive public diplomacy does not pretend that winning favor is realistic although it may be desirable. Its main purpose is "damage control," or to ensure that public opinion is minimally impacted in relation to conditions prior to the event that caused the crisis.

A rudimentary look at some American security and political crises during the 20th century and beyond shows how the United States has relied on reactive public diplomacy in a time of crisis. At the outset of the Cuban Missile Crisis in October 1962, the ad hoc "ExComm" assembled to deal with the matter first did not include the fledgling USIA in its meetings, but this changed once it was realized that communications would play a significant part in its resolution.[39] It would be the USIA Deputy Director Donald Wilson who suggested integrating photographs into the famous speech by Adlai Stevenson before the UN Security Council on 25 October 1962 in which he effectively indicted the Soviet Union for deploying nuclear warheads into Cuba.[40] Returning to a prior example, President Reagan's NSDD 77 specified the need for response-oriented strategies to counter "aggressive political action moves" of the Soviet Union, which he delegated to a sub-committee of the aforementioned SPG.[41]

More recent response mechanisms include the Coalition Information Centers (CIC) shared by the American and British governments, which they jointly created in October 2001 upon the launching of the Afghan military campaign. Emulating the domestic political campaign cultures of both countries, and acknowledging the positive impact of a similar arrangement used by NATO in Kosovo, CIC operations utilized branch offices in Washington, London, and Islamabad to remain engaged at all hours of the news cycle. Created foremost "to reinforce the message that the war is against terrorism, not Islam" on the international front, domestically it compelled an array of government agencies dealing with the press and general public to coordinate messages.[42] The champion of the CIC on the American side, then–White House counsellor Karen Hughes, would subsequently adapt its purposes to form the Rapid Response Unit (RRU) at the Department of State in early 2006. Along with the reproduction of the command center for constant monitoring of international media, the RRU issues daily guidance complete with talking points for American embassies and consulates to respond to emergent matters in the media. In addition, the coordination of talking points creates an "echo chamber" effect by repeating and reinforcing messages originating in Washington.[43]

As is typical of crisis situations, however, it is rather uncommon to find an apparatus like the CIC or RRU in place to anticipate crises before they happen; crises are usually short-lived, as are the temporary offices created to deal with them. Thus practitioners recognize the need to maintain, alongside the response-oriented capacity, a proactive public diplomacy posture that retains far more control of agenda setting, amasses and maintains a stable level of resources to pursue both short- and longer-term agenda items, and permits the practitioner to do so for however long or short the situation requires. In a non-state example, an organization such as the International Committee of the Red Cross prepares for the unpredictable by staffing disaster relief centers and logistical crews standing ready to be called into action, but it also sustains a constant level of activity in what it calls "humanitarian diplomacy" to advance an agenda against what it regards as humanitarian threats and to advocate implementation of international humanitarian laws.[44]

With respect to the agenda-setting capabilities of public diplomacy, the insights of the communications discipline shed light on the relationship between agendas and their potential effects on public perceptions, and further towards the shaping of what Walter Lippmann called the "world outside and pictures in our heads."[45] In this sense, political communications figures try to co-opt international media outlets into telling the public not what to think, but what to think about.[46] Manheim has discussed examples where international actors have successfully steered their agendas for political gains.[47] He raises the instance of a visit to the United States by former prime minister of Pakistan, Benazir Bhutto, whose chief concern was to reverse the declining American interest in Pakistan after the Soviet withdrawal from Afghanistan in 1989.[48] With the aid of an American political consultant, Bhutto approached her visit much like a political campaign and centered her agenda on the theme of a U.S.–Pakistan democratic partnership as a way to remain relevant to U.S. interests in South Asia. By shifting attention away from the geostrategic developments that may have caused the United States to become less interested in Pakistan and placing a spotlight on political partnership, Bhutto won rave reviews in the American media and, as Manheim notes, succeeded in elevating Pakistan's profile among American opinion leaders.

Moreover, with her visit having transpired solely within the month of June 1989, Bhutto's coup over American public opinion shows that proactive public diplomacy may be conducted on a relatively short timescale, and yet the larger portion of public diplomacy scholarship in this area has been devoted to longer-term models.[49] For example, Leonard offers a case study depicting Norway's concentration of public diplomacy resources to cast it as a force for peace and conflict resolution worldwide.[50] Rather than take months, Norway has held to this line for years, and Leonard notes its integral participation in the Middle East peace process (1993 Oslo Accords), extended mediation efforts in the Sri Lankan internal dispute, and even its fortuitous association with the Nobel Peace Prize, which originated in Oslo. What helps in clarifying the general regard for proactive public diplomacy as a long-term effort has to do with defining objectives. While both reactive and proactive forms deal in the currency of messages, the proactive form is more appropriate to the tasks of image and relationship building (or repair), which are invariably time-intensive endeavors.

Matching Sub-traits to Models

New perspectives have been useful for deepening understanding of public diplomacy because they challenge prevailing notions of how it is seen and utilized. For the most part the challenge to

	Advocacy Model		Advisory Model
	Information	Influence	Engagement
Communication Style	Transparent	Propagandistic	Transparent
Timeframe	Long-term/Short-term	Long-term/Short-term	Long-term
Posture Orientation	Reactive/Proactive	Proactive	Reactive/Proactive

Figure 9.1. Sub-traits of Public Diplomacy Matrix

conventional practices is more about redistribution than reinvention. It proposes a movement away from competitive aspects towards the collaborative, from propagandistic to transparent communication styles, and from short-term tactical maneuvers towards an integrated long-term approach.[51] The individual components of the dimensions introduced previously are common to most taxonomies of the public diplomacy "toolkit," and only for the first time are they being assembled in this manner to highlight their relationships to three main approaches of information, influence, and engagement. The matrix provided in Figure 9.1 illustrates these relationships schematically by grouping the three respective columns of approaches against sub-trait rows labeled communication style, timeframe, and posture orientation.

What results from this intersection is the assigning of the dominant sub-trait for each approach. Approaches and sub-traits are then consolidated into two prevailing models of public diplomacy practice: that of "advocacy" and that of "advisory." Some explanation on what these combinations signify follows.

Firstly, the matrix shows transparent communication dominant in the information approach. Information-driven public diplomacy rests on the notion that content used for this approach is based on fact and has not been altered during the process of its delivery to target audiences. According to the U.S. Department of State a high proportion of public diplomacy activity is information-driven and content flows though government-sponsored publications, motion pictures, radio, and television.[52] Of course, government sponsorship raises the question of whether governments can pursue policy objectives while simultaneously upholding full disclosure with its media sources. To deal with this, firewalls are imposed to assure media independence from policymakers, but the "thickness" of firewalls may sometimes be penetrated.[53] The information approach may operate for long or short periods of time and in addition may do so from either a reactive or proactive posture. The information approach is prone to proactive postures mainly in the execution of long-term campaigns, but may also resort to reactive postures when necessary (i.e. in a time of crisis). Many have alluded to the information approach as a "push-down," or "one-way" communication strategy concerned foremost with transmitting content into environments perceived as information-poor, and hardly ever to engage target populations in transnational dialogue.[54]

A shift of a transparent information approach towards the propagandistic exemplifies the second approach, influence. Distinguished by its aggressive nature in steering target audiences toward a certain opinion, influence ranges from gentler forms of persuasion to the manipulation of facts or other intentions to mislead. This approach functions optimally within short- or long-term timeframes. Gregory has said it is commonplace for nations to turn to public diplomacy during wartime, and it is not coincidental that strategists take greater stock of its capacity to influence in order to win the psychological dimension of wars, helped along by a more consenting domestic public galvanized by nationalism.[55] One need only look to the highly orchestrated, but short-lived activities of the Ministry for Public Enlightenment and Propaganda in Nazi Germany, or the extensive psychological contretemps between the United States and Soviet Union during the Cold War. Influence is optimally oriented to a proactive posture by its inclination towards sustained campaigns designed to change deep-seated attitudes and strongly held beliefs. One stream of thought on how to improve post-9/11 U.S. public diplomacy stresses that the key to winning over populations lacking faith in the international goals of the United States is to do a better job of "telling America's story." Motivated by a characteristically exceptionalist groundswell, influence is also infused with the practical mantra of defining oneself to a population before a detractor submits a fractured and unflattering definition in its place.[56] Being proactively persuasive in an overt manner approximates closely with the purposes of "white propaganda," which the U.S. Department of Defense's Dictionary of Military Terms defines as "propaganda disseminated and acknowledged by the sponsor."[57] But in the post-9/11 era, the United States has attempted "black propaganda" as well in which the source of information is completely obscured. Of such efforts, it is hard to surpass the example Office of Strategic Influence that operated at the Pentagon until its revelation by the media forced its closure in early 2002. Media manipulation was discovered to be the prime objective of the Rendon Group, which was contracted by the Department of Defense and alleged to write and distribute falsified reports to international media in support of the Afghan and Iraq wars.[58]

All of this portrays public diplomacy in a rather hawkish light and hardly as the bedrock of media organizations who seek to protect their credibility, and already it has been discussed how some public diplomacy scholars feel it should have nothing to do with the darker arts of communication. However, influence remains a tool at the disposal of a government or organization when communicating with publics *en masse*, albeit employed at great risk to the image and credibility of the sponsor.

Finally, the engagement approach favors a transparent communication style with trust-building central among its objectives. Despite a long predisposition to self-interested, propaganda-style tactics, more recent scholarship in public diplomacy focuses on fundamentals of this approach, which involves multiple stakeholders, and attracts them with the promise of mutual gains. One increasingly typical example of this can be found in Fitzpatrick's relational model of public diplomacy, an adaptation of relationship management familiar to the study of public relations which emphasizes collaboration over competition between public diplomats and counterpart populations, and implies the necessity of a long-term relationship between the two parties to build trust and open communication.[59]

The matrix is completed by labels along the top grouping approaches under the advocacy and advisory models of public diplomacy, and it is here where the essence of the debate on public diplomacy in the U.S. case can be found. While the sub-traits suggest features of approaches, the approaches themselves highlight situations in which one conducts public diplomacy. Reducing forms of conduct into such models shows that the stated goals of public diplomacy do compete with each other in many aspects, and the matrix demonstrates a few of the ways in which this happens. Advocacy is a uni-directional transmission of information, often geared to meet short-term needs, and sometimes moved to communicate in an influence-driven, propagandistic communication style. Proponents of the "new" public diplomacy maintain that states should no longer employ advocacy as the dominant model. Barry Zorthian, a former senior officer in the American foreign service and frequent commentator on the future of U.S. public diplomacy, has said that it is "dependent on basic policies, and we need [public diplomacy] to adjust and articulate them better." Between the twin aims of advising and advocating, Zorthian considers the former to be more critical to the role of public diplomacy officers of the post-9/11 era.[60] A

2003 report of the Council on Foreign Relations concurs by saying that the United States "must take the politics and cultural lenses of others into account as it formulates and communicates its policy."[61]

Conclusions

This chapter launches its analysis of public diplomacy on the basic assumption that it is an act of international communication taking place between a group of public citizens and a state or organization that would not appear to be "domestic". This is not a working definition of public diplomacy, but it does provide the foundation which most scholars and practitioners agree to be true. Rather than become bogged down in long-running disputes among scholars over what comprises, for instance, the "public" or the "diplomacy," or whether propaganda is exclusive to public diplomacy, the point made here is that the nature of these communications between international actors is determined by situations. Situations affect the way actors go about pursuing their interests, they shape agendas and elevate certain norms over others, and they can present actors with unexpected developments. Through its history, public diplomacy has shown an ability to adapt to situations as they arise, and the preceding introduced three dimensions in which this has been seen to occur: communication styles, timeframes, and posture orientations. For definitional purposes, what this offers is a way for scholars to reconcile seemingly opposed sub-traits that practitioners of public diplomacy have occasionally employed. That is, public diplomacy may not be equivalent to propaganda, but there are instances where it has shown a propagandistic communication style. It can operate on two tracks of time, and it has been used to bolster long-term campaigns and manage crises. All of these traits are not irreconcilable, but rather shades of a vast spectrum of activities under one label.

Notes

1 Interview with Henry Loomis, 4 April 1985 in A.M. Sperber, *Murrow: His Life and Times* (New York: Freundlich Books, 1986), 624.

2 John H. Brown, "The Purposes and Cross-Purposes of American Public Diplomacy," *American Diplomacy* (15 August 2002), http://www.unc.edu/depts/diplomat/archives_roll/2002_07–09/brown_pubdipl/brown_pubdipl.html (accessed on 15 July 2006).

3 I have organized public diplomacy activities into two competing models to demonstrate the tension in practitioners' proximity to policymaking. The "advocacy" model describes the role where policy has been made and public diplomats are dispatched for its articulation and defense. The "advisory" model, on the other hand, draws public diplomats to the policymaking table at the formulation stage, and their presence helps to ensure that local concerns have been considered prior to policy implementation. See John Robert Kelley, *From Monologue to Dialogue?: U.S. Public Diplomacy in the Post-9/11 Era.* London School of Economics Doctoral Thesis, 2007.

4 According to the Fletcher definition, public diplomacy "deals with the influence of public attitudes on the formation and execution of foreign policies. It encompasses dimensions of international relations beyond traditional diplomacy; the cultivation by governments of public opinion in other countries; the interaction of private groups and interests in one country with those of another; the reporting of foreign affairs and its impact on policy; communication between those whose job is communication, as between diplomats and foreign correspondents; and the processes of inter-cultural communications . . . Central to public diplomacy is the transnational flow of information and ideas." Edward R. Murrow Center for Public Diplomacy, brochure, http://fletcher.tufts.edu/murrow/public-diplomacy.html (accessed 20 February 2005).

5 Ann Lane, "Public Diplomacy: Key Challenges and Priorities," *Report on Wilton Park Conference WPS06/21* (April 2006), 2.

6 Siobhan McEvoy Levy, *American Exceptionalism and US Foreign Policy: Public Diplomacy at the End of the Cold War* (New York: Palgrave, 2000).

7 Jan Melissen, ed., *The New Public Diplomacy: Soft Power in International Relations* (Basingstoke: Palgrave Macmillan, 2005), 13.

8 Lane, *Report on Wilton Park Conference*, 2.

9 Alan Henriksen, "Niche Diplomacy in the Public Arena: Canada and Norway," in *The New Public Diplomacy: Soft Power in International Relations*, ed. Jan Melissen (Basingstoke: Palgrave Macmillan, 2005), 67–87. For example, Foreign Affairs Canada terms public diplomacy its "third pillar" in pursuing Canadian foreign policy, the other two being "the promotion of prosperity and employment" and "the protection of [Canadian] security, within a stable global framework."

10 See, for example, David Bollier, "The Rise of Netpolitik: How the Internet is Changing International Politics and Diplomacy," *A Report of the Eleventh Annual Aspen Institute Roundtable on Information Technology*, 2003.

11 Joseph S. Nye, Jr., *Soft Power: The Means to Success in World Politics* (New York: Public Affairs, 2004), 107–110.

12 Christopher Ross, "Public Diplomacy Comes of Age," *The Washington Quarterly* 25, no. 2 (Spring 2002): 77–82.

13 Mark Leonard, *Public Diplomacy* (London: The Foreign Policy Centre, 2002), 8–11.

14 Jarol B. Manheim, *All of the People, All the Time: Strategic Communication and American Politics* (Armonk, NY: M.E. Sharpe, 1991).

15 Brian Hocking, "Rethinking the 'New' Public Diplomacy," in *The New Public Diplomacy: Soft Power in International Relations*, ed. Jan Melissen (Basingstoke: Palgrave Macmillan, 2005), 32.

16 R.S. Zaharna, "From Propaganda to Public Diplomacy in the Information Age," in *War, Media, and Propaganda: A Global Perspective*, ed. Yahya R. Kamalipour and Nancy Snow (Lanham, MD: Rowman and Littlefield, 2004), 223.

17 Nicholas J. Cull "Public Diplomacy Before Gullion: The Evolution of a Phrase," USC Center on Public Diplomacy (18 April 2006), http://uscpublicdiplomacy.com/pdfs/gullion.pdf (accessed on 13 June 2006).

18 See, for example, remarks of Nancy Snow, interview by Jerome McDonnell, *Worldview*, 27 November 2006: "There's an ongoing debate amongst scholars as to whether or not the two can be used interchangeably. I tend to use them interchangeably because I view propaganda as a process of mass persuasion that is inherently value neutral. It really comes down to how it's used."

19 Richard Holbrooke, "Get the Message Out," *Washington Post*, October 28, 2001.

20 Michael Macy, interview by author, London, January 26, 2006.

21 Wilson P. Dizard, Jr., *Inventing Public Diplomacy: The Story of the U.S. Information Agency* (Boulder, CO: Lynne Rienner Publishers, 2004), 141–143.

22 Robert Parry and Peter Kornbluh, "Iran-Contra's Untold Story," *Foreign Policy* 72 (Autumn 1988): 3–30; James Dao and Eric Schmitt, "Pentagon Readies Efforts to Sway Sentiment Abroad," *New York Times*, 19 February 2006.

23 Jarol B. Manheim, *Strategic Public Diplomacy and American Foreign Policy: The Evolution of Influence* (New York: Oxford University Press, 1994), 7.

24 See, for example, remarks of Edward R. Murrow, Testimony before the House Subcommittee on International Organization and Movements, March 28, 1963, during which he was quoted as saying, "To be persuasive, we must be believable; to be believable we must be credible; to be credible, we must be truthful. It's as simple as that."

25 Panel on International Information, Education and Cultural Relations, "International Information, Education and Cultural Relations: Recommendations for the Future," *CSIS Special Report Number Fifteen* (Washington, DC: Center for Strategic and International Studies, 1975), 12: "The program must recognize that the communications revolution has educated the world to a greater skepticism concerning things governments say about their societies. Hence, there is a great need today for credibility . . ."

26 Jorge Heine, "On the Manner of Practising the New Diplomacy," *The Center for International Governance Innovation Working Paper 11* (Waterloo, Ontario: The Center for International Governance Innovation, 2006), 7.

27 Advisory Group on Public Diplomacy for the Arab and Muslim World, "Changing Minds, Winning Peace: A New Strategic Direction for U.S. Public Diplomacy in the Arab and Muslim World," *Report of the Advisory Group on Public Diplomacy for the Arab and Muslim World* (Washington, DC: Government Printing Office, 2003), 32 (hereafter "Djerejian Report"); Bruce Gregory, "Public Diplomacy and Strategic Communication: Cultures, Firewalls, and Imported Norms" (paper presented at the American Political Science Association Conference on International Communication and Conflict, Washington, USA, 31 August 2005), 17; Jonathan Alter, "Truth: The Best Propaganda," *Newsweek*, 4 March 2002.

28 James N. Rosenau, *International Politics and Foreign Policy: A Reader in Research and Theory*, New York: Free Press (1969), 167.

29 "Treaty Between the United States of America and the Union of Soviet Socialist Republics on the Elimination of Their Intermediate-Range and Shorter-Range Missiles," Available on Treaties of the U.S. Arms Control and Disarmament Agency website at http://dosfan.lib.uic.edu/acda/treaties/inf1.htm#1.

30 Carnes Lord, "The Past and Future of Public Diplomacy," *Orbis* (Winter 1998), 62–64.

31 Ibid., 64. Also see W. Scott Thompson, "Some Elements of an American Strategy," in William Kintner (ed.), *Arms Control*, Washington, DC: Washington Institute Press (1987), 304–306.

32 Hans Tuch, *Communicating with the World: U.S. Public Diplomacy Overseas* New York: St. Martin's Press (1990), 161.

33 President, "National Security Decision Directive 77: Management of Public Diplomacy Relative to National Security," 14 January 1983. W. Scott Thompson, associate director of the USIA from 1982–1984, writes that the special planning group "gave the [USIA] a voice at the policy level, if only briefly," in Thompson, "Anti-Americanism and the U.S. Government," *Annals of the American Academy of Political and Social Science* 497 (May 1988), 27.

34 "'China threat' fear countered by culture," *China Daily* (29 May 2006), http://news.xinhuanet.com/english/2006–05/29/content_4613721.htm (accessed on November 26, 2006).

35 Cited from Kim Andrew Elliot's letter to a UK public diplomacy review team led by Lord Carter of Coles, January 3, 2005, http://ics.leeds.ac.uk/papers/vp01.cfm?outfit=pmt&requesttimeout=500&folder=141&paper=2182.

36 Shawn Powers, "The Danish Cartoon Crisis: The Import and Impact of Public Diplomacy," USC Center for Public Diplomacy Special Report (April 5, 2006), http://uscpublicdiplomacy.com/pubs/reports/ 060405_powers.pdf (accessed February 22, 2007).

37 Siobhan McEvoy-Levy, *American Exceptionalism and US Foreign Policy: Public Diplomacy at the End of the Cold War* (New York: Palgrave, 2000), 154–156.

38 Mark Leonard, *Public Diplomacy* (London: The Foreign Policy Centre, 2002), 32–38.

39 Wilson P. Dizard, Jr., *Inventing Public Diplomacy: The Story of the U.S. Information Agency* (Boulder, CO: Lynne Rienner Publishers, 2004), 88.

40 Ibid, and corroborated by Walter Roberts in an interview with the author, Washington, DC, December 14, 2006.

41 President, *National Security Decision Directive 77*, 2.

42 Stephen Fidler, "War of words goes hand in hand with war on the ground: Bitter winter nears, and George W. Bush knows he will need to feel the warmth of his close allies," *Financial Times*, November 8, 2001, 22; United States Department of Defense Science Board Task Force on Strategic Communication, *Report of the Defense Science Board on Strategic Communication*, Office of the Under Secretary of Defense, United States Department of Defense (September 2004), 21.

43 Glenn Kessler, "Hughes Tries Fine-Tuning to Improve Diplomatic Picture," *Washington Post*, April 19, 2006.

44 International Committee of the Red Cross, "Humanitarian diplomacy: an introduction," International Committee of the Red Cross, http://www.icrc.org/Web/Eng/siteeng0.nsf/html/57JMAN (accessed February 9, 2007).

45 Walter Lippmann, *Public Opinion* (New York: Macmillan, 1922).

46 Bernard Cohen, *The Press and Foreign Policy* (Princeton, NJ: Princeton University Press, 1963).

47 Jarol B. Manheim, *Strategic Public Diplomacy and American Foreign Policy: The Evolution of Influence* (New York: Oxford University Press, 1994), 127–128.

48 Ibid., 84–91.

49 Some resources on the long-term impact of international broadcasting include James Critchlow, *Radio Hole-in-the-Head: An Insider's Story of Cold War Broadcasting* (Washington, DC: American University Press, 1995) and Donald R. Browne, *International Radio Broadcasting: The Limits of the Limitless Medium* (New York: Praeger, 1982). For some studies on cultural diplomacy, see Yale Richmond, *Cultural Exchange and the Cold War: Raising the Iron Curtain* (University Park, PA: The Pennsylvania State University Press, 2003) and Richard T. Arndt, *The First Resort of Kings: American Cultural Diplomacy in the Twentieth Century* (Washington, DC: Potomac Books, 2005).

50 Mark Leonard, *Public Diplomacy* (London: The Foreign Policy Centre, 2002), 168–175.

51 Shaun Riordan, *The New Diplomacy* (Cambridge: Polity Press, 2003); Mark Leonard, "Diplomacy by Other Means," *Foreign Policy* 132 (2002): 48–56.

52 U.S. Department of State, *Dictionary of International Relations Terms* (Washington, DC: Government Printing Office, 1987), 85.

53 One comparative example lies in the differing relationships of state-sponsored broadcasting outlets with their supervisory bodies, such as the BBC (British Foreign Office) and the U.S. government-sponsored radios (Broadcasting Board of Governors), both briefly described in The Hoover Institution and The

Cold War International History Project of the Woodrow Wilson International Center for Scholars, *Report from Conference on Cold War Broadcasting Impact*, Stanford University, Palo Alto, USA (October 13–16, 2004), 43

54 Ross, "Public Diplomacy Comes of Age," 82; David Bollier, "When Push Comes to Pull: The New Economy and Culture of Networking Technology," *A Report of the Fourteenth Annual Aspen Institute Roundtable on Information Technology* (Queenstown, MD: The Aspen Institute, 2006); Charles Wolf, Jr. and Brian Rosen, "Public Diplomacy: How to Think About and Improve It," *RAND Occasional Paper* (Santa Monica, CA: RAND Corporation, 2004), 5; or Foreign Relations Independent Task Force on Public Diplomacy, *Finding America's Voice: A Strategy for Reinvigorating U.S. Public Diplomacy* (New York: Council on Foreign Relations, 2003), 28.

55 Bruce Gregory, "Public Diplomacy as Strategic Communication," in *Countering Terrorism in the 21ˢᵗ Century*, ed. James J. Forrest (New York: Praeger, forthcoming), 2.

56 Djerejian Report, 16.

57 U.S. Department of Defense. *Dictionary of Military and Associated Terms*, http://www.dtic.mil/doctrine/jel/doddict/ (accessed March 10, 2007).

58 James Bamford, "The Man Who Sold the War," *Rolling Stone*, November 17, 2005.

59 Kathy R. Fitzpatrick, "Questioning the Ethics and Effectiveness of Soft Power: Toward a Relational Model of U.S. Public Diplomacy" (paper presented at the Annual Conference of the International Studies Association, San Diego, USA, 23 March 2006).

60 Barry Zorthian, interview by author, Washington, DC, December 15, 2006.

61 Council on Foreign Relations, 4.

10

Mapping out a Spectrum of Public Diplomacy Initiatives

Information and Relational Communication Frameworks

R.S. Zaharna

Introduction

As evident by this handbook, public diplomacy is rapidly becoming a field of study in its own right. However, the more the field grows, the more unwieldy it appears to become. How does one sort through the mushrooming works on public diplomacy that range from propaganda to nation-building to cultural programs? In an effort to answer this question, I began exploring the communication assumptions and dynamics underlying how political entities try to communicate with international publics.[1] What emerged in the array of public diplomacy initiatives were two underlying perspectives of communication. One perspective tends to view communication as a linear process of transferring information often with the goal of persuasion or control. The other perspective sees communication as a social process of building relationships and fostering harmony. Various dimensions of these two parallel views of communication have been vigorously explored in intercultural communication scholarship.[2]

It is perhaps not surprising that these two perspectives of what it means to "communicate" have surfaced in debates over the nature of public diplomacy. Public diplomacy is as much a communication phenomenon as a political one. The battle of one view trying to win over the other view of communication is reflected in the debates over whether public diplomacy is propaganda or cultural relations, international broadcasts or educational exchanges, tough- or tender-minded, mutual understanding or persuasion.[3] Such debates are likely to continue so long as the underlying assumptions of communication remain unexposed and the legitimacy and strategic value of both views are unacknowledged.

As a preliminary and modest step in public diplomacy theory building, this study uses the two views of communication to construct two complementary communication frameworks for categorizing and analyzing a broad spectrum of public diplomacy initiatives. The information framework focuses on the design and dissemination of messages to advance political objectives. The relational framework focuses on relationship-building and the construction of social structures to advance political objectives. Within the relational framework, education and cultural exchange programs, cultural institutes and cultural relations represent a category of initiatives that use culture as a vehicle for building relationships. However, compared to the wider array of relationship-building initiatives explored in this chapter, culture does not appear to be the only vehicle nor do cultural programs constitute the most sophisticated relationship-building strategies. This chapter seeks to push the boundaries of relationship-building initiatives and broaden the spectrum of public diplomacy initiatives. Some scholars and practitioners have strenuously argued for keeping the different types of initiatives, particularly cultural relations, separate from public diplomacy.[4] My goal in compiling them together is to map out a spectrum of public diplomacy initiatives that display the rich variety of how political entities communicate with publics.

The first section provides a brief overview of the major lines of research underlying the information and relational frameworks of public diplomacy. The next two sections discuss communication features and examples of initiatives within the information and relational frameworks. The relational framework offers a preliminary sketch of three tiers of relationship-building initiatives. The chapter concludes with final thoughts on what appears to be a glaring gap in the spectrum of public diplomacy initiatives and where public diplomacy as an emerging field needs further exploration.

Origins of Information and Relational Public Diplomacy Frameworks

As cultural anthropologists and intercultural communication scholars have long observed, communication is fundamental to all societies, but different societies appear to hold fundamentally different views of what communication is. The origins of the information and relational frameworks stem from a composite of the different perspectives of communication documented in the literature.

Edward T. Hall, often referred to as the father of intercultural communication, proposed the concepts of low-context and high-context cultures to explain where people tend to look for meaning in communication.[5] He described low-context cultures as placing little meaning in the context or setting and instead focusing on the code or message. For high-context cultures, he said, "most of the information is either in the physical context or internalized in the person, while very little is in the coded, explicit, transmitted part of the message."[6] In other words, the context, rather than the message, carries more communication weight.

Another area of research is the collectivism-individualism paradigm. Geertz Hofstede introduced the paradigm in his multi-nation study of IBM employees in the early 1980s.[7] Individualism tends to place the interests of the individual over those of the group, whereas collectivism tends to value group harmony, cohesion and stability over the interests of the individual. Cross-cultural psychologist Harry Triandis called individualism-collectivism the single most important dimension of cultural differences in social behavior and estimated that 70 percent of the world's population held a collectivist view.[8] Psychologists Hazel Rose Markus and Shinobu Kitayama have suggested "independent" and "interdependent," as parallel self-concepts for individualistic and collectivist cultures, respectively.[9] Min-Sun Kim used the contrasting individual/independent and collectivist/interdependent perspectives to explore the cultural underpinnings of dominant communication theories.[10] What she found was "a pervasive Euro-American belief in the autonomous individual" that obscures the social basis of communication found in non-Western societies.

Another line of research that contributed to the framework are the ideas of Canadian scholar Harold Innis and Columbia University professor James Carey. In the early 1950s, Innis, a political economist by training, suggested a distinction between "heavy, durable time-based media" associated with religious empires and their conquest of time and "light, portable space-based media" associated with militaristic empires and their conquest of space.[11] Carey developed Innis' ideas into a 'transmission" and "ritual" views of communication. According to Carey, at the heart of the transmission view is "the transmission of signals or messages over distance for the purpose of control."[12] Whereas the transmission view seeks to "impart information," the ritual view focuses on "the representation of shared beliefs."[13] The ritual view is rooted in the metaphor of religious rituals, or the "sacred ceremony that draws persons together in fellowship and commonality." Rituals, as communication activities, connect and solidify social relations.

These major lines of research highlighting the different views of communication formed the basis for the information and relational frameworks discussed below.

The Information Framework

The information framework is rooted in the view of communication as primarily a linear process of transferring information, often with the goal of persuasion or control. It reflects Carey's notion of transmission, the low-context focus on message, and the individualism ideal. The most dominant feature of the information framework is the central role that designing and disseminating information plays in the initiative. Information is gathered and used in an effort to promote policies, advance political interests, enhance images, or engage publics to achieve the goals of an individual political sponsor. The U.S. definition of public diplomacy captures the information framework: "Public diplomacy seeks to promote the national interest of the United States through *understanding, informing, and influencing* foreign audiences."[14]

Tied to the central role of information are messaging strategies. The first critical questions of information initiatives are: What is our message? And, how do we get our message out? Because messages (information content) carry the communication weight, great emphasis is placed on selecting, structuring, and presenting the information to achieve a desired effect. Many of the prominent reports on U.S. public diplomacy stressed the importance of effective messaging strategies. The 9/11 Commission, for example, called on the U.S. government to "define the message" and offered its suggestion for themes in its 2004 report.[15] The "U.S. National Strategy for Public Diplomacy and Strategic Communication," issued in May 2007, contained a series of "core messages."[16]

A second dominant feature of information initiatives is control. The political sponsor can unilaterally decide on the goal, message, time frame, channels, and target audience. The sponsor can also control the planning, implementation, and evaluation of the initiative. Control over the message is particularly important for information initiatives. Once the message is carefully crafted, the sponsor seeks to control the integrity and consistency of the message over various communication platforms. In an effort to control its message, the White House Office of Strategic Communication issues daily talking points. The U.S. State Department circulates similar talking points to its officials in the field.

A third dominant feature of information initiatives is the restricted or limited interaction between the political sponsor and the public. In information initiatives, the public is construed as the target audience. The audience is separate from the initiative sponsor and plays a passive or limited role. A passive audience plays no role in the planning or implementation of the initiative or the content of the information in a one-way flow of information. Alternatively, the audience may provide feedback, but the sponsor decides whether to incorporate that feedback.

Fourth, most information initiatives use a variety of communication channels to disseminate the information, including interpersonal (designated speakers) such as print (brochures, fact sheets, magazines), audio/visual (films, videos), print and broadcast mass media (newspapers, television, radio), and electronic media (websites, emails, RSS feeds, podcasts). Broadcast and electronic mass media are particularly prized because they are information-efficient (that is, they can deliver the most information to the largest number of people in the least amount of time). A mass media controlled by the sponsor allows for control over message design and dissemination. Several recent broadcasts ventures, such as the U.S. Arabic-language television "Al-Hurra," Russia's English station "Russia Today," or Iran's proposed English-language "Press TV," were developed so that the country could retain control over the information presented to publics.

Finally, the information framework also tends to be goal-oriented or designed to achieve specific objectives such as policy advocacy or image enhancement. Attempts are made to measure an initiative's success based on these objectives. Common measurements of information initiatives include quantifying information output (number of brochures produced or programs aired) and audience reach (how many readers, listeners, or viewers). To measure the impact of the information output, public opinion polls assess changes in the audience's knowledge (i.e., more aware of policy rationale), attitude (i.e., more favorable national image), or behavior (more likely to support policies).

Under the information framework, there are many different types of information initiatives, most of which are readily familiar. While all share a focus on information design and dissemination, the initiatives vary in terms of their level of control, persuasive emphasis, operational context, and communication channels. For example, while most information initiatives strive for control over message content, control message dissemination can vary from relatively little control (i.e., press conference in which the message is passed via the media to the public) to stringent control (propaganda in which competing information sources are jammed, blocked, or distorted). Similarly, persuasive emphasis can range from expressed attempts to disseminate unbiased information (i.e., news broadcasts), to vigorous advocacy (information campaigns), to coercion (propaganda).

Credibility has become a particularly contentious issue for information initiatives. In today's highly competitive information environment, where political entities must compete for audience attention and message acceptance, credibility is becoming a prime determinant of persuasive value. The more credible the information content or source, the more persuasive value it has. Previously persuasion was tied to the manipulation of information. However, with the proliferation of diversified information sources, attempts to manipulate information are often readily detected and vigorously exposed. Today, persuasion appears tied to establishing one's credibility, providing valuable information, and gaining audience trust and confidence. Failure to establish or retain credibility can undermine the effectiveness of information initiatives. Joseph Nye predicted that future communication battles will be "a contest of credibility."[17]

Below is a preliminary sketch of the major types of initiatives within the information framework. I am well aware that some argue against placing some of these initiatives, particularly propaganda and nation branding, under the umbrella of public diplomacy. I myself have argued as much.[18] However, my purpose for doing so here is to explore the range of initiatives and map out a larger spectrum of public diplomacy.

Propaganda

Propaganda is perhaps the oldest and most prominent type of information initiative that political entities use with publics.[19] Political propaganda represents the most extreme form of control over information design and dissemination in an attempt to cross over from public advocacy to coercion.[20] Several of the techniques such as name calling, stereotyping, or scapegoating, add an emotional pressure to reduce the appeal of viable options and heighten compliance.[21] Deception, information control, and manipulation are strategic attributes of effective propaganda. When access to alternative or diverse information sources is limited, the audience is less able to detect discrepancies or determine the validity of the information. Once exposed, propaganda tends to lose its persuasive value. Among the few contexts in which propaganda remains operational are closed communication environments (e.g., dictatorship), or chaotic and conflict-ridden environments (e.g., government coup, civil unrest, or armed conflict). During wartime, circulating misinformation rumors or leaflets can help keep the opponent off-guard, demoralized, or confused, and the local population compliant with military objectives. In today's open communication arena, with its plethora of diverse information sources, propaganda using traditional media may be increasingly difficult to employ. However, research on cyber warfare suggests cyberspace may well be propaganda's new frontier.[22]

Nation-Branding

Nation-branding is another type of initiative that is sometimes viewed as separate from public diplomacy. Simon Anholt, a leading advocate of nation-branding, considers public diplomacy (government communication) as one of four complementary and reinforcing dimensions of a nation brand along with exports, tourism, and foreign direct investment.[23] However, whether one views public diplomacy as a component of a nation brand, or nation-branding as a form of public diplomacy, the practice relies primarily on strategically designing and disseminating information to targeted audiences. The goal of a branding campaign is to differentiate and position an entity in the minds of the audience.[24] A "core concept" or idea is crafted that collects elements of a country's attributes and assets that position the country for internal and external publics.[25] Multiple communication channels and modes (advertising, public relations, and direct marketing) are used to deliver a simple, coherent, and compelling message. Examples of government-sponsored as well as public-private cooperation of nation-branding campaigns are growing more plentiful as the practice spreads.[26] "Dynamic South Korea" and its English-language portal Korea.net are run by the Korean Overseas Information Service (KIOS) of the Government Information Agency.[27] South Africa's "Alive with Possibility" campaign is built on the public-private partnership model and exemplifies the synergy of Anholt's four dimensions operating under a core umbrella concept.[28]

Media Relations

Press offices have long been a stable of diplomatic missions. The "main task of press attachés and information departments . . . is dissemination of information and coordination of public relations with the press."[29] These departments play an important role in being the "point of contact" for international media seeking official information, be it policy statements, quotes, or statistical data. Today, many non-state actors have their press and media relations spokesperson and contact representatives.

International Broadcasts

The British Broadcasting Corporation (BBC) is among the oldest and most prominent example of using radio and television broadcast to disseminate information. Established in 1922, the BBC continues to expand is programming and audience reach. In 2005, it had the largest audience (estimated 163 million weekly listeners) and was broadcasting in 100 languages and dialects (including English).[30] The content, typically news, commentary, and information programming, are developed by the political sponsor and disseminated over sponsor-controlled channels or partner stations. International broadcasts allow a political sponsor to ensure that its message is disseminated unaltered. Russia and Iran and the Arabic language states, concerned that their viewpoint was not being fully presented to European and U.S. public, announced plans for their English-language broadcasts. All international broadcasts tend to reflect the views of their political sponsor either explicitly in their pronouncements or implicitly via the subtle selection, tone, and phrasing of their information content. This a basic feature of communication: the content and style of communication tend to reflect its source, be it an individual or political entity. CCTV International, the 24-hour English language channel of China Central Television, for example, is "dedicated to reporting news and information to a global audience, special focus on China."[31] While politically sponsored broadcasts are often labeled propaganda, they are missing important features such as source deception or coercion. Political sponsors readily and even proudly identify their productions. The Lebanese Hizballah political party touts its station Al-Manar while the U.S. boasts of Al-Hurra. Publics are free to accept their message, or switch the channel.

Information Campaigns

Another familiar information-based initiative includes information campaigns, which tend to be issue-specific, media-driven, and modeled on Western public relations. The U.S. Government Accountability Office included such a model in its recommendations for improving the effectiveness of U.S. public diplomacy.[32] Most models outline in standard public relations text a four-stage model, which begins with research to identify potential audiences and test messages.[33] The planning stage entails outlining key objectives, strategies, and tactics. The implementation stage involves designing and disseminating the information to the target audience. The information products, or "deliverables," can be distributed via a wide range of media. Mass communication channels, however, remain the dominant vehicles for reaching the public. U.S. public diplomacy's first initiative after the 9/11 attacks was an information campaign to link Osama bin Laden and Al-Qaeda with the attacks. The deliverable was a brochure, "The Network of Terror," which was produced in English, translated into a variety of languages, and distributed to publics throughout the Islamic world. The final stage, evaluation, measures the campaign's effectiveness in reaching its stated objectives with the target audience. Public opinion polls such as those by the Pew Charitable Trust have been prominent in U.S. public diplomacy assessments.

Relational Framework

Parallel to the information framework of public diplomacy is the relational framework. Relational framework is rooted in the view of communication that favors the notion of "fellowship" in ritual communication, the high-context focus away from messages, and the collectivist/interdependent concern for social cohesion and harmony discussed earlier. Relationships are the pivotal feature in the relational framework, and public diplomacy initiatives focus on identifying and building relationships. "Public diplomacy . . . is first of all about promoting and maintaining smooth international relationships," noted Jan Melissen.[34] In this respect, building relationships is not a means for enhancing individual national images or policies, but an end in itself that "contributes to a better international environment."[35]

Relational initiatives seek to find commonalities or mutual interests between publics and then ways to link those publics via some form of direct interpersonal communication. Mark Leonard of London's Foreign Policy Centre captured the essence of the relational framework in his definition of public diplomacy as "building relationships, starting from understanding other countries' needs, cultures and peoples and then looking for areas to make common cause."[36] For the relational framework, the critical questions are: What relationships are important? And, how can those relationships be established or strengthened?

A dominant feature of relational initiatives is that they employ primarily relationship-building strategies and tend to downplay messaging strategies. Interestingly, some non-Western public relations models are void of messaging strategies.[37] Rather than having key messages, relational public diplomacy initiatives are often built around specific actions, even symbolic gestures, which

91

demonstrate reciprocity and mutuality. Japan, for example, has literally built "Friendship Bridges" in countries. Scholars who study relationships have also highlighted the importance of demonstrating commitment, building trust, and establishing credibility.[38] A major strength in Britain's 2003 relationship-building campaign in China was its commitment to follow through with the initiative after China was hit with the SARS flu epidemic.

Most relational initiatives tend toward coordination rather than control. To varying degrees, sponsors work with their counterparts in defining, designing, implementing, and monitoring an initiative. As communication scholars have noted, a large part of establishing strong relationships, including relationships with publics, is based on mutuality, reciprocity, and trust.[39] For relationship-based programs to be effective, parties must share in deciding and controlling aspects of the program. Grunig and Hon called this "control mutuality."[40] This requisite is echoed in the public diplomacy literature in descriptions of "mutuality"[41] and "trust-building."[42] Hady Amr suggested the "paradigm of jointness," which he described as "joint planning for joint benefit."[43] Amr suggests that had U.S. public diplomacy adopted a paradigm of jointness, its initiatives in the Arab world might have been more effective.

Another dominant feature is the interactive relationship between the political sponsor and the public at large. In relational initiatives, the public is viewed as active participants, stakeholders, or even constituencies. Relational initiatives stress participation over presentation. In this respect, public diplomacy is more of a process (that is, cultivating connections and coordinating actions) than a product (producing materials for distribution). For example, the U.K. campaign paired its technology expo in China with a public competition to build a robot. Instead of a typical art exhibit, a British sculptor worked with Chinese villagers to create a sculpture garden of 100,000 palm-size figures molded out of the bright red clay native to their region.

Relational initiatives tend to focus on establishing interactive communication channels, and then enhancing or expanding those channels. For example, a British Council initiative for young scientists found that periodic face-to-face contact between collaborators was important for sustaining the relationships, and thus sponsored visits and forums for the participants to meet their counterparts. Communication channels that allow direct interaction, accord a sense of immediacy and facilitate involvement among the participants are favored over mass media channels. Larger initiatives that do use mass communication would tend to rely on the partner's indigenous media rather than creating a new controlled media outlet. Establishing strong media relations and relying on the local media are part of the relationship-building strategy.

Another dominant feature of relational initiative is their focus on continuity and sustainability. Because relationships are by nature on-going and entail continuous monitoring, evaluating the effectiveness of a relational initiative may not be a one-time occurrence. Research on organizational-public relationships suggests the effectiveness of relationship-building strategies is more aptly measured by the duration, strength, and perceived satisfaction among the parties.[44] The value of Britain's relationship-building campaign in China was not reflected in the public opinion polls, but rather in the links created between British and Chinese participants and the foundation the initiative created for future relationship-building activities. The promise of relationship continuity and expansion may be another indication of a successful initiative. For example, an initiative may bring together 45 scientists, 12 of whom begin long-term collaborative research projects.

While scholars and practitioners are increasingly calling for more "relationship-building" in public diplomacy, few have articulated what a relationship approach would entail beyond conducting more exchange programs, more listening or dialogues.[45] Some scholars view relationship-building primarily in terms of cultural programs,[46] and some even argue for keeping cultural relations distinct from public diplomacy.[47] While culture constitutes a prominent vehicle for cultivating relationships, as the variety of examples below illustrate, culture is not the only vehicle, nor are exchange programs the only type of relationship-building strategies. Within U.S.

public diplomacy, relationship-building is primarily thought of as cultural and educational exchange programs. However, such programs may actually be only the very basic level of relational initiatives.

In looking at the various relational public diplomacy initiatives, there appear to be graduated differences such as the level of participation (individuals, institution, or community), degree of coordination (limited, shared, or negotiated), scope (single-issue or multifaceted), time duration (days, months, or years), and policy objective (political or non-political). These graduated differences represent a spectrum of relational initiatives that is much broader and more sophisticated than is usually discussed in current public diplomacy texts and represents an area in need of further exploration. Below is a preliminary sketch of three tiers of relational initiatives based on the relative sophistication of their relationship-building strategies.

First Tier Relationship-Building Initiatives: Exchange Programs and Visits

The first level or tier of relational initiatives includes familiar fixtures in traditional public diplomacy. This tier may be the most elementary because of the circumscribed time frame and levels of coordination and participation. The major limitation of the first tier is that relationship-building is focused at the individual level and as such, an initiative's success is often tied to the personality of the individual participants.

Cultural and Educational Exchange Programs

Cultural and education exchange programs enjoy a long tradition and are well documented within the literature. Since 1946, the U.S. State Department has been sending U.S. students and scholars to foreign countries and bringing their counterparts to the United States under the Fulbright program. The stated goal of U.S. exchange programs is to "foster mutual understanding." Other countries house their exchange programs in their cultural institutes. The Japan Foundation, originally established by the Japanese Ministry of Foreign Affairs in 1973, is now an independent agency. Among the stated goals of its exchange programs is "the maintenance and development of harmonious foreign relationships with Japan." Performance measurements have been a recurring dilemma for exchange programs. While it is possible to quantify the number of participants, officials have struggled to quantify results beyond anecdotal evidence that often relates to specific individuals rather than larger public groupings. Additionally, the circumscribed time frame does not include long-term follow-up or mechanisms for expansion. Although some programs are considering creating a data base of participants to form an "alumni network," the programs were not conceived or designed to be networking initiatives.

Leadership Visits

Visits by heads of state, government, or high-ranking officials represent a relationship-building strategy of traditional diplomacy that dates back to ancient times. There is a wealth of literature on the role such visits play in diplomatic signaling and representation.[48] As Jarol Manheim noted, more than "pomp and ceremony," the welcome accorded to the official guest can signal the importance of the relationship between countries.[49] The timing and length of the visit may also be an indication of the relationship as well as the personal style of the visiting leader. Heads of states can engage directly in public diplomacy by holding joint press conferences, speaking at official ceremonies, addressing the national parliament, or granting media interviews. Direct interaction with the public can speak volumes in terms of public diplomacy. The former Soviet leader Mikhail Gorbachev was particularly adept at public diplomacy.[50] He shattered U.S. images of Russian rigidity when he spontaneously stepped out of his official motorcade to shake hands with pedestrians on a busy Washington street; a scene that was broadcast over and over on U.S. national television.

Second Tier Relationship-Building Initiatives

The second tier represents a graduation in the level of public participation, time frame, partnership coordination, and public diplomacy skills sets. Participation level is expanded from individual-specific initiatives to programs that encompass social groupings such as institutions, communities, or societies. The time frame tends to be open-ended to accommodate relationship growth and continuity. There is a notable difference in partnership coordination between the political sponsor and foreign counterparts, particularly in program planning, design, and implementation. The benefit of integrating foreign participants at this level is that not only do they take partial ownership of the program, but they can provide valuable cultural knowledge and indigenous connections to ensure the program's success. At this level, the public diplomacy skills set focus on establishing interpersonal communication channels, coordinating direct, sustained, and positive contact with counterparts and between participants, as well as nurturing the growth and expansion of relationships.

Cultural and Language Institutes

Cultural and language institutes are another familiar relational public diplomacy initiative with a long tradition. Among the oldest institutes, Alliance Française, established in 1883, currently has more than 1,000 institutes in 135 countries. The British Council, as it is known today, began as the "British Committee for Relations with Other Countries" in 1934. Some scholars see these institutes primarily in terms of their cultural value. Joseph Nye viewed culture as an important soft power resource that a nation can use to enhance its appeal.[51] Culture represents a third dimension of German foreign policy and among the goals of the Goethe-Institut is to "enhance the standing of the Federal Republic of Germany." However, these institutes also constitute important relationship-building structures. They accord channels for direct interaction with publics, allow for coordination between respective counterparts, represent relationship access and commitment, and provide a platform for relationship-building and networking beyond the individual level. China is capitalizing on the relationship-building capacity of its language and cultural Confucius Institutes by partnering with prominent universities in host countries. For example, the Confucius Institute in the U.K. is linked to the prestigious London School of Economics. China's attention to the details of relationship-building is reflected in its stipulation for the locality of a Confucius Institute, which "should be a rather busy business district where there's a large flow of people and a very convenient transportation system."[52]

Development Aid Projects

Relationship-building can also be conducted through development projects. In such initiatives, relationship-building operates on two dimensions. One is the symbolic dimension that the aid or project represents an expression of the ties between two entities. Another dimension is the actual relationship that develops between the personnel of the sponsor and their counterparts as they work together on the project. Some countries have literally built bridges as a concrete expression of a relationship. Japan, with its extensive waterways, has lent its technology and bridge-building expertise to a host of countries. Significantly, Japan stresses relationship-building over politics, as evident in the symbolic nature of their development projects.[53] Among its "major projects to serve the Egyptian people," Japan helped plan and build an Egyptian-Japanese Friendship Bridge in 2001. At the completion of the six-year joint project, Japan emphasized how "mutual friendship was deepened through the joint work with their Egyptian counterparts."[54] Japan has help construct other friendship bridges in Palau, Vietnam, Cambodia, Thailand, and Sri Lanka.

"Twinning" Arrangements

Another relationship-building strategy that is not new but which may be gaining currency are twinning arrangements between towns, cities, or provinces of one country and another country. These arrangements, found world-wide and under various labels such as "partner town," "sister cities," or "brother cities," can be concluded officially by governments or as a form of citizen diplomacy. Among the earliest town twinning arrangements was between the German city of Paderborn and the French city of Le Mans in 836, well before the advent of the nation-state. More recently, the United Arab Emirates signed twinning agreements between Abu Dhabi and Madrid, bringing a "taste of Spain" to the Arab Gulf nation.[55] The Emirates' capital city, Dubai, has already concluded 13 operational agreements with other cities, including Osaka (Japan), Istanbul (Turkey), Geneva (Switzerland), Shanghai (China), and Detroit (USA). These agreements help promote cooperation and exchanges in a variety of areas such as economics, trade, and tourism, as well as education, technology, and sports. However, the major significance in pairing, beyond fostering cross-cultural contact and understanding, is that it serves to institutionalize the relationship-building process.

Relationship-Building Campaigns

Similar to information campaigns, relationship-building campaigns can have a predefined campaign goal, set time frame, specific public, and entail research, planning, implementation, and evaluation, or follow-up stages. However, the primary goal is to build relationships with publics, rather than disseminate information to publics. This would include the campaign sponsor developing in-country partnerships and actively coordinating on the campaign design and implementation. Finally, campaign effectiveness is more aptly gauged by relationship strength and expansion, rather than opinion surveys. Among the few examples of a "relationship-building campaign," is the British Foreign Commonwealth Office 2003 initiative *Think UK, China*.[56] The campaign included more than thirty in-country events, with British and Chinese scientists, sculptors, and writers teaming up for public concerts, exhibitions, competitions, and discussion forums. While the campaign showcased modern art, education, business and cultural achievements of the U.K., the campaign activities were developed through the coordination of more than one hundred Chinese and U.K partner organizations working together and actively engaged the Chinese public. The imaginative public events received extensive coverage by the Chinese media and led to a Chinese television series "U.K.-China Challenge."

Non-political Networking Schemes

Networks have gained increasing prominence for their efficient information-sharing organizational structures. However, networks are fundamentally relationship structures. Robust networks tend to have what Krebs and Holley call a "network weaver," who create links with other members and thus expand the network.[57] In non-political networking schemes, public diplomacy officers in essence become network weavers. Non-political networking schemes build relationships between like-minded individuals or institutions working on a variety of areas such as science, health, environment, or literacy promotion. An example of a non-political networking scheme is the U.K. Science and Innovation Network (SIN) launched by the British FCO in 2000.[58] The initiative consists of a network of SIN attachés in nearly 30 countries who are continuously monitoring scientific developments and opportunities in their assigned countries for scientific collaboration on major projects and research and then facilitating those links. These SIN attachés represent a new breed of public diplomacy network weavers.

Third Tier Relationship-Building Initiatives: Policy Networking Strategy and Coalition Building

A third tier of relationship-building in public diplomacy involves policy networking strategies that incorporate coalition building with other countries and non-state actors to achieve policy objectives. Comparatively speaking, this third tier requires the most intensive diplomatic communication skills because the political entity may have the least amount of control over the direction and outcome of the relationship process, yet the political stakes may be the highest. Brian Hocking spoke about the growing symbiosis between state and non-state activities as "catalytic diplomacy," in which political entities act in coalitions rather than relying on their individual resources.[59] The diplomatic communication skills require facilitation and coordination to establish, monitor, and enhance communication among the parties. Hockings describes these diplomatic roles as "manager, co-coordinator, and integrator" in his catalytic model.[60] Given the policy goals and potential for conflict over competing political interests, this tier also requires advocacy, negotiation, and mediation skills.

Canada and Norway stand out in this diplomatic area of relationship-building. Alan Henrikson described Canadian and Norwegian officials and diplomacy as "master networkers."[61] Among the most prominent case examples of this level of diplomatic relationship-building is that of the Canadian foreign minister Lloyd Axworthy. Axworthy teamed with Jodi Williams of the International Campaign to Ban Landmines (ICBL) to lead the "Ottawa Process" that helped secure ratification of the landmine treaty in an astonishing 18 months by networking and coordinating with other state and nonstate actors. ICBL was awarded the Nobel Peace Prize in 1997. Other examples include the treaty establishing the International Criminal Court[62] and the Kimberly Process that help restrict the trade in conflict or blood diamonds.[63]

Challenges for an Emerging Field

This piece has discussed the origins, features, and types of initiatives of an information and relational framework of strategic public diplomacy. However, the features of these frameworks along with the spectrum of public diplomacy initiatives are in no way complete. Conspicuously absent, for example, are interactive websites such as the virtual embassies planned by Sweden and Maldives on the Second Life platform. Where might they fall? Are there places where the frameworks overlap and are such initiatives better because they employ both communication dimensions?

My goal in laying out the two frameworks and spectrum of initiatives is first to show the wide range of how political entities communicate with publics (my shorthand definition for public diplomacy). Public diplomacy appears heavily weighted under the information framework or split off from the relational framework. For example, while media-driven information campaigns are plentiful and well articulated in the literature, relationship-building campaigns are comparatively rare. This may be because such campaigns are not on the public diplomacy radar screen or because the dominance of the information framework has obscured the panorama of relational initiatives. Subsuming all relations initiatives under "cultural programs" misses the variety of vehicles and strategies for cultivating relationships. Whatever the reason, relational initiatives need to be more vigorously explored and documented. Relationship-building and networking strategies may be particularly important for communicating with culturally diverse publics,[64] and for navigating the changing communication dynamics of the international arena.[65]

Another purpose in identifying the two frameworks is to hopefully expose some of the communication assumptions that fuel public diplomacy initiatives and to prompt Western scholars and practitioners, in particular, to explore those assumptions. The idea that communication equals information and that communication problems can be solved by providing more or better information, countering misinformation, or even trying to build relationships through information, appears to be a dominant Western assumption. Using this assumption to create initiatives for non-Western publics—who may not necessarily share this assumption—may be a recipe for failure. U.S. public diplomacy initiatives in the Arab and Islamic world are a case in point. To be effective, more needs to be understood about the underlying communication assumptions that sponsors and publics bring to the public diplomacy equation.

This chapter concludes with several challenges for public diplomacy scholars and practitioners. The first challenge is to start thinking outside of the "communication = information" box and put relational thinking on the public diplomacy radar screen. However, instead of either/or communication battles that seek to define public diplomacy, public diplomacy needs to redefine its vision of "strategic communication" to include *both* information transfer *and* relationship building. A final related challenge is a need to map out the diversity of initiatives political entities use to communicate with publics and assess their strategic communication and political advantages. Viewing the full spectrum of initiatives is critical for expanding the study and practice of public diplomacy in new directions.

Notes

1 R.S. Zaharna, "Asymmetry of Cultural Styles and the Unintended Consequences of Crisis Public Diplomacy," in *Intercultural Communication and Diplomacy*, ed. Hannah Slavik (Malta: Diplo Foundation, 2004), 133–142.

2 See John Condon and Fathi Yousef, *An Introduction to Intercultural Communication* (Indianapolis: Bobbs-Merrill, 1975); Gou-Ming Chen and William Starosta, *Foundations of Intercultural Communication* (Boston: Allyn and Bacon, 1998), Judith Martin and Thomas Nakayama, *Intercultural Communication in Contexts* (Mountain View, CA: Mayfield, 2000); Larry Samovar, Richard Porter, and Edwin McDaniel, *Intercultural Communication: A Reader* (Belmont: CA: Wadsworth, 2006) for overviews of cultural basis of communication.

3 See Benno Signitzer and Carola Wamser, "Pubic Diplomacy: A Specific Governmental Public Relations Function," in *Public Relations Theory II*, eds. Carl Botan and Vincent Hazelton (London: Lawrence Erlbaum, 2006); Jan Melissen, "The New Public Diplomacy: Between Theory and Practice," in *The New Public Diplomacy: Soft Power in International Relations*, ed. Jan Melissen (New York: Palgrave, 2005), 16–23, for overview of debates.

4 Martin Rose and Nick Wadham-Smith, *Mutuality, Trust and Cultural Relations* (London: British Council, 2004), 5.

5 Edward T. Hall, *Beyond Culture* (New York: Anchor Books, 1976).

6 Edward T. Hall, "Context and meaning," in *Intercultural Communication: A reader*, ed. Larry Samovar and Richard (Belmont, CA: Wadsworth, 1982), 18.

7 Geertz Hofstede, *Culture's Consequences: International differences in work-related values* (Thousand Oaks, CA: Sage, 1980).

8 Harry Triandis, *Individualism and Collectivism* (Boulder, CO: Westview, 1995).

9 Hazel Rose Markus and Shinobu Kitayama, "Culture and the self: Implications for cognition, emotion and motivation," *Psychological Review* 98 (1991): 224–253.

10 Min-Sun Kim, *Non-Western Perspectives on Human Communication: Implications for Theory and Practice* (London: Sage, 2002).

11 Harold A. Innis, *The Bias of Communication* (Toronto: University of Toronto Press, 2003) originally published 1951.

12 James W. Carey, *Communication as Culture: Essays on Media and Society* (New York: Routledge, 1992), 15.

13 Ibid., 18.

14 U.S. State Department, Planning Group for Integration of USIA into the Dept. of State, June 20, 1997.

15 National Commission on Terrorist Attacks, *The 9/11 Commission Report* (New York: W.W. Norton & Company, 2004), 18.

16 U.S. Public Diplomacy and Strategic Communications Policy Coordinating Committee, "U.S. National Strategy for Public Diplomacy and Strategic Communication," Washington, D.C., May 31, 2007.

17 Joseph S. Nye, *The Paradox of Power* (New York: Oxford University Press, 2003), 68.

18 R.S. Zaharna, "From Propaganda to Public Diplomacy in an Information Age," in Y. Kamalipour and Nancy Snow (eds.), *War, Media and Propaganda: A Global Perspective*, (Lanham, MD: Rowman and Littlefield, 2004), 219–225.

19 Jacque Ellul, *Propaganda* (New York: Vintage, 1973); Nicholas J. Cull, David Culbert, and David Welch, *Propaganda and Mass Persuasion: A Historical Encyclopedia, 1500 to the Present* (Santa Barbara, CA: ABC Clio, 2003).

20 Propaganda scholarship is extensive. Early works based on WWI experience include Edward Bernays, *Crystallizing Public Opinion* (New York: Boni and Liveright, 1923), and *Propaganda* (New York: H. Liveright, 1928); and Harold Lasswell, *Propaganda Techniques in the World War* (New York: Alfred A. Knopf, 1927). See Christopher Simpson, *Science of Coercion: Communication Research and Psychological Warfare 1945–1960* (New York: Oxford University Press, 1994), for discussion of the extensive propaganda research in the U.S. following WWII. See Stanley B. Cunningham, *The Idea of Propaganda: A Reconstruction* (Westport, CT: Praeger, 2002) for recent review and analysis. Among the most comprehensive online sources for propaganda studies is maintained by Prof. Philip M. Taylor at The Institute of Communication Studies, University of Leeds, U.K. http://ics.leeds.ac.uk/papers/index.cfm?outfit=pmt.

21 For a discussion of the psychological underpinnings and analyses of communication dynamics, see C. Hovland, I. Janis, and H. Kelly, *Communications Communication and Persuasion* (New Haven, CT: Yale University Press, 1953), J.A.C. Brown, *Techniques of Persuasion: From Propaganda to Brainwashing* (New York: Pelican, 1965).Clyde R. Miller, "How to Detect Propaganda," in *Propaganda Analysis* (New York: Institute of Propaganda Analysis, 1937). Leonard W. Doob, "Goebbels' Principles of Propaganda," *Public Opinion Quarterly* (1950), 14, 419–442.

22 John Arquilla and David Ronfeldt, *Networks and Netwars: The Future of Terror, Crime and Militancy*, Rand MR–1382-OSD, 2001.

23 Simon Anholt, *Brand New Justice* (New York: Butterworth-Heinemann, 2003).

24 Wally Olins, *Wally Olins on Brands* (New York: Thames and Hudson, 2004).

25 Philip Kotler and David Gertner, "Country as a brand, product and beyond: A place marketing and brand management perspective," *Journal of Brand Management* 9, issue 4/5, 249, April 2002.

26 Peter van Ham, "The Rise of the Brand State: The Postmodern Politics of Image and Reputation," *Foreign Affairs* 80 (Sep/Oct 2001): 2.

27 http://www.korea.net/ portal for Dynamic Korea campaign Korea (accessed May 12, 2007).

28 "Alive with Possibility," South African campaign portal, http://www.imc.org.za/ (accessed May 12, 2007).

29 Jan Melissen, "The New Public Diplomacy: Between Theory and Practice," 13.

30 BBC World Service, "Annual Review 2005–2006: A Year in Brief." http://www.bbc.co.uk/world service/us/annual_review/2005/year_in_brief.shtml (accessed April 21, 2007).

31 CCTV International, http://www.cctv.com/english/index.shtml.

32 Government Accounting Office (GAO), U.S. Public Diplomacy: State Department Efforts to Engage Muslim Audiences Lack Certain Communication Elements and Face Significant Challenges, May 3, 2006. GAO-06-535 U.S. Public Diplomacy, 18.

33 See Jerry Hendrix and Darrell C. Hayes, *Public Relations Cases* (Belmont, CA: Wadsworth, 2006) for outline of the ROPE process model (research, objectives, programming, and evaluation).

34 Jan Melissen, "The New Public Diplomacy: Between Theory and Practice," in *The New Public Diplomacy: Soft Power in International Relations*, ed. Jan Melissen (New York: Palgrave, 2005), 21.

35 This is the first stated purpose of the cultural exchange programs operated by the Japan Foundation, established by the Japanese Ministry of Foreign Affairs. www.jpf.go.jp/e/about/program (accessed June 5, 2007).

36 Mark Leonard, "Diplomacy by Other Means," *Foreign Policy* 132 (Sep/Oct 2002): 50.

37 For examples of non-Western models, see K. Sriramesh "Societal Culture and Public Relations: Ethnographic Evidence from India," *Public Relations Review* 18, no. 2 (1992): 202–212; Samsup Jo and Yungwook Kim, "Media or Personal Relations," *Journalism and Mass Communication Quarterly* 81, no. 2 (Summer 2004): 292–306; Basyouni Ibrahim Hamada, "Global Culture or Culture Clash: As Islamic Intercultural Communication Perspective," *Global Media Journal* 3, no. 5 (Fall 2004): article no. 2.

38 James E. Grunig, "Image and Substance: From Symbolic to Behavior Relationships," *Public Relations Review* 19, no. 2 (1993): 121–139. John A. Ledingham and Stephen D. Bruning, "Relationship

Management in Public Relations: Dimensions of an Organization-Public Relationship," *Public Relations Review* 24, no. 1 (Spring 1998): 55–67. Michael L. Kent and Maureen Taylor, "Toward a Dialogic Theory of Public Relations," *Public Relations Review* 28, no. 1 (2002): 21–37.

39 James E. Grunig, "Image and substance: From symbolic to behavior relationships," *Public Relations Review* 19, no. 2 (1993): 121–139. John A. Ledingham and, Stephen D. Bruning, "Relationship Management in Public Relations: Dimensions of an Organization-Public Relationship," *Public Relations Review* 24, no. 1 (Spring 1998): 55–67. Michael L. Kent and Maureen Taylor, "Toward a Dialogic Theory of Public Relations," *Public Relations Review* 28 (2002): 21–37.

40 James E. Grunig and Linda Childers Hon, "Guidelines for Measuring Relationships in Public Relations," *The Institute for Public Relations* (1999), http://www.instituteforpr.org/ipr_info/guidelines_measuring_relationships/ (accessed April 28, 2007).

41 Martin Rose and Nick Wadham-Smith, *Mutuality, Trust and Cultural Relations* (London: British Council, 2004), 8.

42 Mark Leonard and Andrew Small with Martin Rose, *British Public Diplomacy in the "Age of Schisms"* (London: The Foreign Policy Centre), February 2005.

43 Hady Amr, "The Need to Communicate: How to Improve U.S. Public Diplomacy in the Islamic World," The Brookings Institution, http://www.brook.edu/fp/saban/analysis/amr20040101.htm (accessed May 5, 2007): 19.

44 See Walter K. Lindenmann, "Measuring Relationships is Key to Successful Public Relations," *Public Relations Quarterly*, 43 (Winter 1998), 19; and James E. Grunig and Linda Childers Hon, "Guidelines for Measuring Relationships in Public Relations," *The Institute for Public Relations*, Commission of Public Relations Measurement and Evaluation (1999) http://www.instituteforpr.com/measeval/rel_p1.htm; Maureen Taylor and Marya L. Doerfel, "Another dimension to explicating relationships: measuring inter-organizational linkages," *Public Relations Review* 31, 1 (March 2005), 121–129; The Stakeholder 360: Measuring the Quality of Stakeholder Relationships, The Center for Innovation in Management, Simon Fraser University, Canada, www.cim.sfu.ca/folders/research/6-stakeholders (accessed March 6, 2006).

45 See, for example, Mark Leonard, *Public Diplomacy* (London: Foreign Policy Centre, 2002); Marc Lynch, "Taking Arabs Seriously," *Foreign Affairs*, (Sep/Oct 2003); Rhiannon Vickers, "The New Public Diplomacy: Britain and Canada Compared," *British Journal of Politics and International Relations* 6, (May 2004), 182–194; Shaun Riordan, "Dialogue-based Public Diplomacy: A New Foreign Policy Paradigm?," Discussion Papers in Diplomacy No. 95, The Hague, Netherlands Institute of International Relations, *Clingendael*, November 2004; Mark Leonard and Andrew Small, *British Public Diplomacy in the "Age of Schisms"* London, The Foreign Policy Centre, February 2005; Shanthi Kalathil (Rapporteur), *Soft Power, Hard Issues*, The Aspen Institute, Communications and Society Program, Washington, D.C., 2006.

46 Cynthia P. Schneider, "Cultural Communicates: U.S. Diplomacy that Works," in *The New Public Diplomacy: Soft Power in International Relations*, ed. Jan Melissen (New York: Palgrave, 2005).

47 Martin Rose and Nick Wadham-Smith, *Mutuality, Trust, and Cultural Relations* (London: The British Council, 2004).

48 Christer Jonsson and Martin Hall, *Essence of Diplomacy* (New York: Palgrave Macmillan, 2005).

49 In Jarol Manheim, *Strategic Public Diplomacy* (New York: Oxford University Press, 1994), the author provides analysis of official visits by various heads of state.

50 Gorbachev appeared quite adept at public diplomacy; see, for example, Roderic Lyne, "Making Waves: Mr. Gorbachev's Public Diplomacy 1985–6," *International Affairs* 63 (Spring 1987), 205–224.

51 Joseph S. Nye, *Soft Power: The Means to Success in World Politics* (New York: Public Affairs Books, 2004), 8.

52 The Office of Chinese Language Council International, "Introduction to Confucius Institute," The Office of Chinese Language Council International, http://english.hanban.edu.cn/market/HanBanE/412360.htm (accessed May 1, 2007).

53 Karin Gwinn Wilkins, "Japanese Approaches to Development Communication," *Keio Communication Review* 25 (2003), 19, http://www.mediacom.keio.ac.jp/publication/pdf2003/review25/3.pdf (accessed April 22, 2007).

54 Embassy of Japan in Egypt, Economic Cooperation (Official Development Assistance, ODA), "Major Projects to serve the Egyptian People," http://www.eg.emb-japan.go.jp/hompepage_2/e/assistance (accessed June 28, 2006).

55 United Arab Emirates (UAE) Interact, "Twinning Agreement Brings a Taste of Spain to Dubai," UAE. Interact, comment posted on August 30, 2006, http://uaeinteract.com/news/default.asp?ID=328#21927 (accessed May 12, 2007).

56 Think UK, "Final Report, Foreign & Commonwealth Office and British Council," (February 2004), ThinkUKFinal_ReportFebruary2004.pdf (accessed June 15, 2006).

57 Valdis Krebs and June Holley, "Building Smart Communities through Network Weaving," *Orgnet.com* (2002), www.orgnet.com/BuildingNetworks.pdf (accessed May 12, 2007).

58 Foreign and Commonwealth Office, "Science and Innovation Network, Science & Innovation Annual Report," Foreign and Commonwealth Office (July 2006), www.fco.gov.uk/science (accessed April 28, 2007).

59 Brian Hocking, "Catalytic Diplomacy: Beyond 'Newness' and 'Decline,' 12," in *Innovation in Diplomatic Practice*, ed. Jan Melissen, (New York: Palgrave Macmillan, 1999), 31.

60 Ibid., 31.

61 A. Henrikson, "Niche Diplomacy in the World Public Arena: The Global 'Corners' of Canada and Norway," in M. Jan (ed), *The New Public Diplomacy: Soft Power in International Relations*, (New York, NY: Palgrave Macmillan), pp. 67–82, cited at p. 70.

62 D. Davenport, "The New Diplomacy," *Policy Review* 116 (December 2002/January 2003), 17–31, http://www.hoover.org/publications/policyreview/3458466.html.

63 Brian Hocking, "Diplomacy: New Agendas and Changing Strategies," *iMP Magazine* (July 2001), http://www.usip.org/virtualdiplomacy/publications/reports/14b.html (accessed May 19, 2007).

64 R.S. Zaharna, "Public Diplomacy and Islam," paper prepared for the U.S. Senate Committee on Foreign Relations, February 27, 2003, http://foreign.senate.gov/hearings/2003/hrg030227a.html.

65 R.S. Zaharna, "The Network Paradigm of Strategic Public Diplomacy," Policy Brief, *Foreign Policy in Focus*, Vol. 10, No. 1, April 2005. http://www.fpif.org/briefs/vol10/v10n01pubdip.html (accessed May 2, 2007).

11

The Nexus of U.S. Public Diplomacy and Citizen Diplomacy

Sherry Mueller

> Average Americans, in their natural state, are the best Ambassadors a country can have.
> —*The Ugly American*[1]

Introduction

The still pervasive stereotype of U.S. tourists abroad—cameras dangling, loud clothing, and even louder voices—seems to belie William Burdick and Eugene Lederer's assertion in *The Ugly American* that ordinary citizens can be effective ambassadors. However, the stereotypical "Ugly American" is not the only image that America presents to the world. There is much more to the story of U.S. citizen diplomacy and the effort to build international relationships person by person. Citizen diplomacy is a subset of U.S. public diplomacy that—at its best—allows the world a genuine insight into American character, values and institutions. Citizen diplomacy also extends well beyond official government efforts to reach foreign audiences.

History

The idea of supplementing the interaction of government representatives with the involvement of ordinary citizens as "diplomats" has been well established. In fact, wider usage of the concept of citizen diplomacy predates that of public diplomacy. It was in the mid-1960s that Edmund Gullion, Dean of the Fletcher School of Law and Diplomacy, coined the phrase "public diplomacy." Dean Gullion invited Vice-President Hubert Humphrey to speak at the Fletcher School in 1966 to inaugurate the Edward R. Murrow Center for Public Diplomacy. It was at Fletcher that Dean Gullion pioneered the idea that government efforts to influence foreign audiences merited academic attention and scrutiny.

Fully a decade earlier in 1956, President Dwight Eisenhower held a White House Summit on Citizen Diplomacy. This seminal event led to the establishment of People to People International and Sister Cities International, two of a growing number of organizations that have practiced and promoted citizen diplomacy in the decades that followed. These organizations were established and grew, in part, because there was a post-World War II determination to prevent such a cataclysmic catastrophe in the future, and also because advances in transportation technology made travel much more accessible to the average person.

In addition, the concept of citizen diplomacy gained credence as the Cold War evolved. Ironically, the powerful image of an "Iron Curtain" and the stark reality of the Berlin Wall generated the need to surmount those barriers. The superpower standoff produced a variety of exchange programs that facilitated dialogue among groups of individual citizens. Even if official government interactions underscored glaring, fundamental differences, citizens could still forge positive personal relationships and focus on common human aspirations. The formation of organizations such as the Citizen Democracy Corps and the publication of books such as *Citizen Diplomats: Pathfinders in Soviet-American Relations—And How You Can Join Them*[2] illustrate this process. In one historic example of citizen diplomacy in action, the Garst family in Coon Rapids, Iowa hosted Soviet Premier Nikita Khrushchev in September 1959. Coverage of this event in worldwide media reports spread the notion that individual citizens truly do have a role to play in international relations.

Definition of Citizen Diplomacy

Citizen diplomacy is the concept that the individual citizen has the right, indeed, the responsibility to help shape U.S. foreign relations, "one handshake at a time." Citizen diplomats are generally defined as being unofficial ambassadors who participate in exchange programs overseas or host and interact with international exchange program participants in the United States. They build person-to-person relationships—the web of human connections that later serve as the context for official dialogue and negotiations. To the extent that these exchange programs are funded primarily by the U.S. government, citizen diplomacy is a fundamental component of U.S. public diplomacy.

The Impact of U.S. International Exchange Programs

In the United States, public diplomacy and citizen diplomacy inextricably intertwine and overlap in remarkably reinforcing ways. However, there are also many instances in which citizen diplomacy clearly extends beyond and is separate from public diplomacy.

In recent years, the attention directed towards U.S. public diplomacy (in the United States and abroad) has been unprecedented. Authors of a myriad of academic studies, media analyses, and government reports offer many—occasionally conflicting—prescriptions for not-so-quick "fixes." These works, however, share a common theme. Whether focusing on structural issues, message content, or the right mix of public diplomacy tools, the dominant recommendation of these inquiries is that government-sponsored international exchange programs have proven their value and should be expanded. For instance, Lee Hamilton—co-chair of the 9/11 commission—concluded:

> International education is the single most effective tool of American foreign policy. It erodes mistrust, strengthens the bonds of understanding, and encourages reconciliation among peoples.[3]

Moreover, a Congressional Research Service report recapped and analyzed 29 major studies on public diplomacy. The authors highlighted the fact that "more than half of the 29 reports recommend expanding U.S. exchange programs and/or U.S. libraries overseas, making it the most common proposal among this group of reports."[4]

The author of a *Washington Times* article quoted former Under Secretary of State for Public

Diplomacy and Public Affairs, Karen Hughes: "Our education and exchange programs, I'm convinced, are the single most valuable public diplomacy tool."[5] This conclusion—which Under Secretary Hughes often reiterated in her speeches—reinforces the notion that international exchange is a fundamental building block of U.S. public diplomacy.

Unique Public Sector–Private Sector Partnerships

One unique characteristic of U.S. government-sponsored exchanges essential to their success is that they are generally administered through public sector–private sector partnerships. Early on, officials of the U.S. Department of State engaged nonprofit organizations to help implement most U.S. government-sponsored exchanges. These nonprofits have recruited, trained, and recognized the efforts of many citizen diplomats. Examples of these grassroots diplomats at work include: volunteers in Riverside, California, hosting a delegation from their Sister City in Sendai, Japan; state legislators participating in an American Council of Young Political Leaders (ACYPL) trip to Egypt; and families hosting Fulbright graduate students to dinner in their homes for the Institute of International Education Rocky Mountain Regional Center in Denver.

These partnerships endure and have proven their effectiveness over time for three fundamental reasons. First, exchange programs inevitably reflect the culture of the host country. In the United States there has been an historic emphasis on the private sector—a Jeffersonian notion that the government should only do what the private sector cannot do. For example, when the U.S. Department of State first established the Division of Cultural Relations (the antecedent to the Bureau of Educational and Cultural Affairs) in 1938, the Institute of International Education (a private nonprofit organization) had already been in business since 1919, providing services to international students and the universities that host them. Donald Watt founded the Experiment in International Living, now part of World Learning, in 1932. He pioneered the idea of homestays as an integral part of a worthwhile exchange program as he organized cultural immersion experiences in Europe for groups of young Americans. Officials in the new division at the State Department wisely decided to tap the expertise already existing in the private sector as they began to develop a variety of innovative educational exchange programs.

State Department officials were motivated by a second (and perhaps more important) reason to develop partnerships with the private sector. They realized that it would often be advantageous to have private sector nonprofit organizations serve as a buffer between the U.S. Government program sponsor and the program participants. This arrangement preserves the credibility of the program by keeping the government at arm's length. It signals that exchange programs are authentic two-way educational experiences rather than purveyors of brainwashing propaganda. This distance between the U.S. government representatives and the program participants also protects the credibility of the participants, enabling foreigners with a wide range of political persuasions to accept invitations to take part.

Thirdly, there is also a practical economic consideration at play in the decision to partner with the private sector. It is considerably less expensive to provide support for the nonprofit organizations that help implement these international exchange programs than to maintain a comparably sized group of government employees. In addition, these organizations involve many volunteer citizen diplomats who bring remarkable resources to the table. These citizen diplomats contribute time, professional expertise, leadership skills, and their own money to sustain the nonprofit organizations throughout the country that constitute the infrastructure of U.S. citizen diplomacy. Also, they raise substantial funding locally to support their work with the foreign exchange program participants in their communities, as well as to finance American delegations traveling overseas.

Illustration: The International Visitor Leadership Program

In repeated surveys, U.S. ambassadors have ranked the U.S. Department of State International Visitor Leadership Program (IVLP) as the most valuable tool of U.S. public diplomacy at their disposal.[6] Ambassadors appreciate the key role that citizen diplomats play in the IVLP. For instance, at the symposium in Tokyo commemorating the 50th Anniversary of the IVLP with Japan, Ambassador Howard Baker stated:

> Although the IVLP is sponsored by our government, it is actually implemented in the United States by a great network of private citizens, ordinary Americans who volunteer their time and open their homes and their hearts to Visitors from places like Japan. It is precisely this kind of people-to-people linkage that has allowed us to advance our relationship beyond mutual understanding to mutual trust.

Ambassador Walter Cutler, U.S. Ambassador to Saudi Arabia, and (until 2006) President of Meridian International Center for 17 years wrote:

> Whether the International Visitors were journalists emerging in newly-independent Algeria, jurists strengthening civil society in post-war Korea, or public health officials struggling with Ebola fever in the Congo, I have been heartened to see them return from their U.S. visits energized and inspired to build better futures for their own countries. Only recently in Kuwait, a former International Visitor stressed to me how her visit to observe the American elections in 2004 was instrumental in her decision to become one of the first women to run for a seat in her country's parliament.
>
> While most IVLP participants understandably seem to treasure their visits to official Washington and towering New York City, I have found that their time spent "outside the beltway," in "the real America," has often provided them with their most poignant impressions and memories. This, of course, is made possible by the creative efforts of those thousands of dedicated NCIV "citizen diplomats" throughout our country. I salute all of them as, day by day, community by community; they build and maintain the people-to-people bridges that in these troubled times are so critically important and needed.[7]

U.S. Secretaries of State have also acknowledged the indispensable assistance of citizen diplomats in carrying out the International Visitor Leadership Program. In 1965, Secretary of State Dean Rusk told an audience of citizen diplomats: "The government simply can't do what you are doing. We cannot render the kind of individual, sensitive and personalized service such as you can and do render in your own communities."[8]

Almost four decades later, then Secretary of State Colin Powell echoed a similar theme when he observed:

> Your work leverages us in such an important way. When you open your homes, when you open your communities, when you open your hearts to visitors from around the world, you give your guests a chance to see America at our best, to see our warmth and our base for diversity . . . Not only do you help acquaint visitors with what is in American hearts and on our minds, you also help to educate members of our own communities about hopes, fears, and dreams of your visitors. As citizen diplomats, you bring world issues home to the American people in the most direct way possible.[9]

The National Council of International Visitors (NCIV)—the State Department's private sector partner in the administration of the IVLP—estimates that each year approximately 80,000 volunteers are involved in the activities of the 90 community organization members that comprise the NCIV network. These volunteer citizen diplomats serve as local programmers, professional resources, home hosts, board members, drivers, and financial supporters of their organization's work with the IVLP and other exchanges.

In fiscal year 2006, community members of the NCIV network received approximately $2.6 million in federal grants. They raised five times that amount—more than $15 million—to support the work of their organizations with the IVLP and other exchanges. These funds—raised in their communities from sources such as membership dues, special events, corporate sponsorships, and individual contributions—do not include the value of in kind contributions (calculated at $1,825,334) or the estimated value of time donated by volunteers ($8,002,093) that year.[10]

The Power of Citizen Diplomacy

Actual dollars raised by NCIV's 90 community organizations and even the cash value of volunteer time (using nationally accepted figures developed by the Independent Sector) are relatively easy to measure.[11] It is much more difficult to capture the far-reaching impact of their volunteer effort. The following two examples portray the power of citizen diplomacy.

The first example highlights a Liberian participant in the International Visitor Leadership Program and volunteers from the Albuquerque Council for International Visitors (ACIV). Jeff Tarnue had been legally blind since birth. He was part of a group of radio journalists representing six African nations who traveled to the United States in 2006. The group attended a reception hosted by ACIV to welcome them to New Mexico. While speaking with Mr. Tarnue, ACIV volunteers Betty Davis, Carmen Martin, and Susan Severt discovered that he had never been properly treated for his cataracts. They decided to see what could be done to reclaim his vision. To summarize a saga (of tests and surgeries—some provided *pro bono*—and the establishment of a Jeff E. Tarnue Medical Fund to pay medical bills and cover out-of-pocket expenses) that spans more than two months, Jeff regained much of his sight. He came to the United States able to see only shapes and shadows. He returned home able to read large print and use the laptop computer equipped for users with limited vision that ACIV had purchased for him. He commented on this extraordinary gift: "I never expected this when I came here. Words are inadequate. They can't explain how grateful I am feeling."

How does one estimate the immense value to the United States of this story circulating throughout Liberia and beyond? How do you measure the impact of this instance where public diplomacy and citizen diplomacy intersected in such a dramatically positive way? The U.S. Department of State funded the group of participants' trip (as part of the IVLP) to and around the United States. However, the citizen diplomats from this all-volunteer Council in Albuquerque perceived a problem and sought a solution. They acted in the most generous and quintessentially "can do" American way. Their actions and ongoing relationship with Jeff Tarnue convey a powerful and enduring message about the values that motivate U.S. citizens.

A second example spotlights Alan Kumamoto, a volunteer professional resource from the International Visitors Council of Los Angeles (IVCLA). An expert in management and nonprofit governance, Alan often briefs international visitors, sharing his knowledge and professional expertise. Alan has also served as a member of the IVCLA board of directors, and as chair of the NCIV board of directors from 2001 to 2004. After briefing a multiregional group of NGO leaders, Alan was invited to Turkey in 2007 to give lectures and conduct workshops. As a State Department sponsored speaker, his work had a far-reaching impact on the audiences he addressed in Istanbul and Bursa. He also strengthened his relationship with the International Visitor who had first invited him to Turkey.

In writing an article describing the professional and personal rewards of this experience, Alan articulated a metaphor that beautifully evokes the complementary and contrasting nature of public and citizen diplomacy:

Istanbul has two congested suspension bridges that connect the two sides of the city across the Bosporus Strait. There are, however, many small ferryboats rushing across the waterway bringing people together. The suspension bridges represent to me the formal ways our countries practice connecting [public diplomacy], while the ferryboats for me are the smaller personal ways of linking people to people [citizen diplomacy].[12]

Like the massive bridges and agile ferryboats of Istanbul, public diplomacy and citizen diplomacy are making vital connections possible. They are complementary and mutually reinforcing.

Citizen Diplomacy: Beyond Public Diplomacy

While many of the customary citizen diplomacy activities described in this essay can be defined as a subset of public diplomacy, citizen diplomacy also extends well beyond a government's official efforts to communicate with foreign audiences. Many citizen diplomats work with privately funded exchange programs such as Friendship Force International, Rotary International, or People to People International. Youth exchanges, such as those sponsored by the Experiment in International Living of World Learning, AFS Intercultural Programs, Youth for Understanding, and an array of other organizations (both nonprofit and for profit) constitute a critically important category of exchange programs. Although not a part of official U.S. public diplomacy activities, these programs certainly supplement public diplomacy. They enable participants to engage in vitally important efforts to build constructive relationships on behalf of Americans with people around the globe. The *International Exchange Locator*, compiled by the Alliance for International Educational and Cultural Exchange, is an excellent resource that describes many of the international exchange programs available.

We All Are Citizen Diplomats

There is another dimension to citizen diplomacy that is now receiving much more attention. It is the idea that each individual citizen must perceive himself or herself as a citizen diplomat. There is a documentary film on the life of Elvis Presley in which—wearing his army uniform and newly arrived in Germany—he tells reporters: "What we do here will reflect on America and our way of life."[13] While Elvis and citizen diplomacy are certainly not synonymous in most people's minds, clearly he was conscious of the fact that his interactions with foreign nationals would affect their views of the United States. Many leaders have concluded that this consciousness must be cultivated in all U.S. citizens. Whether a student sitting next to a foreign scholar in a university classroom, an athlete competing abroad, an elected official welcoming foreign counterparts, a rock star performing in another country, or a business representative overseas, you are a citizen diplomat. Your actions either increase or decrease foreigners' respect and affection for the United States. As an American you have an obligation to put Uncle Sam's best foot forward.

This is the message that leaders of the international exchange organizations who founded the Coalition for Citizen Diplomacy (CCD) in 2004 want to convey. This loose coalition of like-minded organizations convened the first National Summit on Citizen Diplomacy in July 2006; a second National Summit took place on February 12–13, 2008 in Washington D.C. Most indicative of the grassroots nature of this movement is the fact that more than 65 state or community summits have been held throughout the United States since 2005. Leaders of organizations that share international missions and concern about America's reputation abroad have come together at the national and local level: (1) to recognize the impressive efforts of citizen diplomats; (2) to increase exponentially the number of Americans involved in citizen diplomacy; and (3) to augment the resources—both public and private—devoted to citizen diplomacy.

They are joined by their colleagues in the business community. The ground-breaking work of Business for Diplomatic Action (BDA)—founded in 2004 by DDB Chair *Emeritus* Keith Reinhard is a prime example. He and his BDA colleagues are encouraging business representatives, students, and other Americans interacting with foreign nationals to be aware of their responsibility as citizen diplomats. They have developed and distributed World Citizen Guides, participated in summits on citizen diplomacy and other events, and developed various programs to sensitize Americans to their responsibilities as citizen diplomats.

Many other organizations and individuals are part of this growing effort to increase exponentially the number of Americans engaged in effective citizen diplomacy. For instance, Our Voices Together—an organization founded by families of 9/11 victims—is determined to use that tragedy to help Americans understand the opportunities they have (and must utilize) to build positive relationships with people around the world.

Finally, it is not sufficient simply to be a citizen diplomat; to counter the notion of the "Ugly American," one must be an *effective* citizen diplomat. Greg Mortenson, author of *Three Cups of Tea*,[14] described the lesson that all truly effective citizen diplomats have consciously or subconsciously integrated into their approach:

> That day, Haji Ali taught me the most important lesson I've ever learned in my life. We Americans think you have to accomplish everything quickly. We're the country of thirty-minute power lunches and two-minute football drills . . . Haji Ali taught me to share three cups of tea, to slow down and make building relationships as important as building projects. He taught me that I had more to learn from the people I work with than I could ever hope to teach them.

Notes

1 William J. Lederer and Eugene Burdick, *The Ugly American* (New York: W.W. Norton & Company, Inc., 1999), 108.

2 Gale Warner and Michael Shuman, *Citizen Diplomats: Pathfinders in Soviet-American relations—and how you can join them* (New York, NY: The Continuum Publishing Company, 1987).

3 Lee Hamilton, "New Challenges for the U.S. and Higher Education," Remarks made at National Association of Independent Colleges and Universities Annual Meeting, February 5, 2002.

4 Susan B. Epstein and Lisa Mages, "Public Diplomacy: A Review of Post Recommendations," Congressional Research Report for Congress, September 2, 2005, 11.

5 Nicholas Kralev, "Foreign Ministration," *Washington Times*, July 15, 2007, Specials section.

6 U.S. Department of State, Office of the Under Secretary for Public Diplomacy and Public Affairs, *Field Survey of Public Diplomacy Programs* (Washington, D.C.: GPO, 2000).

7 Walter Cutler, "Personal Message for Sherry Mueller from Walter Cutler," June 11, 2007, personal email July 5, 2007.

8 "COSERV National Conference," *Community Services to International Visitors Newsletter*, IX.4 (1965): 6.

9 Former Secretary of State Colin Powell, speech delivered at the 2002 NCIV National Meeting, March 14, 2002.

10 NCIV, FY2006 Community Impact Summary, July 10, 2007.

11 Ibid.

12 Alan Kumamoto, "International Visitor Invites Professional Resource to Turkey," *NCIV Network News* XLVII.4 (2007): pg. 8.

13 "Remembering Elvis: A Documentary," directed by Richard Bluth, 48 min. Delta, 2001. DVD.

14 Greg Mortenson and Oliver David Relin, *Three Cups of Tea* (New York: Viking, 2006).

Part 3

Public Diplomacy Management

Image, Influence, and Persuasion

Public Diplomacy in International Conflicts

A Social Influence Analysis

Anthony Pratkanis

The typical image of public diplomacy is that it is nice and warm and comforting in contrast to the harsh realities of hardball diplomacy and military action. In the soft power approach to public diplomacy, the United States seeks to promote its interests through attraction (as opposed to coercion); soft power is the use of the attractiveness of a country's culture, political ideals, and policies to get others to admire those ideals and then follow one's lead.[1] This approach to public diplomacy uses such devices as pamphlets, *Voice of America*, books, and other means to explain U.S. policy, cultural exchange programs especially with emerging leaders of other countries to create an appreciation and understanding of American culture, and the sponsorship of American studies programs in overseas schools and universities.[2] In such cases, the goal of public diplomacy is to build long-term relationships and understanding.

While there is nothing wrong with these suggestions, *per se*, even a cursory look at the conduct of public diplomacy in the 19th and 20th centuries reveals that these campaigns can often be quite competitive, nasty, brutish, and even evil. Public diplomacy can consist of propaganda that plays on a target's prejudices and emotions. Hitler and Goebbels marshaled anti-Semitism feelings to promote their notions of Aryan supremacy and a pogram against the Jews. On May 11, 1944 in Cassino, Italy, the Allied troops from Poland, India, the U.S., and Britain were bombarded with Nazi leaflets designed to disrupt the Allied coalition by playing up the British control of India, the Nazi shared interest with the Poles of the defeat of the Soviets, and the fear that American soldiers were sleeping with the wives and girlfriends of British soldiers.[3] During the Cold War, Soviet operatives spread disinformation such as U.S. forces were using chemical weapons in Honduras and Grenada and AIDS was created by the CIA. In Rwanda in the early 1990s, Hutu propaganda portrayed the Tutus as a separate, evil race committing acts of rape and murder. In the mid-1990s, Serbian forces took over major lines of communication and used these media to present distorted accounts of the 1389 Battle of Kosovo and the "Croat genocide" of Serbs in World War II (WWII), thereby creating a belief in the eternal martyrdom of Serbs. Today, in the Darfur region, the Janjaweed preach a propaganda of Arab superiority, resulting in a mission of cleansing the area of Africans. Usama bin Laden blames the United States as a crusader in the Middle East in order to promote terrorism and his personal rise to power. In each of these cases, soft power attracts, not through positive ideals, but by invoking such raw emotions as hate, fear, and insecurity.[4] *Soft power has a very hard edge.*

Another way to look at the hard edge of soft power is to explore the competitive strategies and tactics used in one conflict. The Persian Gulf War of the early 1990s involved three main actors, each trying to influence the hearts and minds of the world's citizens: Saddam Hussein, the Kuwaiti government, and the U.S. government.[5] Saddam attempted to portray to the world that he was a tough dictator who was not guilty of atrocities. He attempted to accomplish this strategy by:

(a) providing tours of supposedly "non-gassed" Kurds, which journalists found unconvincing;
(b) control of information flow via censorship (see CG 4 below);
(c) western hostage-taking to show toughness, which also backfired (see CG 8); and
(d) the stationing of Peter Arnett of CNN to provide vivid accounts of the bombings by Coalition forces.

The Kuwaiti government attempted to portray the image of the good, decent victim. They hired the PR firm of Hill & Knowlton: (a) to depict Kuwait as an open and democratic society that, unlike other Arab countries, allows women to drive cars; (b) to disseminate atrocity stories such as the dubious report of Iraqis soldiers removing babies from incubators; and (c) to control the information flow by serving as the only source of video (much sought-after by Western media) from the Kuwaiti resistance. The U.S. government adopted a strategy of demonstrating leadership of a world united against Saddam's aggression. This strategy was executed by (a) piggy-backing on the efforts of the Kuwaiti government, and (b) showing world leaders opposed to Saddam's actions. The U.S. government also adopted a strategy to strengthen support for the war by (a) reducing expectations for a quick and easy victory (Corollary CG 2a), (b) inoculating the public to possible negative events that could happen in the war (logistical failures, use of chemical weapons), and (c) providing a "troops'-eye-view" of the war via the Hometown News Program. In this battle for hearts and minds, the liberation theme of the U.S. and Kuwaiti governments dominated the "tough" occupier and oppressor strategy of Saddam, as is often the case (see Corollary CG8a).

The purpose of this chapter is to describe a *social influence analysis* (SIA) approach to the use of public diplomacy in international conflict.[6] This approach is based on the science of social influence coupled with historical and case analyses of the use of information and influence in international conflict. The hallmark of a SIA approach is that it appreciates the competitive and often brutal nature of the use of influence in conflict and recommends strategies, tactics, and analyses for countering such propaganda and advancing democratically based national policy and security concerns.

I define public diplomacy as the *promotion* of the national interest by informing and *influencing* the *citizens of other nations*. Two aspects of this definition are critical.

First, public diplomacy is directed towards the *citizens of other nations*. Standard diplomacy is directed at leaders of other governments and political entities. In the best traditions of democracy, public diplomacy is directed at the private citizens of those nations and political entities. As Clausewitz noted, before the French Revolution, most wars in Europe were fought by professional armies of limited size and interests. Rulers were generally unable to involve their subjects directly, and thus, once their forces had been defeated, it was difficult to mobilize a new army. As such, the devastating effects of war tended to be minimized. However, beginning with Napoleon, war "became the business of the people," with their passions and energy stoked and mobilized through rhetoric and propaganda.[7] As evidenced by the U.S. Civil War, two World Wars, the Cold War, and numerous ethnic conflicts and acts of terrorism, the course of war is no longer determined by a rational calculus of interests of elite rulers, but by the prejudices and emotions of everyday people. War is now the business of the people, and thus, in international conflicts, the people must be involved in the diplomacy of war.

Second, public diplomacy is about the promotion of our national interest through *influence*. By influence, I mean changing public opinion, beliefs, behavior, expectations, perspectives, and the like in support of U.S. foreign policy as opposed to merely communicating that policy in the hopes of reaching some understanding. This aspect of the definition is consistent with the change made by John F. Kennedy and Edward R. Murrow in the mission of the U.S. Information Agency (USIA)—one of the chief instruments of public diplomacy at the time—from Eisenhower's goal of "inform and explain" to one of actually "influencing the public attitudes in other nations."[8] Mere communication in the hopes of understanding is just not adequate to counter the propaganda of authoritarians and ethnic hate-mongers; opposing such propaganda requires the efforts of an effective influence campaign. Failure to recognize the influence component of public diplomacy can result in ineffective efforts and a forestalling of a needed discussion of the ethics and legality of public diplomacy (see below).

Public diplomacy can accomplish its mission of promoting national interest through influence through *direct, support,* and *indirect (landscaping and altercasting)* means.

By direct means, I have in mind the use of public diplomacy to change *directly* behavior (especially) but also opinions and beliefs. Typically, this involves bringing public pressure to bear to enact direct change. Some examples of this use of public diplomacy include: the Allied removal of Nazi forces from Rome by countering Nazi pro-Catholic propaganda and bringing to bear an international sentiment that Rome should not be part of the war;[9] Viet Cong infiltration of villages during the Vietnam War; in 1977, President Anwar el-Sadat of Egypt went to Jerusalem to speak directly to the people of Israel and over the heads of Israel's leaders to help mobilize efforts for a change in the direction of peace negotiations;[10] the use of fear-arousing leaflets by coalition forces in the Persian Gulf War to induce Iraqi troops to surrender; and the use of anti-American and anti-Israeli ideology to recruit suicide bombers. Policy makers typically seek these direct effects from public diplomacy, but such effects are often difficult to engineer (especially when the policy is not popular with the target audience).

Public diplomacy can also be used to *support* other tools of foreign policy, such as economic, diplomatic, and military actions. For example, the Soviet Union in the early 1950s, seeking to negotiate a settlement with the U.S. over Austria, coupled its "conciliatory moves coupled with invitation to reciprocate" (or what is often known as GRIT; see below) with a public diplomacy campaign to put additional pressure on the United States to agree to a conference over Austria and eventual settlement of the issues;[11] international public opinion can serve to moderate a nation's extreme demands and positioning;[12] and the success of strategies of deterrence and compulsion often depends on the political situation in a nation, the psychological characteristics of the leaders, and the legitimacy of the deterrence—all factors that can be influenced through public diplomacy.[13]

Finally, public diplomacy can be used in an *indirect* manner to create a situation and common understandings to advance national security objectives. As Joseph Nye puts it: "Moreover, soft-power resources often work indirectly by shaping the environment for policy, and sometimes take years to produce desired outcomes."[14] In the nomenclature of a science of social influence, effective public diplomacy engages in *landscaping* and *altercasting.* Landscaping (or what has been called pre-persuasion)[15] refers to structuring the situation in such a way that the target is likely to be receptive to a given course of action and respond in a desired manner. It commonly employs the influence tactics of definition and labeling, creating a picture of the world through metaphor, story-telling, and similar tactics, framing of issues, setting decision criteria, shared rules and procedures, creating norms, setting expectations, agenda-setting, establishing a choice set, controlling information flow, and creating alliances and coalitions. Some examples of landscaping in international conflict: FDR's use of the four freedoms to set a post-war decision criterion; the establishment of what Graham Allison termed "rules of prudence" to constrain American and Soviet competition during the Cold War;[16] the creation of information channels and procedures to lower the chances of inadvertent war between the U.S. and the Soviet Union;[17] the development of a security regime of principles, norms, rules, and procedures;[18] and the use of public opinion polling and the dissemination of poll results to reach public understanding and consensus in support of a Northern Ireland peace process.[19] Altercasting refers to creating a relationship through social roles with the target of influence such that relationships are formed to promote one's influence goals. The use of cultural exchange and similar programs is an example of one way to implement long-term relationship-building across nations. Glen Fisher provides a fruitful analysis on how to use social roles to understand a culture and develop a public diplomacy effort.[20]

In carrying out its mission to promote national interests during international conflicts, public diplomacy can be asked to accomplish a number of specific tasks and objectives. Some of the more common ones include:

(a) communicate the legitimacy of a course of action;
(b) co-opt a former adversary;
(c) change the mind and behavior of enemies, neutrals, and those who might enter alliances;
(d) win support for ideals;
(e) create and disrupt strategic alliances;
(f) counter the propaganda and deception of dictators, tyrants, and terrorists;
(g) marshal world pressure and condemnation against a rogue regime;
(h) stop ethnic genocide and cleansing (and sadly, in the case of autocratic regimes, to promote it);
(i) encourage belligerents to cease fire;
(j) justify war efforts to significant neutrals;
(k) destroy an enemy's morale;
(l) improve one's own morale;
(m) induce an enemy to surrender;
(n) assist with the conduct of a war (e.g., permission to search a house, gain support of local leaders, solicit information, keep civilians from battle zones, counter rumors, assist with relief efforts);
(o) lessen the perception of a security dilemma (i.e., the increase in security of one nation threatens the security of others);
(p) resolve a conflict and prevent a war in the first place;
(q) change the images and expectations held by those in the conflict to allow negotiations and other means of conflict resolution to take place;
(r) create the basis for reconciliation among combatants so that not just the war but the peace is won as well; and
(s) develop support for international institutions and treaties in pursuit of peace.

Currently, there are two principal and popular models for achieving public diplomacy goals and objectives: (a) advertising; and (b) public relations (PR). Both of these techniques adopt the *sprinkle* approach to public diplomacy—images, photo-ops, and slogans are sprinkled on top of foreign policy and international actions to make those policies and actions taste sweeter and smell better. As such, "sprinkleism" tends to be ineffective (especially in the long run) and is counter to an approach that integrates public diplomacy concerns into overall foreign policy and objectives.

Advertising and Brand Positioning

The goal of advertising is to develop a favorable and positive image of the product (branding) and to position that brand image so that it competes effectively in a product niche or segment (for example, a Lexus appeals to the luxury-minded and the Prius to the energy-conscious). Multiple brands can exist in a product category just so long as each appeals to a unique market segment and gains enough sales to be profitable. A brand is communicated most often through paid media, especially TV, print, and radio ads. Advertising works best under conditions of audience low involvement.[21] A recent example of its use is the Shared Values Initiative (SVI) directed towards the Muslim world in the early winter of 2002 under the direction of U.S. Under Secretary of State for Public Diplomacy and Public Affairs, Charlotte Beers. The campaign consisted of five TV ads describing the life of Muslims in America along with supporting print ads and booklets. The goal of the campaign was to show that America tolerated and respected the Muslim religion.

The problem with using advertising and its philosophy of branding in public diplomacy is that advertising's core goal of brand positioning in a niche market is inconsistent with the major issues faced by a nation involved in an international conflict. In an international conflict, ideas compete head on with other ideas for dominance in a dynamic, competitive, and intensely adversarial environment. Branding a country may be useful in promoting tourism where different segments of the population seek different vacations (sun and fun, family, gambling, and so forth). The public diplomacy practitioner is not seeking to persuade a niche but to influence the attitudes and actions of a range of target audiences, including combatants, neutrals, and allies. (One exception is when a containment strategy is employed which divides the world up into spheres of interest or segments.) Further, an international conflict by its nature *brands* the participants in the minds of targets, if the nation is not already branded by its previous words and deeds.

One of the first critics of the use of advertising in public diplomacy was Martin Herz, chief U.S. leaflet writer during WWII and later a career Foreign Service officer, ambassador, and public diplomacy professor at Georgetown. In an article after WWII for *Public Opinion Quarterly* he develops a metaphor of what it would be like to sell America as if it were the fictitious *Fleetfoot* brand of automobiles.[22] Herz argues that any ad extolling the beauty and grace of the *Fleetfoot* would be immediately countered with a barrage of anti-*Fleetfoot* editorials, ads, and whatever means of communication the adversary had at her or his disposal. As he puts it: "Praising the excellence of our product is not only secondary but rather beside the point. As we have seen, it would be difficult to sell the beauty and stylishness and engineering advances of *Fleetfoots* to potential customers who are day in, day out told that *Fleetfoots* are a danger and a menace."[23] Herz concludes that a campaign based in such puffery would lack veracity and fail.

The problems (and some of the possibilities) of using advertising for public diplomacy can be observed in the SVI. Jami Fullerton and Alice Kendrick have conducted a thoughtful analysis of this campaign in order to separate the heat and hype from the facts.[24] In a set of experiments conducted with Muslim foreign exchange students, they found that viewing the ads increased these students' belief that Muslims were fairly treated in the United States and had positive effects on their attitudes towards the U.S. government and Americans. The U.S. State Department commissioned a market test of the ads in Indonesia and found that the ads had very high recall and playback of the message, indicating that the ads received considerable attention by Indonesians. However, consistent with the Herz critique, Fullerton and Kendrick also found that many of the students thought the ads were misleading, false, one-sided, too good to be true, and too positive.

While the message of the SVI may have been well received among test subjects, the actual placement of the ads met a firestorm in an adversarial climate. Many Arab stations—especially state-run TV and *Al Jazeera*—refused to air the ads, presumably because they thought them to be American propaganda. This not only limited the reach of the campaign, but served as an indicator that the SVI message should not be considered normative in the Arab world. Consistent with the Herz analysis, the SVI provoked an adversarial response. Editorials and commentary in Muslim newspapers frequently ridiculed the campaign. For example, the Tunisian French language newspaper *La Quotidien* wrote: "This is so funny! Because what we understand from this campaign is that Americans just really need a small cloth to polish their image, and that's it!"[25] A

Pakistani newspaper *Ummat* ran a series of "ads" in the same style as the SVI and lampooned the effort. One ad read: "I insisted on the freedom of my country and religion. America killed me and left my five children orphaned" and featured a photo of a dead Afghan. Another ad told the story of the hate-crime killing of a Muslim immigrant in Texas after 9/11.[26]

In addition to these problems, the SVI campaign broke just as the U.S. was indicating that it would invade Iraq. The SVI theme of religious tolerance did not address the core concerns of Muslims ("occupation by an invading crusader") and indeed the campaign's theme of tolerance appeared to be inconsistent with the U.S.'s action in Iraq. Given the lead times in creating ads, advertising was ill-equipped to handle this dynamic aspect of the international conflict.

In fairness to Under Secretary Beers, she did not intend the SVI to be a magic bullet that changed Arabs' minds with an enchanting sprinkle of advertising, but instead viewed it as a first step to creating dialog in the region. Given that there were limited public diplomacy efforts in the region following the campaign and no follow-through on the SVI (especially the development of a Shared Futures campaign), it is impossible to know if her efforts would have been effective in opening up a bridge of understanding between Americans and citizens of the Muslim world.

In evaluating the use of advertising for public diplomacy, advertising should be viewed as a technique not a viable strategy for setting public diplomacy efforts. The philosophy of branding ignores the dynamic, competitive nature of international conflict. As a technique (and subject to the limitations described above), advertising may be useful in providing information in some situations. Other nations, which have free and open access to American advertising markers, often promote the business climate of their lands or use American advertising to get over other points of interest. Advertising may also be used to get over limited pieces of information, such as the dangers of roadside bombs for children in an area of conflict, or the promotion of brotherhood themes, although such messages should not be limited to just 30-second spots but should involve a concerted media campaign as was done in Bosnia beginning in 1998.[27]

Public Relations

The public relations (PR) approach consists of a set of techniques designed to raise awareness of an issue or entity and to create a favorable impression of that issue or entity. PR attempts to accomplish its goals primarily through the creation and dissemination of images and visuals and the establishment and use of relationships and networks to shape a story. Some of the more common techniques include: the staged event, photo-ops, the third party technique (use of front organizations or shills to deliver a message for clients), sponsoring committees, press kits to save reporters the work of reporting, press dinners and junkets, editorial and news placements (via press release or social relationships), video news releases (VNR), lobbying and contact with government leaders, as well as advice on how to fit a client's actions and message to best appeal to a target's psychological motives.[28] A recent example is the Rendon Group's efforts to secure positive news coverage in Iraq and to promote favorable events on behalf of the U.S. government.

PR is frequently used in public diplomacy with both great successes and with devastating failures. A careful appraisal of these successes and failures reveals why this approach is at best inadequate for use in international conflicts.

PR has been successful in promoting causes and changing the public perception of nations and conflicts. In a recent analysis of Third World rebellions, Clifford Bob asks why certain such rebellions become global *causes célèbres* (particularly, American *causes célèbres*) and others do not.[29] For example, the Chinese government opposes the independence of both the Uyghurs and the Tibetans led by the Dalai Lama, but yet few Americans have even heard of the Uyghurs much less adorn their car bumpers with stickers demanding their freedom. Bob finds that PR is a major factor in a Third World cause reaching public consciousness. Similarly, Jarol Manheim and

Robert Albritton have looked at six cases in which a foreign nation hired a PR firm to improve its image with the American public.[30] Manheim and Albritton found that in five of the six cases, the PR firms successfully reduced the amount of negative stories (or visibility) about the nation appearing in the *New York Times*, and for four of the nations coverage became more positive. These results should not surprise us. The first wholesale use of PR to sell a conflict was the very effective efforts of the Committee on Public Information (known as the Creel Commission) to convince the American public on the value of entering the World War I. Indeed, two of the founders of the modern PR method—Eddie Bernays and Carl Byoir—first developed their techniques as members of the Creel Commission.[31]

However, Manheim and Albritton in a separate analysis also identified two cases where PR campaigns failed to improve the public image in America of the sponsoring nations—Iran under the Shah in the mid-1970s and the Philippines under the Marcos in the 1980s.[32] In both cases, despite sophisticated PR technique, negative coverage of the nations increased in the *New York Times*. We can identify five conditions under which PR is and is not an effective tool for public diplomacy.

First, PR is most effective when a nation or cause is little known by a public and the goal is to raise visibility and attract attention. In the cases of Iran and the Philippines, both had received extended treatment in the news before the introduction of PR. Similarly, most wars and conflicts generate extensive public attention, negating this goal of PR.

Second, PR's creation and dissemination of images are most effective in influencing public opinion when those images are accepted with little scrutiny—that is, the public is in a low involvement state or employing a peripheral route to persuasion.[33] In the cases of PR failure, both countries received intensive press scrutiny and thus their attempts to generate a positive image backfired. War generally generates similar scrutiny and also involves an adversarial situation which generates further scrutiny from political competitors.

Third, when a nation or cause is subject to intense negative media coverage, Manheim and Albritton recommend the strategy of reducing visibility (remove the cause from the limelight) before presenting positive images. The attempt to present positive images in a negative context is ineffective and likely to boomerang. Neither Iran nor the Philippines adopted this strategy. In matters of international conflict, it is often impossible to temporarily stop the conflict and put a hold on news coverage in order to adopt this strategy.

Fourth, during the PR campaigns of Iran and the Philippines more negative images were disseminated in the media and these images could not be countered by attempts to replace them with positive images. War and conflict often generate a similar stream of negative images—for example, Serbs made it a point to tour international journalists through NATO bombing sites during the Kosovo conflict, and *Al-Jazeera* has gained ratings through similar coverage in Iraq.

Finally, in a competitive and adversarial situation, it is very likely that someone will point out that PR technique is being used to promote the cause. Such a revelation is almost certainly likely to produce a backlash as people generally do not like to feel manipulated (see CG 8 below), especially in a covert manner (see CG 3d below) such as with the hidden techniques of PR. This is exactly what happened in the Iran and Philippine cases as a firestorm erupted over their use of PR. The history of the use of PR in international conflicts reveals that such backlashes over the use of PR is quite common—for example, PR professionals Ivy Lee and Carl Byoir created controversy (and the Foreign Agents Registration Act of 1938) in their efforts to change the image of Nazis in America, and the Creel Commission fell into disrepute after World War I (WWI) as its techniques were uncovered.[34]

In summary, what is the value of PR in international conflict? It is clear that PR is capable of creating effective visual images and in using social relationships to control mass media agendas (see CG 4 below). These images are most effective when the public really isn't thinking much about those images and in a non-adversarial situation. In adversarial situations, the effective image of one combatant can quickly be replaced by the effective visual image of another on the world's TV screens. Any short-term accomplishments that might be gained through PR often come at a steep long-term price: the erosion of trust. PR is perceived as covert and manipulative and thus results in a backlash when its use is revealed. As with advertising and branding, PR ignores the dynamic, competitive nature of international conflict and is primarily technique and not a strategy.

Before concluding this section, I should note that there are other, more democratic, models of PR than the one presented here. In arguing for more PR in daily life, Bernays advocated a two-way street model of PR—that it was the PR professional's responsibility to change public attitudes but also to change public policy (that is, the client's behavior) in the face of public opinion. More recently, Grunig described a "two-way symmetrical model" model of PR in which the practitioner plays a role in adjusting the behaviors of publics and dominant coalitions for mutual advantage.[35] If ever employed, these models would show less sprinkleism and start to incorporate some of the principles I discuss in another chapter in this book, particularly the principle of "Ed Murrowism" and CG3a (listening). Regardless, these models serve as the ultimate moral and ethical critic of traditional PR practices. Traditional PR relies on a unidirectional authoritarian technique that is antithetical to the type of social influence and persuasion that is the basis of a successful democracy.[36]

So how can we change hearts and minds? At the core, there are really only three ways to change human beliefs and behavior. First, one might employ outright *deception*—that is, to lead a person to believe he or she is doing X but in reality is doing something else. One effective use of deception in international conflict was the Allied ruse that caused Hitler and his generals to believe that the D-Day invasion was coming at Calais and not Normandy.[37] As any magician and fraud criminal can attest, deception can be a powerful means for creating a false reality and manipulating human behavior *in the short run*.[38] Nevertheless, we humans tend to rebel when we feel we are manipulated (see CG 8 below) and thus deception destroys the sense of trust (see CG 3 below) needed to build a public diplomacy campaign. With the exception of some military operations, deception is a poor means for changing hearts and minds in international conflicts.

A second means for changing beliefs and behavior is raw *power* or the control of critical resources to induce another to do as you wish.[39] War is perhaps the most extreme application of power, but the use of power also includes promises and threats designed to induce or deter behavior.[40] History teaches that power is an important tool of statecraft and that such power can serve to change the course of history. Nevertheless, the use of power can come with considerable costs as the exercise of power begets the use of more power by one's adversaries in a spiral of conflict such as the world witnessed in two world wars. Ironically, the destruction of an enemy's physical assets under certain conditions may actually increase the will to fight, as that enemy now has little left to lose and much to revenge.[41] Further, the effectiveness of the use of power is limited if it is not perceived to be a legitimate exercise—a legitimacy that can only be obtained with our third means of influence (see CG 8 below).

A third way to change human belief and behavior is through the use of *social influence*. By social influence I mean any non-coercive technique, device, procedure, or manipulation that relies *on the social psychological nature of human beings as the means for creating or changing the belief or behavior of a target*, regardless of whether or not this attempt is based on the specific actions of an influence agent or the result of the self-organizing nature of social systems. In other words, social influence uses tactics that appeal to our human nature to secure compliance, obedience, helping, and behavior and attitude change. A social influence campaign can consist of propaganda—the use of often short, image-laden messages to play on the target's prejudices and emotions—as well as other forms of persuasion such as debate, discussion, argument, and a well-crafted speech that are more suited to a democracy. *Social influence is the means by which soft power is implemented in international conflicts.*

The 20th century witnessed the development of a science of social influence.[42] This science has used experiments, case studies, surveys, and other research designs to develop the empirical conditions under which social influence is more (and least) effective. This body of scientific analysis allows us to conduct a *Social Influence Analysis* (SIA) of any given situation to understand the types of influence that are used and to gain an understanding of how to intervene in that situation. For example, Doug Shadel and I recently conducted a social influence analysis of how con criminals use social influence to perpetrate their crimes, resulting in policy recommendations and interventions that have been empirically shown to decrease victimization rates.[43]

Formally, a SIA consists of specifying:

(a) the social influence, power, and deceptive tactics used in a given domain;
(b) the strategic goals (the factors that will determine the success or failure of influence in a domain);
(c) how influence is exchanged within a community (social institutions and influence landscape); and
(d) the patterning of influence within and across communities (e.g., communication networks and channels of influence), along with using social-psychological principles and theories (e.g., dissonance, social cognition principles) to understand the dynamics of influence in the situation.

In constructing a SIA of international conflict, I began by looking at information campaigns used in past international conflicts using the lens of a science of social influence.[44] Of particular value in this regard are the liberal democracy campaigns that took place in, around, and after WWII, especially the writings of Wallace Carroll, R.H.S. Crossman, and Ralph K. White. The result of this analysis yielded a set of nine strategic goals common across international conflicts (expressed as a set of centers of gravity) and an understanding of the social influence tactics used in such conflicts. These centers of gravity and influence tactics make up the heart of a SIA of international conflict and are described in detail in the next two sections.

A SIA provides extensive recommendations on the use of influence in conflicts. Before getting into that detail, it is useful to take a step back and see the forest for the trees. As a general guide, Figure 12.1 lists 14 core attributes of the SIA approach to public diplomacy. While many of these core attributes are discussed throughout this chapter, I want to focus on five key aspects of a SIA to contrast it with other approaches.

First, a SIA is empirically-based; its prescriptions are derived from a science of social influence and from historical analysis. As such, the bases for a SIA approach to public diplomacy is the social psychological nature of us humans—human nature, if you will—and not some abstract set of naïve assumptions derived from neo-conservative economic models of self-interest or simple game theoretic models based on a questionable conjecture that actors behave "rationally" in expressing fixed preference among fixed choices that cannot be changed.[45] The value of using a social-psychological analysis for international affairs can be seen in Robert Jervis's analysis of misperception in international politics and similar works.[46] Indeed, Glen Fisher, a career foreign service officer and former Dean of the Center for Area and Country Studies in the U.S. State Department, has argued that social psychology is the most relevant discipline of the behavioral sciences for understanding public diplomacy.[47]

Second, in a world of doves and hawks, a SIA is an eagle clutching in its talons the arrows of war and the olive branch of peace. In contrast to doves, a SIA sees the ugly, brutish nature of conflict. While a "play nice" strategy is effective in winning friends and gaining influence (as China's recent charm offensive can attest[48]), such a strategy is ultimately not enough to deal with menaces of genocide of the Hitler, Stalin, Mao, Milošević, Saddam, and bin Laden ilk. Such cases

119

Figure 12.1: Attributes of Social Influence Analysis Approach to Public Diplomacy in International Conflict

1 Soft power has a very hard edge.

2 Influence campaigns are competitive—a battle of ideas for hearts and minds. Such campaigns are not static but dynamic; not peaceful but full of conflict.

3 Influence campaigns must be based on sound theory and practice; influence campaigns should be based on the scientific principles of social influence and rooted in historical analysis of past campaigns.

4 Influence must be strategic and not tactical. The key to any successful influence campaign is to follow the advice of Sun Tzu: "*Thus, what is of supreme importance in war is to attack the enemy's strategy.*"

5 *Ed Murrowism*: Public diplomacy is at the same level as other sources of national power such as diplomacy, military might, and economic strength; Murrow advocated that public diplomacy be involved at the take-off and not just the crash landing of foreign policy.

6 Think globally, act locally. An influence campaign must be organized around national strategy and objectives, but must also allow for localized feedback and quick, effective implementation at a local level.

7 Goal specificity: it is essential to have specific communication goals tied to the advancement of national security.

8 The use of tactical influence for defensive purposes is the first sign of defeat.

9 Trust is essential for communication. Public diplomacy is impossible without a sense of legitimacy.

10 Listen before speaking (if at all possible); use polls and other devices to understand the audience; let your audience know that you are listening and willing to understand their point of view (regardless of whether or not there is agreement).

11 Full conflict analysis: Public diplomacy campaigns should plan for the peace—the post-conflict period. Public diplomacy campaigns should also prepare for the pre-conflict period and look for ways to prevent and lessen conflict. An ounce of social influence prevention is worth a pound of cure.

12 The means determines the ends; a tactic that is manipulative, raises cynicism, or is perceived as coercive will undermine the long-term objectives of a democratic campaign.

13 The instruments of public diplomacy, that is, the institutions and organizations charged with carrying out an influence campaign, should be designed based on the principles of democracy, especially the principles of transparency and of checks and balances on this sort of power.

14 American influence campaigns should reflect the principles of our democracy.

---

often require hard power and soft power with a hard edge to contain or eliminate these dangers from the world stage. In contrast to the naïveté of hawks, a SIA recognizes the costs and real limitations of hard line tactics. People generally don't like to be threatened or have their family members or neighbors killed and thus rebel from such sources of influence. A SIA acknowledges that social influence can be far more powerful and effective for winning and resolving conflicts than the use of bombs. It provides a nation that finds itself in conflict with a way to understand that conflict and a panoply of options for resolving that conflict in contrast to the one-trick pony of "puffed up chest and threat" (which needs must rarely be backed by action) of the neo-con hawk.

Third, an effective public diplomacy "thinks globally, acts locally." In other words, the social influence campaign must be organized around national strategy and objectives (see CG 1), but must also allow for localized feedback and quick, effective implementation at a local level. The selection of media for delivering the campaign is a function of strategy and the local situation.

Fourth, intelligence is needed to effectively apply a SIA to any given current international conflict. This intelligence includes an understanding of the nature of the audience for public diplomacy and profiling the adversary in terms of their goals, strategy, and influence tactics. It should also include a self-appraisal of one's own capabilities. To facilitate intelligence gathering for an effective public diplomacy, Figure 12.2 lists questions that should be addressed in the planning and execution of an influence campaign.

Figure 12.2: Questions to Ask in Developing a Public Diplomacy Effort in an International Conflict

Who is the adversary or adversaries? (Do not assume a bipolar conflict.)

Who is involved in the conflict or may become involved as adversaries, neutrals, observers, third-party intervention, others?

What is the adversary's overall goal or objective and major sub-objectives? What is your overall goal?

What is the adversary's communication strategy in terms of goals, targets, and means and operations (especially message, tactics, and media channels)? What are the current themes of the adversary's messages?

What is your preliminary communication strategy?

What is the appeal of the combatants' strategy to the targets? What are the negative aspects of these strategies?

Do the strategies of the combatants contain strategic traps such as imply a standard of conduct, exclude certain groups of people, invoke humanitarian outrage, prevent certain courses of action, etc.?

How robust are the strategies of the combatants? Imagine likely and even unlikely scenarios. How do the strategies stand up to these changes in situation?

Has your strategy planned for the peace (or is it only about winning the conflict)? Does your plan contain hidden obstacles that make peace difficult? What does peace look like under the adversary's strategy?

Which of the strategies of the combatants is likely to be on offense and which is most likely to be tactical and defensive?

How will your strategy stand up over the long run? Is it capable of producing a consistent message across targets? How is it related to long-term national strategic objectives?

Which media channels (radio, TV, interpersonal, leaflets, etc.) and techniques (advertising, PR, etc.) are available for delivering your message and the message of your adversary? Can channels be created if needed?

What is the morale beneffectance of those supporting the combatants? What factors are most likely to affect the two components of beneffectance—the goodness of the cause (and the badness of the enemy) and efficacy?

What are the expectations held by those involved in the conflict for its outcome and for major processes (civilian deaths, own casualties, etc.) that may occur during the conflict?

How is your adversary establishing trust, credibility, and legitimacy with the targets? What

---

is your basis for establishing trust, credibility, and legitimacy? Are messages plausible to the target? What social relationships are maintained? Are you prepared to admit mistakes and failures?

Are you listening to those involved in the conflict and are you prepared to act on what you hear in a manner that develops trust?

Are your actions in line with your words? Has your adversary committed inconsistent acts that should be brought to the attention of relevant targets?

Are deceptive actions being taken that can undermine your strategy?

What is the current media agenda for relevant communication channels? How is the agenda set in those channels? What options are available to you for setting the agenda in those channels? What options are available to the adversary?

What attitudes held by your targets will serve as a filter and a frame for interpreting the events of a conflict? What images does each of the combatants have about each other? What is the nature of the "naïve realism" of each of the participants in the conflict?

How are the targets for communication segmented?

How can your supporters and the supporters of your adversary be divided and separated (through segmentation variables, appeals to "waverers," with chop and co-opt)? Is your strategy strong enough to hold together your supporters? How can you divide support for an adversary?

What rationalization traps are likely to occur during the conflict and how can these be used or mitigated during the campaign?

Which segments of the population are relatively deprived and frustrated? How can this frustration be eliminated or mitigated?

Which perceived injustices are likely to be part of the adversary's influence campaign?

What are the sources of reactance that may develop during the campaign? How can these factors be eliminated or mitigated?

How is the fog of propaganda distorting (or potentially distorting) your message? Where are the information vacuums? What rumors and speculation are filling the information voids?

What influence tactics are consistently used by your adversary? How can these influence tactics be countered?

What is the current social influence situation in terms of landscaping (definition and labeling, stories about the conflict, framing of issues, setting a decision criterion, norms, expectations, choice set, information flow, etc.), social relationships (credibility and alter-casts), messages, and emotions? What must change to insure success?

What are the norms and rules (as perceived by the relevant targets) for what are fair and acceptable forms of influence and communication?

Do you have a public diplomacy organization in place capable of developing a coordinated influence campaign that can be tailored to specific regions and situations?

Does your public diplomacy meet your ethical standards? Will the means determine the ends in a negative manner?

Using realistic empathy, answer the questions above as the adversary would answer them about you. How will the adversary attack your strategy?

Finally, before detailing the application of SIA to international conflict, I must make a comment on values. For the most part, the science of social influence is value-neutral—it merely describes what works, how, and with what effects. I do not share this neutrality, and I am an unabashed supporter of the promotion of democracy. My support for democracy is informed by the scientific research on the effects of democratic versus autocratic regimes. Democracies are highly productive and more creative than autocracies;[49] mature democracies do not go to war against each other[50] (although immature ones war more frequently);[51] there are negative psychological effects of oppression on the oppressor;[52] poor democracies are more productive and have better citizen well-being than poor authoritarian regimes.[53] Nevertheless, my support for democracy is ultimately a value judgment that informs (biases) my application of SIA. I have no doubt that an authoritarian—albeit of the left or the right—would reach similar conclusions to the ones I have reached about the basic strategies and tactics that are used in international conflict. Indeed, authoritarians have discovered and rediscovered—often at a faster rate than democrats—these principles as they attempt to manipulate their followers. However, the authoritarian would apply these principles in a much different fashion than I have done. As just one example: the authoritarian regime manipulates racial and ethnic passions by whatever means possible to promote its rule; the advocate for democracy seeks tolerance of all but the intolerant.

Centers of Gravity in Conflictual Social Influence Campaigns

The Prussian military strategist Carl von Clausewitz introduced the term *center of gravity* as a means for military planning. According to Clausewitz, one of the central goals of military planning is to attack the enemy's centers of gravity or—"the hub of all power and movement, on which everything depends."[54] It is the focal point(s) that holds an adversary's force or campaign together and the pivotal point(s) at which a conflict will turn. For this reason, Clausewitz argued that a blow directed against a center of gravity will have the greatest effect in determining the outcome of the conflict.

Although Clausewitz's concept of center of gravity is little known in the social sciences, it provides a very useful way of thinking about the application of social science findings and theory.[55] The typical method for applying the results of the social sciences is to develop a model of the underlying processes complete with boxes (representing variables) and arrows (representing causal relationships).[56] Unfortunately, such models often become overly complex, have arrows going in all and both directions, fall prey to local minima effects, and thus provide unclear direction for a policy maker. In contrast, Clausewitz's center of gravity distills a conflict down to a key or a few key points to focus attention on the most important aspects of the conflict.

Just as in traditional warfare, public diplomacy in international conflict also has certain hubs on which everything depends. In this section, I identify nine centers of gravity for social influence campaigns in international conflict to aid with the development of a strategic plan of influence.[57] I view these nine centers of gravity as "focal points" (and not just principles of social influence), that is, the key points in a conflict in which all of one's social influence is brought to bear to produce a favorable and decisive outcome. The nine centers of gravity (CG) were developed by using the concepts of a science of social influence to analyze and distill historical examples of effective and ineffective international influence campaigns. I offer them as a first approximation that no doubt can be improved.

CG 1: Primacy of Strategic Attack

> Thus, what is of supreme importance in war is to attack the enemy's strategy—Sun Tzu

The first (and most important) center of gravity in public diplomacy is based on the advice of the Chinese military strategist Sun Tzu—attack strategy.[58] The strategy of a social influence campaign in a conflict consists of goals (attitudes, beliefs, and actions to be created or modified), targets (who is to be influenced), and means and operations (messages, tactics, media, and the how of reaching a goal). Just as in physical warfare, a social influence campaign must attack the influence strategy of adversaries and competitors. For example, in WWI, Woodrow Wilson's rally cry, "The war to make the world safe for democracy" trumped Germany's coalition of convenience and naked aggression. (However, when Wilson's idealism did not become a reality, his rally cry served to strengthen post-war cynicism and isolationism.) In WWII, most likely as a result of the cynicism from WWI, the Allied information campaign did not at first provide a grand overarching theme for the war, save for the defeat of Hitler; psychological warfare concentrated on countering Nazi propaganda and strengthening the Allied invasion at Normandy at the tactical and operational level.[59] Frank Capra's war films featured the evil inherent in the speeches and propaganda of America's enemies as a means of mobilizing citizens against the Axis forces as opposed to providing Wilsonian goals of creating democracy. Interestingly, as WWII progressed and ultimately ended, the grand strategy of promoting American-style democracy did emerge in the conference at Bretton Woods, the Nuremberg trials, the Marshall Plan, and FDR's four freedoms.[60] During the Cold War, Radio Free Europe took the strategy of undermining totalitarianism by encouraging independent thinking, fostering evolutionary developments that weaken Soviet control, and supporting nationalistic movements.[61]

In the current conflict between the United States and al-Qaeda with their terrorist affiliates, al-Qaeda has adopted the social influence strategy of portraying America as a crusader that seeks to dominate the Muslim world. This strategy employs an often-used influence tactic (see granfalloon below) of creating a common enemy (in this case, America and its allies) to unite disparate groups (the various factions and coalitions in the Muslim world). The United States has not attempted to counter al-Qaeda's influence strategy and in many ways has fallen for bin Laden's trap by failing to establish a pan-Muslim coalition in support of its activities, invading Iraq, and even using terminology sympathetic to America's enemies.[62] In the separate conflict in Iraq, the United States' influence strategy of "bringing democracy" to the Middle East has been trumped by local tribalism and ethnic coalitions (see granfalloon below).[63,64]

The 20th century is often termed the "American Century" as American economic and political institutions along with American values have spread across the globe, resulting in what can be called a virtual empire. This came to pass in part because of the perceived legitimacy of America's grand strategy of commitment to principles of human dignity, justice, and individual freedoms not only for Americans but for humankind. As General Wesley Clark, former NATO Supreme Commander put it:

> I think it [American legitimacy] comes from the heart of American institutions themselves. I think it's because we formed our institutions with the consent of the governed. We are guided by an adherence to our Bill of Rights, and at least in the last century, we've viewed our conception of mankind and our rights as universal truths. . . . We've advocated the enlargement of these rights to all of mankind. And in many ways, not without exception, but largely we've acted consistently with these principles, and in so doing, we earned the goodwill, the good opinion—legitimacy—in the eyes of mankind.[65]

Clark goes on to note that the exceptions (that is, when America didn't live consistent with these principles) go on to prove the rule: "The coups that we fomented, the politicians we attempted to pay off, the efforts that we made in covert action, our occasional support of expediency over principles—most of them came to a bad end."[66] General Clark's analysis demonstrates that an effective public diplomacy is not about "right" technique (seeking the sprinkleism that magically seduces others to your will) or about "right" policy (seeking a foreign policy that pleases everyone or at least those with power), but about the forthright and honest enactment of core democratic values.

Corollary CG 1a: Strategic Traps

> An effective social influence campaign is one that traps and constrains enemy action and weakens and divides support for the adversary; conversely, an ineffective influence campaign is one that can serve as a trap for one's own cause.

In World War I, the Germans used their technological superiority to dominate North Atlantic shipping lanes through U-boat attacks of ships bringing supplies to England and Europe. The British neutralized this advantage by calling attention to the savagery of these attacks, especially those on civilians (e.g., the *Lusitania*). The Wellington House influence campaign effectively trapped the Germans into a choice: (a) continue the attacks and risk condemnation of world opinion (ultimately bringing the Americans into the war); or (b) abandon their technological advantage. In WWII, Adolf Hitler used the themes of "Aryan superiority" and "Germanic unity" to marshal support for early invasions into Austria and other Eastern European countries, and to encourage appeasement based on the notion that Hitler sought only to consolidate Germanic groups. Despite earlier victories, these themes were not a strong enough platform to support Hitler's goals of world domination and served to motivate opposition in regions without strong Germanic allegiance; thus, Hitler was required to rely on quislings and raw power to advance and maintain the fruits of his aggression. Hitler's information campaign became self-trapping and self-defeating. In the Vietnam War, the Viet Cong were successful in portraying the Americans as the descendants of French colonialism and as imperialistic capitalists seeking domination. Thus, American forces were trapped by this social influence campaign: legitimate efforts to help the Vietnamese were seen as Yankee imperialism, Vietnamese officials sympathetic to America were merely puppets, and the imperialism theme would serve to divide the American populace in their support for the war.[67] Bin Laden's strategy of depicting America as a crusader attempting to dominate the Muslim world effectively trapped American foreign policy into a choice: (a) intervene in the Muslim world and risk reinforcing the crusader label; or (b) abandon this part of the world to al-Qaeda terrorism. America could minimize this trap by legitimizing its actions with the support of world and Muslim institutions (as in the early stages of the U.S. counter-attack of al-Qaeda and Taliban forces in Afghanistan).

Corollary CG 1b: 360° Strategy

> A robust social influence strategy is one that anticipates the direction of the conflict in terms of changing circumstances and develops a general framework capable of adapting to conditions.

A successful influence campaign is one that adopts a general strategy (e.g., "the war to end war;" "stop American imperialism") that can be adapted to fit new targets and situations. It provides a platform for launching a campaign of influence. At any given time, the significant actors in a conflict can change, as the domain of dispute grows and contracts. Coalitions may realign and split; allies may decide it is in their best interest to wage an information campaign against their former allies. A robust strategy anticipates these changes.[68] Over time, objectives and goals may be modified and further developed. Perhaps, most importantly, as Daniel Lerner of the Psychological Warfare Division of SHAEF in WWII points out, victory changes objectives such that winning the peace (and not just the war) comes to the fore.[69]

Corollary CG 1c: Control of Information Strategy

> Strategic influence must be offensive and not following and reactive.

Wallace Carroll, director of the U.S. Office of War Information in London during WWII, observed that for the first two years of the war the Allied information campaign was mostly defensive, countering the Axis propaganda that Britain and Russia would not survive and that the United States would be ineffective in its war efforts.[70] At best, such a campaign is merely a holding pattern (a stalemate of words), but in most cases, the use of tactical influence for defensive purposes is often the first sign of defeat. Typically, unless the enemy makes a strategic mistake, the best that can be hoped for in a defensive maneuver is a tie—the adversary did not gain any ground. (Of course, a defensive campaign is superior to leaving enemy propaganda unchecked and un-countered.) The Allied information campaign met with greater success when it went on the offensive by trumpeting the inevitability of Nazi defeat and raising doubts in the minds of the German public about the war effort.

Corollary CG 1d: Plans and Objectives

Social influence campaigns require a long-range plan with objectives.

The successful influence campaign is one that develops a long-range plan that integrates and advances overall policy objectives. In turn, the influence consequences of state actions (military, economic, or political) need to be considered, either as a reason against such action or, if the action is unavoidable, to develop the means for mitigating the negative impact of the action. As famed journalist and former USIA director Edward R. Murrow once put it, public diplomacy should be included at "the take-offs and not just the crash landings" of foreign policy.[71] An ideal long-range plan should involve specific communication goals organized around national strategy and objectives, but with local input and feedback to allow quick, effective implementation.[72] In an effective public diplomacy campaign, tactics should follow from strategy. Long-range planning also employs a full conflict analysis (from looking for ways to resolve disputes in the pre-conflict period through to the post-conflict plan for peace). Without such long-range planning, influence campaigns may do more harm than good. Conflicting messages from the same source cancel out and undermine the legitimacy of the effort.[73] If not carefully timed, an influence campaign can create false hopes with negative consequences such as the "V sign for Victory" campaign on continental Europe in WWII,[74] the Hungarian uprising of 1956,[75] and the encouragement of a Shiite rebellion in southern Iraq after the Persian Gulf War.

Corollary CG 1e: Inadequacy of Advertizing and Branding and PR

In competitive influence campaigns between nations or other groups, niche strategies of the type suggested by branding theory of advertizing and the techniques of PR are ineffective.

CG 2: Morale Beneffectance

The battlefield in a social influence campaign is the morale of combatants, civilians of belligerents, and neutrals and third parties who may become engaged in the conflict.

Morale is the desire and willingness to start and then continue a cause or action. As with other forms of motivation, it can be described by a principle of beneffectance: Morale is a function of the perceived legitimacy and goodness of the cause or action (beneficence or doing good) and the expectations for success of the cause or action (efficacy or a sense that "I can").[76] The beginning of Mark Twain's *War Prayer* expresses these morale factors—a belief in the patriotic and religious righteousness of the cause and an expectation of victory and personal glory.

At any given moment, morale is determined by events (e.g., execution of nurse Edith Cavell,

Dresden bombing, Tet offensive), public opinion (beliefs, attitudes, stereotypes, wishes, and prejudices of participants; see CG 5),[77] information and propaganda (e.g. the interpretation or "spin" placed on events), the relationship of the individual to the group (e.g., sense of shared purpose and equal sacrifice),[78] and the desire of participants to maintain the self-perception that they are good and effective actors (often accomplished through dissonance reduction; see CG 6). Success in a social influence campaign is measured by the reduction of an enemy's morale (or its components) and the strengthening of one's own morale.

Some common ways of influencing beneffectance in international conflicts include (a) attacking the goodness of a cause through atrocity stories[79] and demonizing the enemy;[80] (b) bolstering the goodness of one's own cause through patriotism[81] and religion;[82] (c) undermining the enemy's perceived efficacy by making defeat appear to be inevitable (for example, in WWII, Allied leaflets reminded German soldiers of their inferior small arms, Allied-sponsored astrologers predicted Nazi defeat, and the Belgium underground ran a "V for Victory" campaign);[83] and (d) bolstering one's own sense of efficacy by concretely demonstrating the enemy's vulnerabilities and specifying a plan of action for success.[84] In shaping morale, it is generally easier to share a hatred than to share an aspiration,[85] especially when that hatred is centered on a perceived injustice (see CG 7).

Corollary CG 2a: Expectations

The perceived success or failure of an action is determined, in part, by whether or not it succeeded or failed to meet expectations.

An expectation is a belief about the future. Expectations serve as a reference point by which events are judged. For example, after an Allied bombing run, Goebbels often spread rumors magnifying the number of German civilian deaths. Later, he would issue an "official" report with correct and lower casualty figures to encourage the German public to view the attack as not so bad after all.[86] In contrast, the Allied invasion at Anzio in WWII was accompanied by a leaflet making specific predictions of success that were not obtained. German propagandists used these leaflets to undermine Allied credibility.[87] George Quester points out that the unexpected German air raids on London of WWI (which dropped 225 tons of bombs to kill 1,300 persons) had a dramatic negative effect on British morale, whereas the far more devastating air raids of WWII did not produce a drop in morale and may have stiffened resolve as Londoners realized it was not as bad as anticipated (the British public had expected the use of poison gas and a more severe attack; a parallel result occurred in German morale as a result of the firebombing of Dresden).[88] In cases where expectations are not met consistently, trust and credibility are undermined and the communicator loses the ability to persuade a target (see Corollary CG 3b).

Expectations play a major role in decisions to go to and stay at war and who has actually won the war. Dominic Johnson has gathered case examples of when nations decided to go and not go to war in support of the thesis that positive illusions—expectations, often overly optimistic, that one's own side will be victorious—increase a decision maker's probability of going to war.[89] Once initiated, support for a war is a function of expectations. For example, U.S. public opinions about both the Korean and Vietnam wars became less favorable when military action was stalemated, that is, when it didn't meet the public's expectations for success;[90] recently, a similar pattern of results has been found for U.S. public opinion on the war in Iraq.[91] Finally, the perception of victory in war is often more a matter of expectations—did one side or the other exceed expectations—than a matter of material gains and loses.[92]

CG 2 is a prime battleground in the war between al-Qaeda and the United States. Bin Laden has created a sense of beneffectance in his supporters by linking his cause to religious fervor (fatwas and support of religious leaders) and nationalist and ethnic pride (e.g., expelling the

127

crusaders from Muslim lands), demonizing the U.S. by attacking its culture, support of Israel, and portraying it as the basis of problems in the Middle East, lowering expectations by creating an extended time-frame where victory occurs in generations not months (e.g., 8 years between attacks on the World Trade Center), puncturing the inevitability of American victory by describing how America, once attacked, left Lebanon and Somalia in disgrace, and championing its victories against America (e.g., WTC attacks, attack on the *USS Cole*, the value of martyrdom) as evidence of al-Qaeda's inevitable victory against the far then near enemy. In contrast, the high expectations for a quick and easy victory set by the U.S. government (e.g., a short war of no more than 5 months, "in the last throes," a few dead-enders, greeted as liberators, "Mission Accomplished") were difficult to meet and even more difficult to exceed to insure a perception of victory. As these high expectations were not met, U.S. public opinion soured on the war. Further, al-Qaeda was aided by these high expectations in advancing its propaganda goals—even a minor al-Qaeda victory looms large against the expectations of an easy, complete American victory. The failure to find weapons of mass destruction in Iraq and a link between Saddam and al-Qaeda, along with the incidents at Abu Ghraib, weakened the perceived legitimacy and goodness of the U.S. cause.

CG 3: Trust

Without trust and credibility a social influence campaign is impossible.

Ralph K. White, a social psychologist and an architect of the United States' Cold War information campaign once stated: "The way into the heart of the skeptical neutralist lies not through artifice but through candor."[93] R.H.S. Crossman, chief of British political warfare in WWII, puts it this way: "These are the things that really matter in propaganda. For it is a combination of candour, integrity, and sympathy which demoralizes a totalitarian state."[94] In other words, trust and credibility are an important platform for any communications campaign, especially those involving a democracy. To succeed in public diplomacy, there must be a sense of legitimacy to a course of actions and policy.

If a communicator's words cannot be depended upon, there is little reason to believe that those words will be accepted by a target on a regular basis (one exception to this rule is rumor and innuendo). Crossman goes on to point out that "crude" propaganda, by which he means unbelievable and untrustworthy messages, does more to raise the morale of the adversary than it does to advance the goals of the communicator.[95] (Think of the effects of Baghdad Bob on the American public in the early stages of the Iraq war.) Trust is a particularly important ingredient in peace operations and conflict resolution; laboratory experiments demonstrate that trust is needed for intergroup reconciliation,[96] and history demonstrates that peace operations require trust and legitimacy (such as the Emperor's support for the American post-WWII occupation of Japan and NATO's endorsement of operations in Kosovo).

How can trust and credibility be obtained and maintained? One of the great lessons of every psychological warfare and strategic influence campaign is the importance of speaking the truth.[97] If a communication is perceived as propaganda and untrue, it loses its effectiveness. However, it should also be noted that truth, if not plausibly true in the eyes of the beholder, can be viewed as incredible. For example, truthful messages such as the provision of desired foods to German POWs in WWII,[98] the mistreatment of their own war dead by the German leadership in WWII,[99] and the valiant actions of Turkish troops in Korea[100] were all rejected by a target audience, even though each was objectively true, because the message was not seen as plausible (plausibility is defined in terms of the experience of the target, especially those principles found in CGs 2, 5, 6, and 7).

Trust and credibility are also obtained and maintained through the establishment of social relationships and roles through altercasting.[101] For example, an expert is trusted (more than, say, a child) when communicating about technical matters such as the existence of a 10th planet in the solar system because we expect experts to know such things. In contrast, a child is more effective in arguing for nuclear disarmament (than an expert) because a child as communicator places the target in the role of "protector."[102] Given their ability to induce the role of "protector," children are often used in posters to recruit warriors and to provide a reason for their continued fighting.[103] Similarly, in the world of international affairs, a bully and tyrant places others in a role that produces both compliance (through fear) and resentment that may boomerang against the bully at some point. Arrogance is rarely, if ever, a satisfactory basis for public diplomacy. In contrast, Radio Liberty attempted to create trust through friendship by having their broadcasters "engage in friendly talks" with their targets as opposed to "talking down to their listeners from a platform."[104] As such, Radio Liberty established credibility with its audience by implementing what White called "respect for the target of the communication."[105]

Corollary CG 3a: Listen

A trust relationship begins by listening to one's audience.

Recently, the Council on Foreign Relations called for an improvement in America's ability to listen to foreign publics.[106] Listening can build trust relationships in at least two ways. First, it is impossible to communicate with others without knowing their thoughts, beliefs, desires, and concerns. During the Cold War, Radio Free Europe and Radio Liberty made a concerted effort to find out how those behind the Iron Curtain felt about key issues and about their broadcasts.[107] In contrast, the Soviet leadership abandoned opinion polling in the 1930s (as a result of Stalin's disdain of negative information) and as a result had no means of assessing the building discontent within their borders.[108] Second, the demonstration of a desire to listen to others opens the door for future communication—if the United States is willing to listen to others, then they should be willing to listen to the United States (see norm of reciprocity below).[109]

Corollary CG 3b: The Significance of Deeds

Actions must be in line with words.

In a social influence campaign, deeds and actions speak louder than words.[110] As Secretary of State Dean Acheson once put it: "what is even more important than what we say to the world is how we conduct ourselves, at home and abroad. The force of example and action is the factor which finally determines what our influence is to be."[111] The failure to act consistently with words can have devastating consequences on trust and credibility. For example, Southern newspapers during the Civil War tended to paint a glowing picture of the successes of the Confederate army, resulting in disillusionment and a demoralized public when deeds did not match the words.[112] Similarly, the U.N. mission in Bosnia-Herzegovina in the early 1990s lost support of the populace when U.N. promises to deliver aid and stop the violence were not fulfilled and the U.N.'s goal of democratic procedures was replaced with authoritarian process, compulsory measures, and editorial supervision. In contrast, the U.S. information campaign in Haiti emphasized that the Haitian National Police force was professional and respectful of human rights and was coupled with extensive selection and training of new police officers.[113]

Corollary CG 3c: Admitting a Flaw

A defeat can be used to increase credibility.

The most unbelievable propaganda is one that consistently paints everything in a positive light, regardless of reality. As Wallace Carroll put it: "Unfavorable news must be reported, even to an enemy, if credibility is to be achieved."[114] Carroll's observation is consistent with experimental research showing that admitting to a small flaw increases one's overall credibility.[115] During WWII, Allied Forces were often quick to report negative news: Allied leaflets often described the "failures" of Allied troops, and the BBC consistently reported bad news, even going so far as to correct Nazi reports in a manner that portrayed the Allies in a less favorable manner. Crossman reports that there was considerable after-war evidence that criticism of Churchill during the war by the British public served to weaken the morale of the German people.[116] The result of admitting these failures can be seen in a diary entry by Joseph Goebbels who concluded that the Brits gain more in morale when the BBC covers a defeat than the Nazis gain in announcing a victory.

Corollary CG 3d: Two Sides of the Mouth

Black propaganda can undermine trust.

Black propaganda consists of messages that are made to appear to come from a source other than the communicator. It is typically used to spread disinformation. According to Herz, such communications have an inherent risk: the detection of black propaganda (or even suspicion of its use) will serve to undermine trust needed for the acceptance of other messages.[117] As Herz states: "No nation can talk out of two sides of its mouth at the same time: we cannot on the one hand speak nothing but the truth and then, with a changed voice and pretending to be someone else—but quite obviously still ourselves—say things which we don't dare to say straight out."[118] The use of social influence is often governed by social norms. While it is acceptable to many people if lies and deceptions are told on the battlefield, many also believe that lies and other unfair practices are not permissible in other settings; those who violate these norms run the risk of loss of credibility.

Corollary CG 3e: Propaganda and Trust

Emotional propaganda can produce short-term results but damage long-term trust.

Social influence that plays on emotions and prejudices can be an effective means of mobilizing behavior in the short term—even if that communication is based on lies and deceptions (so long as the untruth seems plausible to the target). However, such propaganda can negatively affect long-term trust as the target discovers the unseemly manipulation. For example, during WWI, the Creel Commission rallied support for the war through atrocity stories of dubious veracity. After the war, U.S. citizens uncovered this manipulation, creating a sense of cynicism that made it more difficult to believe in the occurrence of actual atrocities in WWII such as the holocaust.

CG 4: Agenda Setting

Control of the topics of discussion impacts public opinion.

Each communication media has an agenda—a list of topics that are the focus of discussion. Issues placed on an agenda appear important and serve to define the criteria used in subsequent decisions. As such, agenda setting becomes an important determinant of public opinion.

The function of agenda setting is best defined by describing an experiment conducted by Shanto Iyengar and Donald Kinder.[119] In their experiment, students watched edited versions of the evening news over a week period. The news shows were altered so that some students received a heavy dose of reports on the weakness of U.S. defense capabilities, whereas others watched shows emphasizing pollution concerns, and a third group heard about inflation and the economy. At the end of the experiment, the students rated the target issue—the one that received extensive coverage in the shows they watched—as the issue most important for the country to solve. In addition, the students supported candidates that took strong positions on their target problem.

Some examples of agenda setting in international conflicts include:

(a) in WWI, the British targeted American opinion-makers with pro-war materials written by H.G. Wells, Namier, and Toynbee, and others as a means of affecting newspaper editorials;

(b) during WWII, Allies delivered their newspaper *Frontpost* each week to Axis troops;

(c) Soviet disinformation campaigns such as the one blaming the AIDS virus on U.S. scientists;

(d) Serbian media tours of NATO bombing sites; and

(e) just after the Afghanistan invasion, Islamic media discussed the issue, "Should there be a continuation of war efforts during Ramadan?" as opposed to other issues (e.g., the cruelty of the Taliban).

The battle of agenda setting can be seen in the recent conflict in the Balkans. In the late 1980s and early 1990s, Slobodan Milošević secured access to the major television networks to spread a message of hate against Croats and Muslims;[120] such messages set an agenda of provoked ethnic conflict that ultimately resulted in genocide. In contrast, after the Dayton Accords, peace-keepers set a mass media agenda of supporting a single, democratic, and multiethnic state in Bosnia.[121]

How is a communication agenda set? In a nutshell, a communicator sets an agenda by consistently and repeatedly "staying on message" and emphasizing constant themes. However, the specifics of agenda setting vary with the communication medium. Each medium—TV news, Internet, rumor mill, etc.—has its own set of rules, norms, and procedures for determining what topics are discussed. For example, American mass media places a premium on stories that are new and timely, involve conflict or scandal, contain visual information, are capable of being made personal and dramatic, concern strange or unusual happenings, and fit a current media theme, among other characteristics.[122] Similarly, Arab media also have rules governing their coverage of events.[123] Some Arab stations are state-sponsored and thus reflect the opinions and procedures established by the ruling regime. *Al Jazeera* is semi-independent and seeks ratings, thereby it produces stories that fit the rules of Americanized media (e.g., emphasis on the dramatic, personal, conflict) and fit themes that draw their target audience (e.g., pro-Palestinian issues). News stories that fit the rules of the media, whether it is *Fox* or *Al Jazeera*, are more likely to be covered than those that don't fit the media frame.

Terrorism is also an agenda setting device. With its emphasis on conflict, visual (the remains of a terrorist act), personal impact (survivor stories), and its unusual nature, terrorism as a news event appeals to Western media[124] and thus gains influence beyond its real strength. The attention-getting power of terrorism can be reduced by minimizing the vivid portrayal of the act and instead concentrating on possible coping responses for dealing with terrorism.

One important mechanism for setting an agenda is entertainment. Entertainment can be used to attract an audience to receive a message—for example, Hitler's use of radio and films to draw an audience,[125] B92's rock music as a means to marshal opposition to Slobodan Milošević,[126] and the dissemination of children's cartoons on Iranian television to promote suicide bombings.

Another method for setting a communication agenda is to control (as opposed to participate in) the flow of information through total information dominance. For example, in WWI, the

British cut the trans-Atlantic cables making it difficult for Germany to communicate with other nations. Information dominance can be obtained through electronic warfare, jamming, computer attack, and taking over a local radio station. Some have argued that information control should be used to thwart genocide campaigns.[127] However, such complete control of information is often seen as a violation of the norms of democracy (save for immediate military operations and perhaps for limited humanitarian goals) and can create resentment (see CG 8) especially among those who are being censored. Agenda setting that violates the norms for a given medium will be deemed unfair, as censorship, or as manipulation, and often results in backlash and a rejection of the message.

CG 5: Attitudinal Selectivity

> An individual uses an attitude selectively to make sense of the world and self.

According to the socio-cognitive model, an attitude (a cognitively stored evaluation of an object) serves two functions.[128] First, an attitude can be used to make sense of the world. As such, an attitude is used as an heuristic to bias judgments, attributions, expectations, fact identification, and memory in an attitude-consistent manner (e.g., good [bad] objects are associated with good [bad] attributes). Second, attitudes are held to maintain self-worth and are expressed to obtain approval from others, one's self, and reference groups. Given that an individual's attitudes are unique (or at least held as part of a unique group membership), attitudes can provide a frame for selective exposure and attention to events, differential interpretation of stimuli, varied responses to communications, selective social affiliation, among other behaviors.

Corollary CG 5a: Segmentation

> Groups of individuals with similar attitudes can be targeted with similar messages.

Individuals with similar attitudes (and other characteristics) often have similar lifestyles, media habits, and perspectives making it cost effective to target such segments with an influence campaign. Further, attitudes and similar characteristics can lead to the formation of strong in-group and out-group boundaries (see granfalloon below); failure to consider such factors in a social influence campaign can produce disastrous results—for example, speaking to a group in the wrong language, dialect, or symbols that are associated with their enemies.

The specific segmentation scheme is dependent on the overall strategy (selection of segmentation variables) and objectives (e.g., targeting decision makers, a majority of the population, etc.). For example, during WWII, the Allies used political attitudes to create segments of the German population as a means of developing effective messages.[129] The British were more successful in stopping insurgents during the Malayan emergency when their information campaign became sensitive to segments in Malayan society. Understanding different segments and developing procedures for targeting those segments was a component of effective peace operations in Bosnia and Haiti.[130] There have been repeated calls for a similar understanding and approach in the U.S. war on al-Qaeda and its war in Iraq.[131]

Corollary CG 5b: The Wedge

> Given that a group of individuals can vary in their opinions, perceptions of events, and need for dissonance reduction, then differential influence can be used to drive a wedge into a coalition and divide support for a cause or action.

One strategy for using a wedge to reduce support for an adversary is to target segments of the population that differ on key psychological dimensions with specific, divisive messages.[132] For example, in WWII, Goebbels attempted to drive a wedge between groups in enemy countries by fomenting suspicion, distrust, and hatred.[133] In contrast, one of Joseph Goebbels's greatest worries, expressed in his diaries, was that Allied propaganda would attempt to divide the German public by attacking "Nazism" but not the German people as a whole.[134] In the Cold War, Radio Free Europe sought to drive a wedge between the citizens of Eastern Europe and Soviet Russia by emphasizing religious differences (e.g., by playing banned Christmas carols) and national pride and between Soviet leaders and workers (e.g., stories on the luxurious lifestyles of leaders; reports identifying corrupt and abusive bosses).[135]

A second wedge strategy is to target what Martin Herz calls the marginal person or potential "waverer"—the person with divided attitudes about the cause.[136] In such cases, appeals are designed to bolster and support those attitudes consistent with one's objectives while ignoring those opposed to one's cause to avoid a defensive reaction (see CG 6).

A third wedge strategy can be termed "chop and co-opt." In this strategy, the leadership of an adversary is removed from the situation and followers are co-opted to one's own cause. The chop and co-opt wedge is often supported by "the black-top" illusion or the tendency to see the enemy's government as evil, but the people of that country as being basically good.[137] A classic example of the use of this type of wedge strategy can be found in the British response to the Malayan emergency.[138] Malaya in 1952 was a multi-ethnic country. The communist insurgents who sought control of the country targeted the unassimilated and landless Chinese (the Min Yuen) as a source for recruits and supplies. The initial British efforts were military in nature and targeted the Min Yuen for assisting the insurgence in a campaign of revenge. Realizing the failure of this approach, the British under the leadership of Lt. Gen Harold Briggs refocused their efforts using a chop and co-opt strategy involving:

(a) the provision of land and resettlement for those Min Yuen who renounced the insurgency;
(b) a rewards-for-surrender program to separate the hard core insurgents from the less committed (with such surrenders trumpeted in leafleting campaigns to use social consensus to induce additional surrenders);
(c) education and information campaigns designed to reduce the significance of ethnic differences and to increase the inclusion of Chinese in Malayan society (see Jigsawing below); and
(d) targeted military strikes on insurgent leaders.

A similar chop and co-opt wedge approach was taken at the end of WWII to separate Nazi leadership from followers by removing leaders through military action and the Nuremberg trials and by providing Nazi defectors with opportunities for inclusion in a new Germany. Such an approach was not followed after WWI, leading to the disastrous rise of the *Freikorps* (the precursors to brown-shirts and other militant supporters of Hitler), nor was it adopted as a means of dealing with Baathists in the first years of the Iraq war.

In making a decision to use or not use a particular wedge strategy, the long-term consequences should be considered. In some cases, the use of a wedge may make later unification of a population difficult, if not impossible. This is most likely to occur when common population segments (religion, ethnicity, class) are used as the wedge. On the other hand, the failure to remove divisive elements can result in negative long-term consequences, as the rise of the *Freikorps* in interwar Germany demonstrates. I discuss below the tactic of jigsaw as an approach to mitigating the negative consequences of wedge strategies.

CG 6: Self-justification

> The tension created by dissonance thoughts produces a drive to reduce that tension and may result in a rationalization trap.

According to a theory of cognitive dissonance, when a person holds two discrepant thoughts (say, "I am a good and moral person" and "I just killed someone") that individual looks for ways to resolve the tension created by this discrepancy.[139] In such cases, a person engages in self-justification and rationalization by doing such things as derogating (e.g., the person deserved to die), bolstering (e.g., looking for ways to prove one's goodness), seeking for external justification (e.g., my religion says it is okay), reframing the action (e.g., it really wasn't murder), among other routes to reduce the dissonance. Effective propaganda often stimulates needed tension states and/or finds a means of reducing dissonance in a manner consistent with the goals of the propagandist.

The potential for self-justification has a number of implications for an influence campaign conducted during international conflicts including the following:[140]

(a) The spreading of rumors and disinformation can serve to resolve dissonance. For example, many in the Muslim world do not believe that 9/11 was caused by Arabs.

(b) Aggression often conflicts with a human's view of him or herself as a moral agent and thus requires justification. For example, al-Qaeda required a fatwa or the justification of religious leaders in order to commit the 9/11 murders.

(c) A direct attack on belief, especially beliefs closely related to the self, can create defensiveness and thus strengthen the morale to fight. For example, there is evidence that the virulent attacks on Hitler and Germans by Soviet propagandists in general served to stiffen the German will to fight.[141]

(d) Discrepant and disagreeable information is often ignored or selectively interpreted. One counter to this tendency is to embed such information in entertaining formats.

(e) One reaction to a failing course of action is to escalate commitment to that failing course of action as a means of convincing one's self that the original action was prudent.[142]

(f) A call for unconditional surrender (and similar outcomes) often stiffens the resolve of adversaries as they are faced with a self-threatening admission of defeat.[143] To end a conflict—both physical and cognitive—it is often important to give the person an easy way out consistent with what you want him or her to do.

(g) The ultimate perception of victory and defeat in an international conflict can also be determined through dissonance as partisans with different ideologies and beliefs attempt to justify their positions.[144]

I should note that policy- and decision-makers are not immune to the rationalization trap of dissonance, which can result in the catastrophic consequences of escalating commitment to a failing course of action and selective inattention to evidence and facts.[145]

CG 7: Seeds of Hatred

> Propaganda is most readily accepted by those who are under threat and relatively deprived.

Relative deprivation occurs when a person's expectations about what he or she is entitled to exceed what that person actually obtains.[146] It is a feeling that "I should be getting more out of life than I am." Relative deprivation can be produced by a number of situations including a decline in economic and social status or the failure to meet rising expectations of improved conditions.

Relative deprivation is experienced as a self-threat (e.g., "perhaps I am not good enough to meet expectations"), and thus the person is open to propaganda that resolves this threat.

The classic demagogue formula for resolving such threats includes (a) blaming a scapegoat for the problem (e.g., the Nazis blamed the Jews; al-Qaeda blames the U.S.), (b) providing a simple solution to the threat (e.g. a Nazi dictatorship or a radical Muslim theocracy), and (c) creating a special identity for the person to restore self-esteem (e.g., "anointed of God"). For example, early Nazi supporters tended to be discontent with their declining economic and social status and included members of the *Freikorps* and those who had lost wages, jobs, and businesses.[147] In the 1950s, those who voted communist in French and Italian elections were likely to feel frustrated that their aspirations and expectations were unfulfilled.[148] In the 1980s, Yugoslavia suffered under mounting debt, spiraling inflation, and high unemployment, a situation that was ripe for the demagoguery of hatred and ethnic strife that led to conflict in the region.[149] Islamic and other terrorists tend to be underemployed for their level of education and feel rejected and second-class before joining their groups.[150] (For domestic examples of the relationship of self-threat to the acceptance of propaganda, see my article with Marlene Turner.)[151] The frustration of relative deprivation serves as a center of gravity to which hate propaganda flows to create the vanguard of extremist groups and movements. (Note: absolute deprivation such as abject poverty is marked by little hope, a sense of learned helplessness, and resignation and does not necessarily lead to militancy.)

Corollary CG 7a: Perceived Injustice

The perception of an injustice is one of the strongest motivations for encouraging attacks including aggression and war.

An injustice occurs when there is a discrepancy between a person's fate and that to which he or she feels entitled.[152] As a core human motivation, people attempt to restore justice including resorting to violence and aggression, especially when the injustice is perceived as a threat to one's self-worth.[153] The history of warfare is the history of the perception of injustice, whether that injustice be real, manufactured, or imagined. For example, the Russian attack of the Turks in the Crimean War was justified by the perceived injustice of being refused the right to protect Christian shrines in the Holy Land and Orthodox Christians living within the Ottoman Empire. Austria's attack (encouraged by Germany) on Serbia, which triggered WWI, was ostensibly motivated by the assassination of the Austrian Archduke Franz Ferdinand. Italy's attack of Ethiopia in 1935, which led to the overthrow of Haile Selassie, was supposedly in response to a border incident in the city of Wal Wal. The Japanese claimed their attack on Manchuria was motivated by treaty violations by the Chinese.[154] The Serbs justified the Bosnia-Herzegovina war of the early 1990s by pointing to the defeat of Serbs by Ottoman Turks (Muslims) in 1804 and in the 1389 Battle of Kosovo. The Serbian sense of felt injustice was expressed in one of their propaganda posters as simply: "You have victims for enemies."[155]

The sense of relative deprivation and injustice (real, manufactured, or imagined) provides one of the greatest challenges to a democracy. Such threats encourage authoritarian responses that undermine democracy. Some steps for reducing this threat include:

(a) establish conflict resolution procedures that are perceived as legitimate and fair by all parties;[156]
(b) reinforce principles of democracy including protection of minority rights;[157]
(c) provide other means to self-worth than derogating a scapegoat;
(d) use a Marshall Plan-style aid to build equal-status relationships and provide realistic hope in the face of relative deprivation;

(e) separate demagogues from those who may be influenced by such appeals; and

(f) reduce intergroup antagonism through the jigsaw tactic (see below) and other means.[158]

CG 8: Psychological Reactance

Coercive influence creates resentment and rebellion.

We humans have a general tendency to react against coercive influence, whether that coercion is based on the use of power, deception, or the result of other manipulative processes. This tendency, termed psychological reactance, occurs when an individual perceives that his or her freedom of behavior is restricted; it is an aversive tension state that motivates behavior to restore the threatened freedom.[159] Although the exact response to reactance varies with the situation, two common approaches in conflict situations are (a) an oppositional response (boomerang) of attempting to do the reverse of the reactance-arousing social pressure (a common response to censorship), and (b) attempts at the direct elimination of the threat to freedom (e.g., attacking the coercive agent).[160] Reactance can be used as a propaganda device by making it look like a target's freedom has been taken away by an adversary (even if that is not the case) and thereby encourage attacks on that adversary. In contrast, psychological reactance is an important social influence process in the establishment of democracy and serves to provide the psychological motivation for throwing off the yoke of oppressive regimes.

Reactance to coercion and the perception of manipulation can seriously impact public diplomacy efforts. For example, despite a reign of terror, Stalin could not stifle dissent in the Soviet Union as everyday citizens found the means to subvert totalitarian efforts.[161] As is often typical in rebellions, the British crackdown (including the execution of guerrilla fighters) of EOKA (Greek patriots in Cyprus) in the 1950s created a political backlash that undermined the British efforts.[162] In its successful efforts to deal with Communist insurgents in the Malaya Emergency, the British switched from a policy of heavy force to one of minimized military force and British occupation, and instead relied on the use of rewards, political means, and social integration. John Nagl's insightful analysis of the Malaya and Vietnam counterinsurgency efforts identifies the minimum use of military force as one of five key factors in a successful counterinsurgency campaign.[163] China has also recently realized the downside of intimidation.[164] Up until the mid-1990s, China used military strength to try to induce its Asian neighbors to abandon alliances with the U.S—a tactic that merely drove these countries further into the U.S. camp. China is experiencing much more success with its policy of "Peaceful Rise" (heping jueqi) involving non-threatening cooperation with other, especially developing, nations. Smart interrogators know that the use of coercive tactics (threats, beatings, humiliations, torture) is likely to result in false and misleading confessions as the detainee attempts to appear compliant but is nonetheless resistant to yielding information.[165] As coercive interrogation methods come to light, they can create further reactance in the public's mind and undermine any democratic effort at public diplomacy.

The potential negative consequences of coercive action raises Machiavelli's famous question, "Is it better for a prince to be loved or feared?" Machiavelli answered that it was clearly better to be feared. A SIA argues, consistent with the analysis of Joseph Nye,[166] that it is important to be both and to follow Teddy Roosevelt's edict to "Speak softly and carry a big stick." Speaking softly (social influence, negotiation, diplomacy) allows conflicts to be resolved without invoking the negative consequences of reactance (along with saving a human and financial toll)—an advantage that accrues to mature democracies, which have established mechanisms for conflict resolution other than war.[167] Coercive bargaining tactics tend to result in increasingly coercive bargaining on all sides as threats and punishments are reciprocated in a potentially escalating spiral.[168]

In some cases it may be necessary to use coercive tactics such as threats, punishments, deterrence, and military action—for example, in dealing with authoritarian regimes that are not responsive to domestic or international opinion, in cases where there is an absence of conflict resolution institutions, in stopping genocide, and in response to threats and attacks. In such cases, it is most effective to couple the coercion with a "carrot" or face-saving mechanism that allows the target the perception of some freedom of choice. Specifically, research on coercion and deterrence finds that it is most effective when:

(a) the effort has limited objectives;
(b) the threat is seen as legitimate (i.e. consistent with social norms that can be potentially made salient through public diplomacy);
(c) the threat is coupled with carrots for desired behavior;
(d) co-operating behavior is reciprocated; and
(e) the target has a way out (preferably the desired behavior) to save face.[169]

Corollary CG8a

There is more advantage to being perceived as a liberator than as a controlling oppressor.

Corollary CG8b

Coercion has time-limited effectiveness.

Given that coercive techniques result in reactance, any effects of such tactics are limited in nature and are likely to wear off if the influence agent is perceived to have lost the power to deliver the aversive consequences and/or is removed from the situation.[170]

CG 9: The Fog of Propaganda

Misperceptions and distortions of information are common in conflicts including wars.

According to Clausewitz, the fog of uncertainty is a fundamental property of military action.[171] The same is true of influence campaigns, which can also add to the fog of military action. The propaganda used to support a war can be based on the stereotypes, irrational beliefs, and wishful thinking of a targeted group, and thus, in turn, reinforce the original erroneous thinking. Information disseminated within a clash is typically leveled and sharpened to fit the bipolar theme of conflict. The arousal of a battle can result in autistic, black-and-white thinking. During conflict, there is an increased need to know and to make sense of the world; any information vacuum will be filled and often filled with rumor and speculation that increases the density of the fog. This differential flow of influence means that belligerents live in different "reality worlds," resulting in naïve realism: a sense that one's own construal (perception and understanding) of the world is real and a failure to correct for the subjective nature of one's own interpretation of events.[172] As such, the fog of propaganda can increase the chances of an inadvertent war[173] and of continuing a war needlessly[174] as well as making it much more difficult to end a war and win a peace.[175]

The chief corrective to the misperceptions of naïve realism is what Ralph White terms *realistic empathy* with an antagonist: an attempt to understand how the conflict looks from the other side's point of view.[176] Empathy is an understanding of the thoughts and feelings of others (in contrast to sympathy or identifying with the feelings of others). Realistic empathy can be achieved by asking such questions as: How would I feel in the situation that now faces my enemy? How do the life experiences and history impact the judgment of my adversary? How would I interpret my behavior if I were the enemy? Realistic empathy is the first step towards cutting the fog of propaganda, identifying the common ground for any attempt at conflict resolution,[177] and comprehending the enemy's influence strategy (see CG 1).

Tactics of Social Influence for Use in International Conflicts

The engine behind every influence campaign is the social influence tactic: a device or procedure that makes use of our nature as human beings to change beliefs and behaviors. Indeed, a public diplomacy campaign can be seen as a series of social influence tactics and counter-tactics hopefully in pursuit of an effective strategy (as described above).

Joseph Nye has analyzed the efforts of Woodrow Wilson, Franklin Roosevelt, and George W. Bush to achieve the goal of spreading democracy to other nations.[178] Nye concludes that critical elements for success as a leader are soft power skills, such as communication, along with other influence-related skills, such as the management of organizations and political acumen. Rod Kramer also identifies the significance of knowledge of influence tactics by leaders and points to social-psychological obstacles that prevent leaders from using influence effectively.[179] I agree with the Nye and Kramer analyses. A knowledge of social influence tactics is imperative for the conduct of an influence campaign including planning (an assessment of available options and their limitations), development (creation of influence devices for the situation), operations, and profiling of the adversary (what tactics are most likely to be used by a foe and how best to counter them).

Recently, I reviewed the experimental literature on social influence to identify 107 empirically tested social influence tactics (plus 18 ways to build credibility).[180] Although space precludes a discussion of all of these tactics, I briefly describe seven tactics that are used in war and international conflict settings as an illustration of a social influence approach. (Table 12.1 lists an additional 14 social influence tactics.) Many examples of the use of these 107 tactics can be found in cases of international influence. These tactics can serve as a way to achieve the goal of educating leaders about the nature of social influence and as a terminology for making sense of the continuous stream of influence that occurs in international conflict (and in other domains that confront a political leader).

Norm of Reciprocity

Every human society (and a few chimpanzee ones too) has a simple rule of reciprocity: If I do something for you, then you should do something for me in return. Invoking this rule triggers a feeling of indebtedness or obligation to the person who has given a gift or performed a favor. A tension state is thus created: Do I live up to my social obligation or not? Conversely, aggression and attack invite motives of revenge and getting even.

The norm of reciprocity is used extensively in international conflicts and in many different ways.[181] First, the norm of reciprocity can be used as a simple compliance device to secure a limited goal, for example, F.D. Roosevelt worried about how his New Deal was being perceived in Britain worked out an exchange of radio time with the BBC in the early 1930s.

Second, the norm of reciprocity can be used to defuse antagonisms between states and to induce cooperation, especially if the norm of reciprocity is used in a manner consistent with GRIT (as opposed to a simple tit-for-tat strategy). According to GRIT, negotiation and cooperation can be fostered between bitter foes if one of the adversaries makes a public announcement that a small, cooperative act will be taken and then is subsequently enacted. The adversary is then invited to reciprocate to induce a series of increasingly cooperative actions.[182] Joshua Goldstein

Table 12.1. Some Additional Influence Tactics Used International Conflict

Tactic	Description
Authority	Authority increases obedience and compliance with commands. Example: In both World Wars, Allied leaflet writers found that the addition of authority cues (embossed seals, signature of Allied Commander) increased surrender rates for safe conduct passes.
Commitment	Binding an actor to a behavior or course of action increases the likelihood that the target will comply and perform that behavior. Examples: Polish Communism Party announced free elections in Poland as a means of locking in this course of action in the face of possible Soviet opposition.
Define and label an issue	How an issue or event is labeled controls and directs thought that then impacts persuasion. Example: Goebbels labeled dissent in Britain in WWII "the creeping crisis" in an attempt to make it appear to the German public that the British were losing their will to fight.
Door-in-the-face	Asking for a large request (which is refused) and then for a smaller favor; typically used in negotiation settings.
Expectations	Options are evaluated by comparison to a reference point. Example: Goebbels would pre-announce to the German public a higher than expected casualty rate for a battle; when the actual death toll was lower, victory would be claimed.
Imagery sells	Imagining the adoption of an advocated course of action increases the probability that that course of action will be adopted. Examples: Effective surrender leaflets encourage imagination of the benefits of ceasing the fight.
Phantom fixation	An unavailable alternative is made to look real to create an emotional attachment that then serves to motivate behavior. Examples: the creation of a Juche paradise in North Korea; al-Qaeda seeks to bring the City of God on earth; both Hitler and Saddam believed that secret, phantom weapons would soon be available to insure victory in their wars.
Repetition	Repeating the same information increases the tendency to believe and to like that information.
Scarcity	Scarce items and information are highly valued. Examples: Marking documents "classified" in Operation Bodyguard led Nazi officials to view them as important; the Soviet attempt to silence Radio Free Europe increased the value of this news source.
Self-generated persuasion	Establish a situation in which the target will persuade her or himself of the arguments for a course of action. Examples: Marshall Plan asked aid recipients to come up with their own plan for a common goal with the U.S.; reconstruction in post-WWII Japan was conducted through small informational and participation groups designed to solve local problems.
Social consensus	If others agree, it must be the right thing to do. Examples: Mao's propaganda posters often show many people engaged in a state-approved behavior; security regimes such as the Metternichean Concert are supported by a consensus among the great powers.
Stealing thunder	A counter-influence tactic to lessen the damage done by an adversary's use of negative information; it consists of revealing potentially damaging information before it can be stated by an opponent.
Story-telling	A plausible story serves to guide thought and determines the credibility of information. Example: bin Laden tells stories about his campaign against the Soviets to build credibility and to frame the fight against America.
Vivid appeal	Vivid (concrete and graphic) images can define and give meaning to a conflict as well as amplify the persuasive impact of a message. Examples: Images such as Robert Capa's *Falling Soldier* from the Spanish Civil War; a Chinese child in the rubble from a Japanese bomb in WWII; a child burned by napalm in Vietnam; and Abu Ghraib.

and John Freeman analyzed bilateral cooperative and antagonistic events that occurred during the period of 1953 to 1982 between China, the Soviet Union, and the United States.[183] They found extensive evidence of bilateral reciprocation between the nations (as opposed to opportunism or taking advantage of an act of cooperation). It typically took two to six months

139

before cooperation was reciprocated and an abrupt change in policy coupled with a clear communication of a willingness to cooperate worked best in overcoming the policy inertia of an adversary. Public diplomacy is particularly important for implementing GRIT as it can be used to make clear the cooperative nature of a concession and the desire for a reciprocating action by an adversary.

Third, the norm of reciprocity is of value in creating social relationships. Glen Fisher describes how gifts, obligations, and reciprocity serve to create a social network of relationships in Japan and the Philippines.[184] Such processes are not limited to these two countries and are captured by Bronislaw Malinowski's concept of *kula* first identified among Trobriand Islanders.[185] In *kula* ceremonial gifts are exchanged among equals to create "a circle" of relationships, which in turn serves as a means of conflict resolution and decision making. (*Kula* is distinct from *gimwali* or economic exchange.) Recently, Jerry Burger and his colleagues have found that the exchange of favors among college students in a laboratory experiment increased the likelihood of compliance with future requests in a manner consistent with *kula*.[186] The use of the norm of reciprocity (*kula* and *gimwali*) to create relationships is more than likely an important ingredient to creating security regimes among nations.

Finally, the norm of reciprocity can be used to emphasize dominance relationships, whether that is the intended goal or not. A gift can establish a dominance relationship when it is unrequited and cannot be returned. Wilton Dillon documents the reaction of French citizens to United States' aid to France in the post-WWII period.[187] While the French appreciated the significance of the aid, they for the most part developed a sense of resentment to the "superior" donor because the aid was a one-way street and there was no opportunity to reciprocate. Marcel Mauss terms such gifts as *potlatch* after a practice of Northwestern American Indian chiefs who give away or destroy large portions of their wealth as a way to outdo others and as a sign of their superiority.[188] China's recent "Peaceful Rise" (*heping jueqi*) campaign couples economic aid to other countries with humility to lessen the resentment of perceived *potlatch*. When foreign aid is given, Chinese officials stress that they (the donors) seek to learn from the recipient of the aid.[189]

Fear Appeals

A fear appeal is one that creates fear by linking an undesired action (e.g., the fall to communism of countries in Southeast Asia like dominos) with negative consequences or a desired action (e.g., surrender of an enemy) with the avoidance of a negative outcome. Fear as an emotion creates an avoidance tendency—a desire to shun the danger. As an influence device, fear has proven to be effective in changing attitudes and behavior when the appeal (a) arouses intense fear, (b) offers a specific recommendation for overcoming the fear, and (c) when the target believes he or she can perform the recommendation.[190] In other words, the arousal of fear creates an aversive state that must be escaped. If the message includes specific, doable recommendations for overcoming the fear, then it will be effective in encouraging the adoption of that course of action. Without a specific, doable recommendation, the target of the communication may find other ways of dealing with the fear, such as avoidance of the issue and message, resulting in an ineffective appeal. The repeated use of fear can habituate a population (especially when the fear is manufactured) and thereby diminish the impact of subsequent fear appeals. The use of fear as an influence tactic can be countered by (a) trumping the adversary's fear appeal with something that is even worse to fear (e.g., Saddam countering U.S. surrender messages by threatening the fate of surrendering Iraqi soldiers' families), (b) switching the doable response provided by an adversary to a doable response you would like to see happen, (c) providing a basis for hope in the face of fear (e.g., Winston Churchill's "finest hour" speech), and (d) decreasing the fear created by an adversary (e.g., there is nothing to fear but fear itself).

140

Foot-in-the-door

In the foot-in-the-door tactic (FITD), a target is first asked to do a small request (which most people readily perform) and then is asked to comply with a related and larger request (that was the goal of influence all along). For example, in one experiment suburbanites were asked to put a big, ugly sign stating "Drive Carefully" in their yard. Less than 17% of the homeowners did so. However, 76% of the homeowners agreed to place the sign in their yards, if two weeks earlier they had agreed to post in their homes a small, unobtrusive 3-inch sign urging safe driving.[191] The FITD tactic works because it creates a commitment to a course of action and self-perceptions that one is the type of person to perform such actions. During the Viet Nam War, the Viet Cong (unknowingly) used this tactic to infiltrate a hamlet. They began by first asking the villagers for a small request such as a drink of water, boys to carry messages, or women to prepare bandages. Using these small commitments, the Viet Cong would then ask for larger requests such as support for their war efforts and acceptance of their propaganda[192]

Granfallooning

According to the novelist Kurt Vonnegut, a granfalloon is "a proud and meaningless association of human beings," such as a Hoosier, Buckeye, devotee of Klee, or Nazi, that takes on great meaning for those involved. Once an individual accepts a social identity, social influence follows in at least two ways. First, the social identity provides a simple rule to tell the individual what to believe: "I am a_____[fill in the blank with an identity] and we do and believe_____[fill in the blank with identity-related behavior and belief]." Second, in specialized cases, some identities become important as a source of self-esteem and locate a person in a system of social statuses. In such cases, influence is based on a desire to stay in the good graces of a positive group and avoid the pain of associating with a derogated identity.[193] Some examples of granfalloons include Nazi brown-shirts, cult of Juche in North Korea, terrorist identities, Slobodan Milošević's pro-Serbian and anti-Muslim/anti-Croat propaganda, and bin Laden's use of the Muslim faith. The British were able to stop the communist insurgency in Malaya with appeals to the majority's Muslim identity.

Jigsawing

Jigsawing is a means of promoting positive relationship among potentially adversarial (ethnic) groups or granfalloons developed by Elliot Aronson and his colleagues.[194] The goal is to create mutual interdependence using the equal status contact principle in which group members (a) possess equal status, (b) seek common goals, (c) are cooperatively dependent on each other, and (d) interact with the support of authorities. This can be accomplished by establishing a situation where people from different granfalloons are required to work together to reach a goal. For example, American aid to war-torn Europe in 1945 (over $9 billion) was originally given piecemeal to previously warring countries and thus served to intensify competition among the factions. Under the Marshall Plan, aid was distributed in a different manner that required collaborative processes (cooperatively dependent), resource sharing (equal status), and joint planning (shared goals) among the various factions.[195] The goal was to create an integrated economy and a United States of Europe that transcended warring sovereignties. Jigsawing provides a framework for distributing aid packages and remains one of the most effective mechanisms for reducing intergroup (ethnic and religious) violence. (As noted above, the British used jigsawing in the Malaya Emergency to reduce ethnic barriers by giving land to disenfranchised members of the Chinese minority and through education and policy to insure their inclusion in mainstream Malayan society.)

141

Projection

One way to cover one's misdeed is to employ the projection tactic—accusing another of the negative traits and behaviors that one possesses and exhibits with the goal of deflecting attention from one's own misdeeds and towards the accused. Derek Rucker and I conducted four experiments in which students were informed that a misdeed was committed (e.g., lying about intentions, invading another country, cheating on a test) and, in the experimental treatments, one of the protagonists in the story accused another of the misdeed.[196] In these four experiments, we found that projection was effective in increasing the blame placed on the target of projection and decreasing the culpability of the accuser. In addition, the effects of projection persisted despite attempts to raise suspicions about the motives of the accuser and providing evidence that the accuser was indeed guilty of the deeds. The projection tactic is a stock technique of authoritarian regimes. For example, in the 1930s, Mussolini accused Ethiopia of provoking Italy as Mussolini invaded the country. The 1939 Nazi propaganda film, *Der Feldzug in Poland* (*Campaign in Poland*) explained the German invasion of Poland as an attempt to stop Polish attacks on Germans. After invading South Korea in June of 1950, Pyongyang's press and radio claimed that the armies of "the traitor Syngman Rhee" of South Korea had attacked first and that the North Koreans were merely acting in self-defense. During the Korean War, North Korea claimed U.S. and U.N. forces were using chemical warfare that caused illnesses among North Koreans when in fact the sicknesses were the result of typhus brought to Korea by Chinese soldiers. The use of the projection tactic is inconsistent with the requirement for truthfulness in a democracy.

Damn it, Refute it, Damn it, Replace it

This counter-tactic for responding to innuendo and disinformation was developed during WWII as a means of rumor control. Specifically, begin and end any refutation of an adversary's disinformation with a clear message that the information is false and negated (damn it). Don't repeat the false information in a memorable manner. The refutation should be logical, short, factually, consistent, conclusive, and presented calmly. If at all possible, replace the false information with positive information about the target of the innuendo or otherwise change the topic of conversation. For example, the British established local and regional rapid response teams during the Malaya Emergency to counter enemy propaganda such as those insurgents who surrendered would be killed or ill-treated.[197] In contrast, U.N. peacekeepers in Bosnia in the early 1990s were subject to a barrage of rumors and propaganda by Serbian forces including personal slurs and attacks on military commanders; this propaganda went uncountered, resulting in an erosion of the credibility of the U.N. and its mission.[198]

The Democratic Use of Social Influence: Ethical and Legal Issues

One consistent point of agreement among those who have practiced the art of public diplomacy is that Americans have a strong dislike and aversion to the use of persuasion and influence to promote national goals. At first blush, this aversion appears to be inconsistent with American practice. Our nation was founded on the principle that citizens use social influence and persuasion to make collective decisions as opposed to other devices such as force, divine right, politburo fiat, or the genes of royalty. We are a nation of sale agents, advertisers, politicians, and lawyers.

A closer inspection reveals that Americans have a healthy fear that their government might "psyop" them—an apprehension that goes back to the founding of the nation. R.H.S. Crossman describes a practice during WWII that serves to justify these concerns. As part of his political warfare efforts, Crossman created rumors to undermine enemy morale. His measure of success was whether or not the rumor was later reported to be true by intelligence and news agencies. In retrospect, Crossman doubted "whether it was wise to deceive ourselves so much in an effort to deceive the enemy!"[199] One attempt to resolve this problem was the passage of the Smith-Mundt ban on domestic propaganda, which endeavored to create a firewall to prevent communications by the U.S. government designed for a foreign audience from reaching domestic ones.[200] However, in an age of cable satellite dishes, Internet, and near instantaneous world-wide communications, such efforts have become rather feeble.

Nevertheless, these legitimate concerns place democracies at a disadvantage. Tyrants, demagogues, dictators, and terrorists do not share these concerns about "psyoping" citizens. Indeed, their whole purpose in life is to gain power, whether through force, propaganda, or other means. As the Council on Foreign Relations concluded, "The United States needs to be able to counter these vitriolic lies with the truth."[201] Indeed, democracies have not just a right but a duty to promote and protect its values. Without a viable public diplomacy effort, responses to tyranny and genocide are reduced to two: ignore it (isolationism) or take military action. To generate discussion on this important topic, I conclude this chapter with a presentation of three suggestions for how to use social influence to promote the national goals of a democracy, along with my own observations on the matter.

Gordon Allport, one of the leading psychologists of his generation and a member of the S.P.S.S.I.'s Committee on Morale during WWII, outlined the basis for maintaining morale in a democracy during a war.[202] For Allport, it was acceptable for a democratically elected government to maintain public support and morale (along with influencing other nations) as long as those efforts were consistent with the unique features and values of democracy. These values included voluntary participation, respect for the person, majority rule, freedom of speech, tolerance, among others. In a paper with Marlene Turner, I take a similar approach and present structural characteristics (see particularly Table 12.1) for promoting the deliberative persuasion of a democracy.[203]

The Allport approach has a number of important advantages including the requirement that a democracy act consistent with its principles (see Corollary CG 3b) and the use of democratic institutions as a check and balance on the conduct of an influence campaign. It falls short in at least three regards. First, it is vague on operational details. For example, is censorship consistent with democratic values if freely chosen (as was the case, for the most part, in WWII)? Second, authoritarian regimes are not constrained in their selection of influence tactics and thus may gain an advantage. However, to engage in the undemocratic influence tactics of authoritarian regimes is an admission of the defeat of the ways of democracy. Finally, the Allport approach places a premium on maintaining the institutions of democracy as the primary safeguard to the illegitimate use of influence by a government, thus requiring ever-vigilant citizens with an intolerance of intolerance. Such vigilance is often difficult to maintain in times of conflict.

Ralph White sees the problem with the use of influence as a failure to distinguish morally questionable from morally acceptable techniques.[204] This creates a double problem. On the one hand, without a clear understanding of what is a dirty, underhanded technique, the propagandist can use certain tactics without a proper feeling of guilt. On the other hand, a persuader may be inhibited from doing a proper job by vague feelings that "influence of any kind is wrong." White's morally acceptable influence tactics include: (a) getting and keeping attention, (b) getting and keeping rapport, (c) building credibility, (d) appealing to strong motives and emotions, and (e) using action involvement (such as the foot-in-the-door tactic). He deems the following techniques as off-limits in a democracy: (a) lying, (b) innuendo, (c) presenting opinion as fact, (d) deliberate omission, and (e) implied obviousness (assuming naïve realism).

White's approach can be seen as a good first step to legitimizing fair, moral social influence. Nevertheless, it runs into problems in implementation. The morality of many influence tactics often depends on the context (e.g., it is generally permissible to lie on the battlefield and to save a

Jew from a Nazi). Some may question whether the use of fear and other intense emotions are acceptable to use in a democracy. White would counter that if the fear is real (as opposed to constructed), then it would be immoral not to warn people. But this begs the question of what is a real versus a constructed fear—a question that is often difficult to answer in the fog of war and propaganda. Finally, as with Allport, White would rule out the use of certain techniques by a democracy that may be employed by authoritarian regimes.

Lt. Gen. William Odom presents another approach to justifying the use of social influence in strategic arenas.[205] Odom agrees with other commentators that Americans have a difficult time accepting the concepts of psychological operations, political warfare, and the like, and argues that we should abandon such terms altogether. Instead, America should concentrate its political efforts on what he sees as the primary foreign policy goal of the United States: to promote democracy where law is primary over even majority parties and serves to protect the rights of the minority. Odom's approach is one of transparency: to be open and up-front that America's goal is to persuade others of the value of democratic institutions. He does not get into the operational details of what is and is not a permissible device, although it can be assumed that his definition of democracy (primacy of law; protection of minority rights) would serve as a check and balance on public diplomacy in manner similar to that of Allport.

In comparing the three approaches above (along with an understanding of the centers of gravity in an influence campaign), we can begin to draw out the characteristics of a public diplomacy organization that both satisfies the need to respond to authoritarian propaganda but yet allays the fears of Americans. These characteristics include: (a) transparency of operations and organization (i.e. Americans see and understand the nature of the influence campaign), (b) reliance on a series of checks and balances to prevent the illegitimate use of influence by the government, (c) use of influence must be consistent with democratic values given that actions speak louder than words (Corollary CG 3b), and (d) the influence campaign has the trust and consensus of the American people.

The democratic legitimacy of any given influence tactic can vary with the context. However, there is one ethical precept that is invariant across situations. In contrast to the "ends justify the means" morality of Hitler, Goebbels, and other autocrats, in reality *the means determine the ends*. If an influence agent uses deceit, trickery, or other nondemocratic means of persuasion, then it is likely to result in resentment, lack of trust, reactance, and ultimately do more damage than good for the cause. As the Chinese philosopher Mencius once argued: immediate goals may be accomplished with devices that produce long-term evil.

Soft power often comes with a very hard edge. Dictators, demagogues, tyrants, terrorists, and other assorted autocrats use the attractiveness of ethnic prejudice and other hatreds coupled with the image of power to get others to follow their lead. Fortunately, in the last century the development of a science of social influence has given us some tools for the defeat of this tyranny. And we are even more fortunate that the last American century showed us how to conduct an effective public diplomacy by basing it on our commitment to democratic values and principles of human dignity, justice, and individual freedoms not only for Americans but for humankind.

Notes

1 Joseph S. Nye, *Soft Power* (New York: Public Affairs, 2004); Joseph S. Nye and William A. Owens, "America's Information Edge," *Foreign Affairs* 75, no. 2 (March/April, 1996): 20–36.

2 Christopher Ross, "Public Diplomacy Comes of Age," *The Washington Quarterly* 25, no. 2 (2002): 75–83.

3 Peter Batty, *Paper War: Nazi propaganda in one battle, on a single day Cassino, Italy, May 11, 1944.* (West New York, NJ: Mark Batty Publisher, 2005).

4 Attraction can be in the eye of the beholder; Nye's attractive force of soft power no doubt appeals to

"your poor, your tired, your huddled masses longing to be free," whereas the propaganda of hatred and fear appeals to those who seek power.

5 For details, see Jarol B. Mannheim. *Strategic Public Diplomacy and American Foreign Policy* (New York: Oxford University Press, 1994).

6 I first outlined this approach to international conflict for a military audience in Anthony R. Pratkanis, "Winning Hearts and Minds: A Social Influence Analysis," in *A Guide to Information Strategy*, ed. J. Arquilla & D.A. Borer, (New York: Routledge, in press). This chapter borrows the core findings from this initial paper but expands the analysis to address issues of state and public diplomacy.

7 Carl von Clausewitz, *On War* (Princeton, NJ: Princeton University Press, 1832/1894): 592. For a similar analysis of the rise of publics in diplomacy in the 20th century, see Glen H. Fisher, *Public Diplomacy and the Behavioral Sciences* (Bloomington, IN: Indiana University Press, 1972).

8 Hans N. Tuch, *Communicating with the World: U.S. public diplomacy overseas* (New York: St. Martin's Press, 1990), 26–27.

9 Wallace Carroll, *Persuade or Perish* (Boston: Houghton-Mifflin, 1948).

10 Janice Gross Stein, "Deterrence and reassurance," in *Behavior, Society, and Nuclear War*, ed. P.E. Tetlock, J.L. Husbands, R. Jervise, P.C. Stern, and C. Tilly (Oxford: Oxford University Press, 1991), 8–72.

11 Deborah Welch Larson, "Crisis Prevention and the Austrian State Treaty," *International Organization* 41 (1987): 27–60.

12 Matthew Evangelista, "Sources of Moderation in Soviet Security Policy," in *Behavior, Society, and Nuclear war*, ed. P.E. Tetlock, J.L. Husbands, R. Jervise, P.C. Stern, and C. Tilly (Oxford: Oxford University Press, 1991), 254–354.

13 Janice Gross Stein, "Deterrence and reassurance," in *Behavior, Society, and Nuclear War*, ed. P.E. Tetlock, J.L. Husbands, R. Jervis, P.C. Stern, and C. Tilly (Oxford: Oxford University Press, 1991), 8–72.

14 Joseph S. Nye, *Soft Power* (New York: Public Affairs, 2004), 99.

15 This concept is similar to Riker's *heresthetics*; William H. Riker, *The Art of Political Manipulation* (New Haven, CT: Yale University Press, 1986).

16 Graham T. Allison, "Primitive Rules of Prudence: Foundations of Peaceful Competition," in *Windows of Opportunity*, ed. G.T. Allison and W.L. Ury with B.J. Allyn (Cambridge, MA: Ballinger, 1989), 9–37.

17 William L. Ury, "Developing Risk Reduction Institutions and Procedures," in *Windows of Opportunity*, ed. G.T. Allison and W.L. Ury with B.J. Allyn (Cambridge, MA: Ballinger, 1989), 69–91.

18 Joseph S. Nye, "Nuclear Learning and the Evolution of U.S.-Soviet Security Cooperation," in *Windows of Opportunity*, ed. G.T. Allison and W.L. Ury with B.J. Allyn (Cambridge, MA: Ballinger, 1989), 131–161.

19 Colin Irwin, *The People's Peace Process in Northern Ireland* (New York: Palgrave, 2002).

20 Glen H. Fisher, *Public Diplomacy and the Behavioral Sciences* (Bloomington, IN: Indiana University Press, 1972), 66–75.

21 Herbert E. Krugman, "The Impact of Television Advertising: Learning Without Involvement," *Public Opinion Quarterly* 29 (1965): 349–356.

22 Martin F. Herz, "Some Psychological Lessons from Leaflet Propaganda in World War II," *Public Opinion Quarterly* 13 (1949): 471–486. For a similar analysis, see R.H.S. Crossman, "Psychological Warfare," *The Journal of the Royal United Service Institution* 97 (1952): 324–325.

23 Martin F. Herz, "Some Psychological Lessons from Leaflet Propaganda in World War II," *Public Opinion Quarterly* 13 (1949): 476–477.

24 Jami Fullerton and Alice Kendrick, *Advertising's War on Terrorism* (Spokane, WA: Marquette Books, 2006).

25 Ibid., 105.

26 Ibid., 106.

27 For a description of this campaign and how to improve it, see Kevin Avruch, James L. Narel, and Pascale Combelles Siegel, *Information Campaigns for Peace Operations* (Vienna, VA: CCRP Publications, 2000).

28 For detailed examples of the modern use of PR technique, see Ken Auletta, "The Fixer," *New Yorker* (February 12, 2007): 46–57; Ken Silverstein, "Their Men in Washington," *Harper's* (July 2007): 53–61.

29 Clifford Bob, *The Marketing of Rebellion* (Cambridge: Cambridge University Press, 2005).

30 Jarol B. Manheim and Robert B. Albritton, "Changing National Images: International Public Relations and Media Agenda Setting," *American Political Science Review* 78 (1984): 641–657.

31 Scott M. Cutlip, *The Unseen Power* (Hillsdale, NJ: Lawrence Erlbaum, 1994).

32 Jarol B. Manheim and Robert B. Albritton, "Public Relations in the Public Eye: Two Case Studies of the Failure of Public Information Campaigns," *Political Communication and Persuasion* 3 (1986): 265–291.

33 Richard E. Petty and John T. Cacioppo, *Communication and Persuasion: Central and peripheral routes to attitude change* (New York: Springer-Verlag, 1986).

34 Scott M. Cutlip, *The Unseen Power* (Hillsdale, NJ: Lawrence Erlbaum, 1994).

35 James E. Grunig, "Symmetrical Presuppositions as a Framework for Public Relations Theory," in *Public Relations Theory*, ed. C.H. Botan and V. Hazelton (Hillsdale, NJ: Lawrence Erlbaum, 1989), 17–44.

36 Anthony R. Pratkanis, "The Social Psychology of Mass Communications: An American Perspective," in *States of Mind: American and Post-Soviet Perspectives on Contemporary Issues in Psychology*, ed. D.F. Halpern and A. Voiskounsky (New York: Oxford University Press, 1997), 126–159; Anthony R. Pratkanis and Marlene E. Turner, "Persuasion and Democracy: Strategies for Increasing Deliberative Participation and Enacting Social Change," *Journal of Social Issues* 52, no.1 (1996): 187–205.

37 For discussions of the use of deception in military operations, see James F. Dunnigan and Albert A. Nofi, *Victory and Deceit* (San Jose, CA: Writers Club, 2001); Thaddeus Holt, *The Deceivers* (New York: Scribners, 2004); Jon Latimer, *Deception in War* (Woodstock, NY: The Overlook Press, 2001).

38 Nathaniel Schiffman, *Abracadabra!: Secret methods magicians & others use to deceive their audience* (Buffalo, NY: Prometheus Books, 1997); Anthony R. Pratkanis and Doug Shadel, *Weapons of Fraud: A source book for fraud fighters* (Seattle, WA: AARP Washington, 2005).

39 Richard M. Emerson, "Power-Dependence Relations" *American Sociological Review* 27 (1962): 31–41; Jeffrey Pfeffer and Gerald R. Salancik, *The External Control of Organizations* (New York: Harper & Row, 1978).

40 Alexander George, *Forceful Persuasion* (Washington, DC: Institute of Peace Press, 1991); Robert Jervis, Richard Ned Lebow, and Janice Gross Stein, *Psychology and Deterrence* (Baltimore, MD: Johns Hopkins University Press, 1985).

41 Nigel Howard, *Confrontation Analysis: How to win operations other than war* (Vienna, VA: CCRP Publications, 1999).

42 For a brief history of this research, see Anthony R. Pratkanis, "An Invitation to Social Influence Research," in *The Science of Social Influence: Advances and future progress*, ed. A.R. Pratkanis (New York: Psychology Press, 2007), 1–15; for descriptions of its core finding, see Robert B. Cialdini, *Influence* (Boston: Allyn & Bacon, 2001); Anthony R. Pratkanis, *The Science of Social Influence: Advances and future progress* (New York: Psychology Press, 2007); Anthony R. Pratkanis, "Social Influence Analysis: An Index of Tactics," in *The Science of Social Influence: Advances and future progress*, ed. A.R. Pratkanis (New York: Psychology Press, 2007), 17–82; Anthony R. Pratkanis and Elliot Aronson, eds., *Age of Propaganda: The everyday use and abuse of persuasion* (Revised edition) (New York: W.H. Freeman/Holt, 2001).

43 Anthony R. Pratkanis and Doug Shadel, *Weapons of Fraud: A source book for fraud fighters* (Seattle, WA: AARP Washington, 2005); for additional examples of the use of SIA in other domains, see Anthony R. Pratkanis, "Propaganda and Persuasion in the 1992 U.S. Presidential Election: What are the Implications for Democracy?" *Current World Leaders* 36 (1993): 341–362; Anthony R. Pratkanis and Marlene E. Turner, "Nine Principles of Successful Affirmative Action: Mr. Branch Rickey, Mr. Jackie Robinson, and the Integration of Baseball," *Nine: A Journal of Baseball History and Social Policy Perspectives* 3 (1994): 36–65; Anthony R. Pratkanis, "How to Sell a Pseudoscience," *Skeptical Inquirer* 19 (1995): 19–25; Anthony R. Pratkanis, "Why Would Anyone Do or Believe Such a Thing? A Social Influence Analysis," in *Critical Thinking in Psychology*, ed. R.J. Sternberg, H. Roediger, III, and D. Halpern (Cambridge: Cambridge University Press, 2006), 232–250.

44 Students of public diplomacy can profit greatly from reading historical examples of past influence campaigns such as can be found in Nicholas John Cull, *Selling War* (Oxford: Oxford University Press, 1995); Philip M. Taylor, *British Propaganda in the Twentieth Century* (Edinburgh: Edinburgh University Press, 1999); Philip M. Taylor, *Munitions of the Mind* (Manchester: Manchester University Press, 2003).

45 It is questionable whether such economic models are useful in guiding economic policy much less international affairs; for an insightful critique, see Max H. Bazerman and Deepak Malhotra, "Economics Wins, Psychology Loses, and Society Pays," in *Social Psychology and Economics*, ed. D. de Cremer, M. Zeelenberg, and J.K. Murnighan (Mahwah, NJ: Erlbam, 2006), 263–280.

46 Robert Jervis, *Perception and Misperception in International Politics* (Princeton, NJ: Princeton University Press, 1976).

47 Fisher's analysis emphasizes social perception processes, whereas I look at social influence. Nevertheless, his analysis anticipates many of my conclusions, particularly CG's 5, 6, and 9; see Glen H. Fisher, *Public Diplomacy and the Behavioral sciences* (Bloomington, IN: Indiana University Press, 1972).

48 Joshua Kurlantzick, *Charm Offensive* (New Haven, CT: Yale University Press, 2007).

49 Ralph K. White and Ronald Lippitt, *Autocracy and Democracy* (New York: Harper & Brothers, 1960).

50 Spencer R. Weart, *Never at War: Why democracies will not fight one another* (New Haven, CT: Yale University Press, 1998).

51 Edward D. Mansfield and Jack Snyder, *Electing to Fight: Why emerging democracies go to war* (Cambridge, MA: MIT Press, 2005).

52 Anthony R. Pratkanis and Marlene E. Turner, "The Significance of Affirmative Action for the Souls of White Folk: Further Implications of a Helping Model," *Journal of Social Issues* 55 (1999): 787–815.

53 Joseph T. Siegle, Michael M. Weinstein, and Morton H. Halperin, "Why Democracies Excel," *Foreign Affairs* 83 (September/October, 2004): 57–71.

54 Carl von Clausewitz, *On War* (Princeton, NJ: Princeton University Press, 1832/1894): 595–596.

55 For an overview, see the excellent analysis of Michael I. Handel, *Masters of War* (London: Frank Cass, 2001).

56 For example, see influence models such as Situational Influence Assessment Module (SIAM); Jeffrey I. Sands and Bradd C. Hayes, "Understanding and Using SIAM," unpublished paper, Naval War College, Center for Naval Warfare Studies, Decision Support Department, 1997, http://www.dodccrp.org/files/Hayes_Doing_Windows.pdf.

57 A different set of centers of gravity may apply to other influence domains. For example, in U.S. Presidential elections important centers include control of the agenda, a positive candidate image, and attack and respond to attack; see Anthony R. Pratkanis. "Propaganda and Persuasion in the 1992 U.S. Presidential Election: What are the Implications for Democracy?" *Current World Leaders,* 36 (1993): 341–362. Anthony R. Pratkanis. "Propaganda and Deliberative Persuasion: The Implications of Americanized Mass Media for Emerging and Established Democracies," in *The Practice of Social Influence in Multiple Cultures,* ed. W. Wosinski, R.B. Cialdini, J. Reykowski, and D.W. Barrett (Mahwah, NJ: Lawrence Erlbaum, 2001): 259–285. However, in most competitive influence domains, CG1 (attack strategy) applies.

58 Sun Tzu, *The Art of War* (Oxford: Oxford University Press, circa 500 B.C.E. /1963), 77.

59 Wallace Carroll, *Persuade or Perish* (Boston: Houghton-Mifflin, 1948); Daniel Lerner, *Sykewar* (New York: George W. Stewart, 1949).

60 Elizabeth Borgwardt, *A New Deal for the World* (Cambridge, MA: Harvard University Press, 2005).

61 Arch Puddington, *Broadcasting Freedom: The Cold War triumph of Radio Free Europe and Radio Liberty* (Lexington, KY: University of Kentucky Press, 2000).

62 Douglas E. Streusand and Harry D. Tunnell, IV, "Choosing Words Carefully: Language to Help Fight Islamic Terrorism," *IOSphere* (Fall, 2006): 4–6.

63 Originally, there was no relationship between the war against al-Qaeda and the war in Iraq. However, as the war in Iraq progressed, al-Qaeda saw a strategic advantage and extended its efforts to that region. This has increased the burden placed on America's public diplomacy as the invasion of Iraq strengthened the al-Qaeda information strategy of portraying America as a crusader and has resulted in competing and unclear national security objectives which must be disentangled before a public diplomacy campaign can be implemented.

64 The Bush administration used a definition of democracy as "majority rule via a vote" in its influence strategy. This definition likely increased the chances for a civil war as those groups excluded from the "majority" perceived that their best course of political action was violence. A more mature and thoughtful definition of democracy consistent with American history as "the protection of minority rights and the fostering of institutions to support those rights" would have lessened the chances for civil war. For details on this definition, see Kurt Lewin, Ronald Lippitt, and Ralph K. White, "Patterns of Aggressive Behavior in Experimentally Created 'Social Climates,'" *Journal of Social Psychology* 10 (1939): 271–299; Abraham S. Luchins and Edith H. Luchins, *Revisiting Wertheimer's Seminars*, Volume 2 (Lewisburg, PA: Bucknell University Press, 1978): 458–465; Anthony R. Pratkanis, "The Social Psychology of Mass Communications: An American Perspective," in *States of Mind: American and Post-Soviet Perspectives on Contemporary Issues in Psychology*, ed. D.F. Halpern and A. Voiskounsky (New York: Oxford University Press, 1997) 126–159; Anthony R. Pratkanis and Marlene E. Turner, "Persuasion and Democracy: Strategies for Increasing Deliberative Participation and Enacting Social Change," *Journal of Social Issues* 52, no. 1 (1996): 187–205; Ralph K. White and Ronald Lippitt, *Autocracy and Democracy* (New York: Harper & Brothers, 1960).

65 Wesley Clark, "Legitimacy: First Task for American Security," speech given at Center for Politics and Foreign Relations, Paul H. Nitze School of Advanced International Studies (SAIS), The Johns Hopkins University, May 16, 2007.

66 Wesley Clark, "Legitimacy: First Task for American Security," speech given at Center for Politics and Foreign Relations, Paul H. Nitze School of Advanced International Studies (SAIS), The Johns Hopkins University, May 16, 2007.

67 For a strategic response to this line of propaganda, see Ralph K. White, "'Socialism' and 'Capitalism:' An International Misunderstanding," *Foreign Affairs* 44 (January 1966): 216–228.

68 As just one recent example of this Corollary CG: in the early 1990s, the U.N.-led coalition intervening in Bosnia was marked by changing goals and shifting priorities; this negatively impacted the U.N. efforts at an information campaign; see Kevin Avruch, James L. Narel, and Pascale Combelles Siegel, *Information Campaigns for Peace Operations* (Vienna, VA: CCRP Publications, 2000). In contrast, the American-led efforts in Bosnia and in Kosovo were able to maintain a coalition with a sustained influence campaign;

for detailed analysis of how to accomplish these goals, see Richard Holbrooke, *To End a War* (New York: Modern Library, 1999); Wesley, K. Clark, *Waging Modern War* (New York: Public Affairs, 2001).

69 Daniel Lerner, *Sykewar* (New York: George W. Stewart, 1949).

70 Wallace Carroll, *Persuade or Perish* (Boston: Houghton-Mifflin, 1948).

71 Quoted in Peter G. Peterson, *Finding America's Voice: A strategy for reinvigorating U.S. public diplomacy* (New York: Council on Foreign Relations, 2003): 8.

72 For discussion on how to organize public diplomacy so that it is both coordinated nationally but responsive locally, see James R. Bortree, "IO During the Malayan Emergency," *IOSphere* (Spring 2007): 24–32; Peter G. Peterson, *Finding America's Voice: A strategy for reinvigorating U.S. public diplomacy* (New York: Council on Foreign Relations, 2003); for a history of the organization of U.S. public diplomacy, see Gifford D. Malone, *Organizing the Nation's Public Diplomacy* (Lanham, MD: University Press of America, 1988).

73 Wallace Carroll, *Persuade or Perish* (Boston: Houghton-Mifflin, 1948).

74 R. H.S. Crossman, "Psychological Warfare," *The Journal of the Royal United Service Institution* 97 (1952): 319–332.

75 Arch Puddington, *Broadcasting Freedom: The Cold War triumph of Radio Free Europe and Radio Liberty* (Lexington, KY: University of Kentucky Press, 2000).

76 Anthony G. Greenwald, "The Totalitarian Ego: Fabrication and Revision of Personal History," *American Psychologist* 35 (1980): 603–618, Anthony G. Greenwald and Anthony R. Pratkanis, "The Self," in *The Handbook of Social Cognition*, ed. R.S. Wyer and T.K. Srull (Hillsdale, NJ: Erlbaum, 1984), Vol. 3, 129–178; for a similar perspective, see Maurice Tugwell, "Terrorism as a Psychological Strategy," in *Psychological Operations and Political Warfare in Long-term Strategic Planning*, ed. J. Radvany (New York: Praeger, 1990), 69–81.

77 Anthony R. Pratkanis, "The Cognitive Representation of Attitudes," in *Attitude Structure and Function*, ed. A.R. Pratkanis, S.J. Breckler, and A.G. Greenwald (Hillsdale, NJ: Erlbaum, 1989), 71–98; Anthony R. Pratkanis and Anthony G. Greenwald, "A Socio-Cognitive Model of Attitude Structure and Function," in *Advances in Experimental Social Psychology*, ed. L. Berkowitz (New York: Academic Press, 1989): 245–285.

78 Goodwin Watson, "Five Factors in Morale," in *Civilian Morale*, ed. G. Watson (New York: Houghton-Mifflin, 1942), 30–47.

79 James Morgan Read, *Atrocity Propaganda 1914–1919* (New Haven, CT: Yale University Press, 1941).

80 Sam Keen, *Faces of the Enemy* (New York: Harper & Row, 1986), Ralph K. White, "Enemy images in the United Nations-Iraq and East-West conflicts," in *The Psychology of War and Peace: The Image of the Enemy*, ed. R.W. Rieber (New York: Plenum, 1991), 59–70.

81 Daniel Bar-tal and Ervin Staub, *Patriotism* (Chicago: Nelson-Hall, 1977).

82 Brad J. Bushman, Robert D. Ridge, Enny Das, Colin W. Key, and Gregory L. Busath, "When God Sanctions Killing: Effect of Scriptural Violence on Aggression," *Psychological Science* 18 (2007): 204–207.

83 Elliot Harris, *The "Un-American" weapon: Psychological warfare* (New York: M.W. Lads Publishing, 1967).

84 Christopher B. Snavely, "Historical perspectives on developing and maintaining homefront morale for the war on terrorism". Unpublished master's thesis. Naval Postgraduate School, Monterey, CA, 2002.

85 Goodwin Watson, "Five Factors in Morale," in *Civilian Morale*, ed. G. Watson (New York: Houghton-Mifflin, 1942): 30–47.

86 George H. Quester, "The Psychological Effects of Bombing on Civilian Populations: Wars of the Past," in *Psychological Dimensions of War*, ed. B. Glad. (Newbury Park, CA: Sage, 1990): 201–214. For an allied example, see page 327 of R.H.S. Crossman, "Psychological Warfare," *The Journal of the Royal United Service Institution* 97 (1952): 319–332.

87 Martin F. Herz, "Some Psychological Lessons from Leaflet Propaganda in World War II." *Public Opinion Quarterly* 13 (1949): 471–486.

88 George H. Quester, "The Psychological Effects of Bombing on Civilian Populations: Wars of the Past," in *Psychological Dimensions of War*, ed. B. Glad (Newbury Park, CA: Sage, 1990): 201–214.

89 Dominic D.P. Johnson, *Overconfidence and War* (Cambridge, MA: Harvard University Press, 2004); for a description of Saddam Hussein's confidence of success in the 2003 Iraqi war, see Kevin Woods, James Lacey, and Williamson Murray, "Saddam's Delusion: The View from the Inside." *Foreign Affairs* 85 (2006): 2–26.

90 Eric V. Larson, *Casualties and Consensus: The historical role of casualties in domestic support for U.S. military operations* (Santa Monica, CA: Rand, 1996); see also the data in John E. Mueller. *War, Presidents, and Public Opinion* (New York: John Wiley, 1973).

91 Christopher Gelpi, "Misdiagnosis," *Foreign Affairs* 85 (January/February 2006): 139–142.

92 Dominic D.P. Johnson and Dominic Tierney, *Failing to Win* (Cambridge, MA: Harvard University Press, 2006).

93 Ralph K. White, "The New Resistance to International Propaganda," *Public Opinion Quarterly* 16 (1952): 540.

94 R. H.S. Crossman, "Psychological Warfare," *The Journal of the Royal United Service Institution* 98 (1953): 358.

95 Ibid.

96 Arie Nadler and Ido Liviatan, "Intergroup Reconciliation: Effects of Adversary's Expressions of Empathy, Responsibility, and Recipient's Trust," *Personality and Social Psychology Bulletin* 32 (2006): 459–470.

97 Leigh Armistead, *Information Operations* (Washington, DC: Brassey's, 2004); Wallace Carroll. *Persuade or Perish* (Boston: Houghton-Mifflin, 1948); R.H.S. Crossman, "Psychological Warfare," *The Journal of the Royal United Service Institution* 97 (1952): 319–332; William E. Dougherty, *A Psychological Warfare Casebook* (Baltimore, MD: The Johns Hopkins University Press, 1958); Elliot Harris, *The "Un-American" Weapon: Psychological warfare* (New York: M.W. Lads Publishing, 1967). Martin F. Herz, "Some Psychological Lessons from Leaflet Propaganda in World War II," *Public Opinion Quarterly* 13 (1949): 471–486; Arch Puddington, *Broadcasting Freedom: The Cold War triumph of Radio Free Europe and Radio Liberty* (Lexington, KY: University of Kentucky Press, 2000); Ralph K. White, "The New Resistance to International Propaganda," *Public Opinion Quarterly* 16 (1952): 539–551.

98 Elliot Harris, *The "Un-American" Weapon: Psychological warfare* (New York: M.W. Lads Publishing, 1967).

99 R. H.S. Crossman, "Psychological Warfare," *The Journal of the Royal United Service Institution* 97 (1952): 319–332.

100 William E. Dougherty, *A Psychological Warfare Casebook* (Baltimore, MD: The Johns Hopkins University Press, 1958).

101 Anthony R. Pratkanis, "Altercasting as an Influence Tactic," in *Attitudes, Behavior, and Social Context*, ed. D.J. Terry and M.A. Hogg (Mahwah, NJ: Lawrence Erlbaum, 2000): 201–226.

102 Anthony R. Pratkanis and Melissa D. Gliner. "And When Shall a Little Child Lead Them?: Evidence for an Altercasting Theory of Source Credibility," *Current Psychology* 23 (2004–2005): 279–304.

103 For examples, see Daoud Sarhandi and Alina Boboc, *Evil Doesn't Live Here* (New York: Princeton Architectural Press, 2001): 33, 55, 113; and G.H. Gregory, *Posters of World War II* (New York: Gramercy Books, 1993): 5, 7, 43, 53, 60, 61, 71, and 114–115.

104 Arch Puddington, *Broadcasting Freedom: The Cold War triumph of Radio Free Europe and Radio Liberty* (Lexington, KY: University of Kentucky Press, 2000): 164–165.

105 Ralph K. White, "The New Resistance to International Propaganda," *Public Opinion Quarterly* 16 (1952): 539–551.

106 Peter G. Peterson, *Finding America's Voice: A strategy for reinvigorating U.S. public diplomacy* (New York: Council on Foreign Relations, 2003); see also Kevin Avruch, James L. Narel, and Pascale Combelles Siegel, *Information Campaigns for Peace Operations* (Vienna, VA: CCRP Publications, 2000): 142 for a discussion of the significance of listening in a case analysis of U.S. involvement in Haiti.

107 Arch Puddington, *Broadcasting Freedom: The Cold War triumph of Radio Free Europe and Radio Liberty* (Lexington, KY: University of Kentucky Press, 2000): 164–165.

108 David Wedgwood Benn, *Persuasion and Soviet Politics* (New York: Basil Blackwell, 1989).

109 For a discussion of the role of listening for current U.S. public diplomacy, see Nancy Snow, *The Arrogance of American Power* (Lanham, MD: Rowman & Littlefield, 2006).

110 Wallace Carroll, *Persuade or Perish* (Boston: Houghton-Mifflin, 1948).

111 Quoted in Ralph K. White, "The New Resistance to International Propaganda," *Public Opinion Quarterly* 16 (1952): 540.

112 J. Cutler Andrews, "The Confederate Press and Public Morale," *The Journal of Southern History* 32 (1966): 445–465.

113 Kevin Avruch, James L. Narel, and Pascale Combelles Siegel, *Information Campaigns for Peace Operations* (Vienna, VA: CCRP Publications, 2000): see pages 40 and 84 for description of U.N. operations in Bosnia; pages 122–123 for U.S. operations in Haiti.

114 Wallace Carroll, *Persuade or Perish* (Boston: Houghton-Mifflin, 1948): 125.

115 Robert B. Settle and Linda L. Golden, "Attribution theory and advertiser credibility," *Journal of Marketing Research* 11 1(1974): 181–185.

116 R. H.S. Crossman, "Psychological Warfare," *The Journal of the Royal United Service Institution* 97 (1952): 319–332.

117 Martin F. Herz, "Some Psychological Lessons from Leaflet Propaganda in World War II," *Public Opinion Quarterly* 13 (1949): 471–486. For a similar perspective see R.H.S. Crossman, "Psychological Warfare," *The Journal of the Royal United Service Institution* 97 (1952): 319–332.

118 Martin F. Herz, "Some Psychological Lessons from Leaflet Propaganda in World War II," *Public Opinion Quarterly* 13 (1949): 483.

149

119 Shanto Iyengar and Donald R. Kinder, *News that Matters* (Chicago: University of Chicago Press, 1987).

120 Richard Holbrooke, *To End a War* (New York: Modern Library, 1999).

121 Kevin Avruch, James L. Narel, and Pascale Combelles Siegel, *Information Campaigns for Peace Operations* (Vienna, VA: CCRP Publications, 2000).

122 Anthony R. Pratkanis, "The Social Psychology of Mass Communications: An American Perspective," in *States of Mind: American and Post-Soviet Perspectives on Contemporary Issues in Psychology*, ed. D.F. Halpern & A. Voiskounsky (New York: Oxford University Press, 1997), 126–159.

123 Mohammed El-Nawawy and Adel Iskandar, *Al-Jazeera* (Cambridge, MA: Westview, 2002); George Emile Irani, "Strategic Communications: Arab Media and the War in Iraq," *IOSphere* (Spring 2007): 35–41; Avi Jorisch. *Beacon of Hatred: Inside Hizballah's al-Manar television* (Washington, DC: Washington Institute for Near East Policy, 2004). Hugh Miles, *Al-Jazeera* (New York: Grove Press, 2005).

124 Brigitte L. Nacos, *Terrorism and the Media* (New York: Columbia University Press, 1994).

125 Leonard W. Doob, "Goebbels' Principles of Propaganda," *Public Opinion Quarterly* 14 (1950): 419–442.

126 Matthew Collin, *Guerrilla Radio* (New York: Thunder's Mouth, 2001).

127 Jamie F. Metzl, "Information Intervention: When Switching Channels Isn't Enough," *Foreign Affairs* 76 (1997): 15–20.

128 Anthony R. Pratkanis, "The Cognitive Representation of Attitudes," in *Attitude Structure and Function*, ed. A.R. Pratkanis, S.J. Breckler, and A.G. Greenwald (Hillsdale, NJ: Erlbaum, 1989): 71–98; Anthony R. Pratkanis and Anthony G. Greenwald., A.G. "A Socio-Cognitive Model of Attitude Structure and Function," in *Advances in Experimental Social Psychology*, ed. L. Berkowitz (New York: Academic Press, 1989): Vol. 22, 245–285; Anthony R. Pratkanis and Marlene E. Turner, "Of What Value is a Job Attitude?: A Socio-Cognitive Analysis," *Human Relations* 47 (1994): 1545–1576.

129 Daniel Lerner, *Sykewar* (New York: George W. Stewart, 1949).

130 Kevin Avruch, James L. Narel, and Pascale Combelles Siegel, *Information Campaigns for Peace Operations* (Vienna, VA: CCRP Publications, 2000).

131 Robert S. Leiken and Steve Brooke, "The Moderate Muslim Brotherhood," *Foreign Affairs* 86 (March/April 2007): 107–121; Vali Nasr, *The Shia Revival* (New York: Norton, 2007).

132 For a discussion of the diplomatic difficulties of talking with oppositional groups, see Martin F. Herz. *Contacts with the Opposition* (Lanham, MD: University Press of America, 1979).

133 Leonard W. Doob, "Goebbels' Principles of Propaganda," *Public Opinion Quarterly* 14 (1950): 419–442.

134 Joseph Goebbels, *The Goebbels Diaries* (New York: Doubleday, 1948).

135 Arch Puddington, *Broadcasting Freedom: The Cold War triumph of Radio Free Europe and Radio Liberty* (Lexington, KY: University of Kentucky Press, 2000), 164–165.

136 Martin F. Herz, "Some Psychological Lessons from Leaflet Propaganda in World War II," *Public Opinion Quarterly* 13 (1949): 471–486.

137 Ralph K. White, *Fearful Warriors* (New York: Free Press, 1984).

138 James R. Bortree, "IO During the Malayan Emergency," *IOSphere* (Spring 2007): 24–32; John A. Nagl, *Learning to Eat Soup with a Knife* (Chicago: University of Chicago Press, 2002).

139 Elliot Aronson, "The Theory of Cognitive Dissonance: A Current Perspective," in *Advances in Experimental Social Psychology*, ed. by L. Berkowitz (New York: Academic Press, 1969): Vol. 4, 1–34; Leon Festinger, *A Theory of Cognitive Dissonance* (Stanford, CA: Stanford University Press, 1957).

140 Albert Bandura, "Mechanisms of Moral Disengagement," in *Origins of Terrorism: Psychologies, ideologies, theologies, states of mind*, ed. W. Reich (Cambridge: Cambridge University Press, 1990): 161–191.

141 Paul M.A. Linebarger, *Psychological Warfare* (Washington, DC: Infantry Journal Press, 1948).

142 Ralph K. White, *Nobody Wanted War: Misperception in Vietnam and other wars* (New York: Doubleday, 1968).

143 Daniel Lerner, *Sykewar* (New York: George W. Stewart, 1949).

144 Dominic D.P. Johnson and Dominic Tierney, *Failing to Win* (Cambridge, MA: Harvard University Press, 2006).

145 Ralph K. White, *Nobody Wanted War: Misperception in Vietnam and other wars* (New York: Doubleday, 1968); Ralph K. White, "Selective Inattention," *Psychology Today* 5 (November 1971): 47–50; 78–84.

146 Faye J. Crosby, "A Model of Egoistical Relative Deprivation," *Psychological Review* 83 (1976): 85–113, James M. Olson, C. Peter Herman, and Mark P. Zanna, *Relative Deprivation and Social Comparison* (Hillsdale, NJ: Erlbaum, 1986).

147 Theodore Abel, *Why Hitler Came to Power* (New York: Prentice-Hall, 1938).

148 Hadley Cantril, *The Politics of Despair* (New York: Basic Books, 1958).

149 Richard Holbrooke, *To End a War* (New York: Modern Library, 1999), 26.

150 Jessica Stern, *Terror in the Name of God* (New York: HarperCollins, 2003); see also the data collected in Marc Sageman, *Understanding Terror Networks* (Philadelphia, PA: University of Pennsylvania Press, 2004).

151 Anthony R. Pratkanis and Marlene E. Turner, "The Significance of Affirmative Action for the Souls of White Folk: Further Implications of a Helping Model," *Journal of Social Issues* 55 (1999): 787–815.

152 Melvin J. Lerner, "The Justice Motive in Human Relations: Some Thoughts on What We Know and Need to Know about Justice," in *The Justice Motive in Social Behavior*, ed. M.J. Lerner and S.C. Lerner. (New York: Plenum, 1981), 11–35.

153 Roy F. Baumeister and Joseph M. Boden, "Aggression and the Self: High Self-esteem, Low Self-control, and Ego Threat," in *Human Aggression*, ed. R.G. Geen and E. Donnerstein (San Diego, CA: Academic Press, 1998), 111–137.

154 Bruno Lasker and Agnes Roman, *Propaganda from China and Japan* (New York: American Council, Institute of Pacific Relations, 1938).

155 Daoud Sarhandi and Alina Boboc, *Evil Doesn't Live Here* (New York: Princeton Architectural Press, 2001), 101.

156 Karl Aquino, Thomas M. Tripp, and Robert J. Bies, "Getting Even or Moving On?: Power, Procedural Justice, and Types of Offense as Predictors of Revenge, Forgiveness, Reconciliation, and Avoidance in Organizations," *Journal of Applied Psychology* 91 (2006): 653–668.

157 Juan M. Falomir-Pichastor, Christian Staerklé, Marie-Aude Depuiset and Fabrizio Butera, "Democracy Justifies the Means: Political Group Structure Moderates the Perceived Legitimacy of Intergroup Aggression," *Personality and Social Psychology Bulletin* 31 (2005): 1683–1695.

158 For a discussion of peace-building efforts, see John Paul Lederach. *Building Peace: Sustainable Reconciliation in Divided Societies* (Washington, DC: United States Institute of Peace Press, 1998); for a discussion of creating the rule of law in conflict situations, see Jane Stromseth, David Wippman, and Rosa Brooks, *Can Might Make Rights?* (Cambridge: Cambridge University Press, 2006).

159 Jack W. Brehm, *A Theory of Psychological Reactance* (New York: Academic Press, 1966); Sharon S. Brehm and Jack W. Brehm, *Psychological Reactance* (New York: Academic Press, 1981).

160 See discussion of the effects of Soviet calls for Nazi soldiers to overthrow Hitler in Martin F. Herz, "Some Psychological Lessons from Leaflet Propaganda in World War II," *Public Opinion Quarterly* 13 (1949): 477–478.

161 Sarah Davies, *Popular Opinion in Stalin's Russia* (Cambridge: Cambridge University Press, 1997).

162 Robert Taber, *War of the Flea* (Washington, DC: Brassey's, 1965/2002).

163 John A. Nagl, *Learning to Eat Soup with a Knife* (Chicago: University of Chicago Press, 2002), 30; Nagl also develops five principles of counterinsurgency that are consistent with the emphasis on strategy in CG 1.

164 Joshua Kurlantzick, *Charm Offensive* (New Haven, CT: Yale University Press, 2007).

165 For a case example of the failure of torture to extract useful information, see the discussion of the interrogation of Nguyen Tai in Merle E. Pribbenow, "The Man in the Snow White Cell," *Studies in Intelligence* 48 (2004): 59–69; for general references on how coercion leads to false confessions, see Lawrence S. Wrightsman and Saul M. Kassin, *Confessions in the Courtroom* (Newbury Park, CA: Sage, 1993); Philip G. Zimbardo, "Coercion and Compliance: The Psychology of Police Confessions," in *The Triple Revolution: Social Problems in Depth*, ed. R. Perruci and M. Pilisuk (Boston: Little, Brown, 1968), 550–570; for an illustration of how to use social influence tactics that are noncoercive but nonetheless extremely effective for obtaining information, see the account of how Nazi Hans-Joachim Scharff interrogated downed Allied pilots in WWII in Raymond F. Toliver, *The Interrogator* (Atglen, PA: Schiffer Military History, 1997).

166 Joseph S. Nye, *Soft Power* (New York: Public Affairs, 2004), 25–30; 67–68.

167 Edward D. Mansfield and Jack Snyder, *Electing to Fight: Why Emerging Democracies Go to War* Cambridge, MA: MIT Press, 2005); Spencer R. Weart, *Never at War: Why Democracies Will Not Fight One Another* (New Haven, CT: Yale University Press, 1998).

168 Russell J. Leng and Stephen G. Walker, "Comparing Two Studies of Crisis Bargaining: Confrontation, Coercion, and Reciprocity," *Journal of Conflict Resolution* 26 (1982): 571–591.

169 Lawrence Freedman, *Deterrence* (Cambridge, MA: Polity Press, 2004); Alexander George, *Forceful Persuasion* (Washington, DC: Institute of Peace Press, 1991); Russell J. Leng, "Influence Techniques among Nations," in *Behavior, Society, and International Conflict*, ed. P.E. Tetlock, J.L. Husbands, R. Jervis, P.C. Stern, and C. Tilly (Oxford: Oxford University Press, 1994): Vol. 3, 71–125; Russell J. Leng and Stephen G. Walker, "Comparing Two Studies of Crisis Bargaining: Confrontation, Coercion, and Reciprocity," *Journal of Conflict Resolution* 26 (1982): 571–591; Russell J. Leng and Hugh G. Wheeler, "Influence Strategies, Success, and War," *Journal of Conflict Resolution* 23 (1979): 655–684; Janice Gross Stein, "Deterrence and Reassurance," in *Behavior, Society, and Nuclear War*, ed. P.E. Tetlock, J.L. Husbands, R. Jervis, P.C. Stern, and C. Tilly (Oxford: Oxford University Press, 1991): Vol. 2, 8–72.

170 Herbet C. Kelman, "Processes of Opinion Change," *Public Opinion Quarterly* 25 (1961): 57–78; B.F. Skinner, *Science and Human Behavior* (New York: Free Press, 1953).

171 Carl von Clausewitz, *On War* (Princeton, NJ: Princeton University Press, 1832/1894), 140.

172 Lee Ross and Andrew Ward, "Naive Realism in Everyday Life: Implications for Social Conflict and Misunderstanding," in *Values and Knowledge*, ed. S. Reed, E. Turiel, and T. Brown (Hillsdale, NJ: Erlbaum, 1996), 103–135.

173 Ralph K. White, *Nobody Wanted War: Misperception in Vietnam and other wars* (New York: Doubleday, 1968).

174 Ralph K. White, *Fearful Warriors* (New York: Free Press, 1984).

175 Paul R. Pillar, "Ending Limited War: The Psychological Dynamics of the Termination Process," in *Psychological Dimensions of War*, ed. B. Glad. (Newbury Park, CA: Sage, 1990), 252–263.

176 Ralph K. White, *Fearful Warriors* (New York: Free Press, 1984); Ralph K. White, "Enemy Images in the United Nations-Iraq and East-West conflicts," in *The Psychology of War and Peace: The Image of the Enemy*, ed. by R.W. Rieber (New York: Plenum, 1991), 59–70; see also R.H.S. Crossman, "Psychological Warfare," *The Journal of the Royal United Service Institution* 97 (1952): 328.

177 Kenneth Arrow, Robert H. Mnookin, Lee Ross, Amos Tversky, and Robert Wilson, *Barriers to Conflict Resolution* (New York: Norton, 1995); Morton Deutsch and Peter T. Coleman, *The Handbook of Conflict Resolution* (San Francisco, CA: Jossey-Bass, 2000); Roger Fisher, William Ury and Bruce Patton, *Getting to Yes* (New York: Penguin, 1991).

178 Joseph S. Nye, "Transformational Leadership and U.S. Grand Strategy," *Foreign Affairs* 85 (July/August 2006): 139–148.

179 Roderick M. Kramer, "Self-Defeating Leader Behavior: Why Leaders Misuse their Power and Influence," in *The Science of Social Influence: Advances and Future Progress*, ed. A.R. Pratkanis (New York: Psychology Press, 2007), 297–319.

180 Anthony R. Pratkanis, "Social Influence Analysis: An Index of Tactics," in *The Science of Social Influence: Advances and Future Progress*, ed. A.R. Pratkanis (New York: Psychology Press, 2007), 17–82.

181 For an excellent discussion of the use of reciprocity in international relations along with conditions that promote and prevent its use, see Deborah Welch Larson, "The Psychology of Reciprocity in International Relations," *Negotiation Journal* 4 (1988): 281–301.

182 Charles E. Osgood, *Alternative to War or Surrender* (Urbana: University of Illinois Press, 1962); for development of these ideas, see Amitai Etzioni, "The Kennedy Experiment," *Western Political Quarterly* 20 (1967): 361–380; for a case analysis of these principles in action, see Deborah Welch Larson, "Crisis Prevention and the Austrian State Treaty," *International Organization* 41 (1987): 27–60.

183 Joshua S. Goldstein and John R. Freeman, *Three-way Street: Strategic Reciprocity in World Politics* (Chicago: University of Chicago Press, 1990).

184 Glen H. Fisher, *Public Diplomacy and the Behavioral Sciences* (Bloomington, IN: Indiana University Press, 1972), 42, 92.

185 Bronislaw Malinowski, *Argonauts of the Western Pacific* (Long Gorve, IL: Waveland Press, 1922/1984).

186 Jerry M. Burger, Alison M. Ehrlichman, Neda C. Raymond, Janet M. Ishikawa, and Joanna Sandoval, "Reciprocal Favor Exchange and Compliance," *Social Influence* 1 (2006): 169–184.

187 Wilton S. Dillon, *Gifts and Nations* (New Brunswick, NJ: Transaction, 1968/2003).

188 Marcel Mauss, *The Gift* (New York: Norton, 1950/1990).

189 Joshua Kurlantzick, *Charm Offensive* (New Haven, CT: Yale University Press, 2007), 17, 35, 53, and 56.

190 Howard Leventhal, "Findings and Theory in the Study of Fear Communications," in *Advances in Experimental Social Psychology*, ed. L. Berkowitz (New York: Academic Press, 1970); Vol. 5, 119–186. James E. Maddux and Ronald W. Rogers, "Protection Motivation and Self-Efficacy: A Revised Theory of Fear Appeals and Attitude Change," *Journal of Experimental Social Psychology* 19 (1983): 469–479. Interestingly, Major Herz identified the same principles of fear in the design of leaflets in WWII and appeals to civilian populations; see Martin F. Herz, "Some Psychological Lessons from Leaflet Propaganda in World War II," *Public Opinion Quarterly* 13 (1949): 471–486.

191 Jonathan Freedman and Scott Fraser, "Compliance Without Pressure: The Foot-in-the-Door Technique," *Journal of Personality and Social Psychology* 4 (1966): 195–202.

192 Ralph K. White, "Propaganda: Morally Questionable and Morally Unquestionable Techniques," *Annals of the American Academy of Political and Social Sciences* 398 (1971): 26–35.

193 Marlene E. Turner and Anthony R. Pratkanis, "A Social Identity Maintenance Theory of Groupthink," *Organizational Behavior and Human Decision Processes* 73 (1998): 210–235.

194 Elliot Aronson, Nancy Blaney, Cookie Stephan, Jev Sikes, and Matthew Snapp, *The Jigsaw Classroom* (Beverly Hills, CA: Sage, 1978).

195 Michael J. Hogan, *The Marshall Plan* (Cambridge: Cambridge University Press, 1987).

196 Derek D. Rucker and Anthony R. Pratkanis, "Projection as an Interpersonal Influence Tactic: The Effects of the Pot Calling the Kettle Black," *Personality and Social Psychology Bulletin* 27 (2001): 1494–1507.

197 James R. Bortree, "IO During the Malayan Emergency," *IOSphere*, (Spring 2007): 24–32.

198 Kevin Avruch, James L. Narel, and Pascale Combelles Siegel, *Information Campaigns for Peace Operations* (Vienna, VA: CCRP Publications, 2000).

199 R. H.S. Crossman, "Psychological Warfare," *The Journal of the Royal United Service Institution* 98 (1953): 356.

200 Allen W. Palmer and Edward L. Carter, "The Smith-Mundt Act's Ban on Domestic Propaganda: An Analysis of the Cold War Statute Limiting Access to Public Diplomacy," *Communication Law and Policy* 11 (2006): 1–34.

201 Peter G. Peterson, *Finding America's Voice: A Strategy for Reinvigorating U.S. Public Diplomacy* (New York: Council on Foreign Relations, 2003), 36.

202 Gordon W. Allport, "The Nature of Democratic Morale," in *Civilian Morale*, ed. G. Watson (New York: Houghton-Mifflin, 1942), 3–18.

203 Anthony R. Pratkanis and Marlene E. Turner, "Persuasion and Democracy: Strategies for Increasing Deliberative Participation and Enacting Social Change," *Journal of Social Issues* 52 (1996): 187–205.

204 Ralph K. White, "Propaganda: Morally Questionable and Morally Unquestionable Techniques," *Annals of the American Academy of Political and Social Sciences* 398 (1971): 26–35. For a similar approach, see Robert B. Cialdini, "Social Influence and the Triple Tumor Structure of Organizational Dishonesty," in *Codes of Conduct*, ed. D.M. Messick and A.E. Tenbrunsel (New York: Russell Sage, 1996): 44–58.

205 William E. Odom, "Psychological Operations and Political Warfare in Long-Term U.S. Strategic Planning," in *Psychological Operations and Political Warfare in Long-term Strategic Planning*, ed. J. Radvanyi (New York: Praeger, 1990), 8–18.

13

Credibility and Public Diplomacy

Robert H. Gass and John S. Seiter

Immediately following the tragic events of September 11, 2001, George W. Bush enjoyed record high public approval ratings in the U.S.A., ranging from the mid 80s to the low 90s, depending on which polls one consulted.[1] His ratings slipped during the invasion of Iraq, then spiked again following his famous "mission accomplished" speech aboard the *USS Abraham Lincoln* on May 1, 2003. Afterwards, his public approval ratings declined precipitously. As of early 2007, Bush was polling in the high 20s to low 30s, the lowest presidential ratings recorded since Richard Nixon during the Watergate era or Jimmy Carter during the Iran hostage crisis.[2]

Some of Bush's lack of popularity can be traced to domestic policy failures, such as FEMA's sluggish response in the aftermath of Hurricane Katrina, domestic eavesdropping on U.S. citizens by the NSA, and the firing of U.S. attorneys for apparently political reasons. However, much of Bush's dismal approval ratings stemmed from shortcomings in his foreign policy—most notably the war in Iraq. Towards the end of his term Bush was not only unpopular at home, he was unpopular abroad. According to a BBC poll, nearly three-quarters of the people polled in 25 countries disapproved of the U.S. policy in Iraq.[3] In a similar vein, Zaharna commented that "U.S. public diplomacy has a much more serious problem. It has a credibility deficit of global proportions."[4] In short, Bush's credibility suffered, in large part, due to ineffective public diplomacy.

As president and commander in chief, Bush's credibility, in turn, rubbed off on the United States in general. As Snow recently lamented, ". . . the American image in the world is now at rock bottom."[5] Likewise, Peterson commented ". . . there is little doubt that stereotypes of Americans as arrogant, self-indulgent, hypocritical, inattentive, and unwilling or unable to engage in cross-cultural dialogue are pervasive and deeply rooted."[6] Thus, from the vantage point of much of the world, "America the beautiful" became a nation of ugly Americans.

This is not to say that the U.S. has ignored efforts to improve its image abroad. The problem is that many such efforts by the State Department simply seem like window dressing. By way of illustration, rap artist Toni Blackman was appointed as the official "Hip Hop" ambassador by the U.S. Department of State, and former Olympic skater Michelle Kwan holds the official title of "American Public Diplomacy Envoy."[7] Moreover, Charlotte Beers, a successful Madison Avenue ad executive was hired to "rebrand American foreign policy" in the Middle East.[8] She resigned 17 months later, having accomplished little. Apparently, selling Uncle Sam's policies on the Arab street proved much more difficult than selling Cheerios on Main Street.

In a more serious move to enhance the U.S. reputation abroad, Bush appointed Karen

Hughes, former White House Communications director, as Under Secretary for public diplomacy in 2005.[9] She was roundly criticized, however, for lacking knowledge of, and experience in, the Middle East.[10] Her lack of experience underscored the U.S. credibility problem. The reality is that no set of talking points from the State Department can undo the damage caused by the Abu Ghraib scandal, the detainees still being held at Guantanamo, and trials involving extraordinary renditions of foreigners by the CIA. Zaharna underscored this point, noting that:

> What U.S. officials don't seem to register is that no amount of information pumped out by U.S. public diplomacy will be enough to improve the U.S. image. The problem, ultimately, is not lack of information but lack of credibility ... Without credibility, no amount of information holds persuasive weight, and U.S. soft power can't attract and influence others.[11]

Aims and Goals

We concur that America has an image problem. Most notably, the United States' credibility is suffering. We also believe that it is difficult to project a credible image without knowing what credibility entails. In this essay we therefore examine the concept of source credibility as it relates to public diplomacy. Specifically, we draw upon recent examples of public diplomacy successes and failures to illuminate key constructs related to credibility. In addition, we argue for an extended conceptualization of credibility that includes not only individuals, but corporations, organizations, institutions, governments, social movements, and other organized collectivities.[12] Thus, Colin Powell's speech before the United Nations on February 5, 2003 affected not only his own credibility, but that of the entire Bush administration. Powell subsequently described that speech as the "lowest point in my life."[13]

In addition to advocating an expanded view of credibility, we argue for an expanded conceptualization of public diplomacy, rather than the traditional view that public diplomacy entails official government-sponsored efforts to shape public perceptions.[14] Our view is consistent with that of Snow and others included in this volume. Public diplomacy, in our view, consists of more than the words or deeds of heads of state and their representatives. Public diplomacy also encompasses civic action, such as actions by social movements, cultural exchange programs, and the involvement of non-governmental organizations. Public diplomacy is essentially a form of national image management, which includes any and all efforts to capture the hearts and minds of others, through official or unofficial means.[15] Thus, the U.S. military's role in the Abu Ghraib scandal can be viewed as an unfortunate act of public diplomacy that severely damaged the U.S. military's credibility in Iraq and America's credibility in the Middle East. In contrast, efforts by Habitat for Humanity International to build homes for poor people across the globe have enhanced the United States' image abroad.

In advocating an expanded view of credibility we also argue for an expanded view of persuasion. We suggest that persuasion may be intentional or unintentional. Accidental influence is, in fact, quite common. Thus, missteps by an organization or institution may inadvertently damage that organization's or institution's credibility and, in turn, its potential to persuade. Missteps by the U.S. in Iraq, for example, have damaged U.S. credibility and, in turn, the U.S. ability to persuade other nations that Iran's nuclear intentions are military rather than commercial.

Tenets of Credibility

Credibility is a Perceptual Phenomenon

Whether a source possesses credibility or not is largely in the eye of the beholder. O'Keefe defines credibility as "judgments made by a perceiver (e.g. message recipient) concerning the believability of a communicator."[16] This definition highlights the fact that credibility is receiver-based. Credibility does not reside in a source. It is bestowed on a source by an audience.

This realization is important because a source westerners might see as lacking in credibility may nonetheless have high credibility in the eyes of his or her followers. For example, Iran's president Mahmoud Ahmadinejad is almost universally disliked by Americans and Brits. Yet among his conservative followers, especially the ideological hardliners, he is extremely popular. He is less popular among Iran's centrists and reformists, which illustrates that within his own country his credibility varies.

Organizational or institutional credibility is a perceptual phenomenon as well. To some, a multinational corporation such as Coca-Cola may be revered, while in the eyes of others it may be reviled. Much the same applies to governments and nations. Some nations—though they are regrettably fewer of late—respect and admire the U.S., while others loathe America and its policies. As Snow opined, "Too often the United States is seen as a benevolent Dr. Jekyll at home and a malevolent Mr. Hyde abroad."[17] Such differences in domestic versus foreign perceptions of the U.S. illustrate the perceptual nature of credibility.

Of course, saying that credibility "resides" in the minds of audience members is different from saying that the source has no control over perceptions of credibility. Indeed, while audience members ultimately decide who is and is not credible, their impressions are affected by the statements and actions of a source. This notion is central to Impression Management Theory, which not only suggests that communicators try to project desirable images but also that credibility is centrally important to this process.[18] For example, while other dimensions (e.g., a source's likeability) may be significant for those attempting to project a positive public image, Tedeschi and Norman noted that credibility was the most important dimension.[19] The implication of this is clear: sources have the ability to influence perceptions of their credibility and will be most successful when they can adapt to their audiences. This theme is so important, we will return to it shortly.

Credibility is Dynamic

Like a bull or a bear market, credibility comes and goes. Popular leaders cannot rest on their laurels. Maintaining credibility is an ongoing effort. As we noted at the outset of this essay, George W. Bush's public opinion polls were saw-toothed, waxing soon after September 11 and waning steadily during his second term in office. Bush remained steadfast in his support for the war, but the swagger he displayed when he proclaimed "Mission Accomplished" aboard the *U.S.S. Abraham Lincoln* in May 2003 was soon gone. Similar ups and downs are experienced by many if not most world leaders. A leader's standing tends to ebb and flow over time.

Such was the case for Kofi Annan. His credibility dipped dramatically in 2005, in the wake of the oil-for-food scandal.[20] Some $64 billion worth of Iraqi oil was illegally sold on the black market. Worse yet, Kofi Annan's son, Kojo, was implicated in the scandal. In light of this and other scandals, a number of sources called for Annan's resignation.[21]

The dynamic nature of credibility holds true for organizations and institutions as well. An institution, such as the U.N. can enjoy high credibility in one decade and low credibility in another. Most recently, the U.N. has been an embattled organization, rocked by scandals and plagued by the perception that it is largely irrelevant.[22] The movie *Hotel Rwanda*, for example, portrayed the U.N. as ineffectual in preventing genocide in Africa. Consider the following characterization of the U.N. that was offered in an editorial in the *Columbus Dispatch*:

> The United Nations gave credence to the charge that it is a useless debating society when it was powerless to stop an Arab militia's slaughter of thousands of Africans in Sudan's Darfur region. Add to that the scandals in the oil-for-food program in Iraq, missing documents in a probe of wrongdoing

by an oil-for-food contractor that employed Secretary-General Kofi Annan's son, sexual abuse of Africans by U.N. peacekeepers and the membership of the worst human-rights violators on the U.N. Commission on Human Rights. The United Nations is damaged goods.[23]

This harsh assessment illustrates the dynamic nature of institutional credibility. The U.N.'s new secretary general, Ban Ki Moon, has an opportunity to restore the organization's image. His personal credibility and that of the United Nations will be tested on such hot button issues as nuclear proliferation in Iran and genocide in Sudan. To restore the world body's tarnished image, he will need to demonstrate that the U.N. is capable of doing more than sending people wearing blue helmets to stand by and do nothing while refugees starve or are butchered.

Credibility is Situation-specific and Culture-bound

Sources must realize that because they are credible in one situation or circumstance does not mean they are credible in all situations or circumstances. A source's credibility is subject to change as she or he moves from one setting to another. By way of example, Bush's credibility soared when he addressed the first responders and the nation via a bullhorn from ground zero on September 14, 2001. It was an iconic moment in his presidency as he stood with his arm around one firefighter. He seemed made for the job. He exuded toughness and fortitude. He also exhibited compassion and reassured a nation that was in shock. "I can hear you" he said to firefighters who shouted their support. "The rest of the world hears you. And the people who knocked these buildings down will hear all of us soon."[24]

Cut to four years later and Bush's response to Hurricane Katrina and the situation was entirely different. Gone was the confidence and fortitude he had displayed at ground zero. The president seemed detached, disconnected, and disengaged.[25] There was no "bullhorn moment." Instead, there was another defining moment of his presidency, when he complimented his political appointee, Michael Brown, who lacked any experience in disaster relief, by proclaiming "Brownie, you're doing a heck of a job." Brown, the head of FEMA, resigned 10 days later following an onslaught of negative publicity.

Not only is credibility situational or contextual, it embodies a cultural component as well. Credibility operates similarly, but not identically, across cultures. We examine cross-cultural differences in credibility in more detail later. For the moment, however, it is worth noting that the importance attached to particular dimensions of credibility may vary from culture to culture. Hayes reported, for example, that the general finding that high credibility sources are more persuasive than low credibility sources held true for international audiences.[26] However, Hayes found that Jamaicans were less suspicious of a low credibility source (Radio Peiping) than Americans or Cubans, while Cubans were more critical of a high credibility source (the BBC) than Americans or Jamaicans. The differences were attributed, in part, to Cold War perceptions of the media.

Credibility is a Multi-dimensional Construct

Those attempting to project a credible image must realize that credibility is not comprised of a single factor or dimension. Credibility represents a confluence of characteristics which have been classified into primary and secondary dimensions. In 380 B.C.E. Aristotle proclaimed that ethos was comprised of "good sense, good moral character, and good will."[27] He was, for the most part, on target. Factor analytic studies conducted since the 1960s have confirmed that there are three basic or primary dimensions of credibility and perhaps a half dozen secondary dimensions.[28] As we'll note later, while the primary dimensions tend to be relevant in almost all contexts, the secondary dimensions are more situation-specific. We now examine each of these dimensions, in turn, as they apply to public diplomacy.

Expertise

An important, primary dimension of source credibility is expertise, which is also referred to in the literature as competence or qualification.[29] Expertise answers the question, "Does the source know his or her stuff?" In the case of an organization or other entity, one might ask, "is there sufficient institutional expertise?" To be viewed as credible a source must be seen as knowledgeable about the issue at hand, competent in dealing with the issue, and capable of making the best decision on that issue.

A clear example of a lack of apparent expertise is illustrated by the fact that the Bush administration got it all wrong when it concluded Saddam Hussein possessed weapons of mass destruction. Various White House officials, from Colin Powell, to Dick Cheney, to Donald Rumsfeld, to Condoleezza Rice, to the President himself all announced matter-of-factly that Iraq had stockpiles of chemical and biological agents and was pursuing nuclear weapons. In 2003, Rumsfeld pronounced "We know where—where the WMDs are. They're near Tikrit and Baghdad, and north, south, east, and west of there."[30] In a now infamous sound bite, Rice stated "We don't want the smoking gun to be a mushroom cloud."[31]

The Bush administration also damaged its perceived expertise by adopting an "anti-science" stance on a number of issues, most notably global warming. Bush withdrew from the Kyoto Accord, claiming the "jury was still out" on climate change. Furthermore, testimony by witnesses at Senate hearings held in February 2007 revealed that administration officials tried systematically to manipulate or withhold information on climate change and to muzzle government scientists who tried to speak out on the issue.[32]

Bush is not the only actor on the world stage who has demonstrated an apparent lack of expertise. Iranian president Mahmoud Ahmadinejad's decision to host a "holocaust denial" conference did little to enhance his perceived expertise. His denouncement of claims that 6 million Jews died at the hands of the Nazis as "a myth" convinced many in the world community that he is not a rational actor.

In the Arab world, the *Al Jazeera* network is viewed as having expertise. The network, which is now more than a decade old, boasts some 50 million viewers and possesses far greater credibility to its viewers than the BBC or CNN. *Al Jazeera*, well-known for airing Osama Bin Laden's videotapes, has a decidedly Muslim bent (using terms like "martyr" rather than "terrorist"). Viewers throughout the Middle East, however, regard it as a reliable alternative to Western media propaganda. Based in Qatar, *Al Jazeera* is seen as offering a more balanced perspective, countering both Western media and more extremist networks such as *Al Manar* (the pro-Hamas station).[33]

Al Jazeera functions as an arm of public diplomacy in the Middle East in the same way that the BBC and CNN do in the Western world. George W. Bush himself may have inadvertently boosted *Al Jazeera*'s credibility on the Arab street. According to a memo leaked to the British press, Bush considered bombing the network at one point.[34] *Al-Arabiya* is *Al Jazeera*'s major rival satellite network in the Middle East. The American-owned and operated satellite channel, *Al-Hurra* ("the Free One"), has attracted only a few million viewers.

Trustworthiness

A second, primary dimension of credibility is trustworthiness.[35] A source may be knowledgeable or possess expertise, but what if the source can't be trusted? Trust is vital for actors on the world stage. Consider George W. Bush's comment about Russia's president Vladimir Putin, when the two met for the first time in 2001. "I looked the man in the eye. I found him to be very straightforward and trustworthy. We had a very good dialogue. I was able to get a sense of his soul."[36] Contrast this with Bush's State of the Union address in 2002 in which he branded Iran, Iraq, and North Korea an "axis of evil" and it is easy to see why he is not trusted by Ahmadinejad and Kim Jong Il, the two remaining leaders of the so-called evil triumvirate.[37]

Trust is a prerequisite for cooperation. Thus, if two leaders or two countries don't trust one another, credibility may be eroded and diplomatic efforts may be stymied. It is safe to say that Hugo Chavez does not trust George W. Bush. When Venezuela's firebrand leader addressed the United Nations General Assembly in September 2006, one day after George W. Bush addressed the same body, Chavez declared "The devil came here yesterday . . . It smells of sulphur still today . . . He came here talking as if he were the owner of the world."[38] It is difficult to imagine much cooperation between these two leaders with so much vitriol in the air.

In the context of public diplomacy, there are deep-seated, long-standing cases of mistrust. One of these involves the media. The phenomenon known as the "hostile media effect" refers to the tendency of observers to perceive that the media is biased and hostile to their own self-interests.[39] Since the media is often viewed as an arm of public diplomacy, observers may see the media as a partisan player in public diplomacy.

By way of illustration, in 2005 a Danish newspaper, *Jyllands-Posten*, published cartoon caricatures of the Prophet Muhammad. The cartoons, one of which depicted Muhammad wearing a turban shaped like a bomb, sparked an international furor that led to riots and the burning of several Danish embassies.[40] Many westerners could not understand why the cartoons were so incendiary. For Muslims, however, the cartoons reinforced a long-standing distrust of Western media.[41] "Correctly or not," noted Ahmed, "Muslims perceive the Western media as hostile."[42] Their distrust may be justified, at least partly.[43] According to a report commissioned by the Kuwaiti government that examined Western media, "the terms Islamic or Muslim are linked to extremism, militant, jihads, as if they belonged together inextricably and naturally (Muslim extremist, Islamic terror, Islamic war, Muslim time bomb)."[44] The Western media, itself, is therefore viewed as an agent of public diplomacy. How the American media in particular covers events in the Middle East and elsewhere affects the credibility of the United States abroad. Distrust is, of course, a two-way street. Many westerners do not trust Middle Eastern news sources, such as the *Al Jazeera* network.

Oddly enough, in some cases it may be an advantage for an international actor to be seen as untrustworthy. Making bellicose statements and using inflammatory rhetoric may actually be to the advantage of a leader. If a leader is too reliable, dependable, or predictable, adversaries may be able to take advantage of him or her. Leaders like Kim Jong Il or Mahmoud Ahmadinejad may purposely cultivate an image of being inscrutable. If the U.S. President or Gordon Brown are uncertain how these leaders may react, they may tread more carefully.

Goodwill

A third, primary dimension of credibility is known as goodwill or perceived caring.[45] To be perceived as credible, a source must convey respect for others and a genuine interest in their well-being. Goodwill was manifested via two former U.S. presidents, in the aftermath of the disastrous tsunami that struck Indonesia in December 2004, which left more than 200,000 people missing or dead. George Bush Sr. and Bill Clinton, a seemingly unlikely duo, partnered up to raise money and spearhead U.S. efforts to provide food, medicine, reconstruction, and other aid to the stricken region. Their efforts helped shore up America's credibility. An opinion poll conducted in March 2005 revealed that 65% of Indonesians viewed the United States more favorably after the relief effort.[46]

If the Indian Ocean tsunami relief was a high point for U.S. goodwill during the Bush Administration, the Abu Ghraib scandal was certainly one of the low points. The photographs documenting systematic abuse of the prisoners being held at the Abu Ghraib prison cost the U.S. dearly. In one photo, private Lindy England, mugged for the camera, a cigarette dangling from her lips, while she pointed at a hooded detainee's genitals. In another, a shrouded Iraqi stood on a box with electrodes connected to his hands and genitals. The photographs became iconic reminders of everything that was wrong with the U.S. policy in Iraq. The humiliating nature of the acts, many of which were designed intentionally to offend Muslim culture and religion, demonstrated ill-will by the U.S. military toward the Iraqi people.

For many Iraqis, Abu Ghraib marked a turning point in their support of America's military involvement in Iraq. As Diehl noted, "The photos from Abu Ghraib prison may have destroyed what was left of the Bush administration's credibility with Arab popular opinion."[47] Indeed, while Bush may have tried to distance his administration from what happened at Abu Ghraib by promising a full investigation and the delivery of justice, the fact remains that, so far, not a single high ranking military official has been punished for what happened in the prison. Moreover, the fallout from the scandal extended beyond the Middle East. As Kenneth Roth, executive director for Human Rights Watch, observed, Abu Ghraib:

> undermined Washington's much-needed credibility as a proponent of human rights and a leader of the campaign against terrorism. In the midst of a seeming epidemic of suicide bombings, beheadings, and other attacks on civilians and noncombatants—all affronts to the most basic human rights values—Washington's weakened moral authority is felt acutely.[48]

Goodwill is much more likely to be communicated via "soft power." At present, more efforts employing soft power are sorely needed. As the Council on Foreign Relations warned, "negative opinions of the United States and its policies have metastasized. Beyond the threat of a direct attack by al-Qaeda and those influenced by that movement . . . the United States is now facing a more fundamental loss of goodwill and trust from publics from around the world."[49] Programs such as the Fulbright Program, the International Visitor Leadership Program, and other educational and cultural exchanges hold considerable promise as a means of spreading American values abroad. Unfortunately, for every dollar that is spent on the military, only one-quarter of one cent is spent on public diplomacy, including educational and cultural exchange programs.[50]

Non-governmental organizations (NGOs) also are particularly good at demonstrating goodwill. Organizations such as Amnesty International, Doctors without Borders (a.k.a. Medicines sans Frontières), Human Rights Watch, and the Land Mine Survivors Network demonstrate perceived caring by taking on difficult tasks which official bodies cannot or will not tackle. NGOs are more adept at such humanitarian missions because they have neither the profit motives of multinational corporations nor the political agendas of government agencies. NGOs are well equipped to tailor their efforts to the particular situational exigencies. And NGOs often partner with local leaders and groups to ensure aid reaches the intended beneficiaries.

Goodwill, then, is an essential ingredient in public diplomacy. Other nations and other people must perceive that the U.S. is acting in their interest, not merely its own self-interest. Too often, official aid seems tied to the White House's political agenda, rather than the genuine needs of the aid recipients. For instance, foreign aid that is earmarked for AIDs programs must include abstinence only education. Such a policy demonstrates that U.S. foreign aid is geared more toward satisfying a domestic agenda, appeasing religious fundamentalists at home, than helping those abroad.

Secondary Dimensions of Credibility

In addition to the primary dimensions of credibility, i.e., expertise, trustworthiness, and goodwill, a variety of secondary dimensions have been identified as well. Space considerations do not permit us to elaborate on all of these secondary dimensions. A few, however, bear mentioning. One such secondary dimension is composure.[51] To be perceived as credible a leader must remain calm, cool, and collected in a crisis. A leader who appears panicky or is easily rattled may lose credibility. A clear example of a lack of composure was George W. Bush's infamous "deer in the headlights" moment on September 11, 2001, when he continued reading "My Pet Goat" to a classroom full of 3rd graders after being informed that the nation was under attack. By way of contrast, Tony Blair appeared steadfast and resolved in his reaction to the capturing of 15 British sailors by Iran in April 2007. Although the manner of their release—Ahmadinejad called it an "Easter gift" for the U.K.—was embarrassing for Britain, Blair was able to maintain that "Throughout we have taken a measured approach—firm but calm, not negotiating, but not confronting either."[52]

Another secondary dimension of credibility is dynamism. At times, it is important for a leader to appear energetic, enthusiastic, and animated. A leader must not, however, appear overly exuberant. The trick is for a leader to "match his or her dynamism with the demands of the particular situation."[53] Presidents Kennedy, Reagan, and Clinton often exhibited dynamism when putting forth their visions for America. Presidents Carter and George Bush Sr., on the other hand, were not known for exuding dynamism. The latter were often seen as too reserved. British prime ministers, such as Blair, Major, and Thatcher, are usually adept at evincing dynamism, because the prime minister must frequently advocate positions and field questions before the House of Commons, where debates can be heated.

Hu Jintao, the current president of the People's Republic of China, is low in dynamism, as are many Asian world leaders. At present there are no Asian leaders with the dynamism of a Mao Tse Tsung or a Ho Chi Minh. Japan's former prime minister, Junichero Koizumi, known for his stylish hair and modern suits, was probably the most colorful of the lot. Kim Jong Il is, of course, known for being eccentric. His eccentricities, however, don't enhance the world community's perception of him as leaderly. Cultural expectations may require Asian leaders to appear more conservative and less flamboyant than their Western counterparts. Indeed, the Japanese maxim "the nail that sticks up gets pounded" illustrates that drawing too much attention to oneself might be frowned upon in some cultures.

Institutions and organizations may exhibit dynamism as well. Some groups, such as Greenpeace and People for the Ethical Treatment of Animals (PETA), are much more active, often relying on "in your face" and "shock" tactics to gain attention and awareness. Other groups, such as Catholic Relief Services and Save the Children are more staid and sedate and do not clamor for media attention. For NGOs a balancing act may be involved: An organization that is seen as too controversial may scare away potential donors or volunteers, but an organization with too low a profile may not attract enough donors or volunteers. Given that credibility is situation-specific and context-bound, the nature of the organization and the cause it is trying to promote will tend to determine how much dynamism is needed. Sometimes it is useful to seek the limelight, at other times not.

Credibility and Culture

We have argued elsewhere that, to be successful, a "persuader doesn't move the receiver to a message, the persuader moves the message to the receiver."[54] In other words, effective influence requires the ability to analyze and adapt to particular audiences. Because public diplomacy, by definition, involves communicating with a vast array of audiences with differing cultural backgrounds, the ability to understand and adapt becomes even more significant in this context. With regard to this article, a question that naturally follows is: do cultures differ in their perceptions of credibility?

Unfortunately, too little research has focused on cultural differences in such perceptions (i.e., most studies identifying dimensions of credibility have used U.S. participants). That which does exist, tends to support what we have said so far. Specifically, the primary dimensions of credibility seem to generalize to most situations, including those in other cultures. For example, King, Minami, and Samovar found that both U.S. and Japanese participants consistently employed the dimensions of competence (i.e., expertise) and character (i.e., trustworthiness) when judging others' credibility.[55] Ward and McGinnies found that sources high in expertise and trustworthiness, compared to those low in these dimensions, were more persuasive in Australia, Japan, Sweden, the United States, and New Zealand.[56]

Even so, the configuration of the primary credibility dimensions may vary from culture to culture. For instance, although Heyman found that Australians employed two distinct dimensions of expertise and trustworthiness, Singaporeans employed only one dimension that seemed to be a combination of expertise and trustworthiness.[57] This suggests that in some cultures, in order to be perceived as an expert, you must also be perceived as trustworthy and vice versa.

As we noted earlier, compared to the primary dimensions, the secondary dimensions of credibility are more situation-specific, suggesting that they may be employed differently across cultures. Some research supports this notion. For example, King et al. found that, when judging credibility, Japanese participants employed two additional factors (i.e., consideration and appearance) that were not employed by U.S. participants.[58]

In addition to playing a role in what dimensions are employed when making judgments about credibility, an individual's cultural background interacts with credibility in other ways. For example, Ruelas, Atkinson, and Ramos-Sanchez found that, when judging counselors' credibility, Mexican-Americans provided higher ratings than did European-Americans.[59] Other research suggests that people tend to rate members from their own culture as more credible than those from a different culture.[60] Finally, in a study on medium credibility, black participants perceived television to be the most credible source of news information, while whites perceived magazines to be the most credible.[61]

Conclusion

Since credibility is in the eye of the beholder, those seeking to project credibility through public diplomacy must adopt an audience-centered approach. Since credibility is dynamic, public diplomacy must be flexible and capable of adapting to changing circumstances. Since credibility is situation-specific and culture-bound, public diplomacy efforts that succeed in one region of the world may not succeed in another. There is also considerable need for diplomatic personnel to be culturally sensitive. As Snow advised, we need to, "Drop the one-size-fits-all attitude toward programs for overseas audiences; tailor outreach to individual countries and regions."[62] Since credibility is a multi-dimensional construct, it is not enough to focus on expertise, trustworthiness, or goodwill alone. All three dimensions are important. We must realize, for example, that projecting power alone does not equate to credibility. Efforts at establishing "hard power" may work in some cases, but building trust and perceptions of goodwill by establishing relationships is also essential.

Following the presidential election in 2008 we will be living in a post-George W. Bush world. A new administration, whether led by Democrats or Republicans, will have an opportunity to reconnect with the world in a less unilateral, more cooperative manner. A new administration will have a chance to deemphasize hard power and reinvigorate soft power as a means of conducting foreign policy. Projecting power isn't enough. America also needs to project credibility. Public diplomacy will become more vital in the next decade as America seeks to restore its tarnished image abroad. Individuals and institutions engaged in public diplomacy would be wise to heed the importance of building and maintaining credibility. We hope the discussion of credibility as it relates to public diplomacy discussed herein provides a step in that direction.

Notes

1 http://www.pollingreport.com/BushJob1.htm.
2 Kim Franke-Folstad, "Unloved presidents may still have their day," *Tampa Tribune*, February 19, 2007, 1; see also Niles Latham, "Bush hits Iraq Bottom: Among least popular presidents of all-time as war takes toll in poll," *New York Post*, January 29, 2007, 9.
3 BBC World Service, "World view of United States role goes from bad to worse," January 23, 2007; http://www.bbc.co.uk/pressoffice/pressreleases/stories/2007/01_january/23/us.shtml.
4 R.S. Zaharna, "The U.S. credibility deficit," *Foreign Policy in Focus*, December 13, 2006, http://www.fpif.org/fpiftxt/3796.
5 See Nancy Snow, *The Arrogance of American Power: What U.S. Leaders Are Doing Wrong and Why It's Our Duty to Dissent*. Lanham, MD: Rowman and Littlefield, 2007. Her book addresses the Brand America debate and public diplomacy efforts to improve America's image in the world.
6 Peter G. Peterson, "Public diplomacy and the war on terrorism: A strategy for reform," *Foreign Affairs* 81, no. 5 (2002): 74–96.
7 Tiffany Jenkins, "Why should artists be agents for the government?" *The Independent*, February 28, 2007, 30.
8 Clay Risen, "Re-branding America: Marketing gurus think they can help 'reposition' the United States and save American foreign policy," *Boston Globe*, May 13, 2005, D1.
9 Morton Kondracke, "Bush aid goes after Islamic hearts, minds," *Chicago Sun Times*, September 19, 2006, 31.
10 Edward Luce, "Bush ally hopes to win over Islamic world," *Financial Times*, January 16, 2007, 6.
11 Zaharna, paragraph four.
12 For further analysis of this extended concept of credibility, see Robert H. Gass and John S. Seiter, *Persuasion, Social Influence, and Compliance, Gaining*, 3rd ed (Boston, MA: Allyn & Bacon/Pearson, 2007).
13 CNN.com, "Former aid: Powell WMD speech 'lowest point in my life'," http://www.cnn.com/2005/WORLD/meast/08/19/powell.un/.
14 See, for example, Hans N. Tuch, *Communicating with the World* (New York: St. Martin's Press, 1990).
15 Jian Wang, "Telling the American story to the world: The purpose of U.S. public diplomacy in historical perspective," *Public Relations Review*, Vol. 33 (2007): 21–30.
16 Daniel J. O'Keefe, *Persuasion: Theory and research* (Newbury Park, CA: Sage, 1990): 130–131.
17 Snow, 62.
18 Barry R. Schlenker, "Identity and self-identification," in *The Self and Social Life*, ed. B.R. Schlenker (New York: McGraw-Hill, 1985), 65–99.
19 James T. Tedeschi and Nancy M. Norman, "Social power, self-presentation, and the self," in *The Self and Social Life*, ed. B.R. Schlenker (New York: McGraw-Hill, 1985), 292–322.
20 See Michael Jordan, "Under fire, the U.N. looks to retool," *Christian Science Monitor*, April 6, 2005, 6; and Conor O'Clery, "New questions on the credibility of Kofi Annan," *Irish Times*, April 27, 2005, 11.
21 See Norman Coleman, "Kofi Annan must go," *Wall Street Journal*, December 1, 2004, A10; Niles Gardiner, "Kofi Annan's shrinking credibility," Web Memo #589, Washington, D.C.: The Heritage Foundation, October 19, 2004, http://www.heritage.org/Research/InternationalOrganizations/wm589.cfm; and Salim Mansur, "Annan should resign," *Toronto Star*, April 2, 2005, 19.
22 Ibid, Jordan, "Under fire."
23 "Clean up the mess," editorial, *Columbus Dispatch*, April 2, 2005, A8.
24 CNN.com, "Bush tours New York devastation. Bush promises terrorists will get message soon," September 14, 2001. See http://archives.cnn.com/2001/US/09/14/america.under.attack/.
25 Judy Keen and Richard Benedetto, "A compassionate Bush was absent after Katrina," *USA Today*, September 9, 2005, A2.
26 Harold B. Hayes, "International persuasion variables are tested across three cultures," *Journalism Quarterly* 48 (1971): 714–723.
27 Aristotle, *The Rhetoric*, W.R. Roberts, Trans. (New York: Random House, 1954).
28 Gary G. Cronkhite and Jo Liska, "A critique of factor analytic approaches to the study of credibility," *Communication Monographs* 43 (1976): 91–107. See also Chanthika Pornpitakpan, "The persuasiveness of source credibility: A critical review of five decades' evidence," *Journal of Applied Social Psychology* 34, no. 2 (2004): 243–281.

29 Different researchers have used slightly different scale items when measuring credibility dimensions. For additional reading, see David K. Berlo, Joseph B. Lemert, and Robert J. Mertz, "Dimensions for evaluating the acceptability of message sources," *Public Opinion Quarterly* 33 (1969): 563–573; Carl I. Hovland, Irving L. Janis, and Harold H. Kelly, *Communication and Persuasion* (New Haven, CT: Yale University Press, 1953); James C. McCroskey, "Scales for the measurement of ethos," *Speech Monographs* 33 (1966): 65–72; James C. McCroskey and Jason J. Teven, "Goodwill: A reexamination of the construct and its measurement," *Communication Monographs*, 66 (1999): 90–103; and James C. McCroskey and Thomas J. Young, "Ethos and credibility: The construct and its measurement after three decades," *Central States Speech Journal* 32 (1981): 24–34. Terminology for the same or comparable dimensions often varies, because the researcher decides what label to attach to a particular set of items that "hang together" in factor analysis. Thus "expertise" is also known as "competence" or "qualification." "Trustworthiness" is also referred to as "character," "safety," or "personal integrity." "Goodwill" is also known as "perceived caring."

30 CNN.com, "Ex-CIA analyst: Rumsfeld 'should have owned up,'" May 5, 2005. http://www.cnn.com/2006/POLITICS/05/04/cnna.mcgovern/.

31 CNN.com, "Top Bush officials push case against Saddam," September 8, 2002. http://archives.-cnn.com/2002/ALLPOLITICS/09/08/iraq.debate/.

32 Luke O'Brien, "Bush ripped on global warming," *Wired*, February 7, 2007. http://www.wired.com/politics/law/news/2007/02/72672.

33 Samantha M. Shapiro, "The war inside the Arab newsroom," *New York Times*, January 2, 2005: 27.

34 Luke Baker, "'Britons on trial over leaked memo' Document claimed Bush threatened to bomb Al Jazeera," *Toronto Star*, April 19, 2007.

35 Ronald L. Applbaum and Karl W.E. Anatol, "The factor structure of source credibility as a function of the speaking situation," *Speech Monographs* 39 (1972): 216–222.

36 CNN.com, "Transcript: Bush, Putin news conference," June 18, 2001. http://archives.cnn.com/2001/WORLD/europe/06/18/bush.putin.transcript/index.html.

37 http://www.whitehouse.gov/news/releases/2002/01/20020129–11.html.

38 BBC News, "Chavez tells UN Bush is 'devil,'" September 20, 2006 http://news.bbc.co.uk/2/hi/americas/5365142.stm.

39 Robert P. Vallone, Lee Ross, and Mark R. Lepper, "The hostile media phenomenon: Biased perception and perceptions of media bias in coverage of the 'Beirut Massacre,'" *Journal of Personality and Social Psychology* 49 (1985): 577–585.

40 Jeffrey Fleishman, "Protesters burn two embassies in Syria over cartoons of Prophet," *Los Angeles Times*, February 5, 2006: A3; and Kevin Sullivan, "Muslims' fury rages unabated over cartoons," *Washington Post*, February 11, 2006, A12.

41 "Media has anti-Muslim bias, claims report," *The Guardian*, November 15, 2005 http://www.guardian.co.uk/international/story/0,3604,1642320,00.html.

42 Akbar S. Ahmed, *Islam in the Age of the Western media*. Excerpted from *Living Islam, From Samarkand to Stornoway* (Wood Lane, London, U.K.: BBC Books 1985) http://muslim-canada.org/livingislam2.html.

43 Brigitte L. Nacos and Oscar Torres-Reyna, *Fueling our Fears: Stereotyping, Media Coverage, and Public Opinion of Muslim Americans* (Lanham, MD: Rowman & Littlefield, 2007).

44 "Media has Anti-Muslim Bias, Claims Report," *The Guardian* (London), November 15, 2005, http://www.guardian.co.uk/international/story/0,3604,1642320,00.html.

45 James C. McCroskey and Jason J. Teven, "Goodwill: A reexamination of the construct and its measurement," *Communication Monographs* 66 (1999): 90–103.

46 D.E. Graham, "Envoy says tsunami relief aids U.S. image," May 21, 2005, *San Diego Tribune*, B6.

47 Cited in Ruell M. Gerecht, "Who's afraid of Abu Ghraib?," May 24, 2004, *The Weekly Standard*, http://www.weeklystandard.com/Content/Public/Articles/000/000/004/096uutti.asp.

48 Kenneth Roth, *Darfur and Abu Ghraib*. Human Rights Watch, 2005. http://hrw.org/wr2k5/darfurand-abughraib/1.htm.

49 Council on Foreign Relations. *Finding America's Voice: A strategy for reinvigorating U.S. public diplomacy* (New York: Council on Foreign Relations, 2003).

50 Ibid, 8.

51 G.R. Miller and M.A. Hewgill, "The effect of variations in nonfluency on audience ratings of source credibility," *Quarterly Journal of Speech* 50 (1964): 36–44.

52 Paul Kent, "Iran frees seized sailors, but . . . Blair insists no deal with devil was made," *The Daily Telegraph* (Australia), April 6, 2007, 15.

53 Gass and Seiter, 81.

54 Ibid., 113.

55 Cited in Kak Yoon, Choong Hyun Kim, and Min-Sun Kim, "A Cross-Cultural Comparison of the

Effects of Source Credibility on Attitudes and Behavioral Intentions," *Mass Communication & Society* 1, no. 3 & 4, 1998: 153–173.

56 C.D. Ward and E. McGinnies, "Persuasive effect of early and late mention of credible and noncredible sources," *Journal of Psychology* 86 (1974): 17–23.

57 Sam Heyman, "A Study of Australian and Singaporean Perceptions of Source Credibility," *Communication Research Reports* 9 (1992): 137–150.

58 Stephen King, Yuko Minami, and Larry Samovar, "A Comparison of Japanese and American Perceptions of Credibility," *Communication Research Reports* 2 (1985): 76–79.

59 Shelley R. Ruelas, Donald R. Atkinson, and Lucila Ramos-Sanchez, "Counselor Helping Model, Participant Ethnicity and Acculturation Level, and Perceived Counselor Credibility," *Journal of Counseling Psychology* 45 (1998): 98–103.

60 Claudia F. Gomez, and Judy C. Pearson, "Students' Perceptions of the Credibility and Homophily of Native and Non-Native English Speaking Teaching Assistants," *Communication Research Reports* 7 (1990): 58–62.

61 Richard M. Durand, Jesse E. Teel, Jr., and William O. Bearden, "Racial Differences in Perceptions of Advertising Credibility," *Journalism Quarterly* 56 (1979): 562–566.

62 Snow, 184.

14

The Culture Variable in the Influence Equation

Kelton Rhoads

Western Concentration of Influence Research

By recent count, I've given over 300 presentations to professional audiences on the topic of influence psychology. Two of the most frequently asked questions I've received are: "Aren't most of these influence studies you're referencing conducted in North America?" followed by "What evidence do you have that these influence tactics will work anywhere else in the world?" These are important questions.

The first question is easier to answer: Yes, most of the studies in the social science canon are from North America. That's due to an accident of history. During the 1920s, Germany was the center of the emerging field of social psychology, and its foremost practitioner was a German Jew named Kurt Lewin who later became known as "the father of social psychology." Having predicted the direction of Germany's future earlier than others, he emigrated to the United States in 1932, where he continued his empirical approach to the social sciences that had such a profound impact on the field. Hitler's loss was F.D.R.'s gain, and soon Lewin's talents were engaged in the American war effort. After World War II (WWII), the study of influence psychology gained critical mass, and a rich scientific literature now exists on topics of persuasion, compliance, propaganda, and indoctrination.

It's difficult to say how much research is conducted in North America compared to the rest of the world, but one telling estimate comes from the number of replications of a classic conformity study conducted by Solomon Asch in the 1950s,[1] which may be the most frequently replicated study within the influence canon, having been replicated 133 times by a recent count.[2] It appears that approximately 73% of the research was conducted in the U.S., the remaining 27% spread across 13 other countries, most of them European. North America and Europe combined account for about 88% of the research in this legacy line of inquiry. If other lines of influence research are similarly apportioned, this gives us a view of the problem faced when attempting to generalize findings to the rest of the world. There are many nations that engage in very little influence psychology research, or none at all.

But there's a potential silver lining when one considers *to what* we are attempting to generalize these psychological findings. Are we attempting to generalize to *cultures*, or to *humans*? Bad news if the former, good news if the latter. And that brings us to the formidable follow-up question: "What evidence do you have that these influence tactics will work anywhere else in the world?"

The Primacy-of-Culture Perspective

The question assumes that culture fundamentally changes cognitive processing. Therefore, the primacy-of-culture approach considers psychological research from any particular culture to be largely inapplicable to other cultures. It argues for indigenous psychologies to be built from the ground up within disparate cultures (however they are demarcated) before we may be confident of the practical generalities that are the stock-and-trade of influence psychology. In practice, nationality, language, and geographic region are frequently substituted for culture.[3]

The idea that psychological research from one culture may be applicable to people of other cultures is seen variously as culturally insensitive, impractical, or psychologically invalid. "People from some other nations differ in cognition," writes Klein. "Practitioners simply cannot apply research findings gleaned from Western research and expect it to help in multinational environments."[4] A recent review of information operations in *Jane's* asserts "We need to give IO officers and commanders comprehensive cultural training so they can tailor the right message to the Iraqi people."[5] A primary recommendation from a recent Department of Defense review of Psychological Operations (PSYOP) effectiveness recommended "greater familiarization with cross-cultural communication techniques," urging PSYOP to concentrate on a "deep understanding of the target audience's culture and subcultures."[6] I have heard top military analysts echo these sentiments, declaring, "When you are dealing with people in another culture, *everything changes.*" The primacy-of-culture perspective implies that people in different cultures process stimuli differently, that they think and feel with different thoughts and feelings that are alien to observers in other cultures—as if people of diverse cultures or geography were, for practical purposes, different species of humans. While currently fashionable in the West, the primacy-of-culture idea is not new.

In the 1950s, an amateur linguist named Benjamin Whorf proposed that language constrained thought.[7] He thought a unique culture with a unique language resulted in unique processes of thought. In the 1960s, Lorand Szalay studied free word associations, and found interesting differences among cultures regarding conceptual associations that were thought to constitute meaning.[8] These theories have been called on to support popular explanations of why Eskimos have more words for snow than do English speakers (which they apparently do not),[9] and questions regarding whether Filipinos, having generic pronouns that don't distinguish between "him" and "her," are unclear on the concept of sexuality (which they apparently are not).[10]

Primacy-of-culture paradigms currently predominate, and are considered by many to be the fundamental ingredient in successful cross-cultural, cross-national, and cross-geographic influence campaigns. For example, the ethnic segmentation of markets is a reflexive practice among many marketers.[11] The cultural lens model, which "captures the nature and origin of cognitive differences" among people of various cultures, enjoys wide acceptance among information operations intelligentsia.[12] Observers of public diplomacy often align with the view that ". . . culture has emerged as the new dynamic in international relations,"[13] and that cross-cultural sensitivity is the essential ingredient of sound public diplomacy.[14]

Cultural awareness, cultural intelligence, and cultural sensitivity are often-repeated mantras among cross-cultural influencers—as they should be. Cultural tuning increases the likelihood of effective persuasion. It's merely axiomatic to say that it's difficult to be influential without a knowledge of the culture in which one is practicing influence.

The problem comes when cultural knowledge is considered *sufficient* or *primary* for successful intercultural influence, and this is a danger associated with the primacy-of-culture approach. If cultural knowledge is the fundamental ingredient in successful intercultural influence, then the people who conduct influence campaigns should excel in cultural expertise above all else. It follows that indigenous influence agents are to be preferred.

Imagine for a moment that you have found a true cultural expert for an Iraqi influence campaign you are conducting—a sympathetic, loyal, reliable Iraqi who works as an engineer in a local manufacturing plant. He can trace his ancestors back to Hammurabi, and personifies his culture accurately. Is he the ideal person to run your influence campaign? Probably not, because it's unlikely he's also a highly skilled influence agent—he might even be a persuasive bungler. His ability to persuade would depend on a set of skills that were entirely separate from his knowledge of the culture. Influence success requires much more than the mere mastery of culture.

Dissenting Primacy-of-Culture

In some quarters, one can find dissent with the idea that culture changes fundamental human cognition, or that cultural sensitivity is in fact the primary ingredient of successful intercultural influence campaigns. Some researchers observe that culture is frequently assumed to be causal, even though other causes may provide better explanations of behavior.

For example, predictable conflicts flare up between certain departments within companies. A perennial quarrel between marketing and production occurs in many organizations, due to their conflicting goals. But Professor Livia Markóczy, also an international management consultant, noticed that these conflicts were often misattributed to differences of national culture within international organizations, when one region was primarily responsible for marketing, and another for production. "In my work," writes Markóczy, "I have found that the actual fault lines in beliefs fall along functional lines and not national ones. . . . The temptation to attribute differences to different cultural mindsets is strong . . . but may pale in comparison to the differences between the production people and the marketing people in that same firm."[15] Elsewhere she writes, "Our view is obscured by our expectation of substantial cultural differences . . . the line between being insensitive and sensitive to cultural differences may be as thin as the line between being sensitive and oversensitive to them."[16]

Accordingly, Markóczy warns against the "cat and dog" problem: Imagine a Chinese observer looks at a cat, and a German observer looks at a dog. When these two people compare notes, should they assume they've seen the same animal and attribute the differences to culture? Or is it more accurate to attribute their differences to dissimilar fields of view?

For example, a recent USAF study asked several subject matter experts to generate a list of commonly employed lines of persuasion, and then to speculate on the influence potential of these themes in various nations where U.S. PSYOP had seen action.[17] The theme of "battle weariness," for example, was thought to be highly effective for Serbs (ranked #1) but ineffective for Rwandans (ranked last place at #14), which led the authors to comment on differences among cultures. But couldn't the differences in perceived effectiveness be attributed to other causes—such as a costly, drawn-out conflict in Serbia, compared to a nascent conflict in Rwanda? If so, cost and duration of conflict might be better predictors of this theme's utility, than nationality.

To the "cat and dog" problem, we should add the "dog and dog" problem: the Chinese observer sees a black dog, the German observer sees a brown dog—should they conclude they've discovered unique, culturally adapted species? Or are they viewing two relatively minor variations of the same type of animal?

One of my military contacts told me about a PSYOP officer who reported that before deploying, he had read, studied, and concentrated on finding whatever he could to improve his cross-cultural communication skills and cultural awareness. Then he deployed to Iraq. When he returned, he reflected on his experience: "What I read was good but largely not useable. What I really needed to prepare me to do the job I did was to watch the first two seasons of *The Sopranos*, because that tells you more about how things work over there than all the culture stuff."[18] The soldier wished he had invested more time understanding small group dynamics, power, negotiation, and compliance tactics—potentially a more useable skill set.

The officer's comment has depth to it. Does an increasing investment in cultural understanding actually pay out in terms of proportionately increasing influence success? Is the relationship linear, or asymptotic? Does the culture variable provide enough "bang for the buck" that it justifies the costs of pursuing it to the detriment of other influence variables?

From soldiers to senators, the efficacy of redoubling U.S. efforts at cultural sensitivity are being questioned. Dr. R.S. Zaharna, a communications professor from American University and contributor to this handbook, was asked to testify before the Senate Foreign Relations Committee. When she explained that the ire of Islamic nations was aroused by American "lack of cultural sensitivity," Senator Biden pounced. Calling her testimony "meaningless," Biden said: "This notion of cultural sensitivity, which is real, obviously doesn't get us much . . . If countries in Europe are less sensitive to Muslim interests in their countries, and yet are viewed better than we are, obviously cultural sensitivity is not a defining element of how we are viewed." Later he added that cultural sensitivity "is always good, but it's marginal."[19]

Al-Qaeda is universally acknowledged for its ability to effectively manipulate the information environment, and many commentators believe they are winning the information war around the world, attracting sympathizers even in the United States.[20] Are they doing this through sophisticated cultural understanding of, and adaptation to, their Western targets? Unlikely. They reject Western culture and Western thought. To our knowledge, they are not utilizing cultural subject matter experts or employing significant Western cultural adaptation in their messaging. Their successes in the influence wars isn't attributable to sophisticated cultural targeting; they are communicating and influencing through simple and crude universals—often speaking in their native tongues and relying on someone else to translate!

In a parallel phenomenon of cross-cultural effectiveness, witness the remarkable popularity of American political consultants and campaign methodology throughout the world. Consultant James Carville managed campaigns for Greek Prime Minister Constantine Mitsotakis; Brazilian President Fernando Enrique Cardoso; Honduran Prime Minister Carlos Flores; President Jamil Mahuad of Ecuador; British Prime Minister Tony Blair; and Prime Minister Ehud Barak of Israel. Consultants Dick Morris and Rob Allyn led Vicente Fox to victory in Mexico. Boris Yeltsin hired three of California Governor Pete Wilson's campaign advisors—George Gorton, Joseph Shumate, and Richard Dresne—who later helped elect Arnold Schwarzenegger to Wilson's previous office. Consultant Mark Mellman has been active in campaigns in Uruguay and Russia, helped elect Cesar Gaviria to the Columbian presidency. Consultant Frank Luntz recently advised Prime Minister Romano Prodi on his successful campaign in Italy. Philippine candidates have been hiring American consultants since Marcos' 1969 campaign.[21] From 1998 to 2000, U.S. political managers and consultants were estimated to make up 58% of the total hired in Latin America, 40% in Eastern Europe, 30% in Western Europe, and 23% in Russia.[22] These consultants were hired based on their effectiveness as influence agents, not their understanding of foreign cultures. Certainly these American consultants employed cultural tuning in their campaigns to some degree, but we can assume they used the influence tactics abroad that worked at home. And indigenous minds were apparently persuaded in large numbers by these consultants' "foreign" tactics.[23]

We should also ask whether indigenous influence tactics, when they can be identified, are necessarily beneficial to winning a global influence war. Tactics which may be locally appropriate can be reviled on the world stage. Three examples come to mind. First, the placement of stories in the Iraqi media by the Lincoln Group, the topic of considerable discussion in December of 2005.

While "pay-for-play" media is considered unethical in the United States (despite notable lapses),[24] it was culturally adaptive to Iraqi media standards, where placed news stories were commonplace. Second, both presidents Bush have held hands with male Arabic friends. While this is culturally appropriate in Arabic countries as a display of friendship, the practice is seen as smacking of homosexuality in the United States—Michael Moore even used hand-holding footage in *Fahrenheit 9/11* to denigrate the president to movie audiences. Third, taunting one's enemy in Arabic cultures is a long-standing cultural practice. However, after an Australian film crew captured footage of U.S. soldiers in 2005 who were using loudspeakers to taunt the Taliban with phrases such as "Taliban, you are cowardly dogs!" "You are the lady boys we always believed you to be!" and "Come out and fight like men!" the issue inflamed world opinion against the U.S.[25] In response, the military banned the use of taunting messages, which had proven both culturally indigenous and effective in provoking the enemy to engage. Pallid, pre-approved, and politically correct pre-recorded messages were substituted (to unknown effect, but the effects of pre-recorded messages are generally less than live messages).[26] Certainly there are significant examples where accurate cultural tuning backfires at home and on the world stage, when local influence tactics are seen as inappropriate. Overhearing audiences apparently do not give influence agents the benefit of the doubt when using culturally tuned tactics, but instead hold influencers to their own cultural standards. It may be that the safest influence tactics are those that share common currency across cultures.

Some observers point to the paucity of cultural message tuning evident in cross-cultural communications from Russia, China, and Islamic countries, and wonder whether the intense focus on culture is unique to Western democracies with ethnically diverse populations, following the U.S. fixation on cultural diversity, racial quotas, ethnic sensitivity, minority set-asides, affirmative action, and other culture-based issues that are notably absent in many (or perhaps most) world cultures, including Islamic ones. Within the American chattering classes, "cultural diversity" is a revered panacea. It may be that the ingrained values of the Western academic echo chamber are responsible for the call to redouble efforts on cultural sensitivity in the information wars. Ironically, the American veneration of culture may be a significant point of cultural non-adaptation—another American oddity that puzzles the rest of the world.

So the question of how much weight to accord the variable of culture in the influence equation deserves consideration. Social psychologist Thomas Pettigrew has documented the human propensity to attribute strange and negative in-group behavior to situational causes. People tend to believe that the external environment dictates an in-grouper's bad behavior. On the other hand, humans tend to attribute an outgroup member's strange and negative behavior to internal (dispositional, racial, or genetic) reasons.[27] Over-attributing causality to nationality or culture may be a parallel human bias. Yet different cultural software doesn't imply different cognitive hardware. In every culture we encounter *humans* who encounter reality in similar ways, whose brains process information in human ways, and who are vulnerable to common biases and errors of thought the world over. And I believe that psychology can offer even more useful information than the first two seasons of *The Sopranos*!

The dissatisfying generality that emerges from studies of culture and cognition is that both commonalities *and* differences are found, supporting the idea of culture as a significant moderator[28] rather than a variable that fundamentally changes the processes of human cognition. R.C. Mishra, a cultural psychologist who studies cognition, writes: "A widely shared view in cross-cultural psychology today is that cognitive processes are universal, shared by all populations, . . . [but] we find evidence in many societies about the existence of cognitive goals that sharply differ from those valued in western societies."[29] This helps explain many interesting culture-difference findings, such as the study that found Liberian rice farmers could estimate different amounts of rice with 1–2% error, whereas working-class American adults were sometimes wildly inaccurate, overestimating the amount of rice in one case by 100%. Occam's razor applies here—we don't need to attribute this disparity to cultural differences in cognitive processing, when differences in experience and goals would suffice.[30]

The common-yet-different compromise to culture and cognition is echoed by many cultural researchers. Peter Smith writes, "General functions are more likely to yield cultural universals, while specific functions are more likely to prove culturally distinctive. A similar distinction can help to make sense of diverse research findings in many areas of cross-cultural psychology."[31]

Professor Nyiti writes: "While children in different cultures may have to deal with different realities, they all apply the same operations or processes of thought."[32] And values researcher Milton Rokeach notes: "All men possess the same values to different degrees."[33] Among cultural psychologists, the idea of universal human cognitive processes are alive and well—they're just not particularly fashionable. So a model espousing that "everything changes" from culture to culture is considered by many to be too simplistic to be useful; to overemphasize selected elements of the whole; and the model's implications—that we must jettison any non-indigenous psychology—to be rash.

Slouching Toward Complexity

Consider the more complex and, I believe, more realistic model put forward by Professors Kluckhohn and Murray: "Every man is in certain respects (a) like all other men, (b) like some other men, and (c) like no other man."[34] This statement implies three important perspectives that the influence agent must master:

(1) "... *Like all other men* ..." refers to universals of human behavior. The famous psycho-therapist Harry Stack Sullivan insisted that humans are much more similar than they are different. Humans share a genetic code—a common human hardware—which makes the entire species vulnerable to certain influence approaches. For example, a long-term study of successful sur-render themes by Johns Hopkins University discovered that physical hardship, group cohesive-ness, and commitment to ideology are trans-cultural predictors of surrender.[35] A recent review of U.S. PSYOP products notes that "The vast majority of them are exceedingly straightforward and demonstrate little guile or cultural specificity."[36] It would be difficult to imagine that many of the stock-and-trade strategies of influence research, such as reward and punishment, or fear appeal, or value alignment, or decontextualization, or narrative, or messages based on dual-process theory, would be rendered inert due to unique cognitive styles found in particular cultures.[37] The cognitive hardware that we share is universal, but the ability to harness it is not intuitive. It does not follow that each of us has an innate, intuitive command of persuasion, simply because we are human (although this is commonly assumed).

By way of analogy: I use a computer every day, so I feel I know how to use my PowerBook pretty well. Yet all I really do is manipulate different software programs. I have no knowledge of how to reprogram or rewire the computer so it will function differently than it does now. I rely on expert programmers to manipulate the hardware so the computer is useable. Likewise, it's been demonstrated with certainty that we humans have limited insight into our own "hard-ware," despite the fact we *feel* we do.[38] Humans show a tremendous capacity for rationalization, if not rationality. Thus, the need for expertise in basic human hardware: the agent who attempts to understand, predict, and control typically human thoughts and behaviors.

(2) "... *Like some other men* ..." refers to the social instinct in humans. We are like others in the many groups to which we belong: our kin, our region, our nation, our religion, our ethnicity, our culture, our gender, our career, our age, our ideology. These similarities are studied by the demographer, the sociologist, the culturalist, and by some anthropologists, who make generaliza-tions at the group level. They offer the influence agent important and useful insights. Each group association provides incremental information that helps predict and control human behavior with additional precision. Although nationality is a grouping method frequently emphasized as vital to the exercise of political and military influence, it is but one of many. For half a century,

the leading practitioners of commercial market segmentation have been advocating segmentation strategies that go beyond simple demographic variables such as ethnicity, geographic location, and nationality, because by themselves they "are poor predictors of behavior and consequently are less than ideal bases for segmentation strategies."[39] Yet persistent cognitive biases cause differences in ethnicity, nationality, and culture to loom large during conflict: "They are so different from us," thinks the typical human embroiled in dispute.[40] This line of thinking is counterproductive to effective persuasion when it causes influence agents to overlook human similarities, because locating commonalities is an important building block of successful persuasion.[41]

(3) "... *Like no other man* ..." refers to each human's unique traits and personality. The clinical psychologist and the personologist excel in understanding humans as unique individuals, and their information is valuable when trying to predict and control the behavior of specific people, such as the opposition's leadership. Person variables often overwhelm universal and group variables. Professor Robert Gass, another contributor to this volume, is the author of several popular influence texts. He writes: "I don't think culture is as important as it is sometimes made out to be. It is a factor, as are gender, socioeconomic status, demographic differences, etc., but culture is not *the* factor. Individual differences almost always swamp gender and cultural differences in persuasion."[42]

These three perspectives—universal, group, and individual—do a good job of triangulating on the human mind. The influence practitioner would add a fourth: the external environment, which is known to have profound effects on behavior. The famous psychology author David Meyers writes:

> Social science's most important lesson concerns how much we are affected by our environments ... when explaining someone's behavior, we often underestimate the impact of the situation ...[43]

While more accurate, this four-part model presents a considerably more complex formula than primacy-of-culture does, which emphasizes cultural understanding as the key to influence success. But complex human behaviors gone awry require sufficiently complex solutions.

Influence Universals Masquerading as Cultural Specifics

Regarding the ability of influence principles to generalize across cultures, it's important to remember that intercultural psychology places a premium on finding differences, not similarities, between cultures. And humans—including researchers—tend to find what they expect to find.[44] Publishing a study that says, "It appears this effect is pretty much the same in every culture we studied" doesn't generate the interest or garner the publicity of a study that says, "Look at these interesting differences between cultures!" You can sometimes see this "difference bias" when the title of a paper trumpets differences among cultures, but a careful read of the paper demonstrates that the cultures studied are remarkably uniform. So it's a safe bet that found differences will be more prominently featured in cultural psychology than found similarities, because of the way that academia rewards the pursuit of statistically significant research.[45] This is not good news for persuasive agents, since commonalities are the coin of the influence realm. Below are a few cautionary examples of the "dog and dog" variety.

A study of value systems among American vs. Japanese citizens concluded: "These data provide further support for the view that people in the West emphasize individualistic values, while those in the East prefer communal values."[46] Yet the correlation of rank ordering of values by Americans and Japanese was reported at $r=.80$, $p<.0001$; that's a whopping correlation supporting similarity, in a field where correlations of $r=.40$ are considered "large." Yet the *differences* were reported! A cultural researcher writes, "Studies of conformity in Japan have found . . . stronger influence among groups who already knew one another than among groups who were previously unacquainted with each other."[47] This finding is common knowledge to the Western influence researcher, since known others with an established track record are more trustworthy and persuasive in Europe and North America, too.[48]

Some cultural researchers believe that the problem of intercultural replicability supports primacy-of-culture approaches, based on an Israeli[49] and a Brazilian[50] program of research that attempted to replicate an across-the-board (i.e., not focusing on influence) sampling of single-study U.S. social psychological findings. The Israeli research replicated 24 of 64 findings (with main effects replicating more frequently than interactions, hinting at statistical power problems).[51] The Brazilian research reported about half of U.S. findings were successfully replicated. At face value, the percentages sound underwhelming, but these numbers likely tell us more about research methodology, than they do about the psychology of humans across cultures.[52] We cannot establish 100% replicability (or anything close to it) as the comparison point for within-culture replications—to which many frustrated researchers can attest. My informal survey of U.S. social psychologists estimating successful replication percentages *within culture* yielded a range from "typical" at 48% to those considering ideal replication conditions, who gave numbers as high as 80%. In this light, the Brazilian program's findings appear to be within the expected range, and could be considered as support for universalism rather than primacy-of-culture. The important point is that there are a number of methodological reasons why we can't assume that failures of single studies to replicate are evidence that people of diverse cultures have different psychologies. Only a sustained research program with multiple successes or failures for each effect, using high-power studies, would be informative.

A cross-cultural review of upward-directed social influence in the corporate world references a study that discovers indigenous Chinese influence tactics "not tapped by prior U.S. measures."[53, 54] Three of the more interesting "indigenous" tactics discussed in the review included praising the target behind his back, showing consideration for the target's face needs, and working overtime. Yet these are hardly unknown tactics to Western influence researchers, who study them under the headings of ingratiation, face, and exchange or reciprocity. And not only are Western influence researchers in the loop; legions of Western employees engage in these same "Chinese" behaviors to influence the boss.

The problem of viewing universals as cultural specifics doesn't just exist in academia. Below are a few examples from public diplomacy and the military.

In citing key problems with U.S. public diplomacy during the Iraq war, an analyst asserts that:[55]

1   U.S.-style mass-media information dissemination programs aren't effective in the Arab world, which prefers relationship-centered, face-to-face communications. However, it is well known that the same effect holds in the U.S.: face-to-face messages trump mass-media appeals when they're compared.[56]

2   U.S.-style one-way messages are less effective in Arab cultures than are two-way, relationship-building approaches. However, the same effect holds in the U.S.; dialog-style influence is superior to monologue for persuasion.[57]

3   the U.S. prefers facts and statistics, whereas Arabs prefer metaphors and analogies. However, the *base-rate fallacy* was discovered by studying Western subjects, and it states a similar principle: that dramatic stories and examples usually trump fact and statistic.[58] In fact, a recent meta-analysis found the overall correlation between evidence and persuasion *in the U.S.* to be a miserly $r = .18$—hardly evidence of a preference for fact and statistic.[59]

4   direct, confrontational speech in public settings is considered face-threatening in Arab cultures, but "cheered" in U.S. cultures. However, U.S. studies indicate that direct,

confrontational, face-threatening communications engender reactance, reduce influence dramatically, and cause it to "boomerang."[60]

As an influence consultant, I would not have recommended any of these four "U.S. preferences" for a U.S. audience, because the research literature does not support any of them. Likewise, culture differences really don't belong in this conversation of preferred influence styles. Occam's razor shaves again.

Regarding the "Shock and Awe" theme in the Iraq war, retired General Anthony Zinni said, "The biggest mistake the United States made in the war was speaking of 'shock and awe.' That was a way to say: 'Your fate is inevitable. We're going to crush you. The might of America will defeat you. Just surrender and throw down your arms.' You don't speak to Arab pride and Arab manhood in this way. That whole psychological business gave them another cause to fight for, more than they would have fought just for Saddam."[61] While General Zinni correctly identified the reactance phenomenon (one of the major and universal engines of influence), his remarks made it sound as if it were uniquely Arab to resist the message: "Just surrender and throw down your arms." In fact, we would expect *most* cultures to react against a message that said, "Your fate is inevitable. We're going to crush you." For example, in 1956, Khrushchev told U.S. ambassadors: "Whether you like it or not, history is on our side. We will bury you!" In so doing, many commentators believe that Khrushchev unwittingly stoked the Cold War, hastening the USSR's eventual demise. Zinni was correct that a heavy-handed threat of force would not appeal to Arab pride and manhood—but to whose pride and manhood (or basic personhood) *would* such a message appeal? Are we humans so different from each other?

At a NATO conference,[62] a speaker from PSYOP strategic studies discussed a "watershed cultural blunder" that occurred in Afghanistan in October of 2005. According to the speaker, two Taliban were killed after they had ambushed a U.S. patrol, and leaders from the nearest Afghani village did not wish to take possession of the bodies. After a few days, the U.S. lieutenant in charge of the bodies decided to incinerate them—health considerations were later given for this decision. The incident infuriated Muslims, for whom the burning of bodies is taboo. The speaker commented that the lieutenant in charge likely had insufficient cultural training, and recommended more cultural training that emphasized "respect, respect, respect." As an audience member, I wondered why this incident was considered a cultural, rather than a human, blunder. Is it uncommon for the enemy's burning of bodies to be psychologically inflammatory? When have U.S. soldiers or citizens ever been cheered by the news that our countrymen have been immolated by the enemy? If a taboo is shared rather universally by mankind, why would we expect cultural training to highlight it?

During a discussion of culture's impact in one of my university classes, a soldier who had completed a tour of duty in Iraq spoke up. "People in Iraq are really different than we are," he said. "When I was in Mosul, I worked with an Iraqi counterpart. We seemed to get along pretty well, despite the differences of culture. Then one day, out of the blue, this guy gives me a bag of vegetables! He just puts them on my desk! Now what was I supposed to do with a big bag of vegetables?" Another student in the class said, "You were probably supposed to reciprocate." "Interesting you should say that," said the soldier. "When I got that bag of vegetables, I had a talk with our cultural expert about what it meant, and that's what she said I should do—give this guy some food in return. So the next day I gave him a box about the same size as the bag he gave me, filled with food. Seemed to work out pretty well." I pointed out that the soldier's story actually highlighted the universal norm of reciprocity,[63] more than the uniqueness of Iraqi culture. In what culture, I asked, would it be *inappropriate* to reciprocate to a peer with a gift similar to the one you received? "That's not my point," he said. "It's that he gave me *vegetables*. Now that's something that would seldom ever happen in the States." Whether or not you agree with the soldier's statement (personally, I've received vegetables as gifts!), here is an unambiguous example where a working knowledge of universal human psychology would have resolved a seemingly mysterious "foreign" behavior. The Iraqi was trying to start a relationship by giving a gift, and with his gift he was speaking in a universal language that the soldier did not understand—another example of the "dog and dog" problem, where a surface difference obscured a deep similarity.

Of psychological universals, culture researchers Smith and Bond write: ". . . In order to establish these universals, theorists have needed to formulate their concepts at a relatively high level of abstraction . . . whether it is the generality or the specificity that can offer greater value to psychology remains open to debate."[64] In my experience, examples *abound* that indicate the practicality and usefulness of generalities that Smith and Bond call "high levels of abstraction" (although I would argue they are actually mid-levels of abstraction). If an influence practitioner were asking my advice, I would recommend understanding the universals of human psychology first, and *then* supplementing them with cultural knowledge—especially when fast action pays dividends. Expensive adjustable sights on a pistol are of little use if the shooter is wobbly. A steady hand and fixed sights are more accurate. A steady hand and adjustable sights are the most accurate. Get in range with universals, and *then* adjust with cultural specifics to increase influence success.

To this point, Dr. Greg Seese, a psychologist who writes doctrine for PSYOP, notes: "Not understanding culture is a barrier, but a bigger barrier is not understanding basic human psychology."[65] We *know* we don't know the other's culture—that's obvious, so we focus on it; but we *don't know* that we *don't know* the reasons for our *own* behavior. That's one reason why culture tends to be overemphasized, and universals tend to be underemphasized, particularly during conflict. We assume the universals of behavior are simple and obvious (when in reality they are neither), and therefore not worthy of investigation. We focus instead on how different the other is.

Examining the Influence Replications

And now for a second way to answer the question: "What evidence do you have that these influence tactics will work anywhere else in the world?"[66] For quantitative answers, we turn to intercultural replications of influence studies, where the same or similar studies have been conducted in multiple cultures. We are of course interested in influence research here, not group dynamics, leadership, or other neighboring areas of social science.[67] Fortunately, Smith and Bond have reviewed a number of influence research lines cross-culturally, and the conclusions I present regarding the experimental replicability of influence paradigms across diverse cultures rely in many places on their excellent work of collecting and reporting these studies.[68]

Cultural replications are valuable but rare, and sometimes my students seem irritated at this fact—as if it's somebody's fault that more intercultural replications are not available! But here are some of the difficulties:

First, nobody in one country can direct someone else in another country to replicate a study. Indigenous researchers do replications if they find the research line to be compelling, for reasons of their own.

Second, there's not much academic cachet in repeating someone else's research, especially if your findings duplicate theirs. In general, academic reputations are not made by successfully replicating others' research, although reputations *can* be made by challenging existing research (the rewards are for finding differences, again). This also explains why many replications will tweak a variable or two, so the researchers don't have a mere replication, but something new to add to the literature. These "tweaks" wreak havoc with the ability to compare apples to apples, interculturally.

Third, the priority of indigenous research is often aimed at pressing local problems—only wealthy countries with time, subjects, and researchers to spare can indulge themselves in large, philosophical questions such as "What are the universals and particulars of influence?"

Fourth, if a replication is conducted, it can't be considered definitive, because no single study is—multiple studies are needed to get an accurate fix on social phenomena, especially since social science research chronically suffers from a lack of statistical power to detect effects.

Fifth, it's hard to tell if the concepts have translated accurately to another culture—intercultural research is prone to the "dog and cat" problem discussed earlier, where two researchers who believe they are studying the same thing, are actually studying different things.

Sixth, because of these reasons, when an intercultural replication does occur, it may be conducted decades after the original study was done. The mills of intercultural social psychology grind slowly, but—well, mostly just slowly.

These are the reasons that intercultural replications are relatively rare and valuable. Caveats aside, let's take a look at three bellwether influence studies, and one study of cultural values that's often referred to by intercultural influence practitioners. Their ability to replicate in diverse cultures should give us a sense of our bearings:

- In the 1950s, Solomon Asch conducted a series of research studies designed to establish a baseline of conformity within the US.[69] Conformity was one of the "hot topics" that was a legacy issue from WWII. A popular conception at the time was that Germans and Italians were racially predisposed to be obedient and conformist—how else could one explain fascism, after all? And so primacy-of-culture explanations loomed large, as they so often do when cultures are in conflict. Asch had set out to establish a baseline of conformity (or its absence) in the US, and was surprised at the high levels of conformity he actually achieved. Asch placed a real subject among six confederates who gave obviously incorrect answers on a simple matching task. The result—about 37% of responses were affected, conforming to the obviously wrong group answer. Approximately three-quarters of subjects gave at least one wrong, conforming answer during the experiment. This research spawned a great deal of interest and many replications. For 98 known replications in North America, the average effect size was calculated at .95—a large effect size.[70] For 19 studies conducted in Europe, an average effect size of .80 was calculated—also a large effect size, but a little smaller than the North American sample, and the smallest regional effect size overall. (Ironically, this group included "those conformist Europeans" that motivated this line of research!) Other regions may be viewed in the table below. In summary, the size of the conformity effect goes from "large" in Western cultures, to "larger" elsewhere. Because of its ease of replication and the interest it generated, the Asch paradigm is probably the most thoroughly replicated influence study in existence.

Nation	# Studies	Effect Size
Europe	19	.80 (large)
North America	98	.95 (large)
Arab	2	1.3 (very large)
South America	3	1.6 (very large)
Asia	8	1.7 (very large)
Africa	3	1.8 (very large)

- Muzafer Sharif, his wife Carolyn, and several other researchers conducted the classic "Robber's Cave" study in Oklahoma, where they took two groups of a dozen boys each to the Robber's Cave State Park.[71] Phase One of the study allowed campers some time to develop in-group friendships. In Phase Two, the two groups were introduced to each other in competitive situations—rivaling for sporting victories, prizes, etc. Hostility between the two groups developed rapidly, and became so intense that Phase Two had to be ended early. Phase Three attempted to create cooperation between the warring groups, utilizing the tactic of superordinate goals. For example, the chuck wagon "broke down" in the mud, and it required the muscle power of both groups to help free it, so the boys could eat; a movie theater could be rented for the boys only if they all contributed money, etc. These super-ordinate goals successfully ignited cross-group friendships, and at the end of the experiment, the boys insisted they all ride home in a single bus. This complex and expensive experiment was replicated in the UK, in Lebanon (with Christian and Muslim children), and in Russia. Unfortunately, the UK experiment utilized pre-existing groups of boys, introducing an experimental confound. However, all four nations found that in-group favoritism intensified in Phase Two, after competitive interaction. Competition increased hostility toward out-groupers in three of the four nations (not the UK, perhaps because the pre-existing groups had already arrived at stable judgments regarding the other group). Superordinate goals decreased hostility in the US, UK, and Russia, but the Lebanese experiment had to be aborted before Phase Three could be invoked, because it was discovered that one group of boys had stolen knives to "settle scores" with the other group during Phase Two. These results are indicative of the challenges encountered in complex cross-cultural research, but the main effects in these studies replicated where the original methodology was followed, and where data were available.

Contains:	US	UK	Lebanon	Russia
Newly Formed Groups Used	Yes	No	Yes	Yes
In-group Favoritism Found	Yes	Yes	Yes	Yes
Competition Increases Hostility	Yes	No	Yes	Yes
Superordinates Increase Cooperation	Yes	Yes	Experiment Ended Early	Yes

- Stanley Milgram studied obedience to authority with a clever series of experiments that asked the question, "On the directive of an authority figure, how much obedience may be obtained from normal people who are asked to do something that increasingly conflicts with their conscience?"[72] Subjects in this study were assigned to be "teachers," whose job it was to punish a "learner" for mistakes on a memory task by giving the "learner" an electric shock. Shocks were to be administered in increasing voltages for successive errors, and the "shock-box" had switches ranging from 15 to 450 volts—the larger voltages more similar to electrocution than corrective shock! The "learner," who was not actually connected to the shock generator, was in fact an actor who had memorized a script, at various voltages telling the "teacher" that he was having heart trouble, later screaming in pain, later demanding release, and later losing consciousness as the shocks got progressively more intense. The smock-jacketed experimenter was also in the room, but his script was limited to a few innocuous sounding phrases, all encouraging the "teacher" to continue with the experiment. The "teacher" subjects were not constrained, and could end the experiment at any time by simply refusing to proceed, or walking out. Psychologists were asked to estimate the number of people shocking the hapless "learner" to the end of the scale; they estimated around 0.1%. Laypeople were also asked to guess, and their responses averaged 1–2%. In striking contrast to uninformed estimations (with professionals an order of magnitude more inaccurate than novices), Milgram obtained 65% compliance in the main condition of his study. These results were so unpleasant, and so against the views that most people held of themselves, that Milgram's research was attacked repeatedly by scientists and by journalists. He therefore engaged in dozens of replications of his research, as did others, to answer the objections that were voiced: "Certainly women would not behave like this" (they did);[73] "Certainly people would not behave like this in more modern times" (they do);[74] "Certainly my nationality would not behave like this" (see the graph of Milgram-like replications); and of course, the perennial and unanswerable objection, "This research is unethical."

Country	Percent Obedient
USA (1963, males)	65%
USA (1963, females)	65%
Italy (1968)	85%
Germany (1971)	85%
USA (1974)	85%
UK (1977)	50%
Jordan (1978)	62%
Spain (1981)	>90%
Austria (1985)	80%

The above list represents the Milgram-like replications that were fairly true to the original.[75] Viewing these results is somewhat like a projective test: Do you see a remarkable consistency of human behavior across time and nationality, as would a universalist? Do you see dramatic differences when comparing selected responses to others, as would a culturalist?[76] Or do you see the "same-yet-different" compromise referred to earlier? Either way, we can agree that these results are fundamentally different from what psychologists and lay-people predicted regarding the average person's behavior, before knowing the results of Milgram's studies.

- Geert Hofstede published a seminal work on values and culture in 1980. His factor analyses of values revealed four fundamental value dimensions that existed among the 53 cultures he had studied.[77] At the time his data was collected, he was unable to obtain data from the USSR or from China, so his analysis was open to criticism for not being representational. A group of researchers called the Chinese Culture Connection[78] thought Hofstede's work, particularly the questionnaire he used, was biased toward Western cultures. So the CCC had Chinese subjects list Chinese values of importance, and the study was replicated with a Chinese-generated questionnaire in 23 cultures. Despite the differences of cultural origins, time, gender ratio, subject pool, and experimenter desire to see cultural differences emerge, the analyses once again yielded four factors, three of which duplicated Hofstede's. The fourth was dubbed "Confucian Work Dynamism" by the CCC, and Hofstede, eventually incorporating it as a fifth dimension, called it "Long Term Perspective."

In addition to replication research, there are also a host of studies that examine cultural influence differences within single studies. While single studies can seldom be considered definitive, they provide important data that moves the field forward. One's impressions of the applicability of influence tactics across cultures is therefore determined by which studies one has read, and one's own biases, so a broad and clear statement of "same" or "different" puts a person on a precarious limb. New research could at any moment sever the limb—and the reputation of the commentator. That aside, my current, subjective call is that the research I have read in the field of intercultural influence does not deviate notably from the variance found within the studies reviewed above. For my own purposes, I have found the "same-yet-different" compromise more useful than either primacy-of-culture or strict universalist approaches.

For reasons mentioned earlier, intercultural research celebrates differences rather than similarities, and the "rock stars" of intercultural research are *reversals*—where the psychological effects of one culture lie in the opposite direction of another. Reversals are rare within intercultural influence research at this time. Currently, we are not seeing research regarding indigenous influence tactics that are unique to certain cultures, and which are unknown or counterproductive in others. This is not to say they don't exist. There are documented reversals in neighboring fields of social science,[79] so we can't expect reversals not to occur within the influence canon. When they are discovered, influence agents will of course need to incorporate them into intercultural influence paradigms.[80]

There is clarity about one point. The data do not support the contention that, when in another culture, *everything changes*. Humans are, after all, humans—the world over. As Harry Stack Sullivan said, "We're all more human than otherwise." It appears that Western influence research can often get us "within range" in other cultures, and perhaps score the occasional dead-on hit.[81] Certainly we have witnessed other cultures scoring influence hits in our culture, without the benefit of sophisticated message adaptation. Misses should not automatically be attributed to a misunderstanding of culture—witness the agonizingly high number of ineffective ad campaigns within cultures, produced by and for people belonging to the same culture.[82] The current evidence doesn't support the idea that culture alters fundamental cognitive processes. Neither does it support discarding existing influence research and starting from the ground-up in each culture.

A Comparison of Predictions

When teaching students about the "same-yet-different" nature of intercultural influence, I have often referred to a study of some notoriety by Morris, Podolny, & Ariel.[83] This study examines the nature of reciprocal obligations in four nations: China, Germany, Spain, and the US, and it asks the question: "Do the laws of obligation and reciprocity work differently in different cultures?" The authors used a primacy-of-culture approach to predict who would most likely be helped by an employee in a multinational retail bank. Using national characteristics to predict with whom a person would most likely engage in reciprocal behavior, the six choices were: a powerful person, a person linked to a powerful person, a friend, someone linked to a friend, a coworker, and a superordinate (the "boss"). The authors considered the following national characteristics when making their predictions:

- Chinese: Obligation is characterized by "sacrifice for the group," showing "a kind of collectivist solidarity." Exchange hinges on the answer to the question, "Do you have power over me or ties to those who do?"
- German: Obligation was thought to be moderated by "a legal bureaucratic orientation," with exchanges depending on the answer to the question, "Am I officially supposed to assist you?"
- Spanish: Obligation is governed by "strong norms of warm sociability," noting that Spanish friendships "are high in affective intensity and longevity." Exchanges depend on the answer to the question: "Are you my friend or a friend of my friend?"
- North American: Obligation is governed by "whether it profits their individual achievement goals," adding, ". . .the paragon of the successful American has been the person who leaves the group or disrupts the social order." The question of exchange hinges on the answer to: "What have you done for me lately?"

Based on a primacy-of-culture approach, the researchers predicted responses for each nationality (standing in for culture), and obtained data. How well did the primacy-of-culture predictions fit the data? The researchers accurately predicted 16 of 24 cells within the experiment, a hit rate of 67%:

Morris, Podolny & Ariel (2001): Comparisons of Prediction & Results (Predictions based on "primacy-of-culture")

	US	HK	Germany	Spain
Powerful		Predicted		
Linked to Powerful		Predicted		
Friend	Predicted			
Linked to Friends				Predicted
Coworker				Predicted
Superordinate	Predicted	Predicted	Predicted	
	US	HK	Germany	Spain
Powerful	Actual	Actual	Actual	
Linked to Powerful	Actual	Actual		
Friend	Actual		Actual	Actual
Linked to Friends	Actual			
Coworker			Actual	
Superordinate	Actual	Actual	Actual	Actual
	US	HK	Germany	Spain
Powerful	Miss	Hit	Miss	Hit
Linked to Powerful	Miss	Hit	Hit	Hit
Friend	Hit	Hit	Miss	Hit
Linked to Friends	Miss	Hit	Hit	Miss
Coworker	Hit	Hit	Miss	Hit
Superordinate	Hit	Hit	Hit	Miss

16/24 = 67% Accuracy

After having taught this study several times, I began to wonder, what would the hit rate of a universalist's predictions be? Several colleagues agreed that a universalist would not make complex cultural distinctions, but would rather make across-the-board, simple predictions for three targets of obligation: Powerful people, friends, and superordinates. So performing a conceptual replication was a simple task of changing the matrix of predictions:

The universalist approach accurately filled 18 of 24 cells, yielding a hit rate of 75%—a few points better than the primacy-of-culture approach. This is only one example, and post-hoc at that, but it illustrates the importance of questioning the utility of cultural generalizations, and the amount of additional predictability actually gained via primacy-of-culture approaches.

Conclusions

Intercultural psychology, even the attenuated portion devoted to influence psychology, represents a massive amount of theory and data. Clearly this behemoth can't be tamed and caged by one person's perspective. The investigation is also young, so we should expect conceptions of intercultural influence to develop in the coming years, refining and changing the generalities of our time. For now, each person must come to his or her own conclusions regarding the amount of weight to accord the variable of culture in the complex equation of human influence. These are the conclusions I've drawn for myself.

Culture looms large as a causal explanation of human behavior, particularly when cultures are in conflict. Other important influence variables are prone to be overlooked when culture domin-

Morris, Podolny & Ariel (2001): Comparisons of Prediction & Results (Predictions based on theories of "universiality")

	US	HK	Germany	Spain
Powerful	Predicted	Predicted	Predicted	Predicted
Linked to Powerful				
Friend	Predicted	Predicted	Predicted	Predicted
Linked to Friends				
Coworker				
Superordinate	Predicted	Predicted	Predicted	Predicted

	US	HK	Germany	Spain
Powerful	Actual	Actual	Actual	
Linked to Powerful	Actual	Actual		
Friend	Actual		Actual	Actual
Linked to Friends	Actual			
Coworker			Actual	
Superordinate	Actual	Actual	Actual	Actual

	US	HK	Germany	Spain
Powerful	Hit	Hit	Hit	Miss
Linked to Powerful	Miss	Miss	Hit	Hit
Friend	Hit	Miss	Hit	Hit
Linked to Friends	Miss	Hit	Hit	Hit
Coworker	Hit	Hit	Miss	Hit
Superordinate	Hit	Hit	Hit	Hit

18/24 = 75% Accuracy

ates the influencer's view. As "difference" is emphasized, the potential of ignoring commonality increases.

Culture is probably best thought of as an important moderator of psychological effects, rather than a variable that fundamentally changes human psychology. We should not expect the established canon of influence psychology to be rendered impotent in the face of a particular culture. Reversals of social influence effects are rare, with some increasing in effectiveness in non-Western cultures. For increased accuracy and predictability within cultures, indigenous research is beneficial and should be pursued.

As humans, we are both similar to and different from each other. But the social sciences have clearly demonstrated the limitations of human intuition when attempting to access our common cognitive and emotive processes; so asking one's self, "How would I respond?" to access these psychological universals falls far short. Programmatic research coupled with practical experience indicates the way forward.

When approaching a culture, of which one has little knowledge or mutual history, it is of course important to locate or develop cultural expertise. When resources allow, culture should be considered in conjunction with other group-level variables, with human universals, with environmental inducements and constraints (and with individual particulars when possible). Universal influence tactics enjoy the advantages of broad application, quantifiable track records, and speedy deployment. The latter is important when the adversary is rapidly capitalizing on events to capture mindshare.

In persuasion, culture becomes increasingly important as the message approaches the target. In other words, the tools of influence used at the home office to create lines of persuasion (such as demonstrating the suffering of innocents in order to put international pressure on an opposing military force) may be based on effective universals. However, the message and messenger benefit from cultural tuning at the point of delivery. But we cannot expect the most brilliantly conceived and delivered message to neutralize a fundamentally disliked product or policy.

This last point serves as a reminder that successful influence requires a blend of theory and methodology, because neither the theoretical checklist nor the empirical questionnaire is as powerful as the two combined.

Notes

1 Solomon Asch, "Effects of group pressure on the modification and distortion of judgments," in *Groups, Leadership and Men*, ed. H. Guetzkow (Pittsburgh, PA: Carnegie, 1951).
2 Peter B. Smith and Michael Harris Bond, *Social Psychology Across Cultures* (Boston, MA: Allyn & Bacon, 1999, 2nd edition).
3 Culture is not synonymous with nationality, or language, or geographic region, but the latter are easier to quantify, and are often substituted in practice. It's difficult to find quality research that actually uses culture, rather than geography or nationality, as an independent variable. Culture is a slippery term: How big or small is a culture? Within any identified culture, can't it be broken down into further unique, homogenous cultures? How far down should the cultural division go—does it reach as far as tribes? Neighborhoods? Families? Individuals? How useful is a term to the sciences if it is not easily quantified?
4 Herbert Klein, "Cognition in Natural Settings: The Cultural Lens model," in *Cultural Ergonomics: Advances in human performance and cognitive engineering research*, Volume 4, ed. Michael Kaplan (Greenwich, CT: JAI Press, 2004), 249–280.
5 T. Skinner, "Shaping Influence," *Jane's Defense Weekly*, August 23, 2006.
6 Christopher J. Lamb, "Review of Psychological Operations Lessons Learned from Recent Operational Experience," National Defense University Occasional Papers, http://www.ndu.edu/inss/Occas-sional_Papers/Lamb_OP_092005_Psyops.pdf.
7 Often subsumed under discussions of "linguistic relativity" today.
8 Lorand B. Szalay and J.E. Brent, "The analysis of cultural meanings through free verbal associations," *Journal of Social Psychology*, 72 (1967): 161–187. See also Lorand B. Szalay and James Deese Hillsdale, *Subjective Meaning and Culture: An assessment through word associations* (Hillsdale, NJ: Lawrence Erlbaum Associates, 1978).
9 Geoffrey K. Pullum, *The Great Eskimo Vocabulary Hoax and Other Irreverent Essays on the Study of Language* (Chicago: University of Chicago Press, 1991).
10 Wikipedia entry for "Gender-neutral Pronoun."
11 Ethnic segmentation is considered to be a crude form of segmentation by sophisticated marketers, who often prefer usage, lifestyle, and value-based segmentation strategies that go beyond less-useful ethnic, racial, and geographic segmentation strategies. See G. Tellis, *Advertising and Sales Promotion Strategy*, (Reading, MA: Addison-Wesley, 1998).
12 The cultural lens model is an interesting amalgam of various theoretical dimensions of variance among cultures, and proposes that cultural lens training "can enable practitioners to see the world through the eyes of someone from a different nation." See Herbert Klein, "Cognition in Natural Settings: The Cultural Lens model," in *Cultural Ergonomics. Advances in human performance and cognitive engineering research* Volume 4, ed. Michael Kaplan, 249–280.
13 R.S. Zaharna, "The Network Paradigm of Strategic Public Diplomacy" (Silver City, NM & Washington, DC: Foreign Policy In Focus), *Policy Brief* 10 no. 1 (2005): 2, http://www.fpif.org/briefs/vol10/v10n01pubdip.html.
14 Kevin Mulcahy, "Interview with former USIA Director Joseph Duffey," *The Journal of Arts Management, Law & Society*, Spring 1999.
15 Livia Markóczy, "Us and Them," *Across the Board* 35 no. 2 (1998): 44–48.
16 Livia Markóczy, "Are cultural differences overrated?" *Financial Times*, July 26, 1996, 10.
17 J. Barucky, B. Karabaich and B. Stone, "Notes from Evaluation of Cross Cultural Models for Psychological Operations: Test of a Decision Modeling Approach," USAF Research Laboratory, 2001. This study asks five subject matter experts to propose several lines of persuasion and then to guess, based on their experience, the extent to which those lines of persuasion would be effective in various cultures.

The study is actually more an investigation into how SME intuition functions relative to culture, than it is a study of cultural differences.

18 Frank Reidy, e-mail message to author, April 27, 2005. Reidy also inspired the paragraph regarding Al-Qaeda's lack of cultural sophistication.

19 American Public Diplomacy and Islam. Transcript from Panel Two of a Hearing of the Senate Foreign Relations Committee, February 27, 2003. http://www.iraqwatch.org/government/us/hearings preparedstatements/us-sfrc-panel2-022703.htm.

20 "Is Al-Qaeda Winning the War?" *Jane's Intelligence Digest*, May 27, 2004. Of course, examples of this thesis abound.

21 Y. Chua, "With a Little Help from (U.S.) Friends," Special Election Issue, The Campaign, http://www.pcij.org/imag/2004Elections/Campaign/consultants.html.

22 Fritz and Gunda Plasser, *Global Political Campaigning: A Worldwide Analysis of Campaign Professionals and Their Practices* (Westport, CT: Praeger Publishers, 2002). See also: S. Bowler and D. Farrell, "The internationalization of campaign consultancy," in *Campaign Warriors: Political Consultants in Elections*, ed. James Thurber and Candice J. Nelson (Washington, D.C.: Brookings Institution Press, 2000), 153–74.

23 This insight came from political consultant, public relations strategist, and reserve PSYOP officer Mark Myers, see http://www.e-magination.com.

24 It's ironic that the *Los Angeles Times* broke the Lincoln Group Iraqi media placement story. In 1999, the *LA Times* arranged a profit-sharing venture with the nearby Staples Center, whereby the *LA Times* promoted the Staples Center in news copy, and then benefited financially from Staples Center revenues. The *LA Times* isn't alone in making questionable arrangements for self-benefit—recall CNN's pre-war agreement to censor all Saddam atrocity stories.

25 "Taliban Burning Claims Probed," *The World News*, October 23, 2005.

26 NATO JSPOC, Hurlburt Field, FL, Dec 5–8, 2006. Nonattribution rules were in place, thus the omission of the speaker's name.

27 Thomas Pettigrew, "The ultimate attribution error: Extending Allport's cognitive analysis of prejudice," *Personality and Social Psychology Bulletin* 5 (1979): 461–476.

28 A moderator is a variable that modifies the relationship between two other variables. For example, an individual finding himself in the close proximity of a cohesive group is more likely to conform to that group, but even more so in Asian cultures than in Western ones. In this case, culture is a moderator of the main effect of conformity.

29 R.C. Mishra, "Cognition Across Cultures," in *The Handbook of Culture and Psychology*, ed. David Matsumoto (Oxford: Oxford University Press, 2001), 119.

30 Occam's Razor refers to a goal in the sciences for simplicity over needless complexity. Explanations of reality should "shave off" assumptions that aren't necessary. The source for the rice study is J. Gay and M. Cole, *The New Mathematics and the Old Culture* (New York: Holt, Rinehart & Winston, 1967).

31 Peter B. Smith, "Cross-Cultural Studies of Social Influence," in *The Handbook of Culture and Psychology*, ed. David Matsumoto (Oxford: Oxford University Press, 2001), 366.

32 R. Nyiti, "The validity of 'cultural differences explanation' for cross-cultural variation in the rate of Piagetian cognitive development," in *Cultural Perspectives on Child Development*, ed. Daniel Wagner and Harold W. Stevenson (San Francisco: WH Freeman, 1981), 146–165.

33 Milton Rokeach, *Understanding Human Values* (New York: Free Press, 2000).

34 Clyde Kluckhohn and Henry A. Murray, *Personality in Nature, Culture and Society* (New York: Knopf, 1948).

35 U.S. Army Operations Research Office, *Psychological Warfare and Other Factors Affecting the Surrender of North Korean and Chinese Forces* (Washington, DC: Johns Hopkins University Operations Research Office, 1953).

36 Christopher Lamb, *Review of Psychological Operations: Lessons Learned from Recent Operational Experience* (Washington, D.C.: National Defense University Press, 2005), 113. Dr. Lamb's comment appears to be an observation on the current state of U.S. PSYOP. It is probably also a criticism regarding insufficient cultural tuning of PSYOP product, when other comments throughout his paper are considered.

37 These are approaches familiar to influence practitioners, and can be found in most influence textbooks. Decontextualization removes an event or behavior from its surrounding context, usually in an attempt to make the event or behavior look bad. Value alignment "repackages" an argument so it aligns with the target audience's value system. Narrative venues are lines of persuasion that have been worked into stories. Dual-process theories, such as Petty & Cacioppo's ELM and Chaiken's Heuristic-Systematic model, propose that humans are persuaded through two fundamentally different routes, depending on how involving the target finds the topic.

38 There are many demonstrations of the failure of human introspection. Nisbett and Wilson 1977 is an excellent example, giving case after case of humans misunderstanding the causes and motivations of their

own behavior. R. Nisbett and T. Wilson, "Telling more than we can know: Verbal reports on mental processes," *Psychological Review* 84 (1977): 231–259. A perpetual embarrassment for the field of psychology is that Freud is considered its modern founder. Freud went off-track in many ways, and some of his difficulties can be traced to his methodology. He employed reflection and intuition, rather than experimentation, as his primary methodology. One of the most interesting themes in psychology is the inability of humans to understand their own cognitive processes by "reflecting" upon them. In a nutshell, humans have little access to their cognitive processes, and it has only been by the slow and agonizing process of experimentation—including random samples, holding variables constant, employing statistical analyses, etc.—has the field made progress.

39 Russell I. Haley, *Developing Effective Communications Strategy: A Benefit Segmentation Approach* (New York: Wiley, 1985). 3. Hayley notes that demographic information (variables such as race, gender, age, geographic location, etc.) accounts for only about 5% of "micro-behaviors" (referring primarily to the consumption of certain brands). Haley claims that psychographic segmentation, which includes more psychological variables, doubles that number. He notes wryly that segmentation "still leaves a substantial amount of room for improvement."

40 Differences loom large during conflict, causing humans to overlook commonalities. "Differentiation is typical during intergroup conflict. Rather than noticing shared similarities, the groups tend to emphasize their differences," Donelson R. Forsyth, *Group Dynamics* (Boston, MA: Wadsworth Publishing) 388.

41 Persuasion—not compliance, which does not have the same common ground needs as persuasion. Regarding the fundamental nature of commonality to successful persuasion, many influence textbooks devote a chapter to the importance of similarity and commonality. *Bargaining for Advantage* by Richard Shell (2006) contains an elegant chapter addressing the importance of finding common ground.

42 Robert H. Gass and John S. Seiter recently published the third edition of their popular textbook, *Persuasion, Social Influence, and Compliance Gaining* (Boston, MA: Allyn & Bacon). The quote is from personal correspondence with the author.

43 David Meyers, *Social Psychology*. In this quote, Meyers is referring to the human bias called the "Fundamental Attribution Error" or the "Correspondence Bias."

44 Thomas Gilovich, *How We Know What Isn't So: The Fallibility of Human Reason in Everyday Life* (New York: Free Press, 1993).

45 The politics of academic publication give an outsized advantage to statistically significant findings over nonsignificant ones. (It's important to note that statistical significance is not the same as importance, although it's often treated that way. It's possible to discover a trivial, yet statistically significant finding.) Statistical significance is merely a way of saying the findings of a study have conformed to a certain level of confidence that the results aren't merely a fluke. A finding that can claim statistical significance is much more likely to be published. Yet nonsignificant findings may be very important, too, but their chances of being published are slim, because a nonsignificant finding may mean either it could be a chance finding (in which case we don't care to know about it) or that the effect in reality is not there (in which case, we'd want to know this information). The problem is, there's no way to determine which of these two options a nonsignificant finding represents. The Achilles heel of social science, sometimes called "the file drawer problem," is that studies not finding effects often get thrown in the file drawer, so nobody knows how many times an effect has been sought and not found. Imagine, for example, that 20 researchers decide to focus on a politically hot topic that's likely to get them attention and media coverage if they can find the effect they seek. Let's say these 20 researchers test to see if women are in fact better than men at math. Now assume 19 of those studies do not show a significant female superiority in math, but one does. Nineteen go into the file drawer and one gets published—perhaps to eventually show up in the media, or as the basis of legislation. This is why I recommend to my students to be very cautious about studies that support highly politicized stances. One never knows how many studies looked for the effect and failed. You never hear the media say, "In tonight's news, one new study that shows women are actually superior in math skills to men . . . but nineteen other studies didn't."

46 D. Akiba and W. Klug, "The different and the same: Reexamining east and west in a cross cultural analysis of values," *Social Behavior and Personality*, 1999, 27(5), 467–474.

47 Peter B. Smith, "Cross-Cultural Studies of Social Influence," in *The Handbook of Culture and Psychology*, ed. David Matsumoto (Oxford: Oxford University Press, 2001), 364.

48 Richard Perloff, *The Dynamics of Persuasion*, (New Jersey: Erlbaum, 2003, 2nd edition).

49 Y. Amir and I. Sharon, "Are social-psychological laws cross-culturally valid?" *Journal of Cross-Cultural Psychology*, 18 (1987), 383–470.

50 A. Rodrigues, "Replication: A neglected type of research in social psychology," *Interamerican Journal of Psychology*, 16 (1982), 91–109.

51 Interactions (where the DV "differences are different," depending on levels of the IV) are less likely to replicate across the board, because they simultaneously represent a higher level of complexity and diminished statistical power to attain them. When interactions don't replicate, but main effects do, the researcher is correct to suspect problems of statistical power.

52 A low replication rate across cultures does not surprise seasoned researchers, for methodological reasons, not psychological ones. Considering statistical power alone, let's be optimistic and imagine the original and replication studies both had power of .80 (a high standard that many studies do not attain). The chances of two studies finding the same real effect would then be 64%, even if the procedures, experimenters, and subjects were identical. The methodologist Jacob Cohen points out that low power (caused primarily by small sample size) is a chronic problem in the social sciences, causing real effects to frequently go undetected. In fact, Cohen calculated that if an effect were really there to be found, the typical social sciences study would have about a 48% chance of detecting it with a single study—chances that are a little worse than a coin-flip. If Cohen's estimate is correct, that means the average chance of two studies finding the same real effect, all else being identical, would be 23%. Small sample sizes, poor operationalizations, non-interval data, less-than-perfect translations, different research conditions, and other methodological differences would only serve to drive the number down—so we cannot expect high replication numbers for purely methodological reasons alone, and it would be erroneous to conclude that a failure to replicate the typical single study supports a "difference-of-culture" conclusion.

53 Peter B. Smith, "Cross-Cultural Studies of Social Influence," in *The Handbook of Culture and Psychology*, ed. D. Matsumoto (Oxford: Oxford University Press, 2001), p. 367.

54 Sun H. and M. Bond, "The structure of upward and downward tactics of influence in Chinese organizations," in J. Lasry, J. Adair and K. Dion (eds.), *Latest Contributions to Cross-cultural Psychology* (1999), pp. 286–299.

55 R.S. Zaharna, "The Unintended Consequences of Crisis Public Diplomacy: American Public Diplomacy in the Arab World," *Foreign Policy in Focus*, June 2003.

56 R. Rice and C. Atkin, *Public Communication Campaigns*, (Newbury, CA: Sage, 1989). This book provides many examples of the effectiveness of FTF appeals, compared to mass media appeals. The caveat here is that mass media appeals, while less powerful compared to FTF appeals, are considerably more efficient in terms of reach, and may be the only tool available when FTF communicators are in short supply.

57 D. Canary, M. Cody and V. Manusov, *Interpersonal Communication* (Boston: Bedford, 2003). The chapter on Listening is particularly germane.

58 R. Nisbett, E. Borgida, R. Crandall and H. Reed, *Popular Indication: Information is not necessarily informative* (1976).

59 J.B. Stiff, "Cognitive processing of persuasive message cues: A meta-analytic review of the effects of supporting information on attitudes," *Communication Monographs*, 53 (1986), 75–89. In J.S. Carroll and J.W. Payne (eds.), *Cognition and Social Behavior* (Hillsdale, NJ: Lawrence Erlbaum, 1986), pp. 113–133.

60 G. Thompson, *Verbal Judo: The Gentle Art of Persuasion* (New York: Harper Collins, 2004).

61 "'The wrong war at the wrong time,' former mideast envoy maintains," *The Buffalo News*, April 4, 2003. See also: http://www.vaiw.org/.

62 NATO JSPOC, Hurlburt Field, FL, Dec 5–8, 2006.

63 Alvin Gouldner's research was seminal in documenting that all cultures conform to the rule of reciprocity. A.W. Gouldner, "The norm of reciprocity: A preliminary statement," *American Sociological Review*, 25 (1960), 161–178.

64 P.B. Smith and M.H. Bond, *Social Psychology Across Cultures* (Boston: Allyn & Bacon, 1999), p. 96.

65 Author's personal correspondence with Dr. Seese.

66 Some readers may be wondering, can an American even address the topic of influence in other cultures? For that matter, can a man be a gynecologist? Can a black attorney represent a white defendant? Can a septuagenarian possibly be a good pediatrician?

67 This is an important point, because some reviews of cross-cultural influence do not appear to distinguish between influence and other types of social research. For example, the chapter found in Matsumoto's 2001 *Handbook of Culture and Psychology*, entitled "Cross-cultural Social Influence," includes group dynamics, leadership theories, explicit negotiation, and conflict resolution—topics which receive scant, if any, attention in mainstream textbooks on influence psychology. Some authors, finding large cultural differences and even reversals in neighboring and non-influence areas of psychology, then argue for primacy-of-culture perspectives on influence as well.

68 P.B. Smith and M.H. Bond, *Social Psychology Across Cultures* (Boston: Allyn & Bacon, 1999).

69 Asch, S. E. (1955). Opinions and social pressure. *Scientific American*, pp. 31–35. Asch, S. E. (1956). Studies of independence and conformity: A minority of one against a unanimous majority. *Psychological Monographs*, 70.

70 Effect sizes tell researchers how "large" the effect is, how much impact it has, or how important it is. One

advantage of effect sizes over measures of significance is that effect sizes are not affected by the number of subjects in the study. A rough guide for these effect sizes: small = .2; medium, = .5; large = .8.

71 Sherif, M., Harvey, O. J., White, J., Hood, W., & Sherif, C. (1961). Intergroup Conflict and Cooperation: The Robber's Cave Experiment. Norman: University of Oklahoma, Institute of Social Relations

72 Stanley Milgram (1963). Behavioral study of obedience. *Journal of Abnormal and Social Psychology*, Vol. 67, pp. 371–378. Also see: Stanley Milgram (2004). Obedience to Authority: An Experimental View. New York: Harper Collins.

73 "Who are more obedient—men or women? Milgram found an identical rate of obedience in both groups—65%—although obedient women consistently reported more stress than men. There are about a dozen replications of the obedience experiment world-wide which had male and female subjects. All of them, with one exception, also found no male-female differences." See http://www.stanleymilgram.com

74 Thomas Blass analyzed the Milgram research available, spanning 25 years from 1961 to 1985, to see if obedience tapered off as humans "become more sophisticated," as so many people like to believe. The answer is 'No'—no correlation between obedience levels and year exists. Humans are humans, after all, despite the passage of time. See: Blass, T. (1999). The Milgram paradigm after 35 years: Some things we now know about obedience to authority," Journal of Applied Social Psychology, Vol. 25, pp. 955–978.

75 Unfortunately, a number of Milgram-like intercultural replications made significant changes in the methodology, such as substituting verbal criticism for shocks, or significantly changing the appearance and similarity of the victim, or asking only women to shock another woman. These changes were probably made to avoid clean replications of the original, which helps the researcher get published, but is problematic when trying to understand intercultural differences.

76 I generally refuse to present this research to international audiences, after bad experiences in the past, where people object strenuously to high compliance scores posted for their nationality. Interestingly, audience objections generally follow those raised years ago to Asch & Milgram's original work.

77 Hofstede G (1980). Culture's Consequences.

78 Chinese Culture Connection (1987). Chinese values and the search for culture-free dimensions of culture. Journal of Cross-cultural psychology, 18, 143–164.

79 For example, the social loafing phenomenon within group dynamics research has been observed to reverse in some Asian countries (Karu & Williams, 1993) and in Israel (Earley, 1993) with participants working harder in groups, than as individuals. However, this effect has also been found in the US, where "social facilitation" is known to occur for simple and well-learned tasks. In negotiation, problem-solving approaches appear to induce reciprocation in some cultures, but provoked other cultures to take advantage. (Graham, Mintu & Rodgers, 1994).

80 Incorporate them how? is the next question. If there *were* unique, indigenous influence tactics, would it necessarily be wise to use them? Given that modern communication technologies make it difficult to influence anywhere in the world without the rest of the world hearing about it, how would those influence tactics play to a world audience? For example, pay-for-placement in the Iraqi media is culturally sensitive—it's how things are done in Iraq. Yet the Western media—despite occasional indulgences in similar practices (*LA Times* profit sharing with the Staples Center, CNN spiking anti-Saddam stories, *NYT's* Jayson Blair, CBS's forged documents)—blew a gasket over this culturally-adapted influence tactic, causing the Allies to lose additional traction in the info wars. Might it be that the universals of influence would still be the safest tools of choice, even if culturally unique influence tactics were discovered?

81 Certainly the reader will distinguish policy from influence technique!

82 This problem is hotly discussed among advertisers in industry magazines and books with titles like: What Sticks? Why Most Advertising Fails & How to Guarantee Yours Succeeds. A current review estimates a 37% failure rate in US advertising campaigns that are designed by and for Americans. See Neff, J. (2006). Half of your advertising isn't wasted – just 37%. Advertising Age, Vol. 77, Issue 32.

83 Morris M, Podolny J, Ariel S. (2001). Culture, norms, and obligations: Cross-national differences in patterns of interpersonal norms and felt obligations toward coworkers. In Wosinska et al. (Eds.), The Practice of Social Influence in Multiple Cultures. Mawah NJ: Erlbaum.

84 Portions of this paper were written while images of the civilian dead of Qana were being broadcast.

15

Military Psychological Operations as Public Diplomacy

Mark Kilbane

To subdue the enemy without fighting is the acme of skill.

—Sun Tzu, 4th century B.C.E.

Public diplomacy (PD) may be defined as how governments manage their presence abroad. The University of Southern California's Center on Public Diplomacy defines PD as traditionally including "government-sponsored cultural, educational and informational programs, citizen exchanges and broadcasts used to promote the national interest of a country through understanding, informing, and influencing foreign audiences." The Center reminds us not to disregard a nation's "soft" power—its oblique yet powerful foreign influence through movies, music, popular culture, and business advertising.[1] It's no secret that the United States is not the most popular team in town in most of the rest of the world—Europeans sneer at us, Islamists condemn us. So American PD may be viewed as the formal effort by the U.S. government to polish its scuffed-up image overseas: to change how foreigners see and understand us.

Five U.S. agencies are responsible for PD. They are the Broadcasting Board of Governors (BBG), the Department of State, the U.S. Agency for International Development (USAID), the White House (through the National Security Council), and the Department of Defense (DoD). A May 2006 Government Accountability Office report reveals where the money goes: "Funding is concentrated in State and BBG, which together received approximately $1.2 billion for public diplomacy in fiscal year 2005. USAID and DOD have relatively small public diplomacy budgets."[2]

Most U.S. citizens are unaware that DoD has both historical precedent and a codified responsibility to influence foreign audiences, a task it handles largely through Psychological Operations, or "PSYOP" (no plural). PSYOP units are tasked to present messages to the indigenous population and foreign combatants in their area of operations—their Target Audience—in order to influence emotion and attitude, and thus behavior. The U.S. military defines PSYOP as "Planned operations to convey selected information and indicators to foreign audiences to influence the emotions, motives, objective reasoning, and ultimately the behavior of foreign governments, organizations, groups, and individuals."[3]

The definitions of PD and PSYOP overlap—both employ information to influence foreigners. How this is accomplished and the end goals of each may differ, however. "U.S. public diplomacy plays an important role in national power," says Lt. Col. Angela Maria Lungu. "[M]ilitary PSYOP can be used to exercise public diplomacy within the scope of military operations."[4]

PSYOP 101

To most people PSYOP is shrouded in mystery known to them only through Hollywood plots. Even veteran journalist Peter Bergen falls into this mold when he refers to Ali Mohammed, the Egyptian with links to al-Qaeda, who enlisted in the U.S. Army. Bergen mentions Mohammed's training with the Special Forces "in such esoteric subjects as 'psy-ops.'"[5] In the film *The General's Daughter*, starring John Travolta, the writers add a dash of intrigue by adorning the dress uniform of the femme fatale officer he falls for with the purple lapels of the PSYOP branch.

Yet the PSYOP operator is an advertising, media, and marketing professional, not James Bond. These missions, like all military operations, are carried out at the strategic, operational, and tactical levels. Overall military authority for PSYOP is derived from the National Command Authority, or NCA, composed of both the President and the Secretary of Defense.

PSYOP teams accomplish their mission at the tactical level by using leaflets, radio and television broadcasts, loudspeakers that can be transported by vehicles or rucksacks, posters, and old-fashioned face-to-face communication to get their points across. Technology has changed how PSYOP personnel do business, and now cell phones and SMS text messages are part of the turf. The internet remains off-limits because the Smith-Mundt Act of 1948 forbids U.S. propaganda from being used domestically, and the internet can be accessed anywhere.

Most U.S. PSYOP personnel are concentrated in the Army—the other services have limited staff. At this writing there are roughly 3500 Army PSYOP personnel in one active and two reserve groups, all under sub-commands of the Special Operations Command. The active duty 4th PSYOP Group at Ft. Bragg, NC constitutes a quarter of the Army's PSYOP force, and is organized into six battalions: four with specific regional expertise, a tactical PSYOP battalion, and a dissemination battalion. The Group also has a strategic studies detachment that includes civilian area experts. The bulk of the remainder of the Army's PSYOP force is divided between the 2nd and 7th reserve Groups, each of which have four battalions scattered throughout the U.S.

Propaganda?

So aren't we talking about that loaded word, *propaganda*? Iconoclast political scientist Harold Lasswell argued in the *Handbook of the Social Sciences* that propaganda "is no more moral or immoral than a pump handle." This will-it-cut-down-trees sentiment aside, propaganda connotes false information disseminated to deceive and demoralize a battlefield enemy, or to twist truth to control naïve masses into committing or accepting any kind of heinous behavior. History has demonstrated that this can be done well: Goebbels and Stalin.

Indeed, the term *propaganda* is ordinarily "associated with armed conflict," according to an Army field manual on PSYOP operations and tactics.[6] So is the U.S. capable of disseminating propaganda? Of course—the U.S. and the Soviet Union engaged in propaganda and counter-propaganda campaigns during the Cold War from the 1950s to the 1980s. The PSYOP manual describes three types of propaganda: white, gray, and black. White propaganda accurately states the source of the piece and delivers factual information, building credibility. With gray propaganda, as its title suggests, the source is ambiguous and thus the veracity of the content is put in doubt. Black propaganda is the most notorious—it is falsely attributed. Although the color scheme refers to the identification of the source itself, when the source is misrepresented the product is likely to be fabricated. Modern technology, such as audio and video editing software, can make all three forms of propaganda sophisticated. Black, white, and gray elements are enshrined on the escutcheons of the three PSYOP groups and the JFK Special Warfare Center itself.

Three of the four crests also declare *veritas*—same as Harvard. A skillfully executed truthful, or white, PSYOP campaign is vastly more useful and effective than black propaganda. Once a government is discovered in a lie, all credibility is lost. Thus, the vast majority of U.S. PSYOP campaigns employ accurate, verifiable information, even if selectively presented. "Truth is always the most powerful tool when using PSYOP in military operations," states the PSYOP manual.[7]

PSYOP Approval and Oversight

"It's called civilian oversight," says PSYOP Col. Jack Summe, commenting on the PSYOP approval process. "Although PSYOP are a military capability—it has political impact," he says.[8] Precisely because the ability of governments to influence masses has been egregiously misused in history, U.S. PSYOP programs are tightly controlled. PSYOP are subject to an armful of laws and regulations, from Geneva and Hague Conventions to Status of Forces agreements, government directives, regulations, official instructions, and host nation laws. Large-scale programs must be approved by the NCA after numerous agencies, Joint Chiefs, Under Secretaries, and ambassadors have had their chops. The programs are very specific about how and to whom authority is given to produce a PSYOP product. "You don't just print a leaflet and hand it out. Everyone has to work together. There are rules," says retired PSYOP expert Sgt. Maj. Herbert Friedman. "There are FMs [Field Manuals] and ARs [Army Regulations] that recommend what may and may not be depicted or discussed. It ain't the 'wild west.'"[9]

Does It Work?

"Many who work in public diplomacy would not be comfortable considering their work as aligned with what 'boots on the ground' may be doing in combat or crisis zones," says Nancy Snow, a senior fellow at the USC Center on Public Diplomacy.[10] The U.S. citizenry have always found PSYOP somewhat distasteful—dirty pool. Yet it is widely accepted that PSYOP played a spectacular role in the 1991 Gulf War by encouraging 70,000 of Saddam's troops to surrender en masse. Leaflets were dropped over their formations with a message stating that the next day at an exact time the mother of all bombs was to be dropped on them. Yet if they were to lay down arms and head toward Mecca they would be fed and spared a senseless death. The next day at the precise time announced, the U.S. dropped several BLU-82 15,000-pound bombs. Then they dropped the same leaflets and hit the loudspeakers, announcing the attack for the following day. Thousands of Iraqi soldiers surrendered, clutching the leaflets high in their hands.

Subtle as a sledgehammer—but it worked. "Overall, PSYOP in Desert Storm was among the most successful media-based campaigns ever undertaken," reads a PSYOP case study. "Coalition determination to stick to truthful overt PSYOP . . . proved successful in inducing thousands of early surrenders."[11] Although it is difficult to ascertain just how effective any PSYOP campaign is, surrendering Iraqi soldiers reported that the PSYOP campaign did influence them.

As far as the quality of PSYOP products is concerned, journalist Collin Berry pokes fun at the cartoonish depictions. "As design documents, PSYOPs range from amateurish to just plain awful—somewhere between a Chick religious tract and a ball-point drawing made on the back of a Pee-Chee folder," Berry says. But he admits that they are hastily mass produced in difficult settings and that "PSYOPs are credited with saving thousands of lives."[12] To be fair, Iraqi cartoons are of similar quality, and PSYOP designers often mimic the style of the host nation.

The military does the job it is created to do quite well, i.e., to fight and win wars, but struggles when tasked with missions outside its core competence. PSYOP radio and television spots in Iraq today are widely known to be ineffective. "Mass media campaigns are notoriously poor at generating attitude shifts," says Nancy Snow. Oftentimes PSYOP has not been effective outside a standup fight, for example, in Somalia and Kosovo. What about PSYOP in Iraq today?

Current Situation

The conflict in the Middle East is the great struggle of our time. For better or worse, the 150,000 coalition troops in the area are the first contact most Muslims have ever had with Westerners.[13] What we do and how we are perceived are critically important. The U.S. military has had to adapt from their conventional warfighting role to a less familiar one of nation building and asymmetrical warfare. The situation in Iraq and Afghanistan today has moved into what the military calls Phase IV, the post-conflict stage, which shifts more from tactical PSYOP into strategic communication, information operations, and PD. In the Middle East today PSYOP personnel often are charting new territory.

PSYOP effectiveness in Iraq has received mixed reviews. Washington national security journalist Jason Vest observed that "PSYOPS weren't all they were cracked up to be. Part of this had nothing to do with quality . . . there weren't enough of them."[14] During a 2005 defense department town hall meeting, former Secretary of Defense Donald Rumsfeld admitted that PSYOP "is not something we do very well in our country."[15] The turgid approval process mentioned above is a serious stumbling block to exploiting opportunities. "Coalition information operations are a shadow of their opponents'," says Andrew Garfield, senior fellow at the Foreign Policy Institute. He claims the coalition "handicaps itself with its own approval process."[16]

There are also charges that American PSYOP do not employ cultural awareness. Anthropologist Edward Kurjack wonders whether PSYOP may have been more useful if its operators were thinking outside of the box: "The American side could claim that it is bringing freedom to the Shiites in southern Iraq. Why were there no appropriate Arabic quotations from the Koran stenciled on the American tanks?"[17]

Operation *Iraqi Freedom* has seen unprecedented levels of outsourcing military missions to civilian contractors in the forward theater. PSYOP branch got on the bandwagon by hiring several PR firms to handle production and dissemination of PSYOP-type material in-theater. These media concerns, including the established Science Applications International Corporation, were contracted and managed by a new outfit called the Joint Psychological Support Element (JPSE), created in 2004 and composed of about 60 people, over half of whom are in Army uniform.

JPSE says it was created to provide a trans-regional element to complement the 4th Group's rigid area-specific expertise. Critics say JPSE was set up to speed PSYOP into the theater and circumvent rigid approval processes by using civilian entities. PSYOP had deniability. Immediately this got the DoD into hot water. One of the contractors, the Lincoln Group, was collecting true positive information, calling it news, and printing it without attribution—gray propaganda. Lincoln Group, led by young executives with somewhat murky origins, has landed multimillion dollar contracts. *Washington Post* reporter Lynne Duke, who interviewed Lincoln Group, claims that we are even in a war *over* the information war, "over techniques such as Lincoln's and the extent to which the U.S. government should or does disseminate propaganda, even pay to publish favorable 'news' stories."[18]

> **Figure 15.1: Why Public Diplomacy Practitioners Should Understand PSYOP**
>
> — *"PSYOP are a vital part of the broad range of U.S. diplomatic, informational, military, and economic activities." (Joint Psychological Operations manual)*
> — *The U.S. military's outsourcing of PSYOP has spawned a burgeoning cadre of experts in media messaging and influence operations with hands-on knowledge of local nuance and language skills. Many of these civilian positions are occupied by former PSYOP officers. These personnel may be staffing positions of leadership in the rest of the federal government's PD operations.*
> — *The conflict in the Mideast and the dichotomy between the West and Islamic fundamentalism isn't going away. The bulk of the U.S.'s PD efforts will be directed toward the Mideast, and PSYOP personnel are already working there.*
> — *The 4th PSYOP Group's Web site states "The ultimate objective of U.S. military psychological operations is to convince enemy, neutral, and friendly nations and forces to take action favorable to the United States and its allies." Doesn't U.S. public diplomacy share this objective?*
> — *3500 PSYOP personnel work presenting U.S. messages in dozens of sovereign nation-states. What kind of forward presence does the rest of the public diplomacy world have?*

Quo Vadis?

PD practitioners have fought an uphill battle in the U.S. "Public Diplomacy is slow and may take years to realise," writes British Lt. Col. Steven Collins. "Even when large sums of money are allocated to the task and skilled personnel recruited . . . positive achievements may be scanty."[19] Charlotte Beers, brought in from Madison Avenue to head the State Department's PD program after 9/11, resigned shortly after running a Middle East media campaign that flopped. Karen Hughes, the energetic and charismatic Under Secretary for Public Diplomacy and Public Affairs, was crippled by a relatively small budget and staff, and has now resigned.

The U.S. needs more than a Michelle Kwan goodwill tour of China as its PD. It needs a large-scale, concentrated effort that combines the best of our culture with the energies of bright personnel in the branches of government most suited to public diplomacy—and PSYOP can be part of that equation.

A comic book about landmine awareness, developed for Central America in 1998, serves as an example of how different entities can cooperate with U.S. military PSYOP in a tangible way overseas. Researched by the 1st PSYOP Battalion from Ft. Bragg, it was produced in collaboration with DoD, Time Warner's DC Comics, and UNICEF. Army Special Forces, U.S. embassies, foreign governments, and the staff of UNICEF distributed the book and printed 170,000 posters in Spanish.[20]

Already deployed in the forward theater, PSYOP troops may provide a stopgap measure to cover the slow pace of conventional PD. Bolstering U.S. interests may occur by combining efforts of a host of actors, including civilian public affairs firms, nongovernmental organizations, private volunteer organizations, Department of State, USAID, host nation officials, ambassadorial staff, and multinational corporations. The integration of all these elements into a cohesive U.S. foreign policy, effected by a decisive presidential mandate, will benefit the image of the U.S. and promote world stability. The deficiencies PD faces with metrics and long-term development may be offset by PSYOP's immediacy and forward presence. Working together, PSYOP can lay the groundwork in a new zone, coordinate with other agencies, and PD can take over in the long term.

Notes

1 University of Southern California, Center on Public Diplomacy website, http://www.uscpublicdiplomacy.com/index.php/about/whatis_pd.

2 GAO Report, "U.S. Public Diplomacy: *State Department Efforts to Engage Muslim Audiences Lack Certain Communication Elements and Face Significant Challenges*," Report to the Chairman, Subcommittee on Science, the Departments of State, Justice, and Commerce, and Related Agencies, Committee on Appropriations, House of Representatives, May, 2006, 5, http://www.gao.gov/new.items/d06535.pdf.

3 Joint Publication 3–53, *Doctrine for Joint Psychological Operations*, September 5, 2003, ix, http://www.dtic.mil/doctrine/jel/new_pubs/jp3_53.pdf.

4 Maj. Angela Maria Lungu, "War.Com: *The Internet and Psychological Operations*," United States Naval War College, Newport, RI, Feb 5, 2001, 2, http://stinet.dtic.mil/oai/oai?verb=getRecord&metadataPrefix=html&identifier=ADA389269

5 Peter L. Bergen, *Holy War, Inc.*, New York: Touchstone, 2002, 130.

6 Field Manual 3–05.301, *Psychological Operations Tactics, Techniques, and Procedures*, Headquarters, Department of the Army, Washington, DC, December 31, 2003.

7 Ibid., 8–18.

8 Col. Jack Summe, interview by author, September 7, 2006.

9 Sgt. Maj. Herbert A. Friedman, personal communication.

10 Nancy Snow, personal communication.

11 Col. Frank L. Goldstein and Col. Benjamin F. Findley, Jr., eds., *Psychological Operations: Principles and Case Studies*, Maxwell Air Force Base, AL, Air University Press, 1996, 350.

12 Colin Berry, "Fighting Words," *Voice: AIGA Journal of Design* online article, December 10, 2004, http://www.aiga.org/content.cfm/fighting-words.

13 Michael E. O'Hanlon and Nina Kamp, Iraq Index: *Tracking Variables of Reconstruction & Security in Post-Saddam Iraq*, Brookings Institution, Washington, D.C., March 19, 2007, 20, http://www.brookings.edu/iraqindex.

14 Jason Vest, "Missed Perceptions," GovernmentExec.com, December 1, 2005. http://www.govexec.com/features/1205–01/1205–01s5.htm.

15 Marty Kauchak, "Winning the War of Ideas," Special Operations Technology online edition, August 16, 2005, http://www.special-operations-technology.com/article.cfm?DocID=1070.

16 Andrew Garfield, "The U.S. Counter-propaganda Failure in Iraq," *Middle East Quarterly*, Fall 2007, http://www.meforum.org/article/1753.

17 Edward B. Kurjack, personal communication.

18 Lynne Duke, "The Word at War: Propaganda? Nah, Here's the Scoop, Say the Guys Who Planted Stories in Iraqi Papers," *Washington Post*, March 26, 2006, D01, http://www.washingtonpost.com/wp-dyn/content/article/2006/03/25/AR2006032500983_pf.html.

19 Lt. Col. Steven Collins, "Mind Games," *NATO Review*, summer 2003, online journal, http://www.nato.int/review.

20 June 1998 DoD press release, in *Field Manual 3–05.30*, 6–8.

Part 4

State and Non-State Actors in Public Diplomacy

American Business and Its Role in Public Diplomacy

Keith Reinhard

Those who think public diplomacy is not the business of business should think again. Even those who believe the only goal of business is to return profit to its shareholders might have to agree that a world in which 18 percent of consumers in G8 countries already say they avoid buying American brands[1] is at least a threat to that primary goal. American business, especially the growing number of American multinationals that derive more than half their revenue from markets outside the U.S., need a world that welcomes American goods and services. That's the first reason U.S. corporations should play a role in public diplomacy. It's in their own self-interest. Whatever U.S. corporations can do to lift America's reputation will eventually lift the prospects for American business.

The second reason U.S. corporations should take up the challenge of restoring our country's battered image is that American business leaders are for the most part American citizens. It is therefore their patriotic duty to address their country's urgent need—call it "Business Patriotism," to borrow a phrase from Pete Peterson, Chairman of the Board of Directors, Council on Foreign Relations.[2] It's also true that in addressing certain public diplomacy challenges business has a great advantage. At least for now, it can be argued that U.S. business is more credible than the U.S. government and more skilled, more efficient, and possessed of more global savvy. When *natural* disasters strike, American business is often the first to respond with goods, services, and money. The same sense of urgency and commitment should drive a business response now to America's *national* disaster, our country's plummeting reputation across the globe.

America's Reputation is at an All-time Low

Numerous global public opinion surveys, from the Pew Center, GFK Roper, Zogby, Harris Interactive, and other firms, have documented the worsening of public attitudes toward America over the past decade or so. A global survey commissioned by the BBC World Service and released in early 2007 confirms how grave the situation has now become.[3] To quote directly from the BBC article that accompanied the survey results:

> The global image of the US has significantly deteriorated over the past 12 months, as the chaos in Iraq has deepened. And in 18 of the countries that were involved in previous polls, the slide in America's standing has steepened . . . This poll underscores conclusions drawn from several other

surveys—that anti-Americanism is on the rise, and the more the US flexes its hard power—the more it deploys troops abroad or talks tough diplomatically—the more it seems to weaken its ability to influence the world.

This, then, raises an obvious question. Is it simply the Bush administration's foreign policy or the whole image of America that is unpopular? Comparable surveys suggest that there is still strong support around the world for the values enshrined in US society. But it looks as though America itself is seen to be living up to those values less and less.

As a result, America's soft power—its ability to influence people in other countries by the force of example and by the perceived legitimacy of its policies—is weakening.

And in a turbulent, globalizing world, where the US—rightly or wrongly—is associated by many with the disruptive effects of globalization, soft power matters more than ever. It is a resource that once squandered is very difficult to build up again.[4]

A Pew Global Attitudes Survey released in June 2007 confirmed the deterioration of America's favorability ratings across the globe over the past five years—see Table 16.1.[5]

The findings of these surveys and others are irrefutable: America is losing her friends around the world, the country's global reputation is in crisis, and it is not improving. The implications for the future are grave.

The Issue is Complicated. Root Causes are Many

The rise in anti-Americanism is the result of a number of complex factors which have converged in recent years. As a result, there are no "quick fixes" to the problem. Instead, it is a long-term issue that will demand attention and concerted efforts for years to come.

It is true that today the most prominent cause of animus toward our country is widespread disagreement with current U.S. foreign policy and a general dislike of the current U.S. administration. The war in Iraq and numerous policies adopted in the name of the broader war on terror, as the BBC study notes, have sparked sharply negative opinions toward America. The 2007 Pew study shows that majorities in many countries reject the current United States foreign policy and express distaste for American-style democracy. According to the report, respondents not only want the U.S. to pull its troops out of Iraq "as soon as possible" but also seek a rapid end to the American and NATO military intervention in Afghanistan.

Table 16.1. Favorable Views of the U.S. (Selected Countries)

	2002	2007	Change
Canada	72%	55%	−17 points
Argentina	34	16	−18
Brazil	51	44	−7
Britain	75	51	−24
France	62	39	−23
Germany	60	30	−30
Russia	61	41	−20
Turkey	30	9	−21
Indonesia	61	29	−32
Israel	78 (2003)	78	0
China	42 (2005)	34	−8
India	66	59	−7
Japan	72	61	−11

But U.S. foreign policy is not the only cause of anti-Americanism today. In fact, several factors that drive anti-American sentiments are unrelated to U.S. politics, policies, or the Iraq war, and were evident in global public opinion trends well before the 9/11 attacks. Resentment, dislike, and outright hostility toward America have been building for quite some time.

One long-term factor is the West's success in the major foreign policy objective since World War Two: victory in the Cold War. America's status as the sole remaining global superpower—or, to some, a "hyper power"—has spawned anxiety, even fear, about the U.S. using its power indiscriminately. Even in Western Europe, widespread worries about American unilateralism and hegemony have been pronounced for years.

Another important factor has been the effect of globalization on local societies, particularly in parts of the developing world but also in advanced economies like Western Europe. There is a perception that the current wave of globalization is U.S.-led, that it has been exploitative, and has left many people as "have nots." Meanwhile, the strong economic performance of the U.S. economy over the past two decades has inspired envy as well as the concern that globalization seems to work well for America but not for others. This atmosphere of both skepticism and expectation toward the United States has also further emboldened others to challenge the U.S. directly and indirectly—politically, economically, and militarily.

Still another factor is the increasing global challenge directed at American popular culture. While U.S. media and entertainment products still dominate the world stage, perceptions of American morality and values are often quite critical, including among young people. And in some non-Western cultures—throughout much of the Islamic world, for instance—American values and lifestyles are seen as immoral and a serious threat to traditional cultural mores.

There is also the "ugly American" phenomenon—the perception that Americans are arrogant, insensitive, ignorant about the world, and that we don't practice what we preach. In the minds of many, Americans are culturally clueless and parochial.

What We Mean by "Public Diplomacy"

There are many definitions of the term, "public diplomacy." Our understanding of the phrase borrows from that published by the USC Center on Public Diplomacy.[6] We agree that "public diplomacy" refers to "all the ways a country can engage the citizens of other societies and influence their opinions for the better." We also agree with the USC Center that effective public diplomacy "starts from the premise that dialogue, rather than a sales pitch, is central to achieving desired results and that public diplomacy must be seen as a two-way street." Having said that, our own stance is that effective public diplomacy for the United States depends on:

1   a compelling and credible representation of America's values, vision, and voice to the world in ways that demonstrate respect for all people and cultures;
2   an acknowledgement that listening and dialogue lie at the heart of the public diplomacy process;
3   the active involvement of nongovernmental actors such as the media, the business community, nonprofit organizations, and individual Americans.

Why Business is up to the Task

Around the world, business is still admired. In the studies we've reviewed and conducted about the negatives and positives of the United States as seen by people throughout the world, "the American way of business" is one of three or four items that still come up positive.[7]

Indeed, when we commissioned Zogby International to interview more than 200 young Arabs, asking about their career aspirations and life dreams, more than 40 percent said they saw themselves in business. Of those respondents, 40 percent named the U.S. as first choice for learning required business skills. The UK was second with 29 percent, France with 18 percent, and Germany with 7 percent.[8]

So business is admired, more admired than governments. According to the Edelman Trust Barometer presented at Davos in 2006, government is the *least trusted* institution in Brazil, Spain, Germany, and South Korea, and trust in government remains low in the U.S. (38%), UK (33%), France (32%), and Canada (36%).[9]

Not only is business more admired and trusted, in many ways it is more relevant than national governments. The vast global reach of multinational companies through their people and their products touches millions of lives throughout the world every day.

Multinational corporations are also more culturally sensitive. For example, six million of the eight million people employed by U.S. companies outside the U.S. are local nationals, and therefore totally sensitive to local cultures and social mores.

Business is more skilled. Multinational companies are expert at building strong brands that generate goodwill, trust, and loyalty—skills that are sadly lacking in many governments today.

By and large, big multinationals are successful. Companies who depend heavily on foreign markets have learned how to get along and work successfully across borders and cultures, and, indeed, could offer many lessons to government. In fact, the *Washington Post* ran an op-ed piece on January 29, 2007, noting that on the same day a BBC poll found that less than a third of people in 25 countries regard the U.S. influence in the world as positive, McDonald's reported its strongest business results in three decades.[10] Brisk sales in supposedly anti-American countries were a large part of the reason. The piece went on to say that "McDonald's changed in ways that reflect the problem-solving grit of American business. It listened to its critics and adapted." The editorial ends by raising the question of whether the American government can mimic the agility of American business.

Business qualifies for a key role in public diplomacy for other important reasons. People who trade with each other tend not to fight with each other. And I hope we can all agree that businesses are at the strategic center of any free society. They provide employment so people can realize their aspirations for themselves and for their families.

In so many ways, business is actually more qualified for public diplomacy than is the government. As Paul Bracken, Professor of Political Science at the Yale School of Management, has said: "Today, the multinational corporation is the most vital institution in economic development, social change, technology, and let's face it, dynamism and new ideas."[11]

What Business Should Do

First of all, American business should admit that it is American. And be proud of its nationality. Given negative opinions of our country, many American multinationals now claim, "We're not an American company, we're a global company." The goal should be dual citizenship—a company proud to be American and proud of its informed and respectful worldview. An American company that hides its national identity denies itself the opportunity to represent the best of American values to the world.

American companies should practice good world citizenship. Every company should educate its employees on the issue, showing them how America's declining reputation around the world affects a company's long-term prospects, our country's security and economic well-being, and how the issue, if not corrected, will greatly complicate our future dealings with the biggest issues facing us as a nation. Multinationals can build relationships of trust and respect with employees, customers, and communities around the world. As it happens, all of these actions are in a corporation's self-interest.

By providing cultural sensitivity training and language training, at least for employees who work and travel abroad, companies can begin to disabuse foreign publics of their perceptions that we are arrogant, ignorant, and totally self-absorbed, even while they emphasize and personify those great American qualities that have traditionally been admired—our youthful enthusiasm, our optimism, our sense of humor, and our cultural diversity. There are many cultural training tools available. Business for Diplomatic Action provides an excellent one-day immersion. It's called Culture Span, designed for business executives of every level.

At the same time companies are acclimating their American employees to foreign cultures, they can help build better understanding of American culture and values by sponsoring cultural exchanges and English language training, and by giving people in other lands easier access to information about the United States through such efforts as the underwriting of distribution of American periodicals and books in foreign universities.

American companies should continue to set the standard for acts of corporate social responsibility that address human needs and improve the lives of people everywhere. There are many examples of companies changing attitudes toward the U.S. while pursuing their own business goals. And they should not hide those acts of benevolence under a bushel—the world needs to hear the myriad untold stories of U.S. corporations doing good. Dick Martin, in his book *Rebuilding Brand America*, cites two outstanding examples.

Cisco established network-training academies in technical schools, colleges, and community-based organizations across more than 150 countries. To date, the Cisco networking academies have prepared more than 1.5 million students for careers in the information technology industries, including several thousand women in Middle Eastern countries such as Saudi Arabia and the United Arab Emirates.[12]

Global accounting giant PricewaterhouseCoopers gives high-performing young partners eight-week assignments helping NGOs with their work in developing countries. Their projects have ranged from helping an NGO in Belize develop an eco-tourism plan to helping a United Nations agency in Tajikistan create a model for micro-financed enterprises. The program has not only helped PWC retain talented managers, it has helped them develop as responsible leaders attuned to cultural differences.[13]

Business should influence the government, demanding that government fix its visa and entry practices, for example. In a recent survey of international travelers for the Discover America Partnership, America's entry process was rated the world's worst by a factor of two to one over the next worst destination.[14] In another survey conducted by the Santangelo Group, it was estimated that U.S. business interests lost $40 billion between 2002 and 2004 because of visa delays, primarily in India and China.[15]

Companies should work in concert with business associations and groups such as the Business Roundtable to support public diplomacy reforms. There is a broad consensus on what needs to be done, but the administration needs encouragement to take bold steps and help in moving its programs through Congress. Business leaders can provide such encouragement.

Business should lend expertise to the federal government: Technology to streamline the visa process; media training for foreign service officers; marketing and communications skills for the many voices of government; analytical and organizational skills to facilitate action and accountability. Many of these skills that business depends on and takes for granted are sadly lacking in Washington.

Conclusion

Should business play a role in public diplomacy? If we agree that American business is still the world's best model of free and successful enterprise, if we acknowledge that "the American way of business" is one of the key positives in our national image, if we see that "creativity, innovation, and the 'can do' spirit" are attractive brand values for our nation, and if we measure the vast reach and impact of American brands on the peoples of the world, then it seems obvious that American business, its brands and its people, must be seen as among the most powerful diplomats our country could have. The question is not whether business should engage in public diplomacy, but whether it will, and to what extent. A creative and coordinated response by business to the current crisis of national reputation would lead to a win-win-win situation. Good for business, good for our country, good for the world.

Notes

1 "Unpopular U.S. Foreign Policies Threaten Revenue, Diminish Global Market Share for Many American-Based Companies," GMI Poll Press Release, October 21, 2004, http://www.gmimr.com/gmipoll/release.php?p=20041021.
2 Peter G. Peterson, "Where Are the Business Patriots? CEOs Need to Be Statesmen Again," *Washington Post*, June 18, 2004, B1.
3 "'Listen more' is world's message to US," BBC News, January 23, 2007, http://news.bbc.co.uk/go/pr/fr/-/2/hi/americas/6288933.stm.
4 Ibid.
5 "Global Unease with Major World Powers," The Pew Global Attitudes Project, June 27, 2007, http://pewglobal.org/reports/pdf/256.pdf.
6 "What is Public Diplomacy?" University of Southern California Center on Public Diplomacy, http://uscpublicdiplomacy.com/index.php/about/whatis_pd.
7 See, for example, "What Do Europeans Like and Dislike about the United States?" Harris Interactive, March 24, 2004, http://www.harrisinteractive.com/news/allnewsbydate.asp?NewsID=780.
8 Sam Rodgers and Sally Ethelston, "Survey of Younger Arab Leaders in the United Arab Emirates," Zogby International, September 2006.
9 "'A Person Like Me' Now Most Credible Spokesperson for Companies; Trust in Employees Significantly Higher Than in CEOs, Edelman Trust Barometer Finds," Edelman, January 23, 2006, http://www.edelman.com/trust/2007/prior/2006/ReleaseTrustBarometer.DOC.
10 Sebastian Mallaby, "Winning Hearts and Stomachs: Hostility to America, but Lines at McDonald's," *Washington Post*, January 29, 2007, A15.
11 Paul Bracken, "The Multinational Corporation Today," *Yale School of Management Working Paper*, No. OB-06, PM-05, OL-19, March 1, 2004, 1.
12 Dick Martin, *Rebuilding Brand America*, New York: American Management Association, 2007, 198.
13 Ibid., 199.
14 "First Homeland Security Secretary Tom Ridge Teams with the Discover America Partnership to Evaluate U.S. Entry Process," Discover America Partnership, December 20, 2006, http://www.poweroftravel.org/release-12–21–06.aspx.
15 "Do Visa Delays Hurt U.S. Businesses?" The Santangelo Group, June 2, 2004, http://www.nftc.org/default/visasurveyresults%20final.pdf.

17

The Public Diplomat

A First Person Account

Peter Kovach

I took a winding road to the Foreign Service and public diplomacy. And the practice of public diplomacy came to me before Foreign Service, in a series of immersions in other cultures as a student, seeker, journalist, researcher, teacher, and TV personality.

Central to my personal pilgrimage is the idea of immersion with the "other," while at the same time being my extroverted and voluble American self. In retrospect, it seems something between ironic and logical that so much of my Foreign Service career should have been devoted to outreach to peoples united by adherence to Islam. From a mixed religious background, two parents doggedly agnostic and deeply suspicious of organized religion, I remain a child driven in good measure by spiritual, religious, ethical instincts; only the latter my heritage.

Having escaped formal religious initiation—no bar mitzvah, no christening or confirmation until adulthood—by my 22nd birthday, I had logged significant time in monastic exercise in Hindu-Christian Indian environments under the benevolent eye of a French Benedictine guru figure, the late Swami Abhishiktananda. And I had my first taste of Buddha dharma which to this day constitutes my core practice of self-cultivation and personal growth.

My political-geographical orientation to the Arab/Muslim world came early, October of 1961 to be precise in the form of a UN Essay Contest my junior year in high school; before the travesty of the June 1967 War. In an innocent suburban environment where a non-Jew's (for despite my mixed Jewish-Catholic heritage I was definitively non-Jewish in all but a vague historical/cultural pride and identity) view of Israel was all *Exodus*, the film—heroic images embodied by Paul Newman, Eva-Marie Saint and Sal Mineo. In the midst of a demanding liberal public high school education, where students researched subjects that interested them came an assigned contest essay: the Palestinian refugee problem. Thirty pages of writing later, my view of the Middle East would never be the same. Looking at the Jewish component of my complex cultural heritage, the ideal of creating a just society stands out at least in memory as the paramount value my parents imbued in me.

From a high school career defined by public stands in defense of civil rights for African Americans, the Palestinian plight struck a nerve that still twinges today.

Years later, in my second "bout" of grad school, unencumbered by a commitment to Asian Studies inherent in my first round, I intuitively gravitated to interest and study of Palestine/Israel. At that point my long-standing reservations about public service in forms other than political organization and protest had fallen away with the conclusion of the Vietnam War. I knew I was preparing for a career in public diplomacy. And my Arab classmates and their receptivity to my extroversion passed a subliminal message. Not only was work in the Middle East good for careers; it was a region whose symbolic issue I understood and whose currency of personal interaction I was totally at home with. My career began in Yemen where I served as Assistant Public Affairs Officer.

To backtrack to India, my junior year abroad in 1966 as a "casual" student at Banaras Hindu University. In addition to my serious studies of Hindi, Sanskrit, classical Hindu philosophy and myths and rituals surrounding the water cycle, I moved around the country with a frisbee—one I affectionately referred to as "Mr. Ambassador." In situation after situation, including walking up river Ganges tracing major pilgrimage routes, I would take the frisbee out and toss it as a tool of introduction. I even invented with friends a game very close to ultimate frisbee (three years before that game was invented according to the Ultimate Frisbee website)—my Al Gore moment.

I moved easily from the lair of mendicants and pilgrims, sleeping on stone steps by the Ganges River, to that of ministers and diplomats and almost everything in between. I enjoyed speaking of my country (one I was and remain very proud of), my politics, and my values—while listening carefully and accepting just about any and all invitations to stand in others' shoes, to drink from their fountains of worldview, if not wisdom.

A few years later in Japan, it was as a "terebi gaijin" (television foreigner) on NHK's educational channel, a professor of American literature, and a counselor to diplomats and executives about to travel to North America for higher studies that I represented my society.

Finally to Israel/Palestine on a summer grant to study Israeli legal culture in relation to the Palestinian minority. Logically and sublimely landing me in Yemen, an almost medieval culture and a panorama so untouched by modernity as to be positively magical. Make no mistake: despite some prejudices towards Yemenis I encountered elsewhere in the Arab world, urban Yemenis spoke a beautiful classical Arabic and their poetry and "oud" playing is up with the very best I've heard over the ensuing decades.

So what did I find in my transition to professional public diplomacy—fresh out of Arabic language school? Adventure unparalleled. Weekend trips to visit mountain-ensconced tribes of friendships forged in the capital; hospitality of potlatch proportions. Celebratory and even ecstatic meeting of minds etc., under the influence of the soporific "khat" leaf, chewed afternoons in a very relaxed social ritual.

Curiously I found that many of my senior colleagues, officers with a much stronger Arabic than mine, consorted mostly with the few Yemenis who shared a Western outlook and education in the Soviet Union or the West. Frustrated by this, and empowered by a great boss, the recently retired James J. Callahan, I ventured to meet some less Westernized types among Sanaa's leaders.

With my background, and my mandate as a public diplomacy practitioner, one set of such encounters was with the editors of weeklies affiliated with the "Ihkwan Muslimeen," the Muslim brothers. I would say that my initial visits were greeted with a kind of bemused astonishment; we agreed that they would receive a USIA product known as the "Arabic Wireless File" on those days that solar storms and other atmospheric imponderables allowed my office to download it by radio (a long forgotten skill of U.S. public diplomacy officers) and that they would consider running some of our articles about American life. We both made good to our promises. A stream of articles describing a variety of facets of America, including Islam in America, began to appear in their journals. Notably, one of the editors eventually allowed that I was the only foreign diplomat to ever call on him.

This small and rather symbolic victory for our outreach efforts had a larger impact in my career—a determination to push the margins in my contacts; to talk to those with less familiarity, greater doubts, or deeper misconceptions about our policies and our society.

The last two months in Yemen, I was in charge of United States Information Service (USIS) operations during the transition between bosses. What should have been a routine time turned out to be far from it. I returned home one night to receive a cryptic note from one of my close Yemeni friends at the hands of a nervous houseboy. It insisted that I visit the friend that night. No phones. So into the car and across town to the friend's apartment. He had gotten wind of a plot by Palestinian extremists and Yemeni sympathizers to attack the U.S. embassy. And had chosen me as a conduit of this threat information.

I went straight to the house of the Deputy Chief of Mission. By eight the next morning, we had an ad hoc security committee convened. My Ambassador asked if I was comfortable being the "worm on the hook," going back to the source of the information. I agreed without a second thought, knowing full well that my friendship was an exclusive conduit of information vital to the safety of the American Mission and U.S.–Yemeni relations. The friend had to cover his flank and the fact that I was a repeated foreign visitor at his place gave my visits a semblance of normality that would have not obtained had anyone else taken my place. The information would have simply dried up.

Presiding over a remotely located office and language school, I beefed up security and removed records that could in any way embarrass our students, put in the wrong hands—all the while gamely pretending that this was part of the value I was adding to the operation during my weeks in charge. I took my administrative assistant, an American officer, into my confidence. In today's environment, an embassy with this kind of verified threat would have to put out some kind of public notice.

In the end, the plotters were arrested and the network behind the planned attacks dismantled. But this was a heady, albeit stressful, experience for a junior officer.

Next stop was Bahrain, where I was given my own USIS operation to run. I was never quite sure whether it was the sweet words I heard about my performance in Yemen, a shortage of interested bidders, or the life experience I had under my belt before joining that netted me this privileged assignment. It turned out to be a huge professional opportunity. In Bahrain I found a quiet, almost bovine pace of life, quickened somewhat by anxiety over nearby revolutionary Iran and the "tanker war" between Iran and Iraq—a war Gulf insiders sometimes refer to as Gulf War I.

A push for broader diplomatic and PD program outreach, imbued in my professional soul from the Yemen, found a fertile field for full expression in Bahrain. Bahrain was a country ruled for two centuries by a Sunni tribe from the Nejd region of Central Saudi Arabia, leaders who presided over a population variously estimated to be about 75% Shia. Among the Shia, probably two-thirds or slightly more were Arabs whom it was presumed migrated South from the Iraqi marshlands around the Shatt al Arab and who considered themselves Bahrain's true sons and daughters of the soil. The other third of the Shia were Persian ethnics who had migrated across the Persian Gulf more recently, along with some of the great Sunni merchant families and Bahrain's small Sunni middle class. My arrival coming just three years after the Iranian Revolution, I found myself literally in an insular city-state whose major communities were newly wary of one another. The Iran–Iraq War was in its early years and the loyalty of Arab to Arab, amply proven in retrospect by the end of the conflict six years hence, was only a hypothesis, a naive one in many eyes.

From an American perspective, or rather from a Shia perspective of America, there were some frankly surprising potentials, especially for reaching the over-25 generation. When an American company had taken over management from British predecessors of Bahrain's huge Bapco refinery a decade earlier, the Americans found a company segregated in an all too familiar pattern from the American South of just two decades earlier: segregated eateries and toilets, even water fountains. Their first day, the Americans totally desegregated the facility—an act that indelibly put the U.S. on the positive side of a line of demarcation in the eyes of a majority of Bahrain's citizens. Second, also in the tumultuous 1970s, the Shia with their strong doctrines of legitimacy in governance marveled at what they generally viewed as "the peaceful overthrow of a corrupt government," referring, of course, to the impeachment and resignation of President Nixon over the Watergate crisis.

These two lingering positives were ensconced in an air of suspicion that the U.S. was totally sided with the Al Khalifa rulers in the wake of the Iranian Revolution, the hostage crisis, due to a discrete American military presence, the not publicly acknowledged but not denied "home port" for the six ships of the U.S. Navy-MIDEASTFOR in the Persian Gulf. My task as PAO and one of only three Arabic-speaking officers in the small embassy (including the Ambassador) was to make sure that America kept an adequate social presence in the village social centers known as Mata'am, attending weddings, funerals and any other occasions generating invites. The other was to make sure that leaders of the Bahraini Shia elites as well as the emerging technocracy dominated by a rising Persian Shia middle class were well serviced by USIA programs, particularly exchanges.

Rather than citing the joys of my personal life, meeting and marrying my wife, an American-educated Thai stewardess/artist, and enjoying many weekends of sailing in a mixed ex-pat/Bahraini club, let me focus on three PD triumphs of those three years, before reflecting on a fourth challenge.

I was very concerned over the 60% of the Shia population then under 25, "kids" who neither had direct memory of BAPCO desegregation or Watergate and whose views of America were colored by suspicions of perceived U.S. collusion with the disliked Sunni leadership and a challenge to their identities posed to some degree by the Iranian Revolution as an assertion of Shia power. In a small state where sports clubs were a great community force, the answer readily suggested itself: sports exchange. In a cable to USIA, I generated the idea of sending out a basketball team to run clinics and scrimmage with club teams. Washington's initial reaction was to buy my idea but to send out a UCLA powerhouse or the like. I rejoined, "No, I want a team that will legitimately lose a game or two," to wit a Division III elite school whose players would be sophisticated enough to understand the importance of the exchange experience beyond sport. In the end, USIA sponsored a team from Case Western Reserve, an elite engineering school in Cleveland, Ohio. And we had a tour marred only by some bad feelings generated by the more physical style allowed under the international rules that Bahrainis play under. Case did drop a game to a leading club and the whole thing was drowned in positive press coverage that my colleagues and I arranged, the vital complement guaranteeing resonance of a program effort beyond the social milieu of its direct beneficiaries.

The second triumph involved teacher recruitment at the Gulf Polytechnic (GP), the only institution of higher learning actually educating folks (majority Shia and male) for the emerging hi-tech banking and petroleum refining and services economy. GP's energetic and idealistic President, a Bahraini intellectual of working-class Persian Shia origins, related a serious concern to me—how to replace a majority of his superannuated faculty, comprised mostly of aging Brits who had "stayed on" after the colonial era came to an end (for Bahrain in 1968 when the UK withdrew from the "East of Suez") and as British influence gradually waned during the ensuing decade. Understanding that Bahrain's most able Minister of Education (from a leading Sunni merchant family) backed him, I proposed a recruiting contract with Amideast, already USIA's contractor for all student advising operations in the Arab world. I sold the approach to Amideast in Amman, Jordan, and Washington by pointing out that this would give them a traction in the ever more prosperous Persian Gulf region where they lacked a foothold. The result, between 20–30 young, energetic, and qualified American teachers arrived at GP within a year, an outcome that sent the British Ambassador demarching the Minister about "falling standards at the Polytechnic." The Minister almost immediately reported the conversation to me in a tone dripping with sarcasm. Our diplomatic corps was small enough so that I could eventually tease the British envoy about his action, and this mini-juggernaut of American influence in Bahrain. At the same time, I used exchange programs to do the same sort of thing with the as socially relevant College of Health Sciences to improve their emergency health and triage services—this in the absence of a USAID or Peace Corps component to the U.S. Mission.

Finally, there was the matter of our naval "Administrative Support Unit" consisting of several score U.S. Navy men and women led by the resident commander of the Middle East Force (COMIDEASTFOR). Along with the Sunni ruling class's paranoia about a Shia majority, a demographic fact never admitted in public, came a restricted press and public information environment that precluded ANY public mention of our naval presence, despite it being a well known and impossible to hide fact of life in this tight island mini-state of 500,000. As embassy spokesperson, it fell to me to dance a disingenuous minuet with the local press who couldn't have published a word of truth in any case without bringing down the punitive approbation of the rulers. With American and other international journalists, this became an even more complex dance. A well-known American journalist who was new to the Middle East beat (one who much later in life became a friend) asked me about the camouflage-bespeckled C-130s at a far end of Bahrain's airport. Since I knew they did not have American insignias, I benignly suggested that they could be from any one of a number of countries that the U.S. sells planes to and that they were perhaps there as a part of a bilateral equipment exchange. I was quoted on the front page of a major American paper in a way that emphasized what the journalist correctly perceived as my deliberately disingenuous quip; a verbal dance that earned me praise. In a similar vein, I had to fire a corrective to Washington when a senior U.S. military official, speaking on the record in the far less restrictive information environment of neighboring Kuwait, was totally open about the home-porting arrangement offered by Bahrain. In a Gulf media market where people up and down the Gulf and in Iran followed the more liberal Kuwaiti press, this was an incendiary interview. My ambassador and I were both called in by the Government of Bahrain to hear vociferous complaints at our respective levels. At my instigation, all my colleagues up and down the Gulf were given guidance on how to describe the Bahrain–U.S. arrangement on an "if asked" only basis. Today, the bilateral U.S.–Bahraini military cooperation is matter of public record. My predicament was really cultural—in some Arab cultures, what is widely known but not mentioned does not need to be acted upon. Once mentioned, an issue involves public face and potential loss of same in a shame-driven culture.

A final Bahraini experience sheds interesting and somewhat ironic light on current international dilemmas. During my years in Bahrain from 1982 to 1985, the Saudi government committed to finance and build the Arabian Gulf University in Bahrain. And build they did in record time. I am not privy to the Saudi's reasoning in making such an investment in Bahrain, with its demographics. What was obvious as the first deans, all Saudis, arrived in Manama was that they were all very religious Sunnis, wearing the characteristic long beards, short "thobes," and simple sandals. What's more, they came armed with PhDs from the best American universities: Stanford, the Ivies and the like. That this was not a wildly pro-U.S. government crowd was evident in the first calls I paid on them as embassy Affairs Officer. After two years of gradually more cordial acquaintance, conversation became more candid. In retrospect I reflect that these were men of Usama bin Laden's generation and social class, with much the same criticism of their positions in their native society. They were, however, men of knowledge and peace whose minds had none of the poison of war and violence of Bin Laden and his ilk. Perhaps their expensive education and high paying jobs had bought their public silence in the face of their feelings of disenfranchisement. One of them shook my hand as I took leave at the end of the traditional farewell calls a diplomat pays on senior contacts. He said in a voice dripping with bitter irony, "Congratulations, Peter. You are about to go to the freest Muslim country in the world." Catching my slightly discombobulated look, he added, "The United States, of course."

Fast forward to Morocco, where I was Press Attaché (Information Officer) running the USIS "information section" from 1986 to 1990. Two moments in that tour exemplify what different PD tools can potentially do to curry grassroots understanding and favor. And one was a conversation that might (or might not) have been a seed for one of the greatest PD efforts emanating from the Muslim world; in my personal view one of the greatest efforts in the world today, period.

My tour, during the dying days of the Cold War, was still etched strongly in Cold War public diplomacy. Early on, through an arrangement I brokered with the sympatico Novosti Bureau Chief, we jointly staged summit scene-setters at Morocco's national press club. Both embassies led with their most French-fluent senior officers in these events, unique in the world, that the Moroccan press hailed as heralding a more sane international order from a third world perspective. Washington's support for these events was not a given. Here I picked up the practice of organizing edgy events and announcing them to Washington just days before by cable prefaced with the line, "unless we hear to the contrary, we plan to . . ."

In a similar vein, I was bothered by the perfunctory press and media treatment our huge Peace Corps, USAID, and cultural programs received, press treatment pretty much centered around ribbon cuttings and the like. We had a huge investment in Morocco, far greater than either the Soviets or the Chinese; and an illiterate majority of a national population to get the news to. One eye opening moment—hiking one weekend in the Atlas mountains cresting a ridge, I found myself staring down at a village. I sat to eat a sandwich. Something about that village just didn't look right. Finally I cracked the code—TV antennas atop every compound, but no electric wiring at all. The Moroccan government wanted their message beamed to these remote rural populations that had historically been in and out of the Moroccan pale and whose support now was the backbone of support for the monarch, a putative descendant of the Prophet Mohammed. They gave folks TVs and batteries that could be recharged for a penny or two at weekly markets. I determined to get the positive message of U.S. support to these folks by TV or radio and to the thinking, reading elites through the widest range of media.

Both the USAID and Peace Corps country directors proved willing allies to an effort I proposed. That every project have a press plan that presaged fulsome media moments when the essence of a project reached a physically tangible fruition. I had my staff work with USAID and Peace Corps to advance events built around such moments, to get articulate, telegenic, and willing beneficiaries of projects to step forward and talk to the camera or mike. We would then typically shape a formal event, like flying in the Ambassador to cut a ribbon with the local governor. For our part, we would marshall several vans and invite selected press along with enticement of a picnic lunch and exclusive interviews.

Suddenly our projects got a public life. Front and center were accounts by simple people, beneficiaries explaining how our aid transformed their lives in the most direct and credible terms possible, often on TV. I asked the Peace Corps Director whether I could conscript a few volunteer teachers during term breaks, to venture to the most far-flung corners of the country to record testimonies, take candid photos and write about projects in places too remote or small to get governors and press vans to attend. The result, a series of amazing articles with great pictures along with radio actualities telling the human story of our projects.

Rural to urban migration was a huge social phenomena in Morocco. The slums burgeoning around Morocco's larger cities teemed with young, underemployed first generation educated youth. The Koran, now accessible but interpreted in large part by a very conservative clergy forged a new, more anti-Western, anti-modern vein of Islamic interpretation. The rural backbone of support the monarchy enjoyed comprised a largely illiterate mass with their less orthodox Sufi practice of "zikr," where an Islam more of the heart was practiced, one that I view as reinforcing the open-minded values of elite circles, intellectuals still invested with the values of Andalusian Spain, ruled by Moroccan princes where Muslims, Jews, and Christians co-exist, creating one of the greatest cultural epochs in human history.

An eccentric but rather enlightened Moroccan prince, the late Moulay Ahmed Alaoui, published the two major French dailies and was the gadfly architect, underwriter (at least politically) of many of Morocco's many ambitious cultural schemes designed to enhance Morocco's international prestige and to attract tourism. During a meeting on a largely extraneous subject, we digressed into chatter about cultural events that had the potential to build bridges among peoples, especially among people identified with the world's great faith groups. I spontaneously shared a fantasy I had concocted during a graduate school retreat with a career counselor: an international festival of spiritual music. He responded with unbridled enthusiasm.

I have absolutely no idea if this conversation was a seed, or even what Moulay Ahmed Alaoui's role was in its creation. (Another Al Gore moment for me?) The Moroccan Fes World Festival of Sacred Music, now about 15 years old, has fulfilled and far exceeded my fantasy, gaining Morocco and the monarchy tremendous prestige while subtly celebrating her interfaith, Andalousian heritage, and spawning a number of off-shoots including one in Los Angeles organized under the aegis of UCLA's Center for World Performing Arts. In a world where civilizational differences are thought by many to underscore current conflicts, this Moroccan festival in my view is THE premier public diplomacy event extant in the world today. All credit to the Kingdom of Morocco and its enlightened people and monarchs.

My last days in Morocco were marked by Saddam Hussein's August 1990 invasion of Kuwait, an event my Moroccan diplomatic contacts had ominously been predicting over the previous six months due to rising acrimony between Kuwait and Iraq in Arab League fora over that time. I was returning to Washington to assume charge of the office shaping and implementing the North African, Near Eastern, and South Asian International Visitors Leadership Program—every American diplomat's favorite exchange program. The shift in the political map of the Middle East after the invasion made changes in the game plan imperative in order to save the budget. The general tenor of my changes was to put more money into supporting joint "normalization" programming among Palestinians, Egyptians, and Israelis, and between Pakistanis and Indians. While on the surface exchanges represent retail programming involving only participants, because our embassies take great care in selecting the best and brightest among the coming generation, these face-to-face encounters with the "other" on our American shores and the humanized perceptions and dialogue that results have great ripple effects in our visitors' home countries when they return.

The next year, I moved up to the public diplomacy bureau as senior policy officer. Working with my colleagues to expand my initiatives in the previous job, we put a generous hunk of grant money in the hands of our embassies in Islamabad and New Delhi to launch what was called the "Neemrana" process to create a context where Indian and Pakistani intellectuals and opinion leaders could encounter each other in the region as well as in the U.S. Seeded with our funding, within a period of two or three years the "Neemrana" process continued in the region, sustained by the South Asians themselves—an ideal PD outcome by any measure.

A lingering passion of mine remained getting our diplomats to move in wider circles within the host societies where they served. My earlier impulses from my Yemen days found their arena in the context of addressing one of Washington's of the early 1990s major obsessions—addressing "political Islam." Fronted by one of my great patrons and role models, Ambassador William Rugh, Assistant Secretary for North African, Near Eastern and South Asian Affairs, Edward Djerejian was persuaded to make a major policy speech reflecting my persistent obsession with wider PD outreach to those that neither knew us well or necessarily agreed with us. I was tasked with writing the talking points—the building blocks for such a speech. Djerejian gave the speech on June 2, 1992 at Meridian House in Washington, DC; a speech that set a policy direction for public diplomacy that was to last until September 12, 2001, when engaging the moderate, "silent" majority of Muslims became an obvious challenge after the 9/11 attacks.

And I got to go out to Jordan as Counselor for Public Affairs to further put my approach, now policy, into practice.

9/11 was an epochal event that fundamentally reshaped the way American public diplomacy approached reaching out to Muslims. The newly established Bush PD structure was not fully stood up at the moment of the attacks. Charlotte Beers, dubbed the "Queen of Madison Avenue," had been named Under Secretary in late spring but had not been confirmed as of the attacks. She quickly was. Her time was marked by some controversy, especially over the now infamous "shared values" campaign. This expensive effort flooded those Muslim countries that consented to run them with television public service announcements (PSAs) touting the freedom in which American Muslims practice their religion and celebrate their varied cultural heritages. To generalize, the reaction was a collective "ho-hum, we know American Muslims are free to practice and lead a full religious life, but what has America done to guarantee the same rights for us in the face of autocracy and other oppressive elements?" The PSAs briefly became an object of derision in the international media; criticism that eventually bounced back to our shores. I would still defend the effort as a best foot forward in the face of intense pressure to do something, anything. Depicting Islam flourishing in America through PSAs reflected an approach that in a calmer past had garnered very positive results.

It is an injustice to her prodigious intelligence and talent to judge Beers' time as Under Secretary of Public Diplomacy and Public Affairs by this one-campaign, pricey mistake that it may have been viewed retrospectively. She came in on the crest of an era-defining crisis. She was a superb listener and empowered her inner circle to think creatively in the face of that crisis. More specifically, she brought an ethos of measurement to the endeavor of influencing foreign audiences, insisting that PD should employ the same rigorous baseline attitudinal measures as does professional advertising and that a program should define the attitudinal change desired and then measure the extent to which it was achieved or not, and why. Unfortunately, Congressional parsimony, she quickly learned, and State's limited ability to influence funding for the diplomatic endeavor under our American system of separation of powers, precluded the kind of funding necessary to really kick start a more quantitatively rigorous analysis of this kind. Rather we still rely on the traditional more intuitive basis of conducting PD based on language proficiency and cross-cultural training prior to going out to work as diplomats in the field.

While she respected the work of the polling operation in State's Bureau of Intelligence and Research, like so many of us in the field, we realize that there isn't a fraction of the necessary money in this endeavor. A positive development in this vein, with respect due to both President George W. Bush and before him to former Vice President Gore, the culture of program evaluation and accountability in government has, despite inadequate funding, taken root in measuring the results of our PD efforts.

In 2005, I turned my back on two attractive senior positions in East Asia to get back out in the field where I knew I could do work that would pack maximum impact in the post-9/11 world. I opted for a year-long tour of duty in Islamabad, Pakistan as Counselor for Public Affairs. My vision was to rethink a program that had not been significantly examined since 9/11, especially in light of developments in Department support over the intervening years, developments I had a hand in shaping. What I didn't bargain for was one of the most significant natural disasters "of the last hundred years," according to relief experts. The South Asian Earthquake of October 8, 2005 at 7.6 Richter was not the biggest, but its epicenter deep in the Himalayas of Kashmir and the Northwest Frontier Province's Eastern border made getting relief to victims an epochal challenge.

The U.S., contributing a fleet which at maximum numbered over 30 Chinook giant helicopters, did the lion's share to alleviate the crisis—getting desperately needed supplies, no matter from what source, into the zone while ferrying out those in need of sophisticated medical interventions in order to survive. Coordinating a motley public affairs crew consisting of my own staff, a team of military public affairs types, and Office of Foreign Disaster Assistance (USAID) public affairs officers, we embedded both Pakistani and international journalists daily on the relief flights to get the story of the quake and the U.S. relief effort to Pakistan and the world. In

Pakistan, the effect was dramatic. In 10 weeks, the local Nielsen polling affiliate documented a doubling of the number of Pakistanis holding positive feeling towards America—remarkable in the suspicion-laden context of the Global War on Terrorism. I personally led a movement, applauded and supported by the Government of Pakistan, to coordinate messages sent through radio and community organizations to victims; especially those displaced from villages of hundreds who traumatically and suddenly found themselves in displaced persons camps of thousands. This effort, focused on areas like sanitation, food supplies, and government rebuilding schemes, helped to staunch rumors and promote functional adaptation—both vital in such crises. Communication "media" ranged from a network of ad hoc FM stations, to Radio Pakistan, Boy Scout runners in the camps, and Imams around makeshift mosques.

On the program side, I closed a previously announced pledge to provide Pakistan with what would be history's largest student Fulbright program, with a painstaking three-party negotiation to arrange funding, this in an environment where all three potential funding partners had somewhat differing visions of the program. The art of this negotiation laid in reconciling these viewpoints within each party's comfort range of compromise. The program is now funded to the tune of $157 dollars over five years. The 150 Pakistanis beginning their graduate studies in the U.S. each year will contribute immeasurably to the upgrade of Pakistan's university system and will train future teachers for generations.

In addition, I established the first four American Corners in Pakistan. An American Corner is an Internet-wired American reading room hosted by a Pakistani library. Corners, backed by State's cadre of first class Information Resources Specialists (aka, "librarians"), provide authoritative information about American policy, government and society, as well as a programming venue often outside the capital city for embassies and consulates. Equally important, another initiative expanded an excellent State post-9/11 initiative, ACCESS MICROSCHOLARSHIP to as many as six sites. ACCESS programs are after-school English teaching programs that provide a vehicle of hope for urban students of limited means. With the additional support of embassy speakers (including Ambassador Crocker) and American materials, the cadre of Regional English Teaching Specialists in the U.S. Foreign Service ensures a first class curriculum and teacher training. It conceivably opens a world of work prospects in the global economy to a rung of society whose children might out of despair be open to the blandishments of jihadist recruitment. The privilege of leading a class of these students in simple unventilated classrooms, in 100 degree heat, may not be apparent to a reader. But the enthusiasm and the broadened horizons of these young Pakistanis made up for all discomforts and obstacles.

There were smaller moments among the many fulfilling encounters of my year in Pakistan. With my interest in religion, I found an easy rapport with the Islamic scholars in Pakistan's major shariah faculties, that train the highest echelons of at least the majority Sunni religious functionaries. Through much listening, I discovered that establishment scholars of even their conservative ilk felt that under the influence of intolerant strains of Islam, well-funded in Pakistan of recent decades since the Afghan struggle against the Soviets in the 1980s, Pakistan had become a far more conflicted, violent, and intolerant society. In the view of my favorite interlocutor among the shariah deans, Pakistan had lost sight of its more tolerant Asian roots that complemented Islam.

To counteract that, the teaching of comparative religion has come into vogue. But with few non-Muslim practitioners to draw upon, he asked my advice on how to beef up the curriculum in a way that might make a significant impact on intra-Muslim tolerance and understanding of the other great faith traditions. I gave him a grant that should bring practitioners to Pakistan of all the major faith groups, including Hinduism, Buddhism, and Confucianism (the latter a harder pill to swallow for Muslims who are enjoined in their Holy Koran to respect only Christians and Jews as people of the same monotheistic religion of the book). And part of the project will lead to recording a series of DVDs where practitioners of each faith tradition explain themselves. Given the power of these faculties, this program should exercise great intellectual and spiritual leverage on a new generation of religious leaders.

Finally, an afterword on engaging Muslim audiences beyond traditional elites. Our post-9/11 PD emphasizes connecting with mainstream Muslims, a relatively silent majority sharing most values with their counterparts in the other great faith traditions of the world. The majority of people of all faiths oppose the lunatic fringes within their own and certainly other traditions; they oppose behaviors that would qualify as "terrorism" by current Department of State definitions—a point worth making with Muslim contacts without elaborating too much. Islam has no monopoly on these kinds of crazies in modern times. Under Secretaries of Public Diplmacy and Public Affairs, Charlotte Beers, Ambassador Marguerite Tutwiler, Patricia Harrison (acting), and Karen Hughes, have each in their own ways emphasized reaching out to "broader, younger, deeper" audiences in the post-9/11 era. More significantly, this is an emphasis that Secretary Rice has picked up as a key component of her "Transformational Diplomacy" campaign—a push to get our diplomats out from behind their computer screens and fortress-like embassies to engage broader (regional), younger, and deeper (non-elite) audiences in advocating U.S. policy and the values that underlie it.

In my time since Pakistan at UCLA as the Department of State's Diplomat in Residence, I have focused my academic thinking on defining a cultural diplomacy appropriate for this historical moment of the United States in the world. Gone are the Cold War days of what I term "Dizzie meets the Bolshoi" cultural diplomacy, where the U.S. and USSR would tour their most appreciated high culture groups. Their presence staring down at audiences from under a Proscenium Arch carried great symbolic baggage—we are defining culture and aiming it down at "you" from under the arch, we are implicitly superior.

With all the doubts Americans today encounter throughout the post-Cold War world regarding our superpower role and our foreign policies, our cultural presence needs to be recast. What I advocate is a kind of peer-to-peer cultural diplomacy whereby the Bureau of Educational and Cultural Affairs would fund the presence on the ground abroad of an artist/musician on a month or two grant. That American would be programmed by an embassy public affairs section to engage in workshops with host country counterparts with a goal of creating a new amalgam—a fusion of vision and artistry expressed in composition, performance, on canvas, etc. And that subsequent to this new creation, a performing tour in country and region would follow. In turn this would be followed by a U.S. tour of the newly created work. This sort of exchange both in symbolism and reality would be a collaboration of respectful peers, it would be put out for appreciation by audiences in the host region and the U.S. Such an exchange would be far cheaper and less burdensome to our missions to run and would invite participating sponsors from both the public sector overseas as well as the private sector.

Recent examples in the heart of the Arab world included the late 2006 travel of jazz "ambassador" Darryl Kennedy. Kennedy, following up on contacts made previously on a State Department-funded tour in Egypt, went back on his own to jam and ultimately cut a CD with a top Egyptian artist. They toured the new music based on their collaboration throughout Egypt. In the same timeframe, a relatively junior State Department political officer serving in Tunis in his spare time exercised his roots as an accomplished musician in the Appalachian tradition by mixing with top local musicians in Tunis. Eventually, he was able to bring some of his former Virgina-based musical partners out and the result, "Kantara," is a terrific amalgam of what the musicians dub "Arab-Appalachian Music." The combined group traveled throughout Tunis and just this spring finished a two-week tour in the U.S., culminating in a Millennium Stage session at Washington's Kennedy Center in May.

Such a series of collaborations by poets, sponsored by former U.S. Poet Laureate Robert Pinsky under the "poetry project," shows equal promise in another universally appreciated medium.

I have advocated such an approach to cultural diplomacy in several speeches including one at LA's Disney Hall to roll out an impressive first volume on Culture and Globalization that is the result of a collaboration among a virtual United Nations of scholars. I consult with a Brookings Institution-Saban Foundation group of thinkers, engaged artists, and progressive Muslims, involved in organizations such as One Nation on an initiative to bridge gaps in cross-cultural engagement with the Muslim world through the arts. The University of Southern California's Annenberg School Center for Public Diplomacy is another significant forum for such discussions, conveniently located 15 miles down "the 10" freeway from UCLA. So I speak, write, and in my own modest way help connect people to engage in such cross-cultural encounters, convinced as I am of their ultimate potential to add value and bridge human gaps.

No matter what program initiatives are on the table at any moment in time, it is the willingness to deploy them creatively by our diplomats, based on personal engagement with audiences, that makes the signature difference. Maybe now, more than ever in an era marked by heightened paranoia and security concern, taking the message "the last three feet" in the words of the immortal Edward R. Murrow is truly of paramount importance. I look back on a career in public diplomacy and engagement in the Muslim world and see that such person-to-person engagement was at the core of everything good I've been associated with as a PD practitioner. I doubt that changes in the communication environment like the blogosphere or the Internet will fundamentally alter this, my bottom line of engagement as a public diplomat.

18

The Case for Localized Public Diplomacy

William P. Kiehl

So Little Known and So Misunderstood

One of the principal reasons that public diplomacy is so little understood and so often misunderstood in the United States of America is the persistent underreporting of public diplomacy tactics, techniques, and procedures undertaken by the public diplomacy professionals abroad. Public diplomacy professionals are trained to stay out of the limelight themselves in order to utilize better the tools of public diplomacy to inform and persuade their audiences. They know that it is the message, not the messenger, that is the key. And to the extent that the messenger is someone other than an American diplomat or official, it is so much the better to provide credibility. Thus there is an "institutionalized reluctance" to speak about what one does. As the Wizard of Oz hastily shouted to Dorothy and her friends, "Pay no attention to that man behind the curtain!" Perhaps even more so, the public diplomat, like so many other professionals, simply does not know how to explain his or her work to the layman. As Lisbeth B. Schorr wrote: "Even the best practitioners often can't give usable descriptions of what they do. Many successful [organizational and societal] interventions reflect the secret the fox confided to Saint Exupéry's Little Prince: What is essential is invisible to the eye. The practitioners *know* more than they can *say.*"[1] In the words of M.I.T. professor Don Schon, they operate with an "iceberg of tacit knowledge and artistry beneath the surface of readily accessible descriptions" of effective practices.[2] This essay then is one practitioner's attempt to provide a glimpse of the subsurface of that iceberg.

The Concept of "Localized Public Diplomacy"

The notion that public diplomacy works best when centrally planned and focused on a single message or set of messages designed in Washington, DC is most assuredly a false premise. Those who believe this—mainly short time political appointees whose background is largely in political campaigning—would have us accept that nothing worthwhile in public diplomacy happens without Washington's direction.

Anyone who has worked in public diplomacy abroad—"in the field"—is aware of how important on-the-ground experience and sensitivity to the local milieu are to successful public diplomacy. Successful public diplomacy campaigns are rarely if ever "invented" in Washington.

Indeed, most of the "brilliant" ideas from inside the Beltway are at best marginally successful in an overseas context. They are too often "old wine in new bottles" as a way of enhancing the personal reputations of the proponents of these programs rather than any creative new approaches. They often presuppose a "cookie cutter" approach to the world—a "one-size-fits-all" policy line which the public diplomats abroad are expected to toe.

If there is one concept that seems to elude the political masters of the Washington bureaucracy it is that in public diplomacy it is all about *context* and *relationships*. Thus a skilled practitioner of public diplomacy must find a way to take the latest "flavor of the month" cooked up by Washington and make it somehow palatable to key contacts in the host country. The skilled public diplomacy officer must find a way to place the message in a context that is both understandable and reasonable (even if not likeable) to the target audience with whom the officer has built a relationship of trust over time.

Several examples which, in the language of the now defunct United States Information Agency (USIA) are "field-driven" public diplomacy, illustrate what is meant by the term "localized public diplomacy." The examples to follow are illustrative of the countless public diplomacy campaigns over the past half century that originated in the field rather than in the Washington bureaucracy.[3] They were conducted by officers and staff members of the U.S. Information Service (USIS) or in the former USSR and Eastern Europe, The Press and Cultural Section of the U.S. Embassy, as USIA offices were known abroad.

There is nothing inherently more profound about the examples chosen versus the many other examples of field-driven public diplomacy. They are all vignettes from this writer's own public diplomacy career and thus he has both the certain knowledge of their accuracy and their authenticity.[4] In addition to four comprehensive programs created in the field, I have included examples of three publications produced and created by field operations. In a modern context, print publications are still useful in much of the world but the same creativity today can be applied to web-based products as well.

Sri Lanka

Sri Lanka in the mid-1970s was a nation whose early promise had been squandered. Emerging from colonialism as Ceylon in 1948, it began life with a high literacy rate (over 80 percent), a prosperous economy (British expatriates actually sent goodies home to England from the shops of Colombo as late as the early 1950s), and a democratic form of government. All seemed to auger well until the 1956 election of S.W.R.D. Bandaranaike's socialist and anti-Western party which, among its other follies, imposed a "Sinhala-only" policy on the government and the schools. Thus, in one blow, Bandaranaike eliminated English as the medium of instruction and government business, and disenfranchised the sizeable Tamil-speaking minority. This act would sow the seeds for the civil war which has continued for more than three decades on the island nation.

By the 1970s successive governments of various political stripes had failed to come to grips with Sri Lanka's growing problems. The government in power was a coalition of the Bandaranaike socialists under the sway of the assassinated S.W.R.D.'s widow; the Ceylon Communist Party, a pro-Moscow variant headed by Peter F. Kenemen, the Minister of Housing; and the Lanka Sama Samajist Party, a Trotskyite party aligned with the Fourth International and led by the Finance Minister, N.M. Pereira. With this constellation in power, the economy fell even further behind its neighbors, exports stagnated, imports were in short supply, and the future looked dismal indeed.

For the United States, obsessed with the Cold War struggle, there were only two strategic interests paramount: First, to ensure that the huge natural harbor at Trincomalee not become a naval base for its arch-enemy, the Soviet Union. And second, that the Voice of America's relay station just north of Colombo continue to function to broadcast its messages to the peoples of Soviet Central Asia, the Urals, and much of communist China.

David Briggs, the Public Affairs Officer at the U.S. Embassy, had a long and distinguished international career from ambulance driver for the American Field Service during World War II (WWII) to diplomat through much of the Cold War era, but he was best known as one of the world's leading numismatists. He knew that he was outgunned in the struggle for "hearts and minds" on the island of Ceylon. The U.S. Embassy, without an AID Mission and with fewer than 40 American staff members was overshadowed by the large Soviet Embassy and the even larger Chinese Embassy. The Chinese fielded more than 500 "experts," who fanned out across the island bringing a modest amount of aid and a large supply of Mao's "little red book" to the rural population.

It was in this context then that Briggs and his small staff of public diplomacy officers supported by their locally employed staff set about to show the people of Sri Lanka that the U.S. cared about them. A year before the 1976 Bicentennial Year, Briggs determined to use this anniversary not just to celebrate 200 years of American independence but to demonstrate American interest in and commitment to Sri Lanka. The concept he chose was "An American Bicentennial Salute to Sri Lanka" complete with a logo which would appear on every U.S. Information Service product from daily news releases and cultural programs to a full-scale book and two 35 mm. theatrical release films. As Briggs explained it to this writer, his newly arrived Press Attaché, no new money would be coming from Washington for programs in Sri Lanka, but if we could link all of the many things we do in cultural, educational, and informational programs under a common theme and logo, the impact of these programs would be maximized. Thus began a series of routine and rather ordinary public diplomacy programs but with a common link and a common purpose to "salute" the people of Sri Lanka on this the 200th anniversary of American independence. Independence was a theme which registered with Sri Lankan across the political spectrum. Their own independence from Britain was still a living memory for the older generations and young people were eager to learn more about their own history. Coincidentally, much of that history had an American connection, from the American theosophist Henry Steele Olcott's role in founding Ananda College and in spurring the Buddhist revival movement, to the American missionaries in the Tamil north who ministered to the needs of the people there despite threats and intimidation from the British establishment to the visits by American clipper ships bringing goods from around the world to the shops of Colombo.

It was the task of USIS Colombo to use these connections to bring Sri Lankans to a greater understanding of the role that Americans had played in their past and could play in their future. Two examples will illustrate how this was accomplished. One will be found in the section relating to publications, the other is described here.

In thinking about a way to pull all the connections between Americans and Sri Lankans together in an easily understood way, the Press Section hit upon the notion of an exhibition of photographs and memorabilia from the earliest days of American independence to the present day. The concept was easy enough to create but one would see that its execution was a daunting task. There was to be no help from Washington except perhaps some photographs from the archives. The content of the exhibition and its physical structure had to be created on the spot in Sri Lanka. While the Press Attaché and his staff combed the island nation for photographs and memorabilia to place in the exhibit, the administrative section commandeered a team of carpenters and workmen to assemble a series of wooden panels and frames for what would become some 300 separate components.

Where to locate this exhibit and when to mount it were two key questions answered by the Public Affairs Officer. Briggs convinced the Ambassador that the best place to open the exhibit was in the Ambassador's own residence on July 4th during the traditional Independence Day Reception. That would guarantee a high-ranking and influential audience and the publicity necessary to draw crowds to the exhibit. Amazingly Ambassador Christopher Van Hollen agreed and gave up his residence's lower level for two weeks of construction of the wooden panels and displays, and several more weeks of tours of the exhibition following the July 4 opening. Of course today in the over-zealous security environment that cordons off U.S. diplomats from the people they need to talk with, such a location for a public exhibition would be unthinkable.

And yes the exhibition was a huge success; the current and future government leaders were in attendance and were stunned by the number and variety of American connections with their history and society. Everything from early photos of American missionaries and visitors to the island to more substantial items like a 600-pound church bell from one of the American churches near Jaffna, trade goods, such as 19th-century Seth Thomas clocks, and even a huge block of ice in sawdust representing the tons of ice shipped to Sri Lanka by clipper ship from the frozen ponds of New England in the 19th century. As the then current and two future Prime Ministers of Sri Lanka took turns ringing the church bell and reading the captions on the photographs, it was evident that this one, of the dozens of events billed as an American Bicentennial Salute to Sri Lanka, had accomplished its mission. The exhibition had a good run in Colombo and a paper show version of the items with a locally produced brochure circulated around the island for years thereafter in village halls and schools in every corner of the nation.

Czechoslovakia

As World War II was coming to an end, the Red Army raced westward to Berlin and the Western allies moved up the boot of Italy and across France to the Rhine. Czechoslovakia, especially hilly western and southern Bohemia, was to become one of the last redoubts of the Nazis. Both the Russians and the Americans moved aggressively to eliminate this potential hold out. The U.S. Third Army under General George Patton moved into western Bohemia and for a time it appeared that the Yanks would be the first to enter Prague and liberate that city. The communist-dominated partisans in Prague, alarmed at the notion that they might be replaced by pro-American administrators, called for the Red Army to liberate the city. With the final decision made at General Eisenhower's headquarters, George Patton's tanks slowed and met up with the Red Army in the town of Rokycany just east of Plzen (Pilsen), an hour's drive west of the capital city. At the end of the war, American GIs occupied western and southern Bohemia and the Red Army occupied the remainder of Czechoslovakia. The Red Army was reluctant to leave these rich lands, so the American GIs also stayed on until there was a mutual withdrawal in 1946. During that idyll, the GIs and the residents of western Bohemia seemed to have formed some close friendships. Indeed after the war, dozens of monuments were erected spontaneously by local townspeople as tributes to their American liberators.

Following the Communist "coup" of February 1948, the hard-line regime wished to create the myth that it was the Red Army alone which had liberated all of Czechoslovakia from fascism. Honoring the American GIs as liberators was actively discouraged. After crushing the Prague Spring with a Russian-led Warsaw Pact occupation of Czechoslovakia in 1968, the authorities took even more drastic measures. Ostensibly in "outrage" over the Vietnam War, local officials had many of the monuments to American liberators removed and/or destroyed. But memories are much harder to erase.

In part to examine the history of the American liberation of Western and Southern Bohemia and in part as a convenient cover for American military attachés' travel to border areas and other districts of military interest, in the late 1970s the Defense Attaché's Office at the American Embassy in Prague began a series of automobile trips each May to towns and villages in Western Bohemia liberated by U.S. forces. A similar series of journeys was organized in November annually to visit crash sites and monuments to fallen U.S. airmen in Slovakia. Initially only Defense Department personnel made these journeys, but in the early 1980s other personnel from the Embassy, including the U.S. Ambassador Jack Matlock, joined the small motorcade to Bohemia in May each year. The visits to the sites where markers once stood and to the small towns and villages was very low key and attracted little notice, except for the ubiquitous STB (*Statny Tanjy Bezpechnosti* or State Secret Security) detail which shadowed the Americans. Where a monument remained, a small wreath "from the American people" was placed on the marker.

In May 1983, the newly arrived Public Affairs Officer (PAO) joined the motor trips in May and November, which by now included a few key Embassy officers. He realized the potential that these events might have for the U.S. to remind the people of Czechoslovakia of America's role in their liberation from the Nazis and also to demonstrate the interest and concern on the part of the U.S. for the oppressed people of this communist state. Thus, beginning in 1984, the Embassy's May and November "wreath-layings"—as they came to be known—took on a much higher profile and a different character. All U.S. embassy employees and their families were encouraged to join the motorcades which grew much larger with up to two dozen vehicles moving through the back roads and byways of Bohemia. Dates and times of the "wreath-laying" ceremonies were announced through the Czechoslovak Service of the Voice of America (VOA)—the most widely listened-to foreign radio station in Czechoslovakia. In those days, VOA was called "Prague Three" by most Czechs since they had two domestic networks. The Czech and Slovak services of Radio Free Europe (RFE) also announced the events. The Press and Cultural Service of the U.S. Embassy (as the U.S. Information Service was called in Eastern Europe and the USSR) was able to obtain thousands of crossed Czechoslovak–American flag lapel pins from a U.S.–Canadian émigré organization the Czechoslovak National Congress, as well as Voice of America bumper stickers, lapel pins, ballpoint pens, and other "souvenirs" for distribution to well-wishers along the route.

By 1986, the Press and Cultural Service was printing special commemorative postcards by the thousands at a USIS facility in Vienna, complete with a photo of GIs liberating Pilsen. This postcard was produced for mass distribution to the by now thousands of Czechs lining the route and participating in the ceremonies at each site. Wreaths from "the American people" were placed in each location where there had been a monument, whether removed or not. The American Ambassador William Luers addressed large audiences in near-fluent Czech recalling the long friendship between Americans and the people of Czechoslovakia. The STB observers were beside themselves. The crowds were now too large to intimidate. The secret police filming and taping the events was hardly a secret but these tactics were largely ignored by the crowds who often displayed American flags and other expressions of support. Detailed reports of the growing crowds and their enthusiasm were broadcast back to Czechoslovakia by the VOA and RFE.

This local initiative, from the early forays into the Bohemian countryside in the late 1970s and especially after 1984 brought the events to the level of a major public diplomacy program, proved to be a huge success. An early indication of the effectiveness of these trips was the repeated and ever more threatening attempts on the part of the Czechoslovak authorities to prevent them from happening. The program reinforced the belief among the people of Czechoslovakia that the U.S. and the West had not abandoned them and was actively demonstrating that fact through the series of "wreath-layings" around the country. After the successful Velvet Revolution in December 1989, which toppled the communist government, the annual May Embassy "wreath-layings" continued into 1990 and culminated in an event in Pilsen at the newly restored Liberation Monument in front of the city hall. More than 100,000 Czechs honored the American liberators of their city and their nation at the event.

Finland

In the year 1638 a small band of Swedish colonists (the majority happened to be Finns, then under the rule of the Kingdom of Sweden) founded New Sweden on the Delaware River, south of today's Philadelphia, Pennsylvania. Nearly 350 years later, a rather low-key but well organized effort was to have commemorated this event in both Sweden and Finland. The two countries and the U.S. postal authorities had approved the issuance of stamps to mark the occasion in 1988 and various Swedish–American and Finnish–American organizations were making plans to commemorate the event on both sides of the Atlantic.

While studying the Finnish language and culture in preparation for his assignment beginning in July 1987, the future Public Affairs Officer (PAO) learned about the 1988 anniversary and it triggered a series of ideas and plans to increase the American profile in Finland and reinforce the positive feelings for the U.S. that existed there. Recalling the "America's Bicentennial Salute to Sri Lanka" from an earlier assignment, the PAO recognized how successful it had been to bring all public diplomacy programs—the routine ones as well as those created just for the event—under a single banner as his PAO had done in Sri Lanka in 1976.

Using this "Salute" formula as a model, the incoming PAO, in discussion with the Finnish Embassy in Washington and the U.S. Information Agency and Department of State, began to focus on 1988 as "The National Year of Friendship with Finland." Upon arrival in Finland he was able to convince Ambassador Rockwell Schnabel and the Country Team of the value of using this event to further U.S. public diplomacy and traditional diplomatic goals in Finland. Within a few months, an elaborate program of the National Year of Friendship with Finland was announced and underway. A logo for the Finnish–American Year of Friendship was adopted by both the U.S. Embassy and the Finnish Foreign Ministry and soon this logo was on everything from cultural presentations to educational exchanges to publications and special events.

The U.S. Information Service alone listed some 38 separate programs in honor of the "Year of Friendship." The agenda included an all-star program at the prestigious *Finlandia* Hall featuring a video address to the audience (and the national TV audience) by President Ronald Reagan on the importance of the relationship between Finland and the United States over the 350 years since the first Finn set foot in the New World. The event also kicked off a five-year $5 million fund-raising campaign to increase the number of Fulbright grantees between Finland and the U.S. The "Year of Friendship" culminated in a visit to Finland by President Reagan, the first-ever by a sitting U.S. president.

Among the benefits of this elaborate program in cooperation with the Finnish Government was an increased favorability rating for the U.S. as a nation and for specific U.S. foreign policies as measured by public opinion polls. The high level of favorability proved to be important as Finland assumed the Presidency of the Security Council just prior to the Gulf War, and Finland played an important and positive role which supported U.S. positions. Shortly thereafter Finland bought their first-ever U.S. military aircraft when a major contract was awarded for the F-16. This era of good feeling between the U.S. and Finland continued as the Baltic States gained their freedom from the USSR and the Soviet Union itself disintegrated shortly thereafter.

Thailand

The Thai economy was one of the fastest growing of the so-called Asian Tigers in the 1990s. Construction cranes (the national bird!) were seen in every direction in Bangkok, which went from a charming backwater to New York on the Chao Priya River in less than a decade. Fifty- and sixty-story buildings replaced wooden houses and tropical gardens in the capital and similar scenes could be seen in other urban centers throughout the country. Thailand became the "Detroit of Asia" as dozens of automobile brands were manufactured there for the Asian market, and auto parts makers proliferated. But this house of cards was built on speculation and what came to be called "crony capitalism" with loose banking practices, slip-shod securities laws and massive corruption, and much of it was about to come crashing down.

The U.S.–Thai relationship has had its ups and downs in the 165-year history of diplomatic relations. Essentially, the relationship in Thai eyes was a classic *pi–non* relationship, that is, an elder brother–younger brother relationship with the U.S. as the *pi* and Thailand as the *non*. It was the *pi*'s responsibility to look out for the *non*, to assist when needed, to protect and to guide the *non*. The *non*'s responsibility was to be loyal to the *pi* and to follow the *pi*'s lead. This *pi–non* relationship survived the military dictatorships in Thailand's post-war era, the Vietnam War, and American withdrawal from Southeast Asia, and seemed unshakeable in July 1997.

Earlier in the year there had been "runs" on several international currencies by hedge fund operators, the most famous being George Soros' run on the British pound which netted him hundreds of millions of dollars in profit. In July 1997 it became the Thai *baht*'s turn to be attacked by currency traders and it proved to be the beginning of a cascade of economic troubles that caused first the Thai *baht* to crumble and then the Thai financial system to crash and eventually the Thai economy to come tumbling down. A run on a country's currency can be overcome easily if the underlying fundamentals of the economy are sound. But in Thailand's case the fundamentals were in a shambles thanks to the crony capitalism and corruption of the banking and securities sectors.

Thailand became the first of the Asian Tigers to fall, but it soon had plenty of company. Indonesia and then South Korea followed in Thailand's footsteps and for many of the same reasons. When the dust had settled the Thai *baht* went from about 24 to the dollar to about 55 to the dollar. Thousands of workers in the financial sector were suddenly without a job when their banks and securities firms closed their doors overnight.

This is essentially an economic story but it relates to public diplomacy because at its heart is the *pi–non* relationship. When Thailand's economy crashed, it looked to the U.S. for help. But the U.S. Treasury Department, looking through the framework of economics and finance, not public diplomacy or diplomatic relations, examined Thailand and saw that it basically got what it deserved for not having its house in order. The State Department then and now defers to the Treasury in all things having to do with economics and finance. So the U.S. did absolutely nothing when Thailand's crash came. Puzzled and resentful, the Thai saw the U.S. as abandoning Thailand and renouncing the *pi–non* relationship just when the going got tough.

Newspaper editorials pointed to the U.S. as the "real" cause of Thailand's woes. George Soros and other Western currency traders were vilified, and by implication Western governments, especially the U.S., were seen as responsible for the collapse throughout Asia. As if this was not bad enough, the U.S. Government decided that things were indeed beginning to get out of hand in Asia, and the White House announced that it would bail out Indonesia and South Korea with billions of dollars in credit. This was like throwing gasoline on a fire in Thailand. The Thai media and influential Thais across the spectrum of society exploded in indignation. The U.S. would not help Thailand but would help Indonesia! Thailand was one of the five treaty allies of the U.S. in the Pacific; it was a functioning democracy; Thailand was a loyal ally of the U.S. and took its lead from the U.S. Indonesia was none of these things—not a treaty ally nor even an informal ally, a dictatorship not a democracy, and Indonesia, more often than not, was at odds with the U.S.

A major financial decision had been made in Washington without input from two very important sources—first there was no consultation with regard to the public diplomacy dimension of this decision in Thailand or indeed in any of the countries affected, and, second, there was no consultation with the Embassy in Bangkok which actually understood the situation in Thailand. Even before this unfortunate decision was made, the Public Affairs Officer had outlined a series of public diplomacy strategic and tactical measures to explain U.S. policy to the Thais and limit the damage to the bilateral relationship. Following the announcement about aid for Indonesia, Ambassador William Itoh and his Country Team met to develop an overall strategy to cope with this near rupture of the relationship.

Public diplomacy naturally was a central part of the strategy, which also included convincing

State and Treasury to reverse course and provide an aid package for Thailand at least proportional to the aid package proposed for other countries. The Department of Defense was called upon through the Defense Attaché's Office and the Joint US Military Assistance Group to cancel an outstanding contract for F-16 aircraft and parts which would free up hundreds of millions of dollars for the Thai Government.

The U.S. Information Service's public diplomacy strategy focused on several fronts. Because of the crash of the Thai economy and currency, many of the 8,000 Thai students then in American higher educational institutions were suddenly without the financial means to continue their education. For the U.S. this meant well publicized and immediate assistance from both public and private sector sources to provide work-study and loan opportunities for Thai and other Asian students, and the Institute for International Education and a host of American higher educational institutions took the lead. In addition, the Public Affairs Section proposed to Washington that a special high profile scholarship program be established for 165 students selected by the Thai Government for three years to attend U.S. universities. The 165 were linked to the 165 years of diplomatic relations between the two countries, and the total funding for the scholarship program provided through Economic Assistance Funds and administered by USAID came to about $3 million. This is a tiny sum when compared to the $4 billion in loan guarantees provided to Thailand or the nearly $1 billion in debt cancelled by recalling the F-16 contract, but because it involved people not hardware or loans it registered with the Thai public as real help from America. Other smaller exchange programs, too, were augmented, like the Fulbright Program and other government-funded internships, but the 165 scholarships made the biggest headlines.

Determined to demonstrate that the U.S. had not abandoned Thailand, the Embassy encouraged as many high level visitors as possible to visit Bangkok. For its part the U.S. Information Service used each of these cabinet level or equivalent visits to get the message out that the U.S. was interested in Thailand and would do whatever it could to ease the burden during a difficult economic time. Every high level visitor held a press conference and interviews with Thai media, made highly visible public appearances, and consistently expressed the deep concern of the U.S. for Thailand and the Thai people. It was a rare week in 1998 when a U.S. cabinet-level official, congressional delegation or senior military officer did not visit Thailand with a full public diplomacy program.

Recognizing that there was a reservoir of good will in Thailand built up over many years and reinforced by the visit by U.S. President Bill Clinton in 1996, another key component of the public diplomacy strategy focused on reaching out to the gate-keepers of information and the "influencers" in the society to make the case for the United States. The PAO arranged a series of lunches with key editorial boards and influential columnists to provide them with Embassy-produced briefings on the complexities of international finance and currency speculation. U.S. Ambassador Itoh, the fluent Thai-speaking Deputy Chief of Mission Ralph Boyce, the Embassy's entire economic reporting section, and public diplomacy officers were all mobilized to this effort. In the end, it was Thai columnists, commentators, and editorial writers who put the Asian financial debacle in context and into the proper perspective for their readers, listeners, and viewers.

The U.S. emerged not as the villain it appeared to be when it had ignored Thailand's crisis in the summer of 1997 but rather as the prime mover in rectifying a corrupt and mismanaged financial system in Thailand and in other Asian countries. This was seen as an act of responsibility worthy of the *pi*. Ironically, despite their own best efforts in aiding Thailand, it was Japan which was blamed for the instability in the Asian financial world because it continually postponed reforms to their own banking and financial sector. In opinion polling following the resolution of the financial crisis, the U.S. favorability level was nearly identical with the high mark it had reached immediately after the Clinton visit in 1996.

Publications[5]

The importance of a permanent record cannot be overestimated. U.S. Information Service posts in many parts of the world have used print publications to provide this permanent record and to reach many potential members of the targeted audience which would otherwise not have been able to receive the message. And what was that message? In most cases it was a very simple one. "We may be a superpower and we may be quite a different society from yours, but we share common values; we are interested in your nation and we care about you."

There were other messages as well, of course, but the overriding theme of post-produced publications so often echoed this simple statement.

Print publications were not the only media used by field operations to reach a wider audience. Films, TV, and radio programs were conceived, produced, and distributed locally by the U.S. Information Service as well. This writer recalls with great pleasure a series of radio readings of the works of American authors undertaken by the U.S. Information Service and its employees, and aired on the Sri Lanka Broadcasting Corporation's English language service. The author was among other roles "Henderson the Rain King" from the Saul Bellow classic broadcast to millions from the SLBC studios in Colombo, Sri Lanka in the mid-1970s. Other USIS staff portrayed other literary characters for the avid radio audience in a nation that was not to broadcast its first television program for another two years. That same year, the Cultural Attaché Richard Ross portrayed the American theosophist and revered Buddhist revivalist Henry Steele Olcott in a film entitled "Henry Steele Olcott, Searcher After Truth," a USIS film produced in Sri Lanka to introduce the public to an American who was key to the national revival movement and ultimately to the independence of Sri Lanka. As Press Attaché, this writer and his staff ensured the distribution of this film in nearly every community on the island nation in 16 and 35 mm and in English, Sinhalese, and Tamil versions. There was hardly a Sri Lankan unfamiliar with Colonel Olcott and his role in Sri Lanka's revival by the end of the film's run in local theaters.

The examples of print publications below are taken from Sri Lanka, Thailand, and Finland, but similar examples could be found in many other counties around the world.

Images of Sri Lanka Through American Eyes

H.A.I. Goonetileke was the distinguished Librarian at the Peradynia Campus of the University of Ceylon near the ancient capital of Kandy. Author of a two-volume bibliography of Sri Lanka, he had been a 1974 recipient of the a JDR III Fund Fellowship to the United States and, moved by the upcoming American Bicentennial in 1976, determined that he wanted to do something to bring Sri Lanka and America closer together. He approached the American Ambassador, Christopher Van Hollen, with an idea for a book about the impressions of Sri Lanka by visiting Americans over the course of the past 200 years. Goonetileke had already acquired an impressive bibliography of works by a wide range of well-known Americans who had written their opinion of the island and its peoples based on visits brief or lengthy from the earliest days of the American Republic through the early 1970s. Van Hollen was wise enough to know what a contribution this would be to David Briggs' "Bicentennial Salute to Sri Lanka," and immediately put Goonetileke in touch with Briggs and his Press Attaché, whose task it would be to be the text editor/publisher of this volume. It was decided early in the effort to include a series of black and white photographs depicting aspects of Sri Lankan life taken by an American Fulbright grantee in photography, Yvonne Hanemann, and each chapter of the book contains one or more of these stunning photographs of village life from the 1960s. The cover art of Galle Harbor in the early 19th century is by Sri Lankan artist Stanley Kirinde. As the Bicentennial year began, the book, a joint project of a Sri Lankan compiler and editor, an American text editor and publisher, and a USIA printing facility in Manila, emerged in an edition of 5000 copies for presentation and sale throughout the island as part of the American Bicentennial Salute to Sri Lanka. Presenting essays and descriptions of Ceylon over the period 1813 to 1972, the book includes writing from such notables as Mark Twain, Thomas Merton, and Andrew Carnegie, and others perhaps known best for their connection to Ceylon/Sri Lanka like Henry Steel Olcott, Paul Bowles, and Philip Crowe. From the beginning the book was an outstanding success and in the view of many of the reviewers it told as much about the evolving nature of American perceptions of the world as it did of the nature of Ceylon over 200 years. The prevailing view was one which was in harmony with the aim of the publication, that America and Americans have become more perceptive, more sophisticated, and more accepting of differences over the 200 years of the nation's existence. The book was a financial success as well. Deliberately priced as to be in reach of modest incomes, the book had to be reprinted in 1978 and again in 1983. A second edition was produced to commemorate the 50th anniversary of Sri Lanka–U.S. diplomatic relations in 1998. It is this edition's cover that is reproduced in Figure 18.1.

The Eagle and the Elephant: Thai American Relations Since 1833

Perhaps one of the most successful post-produced USIS publications of all time is the coffee-table sized book (279 pages) *The Eagle and the Elephant: Thai American Relations Since 1833*, the cover of the fourth edition (1996) of which is pictured in Figure 18.2. Originally produced in November 1982 to commemorate the 150th anniversary of Thai–American diplomatic relations in 2300 copies, the book was reprinted in another 2000 copies in 1983, and 3000 copies in 1987. The volume was thoroughly revamped, reorganized, and updated with a new cover illustration for the latest edition in 1997.

The 1997 edition of 3000 copies was used for limited presentations to VIPs and leading Thai institutions, but for the first time was also on sale through a local Thai bookseller and thus was able to more than recoup its costs. Importantly, the book was printed in English and Thai side by side so it could be used as an aid to language learning. Although much of the credit for the book must go to those who produced the original, including the then PAO Herwald (Hal) H. Morton, the USIS staff of 1996–97, including editor Patricia Norland, greatly improved the book for the modern reader by combining some of the previous substance of the book with much new material and organizing it into two sections: "I. The Past: 1833–1976" and "2. Current Cooperation: 1976 to the Present." The 1997 edition included material up to and including the visit of President Bill Clinton to Thailand in November 1996. Containing a remarkable collection of photographs relevant to Thai–American relations over 165 years, including rare photos of Thai royalty and the impressive cover photo of the Eagle and Elephant sword presented on behalf of U.S. President Andrew Jackson by his envoy Edmund Roberts to King Rama III in 1833. These "royal connections" mean a tremendous amount to the Thai people who so greatly revere their present monarch.

Seventy Years of Finnish–American Diplomatic Relations

The third and last publication also concerns an anniversary in bilateral relations, always an opportunity to renew the positive aspects of a relationship with the host country. As with the previous book, this volume was printed side by side in English and the host nation's language. As fate would have it the very next year following the National Year of Friendship with Finland (described earlier) would mark the 70th anniversary of Finnish–American diplomatic relations and the USIS Public Affairs Officer was not about to let that opportunity slip by unnoticed. Hastily preparing a selection of locally obtainable photos, a request was cabled to the Office of the Historian of the Department of State for photographs of relevance to Finnish–American relations and a brief history of the 70 years. Washington was able to pull together a modest

Figure 18.1.

photographic collection and use one of the Department's interns to research the project for a short history of diplomatic relations with Finland. While not compelling reading, the history served the purpose admirably, as did brief statements by then Secretary of State James Baker and by William Slany, Director of the Office of the Historian, Department of State. The book, printed locally in a modest 3000 copies, was presented to Finnish officials, leaders, and educational institutions.

Proving its worth, in 1999, on the 80th anniversary of diplomatic relations, the U.S. Embassy reprinted the book with an introduction by U.S. Ambassador to Finland Eric Edelman, along with a commissioned analytical article on the 10 years since the printing of the original book by former Finnish Ambassador to the U.S. and foreign policy expert Jaako Iloniemi. So much history had passed in the interim, including the dissolution of the Soviet Union, the independence of the Baltic States, and the overthrow of communism in Eastern Europe, that an update was

222

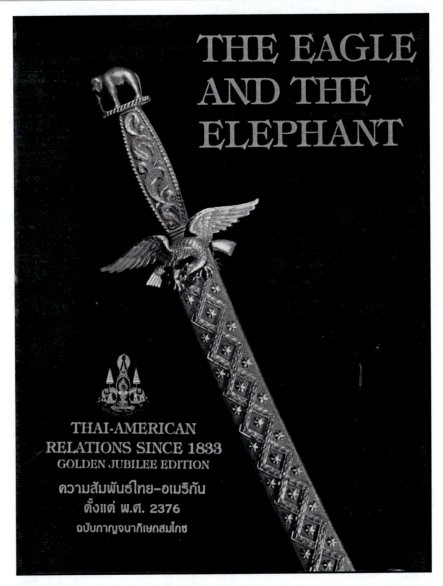

Figure 18.2.

thought absolutely necessary. Indeed, 10 years before no one would have predicted the events in Europe or the accession of Finland to the European Community, much less the use of U.S.-built fighter aircraft in the Finnish Air Force.

And a Lesson Drawn

One might dismiss these seven examples of "localized public diplomacy' as products and processes of an earlier age not so applicable today. Nothing could be further from the truth. Today more than ever before the United States should be relying on its experts in the field for ideas on how to engage foreign audiences on issues of *mutual* concern. Public diplomacy professionals know the answers, not Washington "insiders" who are most decidedly "outsiders" when it comes to global thinking. Whether or not a Bicentennial salute, a series of wreath-laying cere-monies, a scholarship program, an historic anniversary, or a one-off publication is what is needed will be best answered by the people who know the country best, the public diplomacy officers and their locally engaged staff abroad.

There is room for sound and thoughtful initiatives from Washington, and when speaking of foreign policy certainly it is best to speak with one voice or at least with voices in concert. Some programs, particularly exchanges of persons, whether academic or professional, benefit from a Washington perspective.

The cultural programs—now unfortunately mostly a thing of the past—were dependent on Washington recruitment of the big names who would tour the world bringing American dance or theater or jazz music to millions. But at hundreds of overseas posts, at America Houses in Germany, and at American cultural centers and libraries the world over, "entrepreneurial" Cultural Affairs Officers and PAOs managed to enlist a glittering array of talent for small pro-grams, often followed by a social opportunity between the American performing artist and local counterparts.

The traveling exhibitions that toured Soviet and East European cities for a year or longer and U.S. participation in major international festivals of various kinds could perhaps only be organ-ized from Washington, but there are countless examples of locally organized cultural and artistic exhibits and participation in film, arts, and music festivals put together from post and local resources by USIS often in close cooperation with local host organizations.

One thing nearly all localized public diplomacy efforts have in common is that they work. They accomplish what they set out to do. Regrettably, the reverse has been true of many of the Washington-generated one-size-fits-all schemes to make the world love us—or else.

Notes

1 Lisbeth Schorr, *Common Purpose* (New York: Anchor, 1998), 28.
2 I am grateful to Professor Matthew Hartley of the Graduate School of Education, University of Pennsyl-vania for the sources of both of these perceptive quotations.
3 Some of these vignettes have been used in a different format and context in the author's "Seduced and Abandoned: Strategic Information and the National Security Process," in *Affairs of State* ed. G. Marcella (Carlisle, PA: Strategic Studies Institute, U.S. Army War College, Forthcoming).
4 For additional details, see William P. Kiehl, "Oral history interview," *Foreign Affairs Oral History Collection* (Arlington, VA: The Association for Diplomatic Studies and Training, 2005), especially 68–87; 133–160; 165–220; 279–321.
5 The illustrations contained herein are reproduced from the author's personal collection. As they are USG publications, no copyright is claimed or implied by the use of these images.

19

The Distinction Between Public Affairs and Public Diplomacy

Ken S. Heller and Liza M. Persson

American traditions and the American ethic require us to be truthful, but the most important reason is that truth is the best propaganda, and lies are the worst. To be persuasive, we must be believable; to be believable, we must be credible; to be credible, we must be truthful. It is as simple as that.

Edward R. Murrow, Director, USIA, 1963

Strategic Communication entails synchronizing Public Affairs (PA) and Public Diplomacy (PD) in an attempt to unify words and messages. So why is it necessary? What are the distinctions between PA and PD that require such an effort and what would be the effects of such an action?

Originally, the two channels of communication between the U.S. Government and the world's publics were established structurally and doctrinally separate. They each have different commitments, purposes and intended audiences. Yet this is not the first attempt at such a bonding and manipulation.

The purpose of the Office of Strategic Influence (OSI) was to synchronize PA, PD, and Information Operations (IO), specifically that portion of IO known as Psychological Operations (PSYOP), so that messages coming from each would be mutually supportive and validating, regardless of the target audience. However, it was publicly aborted in 2001 due to the suspicion as to the lack of public insight. However, former Secretary of Defense Donald Rumsfeld suggested in November 2002 that only the name of the office had been abolished. In different forms and under different names, the functions were still carried out fulfilling the intended purposes.[1] Few knew the closing of the OSI was due to a whistle blown by a long-time PA officer who objected to the alleged OSI intention of releasing false news to the international media.

Historically, the science and systematic use of psychological means as a tool of statecraft have been around for quite some time. It arose tentatively before World War I (WWI), when the U.S. Government began funding and making use of the research that up until then had been driven by private organizations. It came of age before the nation's entry into WWII when it was used to sway the American people towards entering the war. It is reported to have been used systematically by the U.S. Government at home and abroad ever since, the most recent example being the manipulation of public sentiment in favor of an invasion of Iraq, the creation of heroes and the continued distortions of truth.

It is both necessary and interesting to compare PA and PD. Their individual commitments of enabling the right of a people of a democratic nation to be kept informed about the actions and motives of their government, for PA; and the manipulation of the perceptions of people around the world to facilitate the "interests" of a nation, for PD, would seemingly be replaced by a shared commitment to the communication of a cohesive and consistent presentation of the nation both internally and externally. This should be of great concern.

Fundamental divisions between PA and PD can be found by the comparison of core commitments, purposes and primary audiences.

PA agencies' and operations' core commitment is to fulfill both a pragmatic and democratic need for accurate and timely information. In a democratically governed nation, the public, its political representatives and military community service members have a right to be kept informed about how the resources they make available are used. PA's core purpose is that of **Informing**, and the intended audience is the domestic population.

PD's core commitment is to shape the global mental environment in such a way as to shape the opinions, actions and perceptions of people of other nations to be more in line with U.S. national interests, such as defined by the administration at any given time. The core purpose of PD is that of **Influencing** and the intended audience is the public and leaders of foreign nations.

In 1997, The Planning Group for Integration of United States Information Agency (USIA) into the Department of State used the following definitions (until the merging, USIA was the agency that practiced PD for the Department of State): PD seeks:

> to promote the national interest of the United States through understanding, informing and the influencing of foreign audiences. Public Affairs is the provision of information to the public, press and other institutions concerning the goals, policies and activities of the U.S. Government. Public Affairs seeks to foster understanding of these goals through dialogue with individual citizens and other groups and institutions (through its Community Relations programs), and the domestic and international media. However, the thrust of public affairs is to inform the domestic audience.

Both PA and PD make use of the variety of information technologies available today. Film, television, radio (such as Voice of America and Radio Free Europe), the World Wide Web and video games are important vessels for advancing a national image abroad. New teams such as the State Department's "Digital Outreach Team" or the Department of Defense's "New Media Operations" are exploiting these avenues of approach including the YouTube and MySpace websites as well as the blogosphere, which the United States Central Command (USCENTCOM) Public Affairs Office has also actively engaged in order to reach new publics. PD advocates and practitioners see activities such as sports, cultural events and exchange programs as important avenues for otherwise diverse citizens to understand and interact with each other, and integral to international cultural understanding, which is stated as a key goal of modern PD. These efforts involve not only communicating the message(s) that a country wishes to present abroad, but also analyzing and understanding the perceptions of the nation and the ways that the message is interpreted by diverse societies. They develop and improve tools and skills for effective persuasion and attraction.

> Public Diplomacy includes additional kinds of interaction with foreign publics such as arranging student exchange programs, hosting seminars and meeting with foreign business and academic leaders. Indirect PD includes the activities of citizens internationally, to include the everyday consumption of cultural activities and products such as films, tourism, theater and Internet discussion.

The Smith-Mundt Act of 1948 formed the basic charter for PD after World War II and established the USIA. The Foreign Relations Act of 1972 amended the Smith-Mundt Act to ban the dissemination of any "information about the U.S., its people and its policies" prepared for distribution overseas within the United States. The Zorinsky Amendment further restricted PD by prohibiting any funding of material used "to influence public opinion in the (United States), and no program material . . . shall be distributed within the (United States)."

In short, PD is not to target any part or member of the U.S. public. For example, today the English-language website of The Office of International Information Programs (formerly USIA) still differs from their French and Spanish sites, primarily in that the non-English language sites contain links to articles on human rights (specifically centered on Cuba and Peru), drugs, and corruption, as well as reports on democracy and the AIDS epidemic, none of which appear on the English site. Of particular note is that French and Spanish sites are also linked to the Voice of America, which by law cannot be broadcast into the United States.

Because of rapid changes in the information technology environment and outdated relevant legislature, explicit regulations as well as principles of international laws may inadvertently present both constraints and opportunities.

A point of contention derives from the difficulty of sending one message to international audiences and another to a domestic media in an information environment without territorial borders. Due to the Internet and other communication technologies, it is almost impossible for governments to regulate the flow of information across their borders with the precision of targeting specific groups abroad. The information dimension has become a battlefield in a war that knows no boundaries. Its offensives are directed not just at adversaries in Iraq and Afghanistan or at regimes that obstruct and reject U.S. policy, but also at the world at large. At the same time technological advances have made access to information instantaneous and ubiquitous, eroding and erasing longstanding barriers, legal and otherwise, that in the past protected the American public and press from collateral damage in propaganda campaigns. As a senior military official with knowledge of American psychological operations in Iraq said, "There is no 'local' media anymore. All media is potentially international. The web makes it all public. We need to eliminate the idea that psychological operations and information operations can issue any kind of information to the media ever. Period."[2]

In an article about the U.S. Government's payments to Iraqi journalists to place pro-American news stories in the Iraqi media, defense officials stated that the U.S. public is at risk of being influenced by communication and information operations seeking to manipulate the perceptions of a foreign audience, techniques that the U.S. military is only allowed to use against foreign governments and populations.

So why the temptation to fuse these two modes of communication?

PA is responsible for developing working relationships with reporters and other national and international media representatives to include bloggers who lie in the gray area between being journalists and citizens. It also maintains connections to America's film and publishing industry via liaisons in Los Angeles and New York. It is expected to maintain a robust community relations program in the United States and keep contact with other government agencies.

In its Command/Internal Information program, PA produces military newspapers, magazines, staffs and runs an entire overseas television and radio network, known as American Forces Network, while maintaining oversight of trained broadcasters, videographers, print journalists and photographers. All this to keep military service members and their families abroad informed and entertained. These products were "so successful the broadcast service quickly proved a better purveyor of the American way of life than the more propagandistic Voice of America."[3] PA also authors and reviews materials such as speeches, and its news articles, as well as its radio and television shows for security, accuracy, propriety and policy violations.

The commitment of PA to democratic principles obligates it to provide information to the public under its Public Information program allowing the evaluation of the policies, decisions and functions of their government. This important role of enabling a public to take an active and educated part in evaluating and affecting their governing and representation as a nation around the world explains the demand on PA to deliver information free from attempts at manipulating the audience through misleading, false or suggestive information.

Considering the capabilities, tools, and the scope of PA and PD, it is apparent that making them both "tactics" of national communication strategies would create an information dominance element the world has never seen. Some recognize the gravity of this issue.

In 1991, upon assuming office, Britain's Prime Minister Tony Blair and his media advisor Alistair Campbell commissioned a report on improving management of government communications.[4] The Mountfield Report, accepted by the Prime Minister in November 1997, suggested the government ought to improve the coordination of communication between and from governmental agencies. This action would make communication more consistent, coherent and effective in making the government's key themes and messages come across to the public. One of the ways in which this would be facilitated was through the establishment of a new strategic communication unit which would serve as a "hub" for consolidating communication and include key policies and messages. Experts would provide the leadership and guidance in making communication coordinated, cohesive and internally consistent in promoting national interests and core strategies of communication.

In 1999, U.S. President Bill Clinton established the position of Undersecretary of Public Diplomacy and Public Affairs within the State Department to "help ensure that the communication efforts of Public Diplomacy are practiced in combination with those of public affairs and traditional diplomacy to advance U.S. interests and security."[5]

Shortly after the attacks in America on September 11, 2001, the Office of Strategic Influence (OSI) was established. It was committed ultimately to the executive branch of the U.S. Government. Its purpose was to generate public sentiment and perceptions favorable to U.S. foreign policy by using the full spectrum of both civil and military communication and information. OSI, headed by Air Force Brig. Gen. Simon P. Worden, began "circulating classified proposals calling for aggressive campaigns that used not only the foreign media and the Internet, but also covert operations." Worden envisioned "a broad mission ranging from 'black' campaigns that would use disinformation and other covert activities to 'white' public affairs that relied on truthful news releases," according to Pentagon officials. "It goes from the blackest of black programs to the whitest of white," a senior Pentagon official said.[6]

In September 2004 a report[7] by the Defense Science Board task force outlined the critical role played by what it calls strategic communication, and recommended steps that the U.S. executive branch leadership and agencies, in collaboration with the private sector, should take in order to make recommended changes in information transactions, structures, and practices to make communication more efficient, coordinated, coherent, and internally consistent across government agencies and relative to overarching national strategies for communication in a "generational and global struggle about ideas." It stated, "We need to move beyond outdated concepts, stale structural models, and institutionally based labels. Public Diplomacy, PA, PSYOPS and open military IO must be coordinated and energized."

Based on the described attributes, a number of observations can be made if PA and PD are placed in relation to Strategic Communication. Optimally PA tells the whole truth, to all the people at all times. Truth is a requirement. National interests are defined by military and political leaders who then set restrictions that "chip away" from the "what, to whom, how and when." **Public Affairs is not, in itself, strategic in the classical sense of the word**. PD, on the other hand, has national interests as its *raison d'être*. They shape the activities of PD—not what restricts them. **Public Diplomacy is strategic in itself**.

PD can alter messages, target groups, timing and means much more than PA without violating its commitment or purpose. It not only can, but is supposed to change the forms, targets, timing and content of messages according to its communication strategy.

PA operations must not intentionally deceive and must present statements about events without speculation, subjective or value-based terminology, or other attempts of "packaging" that is to elicit certain effects in an audience. Therefore it can support a communication strategy through altering form, timing and intended audience but not by violating these demands on the content of the communication.

PD, on the other hand, has an emphasis on precisely such "effect-based" communication. Communication to spread non-objective values, ideas and perspectives is not just allowed, but a central dimension of PD.

In his master's thesis for the Naval postgraduate school in Monterey CA, *The Role of Public Diplomacy, Public Affairs and Psychological Operations in Strategic Information Operations*, Bryan R. Freeman describes the potential problematic position of PA. The effectiveness of the strategic influence "toolkit" of PD, PSYOP and PA depends largely upon the synergy of all three components. "Duplication of efforts, inconsistent themes, and the lack of a long-term, strategically focused, integrated information strategy have been an inhibiting factor to American foreign policy success."[8]

Of these three "tools" (PA, PD and IO/PSYOP), PA activities distinguish themselves by being restricted from not focusing "on directing or manipulating public actions or opinion." PA cannot be used as military deception or as disinformation for domestic or foreign audiences, nor can "propaganda or publicity designed to sway or direct public opinion be included in [Department of Defense] PA programs."[9]

Yet, as Freeman writes, "The primary means [for Department of Defense] of communicating with foreign audiences is through PA messages. Its messages should be conducted in concert with PSYOP [and PD] programs. The Department of Defense's PA programs are generally coordinated in accordance with and are intended to support, the Department of State's PD efforts."

As the channel for communication with people outside the Department of Defense and Department of State with the most extensive connections with national and international media, PA seems a tempting tool to use when a shift in public opinion and perception is desired.

An aggressive approach by the George W. Bush administration, driven by the need to achieve positive wartime accounts to enable support, led to a deviation from the norm of PA procedures over the last 30 years. The embedding of reporters directly into combat units had not occurred since the Vietnam era. For some journalists, the results were something that felt close to using the media as a propaganda machine, but the technique was successful from the government's perspective as America stayed glued to multimedia accounts and public support remained high for the first televised war.

Another example is in which Multi-National Force Iraq maintains a website and a YouTube channel for Operation Iraqi Freedom featuring selected multimedia from the military in Iraq. If these venues are PA efforts, then they are a part of a pro-active information campaign and require clear marking as such to maintain transparency. However, as they are reaching publics both domestic and foreign, the fact that they are not easily identified as PA products makes them instead potential violations of U.S. military regulations.

Additionally, there are also instances in which PA officers have been pushed by others to release information that fell in gray zones, that which may not be proved by observable facts but neither could they be easily disproved. For instance, how would a PA officer be able to release information describing the value of a currency and its stability, one from which the ink rubs right off with just a bit of moisture, originating in a country that has just sustained an invasion? Is not the economy one of the first things to collapse?

People wanting to stretch limitations can exploit many other gray areas. Can the choice of what to tell, to whom, and when be considered a violation of telling the truth without hidden agendas? How about the choice of words—can saying "the dropping of our ordnance resulted in collateral damage" rather than "our bombing killed people" be said to be "directing or manipulating public opinion?" Can any one account of an event ever be anything but a product of subjective selection and perception, if only to the extent of choosing what to say and how to say it? How about the difference between truth and accuracy? Matt Armstrong, the author of *Mountainrunner—Public Diplomacy, Unrestricted Warfare, Privatization of Force, and Civil-Military Relations*,[10] a blog exemplifying that the blogging community contains many hard working and devoted subject matter experts, provided a good example: A story can be precisely accurate ("We won't apologize because we don't know who shot that man") or truthful ("We apologize. We don't know who shot that man, but we know it was one of ours").

Problems can also arise from the relation between PA and political policies. The question is whether or not it is the job of military PA to define the political policies and motives for military operations, which will necessarily mean conveying a selective world view, or if they should simply inform the public about the actions and events directly linked to military activities.

Former Marine PA spokesman Josh Rushing said in a recent interview on the program *Democracy Now*:

> . . . as a military spokesperson, you do not talk about policy. You talk about the way you are going to conduct an action, not why you are going to conduct an action. So if someone were to ask me before the war, "Why are you going to invade Iraq?", and reporters did, the only honest answer I could give is, "We'll invade Iraq if the President orders us to and we won't if he doesn't. We don't get to pick and choose our battles." That way, it is left to a politician in a suit behind a podium at the White House to explain why they made that decision. Instead, we had a Republican operative who was put in charge of our office (at USCENTCOM) displacing a colonel that had started doing media liaison when this operative was about five years old. What this guy knew how to do was run a campaign, so we were run like a political campaign. The first step in that political campaign was to sell the product, and that was selling the invasion. He gave the reasons down to the young troops, guys like me, to go out to the reporters and tell them "we're going to invade a sovereign nation."[11]

Nevertheless Public Affairs and Public Diplomacy can also use their differences to create synergy and a greater effectiveness of a common and overarching strategy. The key lies in the difference between **coordinating** and **complementing**.

A coordination of PA and PD, given their different commitments and purposes, could lead to reoccurring choices between having to choose which to give priority over the other. As reflected in the accounts of many PA officers in the Iraq and Afghanistan theaters they were the only ones upholding the tenants of PA against the pressure to make use of its wedge of the credibility. They were directed to use the reach of PA in a frustrating situation, or under unclear or insufficient directives and clearly expressed inclinations from political and military leadership to "shape the truth rather than the message."

Coordination of PA with PD also holds some potential challenges for PD efforts. A consistent and substantial "gap" between the presentation a nation makes of itself through PD and the information about the reality of the power projected by that nation as communicated by PA, undermines current and future efforts to generate and use soft power. Such a gap can only be closed by what 18-year State Department veteran Price Floyd pointed out as the lacking component of the attempt at influencing the opinions of the peoples of the world: "Our actions and our words don't match up. We don't have a marketing problem—it's the product."[12] Instead a focus on the complementing abilities might be a better venue.

If successful, the two will complement each other. Presenting the values and good intentions without disclosing any actions that can lead to questions or objections undermines the credibility and sacrifices the very same values and ideals that are supposedly justifying the costs. Presenting only the actions without the motivational framework will make the actions speak for themselves, out of context.

However, according to surveys, trust in governments, both their own and those of other nations, is decreasing among people.[13] Communication and information perceived as originating from government sources are likely to be met with suspicion.

In his book *Soft Power*, Joseph Nye writes about how "postmodern publics are generally skeptical of authority and governments are often mistrusted." Credibility becomes a crucial resource, a force multiplier, when trying to reach people's hearts and minds. Any dent in credibility is hard to repair, especially as it tends to create a bad circle of negative perception in which attempts at restoring credibility, like strict claims of having "corrected the mistakes" or of being misunderstood or taken out of context, are either ignored or interpreted as further attempts to deceive.

A thesis paper entitled "Information Warfare: An Air Force Policy for the Role of Public Affairs," written by U.S. Air Force Major Robin K. Crumm at the School of Advanced Airpower Studies in Alabama, suggests that PA could be the ultimate information warfare weapon since it is "so stalwart in its claims of only speaking the truth." It quotes an unnamed information warrior who says, "The reason I tell you the truth is so that when I lie, you will believe me."[14]

If the reality of implications of U.S. policies could damage the perceptions of the nation abroad or of political leaders before their constituency, democracy demands accurate accounts be given to the American people even if they may "leak" to people elsewhere in the world. If it means damage to efforts of leveling the global mental topography in favor of national interests, then it lies with the United States to prove that it is capable of what Nye writes as being the most fundamental cornerstone: "Actions speak louder than words and public diplomacy that appears to be mere window dressing for the projection of power is unlikely to succeed."[15] I saw the same basic phrase spray painted in English on the wall of a Southern Iraqi community in early 2003 during the invasion. The lessons are not lost on those who speak other languages, which answer the question: Why do they hate us?

Notes

1 Secretary Rumsfeld Media Availability En Route to Chile, transcript from United States Department of Defense News Transcript, http://www.fas.org/sgp/news/2002/11/dod111802.html (accessed June 30, 2007).

2 Laura Rozen, "Blowback," *War and Piece*, http://www.warandpiece.com/blogdirs/003180.html (accessed June 30, 2007).

3 Answers.com Online Dictionary, "American Forces Network," http://www.answers.com/topic/american-forces-network?cat=technology (accessed June 30, 2007).

4 Information Warfare Monitor, "Information Warfare Timeline," http://www.infowar-monitor.net/modules.php?op=modload&name=Sections&file=index&req=viewarticle&artid=18 (accessed June 30, 2007).

5 Answers.com Online Dictionary, s.v "Undersecretary of Public Diplomacy and Public Affairs," http://www.answers.com/main/ntquery?s=public+diplomacy+and+public+affairs&gwp=13 (accessed June 30 2007)

6 Sourcewatch, "Office of Strategic Influence," http://www.sourcewatch.org/index.php?title=Office_of_Strategic_Influence (accessed June 30, 2007).

7 Report of the Defense Science Task Force on Strategic Communication, (September 2004), http://www.acq.osd.mil/dsb/reports/2004-09-Strategic_Communication.pdf (accessed June 30, 2007).

8 Bryan R. Freeman, "The Role of Public Diplomacy, Public Affairs and Psychological Operations in Strategic Information Operations," Defense Technical Informations Center, http://stinet.dtic.mil/oai/oai?&verb=getRecord&metadataPrefix=html&identifier=ADA435691 (accessed June 30, 2007).

9 Joint Publication 3–61, *Public Affairs*, May 9, 2005, DOD Directive 5122.5, Public Affairs Program, February 12, 1993, III-18.

10 Mountainrunner.us, http://mountainrunner.us/ (accessed June 30, 2007).

11 *Democracy Now*, Wednesday June 20th 2007, transcript from interview with Josh Rushing, http://www.democracynow.org/article.pl?sid=07/06/20/152255 (accessed June 30, 2007).

12 Yochi Dreazen, "A cooperative Bush leaves Allies Wary," *Wall Street Journal*, http://online.wsj.com/public/article_print/SB118152064261530702.html (accessed June 30, 2007).

13 BBC/Reuters Media Poll: Trust in the Media, Globescan, http://www.globescan.com/news_archives/bbcreut.html (accessed June 30, 2007); Edelman Trust Barometer, 2007, "Business and media more trusted than government in every region of the Globe," Edelman, http://www.edelman.com/news/ShowOne.asp?ID=146 (accessed June 30, 2007); G. Shabbir Cheema, "Building Trust in Governments: Findings from Major Surveys," United Nations Online Network in Public Administration and Finance, http://unpan1.un.org/intradoc/groups/public/documents/UN/UNPAN025132.pdf (accessed June 30, 2007).

14 Air University, "Information Warfare—An Air Force Policy for the Role of Public Affairs," http://aupress.maxwell.af.mil/saas_Theses/Crumm/crumm.pdf (accessed June 30, 2007).

15 Joseph Nye, "Public Diplomacy in the 21th Century," *The Globalist*, http://www.theglobalist.com/StoryId.aspx?StoryId=3885 (accessed June 30, 2007).

20

Valuing Exchange of Persons in Public Diplomacy

Nancy Snow

A Personal Introduction to Exchanges

From 1984 to 1985, I spent a year as a Fulbright scholar in the Federal Republic of Germany. With a B.A. in political science fresh out of Clemson University, a land-grant state university in South Carolina, I was delighted to receive this pre-doctoral fellowship grant to live abroad for 12 months (with a three-month extension award) to advance my German language comprehension and investigate my proposed political science study of German foreign aid and its image abroad. It was not my first trip overseas. In 1982 I had spent several weeks traveling with two German language professors and a handful of German language students to East and West Germany, Czechoslovakia, Austria, and Switzerland. Our summer sojourn to Europe was very much in keeping with the typical study abroad experience for American college students. We traveled briefly to mostly Western European countries and toured around more like tourists visiting the Louvre than as purposive exchangees in support of national interests. To their credit, the German language faculty leading this tour arranged sit-down meetings with artists and students in East and West Germany, so not all was oriented toward Bratwurst and *Biergartens*! This short trip gave me the incentive to get back overseas for another go-round.

The distinguishing mark that separated my Fulbright year from my first trip overseas was that it was a sponsored exchange and thus tied, whether explicitly or implicitly, to larger U.S. foreign policy goals and outcomes. These larger goals were oblivious to me at the start of my application process. I was made aware of the Fulbright international educational exchange program when I went to discuss off-campus housing options with the housing coordinator. He happened to wear another hat—that of Fulbright Program advisor—and interrupted our housing conversation with a "Have you ever thought about applying for a Fulbright?" to which I answered, "What's a Fulbright?" He explained that with my German language minor proficiency I could apply to study in West Germany and that the U.S. and German governments would partner in paying for the fellowship. Several months later I received my letter of congratulations. The return address was from the Institute of International Education (IIE), 809 United Nations Plaza, New York City. As a somewhat sheltered Southern young woman who had experienced brief travel overseas, I felt something take hold of my sense of self that day. Like Mary Tyler Moore, I was going to make it after all, if not in the Big City, then across the Big Pond. I was unaware of the administrative, legislative, and appropriations oversight functions held by the U.S. Information Agency, the independent government agency responsible for public diplomacy activities of the U.S. Government, including government exchanges. That would come much later in my academic study and professional career.

The Fulbright Brand

It was clear that by the mid-1980s the Fulbright Scholar moniker was becoming its own major brand in credentialing academicians and their universities. It was by no means the Gold Standard in academic exchange scholarships. That title had long been applied to the Rhodes Scholarships. A Rhodes Scholar remains to this day the most famous and prestigious academic scholarship title in the world that promises a lifetime of the most elite social networks. It is offered each year to a very exclusive group of 32 American university students who spend up to three years in graduate study at Oxford University in Great Britain. Until 1976, the Rhodes Scholar recipients were referred to solely as "golden boys" and it counts among its alumni politicians J. William Fulbright and Bill Clinton, the writer Robert Penn Warren, and actor/musician Kris Kristofferson.[1] In his book, *I Am Charlotte Simmons*, writer Tom Wolfe illustrates how these notable international exchange programs have made their way into the collective American consciousness:

> Charlotte said, "There are only thirty-two Rhodes scholarships?" Adam nodded yes.
> "Well, golly, that's not very many. What if . . . that's what you're counting on and you don't get one?" "In that case," said Adam, "you go after a Fulbright. That's a pretty long way down from a Rhodes, but it's okay. There's also the Marshall Fellowships, they're the last resort. I mean, that's bottom-fishing. During the cold war a bad-ass couldn't have accepted a Fulbright or a Marshall, because they're government programs, and that would've made you look like a tool of imperialism. A Rhodes was okay because there was no British Empire left, and you couldn't be accused of being a tool of something that wasn't there anymore. Today the only empire is the American empire, and it's omnipresent, and so if you don't get the Rhodes you have to make use of it, the new empire. It's okay as long as you're using it for the sake of your own goals and not theirs."[2]

The Rhodes scholarships remain out of reach but for a handful of recipients. The Fulbright is attainable to a far greater number of applicants and yet prestigious enough to elevate a university's reputation among other institutions of higher education as well as potential applicants. In 2006, the *Chronicle of Higher Education* published a series on the 60th anniversary of the Fulbright Program, accompanied by a list of the colleges and universities with the highest number of Fulbright scholar recipients. It is not uncommon for universities to publicize on their websites the names of faculty who have received Fulbright fellowships. In my Fulbright year, the Clemson university media relations office aired a regional TV commercial during televised sports competitions that exalted the academic prowess of Clemson, including its six Fulbright recipients. When we returned from our year abroad, we were invited by Clemson University to dot the "I" in the "Tiger" formation created by the Clemson marching band during an alumni football game. The university was thrilled that our Fulbright class had exceeded the combined number of student fellowships from Yale and Harvard. Such an Ivy League level academic achievement by a land-grant public university is still included today in the university's timeline for 1984: "Clemson scored 100%—six out of six—in awards to seniors who applied for Fulbright scholarships and grants for international study. The 1984 Clemson soccer team won its first national soccer championship with a 2–1 victory over Indiana."[3]

Valuing the Mission of Exchanges

By the mid-1980s the Fulbright brand was 40 years old and its then octogenarian visionary, Senator J. William Fulbright, was making the rounds in support of what he had once said in the *Annals* was "the most significant and important activity I have been privileged to engage in during my years in the Senate."[4] Fulbright viewed his namesake alumni as:

> scattered throughout the world, acting as knowledgeable interpreters of their own and other societies; as persons equipped and willing to deal with conflict or conflict-producing situations on the basis of an informed determination to solve them peacefully; and as opinion leaders communicating their appreciation of the societies which they visited to others in their own society.[5]

This Fulbright messianic vision was inspired by Fulbright's Rhodes Scholar days at Oxford, as Randall Bennett Woods makes clear:

> The Fulbright exchange program was undeniably a reflection, a projection, of J. William Fulbright's personal experience. What he proposed in 1946 was the institutionalization of his own overseas odyssey. It would do for thousands of young people what it had done for him—remove cultural blinders and instill tolerance and a sense of public service. The program was also a natural corollary of Fulbright internationalism. It was the cultural equivalent of collective security and multilateralism.[6]

Fulbright's philosophical support for the human dimension in foreign affairs included a lament that such a dimension was a "low priority add-on to the serious content of our international relations."[7] This benign neglect reflected the conclusions of two influential books that emerged in the 1960s. In 1964, Philip M. Coombs published *The Fourth Dimension of Foreign Policy: Educational and Cultural Affairs* in which he described the human side of foreign policy as:

> concerned, in short, with the development of people, both within and beyond our borders—their skills and knowledge, insights and understanding, attitudes, and values, and all their creative potentialities. It is concerned also with the development of knowledge and creative works—with scholarly research and scientific discovery, with the cultivation of arts and humanities. And it is concerned with the transmission and application of ideas and knowledge in myriad forms and ways.[8]

Coombs sought balance between private intellectual pursuits endeavored by educational and cultural exchanges and their obvious value to national political objectives. But he recognized that those involved in the fourth dimension were often skeptical toward too much government oversight or the overt mixing of their individual intellectual pursuits with short-term U.S. foreign policy goals. Coombs asserted that the U.S. Government must never exploit private individual initiative in defense of short-term U.S. policies, but rather use our educational and cultural strengths like the Fulbright Program in support of broader long-range transnational goals. In a word, educational and cultural affairs, where exchanges have their home, are the positive forces in foreign affairs. They work to unite the community of developed democracies; they assist the underdeveloped nations in becoming more viable and independent; they expand areas of mutual interest and mutual understanding; and they can help to build and strengthen global civic society.

A year later, Charles Frankel released *The Neglected Aspect of Foreign Affairs: American Educational and Cultural Policy Abroad.* Like Coombs, Frankel was a noted assistant secretary of state for educational and cultural affairs. Frankel did not share quite the same sanguine view that Fulbright held about exchanges, arguing that much of the expected and hoped for outcomes of exchanges are driven more by folklore than by fact. These include emotionally-driven myths that goodwill follows from understanding, that face-to-face communication guarantees sympathetic outcomes, or that close contact among peoples from varied backgrounds is enough to keep the peace.

> Even when the United States policies are right, and even when others understand them, they may still not like them because they find them opposed to their interests. In fact, the hard choice often has to be made between promoting goodwill toward the United States and promoting objective understanding of the country and its policies.[9]

Frankel said that exchange programs need to separate promotion of goodwill from understanding for they are not one and the same. If exchanges alone led to liking, then the largest exchange of persons programs—that of military personnel and tourists—would have far friendlier and more sympathetic outcomes than experience shows. Gaining understanding across cultural divides can lead to enmity as well as liking. While Fulbright had once asked, "Can We Humanize International Relations Before We Incinerate Them?,"[10] by the Reagan years he said that exchanges and intercultural education were more significant to national survival than nuclear weapons or the Strategic Defense Initiative.[11] He ultimately recognized that, practically speaking, exchange of persons programs lead more often to understanding than affection. This was reason enough for Fulbright to call for an expansion in exchanges if such an expansion could lead to nations producing an elite cadre who had the knowledge skills set to negotiate skillfully and possibly prevent nations from going to war.

Beverly Lindsay summarized three historical perspectives[12] about international educational and cultural exchange programs that still prevail and help to explain how we view exchanges and their place in public diplomacy dialogue today. The first perspective is to view exchanges as autonomous entities. The second is to view them as playing an integral part in public diplomacy. The third is to see sponsored educational and cultural exchange programs as products of American propaganda efforts. The first approach is generally attached to the ideal of "mutual understanding" expressed in the 1948 Smith-Mundt Act. Not only did this Act create the Board of Foreign Scholarships (BFS), a separate autonomous body outside of government to oversee the selection of the grantees, but also the BFS works to this day in conjunction with a number of subcontracting and yet autonomous agencies of the U.S. Government, most notably the Council for International Exchange of Scholars (CIES) and the Institute of International Education (IIE). As stated earlier, when I received my Fulbright letter of acceptance, it was not from the U.S. Information Agency but from IIE, a hands-off approach to peer review and selection that preserves the integrity of the Fulbright name outside of the direct control of the government.

Many academics tend to view educational exchanges from the first perspective. With an almost faith-based belief, exchanges are seen as private people-to-people transactions that should not be attached directly to the immediacies of day-to-day formal policy considerations or efforts to restore a nation's image in a host country or region. Sussman writes that:

> the principal focus of the Fulbright program has been and should be the enhancement of the individual intellect. Fulbright exchange cannot realistically be based on the export of American systems or institutions; just as the current "U.S. democracy initiative" cannot expect to transfer American political forms to other culture . . . Academics best serve the national interest by being free of the temporal political concerns by whomever defined, and concentrating instead on linkages of understanding with peers abroad.[13]

The value of the Fulbright program to this day is that it celebrates the first perspective in its practice. It maintains mutual understanding and reciprocal exchange at its heart; it is as much about learning from those Fulbright students and teachers who come to the United States as it is about teaching to and learning from the American overseas counterparts. Indeed, perhaps learning on the part of those who originate from outside the United States predominates. In its 60-year history, two-thirds of the nearly 300,000 alumni have originated from outside the United States while one-third of Americans have ventured abroad. No other program, including Rhodes, Marshall, or Rotary, has this unique feature of a double flow of scholars coming to and going from the United States.

Exchanges and Public Diplomacy: Marrying a Mission

The Fulbright program's strength in international institutional partnerships and binational commitments is in part its liability. At a time in which so many exchanges are tied integrally to short-term national security and foreign policy outcomes, the Fulbright program lacks a grander strategy to build global civil society or promote international education. Fulbright's vision to humanize international relations was certainly not what motivated me at the time I applied for this government-sponsored exchange grant. As a student, I had far more practical goals. The Fulbright fellowship was an opportunity for professional development, foreign language immersion, and a "ticket" to the best graduate school. It wasn't until I studied the history of the program and its emphasis on building mutual understanding that I began to fully appreciate the possibility of educational exchange diplomacy or the role of Fulbright scholars as cultural mediators.[14] It must still be acknowledged that many Fulbright scholars, like most exchange scholars, are most interested in academic excellence and personal success rather than in broader, more far-reaching goals of building mutual understanding and empathy which cultural mediation brings. While an academic sojourn has an impact upon every student, it may not come in the form of impacting the role of the Fulbright student as a cultural mediator. Some students may be totally uninterested in becoming links between cultures, while still others may think themselves incompetent in functioning in such a capacity. Some students may also find that they have little opportunity for enacting the role of a mediator due to limited contacts with host nationals or lack of interest from hosts for information about their ways of life back home. It may be safe to say, however, that if Fulbright students were made more aware of the mediating function in exchange then more students would undertake this role as part of their sojourn.

The Council for International Educational Exchange recognizes this need for more intercultural communication competence educational training as part of every sojourn:

> Most students never meet anyone who is a spokesperson for the "other side," those who see Americans in a less-than-attractive light. There is no shortage of these people around the world. Many of them are intelligent, well-educated, and hardly radical. They simply see the world differently than we do. Inviting some of these people as speakers at cross-cultural development sessions is a great way to provide controlled exposure to study abroad students. We should seek and promote these opportunities in our programs. This is not subversive, it's educational. A required cross-cultural learning course or segment should exist in every study abroad program.[15]

The practical motivations of sponsored exchangees do not exclude fulfillment of some public diplomacy goals like those intercultural competence skills promoted by the CIEE, but in a more open and independent manner than traditional message-centered public diplomacy efforts like international broadcasting or short-term targeted international visitor exchanges.

The Cultural Mediator as a Public Diplomacy Measure

A program that is touted for contributing to intellectual pursuits, reinforcing one's role as a global citizen, and working to share ideas and knowledge in pursuit of peace and global cooperation should have a strategy that would reinforce the Fulbright spirit of idealism. In my 1992 doctoral dissertation, I attempted to measure the cultural mediator roles and functions of a group of 290 foreign Fulbright scholars who were in the United States for two years. A majority of those Fulbright scholars surveyed indicated a willingness to serve as more active contributors to the Fulbright network of international scholars through acting as cultural mediators. A cultural mediator is a link or bridge between cultural systems who exhibits an ability to accurately represent and reconcile differences between two or more cultures.[16] Bochner notes: "Only the mediating response provides a genuine framework for acquiring multicultural attitudes, skills, and self-perceptions. At the sociological level, only a mediating framework can provide a basis for a genuinely pluralistic society."[17] In my dissertation, those Fulbright international scholars who exhibited closer ties to American host nationals and larger multicultural networks correlated strongly to an outcome of cultural mediation in both the U.S. host culture and home culture. Scholars who had preacademic training in the U.S. and who knew Americans previously were also more predisposed to anticipate engaging as cultural mediators when they returned home. Nevertheless, my study could only anticipate, but not measure, what these scholars would actually do when they returned to their home countries. It would make sense for the Fulbright program, long touted as America's premier flagship international exchange program, to become a separate global identity that transcends national boundaries. The Rhodes motto, "Once a Rhodes Scholar, always a Rhodes scholar," should likewise apply in kind to the international network of Fulbright scholars. "To have Fulbrighted" could come to mean anyone who supports interpersonal interaction in the service of global understanding and cooperation.

When I returned from my Fulbright fellowship to the Federal Republic of Germany, I heard nothing from either the Fulbright Association or the Institute of International Education, much less the government agency responsible, USIA. I half expected to be asked to give a lecture or write an article about my experience, but it wasn't until I directly contacted the Fulbright Association in Washington, D.C. that I became a member and started receiving quarterly newsletters about Fulbright activities and alumni news. The Fulbright Association celebrated its 30th anniversary in 2007. Its database of Fulbright alumni represents a small minority of the nearly 300,000 alumni scattered throughout the world. The Fulbright Program might want to consider exploiting the energy and interest in giving back to the program illustrated by my study of Fulbright international scholars.

The U.S. State Department released an outcome assessment of the U.S. Fulbright Student Program in 2005 that indicated a nearly unanimous belief that participation in the Fulbright program promotes mutual understanding (97%) and builds leadership traits such as self-reliance and self-confidence (92%); ability to work closely with people from other cultures (89%); ability to lead others (71%); and willingness to lead others (70%). A full 100% developed a deeper understanding of their host country and 93% of the American students reported a deeper understanding of U.S. society and culture as a result of seeing it through the eyes of their host country citizens. Strong evidence for the multiplier effect was in evidence with two-thirds of the grantees maintaining collaborative ties with host country colleagues; nearly all encouraged friends and colleagues to participate in international exchange programs or to apply for a Fulbright grant.

Is It All Propaganda, Anyway?

Beverly Lindsay's study points out that the cultural attaché of the State Department was for 30 years (1948–1978) the key person in the American Embassy who worked with local binational commissions, the State Department's Bureau of Educational and Cultural Affairs, and U.S. exchange agencies to preserve the autonomy of the Fulbright Program. A typical cultural attaché was not unlike a college professor working inside an embassy with both academic experience and advanced degrees. While the cultural attaché worked within a Cold War matrix, by 1978, when exchanges merged with the U.S. Information Agency, the U.S. Government's independent information agency whose motto was "telling America's story to the world," many academics worried that propaganda and public relations efforts would override educational and cultural affairs. Congress addressed these worries when it passed the Foreign Relations Authorization Act of 1979, which underscored President Carter's view that Americans have as much to learn about the history, culture, and attitudes of people in other countries, as they have to learn about us. For a short time, the U.S. Information Agency was revamped as the U.S. International Communication Agency to reflect this new spirit of two-way communication over the more one-way propaganda style. Against a background of domestic inflation, national malaise and a one-term presidency, the USIA moniker was restored. Roth and Arndt argue that American ambivalence about doing propaganda persists despite these three clear functions of Edmund Guillion's "catchy euphemism" public diplomacy: information, cultural affairs, and propaganda. To this day, the U.S. State Department engages in a mix of all three.[18] "American propaganda will probably remain a fluid and expedient mixture of education, culture, and information, of soft-sell and hard-sell, of loud-talk and soft-talk, of short-range tactics and long-range strategies."[19]

Waging Peace and Fighting Terror: Twin Pillars of Official Public Diplomacy

U.S. Government-sponsored international educational and cultural exchanges are considered a pillar in U.S. public diplomacy efforts to inform, influence, and engage overseas publics in pursuit of national interest objectives. The U.S. Government's war on terror that followed the attacks of September 11, 2001 raised the profile of public diplomacy, including the value of exchanges, in the overt promotion of national security objectives. Despite the major role exchanges played during the American Century and Cold War period, exchanges remain sidelined today as slow media efforts while fast media government broadcasting, targeted public relations, and Rapid Response Units proliferate. When exchanges have been utilized in public diplomacy, it is generally in the context of vital national security programs that support the executive branch of the U.S. Government, particularly those that target the Islamic and Arab regions of the world. The Rapid Response Unit at the State Department monitors foreign media coverage from the Middle East to Latin America, and provides a daily e-mail to thousands of senior government and military officials with U.S. position responses to the coverage. In her report card to Congress April 2007, former Undersecretary of State for Public Diplomacy Karen Hughes said that "our public diplomacy programs are reaching more people around the world more strategically than ever before, and public diplomacy is now viewed as the national security priority that it is. Because our efforts against terrorism are more than a military or intelligence matter, but also an ideological struggle, we are asking you to fund urgent public diplomacy programs in this year's war on terror supplemental request, and to support increases for vital programs in our 2008 budget request." Hughes told Congress that the State Department was in the process of creating an interagency counter-terrorism communication center to develop "culturally-sensitive messages to undermine ideological support for terror."

These military-style strategic communication approaches from rapid response units to counter-terrorism communication centers suggest a preference for words that emulate bullets and show lack of understanding about the effectiveness of such measures. As John Nichols noted in "Wasting the Propaganda Dollar," an influential article about the Reagan administration's view of U.S. propaganda, in times of military engagement like the then Cold War or today's war on terror, the tendency is to respond with a magic bullet theory of persuasion.[20] It assumes that foreign audiences are easily malleable to a source's message, especially when the aim is good and the bullet (message) hits its mark. Even the Broadcasting Board of Governors (BBG) 2008 annual report harkens to this outmoded theory of communication. It reports that weekly audience ratings for Alhurra range from a low in Egypt (4.9%), to mid range in Kuwait (26%) and urban Morocco (26%), to much higher ratings in Iraq (42.3%) and Qatar (64.1%), but such numbers say nothing regarding viewer attitudes toward U.S. policy. Social influence scholars Oskamp and Schultz challenge mass communication preferential approaches.[21] The BBG prevailing view is that increasing audience size can produce opportunities for positive attitude shifts toward the U.S. This may have been conventional wisdom in media effects theory when it was thought that mere exposure to mass media produced a change in attitudes. Today other factors like source credibility and audience bias filter source content. Existing attitudes are reinforced more often by mass media and when attitude change does take place, it is often a minor change in intensity than an overall conversion to the other side. Mass media's greatest impact is in creating new opinions on issues when there are no preexisting attitudes. Today there is general agreement among researchers that personal communication has a stronger influence on people's attitudes than mass communication.

The U.S. State Department has long been adept at telling personal anecdotes about how exchange programs like the International Visitors Leadership Program impact. In an April 2007 interview with the *Dallas Morning News*, Assistant Under Secretary for Public Diplomacy Dina Powell responded to a series of questions that exposed the American reluctance to acknowledge anything our government engages in as propaganda.

> Q: "What is public diplomacy?" A: "It's an effort to promote and communicate America's ideals and principles." Q: "Some will call that propaganda. How do you rebut them?" A: "Let me offer an example. Leonard Marks, LBJ's public diplomacy chief, told me about the president meeting with young Egyptians who had traveled here. One said he had been scared to come and anti-American, but he realized that was the propaganda he had heard. When I return to Egypt, he said, 'I plan to tell people this is a freedom-loving nation.' Mr. Marks replied, 'Mr. Sadat, I am so honored you came.' That was Anwar Sadat's first trip here. He saw everyday Americans, so when he had to choose later between the U.S. and the Soviets, he chose us. That's one tool of public diplomacy. You can't bring everyone here. So, we're sending delegations abroad."[22]

The Golden Age of international educational exchange parallels the Cold War period of 1946–1991. For over 60 years, U.S. public diplomacy placed a high priority on cultural and educational exchange activities in the national interest across a continuum that included both hands-off and hands-on approaches. The events of September 11, 2001 have revamped interest in international exchanges and their importance to national security and foreign policy objectives, though not even the subsequent launch of a Global War on Terror could elevate exchanges to the height reached during the Cold War. Secretary of State Dr. Condoleezza Rice, herself an exchange scholar to the Soviet Union, acknowledged this high water mark for intellectual investment in exchange of peoples at the 2006 Summit of U.S. University Presidents on International Education: "We have not as a country made the kind of intellectual investment that we need to make in the exchange of peoples, in the exchange of ideas, in languages and in cultures and our knowledge of them that we made in the Cold War."[23]

Public Diplomacy Under Secretary Hughes described her efforts as "waging peace," whose three strategic imperatives are to "foster a sense of common interests and values between Americans and people of other countries, to isolate, marginalize and discredit violent extremists and to foster a positive vision of hope and opportunity that is rooted in our values: our belief in freedom, equality, the dignity and worth of every human being." In her first speech to Congress in 20 months since her appointment in September 2005, she referenced exchanges like the

Gilman program, Edward R. Murrow journalism program, including a boast that the flagship Fulbright program awarded a record high number of 1,300 student grants in 2006. But these boasts are more window dressing than reality of the U.S. Government's priorities. In annual appropriations, though exchange funding has increased, they still fall short to government international broadcasting efforts, including Middle East Broadcasting Networks such as Al Hurra, Radio Sawa, and Radio Farda, all created since 9/11. The BBG includes Voice of America, Radio Free Europe/Radio Liberty, Radio Free Asia, Radio and TV Marti, and Middle East Broadcasting Networks, and reaches a worldwide audience of 140 million in 58 languages via radio, television, and the Internet.

> New programming proposed in FY 2008 will counter the misinformation and dangerous ideology in East Africa, particularly Somalia; provide expanded broadcasts to North Koreans who seek greater access to unbiased information in their repressive, closed society; and enable Alhurra to enhance its programming, focus the agenda in the Middle East's media market, and reach this critical audience.[24]

The BBG's annual budget is about $645 million and calls for an increase to $668 million in its FY2008 request. Sponsored U.S. Government international educational and cultural exchange programs run by the State Department account for $451 million. Broadcasting gets the larger slice of the public diplomacy resource pie because the bipartisan presidentially-appointed members have the political weight and savvy to lobby on behalf of the BBG interests that are cast largely in terms of national security, supporting the war on terror, and expanding American leadership. The 2008 annual report begins with these words from the Commander-in-Chief:

> Our national security strategy is founded upon two pillars: The first pillar is promoting freedom, justice, and human dignity—working to end tyranny, to promote effective democracies . . . Peace and international stability are most reliably built on a foundation of freedom. The second pillar of our strategy is confronting the challenges of our time by leading a growing community of democracies . . . history has shown that only when we do our part will others do theirs. America must continue to lead.[25]

The BBG calls for an expansion of market areas important to winning the war on terror. These include Radio Sawa, a 24-hour radio network launched in 2002, and Alhurra, the 24-hour TV network based in Northern Virginia launched in 2004. The BBG 2008 budget request for Alhurra recommends the creation of a three-hour daily program in the style of American morning shows like *Today* and *Good Morning America*. The price tag for this expansion is $11.1 million and 150 new employees, this despite a region with competition from more than 200 broadcast channels and the influence of the far more popular indigenous satellite TV networks, Al Jazeera and Al Arabiya.

A 2007 GAO report about U.S. public diplomacy criticizes the BBG for measurement data that do not confirm that larger audience targets in priority markets are being met.[26] This underscores the conclusions of the 9/11 Commission Report that said in the area of international broadcasting, "we need to move beyond audience size, expose listeners to new ideas and accurate information about the U.S. and its policies, and measure the impact and influence of these ideas."[27] The same report gave a grade of "D" to U.S. Government support for scholarship, exchange, and library programs; while noting that spending for exchanges has grown, American libraries are closing and fewer foreign students from the Middle East are electing to study in the United States. Thomas Kean, chair of the 9/11 Commission, and co-chair Lee Hamilton conclude:

Public diplomacy is not a one-way street. It is not delivering a message: It is communication. At its heart, public diplomacy is a process of engagement and developing relationships. We must reach out boldly, broadly to all elements of society, especially to young people. We must combat misinformation, and communicate our ideals with force and eloquence. We see a vigorous and significant expansion of U.S. broadcasting, through Radio Sawa and the satellite TV station al-Hurra. We want to see a similar vigorous and significant expansion of scholarship, exchange, and library programs that reach out to young people and offer them knowledge and hope. Our core values and America's culture of education, equal opportunity, and tolerance still have a powerful appeal around the world.[28]

Their call for a "significant expansion" in international exchanges and library programs reflected a summary report from the Congressional Research Service. The 2005 report, "Public Diplomacy: A Review of Past Recommendations," found that the most common recommendation for U.S. public diplomacy efforts since the attacks on September 11, 2001 was the expansion of U.S. exchange programs and/or U.S. libraries overseas.[29]

A Case for Valuing Exchanges

I have participated in sponsored educational exchange as an autonomous graduate student involved in intellectual pursuits overseas; as a doctoral candidate writing about the need to reinforce the cultural mediator roles of Fulbright scholars in the public diplomacy paradigm of two-communication and relationship building across cultures; and finally, as a USIA governmental official aware of the tendency to propagandize exchanges in support of U.S. foreign policy and national security goals. As one who has been part of all three perspectives on international educational exchange, it continues to perplex that while there is very little evidence that mass media approaches to shifting attitudes are very effective, the U.S. Government continues to fund such approaches to the detriment of exchanges. So why shift preferential preference to exchanges? At a 15th anniversary ceremony of the Fulbright program, President Kennedy said that "of all the examples in recent history of beating swords into plowshares, of having some benefit come to humanity out of the destruction of war, I think that this program in its results will be among the most preeminent."[30]

Such peacebuilding measures are long-term and in that regard, won't necessarily impress Congressional appropriation oversight committees the way market research on audience listening and viewing habits might. As Senator Fulbright once said, "Education is a slow-moving but powerful force. It may not be fast enough or strong enough to save us from catastrophe, but it is the strongest force available."[31] Nevertheless, even if the emphasis is on peace and global security, there is really no question that all nations need to address exchange diplomacy efforts as serious pillars in public diplomacy campaigns. The 21st-century emphasis on exchange reflects a shift from an exchange paradigm that viewed exchanges as an autonomous value unto themselves to a more urgent call for global competence and competition. As Altbach and Teichler explain: "The exchange paradigm was based on the value of hard-to-measure long-term benefits: the virtue of reciprocity, mutual trust, transparency, improvement through cooperation, joint efforts for cost reduction, learning through mutual understanding, and so on."[32] My own doctoral dissertation analysis of the literature on educational exchange programs showed that such contacts do generally translate into greater tolerance in general and such tolerance can serve as a reservoir of goodwill from which one can draw in times of international crisis. There is also evidence that increased diffusion of international knowledge and intercultural contact results in a more interdependent world. Another outcome of exchange is that in the process of increasing knowledge about others, one will see oneself in a clearer light. Exchange thus translates into a process by which an individual enriches a picture of oneself. Finally, the meeting of cultures and minds should further the development of both or either participating countries and thereby better living conditions everywhere. All of these outcomes are still used by sponsored exchange administrators to give a strong rationale for continued or even increased funding of educational exchange programs like the Fulbright program which often cites an intrinsic link between cultural exchange and peace and development.[33]

A shift from the exchange paradigm to a competition paradigm is reflected in the 2005 report released by the Lincoln Commission:

> On the international stage, what nations don't know can hurt them. In recent generations, evidence of that reality has been readily available. What we did not know about Vietnam hurt the United States. What we did not understand about the history and culture of the former Ottoman Empire has complicated our efforts in the Middle East for decades. Mistakes involving the Third World and its debt have cost American financiers billions of dollars. And our lack of knowledge about economic, commercial, and industrial developments in Japan, China, and India, successively, has undermined American competitiveness. Global competence costs, but ignorance costs far more.

The Abraham Lincoln Study Abroad Fellowship Program is an ambitious effort to establish a national study abroad initiative that would eventually increase the number of American students studying abroad annually to 1 million. At present, about 200,000 undergraduate students participate in study abroad each year. If Congress passes legislation to establish a national study abroad program, then international exchange may become more of a norm than an exception. The rationale for such study is to make the United States globally competitive through educating its young people in the ways of the world. "Making study abroad the norm and not the exception can position this and future generations of Americans for success in the world in much the same way that establishment of the land-grant university system and enactment of the GI Bill helped create the 'American century.'"[34]

The Bureau of Educational and Cultural Affairs (ECA), for which I worked in the U.S. Information Agency from 1992 to 1994, is today part of the U.S. Department of State's public diplomacy agenda. Its mission from USIA to State is the same: to foster "mutual understanding between the people of the United States and the people of other countries," a directive that follows from the 1948 U.S. Information and Educational Exchange Act (Public Law 402). Known better as the Smith-Mundt Act for its two principal sponsors, Senator H. Alexander Smith (R-NJ) and Representative Karl E. Mundt (R-SD), it remains the legislative basis for America's foreign informational and cultural exchange programs. The Smith–Mundt Act also prohibits the propagation of the American people by banning the domestic distribution of official state materials produced for overseas audiences, an anachronistic feature that is continually challenged by this and other scholars.[35]

If the State Department as the official face of public diplomacy wishes to emphasize more exchanges, then it will need to emphasize the mutuality and relationship building features that only person-to-person exchanges can deliver. Secretary of State Rice has said that public diplomacy is a conversation, not a monologue. In order to extend that conversation, more students will have to travel and study abroad. So far, it is private international exchange organizations like the Lincoln Commission, the Institute of International Education, and CIES that are leading the charge for more emphasis on international education. Allan Goodman, president of the Institute of International Education, said at the time of the 2007 Academy Awards:

> For citizens of a global power, Americans are woefully uneducated about issues beyond our borders. The average adult American doesn't have a passport and can't locate France, let alone Iraq, on a map. Our TV networks devote less than five minutes a night to international news. Less than 1% of all Americans in college study abroad each year.[36]

Despite these woeful statistics, Altbach and Teichler argue that the "21ˢᵗ century may eventually be called the century of education."[37] They acknowledge the efforts by long-standing exchange organizations like the Institute of International Education (IIE), founded in New York in 1919, the German Academic Exchange Service (Deutscher Akademische Austauschdienst [DAAD]), founded in 1925, and the Fulbright Student Program, administered by the IIE, to increase awareness of exchange opportunities and to serve as leaders in both policy development and management of exchange programs. Despite the efforts by these organizations and the fact that the U.S. remains the largest host nation for international students, there

> remains scant interest in the United States in genuine reciprocal international exchanges and genuine internationalization of higher education … American scholars and students are comparatively weak in knowledge of foreign languages and cultures. These factors, combined with the unwillingness of American academic institutions to invest in international initiatives, meant that the United States fell behind in the internationalization that characterized Europe in the 1980s.[38]

My own experience is that while most every college and university acknowledges a global education mission, overall commitment in real dollars to international education is insufficient. The funding increases are not there, nor are the exchange program initiatives, much less internationalization of the curriculum. The Modern Language Association reports that just 9% of U.S. college students participate in foreign language instruction, while the majority of international students are required to learn English, the language of international commerce, business, and the Internet. Uhlfelder reports that over 600,000 citizens from global competitor countries like China and India studied in the U.S. in 2006, while just 8,200 American students went to China and India in the same time period.[39] Sponsored educational and cultural exchanges remain a largely elite and exclusive undertaking representing about 5% of all exchanges. My own study abroad experiences reflect the usual pattern of an American student coming from a Western industrialized nation. I traveled abroad from a North American nation to a Western European nation, and while I did take foreign language classes and enroll in political science courses, I did not earn an academic degree as the majority of student exchangees from non-Western countries do. The overwhelming majority of exchange students finance their study, and this may explain why so few U.S. students (estimated at 1–3%) enroll in a study abroad program each year. The U.S. State Department Gilman Fellowships are an effort to overcome some of these traditional patterns by offering study abroad fellowships to students from financially-needy families. In return, these students must agree to study in non-traditional destinations like Latin America and Asia.

In the fall of 1993, I participated in a panel convened by the American Political Science Association to analyze the future of Fulbrights in the post-cold-war era. We were eight years away from the post-9/11 era. Beverly Watkins of the *Chronicle of Higher Education* reported on our panel, which greatly pleased the higher ups at the United States Information Agency who felt often hamstrung by the Smith-Mundt prohibitions that prevented domestic publicity of our programs.[40] Fulbright was unique because it was a two-way exchange that lacked an overly political agenda (Tom Wolfe's conclusions excepted) and had a domestic constituency in the form of the American Fulbright alumni who represented one-third of all Fulbrighters. As the Fulbright desk officer for Germany, Spain, and the former Yugoslavia countries, I spoke to the role of Fulbright scholars as cultural mediators: "The great ideas of this country about liberty and economic and political freedom that are taken for granted by those who live here are better appreciated by those who visit us. When students and scholars return to their countries, they take with them those ideas. In the process, we hope they gain a more favorable impression of our nation." With that said, I reminded the gathering that "we as Americans have as much to learn from other nations as they have to learn from us." Ted Lowi, professor of political science at Cornell University, added that he "would like to see the Fulbright program become the moral equivalent of empire. We have never had an adequate substitute for that routine way to get experience abroad. We need a routine way to create a corps of people whose life is international." All of the panelists, including Alice Ilchman, president of Sarah Lawrence College, and Leonard Sussman of Freedom House, agreed that cultural ignorance is a killer, as the Lincoln Commission Report concludes.

As the Fulbright Program enters its seventh decade as America's flagship educational program, and as self-financed cultural and educational exchanges proliferate and dominate, it is my hope that educational ideals will become self-perpetuating realities of more than the single digit participation we see today. It is unconscionable that the world's sole superpower is not the leading light in exchanges. So far we have let our better selves get eclipsed by our urgent selves. We cannot allow our national insecurities to overrule our ability to become a leader in international dialogue and negotiation. Such leadership is strengthened by tapping into the resources that exchange scholars and students offer. Not all may wish to actively participate in mediation and mutual understanding, but how many will do so if never asked? More than 20 years ago, Roth and Arndt asked the right questions, still unanswered:

> With the greatest media and communications systems the world has ever known, what could we not achieve by an effort geared to extending the reach, through this powerful informing resource, of the American dialogue with other nations? With the world's greatest collection of universities, research institutions, libraries, hospitals, enlightened businesses, museums, theatres, and concert halls, and with the professionals to fill them, how far could America go if we focused all our efforts on the outreach of American intellect and knowledge, science, and know-how, of information and culture, while strengthening our own cultural heritage through dialogue with all cultures of the world? How long could certain of the world's technical problems—e.g., hunger—resist an American-fed multilateral attack? If we set out through dialogue not to dominate but to help, through information and educational generously shared, could there be a truer agenda for world peace? Could there be a better, a more American style of "propaganda?"[41]

Whatever we want to call it—propaganda or public diplomacy—we need to not just value exchanges in principle but expand them in practice. Let's give the best, brightest and boldest among us an opportunity to become nonviolent instruments for waging peace and citizen ambassadors for international education.

Notes

1 Thomas J. and Kathleen Schaeper, *Cowboys Into Gentleman: Rhodes Scholars, Oxford, and the Creation of an American Elite* (New York and Oxford: Berghahn Books, 1998), xi.

2 Tom Wolfe, *I Am Charlotte Simmons* (New York: Farrar, Straus and Giroux, 2004), 258.

3 Clemson University website, Welcome message from university with historical milestones timeline, http://www.clemson.edu/welcome/history/timeline.htm.

4 J. William Fulbright, "The Most Significant and Important Activity I Have Been Privileged to Engage in during My Years in the Senate," *Annals of the American Academy of Political and Social Science*, International Exchange of Persons: A Reassessment 424 (1976): 3.

5 Ibid.

6 Randall Bennett Woods, "Fulbright Internationalism," *Annals of the American Academy of Political and Social Science*, The Fulbright Experience and Academic Exchanges 491 (1987): 35.

7 Ibid., 4.

8 Philip H. Coombs, *The Fourth Dimension of Foreign Policy: Educational and Cultural Affairs* (New York: Council on Foreign Relations, 1964), 17.

9 Charles Frankel, *The Neglected Aspect of Foreign Affairs: American Educational and Cultural Policy Abroad* (Washington, D.C.: Brookings Institution, 1965), 83.

10 Fulbright, 1976, 5.

11 William J. Fulbright, "Preface," Annals of the American Academy of Political and Social Science, The Fulbright Experience and Academic Exchanges 491 (1987): 10.

12 Beverly Lindsay, "Integrating International Education and Public Diplomacy: Creative Partnerships or Ingenious Propaganda?" *Comparative Education Review* 33, no. 4 (1989): 424.

13 Leonard R. Sussman, *The Culture of Freedom: The Small World of Fulbright Scholars* (Lanham, MD: Rowman & Littlefield, 1992), 4, 13.

14 Nancy Snow, Fulbright Scholars as Cultural Mediators: An Exploratory Study. Ph.D. diss. (Washington, D.C.: The American University, 1992).

15 Council on International Educational Exchange, "Down with America: Anti-Americanism and Study Abroad," 9, http://ciee.org/images/uploaded/pdf/Down%20with%20America.pdf.

16 Stephen Bochner, *The Mediating Person: Bridges Between Cultures* (Cambridge, MA: Schenkman Publishing Co., 1981).

17 Stephen Bochner, "Coping with Unfamiliar Cultures: Adjustment or Culture Learning?" *Australian Journal of Psychology* 38, no. 3 (1986): 350.

18 Lois W. Roth and Richard T. Arndt, "Information, Culture, and Public Diplomacy: Searching for an American Style of Propaganda," in *The Press and the State: Sociohistorical and Contemporary Interpretations*, ed. Walter M. Brasch and Dana R. Ulloth (Lanham, MD: University Press of America, 1986), 723.

19 Ibid., 744.

20 John Spicer Nichols, "Wasting the Propaganda Dollar," *Foreign Policy* 56 (1984): 129.

21 Stuart Oskamp and P. Wesley Schultz, *Attitudes and Opinions* (Mahwah, New Jersey: Lawrence Erlbaum Associates, 2005): 181–206.

22 "Q and A with Dina Powell," *Dallas Morning News*, April 22, 2007.

23 Condoleezza Rice, Remarks at the Summit of U.S. University Presidents on International Education, January 5, 2006, http://www.state.gov/secretary/rm/2006/58735.htm.

24 Broadcasting Board of Governors, Broadcasting Board of Governors Fiscal Year 2008 Budget Request, 2007, http://www.bbg.gov/reports/bbg_fy08_budget_request.pdf.

25 Ibid., 2.

26 Jess T. Ford, "U.S. Public Diplomacy: Strategic Planning Efforts Have Improved, but Agencies Face Significant Implementation Challenges," GAO-07-795T. Washington, D.C.: United States Government Accountability Office, April 26, 2007, 13.

27 Thomas H. Kean and Lee H. Hamilton. Opening Remarks of Thomas H. Kean and Lee H. Hamilton, Chair and Vice Chair of the 9/11 Public Discourse Project, Report on the Status of 9/11 Commission Recommendations. Part III: Foreign Policy, Public Diplomacy and Non-Proliferation, November 14, 2005, 5, http://www.9-11pdp.org/press/2005-11-14_remarks.pdf.

28 Ibid., 8.

29 Susan B. Epstein and Lisa Mages, "Public Diplomacy: A Review of Past Recommendations," Congressional Research Service Report RL33062 (Washington, D.C.: Congressional Research Service, 2005).

30 John F. Kennedy, Remarks by President Kennedy at ceremony to mark the 15th anniversary of the Fulbright Program, Washington, D.C., August 1, 1961; see "The Fulbright Program, 1946–1996: An Online Exhibit," http://www.uark.edu/depts/speccoll/fulbrightexhibit/intro.html.

31 John Brademas, "A World No Longer Narrow: Bringing Greece to American Universities," *PS* 20, no. 4 (1987): 875.

32 Philip Altbach and Ulrich Teichler, "Internationalization and Exchanges in a Globalized University," *Journal of Studies in International Education* 5, no. 5 (2001): 21.

33 Nancy Snow, "Cultural Mediation and the Fulbright Ideal," *FRANKly*, newsletter of the German Fulbright Alumni Program (Der Newsletter des Fulbright Alumni e.V. 7): 16–20.

34 Commission on Abraham Lincoln Study Abroad Fellowship Program, *Global Competence and National Needs: One Million Students Studying Abroad*, Washington, D.C., 3.

35 See Nancy Snow, "The Smith-Mundt Act of 1948," *Peace Review* 10, no. 4 (1998): 619–624; and Stephen Johnson and Helle Dale, "How to Reinvigorate U.S. Public Diplomacy, Backgrounder #1645," (Washington, D.C.: The Heritage Foundation), April 23, 2003, http://www.heritage.org/Research/NationalSecurity/bg1645.cfm.

36 Allen E. Goodman, "International IQ Test, Special Oscar 2007 Edition, http://www.iienetwork.org/?p=OscarQuiz.

37 Altbach and Teichler, 7.

38 Ibid., 12.
39 Steve Uhlfelder, "Sending students overseas is a ticket to a better image," *St. Petersburg Times*, March 31, 2007, http://www.sptimes.com/2007/03/31/Opinion/Sending_students_over.shtml.
40 Beverly T. Watkins, "Fulbrights in the Post-Cold-War Era," *The Chronicle of Higher Education*, September 15, 1993, A43.
41 Roth and Arndt, 744.

Part 5

Global Approaches to Public Diplomacy

Four Seasons in One Day

The Crowded House of Public Diplomacy in the UK

Ali Fisher

Public diplomacy (PD) in the United Kingdom can be viewed both in terms of the core structure and those organizations which fall outside this structure but fall within the spectrum of PD activity. While numerous definitions of PD have been offered by both practitioners and theorists, the definition offered by the last PD review stated it was:

> Work aiming to inform and engage individuals and organisations overseas, in order to improve understanding of and influence for the United Kingdom in a manner consistent with governmental medium and long term goals.[1]

More recently the Foreign and Commonwealth Office have begun using the definition that PD "is what we use to achieve our Strategic International Priorities (SPs) through our work with the public overseas."[2]

These and further politically motivated iterations will continue to be produced with the focus on a specific institutional use. Definition is useful when part of conceptual clarification, but when it is used as part of territorial demarcation in increasingly introspective internecine struggles it has less practical purpose.[3] Neither the UK definition nor the official PD structure covers the full range of activities which could be considered PD by the vast majority of definitions.

While some countries might be characterized as having a particular approach to PD, this article demonstrates the very British tendency to develop a wide range of approaches. In the British system the official and unofficial worlds of PD interact across the spectrum of activity in the UK.[4]

The Spectrum of Activity in the UK

In response to *The 9/11 Commission Report* Bruce Gregory argued that a "'reinvigorated inter-agency process' must deal with stovepipes: tribal cultures, firewalls, multiple agencies, numerous Congressional committees, and a decentralized budget process."[5] Dealing with the internecine bureaucratic conflict and the difficulties of a silo or stovepipe approach is one part of dealing with an interagency process. However, it is equally important to ensure a clear link between the practical considerations and the different approaches available to a country or PD organization. The creation of a spectrum of activity organizational roles can be aligned against would provide a means to divide roles into different areas, reduce duplication and conflict, or identify areas in which cooperation could be particularly fruitful due to shared approach. Clearly tensions will always exist, but a common understanding of the range of activity provides a means to identify both potential areas of cooperation and points of difference in approach.

The spectrum of PD activity can be viewed on a scale which ranges from primarily "listening" to predominantly "telling." While a degree of listening is required in all PD to ensure that activity is tailored to the audience, it is the degree to which listening is part of the activity rather than merely part of crafting the message which defines the spectrum.[6] Nation branding and tourism or trade promotion, which are in effect Government-sponsored international advertising, appear at the "telling" end of the spectrum and can be generally considered along side policy advocacy or information correction. PD largely based on the facilitation of the aims of the audience, for example programs associated with development work, reside closer to the listening end of the spectrum. A full range of these activities is represented in Figure 21.1.

Listening

Consciously and publicly listening to the perspective of others can be a PD act in itself; in PD it may be the way you act rather than what you say that changes the behaviour of others. Listening is more than just polling; it is demonstrating that views of those overseas are taken seriously and consideration is given to those perspectives. Clearly there is a danger that such listening exercises will not be perceived to be credible if it is believed listening is merely for show, and a pre-ordained action will be taken regardless of what is said.[7]

Facilitation

Providing others with the means of achieving their goals can allow a PD organization to change the way the target audience acts. Effective facilitation cannot be conduced without *genuine* listening and entails the provision of projects which are tailored to the needs of the recipient audience through negotiation or dialogue. The construction of plans with representatives of the recipient audience provides for the realization of specific objectives in a manner the audience both welcomes and over which they feel ownership. This ties the audience to the realization of PD goals because they are viewed as being developed in an endogenous rather than exogenous manner. This type of activity has also been evident in the niche diplomacy adopted by countries such as Norway and Canada in recent years.[8]

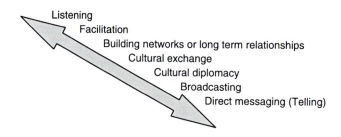

Figure 21.1.

Building Networks or Long-term Relationships

R.S. Zaharna argued, "networking has replaced information dominance as the new model of persuasion in the global communication era."[9] Creating networks for the long term must engage people on the basis of their priorities. However, it can also create a network of advocates working in the same direction as the PD organization. As such, both traditional physical and virtual networks have become increasingly recognized as an important part of PD. This type of activity is based on identifying individuals or groups who will be influential in the future and taking a long-term view of the relationship with them. Clearly one tension of acting for the long term is the increasing pressure to show results in the short term. Without clear evidence of what long-term success might look like in the short term, this type of work may become distorted and increasingly myopic.

Cultural Exchange

The midway point between "listening" and "telling," cultural exchange aims to be a genuine exchange of people, cultural goods or ideas, based on reciprocity and a symmetrical relationship. This exchange may be physical, but with the increasing use of virtual worlds, online communication, and collaboration, exchange is no longer the sole preserve of the traditional travel-based programs. "Success requires listening to others, recognizing the 'value of other cultures,' showing a desire to learn from them, and conducting programs as a 'two-way street.'"[10] If it is one way, it is merely advocacy under another name, which poses the danger of raising expectations of reciprocity which will not be fulfilled, and should be considered cultural diplomacy.[11]

Cultural Diplomacy

As the emphasis shifts away from listening and increasingly towards the promotion of a particular perspective, cultural diplomacy is the act of presenting a cultural good to an audience in an attempt to engage them in the ideas which the producer perceives to be represented by it. Some, such as Milton Cummings, attempt to combine cultural diplomacy with the language of cultural exchange by using phrases such as mutual understanding. However, as Milton Cummings notes, cultural diplomacy "can also be more of a one-way street than a two-way exchange, as when one nation concentrates its efforts on promoting the national language, explaining its policies and point of view, or 'telling its story to the rest of the world.'"[12] Whatever the language, the key difference between exchange and diplomacy is power dynamic; reciprocity and a symmetrical relationship characterize exchange, presentation and one-way communication are a greater part of cultural diplomacy.

Broadcasting

Media production, mainly news, for mass consumption is one-way communication, but rather than total messaging it presents a particular perspective, e.g. Al Jazeera, The Guardian, or Fox News. It has to balance perspective and content to maintain the credibility of the broadcaster with the target audience. This may be classic state-based broadcasting, though may also take a particular regional, political, or religious perspective. Equally, the movement away from the classic broadcasting includes increasing emphasis on web-based content. While clear divisions between "world" and "home" services used to be possible, the advent of online "listen on demand" services have opened domestic content up to audiences overseas. Distinctions between cultural diplomacy and broadcasting may be small as it provides a cultural perspective through a form of one-way communication.

Direct Messaging

Direct messaging is constructed to achieve a particular PD aim and is pursued without reciprocity. It is the "telling" end of the spectrum and attempts to leave as little space for alternative interpretations as possible. There are a range of methods within this area including nation branding, strategic communication, or marketing including promotion of universities, tourism or trade in general.[13] This approach usually emphasizes the "need to be simple" as "the people you're talking to are usually far less interested in you than you are."[14] While lack of interest applies more to nation branding than information correction, direct messaging it is not a negotiation, it is not symmetrical. It is one-way communication designed to change the way the audience acts, without the need for reciprocity. It does, however, come with the danger that, should the producer become too fixed on purely telling the message they produce, it could well be understood by the audience in a totally different way from the original meaning.[15]

Relating the Spectrum to UK Public Diplomacy

The spectrum of activity, from listening to telling, allows the relative roles of the different organizations conducting PD in the UK to be recognized. Just as countries have become known for an emphasis on a particular approach so UK organizations in general terms have a *tendency* toward certain areas of the spectrum. This provides a framework through which to identify the areas of overlap and tension that exist within the system. In doing so the role of those organizations who exist outside the official definition, but which fall within most conceptual definitions also becomes clear.

The core of the UK PD structure is recognized through membership of the Public Diplomacy Board.[16] The organizations represented on the board are: "Foreign and Commonwealth Office, British Council and BBC World Service (with observer status in view of the BBCWS' editorial independence)."[17] The board was created following the Carter Review to "improve public diplomacy effectiveness" through "setting the strategic direction of UK public diplomacy."[18] This initially creates a hierarchical approach, as the objectives are set and then passed down to organizations. However, as Lord Triesman noted recently, this created a tension.[19] Could the various PD organizations "create shared objectives without interfering, for example, with the BBC World Service's complete editorial independence or the British Council's operational decision-making?"[20] This question accurately highlights the way the priorities are applied in different ways by the different members of the UK PD structure, demonstrated by the different positions they occupy on the spectrum of PD activity.

British Council

Placing the core members of British PD on the spectrum of activity, the organization which occupies the area closest to "listening" is the British Council. However, it should be recognized that the British Council operates across a broader range of the spectrum than its PD partners. The emphasis in institutional nomenclature on "mutual benefit" reflects Jan Melissen's argument: "(m)odern public diplomacy is a 'two-way street,' even though the diplomat practicing it will of course always have his own country's interests and foreign policy goals in mind."[21] In conceiving of its work as "Cultural Relations" the British Council places emphasis on the use of culture to develop a "multi-layered network of relations," to use Shaun Riordan's phrase.[22]

The British Council adopts a facilitative approach through programs such as HE Links. HE Links, funded by DFID and delivered in partnership with the British Council, supports "capacity building in higher education in developing countries."[23] Facilitative programs, along with listening exercises, have the inherent difficulty that they rarely seek to promote the nation that is paying for the operation. In an environment of increased pressure for measurable results, efficiency, and valorization, the impact or value for money of these programs is harder to demonstrate in terms of nation promotion.

The criticisms of this type of approach, however, misunderstand a fundamental dichotomy of PD development. PD is not merely about selling policy, it is about achieving specific objectives; it is about changing behavior rather than just perceptions.[24] This facilitative approach is increasingly being recognized as part of UK Public Diplomacy strategy, as Lord Triesman argued:

> I do not believe it is necessary for the UK to get credit for its role in raising consciousness or nudging a foreign government towards a new policy. I want to see the change take place. I don't mind if there are no bouquets.[25]

Moving further along the spectrum, the British Council engages in the development of long-term relationships or networks, through programs such as *The Network Effect*, which focuses on the high degree of "interconnectedness" between civil societies and functions in an environment of greater "openness and transnational cooperation."[26] The network-based approach, in which participants seek mutual benefit through dialogue, ensures that a program maintains relevance to the various local groups engaged within a transnational project. In this type of work the emphasis is on the promotion of free exchange of ideas, rather than advocacy of a specific perspective. However, networks must also need a purpose or issue around which to unite. Laurie Wilson's leaking boat analogy is important here: "It is like being trapped in a leaky boat: If you spend all your time bailing and none of it rowing, you will never get to shore."[27] To provide a dynamic for discussion *The Network Effect* has focused on issues such as "Social Diversity and Cities" or "Media and Legitimacy in European Democracy."

Cultural exchange sits at the center of the spectrum, if based on a symmetrical relationship, in which both sides are engaged in listening and telling. This type of work is fulfilled by *Connecting Classrooms* and *Global Xchange* projects providing different digital or physical approaches to the concept of cultural exchange.[28] However, should an exchange program be based on a one-way engagement, it would be better considered cultural diplomacy, alongside the production of exhibitions such as *Turning Points* held in Tehran in 2004.[29]

The wide range of British Council activity reaches direct messaging or advocacy, in a limited number of cases. In Uganda "[a] cross-section of people, including the government's Ministry of Gender, were invited to contribute research" on "diversity issues facing people and organisations."[30] Within three months the Equal Opportunities Act was adopted in Uganda. Other examples include work on Climate Change.[31] The approach may be based on building a network and developing relationships, but these relationships also have the purpose of promoting a specific position. Equally, the education reform work conducted by the British Council has a specific purpose. The advocacy work creates a potential for tension as the British Council states its mission in the Annual Report; "to build beneficial relationships between people in the United Kingdom and other countries."[32] Mutual benefit defined by one actor, as in the case of policy advocacy or direct messaging, creates a tension with the concept of mutuality, particularly if linked to the focus on dialogue. Some audiences may feel that dialogue with a predetermined purpose is not genuine dialogue, but persuasion by another name.

In addition to the challenges specific to certain types of operations, the British Council also faces the challenge of clearly articulating its approach to PD given the vast range of activity in which it engages. The spectrum of activity in which the British Council is engaged, from facilitation, through cultural diplomacy and cultural exchange to direct messaging, makes any single articulation difficult. This has the potential to have an impact on the practical level; programs with different emphasis on "listening" or "telling" can exist within British Council engagement with a single target audience. Furthermore, without clear articulation there is the danger of programs containing assumptions which are inappropriate to the type of approach. Such a situation could limit the impact of the program and the efficiency of the organization. However, this challenge is not limited to the British Council; any PD organization which adopts a mixed approach across the spectrum of activity must negotiate this challenge either through clear articulation of assumptions or the construction of internal firewalls between the different approaches.

BBC World Service

While the British Council occupies a wide range of PD activity, the focus of the BBC World Service (BBCWS) is much narrower. The nature of broadcasting, particularly by radio, causes it to be largely one-way communication, and as such places the emphasis on "telling." However, broadcasting is about presenting a credible perspective rather than the production of direct messaging. As such, BBCWS seeks "to provide the most trusted, relevant and high quality international news in the world, and an indispensable service of *independent* analysis, with an *international* perspective, which promotes greater understanding of complex issues."[33] The appearance of editorial independence is a vital part of the credibility of BBCWS. Despite the emphasis on independence, the decision to broadcast in a particular language is based, in part, on the region in which a language is spoken and "the strategic importance of that region for Britain." This is of such importance that the "Foreign and Commonwealth Office of the British government, which funds BBC World Service . . . takes part in the decision-making process."[34]

Changes in international priorities and the growth of satellite TV, including Al Jazeera, have caused an increased emphasis on products such as the BBC Pashtu service broadcast in Afghanistan.[35] Lord Triesman has argued that it "is a vital tool . . . and crucially reaches Helmand, where our armed forces face Taliban fighters. Through PD, we hope to make their job easier by making it harder for the Taliban to find safe haven."[36] Other services have experienced a return to prominence, such as BBC Arabic Service, originally launched in 1938; it features programs such as *Al alam hatha al sabah* (The World This Morning).[37]

However, there is a potential tension between seeking recognition as a broadcaster with "*independent* analysis, with an *international* perspective" and achieving specific PD objectives. In this sense, BBCWS has a Janus-faced identity, caught between the hierarchical approach of top down, one-way communication and the production of a multilateral understanding of news broadcasting through the emphasis on producing an international perspective. With one face it feeds into a conception of PD which thrives in highly interdependent regions and between countries that are linked by multiple transnational relationships and a substantial degree of interconnectedness between their civil societies.[38] However, this network approach is limited by the other face, represented by the one-way nature of international broadcasting, despite the inclusion of local perspectives and interactivity. The crux of the tension between the two faces of BBCWS is the tension between the independence and international reputation on the one hand and the realization of certain PD goals on the other. In organizational terms this had been recognized by the "observer status" BBCWS holds on the UK Public Diplomacy Board.[39]

Foreign and Commonwealth Office

As a government department, the Foreign Office approach to PD is dominated by direct messaging, particularly policy advocacy, at the "telling" end of the spectrum. Brian Hocking has described the hierarchical approach as one in which "the foreign ministry and the national diplomatic system over which it presides act as gatekeepers, monitoring interactions between domestic and international policy environments and funnelling information between them."[40] It is focused on the one-way streaming of selected information to an audience. There may be interaction with members of a target audience, but the output of that interaction is largely limited to the content approved by the gatekeeper.

This direct messaging approach can be seen in a competition to be run by one of the diplomatic posts. The competition, to be run on YouTube, was "for a short film on climate change from the perspective of youth. They will then produce a DVD of the winning entries and circulate this to business leaders for whom the youth market is vitally important."[41] While the material produced is likely to be generated from within the target audience, the insertion of a competitive element provides a means for discrimination. Furthermore, the retreat from the technological frontier caused by the change in media platform from the unmediated mêlée of Web 2.0 to the polished DVD allows the gatekeeper function to operate by separating out the preferred or approved content and funnelling it to targeted recipients. Despite the flirtation with the user-generated media this still maintains the commitment to direct messaging.

The telling approach has explicit policy objectives, and the Foreign Office also supports projects through other means such as the Global Opportunities Fund which "aims to promote action on global issues in areas of strategic importance to the UK."[42] While this program is explicitly linked to strategic priorities, it funds "NGO projects, technical assistance to foreign governments, funding for UN activity."[43] This provides the means to vary the method of delivery of the particular activity which has included counter-narcotics in Afghanistan, along with work on human rights and counter-terrorism.[44]

Outside the Public Diplomacy Board

The Public Diplomacy Board includes "the three *main* public diplomacy partners."[45] There are, as the terms of reference indicate, more organizations involved in UK PD than those which comprise the Public Diplomacy Board. These organizations, while they do not make up the core of British PD policy, make an important contribution and the spectrum allows their activity to be represented alongside Public Diplomacy Board members. These organizations are recognized though the Public Diplomacy Partners Group. This group provides a forum for sharing information about activities. In addition, group members also provide advice and "delivery outcomes on specific public diplomacy initiatives."[46]

The Public Diplomacy Partners Group includes the members of the Public Diplomacy Board, and in addition includes: VisitBritain, UKTI, DFID, DCMS, Scottish Executive, Welsh Assembly, MoD, DfES, Northern Ireland and UK Sport. The predominant PD contribution of many of these organizations can be characterized as direct messaging either for specific policies, or sectoral and regional interests. Many approach their contribution to PD from an image, marketing, or branding approach, though there has also been a move toward understanding the contribution of strategic communication.[47]

While generically perceived as promotion of Britain, many of the regions, far from developing a unified image of Britain, are engaged in active competition. University promotion is a clear example; attendance at a Welsh University will in the vast majority of cases eliminate the chance of also being registered on a course at a Scottish University in the same academic year. Tourism is less clear-cut, as visitors could travel to both, yet there is still benefit to one region in drawing tourists away from an alternative, leading to competition.[48]

The Department for Culture, Media and Sport (DCMS) entered into a funding agreement starting in 2001 with the British Tourist Authority (BTA) in response to "the areas of market failure which result from its fragmentation."[49] However, this is not merely an issue of fragmentation in the tourism industry. The stated aim of DCMS is "to improve the quality of life for all through cultural and sporting activities, support the pursuit of excellence, and champion the tourism, creative and leisure industries."[50] The potential for overlap between the development of domestic culture and projection abroad, through cultural diplomacy, creates a complex relationship between the official PD structure and PD activities under most broad definitions.[51] The possibility of duplication and inefficiency is evident, if conducted without the appropriate coordination or firewalls.[52]

The Department for International Development (DFID) presents an important case. Its role in "leading the British Government's fight against world poverty" requires a combination of approaches. Much of the work is facilitative with changes in behaviour the result of support provided to the target audience. However, at the other end of the spectrum, DFID also places some emphasis on strategic communication to support its facilitative function. As such, while it occupies the relatively sparsely populated facilitative end of the spectrum it also joins many other organizations in producing messages originating from Britain which are intended to be consumed overseas.

Conclusion

The dissemination of multiple messages from numerous organizations presents many problems and possibilities. The existence of multiple identities and a lack of homogeneity within a target audience create the need to recognize the development of a "multi-layered network of relations."[53] As a result, there is logic to the use of a range of approaches or multiple messages. However, this conceptually argues for a coordinated structure in which all areas of overlap are developed in cooperation between PD organizations. Conversely, practitioners may consider it preferable to construct firewalls between different areas of activity, thereby acknowledging divergent organizational priorities. Whichever approach a PD structure chooses to adopt, negotiation will occur either over the location of the firewalls or over the priorities of any coordinated approach. This is in part due to the influence of financial considerations. As Lord Triesman said in his capacity as Parliamentary Under-Secretary of State, Foreign and Commonwealth Office: "in the lead-up to every Comprehensive Spending Review, a large number of people compete for funds, and I am not afraid or ashamed to say that I compete along with them. That is the nature of the work that we do, and I am doing it."[54]

Whether a system is constructed on the basis of cooperation or clearly defined and firewalled activity, the recognition of a spectrum of activity and the position of different actors on it is central to ensuring a clear articulation of organizational priorities.

Notes

1 Lord Carter of Coles, Public Diplomacy Review, December 2005, http://www.britishcouncil.org/home-about-us-governance-funding.htm; also quoted in Public Diplomacy Board: Terms of Reference, http://www.fco.gov.uk/servlet/Front?pagename=OpenMarket/Xcelerate/ShowPage&c=Page&cid=1035898725758. For alternatives, see, for example, Karen Hughes; Nominee for Under Secretary for Public Diplomacy and Public Affairs Testimony at confirmation hearing before the Senate Foreign Relations Committee, Washington, DC—The mission of public diplomacy is to engage, inform, and

help others understand our policies, actions and values—but I am mindful that before we seek to be understood, we must first work to understand, http://www.state.gov/r/us/2005/49967.htm; Paul Sharp, "Revolutionary States, Outlaw Regimes and the Techniques of Public Diplomacy," in *The New Public Diplomacy* ed. Jan Melissen (New York: Palgrave Macmillan, 2005), 106.

2 Foreign and Commonwealth Office Annual Report 2006/2007, May 9, 2007 http://www.fco.gov.uk/ servlet/Front?pagename=OpenMarket/Xcelerate/ShowPage&c=Page&cid=1176454609076. This definition has not been agreed with by other UK public diplomacy organizations.

3 I am indebted to Nick Wadham-Smith for clarifying this difference.

4 The construction of the spectrum owes much to the taxonomy produced by Nick Cull in *Public Diplomacy: Lessons from the Past*, Report Commissioned by the Public Diplomacy Board, April 2007. This taxonomy, however, compartmentalized the activities, rather than conceiving them on a continuous spectrum of shifting emphasis and omitted concepts such as facilitation.

5 Bruce Gregory, "Public Diplomacy and Strategic Communication: Cultures, Firewalls, and Imported Norms," paper presented at the American Political Science Association Conference on International Communication and Conflict, August 31, 2005, 30.

6 For listening as a part of message creation, see Simon Anholt, *Another One Bites the Grass: Making Sense of International Advertising* (New York: John Wiley & Sons 2000).

7 See, for example, Ilana Ozernoy, "Ears Wide Shut," *The Atlantic Monthly*, November 2006.

8 Alan Henrikson, "Niche Diplomacy in the Public Arena: Canada and Norway," in *The New Public Diplomacy* ed. Jan Melissen (New York: Palgrave Macmillan, 2005); Kishan S. Rana, "Singapore's Diplomacy: Vulnerability into Strength," *The Hague Journal of Diplomacy* 1 (2006): 81–106. See also Tommy Koh's essay in *Singapore: Re-engineering Success*, ed. Arun Mahizhnan and Lee Tsao Yuan (Singapore: Singapore Institute of Policy Studies, 1999).

9 R.S. Zaharna, "The Network Paradigm of Strategic Public Diplomacy," *Foreign Policy in Focus*, Policy Brief 10, no. 1, April 2005, http://www.fpif.org/briefs/vol10/v10n01pubdip.html. See also Jamie Metzl, "Network Diplomacy," *Georgetown Journal of International Affairs*, Winter/Spring 2001, http://www.carnegieendowment.org/publications/index.cfm?fa=view&id=681&prog=zgp.

10 Bruce Gregory, "Public Diplomacy and Strategic Communication: Cultures, Firewalls, and Imported Norms," paper presentation at the American Political Science Association Conference on International Communication and Conflict, August 31, 2005, 11; quoting *Cultural Diplomacy: Recommendations and Research*, Report of the Center for Arts and Culture, Washington D.C., July 2004, 8–9. While the report is entitled Cultural Diplomacy, this section fits more closely the concept of exchange.

11 For further discussions of a two-way, non-hierarchical approach, see Jan Melissen, "The New Public Diplomacy: Between Theory and Practice," in *The New Public Diplomacy*, ed. Jan Melissen (New York: Palgrave Macmillan, 2005), 18; Ali Fisher "Public Diplomacy in the United Kingdom," from *The Future of Public Diplomacy A European Perspective. Working Paper*, The 2006 Madrid Conference on Public Diplomacy, Real Instituto Elcano, Madrid, Spain, November 2006; http://www.realinstitutoelcano.org/ documentos/276.asp; John Arquilla and David Ronfeldt, *The Emergence of Noopolitik: Toward an American Information Strategy* (Santa Monica, CA: RAND, 1999); R.S. Zaharna, "The Network Paradigm of Strategic Public Diplomacy," *Foreign Policy in Focus*, Policy Brief 10, no. 1, April 2005; Jaimie Metzl, "Network Diplomacy," *Georgetown Journal of International Affairs*, Winter/Spring 2001, http://www.carnegieendowment.org/publications/index.cfm? fa=view&id=681; Shaun Riordan, *The New Diplomacy* (Cambridge: Polity Press, 2003):130; Brian Hocking, "Rethinking the 'New' Public Diplomacy," in *The New Public Diplomacy*, ed. Jan Melissen (New York: Palgrave Macmillan, 2005), 36.

12 Milton Cummings, *Cultural Diplomacy and the United States Government: A Survey* (Washington, D.C.: Center for Arts and Culture, 2003) http://www.culturalpolicy.org/pdf/MCCpaper.pdf.

13 Simon Anholt and Jeremy Hildreth, *Brand America* (London: Cyan, 2004); Jan Melissen, "How Has Place Branding Developed? Opinion Piece," *Place Branding* 2, no. 1 (2006); Jan Melissen, "Wielding Soft Power: The New Public Diplomacy," *Clingendael Diplomacy Papers* no.2 (May 2005): 22–24.

14 Simon Anholt and Jeremy Hildreth, *Brand America* (London: Cyan, 2004), 29.

15 See Simon Anholt, *Another One Bites the Grass: Making sense of international advertising* (New York: John Wiley & Sons, 2000).

16 The Public Diplomacy Board also has two independent advisors, at this writing in 2007, Simon Anholt and Chris Powell.

17 Public Diplomacy Board: Terms of Reference, http://www.fco.gov.uk/servlet/Front?pagename- =OpenMarket/Xcelerate/ShowPage&c=Page&cid=1035898725758.

18 Lord Carter of Coles, Public Diplomacy Review, December 2005, http://www.britishcouncil.org/ home-about-us-governance-funding.htm; Public Diplomacy Board Terms of Reference FCO Website; http://www.fco.gov.uk/servlet/Front?pagename=OpenMarket/Xcelerate/ ShowPage&c=Page&cid=1035898725758.

259

19 Lord Triesman, Parliamentary Under Secretary of State with responsibility for Public Diplomacy (as of June 27, 2007).

20 Lord Triesman, "Public Diplomacy: Steps to the future," speech at *The Future of Public Diplomacy* conference held at Wilton Park, March 1, 2007.

21 Jan Melissen, "The New Public Diplomacy: Between Theory and Practice," in *The New Public Diplomacy*, ed. Jan Melissen (New York: Palgrave Macmillan, 2005), 18.

22 Shaun Riordan, *The New Diplomacy* (Cambridge: Polity Press, 2003), 130.

23 Terry Allsop, Paul Bennell, and David Forrester, *DFID's Higher Education Links Scheme: Review and Possible Future Options for Higher Education Partnerships, Report,* commissioned by the Department for International Development (DFID), March 2003, www.dfid.gov.uk/pubs/files/higheredlinksfull.pdf.

24 For examples of this type of work, particularly niche diplomacy, see Alan Henrikson, "Niche Diplomacy in the Public Arena: Canada and Norway," in *The New Public Diplomacy*, ed. Jan Melissen (New York: Palgrave Macmillan, 2005), 67; Mark Leonard, *Public Diplomacy* (London: Foreign Policy Centre, 2002), 170; and Kishan S. Rana, "Singapore's Diplomacy: Vulnerability into Strength," *The Hague Journal of Diplomacy* 1 (2006): 81–106.

25 Lord Triesman, " 'Public Diplomacy: steps to the future," London School of Economics, April 23, 2007, http://www.lse.ac.uk/collections/LSEPublicLecturesAndEvents/events/2007/20070328t1042z001.htm.

26 Jan Melissen, "The New Public Diplomacy: Between Theory and Practice," in *The New Public Diplomacy*, ed. Jan Melissen (New York: Palgrave Macmillan, 2005), 10; Robert Cooper, *The Breaking of Nations: Order and Chaos in the Twenty-First Century* (London: Atlantic Books, 2003), 76; British Council Slovakia, http://www.britishcouncil.org/slovakia-society-bratislava-network-effect.htm.

27 Laurie J. Wilson, "Strategic Cooperative Communities: A Synthesis of Strategic, Issue-Management, and Relationship-Building Approaches in Public Relations," in *International Public Relations: A Comparative Analysis*, ed. Hugh M Culbertson and Ni Chen (Mahwah, N.J.: Lawrence Erlbaum, 1996), 78.

28 Global Xchange is run in partnership with VSO and CSV and is a six-month exchange programme which gives young people from different countries a unique opportunity to work together, to develop and share valuable skills and to make a practical contribution where it is needed in local communities, http://www.vso.org.uk/globalxchange/; Connecting Classrooms provides cluster groups of 3 schools with the chance to partner with schools from two different countries in sub-Saharan Africa and the UK. The schools will link for intercultural dialogue and to increase knowledge and understanding of each other's societies, http://www.britishcouncil.org/learning-connecting-classrooms.htm.

29 Contemporary art from British collections brought to Iran for the first time to mark the 25th anniversary of the founding of the Islamic Republic of Iran, The Museums, Libraries and Archives Council website, http://www.mla.gov.uk/webdav/harmonise?Page/@id=73&Document/@id=24086&Section[@stateId_eq_left_hand_root]/@id=4302.

30 Lord Triesman, "Public Diplomacy: steps to the future," London School of Economics, April 23, 2007, http://www.lse.ac.uk/collections/LSEPublicLecturesAndEvents/events/2007/20070328t1042z001.htm.

31 ZeroCarbonCity Website http://www.britishcouncil.org/zerocarboncity; See also http://www.scenta.co.uk/Search/518600/zerocarboncity.htm.

32 British Council Annual Report 2005–2006, http://www.britishcouncil.org.

33 Nigel Chapman, "Transforming BBC World Service for a digital age: a strategy for 2010 and beyond," Speech to staff, October 25, 2005, http://www.bbc.co.uk/worldservice/faq/news/story/2005/10/051024_ws2010.shtml.

34 "Why isn't my language included?" BBC World Service website, http://www.bbc.co.uk/worldservice/faq/news/story/2005/08/050810_languages.shtml.

35 Lord Triesman, April 23, 2007.

36 Lord Triesman, April 23, 2007.

37 BBC World Service language services, BBC Press Office, http://www.bbc.co.uk/pressoffice/keyfacts/stories/ws_langs_arabic.shtml.

38 Jan Melissen, "The New Public Diplomacy: Between Theory and Practice," in *The New Public Diplomacy*, ed. Jan Melissen (New York: Palgrave Macmillan, 2005), 10.

39 Public Diplomacy Board Terms of Reference, http://www.fco.gov.uk/servlet/Front?pagename==OpenMarket/Xcelerate/ShowPage&c=Page&cid=1035898725758.

40 Brian Hocking, "Rethinking the 'New' Public Diplomacy," in *The New Public Diplomacy*, ed. Jan Melissen (New York: Palgrave Macmillan, 2005), 35–36.

41 Lord Triesman, April 23, 2007.

42 Global Opportunities Fund Foreign Office Website, http://www.fco.gov.uk/servlet/Front?pagename=OpenMarket/Xcelerate/ShowPage&c=Page&cid=1059131211423.

43 Global Opportunities Fund, FAQ, Foreign Office Website, http://www.fco.gov.uk/servlet/Front?pagename=OpenMarket/Xcelerate/ShowPage&c=Page&cid=1070989717443.

44 Global Opportunities Fund, Foreign Office Website, http://www.fco.gov.uk/servlet/Front?page name=OpenMarket/Xcelerate/ShowPage&c=Page&cid=1059131211423.

45 Public Diplomacy Board Terms of Reference, http://www.fco.gov.uk/servlet/Front?pagename=OpenMarket/Xcelerate/ShowPage&c=Page&cid=1035898725758.

46 Public Diplomacy Partners Group, VisitBritain Website, http://www.visitbritain.com/corporate/stakeholders/public_diplomacy/PublicDiplomacyPartnersGroup.aspx.

47 For alternative views of image and branding, see Simon Anholt and Jeremy Hildreth, *Brand America* (London: Cyan, 2004); Jan Melissen, "How Has Place Branding Developed? Opinion Piece," *Place Branding* 2, no. 1 (2006).

48 Examples of regional attempts to attract tourism include http://www.visitwales.co.uk/ and http://www.visitscotland.com/.

49 Funding Agreement between the Department for Culture, Media and Sport (DCMS) and The British Tourism Authority (BTA) For The Period 2001–02 to 2003–04, DCMS website: www.culture.gov.uk/NR/rdonlyres/9ED54D6C-7E09-4236-A6D9-A696CD2F2E43/0/BTAfundingagreement200102to200304.pdf.

50 Department for Culture, Media and Sport Departmental Annual Report 2006, Presented to Parliament by the Secretary of State for Culture, Media and Sport and the Chief Secretary to the Treasury by Command of Her Majesty, May 2006, http://www.culture.gov.uk/Reference_library/Annual_Reports/ar_2006.htm.

51 Kirsten Bound, Rachel Briggs, John Holden, and Samuel Jones, *Cultural Diplomacy*, DEMOS, February 28, 2007; and Lord Triesman, Lords Hansard, March 6, Column 115–117, http://www.publications.parliament.uk/pa/ld200607/ldhansrd/text/70306-0002.htm.

52 Bruce Gregory, "Public Diplomacy and Strategic Communication," August 31, 2005.

53 Shaun Riordan, *The New Diplomacy* (Cambridge: Polity Press, 2003), 130.

54 Lords Hansard, March 6, 2007, Column 117, http://www.publications.parliament.uk/pa/ld200607/ldhansrd/text/70306-0002.htm.

22

German Public Diplomacy

The Dialogue of Cultures

Oliver Zöllner

Since 1990, the united Federal Republic of Germany has been grappling with the task of defining the country's new role in the world: is it still a giant in economic terms (the world's number three as per gross domestic product), but a dwarf in the political arena?[1] What should Germany's currently carefully limited contributions to international military interventions (in Afghanistan and elsewhere) look like in the future? What will become of the country's recently failed aspirations towards a permanent seat on the UN Security Council? Will a united Europe be dominated by Germany, the European Union's most populous member state (82 million inhabitants), economic powerhouse, and cultural bridge between western and eastern Europe? And what is, or should be, Germany's modern identity, her image, and her message to the world?

It's a reminder of the country's grim past that Germany is often most associated with the Nazi dictatorship (1933–45), World War II, and the *shoah* genocide, as image surveys indicate.[2] Other studies, undertaken in the context of nation-branding and marketing, point at the predominance of cars as the central item of association: "The extent to which Germany and automobiles are currently perceived as a single entity is really quite astonishing."[3] These perceptions clearly are challenges for German public diplomacy which has officially been described as the "third pillar" of the country's foreign policy since the 1960s.[4]

Terminology and Concepts of German Public Diplomacy

The term "public diplomacy" is a relatively recent addition to political terminology in Germany and is gradually being implemented. It is used in the English original since previous German-language terms such as *aussenpolitische Öffentlichkeitsarbeit* (foreign-policy public relations) or *auswärtige Kulturpolitik* (foreign cultural policy) did not match the full meaning of "public diplomacy," while the straight translation *öffentliche Diplomatie* simply failed to catch on. To date, *public diplomacy* is a term that is basically confined to diplomatic and academic circles. The German Foreign Office still uses the term *auswärtige Kulturpolitik* alongside *public diplomacy*, with the latter gradually replacing the former.[5] Published literature on the subject in the German language is rare and mainly covers US examples or draws on US theory development.[6]

The fuzzy terminology points at conceptions of German public diplomacy that are developing but are far from being clear-cut. The gist of the ongoing debate may be formulated as follows: presenting Germany as a modern European nation of culture and a "Land of Ideas," as the slogan of a public-private-partnership-sponsored marketing campaign asserts which seeks to promote Germany as a suitable location for business and industry:

> The main message is "Germany—Land of Ideas." The wording expresses a wealth of positive arguments associated with Germany both within Germany and abroad: nation of science and culture—the land of poets and thinkers, innovative products "made in Germany."[7]

On top of these clearly self-congratulatory claims, engaging foreign target groups in "dialogues" is the fashionable current leitmotif of German public diplomacy and is employed by various actors.

Main Actors of German Public Diplomacy

Foreign Office

Not surprisingly, a major protagonist of German public diplomacy is the country's Foreign Office (*Auswärtiges Amt*, AA) based in Berlin. The ministry's specialist department is the Directorate-General for Communication, Public Diplomacy and the Media (*Abteilung für Kommunikation, Öffentlichkeitsarbeit und Medien*, internally known as the "K" Department). According to their website copy, the K Department seeks to "stimulate interest in Germany, to explain German foreign and domestic policy, to provide information on and discuss developments in society, to promote understanding of our value system through dialogue and to build up lasting ties with Germany."[8]

The dialogic principle is given additional emphasis on a German-language web page of the AA which states that "modern public diplomacy goes beyond one-way transmission of information and stands for dialogue and discussion. . . . It is about reaching the hearts and minds of people."[9] However, the "dialogue" conceptualized by the AA does not seem to be action of a discursive or communicative type as modeled by German theorist Jürgen Habermas; rather, it is seemingly strategic action "oriented to success."[10] This is made obvious in a stated objective which is to promote Germany:

> across the world as an economic partner, a land of culture and an attractive location for investment, education and research. "Promoting Germany" means communicating the modern, multifaceted identity of Germany. Not hiding flaws, but emphasizing strengths and advantages. Germany has many positive sides—but one has to know about them and become familiar with them.[11]

Target groups of this endeavor are the usual decision-makers in the political, business, and cultural spheres, journalists as key multipliers, "senior representatives of parties and civil society organizations, representatives of universities and scientists. The young elites are particularly important."[12] Instruments include Internet resources, print media, tailor-made themed visits for specialist groups (e.g., journalists), and so-called media dialogue events: "The role of the media in a pluralistic, liberal society in a democratic state based on the rule of law is highlighted. Freedom of opinion and of the press are of particular importance."[13]

The AA's central web site (http://www.auswaertiges-amt.de) has versions in five languages (German, English, French, Spanish, and Arabic). German embassies and consulates worldwide plus (as of 2007) five *German Information Centers* (in Brasília, Cairo, Mexico City, Paris, and Washington, DC) offer additional locally relevant information through their websites in 43 languages. Other AA-sponsored web resources draw on topical attractive events such as a website in nine languages on football (soccer) in Germany or feature online editions of the *Deutschland* magazine and the *Facts about Germany* handbook in various major languages. The printed version of *Deutschland* magazine is issued six times a year in 11 languages (total print run: ca. 400,000 copies), while the *Facts about Germany* handbook is published in 13 idioms and likewise has a circulation of 400,000 copies.[14]

In 2006, a key topic in Germany's public diplomacy which saw intense coverage in all the above-mentioned channels was the country's hosting of the football World Cup (a massive media event); during the first half of 2007, special emphasis was given to Germany's presidency of the European Union.

Ever since 2001, a long-term focus of German public diplomacy has been a much-proclaimed "Dialogue with the Islamic World."[15] Engaging in dialogues with Arabic-speaking nations has in fact been a critical feature of Germany's foreign policy approximately since the 1970s when, after several terrorism-related incidents (among them the massacre at the Munich Olympics in 1972), the country started to position itself as a credible mediator and unbiased broker between the West, Arab countries, and Israel. These efforts had been stepped up even before September 11, 2001: in April 1999 the Federal President's Office issued a declaration on the "Dialogue of Cultures" (with a high priority given to the Arab World) which some commentators view as a "new paradigm" of German public diplomacy.[16] An important partner of the AA in this and other contexts is the quasi-public, Stuttgart-based *Institute for Foreign Cultural Relations* (*Institut für Auslandsbeziehungen, ifa*) which is to a large extent funded by the AA itself and the *Press and Information Office of the Federal Government*, the German government's public relations department.

The Foreign Office has developed a partnership with the media through its largely independent relationship with *Deutsche Welle* (DW), Germany's international broadcaster. Since 2001, this relationship has been intensified in the context of the "Dialogue with the Islamic World."

International Broadcasting

Deutsche Welle, Germany's international broadcaster, was founded in 1953 as a radio service to inform audiences abroad about the new, post-Nazi Germany. Today, DW offers radio, television, and online services in 30 languages (see http://www.dw-world.de). At the time of writing, focal broadcast languages are German, English, Spanish, Farsi, Russian, Brazilian Portuguese, Chinese, and Arabic. The station claims to have a total global weekly audience of some 65 million listeners and 28 million viewers.[17] All programmes are produced at facilities in Bonn and Berlin and studios in Brussels, Moscow, and Washington, DC, with additional input from local stringers in various countries.

The German federal government fully funds DW which is an autonomous public-service corporation. The station's journalistic mission is a credible and serious one. In countries where media censorship is rampant and where unbiased reporting of domestic or international news is an exception, DW and other international broadcasters play an important role as a reliable news source. Reflecting its journalistic mission, DW is designed to remain editorially independent; a status which is ensured by an elaborate system of regular parliamentary accords.

The station's mission, as defined by the recently expanded and updated DW Act, is worth a closer look as it reflects Germany's preferred reading of the country's current role and self-identity. According to that legal norm, DW programmes "shall make Germany comprehensible as a culture nation rooted in Europe, and a liberal, democratic nation ruled by law. [Programmes] shall give a forum, both in Europe and on other continents, to German and other views on key topics mainly in the spheres of politics, culture and the economy, the objective being to promote understanding and exchange between cultures and nations."[18]

Following this dialogue and exchange postulate, DW produces, to name but one telling example, a five-hour daily Arabic radio service, an extensive Arabic website (http://www.dw-world.de/arabic) which was considerably expanded and relaunched in 2004, and a total of eight hours daily of Arabic-language slots (alongside English, German, and Spanish segments) on the television service *DW-TV* that were introduced in 2002 and further expanded in 2005. From 2005 to 2007, *DW-Radio* co-produced *Al-Iraq Al-Yawm* ("Iraq Today"), a special format that targeted young Iraqi listeners and was broadcast via Baghdad-based talk radio *Radio Dijla*. The project, which was funded by the Foreign Office, ended abruptly when Radio Dijla's studios were bombed. Plans for a continuation of the service are underway. Since 2005, DW-TV has been co-producing *Liqu'a Oropa* ("Meet Europe"), a monthly Arab–Western discussion format broadcast on *Abu Dhabi TV*. Targeting audiences in Afghanistan, DW-TV produced news bulletins in Dari and Pashto which were broadcast by Afghan state television from 2002 to 2005. This special project, however, ended when funding by the Foreign Office ran out.

Cultural Institutes

"Germany turned to culture to help restore relationships after the Second World War"[19] and in 1951 founded the Goethe Institut (GI) for this end. The Munich-based GI is organized as a private association in which the Federal Republic of Germany and, among others, political functionaries are part of the membership assembly, thereby making the GI a quasi-public service institution. Its budget is mainly allocated by the Foreign Office and the Press and Information Office of the Federal Government. The GI's core activities—German-language teaching, cultural cooperation and promoting the image of Germany abroad through cultural events—are coordinated with the institute's financiers. Well in line with other actors of German public diplomacy, fostering dialogue and understanding between nations and cultures is the GI's main philosophy.[20] There are Goethe Institutes of various sizes in 81 countries. Considerable budget cuts over the last couple of years have forced the GI to close branches or reduce services.

The organization collaborates with the Foreign Office and DW. One joint project is the multi-language website *Campus Germany* (http://www.campus-germany.de) which seeks to attract students to German universities. Another GI partnership—with AA, DW, and the Institute for Foreign Cultural Relations *(ifa)*—is the website *Qantara* (literally: "Bridge," http://www.qantara.de; in Arabic, Turkish, English, and German), an Internet resource dedicated to the aforementioned dialogue with those world regions influenced by Islam.[21] A "dialogue of cultures" by way of exhibitions, conferences, publications and related events has also been the *ifa*'s focus for decades. Since 2003, *ifa* and a private cultural organization, with funding from the *Federal Cultural Foundation* (Kulturstiftung des Bundes) edit the online magazine *Nafas* (literally: "Breath") which focuses on art in the Muslim world and is available in Arabic, English, and German. *Nafas*, the editors' mission statement reads, "aims to contribute to a real dialog[ue] among cultures, understood as communication between individuals from different cultural realms who grant each other self-determined and also changing identities, and who do not deduce these, as rigid constructs, from the mere origin of the other."[22]

Taking into account all these projects, one may guess that a "dialogue of cultures," especially one with the Muslim world, is a high priority of the official German cultural organizations.

Academic Exchange and Scholarships

Activities of the *German Academic Exchange Service* (*Deutscher Akademischer Austauschdienst*, DAAD) partly overlap with those of other institutions of German public diplomacy. The focus of the DAAD, however, is on providing exchange scholarships for German and non-German students, teachers, researchers, and scientists, and the promotion of research cooperation between German and foreign universities. The aim is to recruit and win young elites abroad "as partners and friends of Germany" and to "strengthen German as a major international cultural language and lingua franca and to advance interest in, knowledge of and understanding for Germany."[23]

265

The emphasis is on investing in minds and showcasing Germany as a "Land of Ideas," as expressed in a recent marketing claim. Another goal of the DAAD is supporting economic and democratic reforms in developing countries through the promotion of academic and scientific advancement. The DAAD is mainly funded through the Foreign Office, the Ministry of Education and Research, and the Ministry for Economic Cooperation and Development. For these ends, some 200 programmes are in operation. As part of the general German objective to promote a Western–Muslim dialogue, the DAAD is one of the sponsors of the *German University in Cairo* (GUC) which was founded in 2003 as the first German university abroad. Another actor in the field of international scholarships for academics and scientists is the *Alexander von Humboldt Foundation*, a civic, quasi-public foundation established by the Federal Republic of Germany. In line with other public diplomacy actors, this organization emphasizes "winning hearts and minds" which includes target groups in world regions dominated by Islam.[24]

Other Public Diplomacy Actors

The *Federal Agency for Technical Relief* (*Technisches Hilfswerk*, THW) is a little-known, but certainly noteworthy public diplomacy actor. It operates both nationally and internationally. For its missions abroad, the organization explicitly defines itself as a "humanitarian ambassador" of Germany.[25] As part of an international network of similar institutions and in collaboration with United Nations agencies, it supplies relief assistance in the contexts of natural disasters, wars, violent conflicts, and other man-made disasters. The THW deploys its own expert personnel and trains local staff as well. Recent aid projects include work in Bolivia, Indonesia, Liberia, Lebanon, and Pakistan. One may see these activities as an overlap of public diplomacy and economic development aid. Other actors in this area are the *German Society for Technical Cooperation* (*Deutsche Gesellschaft für Technische Zusammenarbeit*, GTZ), a federally-owned, government-sponsored private company, and the *German Development Service* (*Deutscher Entwicklungsdienst*, DED), a not-for-profit public-private partnership which has various federal ministries as Board members overseeing the operations of the organization.

The *German National Tourist Board* (*Deutsche Zentrale für Tourismus*, DZT) promotes Germany abroad as a vacation destination. It has offices and agencies in 30 countries, and offers a bilingual website (http://www.Germany-tourism.de). As a quasi-public institution mainly funded by the German federal government, it may be seen as an institution of public diplomacy, or nation-branding, albeit one dedicated to straight marketing.

Other German government-sponsored activities that target foreign civilians contribute to a further blurring of the boundaries of public diplomacy and other areas. Alongside their military tasks, the *German Armed Forces (Bundeswehr)*, currently deployed in Afghanistan, in Bosnia-Hercegovina, and in Kosovo province, deliver political education programmes which address local civilians—activities that go beyond military operations as such. The Bundeswehr's *Psychological Operations Battalion 950* edits general interest/political message magazines for Bosnian and Kosovar civilians, produces the Kabul-based radio service *Sada-e Azadi* ("Voice of Freedom") that aims to deliver the message of democracy and political dialogue, and uses kites (kite-flying used to be a popular sport in pre-Taliban Afghanistan) embroidered with peace logos and slogans to reach the "hearts and minds" of Afghans and show them a softer side of the International Security Assistance Force (ISAF).[26] Such activities point to the fact that public diplomacy may come in many different forms, and that today military organizations such as NATO have a Public Diplomacy Division as well.

Conclusion

Germany's public diplomacy is performed by a number of institutions on different levels, and not always in unison. In the past, it often was difficult to see a concerted effort or a unified approach. Lately, the "Dialogue of Cultures," especially one with the Muslim world, has emerged as a common denominator of German public diplomacy activities. If Germany today positions herself as a broker of mediation and dialogues, this is in stark contrast to, and an ostentatious move away from, her dictatorial Nazi past and its cultural imperialist and propagandistic approach.[27]

All in all, this dialogic approach is well in line with concepts of other Western nations. "The new public diplomacy moves away from—to put it crudely—peddling information to foreigners and keeping the foreign press at bay, towards engaging with foreign audiences."[28] Perhaps, then, we should also move away from the old concept of the "audience" as an entity that mainly listens, and conceptualize those target groups of public diplomacy as "stakeholders" (to borrow a term from economics) that may have interests other than one's own organization but who have the capacity to talk back, and do so. Public diplomacy's move towards proclamations of "dialogue" may reflect a general awareness of the need for a global culture of participation. This, in turn, may have to do with the changed nature, and the increasingly uncertain role, of the traditional nation-state under the conditions of globalization.

Realistically speaking, however, it's probably still a long way to a truly symmetrical—and thereby potentially risky—dialogue of cultures and nations. Still awaiting further scrutiny and analysis are the following questions: is "dialogue" as one of the leitmotifs of German public diplomacy truly implemented or is it simply a catchy buzzword? What might be the overall impacts of such an endeavour or disposition—internally and externally? What kinds of (cultural) meaning are produced in the process? And how can possible impacts of dialogue-oriented public diplomacy be evaluated? Perhaps one should at least consider a position held by an institution of German public diplomacy that dialogues of a truly symmetrical nature are difficult to perform:

> It must be accepted that "Western-Muslim dialogue" can essentially not be a dialogue (i.e., an exchange between two sides), but must on both sides integrate a large number of mutually contradictory actors and positions if it is to be meaningful.[29]

The German example also points to the fact that public diplomacy, despite all its glossy packaging and its benevolent emphasis on intercultural dialogue, is about "selling" a positive image of Germany and promoting the country's economic, scientific, and cultural resources. It is easy to imagine that this kind of international relationship is not intended to be lopsided in favour of some other party: the logical objective is to make Germany benefit from her public diplomacy.[30] If that is the case, it is not a communicative, discursive process in Habermasian terms. Rather, it is to be seen as strategic action oriented to success.[31] All in all, Germany's public diplomacy remains ambiguous in this context.

Notes

1 Andrei S. Markovits, Simon Reich and Frank Westermann, "Germany's Economic Power in Europe," in *The German Predicament: Memory and Power in the New Europe*, ed. Andrei S. Markovits and Simon Reich (Ithaca: Cornell University Press, 1997), 150–82.
2 Roland Schürhoff, "Image of and Sympathy Towards Germany Abroad: Does Using Deutsche Welle Programmes Reflect Attitudes vis-à-vis Germany?," in *An Essential Link with Audiences Worldwide: Research for International Broadcasting*, ed. Deutsche Welle and Oliver Zöllner (Berlin: Vistas, 2002), 146.

3 Wally Olins, "Making a National Brand," in *The New Public Diplomacy: Soft Power in International Relations*, ed. Jan Melissen (Basingstoke, New York: Palgrave Macmillan, 2005), 173.

4 Kurt-Jürgen Maaß, "Überblick: Ziele und Instrumente der Auswärtigen Kulturpolitik" [Overview: Objectives and Instruments of Public Diplomacy], in *Kultur und Außenpolitik: Handbuch für Studium und Praxis*, ed. Kurt-Jürgen Maaß (Baden-Baden: Nomos, 2005), 23; Federal Republic of Germany, Deutscher Bundestag [Federal Parliament], 16. Wahlperiode, Drucksache 16/2233 (July 17, 2006), "Große Anfrage zur Auswärtigen Kulturpolitik" [Grand Inquiry into Public Diplomacy], http://dip.bundestag.de/btd/16/022/1602233.pdf; Federal Republic of Germany, Deutscher Bundestag [Federal Parliament], 16. Wahlperiode, Drucksache 16/4024 (January 11, 2007), "Antwort der Bundesregierung" [Federal Government's Reply], http://dip.bundestag.de/btd/16/040/1604024.pdf; Federal Republic of Germany, Deutscher Bundestag [Federal Parliament], 16. Wahlperiode, Protokoll Nr. 16/11 (May 17, 2006), "Ausschuss für Kultur und Medien: Kurz-/Wortprotokoll" [Standing Committee on Culture and Media: Protocol], http://www.bundestag.de/ausschuesse/a22/oeffentliche_sitzungen/17_05_2006/protokoll.pdf.

5 Federal Republic of Germany, Bundesregierung [Federal Government], *Bericht der Bundesregierung zur Auswärtigen Kulturpolitik* (2003) [Report by the Federal Government on Public Diplomacy (2003)]. Internal document (Berlin: Federal Government, 2004); Auswärtiges Amt [German Foreign Office], "Grundlagen und Ziele der Public Diplomacy" [Foundations and Objectives of Public Diplomacy], http://www.auswaertiges-amt.de/diplo/de/Aussenpolitik/PublicDiplomacy/PublicDiplomacy.html.

6 Holger Ohmstedt, "Von der Propaganda zur Public Diplomacy: Die Selbstdarstellung der Vereinigten Staaten von Amerika im Ausland vom Ersten Weltkrieg bis zum Ende des Kalten Krieges" [From Propaganda to Public Diplomacy: The United States' Self-Representation Abroad from the First World War to the End of the Cold War] (Ph.D. diss., Munich University, 1993); Thomas Klöckner, *Public Diplomacy: Auswärtige Informations- und Kulturpolitik der USA. Strukturanalyse der Organisation und Strategien der United States Information Agency und des United States Information Service in Deutschland* [Public Diplomacy of the USA: A Structural Analysis of the Organisation and Strategies of USIA and USIS in Germany] (Baden-Baden: Nomos, 1993); Benno Signitzer, "Anmerkungen zur Begriffs- und Funktionswelt von Public Diplomacy" [Notes on Terminology and Functions of Public Diplomacy], in *Image und PR: Kann Image gegenstand einer Public Relations-Wissenschaft sein?*, ed. Wolfgang Armbrecht, Horst Avenarius and Ulf Zabel (Opladen: Westdeutscher Verlag, 1993), 199–211.

7 Germany—Land of Ideas, "Welcome to the Land of Ideas!," FC Deutschland GmbH, http://www.land-of-ideas.org/CDA/the_initiative,239,0,,en.html (accessed May 20, 2007). The campaign has been initiated by the Federal Government and the Federation of German Industries; partners include the Federal Foreign Office and Deutsche Welle.

8 Auswärtiges Amt [German Foreign Office], "Communication, Public Diplomacy and Media Directorate-General," http://www.auswaertiges-amt.de/diplo/en/AAmt/AA/Kommunikation.html.

9 Auswärtiges Amt, "Grundlagen und Ziele . . .," trans.

10 Jürgen Habermas, *The Theory of Communicative Action. Volume 1: Reason and the Rationalization of Society*, trans. Thomas McCarthy (London: Heinemann, 1984), 279–88, 285.

11 Auswärtiges Amt, "Communication . . ."

12 Auswärtiges Amt, "Communication . . ."

13 Auswärtiges Amt, "Communication . . ."

14 Auswärtiges Amt, "Communication . . ."

15 Auswärtiges Amt [German Foreign Office], *Dialogue with the Islamic World; Dialog mit der islamischen Welt* (Berlin: Federal Foreign Office/Edition Diplomatie, n.d.).

16 Hans J. Kleinsteuber, "Auslandsrundfunk in der Kommunikationspolitik: Zwischen globaler Kommunikation und Dialog der Kulturen" [International Broadcasting and Communication Politics: Between Global Communication and the Dialogue of Cultures], in *Grundlagentexte zur transkulturellen Kommunikation*, ed. Andreas Hepp and Martin Löffelholz (Konstanz: UVK, 2002), 350.

17 Oliver Zöllner, "A Quest for Dialogue in International Broadcasting: Germany's Public Diplomacy Targeting Arab Audiences," *Global Media and Communication* 2 (2006): 170.

18 Deutsche Welle, *Deutsche-Welle-Gesetz* [Deutsche Welle Act]: *Gesetz über die Rundfunkanstalt des Bundesrechts "Deutsche Welle" vom 16.12.1997 in der Fassung vom 15.12.2004* (Bonn: Deutsche Welle, 2005), 8, http://www.dw-world.de/popups/popup_pdf/0,,1275486,00.pdf (accessed May 11, 2007), trans.

19 Cynthia P. Schneider, "Culture Communicates: US Diplomacy That Works," in *The New Public Diplomacy: Soft Power in International Relations*, ed. Jan Melissen (Basingstoke, New York: Palgrave Macmillan, 2005), 158.

20 For an analysis, see Antje Scholz, *Verständigung als Ziel interkultureller Kommunikation: Eine kommunikationswissenschaftliche Analyse am Beispiel des Goethe-Instituts* [Understanding as an Objective of

268

Communication: An Analysis of the Goethe Institute from a Communication Perspective]. (Münster: Lit, 2000).

21 Zöllner, "A Quest . . .," 174–175.

22 Universes in Universe—Worlds of Art and Institute for Foreign Cultural Relations, "Nafas: Art Magazine—Editorial," http://universes-in-universe.org/eng/islamic_world/editorial.

23 Deutscher Akademischer Austauschdienst [German Academic Exchange Service], "Goals and Roles," http://www.daad.de/portrait/en/1.1.html.

24 Erin Taylor, "Winning Hearts and Minds," Humboldt Kosmos 11/2006, Alexander von Humboldt Foundation, http://www.humboldt-foundation.de/kosmos/titel/2006_011_en.htm.

25 Technisches Hilfswerk [Federal Agency for Technical Relief], "A Humanitarian Ambassador— Officially and Traditionally," http://www.thw.bund.de/cln_036/nn_932064/EN/content/about __us/general__information/human__ambassador/human__ambassador__node.html__nnn=true.

26 Psychological Operations Battalion 950, "Products: The Secret Is in the Media Mix," Bundeswehr [German Armed Forces], http://www.opinfo.bundeswehr.de/portal/a/streitkraeftebasis/kcxml/ 04_Sj9SPykssy0xPLMnMz0vM0Y_QjzKLt4j39HcDSYGYJm7B-pEwsaCUVH1fj_zcVH1v_QD9 gtyIckdHRUUApKS78Q!!/delta/base64xml/L0lKWWttUSEhL   3dITUFDc0FJVUFOby80SUVh REFBIS9lbg!! It is worth noting here that the Battalion's official English website refers to "Psychological Operations" and "PSYOPS" whereas the German version sticks to the official term "Operative Information" (Operational Information), a nomenclature in use since 1990.

27 Kurt Düwell, "Zwischen Propaganda und Friedenspolitik—Geschichte der Auswärtigen Kulturpolitik im 20. Jahrhundert" [Between Propaganda and Peace Politics: The History of Public Diplomacy in the 20th Century], in *Kultur und Außenpolitik: Handbuch für Studium und Praxis*, ed. Kurt-Jürgen Maaß (Baden-Baden: Nomos, 2005), 64–66.

28 Jan Melissen, "The New Public Diplomacy: Between Theory and Practice," in *The New Public Diplomacy: Soft Power in International Relations*, ed. Jan Melissen (Basingstoke, New York: Palgrave Macmillan, 2005), 13.

29 Jochen Hippler and Barbara Kuhnert, "Foreword," in *Der Westen und die islamische Welt: Eine muslimische Position; The West and the Muslim World: A Muslim Position; Al Garb wa-'l-'ālam al-islāmī nazra islāmīya*, ed. Institute for Foreign Cultural Relations (Stuttgart: ifa, 2004), 98.

30 Volker Rittberger and Verena Andrei, "Macht, Profit und Interessen—Auswärtige Kulturpolitik und Außenpolitiktheorien" [Power, Profit and Interests: Public Diplomacy and Theories of Foreign Policy], in *Kultur und Außenpolitik: Handbuch für Studium und Praxis*, ed. Kurt-Jürgen Maaß (Baden-Baden: Nomos, 2005), 31–52.

31 Habermas, *Theory of Communicative Action*, 285; Zöllner, "A Quest . . .," 169.

23

Origin and Development of Japan's Public Diplomacy

Tadashi Ogawa

Prime Minister Shinzo Abe closed his inaugural policy speech to the Japanese Diet (Parliament) on September 29, 2006, with the following statement:

> It is quintessential for Japan to present its "country identity" to the world so that many countries and many people will regard Japan as a good model to emulate. Moreover, I will place emphasis on creating an environment that will attract such people to come to Japan.

No other prime minister of Japan had ever expressed in such a clear manner his concern for public diplomacy. "Public diplomacy" is not a term that is heard often in Japan, and still it is not a concept that is shared as social consensus except among a small diplomatic community. However, it has been increasingly highlighted as a tool for strategies of diplomacy, cultural promotion, trade, tourism, and urban planning.

In 2004, structural reform of the Ministry of Foreign Affairs (MOFA) led to the integration of units for external public relations and cultural exchange into a newly established Public Diplomacy Department (PDD). This structural reform meant that MOFA, which had long maintained a policy of separation between public relations and culture, had decided to adopt a "public diplomacy" approach by dealing with culture more strategically as a diplomatic resource.

In the 1990s, the Japanese economy, which had garnered a significant global presence, lost impetus and began staggering. Seeking an alternative mechanism for maintaining its presence other than its economy, Japan became concerned about "Soft Power," looking to Tony Blair's "Cool Britannia Policy" as a model for Japan's public diplomacy.

Nowadays, the Japanese mass media is abuzz with discussions of China's emerging public diplomacy, which led the Chinese government to establish more than a hundred Confucius Institutes promoting Chinese language and culture all over the world and to organize large-scale cultural events. Some in the media warn that a rapid growth in China's global cultural presence would cause the Japanese cultural presence overseas to erode. However, strong arguments have also been made that it is not appropriate to presume that China would be a rival for Japan in the field of culture, and that Japan should make efforts to engage China as a responsible member of the global community through communication.

In this chapter, after providing a sketch of the present structures of Japan's public diplomacy, I describe how public diplomacy was implanted and developed in the process of Japanese modernization. I also show the commonalities and differences between the vision for and approach to Japan's public diplomacy and those in the West.

Main Actors of Japan's Public Diplomacy

In Japanese diplomatic history, the idea of promoting familiarity and intimacy with people from other countries and creating deeper perceptions about Japan as a coherent concept and coordinated policy through public relations and cultural exchange—in other words, public diplomacy—is a relatively new one. After World War II, the bitter memories of the state's excessive intervention and censorship of culture during the war-time military regime prompted governmental organizations such as MOFA, the Japan Foundation, the Japan Broadcasting Corporation (Nihon Hoso Kyokai: NHK), the Agency for Cultural Affairs (ACA), and others to operate a variety of activities while maintaining a certain level of autonomy.

In that sense, Japan's post-war public diplomacy is similar to the British model, whose organizations are loosely coordinated. In the following sections, I wish to outline the main actors in Japanese public diplomacy, namely, MOFA and the Japan Foundation.

MOFA

MOFA is supposed to be a flagship of Japanese public diplomacy. It carries out public relations activities targeted at foreign citizens and overseas media, as well as cultural exchange programs through its own operations and 189 embassies and consular offices overseas. However, there is no inter-ministerial coordination system within the Japanese government to discuss overall public diplomacy strategies or advise on resource allocation, performance, management, and evaluation, such as the UK's Public Diplomacy Board.

MOFA's PDD deals with external public relations, introduces Japanese culture and society around the world, conducts people-to-people exchange, promotes Japanese language study and Japanese studies overseas, carries out artistic and intellectual exchange, and cooperates with international agencies such as UNESCO.

The PDD's annual budget in 2005 was JPY27.5 billion (4 percent of MOFA's total budget). However, because most of its budget consists of subsidies to the Japan Foundation and donations to UNESCO, its own disposable budget is limited to JPY6 billion. MOFA extends its public diplomacy through 189 embassies and consular offices all over the world. As many as 47 of these foreign missions operate cultural and information centers. Most of these missions create their own homepages to report on Japanese foreign policy and provide information on Japanese culture in local languages. This is in addition to MOFA's homepage and Web-Japan, which was launched with the aim of helping people around the world get to know more about Japan and the Japanese people.

Embassies and consular offices have their own budgets for cultural programs. They hold various cultural events such as concerts, seminars, exhibitions, and films, and provide assistance to Japanese language educational institutions and other organizations. In 2005, the total number of these cultural events organized by Japanese foreign missions reached 1,609 projects, and they extended financial assistance to 1,374 other projects.

The Japan Foundation

The Japan Foundation was established in 1972 to undertake international cultural exchange. Its stated purpose is "to contribute to a better international environment, and to the maintenance and development of harmonious foreign relationships with Japan, through deepening other nations' understanding of Japan, promoting better mutual understanding among nations, encouraging friendship and goodwill among the peoples of the world, and contributing to the world in culture and other fields through the efficient and comprehensive implementation of international cultural exchange activities" (*Independent Administrative Institution Japan Foundation Law*, Article 3).

The Japan Foundation carries out programs and activities in three major categories:

1 arts and cultural exchange;
2 Japanese language education overseas; and
3 Japanese studies overseas and intellectual exchange.

The foundation's head office is in Tokyo, and it has 19 overseas offices in 18 countries, mainly in Asia, the United States, and Europe. The Japan Foundation's annual budget in 2004 was JPY16.8 billion. Of this, JPY13.7 billion comes from governmental subsidies, JPY1.8 billion from interest on the endowment, JPY900 million from donations, and JPY100 million from income-generating activities. When the Japan Foundation was established, the Japanese Diet (parliament) guaranteed a certain level of autonomy by allowing the Japan Foundation to maintain its own funds in order to stabilize its finance. Since its initial endowment of JPY5 billion, the Japanese government has made additional contributions, amounting to a total of JPY113 billion.

The Japan Foundation, as an organization carrying out the public diplomacy policy goals set by MOFA, plans and organizes its own programs and supports individuals and institutions with shared visions. Working in close coordination with MOFA, the foundation maintains a certain level of autonomy from the ministry in order to play an intermediary role between the government and the private and civil society sectors.

History of Japanese Public Diplomacy

It is possible to recognize some diplomatic operations as public diplomacy since the time that Japan began its process of modern nation building in the 1860s. This would include its participation in World Expositions and public relations activities appealing to the American public during the Russo-Japanese War. However, these were just temporary operations, neither institutional nor systematic. It was after World War I that the Japanese government fully committed to external public relations and cultural diplomacy. Previous to this move by Tokyo, during World War I, U.S. President Woodrow Wilson created the Committee on Public Information to make the world understand U.S. war aims. Diplomatic communities in Europe and the United States began to realize how important it was that they obtain support from the public in their appointed countries.

Noticing that the Western powers consolidated their propaganda efforts during World War I, Prime Minister Takashi Hara and his staff started to study the setup of machines for external public relations within the Japanese government. It was the eloquent Chinese delegation in the Paris Peace Conference charging Japanese expansionism in China that made the Japanese leaders feel it was necessary to consolidate external public relations. Ayamaro Konoe, a young aide to the ambassador to the Paris Peace Conference—later Prime Minister of Japan—in his publication on the Paris Peace Conference, emphasized the indispensability of propaganda in post-World War diplomacy, saying that "it is urgent that we create and consolidate a new propaganda organization in our diplomacy with more chaotic-driven China to maintain our present honorable status and interests."

In 1920, MOFA established the Department of Information, which, although it experienced some structural changes several times, became the basis for the present Public Diplomacy Department in MOFA. In addition to this structural reform, MOFA adopted another important policy. It started new programs of cultural exchange with China. Since the 1910s, Japan had suffered from growing anti-Japanese sentiment among young Chinese intellectuals such as was seen in the May Fourth Movement. In order to improve Chinese sentiment toward Japan, MOFA, in 1923, founded a unit for promoting Japan–China cultural exchange supported by reparations for the Boxer Rebellion from the Chinese government. MOFA carefully avoided criticism of its activities as one-way pressure by Japan on China by making sure that the program was managed equally by both sides. For instance, in order to reflect upon opinions from Chinese intellectuals, an advisory council was set up, consisting of ten members each from Japan and China. A year later, the unit for promoting Japan–China cultural exchange was expanded into the Department of Cultural Affairs within MOFA.

In the 1920s and 1930s, the various world powers created structures to promote international cultural exchange as tools of diplomacy. It was in this era that prestigious public international cultural exchange organizations were founded. Germany established the Goethe Institute in 1932. The U.K. established the British Council in 1934. In order to confront cultural propaganda offensives from Nazi Germany, U.S. President Franklin D. Roosevelt, in 1938, created the Interdepartmental Committee for Scientific Cooperation and the Division for Cultural Cooperation in the State Department and appointed cultural affairs officers to several Latin American countries.

In 1934, the same year as the creation of the British Council, Japan became the first and only non-Western nation to establish a modern international cultural exchange organization. The Society for International Cultural Relations (Kokusai Bunka Shinko-kai, or KBS) was established with donations from the private sector and subsidies from the government. KBS programs included dialogues among prominent cultural leaders, dispatch of cultural missions, and publications on Japan, among other activities.

The motivation for the establishment of the KBS in some ways resulted from Japan's diplomatic isolation in the 1930s after it chose to drop out of the League of Nations, which had condemned Japan for the Mukden Incident. Because political and military channels were staggered, Tokyo felt it necessary to activate cultural channels to the world and to improve its damaged national image through the KBS.

Afterwards, the Sino-Japanese War and World War II made Japan's public diplomacy more of a one-way track, with more wartime-natured national propaganda. As a result of merging of units on information, public relations, and international cultural exchange, the Cabinet Bureau of Information was established to take the place of MOFA's departments of Information and Cultural Affairs, while the Japanese Navy and the Army maintained their own propaganda machines until the end of the war. The Cabinet Bureau of Information not only dealt with public relations, but it also gathered intelligence, analyzed information, and provided information controls for the wartime regime. Its administrative powers reached overseas to Japanese occupied territories.

In the 1930s, the KBS's priority was on the United States and European nations. Once World War II broke out, under the guidance of the cabinet, the KBS's priority shifted to China and Southeast Asia to win the hearts and minds of local residents in these areas that were suddenly occupied by Japan.

Looking for a New National Identity

Japan lost its sovereignty in its unconditional surrender to the Allied Forces and the occupation that followed. External public relations and cultural exchange activities were suspended. The Cabinet Bureau of Information was abolished in December 1945. MOFA reestablished the Department of Information, which was in charge of cultural exchange, when it underwent a restructuring in 1946. But it had too few staff and too little budget to resume its pre-war activities. At the same time, Japan was required to neglect its state-controlled cultural policies and abandon its self-image as a military-state by expressing a fresh vision for its own national identity. Prime Minister Tetsu Katayama, in a policy speech, advocated the "construction of a culture state" in order to restore national pride and international credibility.

As a first step toward restoring its sovereignty, Japan aimed to obtain membership of UNESCO and successfully became a full member in July 1951, two months before the San Francisco Peace Treaty was signed between Japan and the Allied Powers in September 1951.

In the 1950s, the Japanese government could not afford to promote external cultural exchange activities for financial reasons. The budget for cultural exchange was quite limited and most funds were continuously allocated for grants to the KBS, which, in the 1950s, only covered the United States by introducing traditional Japanese culture. In the 1960s, Japan entered a new period of high economic growth and started to become a world economic power. The 1964 Summer Olympics in Tokyo and the 1970 EXPO in Osaka symbolized the emergence of Japan on the international scene as a nation with a strong economy and advanced science and technology capabilities. There were several important policy changes that took place during this period. In the post-war period, the Japanese government had restricted overseas travel by Japanese citizens because of the shortage of foreign currency reserves. In 1964, those restrictions were lifted. After that, in the 1970s and 1980s, grassroots-level international exchange began to boom for the first time in the long history of Japan. This boom fundamentally changed the Japanese general public's perceptions of the world as well as its own self-image.

With self-pride as a global economic power, the Japanese public increasingly argued that the Japanese government should make efforts to enhance its culture as a mature nation-state like France. Reflecting with self-criticism upon the excessive control of culture by the central government during the war, the Japanese government hesitated to play a strong role in cultural administration and cultural exchange. In 1968, the establishment of the Agency for Cultural Affairs was a sign that the government had gradually recovered from the wartime traumatic experiences, and it started to create new policies in the 1970s. MOFA also consolidated the Division of Culture, which had been established in 1958, into the Department of Culture in 1964.

Consolidating Cultural Diplomacy with Emerging Economic Power

Japan, which obtained international status as an economic superpower, experienced several changes in its international relations, illustrated by such crises as the Nixon Shocks. The term "Nixon Shocks" refers to two unexpected policy changes taken by U.S. President Richard Nixon in 1971 and 1972. The first Nixon Shock was when he cancelled the Bretton Woods system and stopped the direct convertibility of the U.S. dollar to gold in 1971. The second Nixon Shock was his surprise visit to Beijing and the termination of the U.S. confrontation policy without consultation with Japan, following his secret negotiations with China in 1972. These shocking experiences reminded the Japanese leaders of their catastrophic isolation in the 1930s and 1940s.

Other challenges included the emergence of anti-Japanese sentiment. Japan's rapid economic growth and success aroused worldwide concern about Japanese society and culture as resources of remarkable success. However, criticism and misunderstanding also grew during this period. Responding to these fundamental changes, the Japanese government began to take measures to consolidate cultural diplomacy and external public relations. In this period, the framework for Japan's present public diplomacy was formed with the creation of the Japan Foundation, a central actor in public international cultural exchange. Suffering from a series of Japan–U.S. frictions over trade imbalances and the Nixon Shocks, the Japanese diplomatic community began to recognize combating misunderstanding about Japanese culture and behavior as an urgent diplomatic agenda.

The creation of the Japan Foundation became a crucial point in the history of Japanese cultural diplomacy. Then Foreign Minister Takeo Fukuda instructed MOFA to start feasibility studies for the establishment of a large-scale international cultural exchange organization mainly targeting relations with the United States. In 1972, the Japan Foundation Law was approved by the Diet. The Japan Foundation was funded by the government (JPY5 billion) with a token contribution (JPY6 million) from the business sector.

The Japan Foundation operates under the supervision of the Cultural Division of MOFA. According to the Japan Foundation Law, the foreign minister has the authority to appoint the president of the Japan Foundation and MOFA has some veto powers. The foundation started a variety of programs dealing with exchange among prominent academic and cultural leaders, promotion of Japanese language education and Japanese studies overseas, concerts, exhibitions, Japanese film and television showings, and publications.

The United States was initially a high priority target country, but Southeast Asia became another important area for the Japan Foundation soon after the anti-Japan riots broke out in Thailand and Indonesia during the official visit of Prime Minister Kakuei Tanaka in January 1974. Japan realized how deeply embedded Southeast Asia's negative emotions were regarding the bitter experiences during the Japanese occupation and post-war Japanese economic dominance. In response to the situation, the Japan Foundation shifted much of its human and financial resources into Southeast Asia.

During this era, the Japanese government realized that culture and education should be a priority area for aid programs to developing countries such as Southeast Asia. MOFA started its Cultural Grant Aid Program in 1975 and made contributions to the preservation and restoration of cultural heritage sites in Southeast Asia. MOFA gave special consideration to Southeast Asia by donating JPY5 billion to the ASEAN Cultural Fund established in 1978 with the aim of promoting cultural exchange within ASEAN.

Mushrooming Main Actors

With its greater international status and responsibilities, Japan, in the 1980s, tried to reinvent itself as an "international state" to take global leadership in various fields besides the economy, while the United States insisted that Japan should fulfill its international responsibility commensurate with its economic power. Under these pressures, the Japanese government decided to consolidate its cultural diplomacy.

As written in this article, the Second Provisional Commission on Administrative Reform (PCAR) of 1983 made recommendations on diplomacy because Japanese cultural exchange lagged behind the major developed nations. Motivated by this recommendation, MOFA established the Department of Cultural Exchange in 1984. In the 1980s, MOFA and the Japan Foundation were required to respond to the rapid spread of interest in Japanese language education overseas. Support for Japanese language education overseas became a top priority for the Japan Foundation in the 1980s. The Japanese language boom still continues, although the growth rate has been slowing down. According to a survey by the foundation in 2003,

"Japanese-language education is under way in 127 countries. More than 2.35 million students are studying Japanese. This number does not include those studying Japanese using language lessons broadcast on TV or radio, via the Internet, or private lessons. Over the period from 1979 through 2003, the number of students increased 18.5 times."

In the 1980s, China increasingly became a priority state for the Japan Foundation. The Japan Foundation, based upon an agreement with the Chinese government, started a special program in China to provide intensive training for Chinese instructors of Japanese language. Starting in 1982, the Japanese government funded the Japan Foundation's Japanese language programs through its official development assistance (ODA) budget. By 1987, the ODA portion reached 30 percent of its operating costs.

The Japan Exchange and Teaching (JET) program, one of the largest and most successful cultural exchange programs in Japan, was launched in 1987. Supported by MOFA and the Ministry of Education, local governments invite young university graduates from overseas to participate in international programs or foreign language education throughout Japan. The number of current JET participants has reached over 5,500 from 44 countries. Follow-up and network building among participants in the JET program have been remarkable. The JET Alumni Association has 20,000 members and 50 local chapters in 15 countries. The program was started with the purpose of internationalizing Japan's local communities by helping to improve foreign language education. But it also creates grassroots channels between Japan and the rest of the world and develops the next generation of supporters of Japan.

In the late 1980s, the Japanese government accelerated the buildup of cultural exchange programs. Expansion of cultural exchange was one of three pillars of the Global Initiative that Prime Minister Noboru Takeshita advocated in 1988. It was the first time in Japanese diplomatic history that cultural exchange was made a top priority. The prime minister requested the Advisory Group on International Cultural Exchange to examine how to promote international cultural exchange. The advisory group report presented to the prime minister in 1988 emphasized that it was an urgent national task for Japan to strengthen international cultural exchange at a time when greater contributions to the international community were demanded of it. Specifically, the report made proposals on important policies, such as the strengthening of the budget and personnel for the Japan Foundation, and pointed out the need to pay special attention to enhancing the government budget.

In response to the report, the Conference for the Promotion of International Cultural Exchange was created by the cabinet in June 1989 to promote cultural exchange in general from a wide range of views across government agencies. The conference drew up the Action Program for International Cultural Exchanges in September 1989. Based upon the action plan, the government increased its contribution to the Japan Foundation by JPY5 billion in 1989 and, from then to 1995, the budget and number of personnel doubled.

This expansion of cultural exchange included a new approach and idea. The Japan Foundation ASEAN Culture Center, opened in 1990, was operated under the ideal that cultural exchange should be a two-way track carried out in a nonhierarchical manner; therefore, Japan would make efforts to introduce the cultural richness of ASEAN countries into Japan. The ASEAN Culture Center was expanded in 1995 into the Japan Foundation Asia Center, which dealt with intellectual exchange, promotion of Asian cultures, and better understanding of Asia among the Japanese.

Harmony with the international community was a keyword of Japanese diplomacy from the late 1980s to the early 1990s as the enormous trade imbalance with Japan caused friction not only in the economic field but also in social and cultural areas. Japan needed to show its willingness to contribute to the world in order to help pacify the spreading sense of distrust and fears of Japan as an economic superpower. The Japanese Trust Fund for the Preservation of the World Cultural Heritage established within UNESCO in 1989 was one response to these needs. The MOFA Bluebook 1989 made the following statement:

An absence of understanding of the conception structure and sense of value of a country which can influence the world trend may produce an international image of Japan as a "mysterious power." Moreover, Japan's economic image is feared to be stressed too much.

In response to the economic friction, the Japanese government was required to consolidate external public relations explaining trade policies and their background. MOFA took measures to restructure itself and established a new post of press secretary. Before this, there was no good coordination in public relations other than the director general of the Bureau of Information and Culture holding weekly press conferences for foreign correspondents while other ranking officials held casual meetings. By establishing the post of press secretary, the controls in public relations were unified and coordinated.

Consolidating Global Partnership and Multilateral Approaches

Japan–U.S. relations were put on trial in the early 1990s because the U.S. Congress, irritated by the huge trade imbalances, pressured its government to take tougher measures toward Japan. By the time the Soviet Union collapsed, there had been an increasing sense of threat in the United States from Japan's economic power instead of Russian military power. "Revisionist thinking" and "Japan bashing" were gaining attention. The revisionists argued that the United States should adopt different rules against Japan because Japan is entirely different from the rest of the world in all aspects of life, be it economy, society, or culture. They insisted that, because Japan was a closed society, American firms could not compete fairly with Japanese firms. Such an argument raised serious questions about the mutual understanding of both nations. The limited presence of Japan in international cooperative actions at the time of the Gulf Crisis in 1990–1991 exacerbated the American perceptions that Japan was avoiding its responsibility as a world power and, therefore, was a free rider on the world order.

In order to overcome these challenges, MOFA realized that Japan's foreign policy had come to a point at which it should be showing a new face. The Japanese government promoted Takeshita's "international cooperation initiative" with the three pillars of "cooperation for peace," "enhancement of ODA," and "strengthening international cultural exchange," because this initiative fit Japan's diplomacy requirements in the changing international community.

One of the intellectual reflections on this transformation of diplomacy was the establishment of the Japan Foundation Center for Global Partnership (CGP) in 1991 with an additional endowment of JPY50 billion to the Japan Foundation. Following a proposal made by former Foreign Minister Shintaro Abe, father of the 2006–2007 Prime Minister Shinzo Abe, CGP's mission is to promote collaboration between Japan and the United States with the goal of fulfilling shared global responsibilities and contributing to improvements in the world's welfare, and to enhance dialogue and interchange between Japanese and U.S. citizens on a wide range of issues, thereby improving bilateral relations.

To carry out its mission, CGP operates grant programs as well as self-initiated projects and fellowships. CGP has supported an array of institutions and individuals, including nonprofit organizations, universities, policymakers, scholars, and educators. CGP's mission and operations were innovative because it shifted from the conventional idea of introducing Japanese ideas and high culture overseas into a collaborative problem-solving approach.

In the 1990s, as East Asia achieved remarkable economic development, the idea of a new regionalism gained attention in Asia. The report of the second "Conference for the Promotion of International Cultural Exchange" in 1994 recommended "exchange that will build the future of the Asia-Pacific region" in order to foster a sense of community spirit in Asia. In order to create a new identity, "we, Asians," advocated multilateral approaches rather than bilateral approaches. The Japan Foundation Asia Center was a key player in promoting the new multi-lateral cultural exchange policy. In the late 1990s, the center promoted intellectual exchange and artistic collaboration on a multilateral basis.

Prime ministers in the 1990s provocatively adopted new cultural exchange approaches toward Asia. Prime Minister Tomiichi Murayama's Peace, Friendship and Exchange Initiative in 1995 aimed at overcoming unsettled disputes on Japanese colonization and military occupations from 1910 to 1945. His statement on the occasion of the 50th anniversary of the end of the war (15 August 1995) included obvious words of apology. Based upon his statement, the Peace, Friendship and Exchange Initiative consisted of two parts promoting support for historical research in modern-era relations between Japan and its neighboring Asian countries and rapid expansion of exchange with those countries. The Japan Foundation Asia Center was created by an increase in the cultural exchange budget as a part of the Murayama Initiative.

Prime Minister Ryutaro Hashimoto, successor to Murayama, accelerated the "rapid expansion of exchange with the neighboring Asian countries through multilateral cultural exchange involving the private and civil society sectors." In January 1997, he proposed the creation of Multinational Cultural Missions composed of government and private-sector representatives from Japan and ASEAN countries. At the concluding meeting held in April 1998 in Japan, the action agenda for cultural exchange was proposed, aiming to create multilateral networks and build a sense of community between Japan and the ASEAN countries.

Keizo Obuchi was inaugurated prime minister after Hashimoto in 1998. His remarkable achievement in public diplomacy was the improvement of relations with the Republic of Korea (ROK). Obuchi and Korean President Kim Dae Jung's most important decision was their agreement to designate 2002—the year of the FIFA World Cup co-hosted by the two countries—as the Year of Japan–ROK National Exchange and to promote exchange in fields such as culture, sports, youth, regional exchange, and tourism. The Japanese perception of Korea was dramatically improved by these epoch-making events and, since then, Japan–ROK relations have been relatively stable, based upon a huge number of people-to-people exchanges in spite of a series of later diplomatic turbulence.

Culture Attracts the World Instead of Economy

Following structural reform of MOFA in August 2004 the Public Diplomacy Department was created as a result of integration of external public relations and international cultural exchange units, which had been separated in the 1980s. The Public Diplomacy Department is in charge of implementing international agreements to promote cultural exchange, cooperating with international cultural organizations, and introducing Japanese culture abroad and promoting cultural exchange with foreign countries, as well as supervising the Japan Foundation. Concerning the division of labor between MOFA and the Japan Foundation after this structual reform, MOFA is responsible for strategy building and long-term policy planning while the Japan Foundation implements MOFA's policies at the operational level. Considerable autonomy in its operations is given to the Japan Foundation.

In December 2004, Prime Minister Jun'ichiro Koizumi launched the Council on the Promotion of Cultural Diplomacy. The council pointed out that "understanding Japan by the public of a country may be the most influential factor for the government of that country in deciding policies and actions toward Japan." Given that cultural exchange may seem to be a circumstantial approach to improving the image of Japan, the council admitted that "it is a very effective way to sow seeds for deepening understanding of Japan in the next generation."

Thus, the council provided recommendations on the challenges and strategies of Japanese cultural diplomacy. The council recommended that "Japan should try to actively cultivate a

'Japanese animation generation' across the globe, seizing interest in the Japanese language and pop culture as an opportunity to encourage further interest in other aspects of diverse Japanese culture." In the accelerated globalized international community of the 21st century, Japan feels strongly that it should be proactive in conveying its message to the public overseas. In particular, the increasing presence of China in the Asia Pacific region makes the Japanese feel that public diplomacy is necessary to consolidate public relations and cultural exchange in order to balance its presence. In addition, the anti-Japanese demonstrations that took place in China and Korea in 2005 strengthened Japan's motivation for public diplomacy toward Asia.

The terrorist attacks on the United States in 2001 and the following wars in Afghanistan and Iraq also had tremendous impacts on Japanese public diplomacy. Strategic priorities on the Middle East, which had traditionally been given less priority in Japanese public diplomacy, were increased. While dispatching the Self Defense Forces to Iraq, it needed to maintain positive images of Japan and to win support from local communities in the area to which they were dispatched.

Japan's Current Public Diplomacy Toward the Middle East

Public diplomacy strategies in the Middle East are most critical for the Western public diplomatic communities. Because of differences in historical backgrounds, Japan has adopted certain unique approaches on this matter, although the financial allocations to the region were relatively small in comparison with the Western countries. (The Japan Foundation's 2005 budget for the Middle East and North Africa is JPY510 million.)

Japan, in its long history of cultural exchange with China, Korea, Southeast Asia, India, and the West, has created its own traditions. In particular, since the beginning of modern times, facing the powerful Western civilization, Japan has been a front runner of modernization among non-Western countries, and it has kept a balance between tradition and modernity through processes of trial and error. The historical experiences can be assets for Japan's public diplomacy.

The report of the Council on the Promotion of Cultural Diplomacy, submitted to Prime Minister Koizumi in 2005, suggested the following:

> Cultural exchange was an important factor in the process of Japan's modernization. It is Japan's experience in conciliating and mediating the irreconcilabilities and conflicts between different civilizations that enables it to understand the difficulties facing the current non-Western societies that are struggling to achieve modernization. By taking advantage of its position, Japan can promote mutual understanding between the East and the West, the North and the South, nations, regions, civilizations, or cultures without becoming entangled in clashes between civilizations, ideologies, or religions.

It may be difficult for Western modernists to imagine that modernization for non-Western countries involves traumatic experiences. Japan's 19th-century decision to promote modernization was not a self-initiated choice, but the only solution to avoid colonization by a Western power and to maintain its sovereignty in the era of Imperialism. In order to achieve modernization, it was essential for Japan to dissolve the traditional local kindred communities into more industry-wise organizations. In that process, numerous small traditions were lost. Some suffered from an identity crisis. Because of such embedded spiritual identity crisis, modern Japan sometimes inclines toward a quest for self-assurance through nationalism. It was this trauma that caused the sudden upheaval of fundamentalist movements emphasizing Japan's own traditions and values, such as the ultra-nationalist movements from the 1930s to 1945.

Therefore, Japan can understand the unproductiveness of one-way diplomacy imposing values of militarily or economically dominant forces. The goals of public diplomacy in the Middle East should include recovery of traumatized self-pride in this region in the process of modernization through multi-dimensional dialogue based upon mutual respect for culture and traditions. In such a sense, the goals of Japan's public diplomacy toward the Middle East should be to differentiate itself from Western public diplomacy.

Considering such perspectives on Japan's position toward the Middle East, the Japan Foundation began consolidating its programs dealing with the Middle East in 2003, creating three pillars of activities: intellectual exchange; support for cultural promotion in the Middle East; and promotion of better understanding of the Middle East among the Japanese. Through these activities, the Japan Foundation is careful to respect the honor of the people of the Middle East.

The Japan Foundation's initial measures were projects contributing to rehabilitative treatment for wounded pride in the war-damaged countries. In cooperation with MOFA, the Japan Foundation gave a grant to cover travel expenses for the Japan Football Association (JFA) to invite the Iraqi national soccer team to Japan. With this assistance, the JFA organized a match between Japan and Iraq in 2004. The game was broadcast worldwide, because this was the first international game for the Iraqi soccer team since the Iraq War began. MOFA worked with the Iraqi government to provide intensive training for the national athletes and coaches. The Iraqi people applauded their good performances in international games such as the Athena Olympics while healing their traumatized national pride.

In cultural exchange with Afghanistan, healing through culture has been a consistent agenda. In 2003, the Japan Foundation held an exhibition of paintings and crafts made by street children from Kabul at the Japan Foundation Forum in Tokyo. The exhibition offered opportunities for street children who were deprived of chances to express themselves because of the civil wars and the Taliban regime. The exhibition also had an educational function for the Japanese who were able to gain high respect for the Afghan children because of their artistic creativity and rich personalities instead of mere commiseration.

The Japan Foundation has paid much attention to the idea of mutuality, which means keeping a balance in flows of information and knowledge between Japan and the Middle East. Therefore, one of three pillars of the new Middle East programs is to promote better understanding of the Middle East among the Japanese. Reflecting on this idea, the Japan Foundation held a series of cultural events related to the Middle East in Japan, including film screenings, contemporary drama performances from the Middle East, and invitations for prominent Middle Eastern cultural leaders to Japan.

This approach, which fosters better understanding of foreign cultures among the Japanese, has already been utilized and expanded as a cultural exchange tool with Southeast Asia since the late 1980s. This can be interpreted as support to outward-looking activities of intellectuals and artists in Southeast Asia, which had suffered from an imbalance of culture and information with developed countries because their governments could not afford to promote external public relations or cultural exchange. By adopting this approach with large-scale ODA programs, Japan succeeded in extinguishing the anti-Japanese sentiments that existed in the 1970s.

According to a BBC World Service Poll, Japan is one of the most positively viewed countries worldwide. In particular, Southeast Asia has quite a positive view of Japan, including Indonesia (84 percent) and the Philippines (70 percent). Self-censoring of one-sided impositions of Japanese culture has contributed to improvements in these public diplomacy perceptions.

References

Hirano, K. editor. 2005. *Sengo Nihon no Kokusai Bunka Koryu* [Japan's Post-war International Cultural Exchange]. Tokyo: Keiso Shobo.

The Japan Foundation, Annual Report. 1983, 2004.

Katzenstein P. 2005. *A World of Regions: Asia and Europe in the American Imperium*. Ithaca, New York: Cornell University Press.

Matsumura, M. 1996. *Kokusai Koryu-shi: Kingendai no Nihon* [The History of International Exchange: Japan in Modern and Contemporary Times]. Tokyo: Chijinkan.

The Ministry of Foreign Affairs of Japan, Diplomatic Bluebook. 1971–2006.

Shibazaki, A. 1999. *Kindai Nihon to Kokusai Bunka Koryu: Kokusai Bunka Shinkokai no Sousetsu to Tenkai* [International Cultural Relations and Modern Japan: History of Kokusai Bunka Shinkokai 1934–45]. Tokyo: Yuushindo Kobunsha.

Tuch, Hans. 1993. *Communicating with the World: U.S. Public Diplomacy Overseas*. New York: St. Martin's Press.

24

China Talks Back

Public Diplomacy and Soft Power for the Chinese Century

Gary D. Rawnsley

The story of the so-called Chinese miracle is well known: unprecedented growth rates; an "open door" policy that has attracted extraordinary amounts of foreign investment; a determination to reap the economic rewards of globalization; an apparent commitment to a benign and responsible foreign policy; and a greater involvement in international regimes, including the World Trade Organization (WTO) and United Nations peacekeeping operations.[1] In short, the People's Republic of China (PRC) is no longer an insular power constrained by an ideological straitjacket that prevents full engagement with the international system, but is now firmly embedded within, and more tolerant of the interdependent global environment.

Globalization has forced the Chinese government to pay more attention than ever before to public diplomacy and soft power, and a close reading of Chinese newspapers and reports reveals the existence of an elite level discourse on these subjects. When essays appear in the *People's Daily* newspaper, the official mouthpiece of the Communist Party (known colloquially throughout China as *dangbao*, literally "party newspaper")[2] it is a clear indication of elite opinion and approval. One such article was written by Zhao Qizheng, the deputy director of the Foreign Affairs Committee of the Communist Party's Central Committee and emphasized that China "must represent an accurate picture of itself to the world . . . China should not only listen, but talk back."[3] The President of China, Hu Jintao, is also an advocate of "talking back," of integrating a public diplomacy strategy with China's foreign policy ambitions, and of finding better ways to sell China to the international community.[4] Zhao's essay in the *People's Daily* reflected this core elite opinion when he described how "Public diplomacy spreads Chinese culture and political influence more efficiently, improving the world's opinion of China and safeguarding national interests."[5] In other words, China's public diplomacy, created and managed by the government, informs and is informed by a specific political agenda and a determination to project an image of strength, affluence, and political responsibility that surmounts the popular impression of China as a state which routinely violates human rights and threatens global stability.[6] The appointment in 1984 of a spokesman for the Ministry of Foreign Affairs and the launch of regular press conference, the creation of the Information Office of the State Council in 1991 (that since 2003 trains central and provincial-level spokespersons), and the re-branding in English of the Communist Party's Propaganda Department ("*xuanchuan*") as the Publicity Department, all indicate China is being ever more sensitive to the need for the institutional frameworks of public diplomacy—for the medium as well as the message.[7]

The Chinese use both soft power and public diplomacy to engage with international audiences and it is sometimes difficult to differentiate the one from the other. I shall argue in this chapter that the success of this multifaceted strategy is limited. Joseph Nye based his description of soft power on values. Soft power, he said, includes "attractiveness of a country's culture, political ideas and policies. When our policies are seen as legitimate in the eyes of others, our soft power is enhanced."[8] Despite its remarkable economic success, China still attracts severe rebuke from the international community because its leadership remains committed to the preservation of authoritarian rule, including the absence of human rights and democratic institutions and processes. China must also face the challenge of squaring its foreign policy, based on a realist approach to international relations and alliances with vilified regimes such as Sudan, Burma, North Korea, and Zimbabwe, with its promotion of soft power and its more global-oriented foreign policy ambitions.

So far, the PRC's approach to public diplomacy—"talking back"—has focused on two areas, namely the economy and culture.

Economics and Public Diplomacy

The first is a familiar story. By 2006, China had become the world's second largest economy after the United States with an average growth rate of 9 percent. This represents a more than tenfold increase since the economic reforms started in 1978. It is not surprising the so-called "Chinese model," emphasizing market-led development and authoritarian politics, has proven attractive to many developing nation-states around the world, especially Cambodia, Laos, and Vietnam, and in Latin America, where Hugo Chavez has referred to the "great Chinese fatherland."[9] Sutter and Huang state that "Beijing's ability to present an alternative political and economic model is said to be a telling indicator of a growing Chinese ideological influence that is countering Western perspectives that insist democratic principles are a requisite for economic prosperity."[10] The export of the Chinese model suggests the success of soft power as this approach to development connects an attainable economic paradigm with a set of specific political and cultural values—authoritarian state-led management, "Asian values," etc. However, this means that the Chinese model is attractive only to a particular set of regimes which are already practised in authoritarian-style government. Hence China is successfully exporting the economic imperatives behind its growth, but has difficulty in selling its political values except to governments in need of, or experienced in, undemocratic politics. The liberal democratic world, by contrast, is not yet convinced by the political dimension of the Chinese model. As Huang and Ding have noted, "A country's economic clout reinforces its soft power if others are attracted to it *for reasons beyond trade, market access, or job opportunities* [emphasis added]."[11] So far, there is little evidence that political or ideological motivations trump the economic benefits of associating with China.

Other features of the model are also costing China's public diplomacy. While Chinese workers and investment, especially in construction, venture into the developing world, local communities who should be the principal beneficiaries are increasingly vocal in their criticism of the "Chinese tsunami." While international monitors focus on the neglect of worker health and safety and workers' rights, local communities protest against the loss of jobs and the closure of factories. This is a familiar story to manufacturers across the world, and the economic sense of open markets and cheap Chinese imports and production costs conflicts with the economic reality for those whose livelihoods disappear under the weight of competition from China. Clearly this has consequences for Chinese public diplomacy as it tries to square such criticism with its commitment to an interdependent global economy.

In addition to investment and trade, China has devoted considerable resources to foreign aid, also a valuable instrument of public diplomacy. While the actual size of China's foreign aid budget is unknown, estimates place the total in 2004 anywhere between $731.2 million and $1.2

billion depending on which definition of "aid" one accepts.[12] Moreover, between 2000 and 2007 China donated to Africa an estimated $5.4 billion and cancelled more than $10 billion of debt. In 2002, Beijing pledged $5 million to Afghanistan, and donated $2.6 million to the victims of the December 2004 tsunami. It also contributed $2 million in cash as aid and despatched a 44-member team of experts following the earthquake in Java, May 2006. In a public diplomacy *coup de grâce*, China even pledged $5 million of aid and over almost $620,000 in emergency supplies to those parts of the US hit by Hurricane Katrina in 2005. We should not be surprised that China pursues a political agenda through its aid programme: In September 2005 while on a visit to New York, President Hu Jintao promised $10 billion in Chinese aid over the next three years to the poorest countries with diplomatic ties to China, suggesting that countries which recognize Taiwan would reap substantial economic benefits if they switched their recognition to Beijing.

The status of Taiwan is a crucial factor in China's relations with other countries, and the diplomatic "de-recognition" of Taiwan is a fundamental precondition for those areas of the developing world which wish to receive Chinese aid. The strategy has worked: only 24 countries maintain full and formal diplomatic relations with Taiwan including Burkina Faso, Swaziland, the Solomon Islands, and the Vatican. As Ian Taylor has observed, "It is probably true that most Africans do not care much who is the 'real' China or with whom official diplomatic ties should be established. . . . However, astute state elites . . . have become conscious of the fact that the diplomatic competition between the two countries is a diplomatic spat that elites in economically depressed countries . . . are able to profit from."[13] In other words, we see here a clear reason to be apprehensive of claims that Chinese public diplomacy is working. The motivation for small and/or developing nations to switch their allegiance from Taiwan to China has little to do with convincing them of the intricate political and legal arguments for doing so and almost everything to do with the promise of more financial rewards than Taiwan can offer. As Taiwan's *Free China Review* noted in 1998, "in diplomacy, you can't buy friends, you only rent them."

Culture and Public Diplomacy

In addition to its wealth and economic projection, history also provides cultural capital for China's public diplomacy and soft power. This is not a recent development: we should not overlook how China has long added a cultural dimension to its engagement with foreign powers, with its self-belief and self-confidence in *zhong guo* literally "the middle kingdom" at the strategy's core. Andrew Scobell describes how dynastic China practiced public diplomacy by "in reach" whereby foreign guests were "permitted" to make "pilgrimages to the center of the civilized world."[14] Once there, the guests were "surrounded by all the glories of Chinese civilization and the refinements of its culture." The Chinese clearly believed that such exposure to Chinese civilization could yield tangible results: "At the end of their usually extended stay, these guests departed with, at the very least, a greater appreciation of the wonders of the Middle Kingdom and the benefits of participating in the Sino-centric world order."

In the centuries that followed, the West appropriated Chinese culture for its own satisfaction. During the 17th and 18th centuries *Chinoiserie*, a fascination with all things Chinese, was extremely fashionable throughout Europe,[15] though we should note that this was a specifically Western—"Orientalist"—interpretation of China and bore little resemblance to the "authentic."[16] This appropriation was not motivated by Chinese interests, so its role in public diplomacy was limited. Nevertheless, it did provide the focus of a complex cultural and political discourse that brought China to the attention of the international community and inspired further engagement.[17]

After the triumph of the Communist Party in 1949, China's pursuit of cultural diplomacy diminished in favour of exporting the Chinese model of revolution and development (especially when China became the unofficial leader of the non-aligned movement in 1955 and thus specifically targeted the developing world), though the salesmanship used techniques associated more with propaganda than diplomacy. China turned its attention again to cultural public diplomacy in the early 1970s following the restoration of diplomatic relations with the United States. After the success of "ping-pong diplomacy" (when in 1971 the US table tennis team visited the PRC and thus became the first Americans to set foot in Beijing since 1949), Mao Zedong tried "panda diplomacy" whereby pandas were despatched across the globe as a sign of goodwill. The arrival in the US of Hsing Hsing and Ling Ling, and of Chia Chia and Chin Ching in the United Kingdom sealed the desire for a more cordial relationship with Washington and London (the practice has now ended because the panda is an endangered species, though pandas are still loaned or rented to zoos around the world). In engaging in "panda diplomacy" Mao was drawing on a centuries-old practice: pandas were first presented to the Japanese court during the reign of the empress Wu Zetian (624–705). In September 2007 an exhibition of Xian's famous Terracotta Warriors arrived at the British Museum and organizers predicted it would have the same impact as the legendary Tutankhamen exhibition there in the 1970s, demonstrating again the value of history as an instrument of China's out-reach.[18]

Today, the cultural approach is centred within the new Confucius Institutes, established by China's Ministry of Education and privileging Mandarin language tuition. Modeled loosely on non-Chinese equivalents such as the British Council and the Maison Française, these Confucius Institutes are designed for the specific aim of selling Chinese culture. I use the term modeled loosely because, unlike their foreign counterparts, the Confucius Institutes are joint ventures, are located within a university, and the partner school in China sends teachers to participate. Their teaching programs are given a stamp of approval by *Hanban*, the China National Office for Teaching Chinese as a Foreign Language. The aims of Confucius Institutes include forging "strategic alliances with business, industry, government and other institutions with an interest in closer and more productive ties with China and the global Chinese diaspora.... [Working] with the academic faculties in encouraging students to develop a sound knowledge of China," and promoting "an awareness of the Chinese language and culture amongst the wider community."[19] Confucius Institutes are at the forefront of efforts promoted by the Chinese Premier, Wen Jiabao, to link culture with foreign policy: "Cultural exchanges," he said, "are a bridge connecting the hearts and minds of all countries and an important way to project a country's image."[20] China plans to have helped create 200 Confucius Institutes by the end of 2007: "The number of teachers China is sending abroad is also increasing; in 2006 China sent 1004 teachers to 80 countries and 1050 volunteer teachers to 34 countries. Furthermore, in 2006, the number of foreigners who undertook Chinese language examinations doubled from 2005."[21] Clearly the Confucius Institutes play an important strategic role in Chinese foreign policy because they provide the architecture for selling the "software" required to engage with China, but it is still too early to assess their impact.[22]

Sport and entertainment too are increasingly important exports of Chinese culture. A recent wave of Chinese films has enjoyed unprecedented success among global audiences (and outside art-house cinemas, their traditional home), while Yao Ming, basketball player for the Houston Rockets has helped project a new softer image of China: "a new demographic of Asian fans has flocked to stadiums to watch the giant stride across court, offering an image of China that has nothing to do with Chairman Mao or massacres at Tiananmen Square."[23] The author of this article, Brook Larner, notes: "the new generation of Chinese leaders still sees sports not so much as business, recreation or entertainment, but as a projection of national ambition . . ."[24] I do not need to rehearse here the importance of the 2008 Beijing Olympics as an important landmark event in China's public diplomacy, but the games—the glitz and glamour and the gold medals that Chinese athletes are sure to win—are not as important as the story that runs parallel as foreign journalists (most of whom will know nothing about China) descend on Beijing: the human and financial cost of the Olympics; the greater attention to the lack of human rights; and the price of China's economic modernization. China can and will control coverage of the Olympic Games, but will have a more difficult time trying to control the human interest stories that foreign journalists are sure to uncover.

The cultural approach to public diplomacy is also represented by international broadcasting. China Radio International continues to broadcast to the world on short-wave, medium-wave, and now the internet, while CCTV 9, launched in 2000, remains China's only English-language television service carried by satellite across the world (CCTV 4 carries Mandarin-language programming to an international audience, though Hong Kong-based Phoenix Television, part owned by News Corporation and with ties to the Communist Party, appears to be the preferred channel for overseas Chinese). In 2004 CCTV also started two new channels, CCTV E (Spanish) and CCTV F (French). Without a doubt CCTV International (the collective name for CCTV 9, E and F) is a political instrument: it receives instructions from the Ministry of Foreign Affairs about what to include in its programming, based on guidance provided by embassies in the target areas. Programs are designed around the news broadcasts to sell Chinese business, culture, tourism, and even language.[25] The problem, however, is that it is impossible to determine the effect of these broadcasts or even the size of their audience. CCTV International is confident about the size of its *potential* audience—those who merely live in target areas or who subscribe to satellite and cable packages that include access to the station (45 million subscribers outside China via six satellites[26])—but I suspect that the *actual* audience remains small and consists mostly of Chinese who wish to improve their English (a survey published in 2002 found that 90% of CCTV 9 viewers lived in China, only 4% of whom were foreigners; 80% watched to develop their understanding of English[27] or were expatriates in China who do not have access to other English-language programming.

The Public Diplomacy Strategy

For those of us who follow China's practice of public diplomacy there is little here that is new, exciting, or unexpected. As other contributors to this volume make clear, public diplomacy has always drawn on culture, heritage, and language, international broadcasting has long been a core component of national projection, and the economic dimension of public diplomacy walks a perilous tightrope between providing a blueprint for development and justifying authoritarian politics (which can be judged good or bad depending on the audience).

What is important to address is not the novelty of the approach but its effect. In other words, we need to examine how these public diplomacy resources might contribute to realizing China's foreign policy objectives, and the PRC is starting to demonstrate a more mature and nuanced understanding of how public diplomacy may connect in a profitable way with China's international ambitions. This conclusion emerges from the reports of a meeting organized by the Communist Party Propaganda Department in early 2007.[28] In addition to the expected inventory of directives to the media on what they may or may not publish ahead of the important 17th Party Congress in 2007 (reinforcing Hu Jintao's leadership and mobilizing the next generation of leaders who will assume power in 2012) and the Beijing Olympics in 2008, the meeting of the Propaganda Department provided a series of recognizable indicators of how China's practice of public diplomacy and soft power may develop. I take each in turn:

(1) "Do not criticise foreign affairs without prior authorisation. Everything needs to be considered for possible domestic or international impact . . ."

This is a customary practice in public diplomacy that highlights the relationship between foreign policy and public opinion. It suggests the need for a centrally co-ordinated message and for an appreciation of how foreign policy decisions will be received by different audiences including, in the Chinese case, the domestic constituency. Until the Tiananmen Square massacre of 1989 destroyed China's global image, and even during the first outbreak of SARS in 2003, Beijing did not appear to recognize this correlation. A progressive understanding of public diplomacy surfaced only after the public relations disaster of 1989 and with the determination of a new generation of leaders in Beijing to counteract the global negative reaction to its violent suppression of the student protestors. It is not a coincidence that in 1990 the Chinese Communist Party restored the Propaganda and Education Leading Group that had been suspended in 1988, and that one year later the Information Office was established by the State Council.[29] The aftermath of Tiananmen also saw the first publication by the Information Office of white papers discussing the issues on which China is most often criticized abroad, including human rights, Tibet, freedom of religious belief, family planning etc. The Chinese leadership clearly saw the need to create an institutional framework to manage better the release and control of information to domestic and international audiences.

(2) "Care needs to be paid to propaganda regarding 'the year of the pig' in the traditional calendar; extra effort needs to be made to prevent hurting the feelings of the Islamic brotherhood nations."

China has not yet played an active role in the so-called war on terror, but given its problems with Muslim separatists in Xinjiang, sensitivity of China's borders with Islamic countries, and the potential instability that would undermine China's goal of regional stability, Beijing is here perceptive of the possible consequences of aggravating Islamic extremism.

(3) "China is currently making diplomatic efforts to break the stalemate with Japan. For this reason, propaganda declarations must be careful, very careful, not to stir up anti-Japanese sentiment."

This is particularly interesting for it demonstrates an explicit connection within Chinese foreign policy between public and non-public diplomacy, and recognizes how misguided remarks can have serious consequences for foreign policy, especially when state and non-state relations are erratic. Despite the importance of memory and the theme of victimhood in popular discourse,[30] and even though the Sino-Japanese war continues to structure Chinese popular attitudes towards their neighbor, China is determined not to publicly aggravate Japan. This is a dramatic turnaround from the government-encouraged pro-nationalist anti-Japanese sentiments in 2005 against Tokyo's application to become a permanent member of the United Nations Security Council and the then Japanese Prime Minister's frequent controversial visits to the Yasukuni war shrine. Other indicators of a commitment to better relations include Chinese Premier Wen Jiabao's visit in April 2007, becoming the first Chinese Premier to visit in seven years; and muted Chinese reaction to the election of nationalist Shinzo Abe as Japanese Prime Minister and his reported intention to revise Japan's pacifist constitution and turn the defense agency into a Ministry.

This new style of Chinese public diplomacy is not aimed at Japan alone. Having a distinct regional focus it is also designed for consumption by China's other regional neighbors. This is a particularly important issue as China is determined to reinforce its commitment to a peaceful foreign policy in Asia, principally for mutual economic benefit but also to demonstrate China's credentials as the region's political superpower. Public diplomacy must promote the principles: "do good to our neighbors, treat our neighbors as partners" (*yulin weishan, yilin weiban*), and "maintain friendly relations with our neighbors, make them feel secure, and help to make them rich" (*mulin, anlin, fulin*) (*People's Daily*, December 14, 2005). The economic and humanitarian dimension was discussed earlier. The political commitment is most apparent in China's active membership in regional organizations, especially the Shanghai Cooperation Organization and ASEAN. China also initiated the Six-Party Talks on North Korea's nuclear ambitions in 2003 and its intervention was crucial in defusing a potential nuclear crisis in the Korean Peninsula in

October 2006. "China continues to reassure its neighbours that its rising military and other power will not endanger their interests as Chinese officials remain well aware of the concern among many Southeast Asian governments regarding China's long-term intentions."[31]

Even in its relations with the "renegade province" of Taiwan, China has combined the notorious "stick"—700 missiles aimed at the island and anti-secession legislation that guarantees a military response if Taiwan moves towards independence—with "carrot," including inviting prominent Kuomintang (Nationalist party) leaders from Taiwan to visit China, granting extra tuition benefits for Taiwanese students, removing tariffs on imports of fruit from the island, and providing Taiwanese investors and businesses with a range of perks and incentives.[32]

It is important to note here that such measures do not accomplish China's ultimate policy objective of the (re)unification of Taiwan with the mainland. Neither do they go any way towards making public opinion in Taiwan more sympathetic to China. In fact it is possible to argue that in this case the effects of the carrot are neutralized by the presence of the stick and China's consistent promise to wield it should politics in Taiwan move in an undesirable direction.

The Personal Touch

In discussing China's public diplomacy strategy it is important not to neglect the personal touch. Chinese tourists and students are flocking overseas in ever greater numbers: in 1992 just 6,540 Chinese students studied abroad; by 2002 that number had increased to 125,179.[33] By 2007, more than 100,000 students were studying abroad annually,[34] making China the largest exporter of students. This is "outreach": in terms of "in reach" the figures are similarly impressive. China received more than 162,000 students from 185 countries and regions in 2006, three times the number in 2000. Between 1978 and 2005, the total number of foreign tourists in China increased from 0.23 million to 20.26 million.[35] Beijing alone received just 1.9 million foreign tourists in 2003; in 2008, Beijing will attract an estimated 4.6 million, largely because of the Olympics.

China's leaders are also increasingly accomplished in personal public diplomacy as they venture overseas. Deng Xiaoping was the first to make an impression on the international stage, partly because of his commitment to development and opening up, but also because he was so conscious of his image. *Time* magazine's Man of the Year in 1979, Deng was the first Chinese leader to visit the United States the same year, appearing on television in a ten gallon hat during a stop-off in Houston. However, his image irrevocably suffered along with his country's when Deng ordered troops to end the student protests in Tiananmen Square in 1989. Coverage of the ensuing massacre brought home to the Chinese leadership the consequences of the international media relaying damaging images worldwide and then transmitting them back into China for domestic consumption.

President Jiang Zemin, head of the so-called Third Generation leadership (following Mao Zedong as the First and Deng as the Second) assumed power with a number of advantages over his predecessors that could feed into China's public diplomacy: He was not Deng Xiaoping, which means for an uninformed international audience unaware of the minutiae of elite decision-making in Beijing's Zhongnanhai that Jiang is less accountable than Deng for the deaths in Tiananmen Square. Jiang Zemin, Zhu Rongji (Jiang's Vice Premier and later Premier) and others represented a younger and more technologically sophisticated leadership (Jiang was trained as an engineer) that was more receptive to new ideas. They were also more attentive to the requirements of conducting foreign policy in a 24/7 international media environment. On trips abroad both Jiang and Zhu appeared regularly on local television. In the US Zhu spoke in English and was not afraid to answer unscripted questions from journalists, some of whom were predictably hostile to China. Moreover, rather than being forced on to the defensive, Zhu repeatedly seized the initiative and brought up for discussion before his questioners sensitive topics such as Tiananmen and human rights. This allowed him to control the agenda of the interview and present an image of a statesman confident enough to tackle difficult issues head on. When in 1999 the final negotiations about China's entry to the WTO stalled, Zhu organized a public diplomacy offensive in the US that included interviews on CNN and meeting relevant constituencies to convince them that China's membership of the WTO was a win–win scenario. Talking back indeed!

Conclusions

Clearly China has a long tradition of public diplomacy and has exercised its soft power for many centuries. After the Communist Party won power in 1949, public diplomacy took a back seat to international propaganda, although China's pursuit of friendship with the non-aligned bloc of states since the 1950s demonstrated that it was prepared to engage in public diplomacy for political and economic profit. Only after the demise of the Cultural Revolution, a period when China turned in on itself, and the US started to make overtures to Beijing at the beginning of the 1970s, did China begin to re-think its public diplomacy strategy. With the rise of Deng Xiaoping, public diplomacy was indelibly tied to China's drive for modernization. In other words, the public diplomacy strategy shifted from the political struggles associated with the Cold War to securing economic benefit, investment, and trade. "In reach" combined with "out reach" as more and more Chinese ventured overseas—as students, workers, investors, and now increasingly as tourists. China has been particularly successful in generating interest by exporting its culture: exhibitions, culture fairs, and most recently the Confucius Institutes. This success challenges assumptions made by Huang and Sheng, who, paraphrasing Joseph Nye, have written that "culture is more likely to attract people and produce soft power in situations where cultures are somewhat similar rather than widely dissimilar."[36] I disagree since the exotic "other" has proven tremendously alluring to dissimilar cultures, and China's successful use of the cultural approach to public diplomacy has brought that nation and its history to the attention of the West.

Today, ahead of the Olympic Games in 2008, the Chinese political elite are openly discussing the need for a more effective public diplomacy that involves more openness, transparency, and freedom of movement for foreign journalists. However, the "Regulations on Reporting Activities in China by Foreign Journalists during the Beijing Olympic Games and the Preparatory Period" which promises greater freedom of movement and access for foreign journalists may provide the context for more critical reporting of China, especially by journalists with little experience or background in the country. The Olympic Games will be only one small part of the China story they convey. Besides, the regulations are having limited effect, especially at the local level where journalists are still routinely prevented from covering stories.

It is not yet clear if China has the capacity to convert public diplomacy resources and effort into achievable foreign policy aspirations. China bestows upon its distinct approach to public diplomacy an extraordinary amount of hard and soft capital—in selling Chinese language and culture; in humanitarian assistance; and in persuading its neighbors of China's commitment to a stable, peaceful, and prosperous Asia-Pacific. China's economic and commercial power is undeniable, and as we have seen, this makes it an attractive destination for global investment and entrepreneurship. However, convincing the liberal democratic international community to look beyond trade and economics and to accept China as a credible diplomatic and political power is a considerable challenge for China's public diplomacy. Cultural and economic diplomacy neither easily nor necessarily translate into foreign policy success.

The principal problems for public diplomacy are the contradictions in Chinese foreign policy.

On the one hand, China yearns to be part of an interdependent world and to spread the benefits of political, economic, and cultural engagement with China. On the other hand, Chinese political discourse is often characterized by a fierce nationalist rhetoric that is reinforced by the Communist Party's determination to maintain authoritarian rule. Together with China's unconditional friendship of ostracized and dubious regimes, especially Zimbabwe and Sudan,[37] and the use of the military threat against Taiwan, this undermines the idea that Chinese soft power is all about selling national and cultural *values*. Until they are able to overcome such contradictions it is unlikely that Chinese public diplomacy will break out of its narrow success in the few friendly areas of the world where Beijing now operates.

Notes

1 D. Shambaugh, "China's propaganda system: Institutions, processes and efficacy," *The China Journal* 57 (January 2007): 25–58; G.D. Rawnsley, "May you live in interesting times," in *Major powers and peacekeeping: Perspectives, priorities and the challenges of military intervention* ed. R. Utley (Aldershot: Ashgate, 2006), 81–98.

2 Its authoritative status is confirmed by its availability: The *People's Daily* (*Renmin Ribao*) is incredibly difficult to acquire and impossible to buy on the streets, being available by subscription only. Before leaving China in February 2007 after living there for 18 months, I tried to find and buy a copy. It was impossible. My contacts within the Communist Party eventually found me some copies and explained my difficulty by telling me that "no-one wants to read it."

3 Qizheng Zhao, "Better public diplomacy to present a truer picture of China," *People's Daily*, March 30, 2007, http:<//english.peopledaily.com.cn/200703/30/eng20070330_362496.html.

4 "Premier: Building prosperous China," *People's Daily*, March 6, 2006, http://www.chinese-embassy.org.uk/eng/zyxw/t301582.htm, accessed 26 September 2007).

5 Zhao, 2007.

6 R. Bernstein and R.H. Munro, *The Coming Conflict with China* (New York: Vintage, 1998); Samuel Huntington, *The Clash of Civilizations and the Remaking of the World Order* (New York: Simon and Schuster, 1996); G.C. Chang, *The Coming Collapse of China* (New York: Random House, 2001).

7 Shambaugh.

8 Joseph S. Nye, *Soft power: The means to succeed in world politics* (New York: Public Affairs, 2004), x.

9 J. Forero, "China's Oil Diplomacy in Latin America," *New York Times*, March 1, 2005, http://www.nytimes.com/2005/03/01/business/worldbusiness/01oil.html?_r=1&position=&adxnnl=1&fta=y&pagewanted=all&adxnnlx=1194087711-YI0P4DAXsclZ5vzWaWlX1g&oref=slogin, accessed November 3, 2007.

10 R. Sutter, and C.H. Huang, "Military diplomacy and China's soft power," *Comparative Connections* 8, no. 2 (2006): 75–84.

11 Y.Z. Huang and S. Ding, "Dragon's underbelly: An analysis of China's soft power," *East Asia* 23, no. 4, (2006): 22–44.

12 G. Pehnelt, "The political economy of China's aid policy in Africa," JENA Economic Research Papers, 2007–051, http://zs.thulb.uni-jena.de/servlets/MCRFileNodeServlet/jportal_derivate_00039789/wp_2007_051.pdf, accessed September 26, 2007.

13 Ian Taylor, "Taiwan's foreign policy and Africa," *Journal of Contemporary China* 11, no. 3 (2002).

14 Andrew Scobell, "China's soft sell: Is the world buying?" *The James Town Foundation China Brief*, http://jamestown.org/terrorism/news/article.php?articleid=2373263, published January 24, 2007, accessed October 6, 2007.

15 J. Spence, *The Chan's Great Continent* (London: Allen Lane, 1999).

16 See Edward Said, *Orientalism: Western Conceptions of the Orient* (London: Penguin, 1985).

17 Spence, 1999.

18 "The last time they [the Terracotta Warriors] were loaned out was to Taiwan, where, having failed so far at traditional diplomacy, it was claimed China was now practising 'terracotta diplomacy.'" Tim Adams, "Behold the Mighty Qin," *The Observer*, August 19, 2007.

19 S. Ding and R.A. Saunders, "Talking up China: An analysis of China's rising cultural power and global promotion of the Chinese language," *East Asia* 23, no. 2, (2006): 3–33; S.H. Donald and R. Benewick, *The State of China Atlas* (Berkeley, CA: The University of California Press, 2005).

20 *People's Daily*, March 6, 2006.

21 *People's Daily* online (22 March 2007). Number of Confucius Institutes to reach 200 in 2007, http://english.peopledaily.com.cn/200703/22/eng20070322_359963.html, October 10, 2007.

22 Anecdotal and critical evidence revealed to the author suggest their limited effect beyond raising in the short term the profile of China in the host university. See Shepherd, "Not a propaganda tool," *The Guardian (Education Section)*, 6 November 2007, p. 12, p. 18 note 35.

23 B. Larner, "The centre of the world," *Foreign Policy* 150 (Sept/Oct 2005): 66–74.

24 Ibid.

25 J. Jirik, "China's new media and the case of CCTV-9," in *International news in the twenty-first century* ed. C. Paterson and A. Sreberny (Eastleigh: John Libbey, 2004), 127–146.

26 "The deals [between CCTV 9 and American satellite/cable distributors] are largely meaningless from a short-term economic point of view . . . they give several cities one more cable channel to choose from. . . . The significance of the deals lay in Beijing's decision to grant the transnationals limited access to China's huge domestic market . . . in exchange for overseas distribution of CCTV-9." (Jirik, 2004)

27 W. Qian, *Politics, market and the television system—study on changes in China's television system* (Henan: Henan People's Press, 2002).

28 J. Paradie, "Can China's soft power offensive succeed?" AsiaMedia, March 5, 2007, http://www.asiamedia.ucla.edu/article.asp?parentid=65078, accessed 2 July 2007.

29 Shambaugh, 2007.

30 N. Renwick and Q. Cao, "Modern political communication in China," in ed. G.D. Rawnsley and M.Y.T. Rawnsley, *Political communications in Greater China: The construction and reflection of identity* (London: RoutledgeCurzon, 2003): 62–82; P.H. Gries, *China's New Nationalism: Pride, Politics and Diplomacy* (Berkeley, CA: University of California Press, 2004).

31 Sutter and Yuang, 2006.

32 C.Y. Lee, "When private capital becomes a security asset—the pattern and evolution of the relations between Taiwanese businessmen and Chinese local government, 1987–2004," *American Journal of Chinese Studies* 13, no. 2 (2006): 149–176; C.Y. Lee, "The Changing Interaction Between Taiwanese Businessmen and the Chinese Government, 1987–2004." Unpublished Ph.D. thesis, University of Nottingham, 2007.

33 Donald and Benewick, 2005.

34 "Foreign students drawn to China's schools," *People's Daily*, October 12, 2007, http://english.people.com.cn/90001/90776/6281460.html, accessed October 13, 2007.

35 Huang and Sheng, 2006.

36 Huang and Sheng, 2006.

37 As international criticism of its position on Darfur clearly demonstrates (Chinese oil companies have invested over $2 billion in Sudan despite US sanctions) China does pay a price in terms of its public diplomacy. China's special envoy on Darfur, Liu Guijin, maintains the official line: "It is not China's Darfur, it is first Sudan's Darfur and then Africa's Darfur" (Bezlova, 2007).

25

Central and Eastern European Public Diplomacy

A Transitional Perspective on National Reputation Management

György Szondi

Introduction

Public diplomacy theory and practice have been dominated by American, Canadian, and British experiences. Western public diplomacy traditionally targeted regions of conflicts, closed systems with significant information deficiencies behind enemy lines. The evolution and practice of public diplomacy were significantly shaped and contextualized by the Cold War and the political environment in which Central and Eastern European (CEE) countries were on the receiving end of Western public diplomacy for decades. Scholars and Cold War public diplomacy practitioners are cautious of attributing the fall of communism entirely to the success of American and Western European public diplomacy,[1] but it is without doubt that radio broadcasting (such as the BBC, Voice of America, Radio Free Europe, or Radio Liberty), cultural and educational exchange programmes, and other public diplomacy tools were nails in communism's coffin. After the fall of the Berlin Wall traditional public diplomacy has gradually been fading away in Central and Eastern Europe[2] and was replaced by economic assistance, knowledge, and skills transfer to facilitate political and economic transition.

The very notion and "invention" of Eastern Europe dates back to the Enlightenment period when East and West were created by Western European philosophers and other intellectuals.[3] Since the Enlightenment *Western Europe* and *Eastern Europe* have existed as complementary concepts defining each other by opposition and adjacency. This conceptual division became a physical one with the descent of the Iron Curtain resulting in ideological polarization too. During the Cold War CEE countries had little space and opportunity to promote themselves and their interests beyond the Iron Curtain where the mental picture was that of a homogeneous "block" of communist countries. The Iron Curtain sealed off a culturally diverse and colorful territory, which was homogeneous only in the ideological sense.

After the fall of the Berlin Wall the CEE countries seized the opportunity to invent themselves, rather than being invented by others. Since 1989, 29 countries have emerged out of the eight former communist countries in Eastern Europe and have engaged in positioning themselves on to the geographical and mental map of Europe and the entire world as democratic, politically stable countries with emerging and promising market economies. Various responses and alternatives have been used in a rather unsystematic way to promote political and economic interest abroad: nation branding, image projection, reputation management, public diplomacy, or

292

country promotion have been utilized to develop and communicate identities that would result in positive "country images."

This chapter focuses on those Eastern European countries that are members of the European Union (EU);[4] however, references are made to other countries of the region which are at earlier stages of their political and economic transitions. Special attention is devoted to Poland, Hungary, and Estonia since the author of this chapter was living in these countries and speaks their languages to different extents.

Public diplomacy so far remains in the realm of international relations, especially within diplomacy. Diplomats' and diplomacy's monopoly on public diplomacy is, however, seriously challenged by other disciplines and practitioners such as international communication, branding, or international public relations. This chapter views public diplomacy as an interdisciplinary area of study, which can draw upon a variety of disciplines to develop concepts and practices. Besides the traditional approaches to and conceptualization of public diplomacy as a foreign policy tool or as international communication, new approaches include the theorization of public diplomacy as branding or as public relations. The conceptual framework for this chapter is *international public relations*, defined as "the planned and organised effort of a company, institution or government to establish mutually beneficial relations with the publics of other nations."[5] Public diplomacy, together with country branding, are conceptualized as pillars of national reputation management.

The Challenges and Special Characteristics of Central European Public Diplomacy

Making impressions and competing for attention and influence have been important for CEE countries, the majority of which are relatively small in size. Limited financial and human resources to promote identities, policies, and interests abroad can seriously restrict the conduct of public diplomacy, especially if sponsored entirely from central budget. As a consequence, Eastern European public diplomacy efforts focus on well-defined countries of geopolitical and geographical positions and importance. These states need to be creative to make their voice heard and try to identify "niches" in foreign policy orientations.[6]

CEE countries have little coverage in the Western media and had little success in influencing the European policy and media agendas before EU accession. Getting positive media coverage presents a further challenge, as coverage is usually linked to political crises (the Orange revolution in Ukraine in 2005), national elections, catastrophes (the sinking of the ferry *Estonia* in 1994; the collapse of an exhibition center's roof in the Polish town of Katowice in 2006), anniversaries (50th anniversary of the 1956 Hungarian Revolution), or unique events (NATO summit in Latvia in 2006; the death of Pope John Paul II and Poland's mourning). When these countries hold the rotating EU presidency, they will get significantly more media attention which will also raise the country's international profile.[7]

Western public and cultural diplomacy is often rooted in those countries' imperial and colonial past, as both concepts have been significant in exerting influence after decolonialization. Central European countries did not have colonies, but due to being the subject of many European treaties and pacts during their turbulent histories, the borders of many Eastern European countries do not follow the ethnic and linguistic borders of a nation; therefore it is of crucial importance to distinguish between a "nation" and a "state" in the Eastern European context. This distinction is often ignored or the terms are used interchangeably by many Western European scholars. About three million Hungarians are scattered in seven countries around Hungary, while half a million Poles live in Belarus, 150,000 in Ukraine, and 240,000 in Lithuania. These people have lived in these territories for centuries and are not migrant minorities (such as the Russians living in the Baltic states due to forced Sovietization during the Communist Soviet era). CEE governments have always considered cultivating relationships with these communities living in neighboring countries as a primary foreign policy goal. Preserving their language and culture, supporting and protecting the rights of these people are important goals of Eastern European public diplomacy. Romania, for example, does not maintain universities in Hungarian language despite the fact that some 1.5 million Hungarians live in Transylvania. It is the Hungarian government that funds a university in Romania where different programmes and degrees are taught in Hungarian. How minorities in Romania or Belarus are treated is not simply a domestic affair issue for the Romanian or Belarus governments, but becomes a foreign affairs issue for the Hungarian or Polish governments. During the decades of communism millions of dissidents left Central and Eastern Europe and started new lives in Western Europe or in the USA. The Polish community in the USA is an estimated 10 million people and about a million Hungarians live in the USA. These communities and expatriates are also important targets and means of Central European public diplomacy.

Small nations can also join efforts and cooperate closely in order to achieve common foreign policy or economic goals and to speak "with a single voice." The Visegrád Group was formulated by Hungary, Poland, the Czech Republic and Slovakia in 1991 to facilitate the countries' transition and to achieve EU and NATO membership[8] and represent their interests jointly. The organization has played an important role in facilitating discussions about a Central European identity and enhancing this regional identity. Another example of regional co-operation is the Baltic Sea Region initiative, which is an economic rather than a political co-operation with the aim of increasing economic development, including investment attracting and export promotion. Public diplomacy for intergovernmental organizations, such as the Visegrád Group, the European Union, ASEAN, or the UN, has so far received little attention, and these organizations will need to engage in more strategic public diplomacy when promoting supranational interests on a global scale.

A further challenge is the languages of the region as they do not belong to the most popular languages learnt by foreigners; therefore any attempts to influence foreign audiences through language can have rather limited impact, unlike American, British, or Canadian public diplomacy activities, which can heavily rely on English, as the most widely studied second language.[9] There are attempts, however to promote language learning. These include the Polish Radio, grouped together with Deutsche Welle and Radio France Internationale, that launched a new interactive initiative in 2007 to promote Polish, German, and French language study among young audiences.[10]

After the fall of communism, Eastern European countries underwent radical economic and political changes. The transition from central planning to a market economy and from an authoritarian, one-party system to a pluralistic and democratic society presented huge challenges to the countries. The transition involved a systematic identity and image transformation as well and public diplomacy has played a significant role in this process. The functions of public diplomacy in transitional countries are as follows:[11]

- *To distance the country from the old economic and/or political system, which existed before the transition.* Public diplomacy together with country branding have been the primary tools of distancing these countries from communism and the negative connotations evoked by "Eastern Europe," which often meant backwardness, despair, something poor or inferior. During the Cold War Eastern Europe and communism became synonyms and have been used interchangeably; therefore many countries in transition have consciously defined and position themselves as Central European countries. Estonia, Latvia, and Lithuania had to make further efforts to get rid of the burdens of and associations with the Soviet Union while Slovenia, Croatia, or the newly independent Montenegro consciously distance themselves from Yugoslavia or even the Balkans. Estonia has positioned itself in international relations as "the only post-communist Nordic country."

- *To position the country as a reliable and eligible "candidate" of the new system that the transition is aiming for, or that of the international community.* The aim is to portray the country as a credible and trustworthy partner in international relations.
- *To change negative or false stereotypes or reinforce some positive stereotypes associated with the country and its people.*
- Countries in transition rely on the moral, financial, and political support of more developed regions or nations, called "center nations," such as the Western European countries. The less developed or transitional countries are often situated on the "periphery" or "semi-periphery." In their orientation the transitional countries are moving from the periphery towards the center position and *the function of public diplomacy is to support and justify this "move" and demonstrate that these countries are worthy of the center nations' support.* The primary target of periphery countries' public diplomacy campaigns are nations situated in the center and those of geopolitical importance.
- *To position the country as the center of the region or as a regional leader.* The periphery countries are competing with each other to become the center and/or the leader of the region/periphery. Competition for the political, financial, commercial, logistical, tourist, or cultural center positions has been strong among Hungary, the Czech Republic, and Poland. Following NATO and EU membership in 2004, Lithuania expressed its new foreign policy vision to become the regional leader and "to become an active country, visible in the world and influential in the region."[12] An interesting expression of the country's ambitions and visibility was when on the eve of EU accession Lithuania became the "brightest" country in Europe. Citizens were asked to light every possible source of light and direct them towards the sky at a particular time to becapturd by a satellite to show the world how bright Lithuania was. Poland also expressed its ambitions to become a regional leader both economically and politically.[13]
- *Public diplomacy can also facilitate (re-)defining and (re-)constructing national identities as identity is also changing during transition.* The countries and their peoples often faced the questions of "who are we?" and "how do we want to be seen by others?" Countries in transition or peripheries are often defined by center nations who also construct periphery nations' and their peoples' images. Creating "Euro conform" identity was of crucial importance for most countries aiming for EU membership. "Europeness" and "Returning to Europe" have been central themes for each country that joined the European Union.[14]

The Institutionalization of Reputation Management

Institutionalizations meant that special governmental organizations, departments, or positions were created to research and evaluate existing country images in the different target countries; to develop communication policies, strategies, and tactics to promote political and economic interests abroad; and to co-ordinate efforts of different organizations. In Poland, for example, the Ministry of Economy, the Ministry of Foreign Affairs, the Ministry of Culture, as well as a the Polish Chamber of Commerce, the Institute of Polish Brand, the Polish Institutes, and the Mickiewicz Institute have all been involved in promoting Poland, sometimes communicating different and uncoordinated messages about the country.

In 1998, the Hungarian government set up the Country Image Centre to manage Hungary's reputation abroad. The Centre's aim was "to develop a concept for the new image of the country and to build this new image both inside and outside the country." The Latvian

Institute was also established in 1998 by the government "to help the globalised world community better understand Latvia today by providing essential and useful information on all aspects of Latvia's history, culture and society." The Czech Centres' main mission is "to develop a good name and positive image of the Czech Republic abroad, to actively promote the Czech Republic's interest and to exercise public diplomacy in line with the state's foreign policy priorities."

Poland was the first country in the region to set up a public diplomacy department within the Ministry of Foreign Affairs, which initiated several public diplomacy programs and campaigns in the early years of 2000. The very term "public diplomacy" has been consciously used in Poland where the Ministry of Foreign Affairs has a Department of Public Diplomacy.[15] The Department is in charge of promotion of the Republic of Poland abroad and elaborates appropriate strategies serving that end; encourages contacts with various social groups in foreign countries, focusing on opinion-forming circles; and is responsible for creating a positive image of Poland abroad.[16]

In many Central European countries the newly elected governments have erased the efforts of the previous government resulting in discontinuity of reputation management. Soon after, however, the new government also "realizes" that there is an "image problem" abroad and tries to set up (new) institutions and develop strategies to deal with them. As a result "reputation management" has been shifted around among different ministries and governmental departments. Hungary's Country Image Centre was heavily criticized by the opposition and seen as the "propaganda machine of the government" both within and outside the country. Despite the relevance and necessity of an organization as such, it was abolished once a new government was formed in 2002. It is—and probably will always be—easy to discredit any of the institutions and organizations involved in reputation management as propagandists. Involving communication practitioners from a range of backgrounds and adopting strategic approaches, based on ethical two-way communication and with the consent of the domestic public can legitimize the existence of such organizations and their practises.

International Public Relations: The Framework

Public Relations Defined

The conceptual framework for describing and analyzing reputation management for countries is international public relations. Public relations (PR) is often misunderstood and misinterpreted by international relations, international communication, marketing, or branding scholars as well as practitioners who often use the term as a synonym for hype, deception, lies, or propaganda. The British Institute of Public Relations defines PR as "the planned and sustained effort to establish and maintain goodwill and mutual understanding between an organisation and its publics."[17] Its aim is to establish and maintain mutually beneficial relationships between an organization (government or country) and the publics on whom its success or failure depends.[18] Public relations is about building and maintaining long-term relationships and trust with key stakeholders and publics in order to create mutual understanding.

Nessmann[19] summarized the following aims and functions of public relations:

- creating trust, comprehension, and sympathy;
- arousing attention, interest, and needs;
- creating and cultivating communication and relationships;
- creating mutual understanding and agreement;
- articulating, representing, and adjusting interests;
- influencing public opinion;

- resolving conflicts; and
- creating consensus.

It is not difficult to see how these concepts are core to any public diplomacy aims and strategies. Adopting a public relations approach to public diplomacy can:

- contribute to the growing body of knowledge of public diplomacy;
- position public diplomacy as a strategic function and activity since public diplomacy activities often remain tactical and situational in many countries;
- provide guidelines on how best to conduct ethical public diplomacy through two-way symmetrical communication,[20] as well as develop and maintain relationships between a government and foreign publics;
- help develop and maintain mutually beneficial relationships between a government and foreign publics, emphasizing relationship building over "creating and promoting a positive image" as the ultimate public diplomacy goal;
- help research, plan, and implement strategic public diplomacy campaigns;[21]
- contribute to identifying and formulating specific and measurable public diplomacy objectives since national public diplomacy objectives often remain vague, elusive and unspecific;
- contribute to identifying, prioritizing, and segmenting publics and stakeholders, which are core concepts to both public relations and public diplomacy;
- provide a conceptual framework and guidelines to evaluate public diplomacy since assessing the impact and effects of public diplomacy programs remains under-researched and often neglected;
- anticipate, identify, and analyze domestic as well as international "issues" that have consequences on a country's reputation.[22] Depending on the nature of these issues, proactive or reactive strategies can be developed to strategically address them.

International public relations consultancies are often engaged in public diplomacy campaigns on behalf of governments to promote a country's economic and political interests abroad. Central and Eastern European governments have often used the services of PR consultants and agencies, which offer strategic advice, media relations, media monitoring, public affairs, lobbying, events management, online PR, issues and crises management as part of public diplomacy campaigns.[23]

In public diplomacy theory and practice *image* and *image management* are recurrent terms. Image management for countries is not a new phenomenon, nations throughout the world have long engaged in image cultivation.[24] The role of images of nations has been widely discussed in a variety of disciplines including history, international relations, diplomacy, literature, social psychology, sociology, communication studies, marketing, and public relations. It is only recently that these disciplines have started to cross-fertilize, testing the boundaries and the validity of each discipline, often encroaching upon each other's territory.[25] The concept of image in these areas has been used in a plethora of contexts but often without appropriate conceptualization and operationalization.

Public diplomacy, international relations, and branding scholars and practitioners tend to attribute too much importance to image and usually make the assumption that there is a single and uniform "image." Creating and promoting "a positive image" of a country remains the ultimate—albeit immeasurable and intangible—goal of public diplomacy. As James Grunig, a recognized public relations scholar, argued, image is an overused term in marketing, branding and public relations—and one can add international relations and public diplomacy as well—and it is often used as a synonym for concepts such as message, reputation, perception, credibility, attitude, or relationship, disguising these more precise concepts.[26] Image can also be interpreted as the opposite of reality, and image management can easily boil down to impression management.

Instead of a positive image it is more appropriate to identify *positive reputation* as the overall goal of international public relations for countries. Reputation must be earned while images can be created, manipulated, and they do not always reflect or represent reality. Depending on the subject of communication, Figure 25.1 and Table 25.1 summarize the several specializations of national reputation management, including aims, actors, and some examples from Central and Eastern Europe:

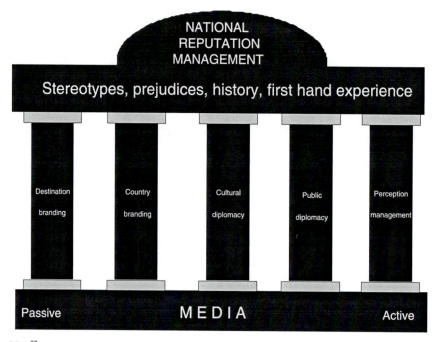

Figure 25.1.[27]

These specializations of national reputation management are not distinct but interact, influence, and reinforce each other. Countries can engage in these specializations to different extents and the emphasis may also vary. What is crucial, however, is the strategic approach to and the co-ordination of branding, cultural and public diplomacy to achieve synergy. A crisis in one dimension can have consequences on other dimensions and can result in the further escalation of the crisis. A country can be more successful in one of the above dimensions but rather poor at others. Croatia is a good example: it has been a very popular tourism destination but has been unsuccessful in public diplomacy.

The media are vital tools in each specialization, however, their role may vary. In the case of *destination* and *country branding*, print and electronic media carry sponsored advertisements and spots about a country, but the media are not the sole channel and tool of communication. Government-sponsored country advertisements to attract investors or raise the profile of the country in national and international print publications are on the increase, together with country advertising spots in electronic media, such as BBC World, Deutsche Welle, or CNN. Poland's Prime Minister, Lach Kaczynski for example, featured in a high profile advertising campaign in 2007 "to raise the international profile and image of Poland." Leading European publications, such as the *Financial Times* or *The Economist* often publish country reports or special supplements

Table 25.1. The Specializations of Reputation Management

Subject	Specialization	Aim	Examples	Actors
Tourism	**Destination branding**	Attract visitors; boost tourism	Croatia—"The Mediterranean As It Once Was," Latvia—"The land that sings" Hungary—"Talent for Entertaining"	National and regional tourist boards, travel agencies; marketing and branding agencies
Economic policy	**Country (nation) branding**	To create a "country brand" which will sell products abroad as well as advance commercial interests abroad; to attract investors; to gain competitive advantage; export development; to advance "country-of-origin" effect	Estonia—"Positively Transforming" Poland—"Creative Tension" Czech Republic— "Czech★Idea" Hungary—"Talent for . . ."	Ministry of Economics, investment promotion and export agencies; trade boards, chambers of commerce, multinational organizations
Culture (heritage, language, arts, films, etc.)	**Cultural relations (Cultural diplomacy)**	Promote culture, language learning; educational exchange, create a favorable opinion about a country; to change negative or false stereotypes; to create mutual understanding between cultures	Polish Year in Sweden; "Czech Music 2004;" "Czech Seasons;" Eurovision Song Contest; 50th anniversary of the 1956 Hungarian Revolution; "Magyar Magic" in the UK; exhibitions; international film festivals	Ministry of Culture; Ministry of Foreign Affairs, Cultural Institutions, embassies' cultural attachés, cultural and media organizations
Foreign policy and external relations	**Public diplomacy**	To create a receptive environment for foreign policy goals; to advance these goals; to get countries to change their policies towards others; raising international profile of countries, their politicians, governments.	Becoming EU, NATO members; supporting or opposing the war in Iraq; to promote democratization	Government, Ministry of Foreign Affairs, NGOs, media outlets broadcasting abroad
Domestic and foreign unethical policies, and actions; images	**Perception management**	To create images that are not aligned with reality; to create and promote negative images; to discredit regimes, countries, governments; create crises situations	Russia's efforts to discredit the Baltic states; Russia's efforts to manipulate ethnic Russians living in the Baltic states; Romanian government's campaigns; Albania's image campaign	Ministries of Defense, government, foreign governments, secret agencies

on countries,[28] reviewing the current political and economic state of the country. Governments of the specific country usually sponsor advertisements in these sections.

In *perception management* the media is the main tool and field where perceptions are "managed." In *public diplomacy* the following factors influence the role of media. First, with the exception of some major powers and some rogue states, public interest in other nations' foreign policy is of little interest. Second, media ownership can have a bearing on representing other countries and their foreign policies. In Central and Eastern Europe many media outlets are owned by foreign (Western) companies and the media are often politicized, openly supporting political parties and interests. There are several examples when political parties use the international arena for domestic issues and take home affairs abroad in the hope that international media attention and pressure will result in change of government policies. The Hungarian opposition have often used this "reversed public diplomacy" to alter domestic as well as foreign policies.

Politicians often use the foreign mass media to mobilize foreign public support for their country's policies. Former Polish president Aleksander Kwasniewski published several articles in British quality newspapers about Poland and its aspirations for EU membership to generate more support for EU enlargement among British citizens. These attempts can be classified as media diplomacy under the auspice of public diplomacy, though traditionally media diplomacy referred to conflict resolutions.

Destination and Country (Nation) Branding

The two specializations of national reputation management are destination and country branding. Applying the concepts of branding to places, such as cities, regions, or countries does not have a long tradition and place branding is still an emerging field. Nation branding, however, has become a powerful metaphor as well as reality during the last decade or so, resulting in heated debates whether it is possible or feasible to brand countries in the first place. As Wally Olins, a British branding expert argues, companies and countries are becoming more like each other: "As countries are developing their 'national brands' to compete for investment, trade and tourism, mega-merged global companies are using nation-building techniques to achieve internal cohesion across culture."[29] Nation branding has been used in a plethora of contexts without clear conceptualization and is therefore not always appropriately understood and interpreted.

The tools of marketing and branding have long been used in domestic political communication to raise awareness of or increase support for—or sometimes to discredit—political ideas, parties, or politicians; however, these concepts and strategies have made their way into the international political communication arena only recently. During the late 1990s and 2000s domestic governmental and public sector communication in many countries were strongly influenced by branding and marketing, an approach which has slowly been penetrating into international governmental communication.

The aim of *destination branding* is to attract visitors and boost tourism while *country branding* promotes economic and commercial interests at home and abroad.[30] Country brands have both intangible and tangible elements, such as the products or services of the particular country. The more specific aims of country branding are to create or advance the "country-of-origin" effect, to promote exports (outward direction), or attract investors or a skilled workforce (inward direction). Country brands can serve as a sort of umbrella under which further sub-brands can be developed. Many Central European countries have become successful destination brands, attracting tourists from Western Europe and all over the world. Poland and Estonia were the first countries to go further and develop coherent country brands. Poland has made several uncoordinated efforts to promote the country abroad between 1998 and 2004 until British branding "guru" Wally Olins and his company, Saffron arrived to rescue the initiative and coordinate the branding process in 2004. Commissioned by the Ministry of Foreign Affairs, Saffron developed a country brand for Poland with the core theme "Creative Tension." The government's involvement was also significant in Estonia's country brand ("Positively transforming") launched in 2001. It is interesting to note that change and contrast between past and present, paradox of characteristics in the country and its people have been a common theme of country branding in the region, reinforcing the intellectual invention and framing of Eastern

Europe. The majority of Central European countries are engaged in some kind of nation branding activity with different degree of success, however.

In Poland it was suggested that another brand be used in country branding in 2005: "Solidarity," a well known Polish political brand. The initiative to use it as an overall brand for Poland met some criticism as this brand could be seen as outdated, lacking dynamism, and very abstract. Poland's example demonstrates, however, that a country brand can consist of different brands, such as a destination brand, an export brand, an investment brand, and a political brand, which can be all different rather than having a central, all-encompassing country brand.

In 1999, four Hungarian companies founded the Hungaricum Club with the aim of creating a stylish "calling card" for Hungary. The founders aimed at contributing more to Hungary's image by their own means and through their joint appearance and at "furthering Hungary's progress towards membership of the European Union, while retaining their traditional identities as Hungarian brands." Members of the club put together a boxed set called "A Taste of Hungary" featuring selected samples of their products, Herend Porcelain, Pick Salami, Tokaj Aszu Wines, Zwack Unicum liqueur, and the Halas sewn lace, all linked to traditional dining.[31]

There are different and sometimes inconsistent views on the relationship between nation branding and public diplomacy.[32] One of the reasons for the inconsistency is that both nation branding and public diplomacy are ubiquitous terms, which have been poorly conceptualized. *Place Branding*, a British journal, was launched in 2004 as a "quarterly review of branding, marketing and public diplomacy for national, regional and civic development." Managing editor Simon Anholt initially viewed diplomacy as a subset of nation branding.[33] To incorporate the growing field of public diplomacy as a discipline, in 2007 the journal changed its name (rebranded itself) to *Place Branding and Public Diplomacy*, inviting international relations scholars onto its editorial board. This journal has become the prime source of advocating and advancing a branding approach to public diplomacy.

Applying the concepts of branding and marketing to foreign policy has been a recent phenomenon demonstrating both the encroachment of different disciplines and the "commercialization" of foreign policy and public diplomacy. Foreign policy advisors and government officials (e.g. Charlotte Beers) as well as International Relations scholars[34] jumped on the "b®andwagon," adopting the view that foreign policy can also be the subject of branding. Branding practitioners, on the other hand, have become foreign policy specialists and advisors. A branding-driven foreign policy approach created business opportunities for British branding gurus Simon Anholt and Wally Olins, and agencies such as Interbrand, that rushed to Eastern Europe to sell their expertise to CEE governments, and ministries of foreign affairs often presented branding as the "panacea" of communicating with foreign audiences. This British nation branding "know-how" was present in the Estonian, Polish, Latvian, Croatian, Slovenian, Bulgarian, and Lithuanian nation branding campaigns, while Hungary used its own resources.[35] Outsourcing foreign policy and public diplomacy to external (foreign) agencies in a nation branding format can have several drawbacks, however. Eastern European government officials had high expectations from nation branding but quickly became disillusioned when it did not produce the desired short-term results and expectations or the final invoice was presented.

In conceptualizing national reputation management, both country branding and public diplomacy are important elements, which should complement rather than replace each other. Branding is relevant when there is a choice to be made by the "consumers" whose choice can be influenced by a strong brand name and brand value. When choosing a holiday destination or deciding where to invest, the options are endless. However, the foreign policy of a country is unique; there are certain policy goals but these are not competing with each other for the attention of foreign publics. Branding is very much image-driven, with the aim of creating positive country images. Branding is foremost one-way communication where the communicator has control over the message, which tends to be simple and concise and leaves little space for dialogue and interactions. A branding-driven approach can also dilute the essence of public diplomacy as the diplomacy component fades away. Branding targets mass audiences in the target nation—who are largely passive—while public diplomacy targets well-defined publics such as the cultural or political elites, opinion formers and leaders, those interested in foreign news or policy. Sproule's view is more relevant to branding than public diplomacy: "Mass audiences respond to conclusions, not reasons; to slogans, not complexities; to images, not ideas, to pleasing, attractive personages, not expertise or intellect; and to facts created *through* suasion, not suasion *based on* facts."[36]

Attributing too much importance to brand names (country names) and (brand) images has led so far that Lithuania is considering changing its name in English to something easier to pronounce as an attempt "to raise the country's profile." The Polish government made significant efforts to dissociate Poland's name from the concentration camps as the international media have often referred to the "Polish concentration camps" when speaking of the former Nazi death camps in the south of Poland. In 2006, the governments efforts bore fruits as UNESCO agreed to rename the camps as "The Former Nazi German Concentration and Extermination Camp Auschwitz Birkenau." Romania is also struggling with its name as it includes "Roma" which evokes images of Roma gypsies rather than those of the "eternal city."

Cultural Diplomacy and Relations

Cultural diplomacy has always been one of the pillars of foreign policy in many Central European countries. Cultural diplomacy is closely related to the government of a country and to achieving foreign policy goals as it seeks "to present a favourable image so that diplomatic operations, as a whole, are facilitated."[37] Culture in this sense serves as an instrument of achieving foreign policy goals and thus is politicized. Cultural relations are concerned with promoting cultural "products" such as literature, films, TV, and radio programs, arts, science, music as well as languages abroad. The ultimate goal is to make foreign publics familiar with a nation, its people, culture, and language, and to create a favorable opinion about the country through its culture. While cultural diplomacy tends to be a one-sided activity, cultural relations aim at achieving "understanding and cooperation between national societies for their mutual benefits."[38] Cultural relations is the best way to change negative or false stereotypes as they have deeper impact and carry more credibility than other forms of reputation management.

The *Magyar Kulturális Intézet*, the *Instytut Polski*, the *Eesti Instituut*, or the *Latvijas Institūts* are the leading institutions of cultural promotions for Hungary, Poland, Estonia, and Latvia respectively. The Estonian Institute's main goal is "to spread information about Estonian society, culture and education both at home and abroad; to introduce Estonian culture to other countries and to promote cultural communication between Estonia and other countries; and to support the teaching of Estonian language and culture-related subjects in the universities abroad."[39] These institutions are closely linked and dependent on funding from the governments or ministries of culture unlike the Western European counterparts, such as the British Council or the Goethe Institut, which have more independence and are not associated with the governments. CEE cultural institutions are located in "strategic countries" only: lack of funding prevents these countries from setting up cultural institutions in too many countries. Table 25.2 summarizes the leading cultural institutions of those Eastern European countries that are members of the European Union.

Educational exchange programs are crucial factors in building cultural relations. Western European students rarely choose Central and Eastern European countries for study or to do a degree there and these countries can never compete with the English-speaking countries' universities where foreigners are flooding to study. This is partly due to the fact that CEE countries

Table 25.2. Cultural Institutions of those Eastern European Countries that are EU Members

Country	Cultural institutes and their numbers abroad
Bulgaria	Bulgarian Cultural Institutes (10)
Czech Republic	Czech Centres (18)
Estonia	Estonian Institute (4)
Hungary	Hungarian Cultural Centres (19)
Latvia	Latvian Institute (only in Latvia)
Lithuania	Lithuanian Institute (only in Lithuania)
Poland	Polish Institute (14)
Romania	Romanian Cultural Institute (15)
Slovakia	Slovak Institute (8)
Slovenia	None

offer only limited courses and degree programs in English and/or German and the language barrier prevents many foreign students from pursuing their studies in the region. African and Asian students, however, often choose Central European countries, whose education standards and affordable degree programs are well known all over the world.

The European Capital of Culture has been an initiative by the European Commission since 1985 which presents a chance for cities and regions to showcase their cultural lives and cultural developments. In 2000, Krakow and Prague were the first cities from Central Europe designated together with seven other Western European cities as Capitals of Culture. Given the symbolic importance and the positive impact of the "European Capital of Culture" event, from 2009 each year a country from CEE can also designate a city besides the "old" member states, Lithuania being the first together with Austria.

One of the most efficient and best-known ways of reputation management is the Eurovision Song Contest where millions across Europe tune into the singing contest. In 2005, Ukraine hosted the event and seized the opportunity to communicate the values, hopes, and visions of the country to a Europe-wide audience. When Estonia won the song contest in 2001 and hosted Eurovision in 2002, the country used it to kick off the "Branding Estonia" initiative and showed the 166 million viewers how the country had transformed from a Soviet Republic to an EU and NATO contender. In 2007, Serbia won the competition together with the right to organize the event in 2008. Serbia used the song contest as a public diplomacy tool to showcase the country's "European values." The old member states—especially the UK—may attribute little significance to Eurovision but it has meant a great deal for many Central and Eastern European nations to express themselves and boost their confidence. As *The Economist* magazine commented: "The biggest single lesson of Eurovision is that Europe's centre of gravity is moving east."[40]

Hosting international sports events is another important tool of reputation management for countries. Poland and Ukraine will host the European football championships in 2012.

Public Diplomacy

The next pillar of reputation management is public diplomacy, which can be defined as foreign policy's communication dimension. Influencing foreign public opinion to achieve national goals and advancing and protecting national interest have always been of key importance for any nation. Before outlining public diplomacy in the Eastern European context, it is worth reviewing some changes and trends in pubic diplomacy. Earlier definitions of public diplomacy evolved around strategies of promotion and persuasion and were closely related to self-interest and impression management. Public diplomacy was defined as "direct communication with foreign peoples, with the aim of affecting their thinking and ultimately, that of their governments."[41] As for the content of public diplomacy, it described activities, directed abroad in the fields of information, education, and culture, whose objective is to influence a foreign government, by influencing its citizens.[42] This definition also demonstrates that for many American writers cultural diplomacy forms a part of public diplomacy. Analysing the past and current definitions and practice of public diplomacy, the following changes can be observed. The objectives of earlier definitions of public diplomacy were two-fold: to influence the "general" public of the target nation and by doing so to get them to pressure their own government to change foreign or domestic policy. These definitions well represent the international political environment—the Cold War—in which public diplomacy was contextualized, making the assumptions that public opinion can actually influence foreign policy. Recent definitions of and approaches to public diplomacy hardly make any reference to the target countries' governments; influencing the public opinion to create a receptive environment for foreign policy goals and promote national interests have become the ultimate goal. Traditionally public diplomacy was closely linked to conflicts and tensions between countries. Frederick positioned public diplomacy as one of the means of low intensity conflict resolution. According to this approach, public diplomacy is not practised in peaceful relations but in certain degree of conflict in order to "convey positive American values to foreigners, to create a climate of opinion in which American policies can be successfully formulated, executed and accepted."[43] This still might be true for American public diplomacy—which in many respects remains traditional—but certainly not for Central European countries, for which public diplomacy can flourish only in peaceful conditions.

The objectives of public diplomacy have shifted from a behavioural dimension—to get citizens to do something—towards an attitudinal objective, such as supporting—or at least not opposing—another country's foreign policy goals. Another change is the move towards understanding and dialogue replacing the monologue and promotional nature of earlier definitions and strategies. During the Cold War, public diplomacy was concerned with achieving change in the target countries' political environment while 21st-century public diplomacy embraces and supports economical goals too. The expansion of target audiences is also a characteristic of 21st-century public diplomacy, as the support of the domestic audiences for foreign policy actions has also become crucial, especially with the emergence of "intermestic" affairs when international and domestic affairs merge and encroach in each other.[44]

Table 25.3 further compares traditional public diplomacy and 21st-century public diplomacy, however, it is important to acknowledge that many states' public diplomacy still follows the traditional model. The European Union's emerging public diplomacy is another example of the 21st-century PD.

While branding is not necessarily linked to the government, cultural and public diplomacy—together with perception management—are the most closely linked to the government of the particular country. Direct or indirect government involvement, support and control are core to many public diplomacy definitions and programmes, albeit the government is not always the "official face" of public diplomacy campaigns as the role of non-state actors in public diplomacy is also on the increase. The extent to which the government is visible and recognisable as the sponsor, initiator or source of communication may vary from campaign to campaign. The government's role in communicating with foreign publics is crucial as foreign policy priorities can change with the change of government and public diplomacy can easily boil down to promoting a government (and its foreign policy) abroad rather than promoting the country and its interests.

For the Central European countries the most important foreign policy goal right after the collapse of communism was accession to the European Union and joining NATO. Public diplomacy was utilised to induce more support for membership among EU citizens as well as to counteract the negative stereotypes and prejudices that the countries were associated with.

Table 25.3. Traditional and 21st Century Public Diplomacy Compared

	Traditional public diplomacy	*21st-entury public diplomacy*
Conditions	Conflict, tensions between states	Peace
Objectives	To achieve political change in target countries by changing target audiences' behaviour	Political and economic interest promotion to create receptive environment and positive reputation of the country abroad
Strategies	Persuasion Managing publics	Building and maintaining relationships Engaging with publics
Direction of communication	One way communication (monologue)	Two-way communication (dialogue)
Research	Very little, if any	PD based on scientific research where feedback is also important
Message context	Ideologies Interests	Ideas Values
Target audiences (publics)	"General" public of the target nation; sender and receivers of messages	Segmented, well-defined publics + domestic publics; Participants
Channels	Traditional mass media	Old and new media; often personalized via networks
Budget	Sponsored by government	Public and private partnership

During the 1990s the precise date of accession was not set, the date was floated by the EU. Initially, enlargement was subject to public referendums in some of the old member states. In the end, however, the Accession Treaty was ratified by the national parliament of each member state and by referendums in the accession states.[45]

Support for a candidate country's membership in the EU has always been of critical importance. Former European Enlargement Commissioner, Günter Verheugen called for developing and launching an enlargement communication strategy that would facilitate dialogue between future and present citizens. Eurobarometer, which monitors EU citizens' opinions on a variety of issues, clearly demonstrated that there had been serious gaps in the acceptance of certain candidate countries by the citizens of many member states. France, Germany and Spain were among the top countries that opposed Poland's membership. In 2000, the Council of Ministers in Poland adopted the "Framework Programme of Foreign Promotion of the Republic of Poland's Accession to the European Union." This document outlined the strategies and tactics for the years 2000–2002 as the date of accession was first set by 2002. To further promote Poland in the member states and to achieve the ratification of the Accession Treaty a second programme was drawn up in 2002 with the title: "Programme of Promoting Poland in the Member Countries of the European Union during the Ratification of the Accession Treaty." Image building and promotion are identified in both programmes as overall goals, gaining membership support and credibility being the more specific—and certainly more measurable—objectives. These programmes aimed at the "general public" as well as the members of the parliaments who would, in the end, ratify the Accession Treaty. The program included The Polish Year in Spain (2002), in Austria (2002–2003), Sweden (2003) and the Polish Cultural Season in France 2004.[46]

Central and Eastern European countries have often concentrated on their past rather than on their future in their public diplomacy efforts. Politicians often portrayed these countries as victims of the Soviet era that needed aid and support. Past or future orientation can have a significant bearing on the acceptance and credibility of these countries and their rhetoric. Contemplating the past or looking into the future is demonstrated by two Baltic countries' attitudes. As a Latvian journalist observed: when an Estonian diplomat goes to a conference, he says: "We have an idea." When a Latvian diplomat goes to the same conference, he says: "We have a problem."

A country's prime minister, its president and the minister of foreign affairs are the main figures who represent a country in foreign relations. They are the "official faces" of a country and their communication and actions generate foreign media coverage. They can boost as well as damage a country's reputation. The Kaczynski twins' actions and ideas often dominated the international headlines in 2006, influencing Poland's reputation abroad. Hungary's socialist prime minister, communist-turned-billionaire Ferenc Gyurcsany made the international headlines a few times during 2005 and 2006. He praised the Hungarian national soccer team's performance in a friendly game against Saudi Arabia in February 2005: "I think that there were very many terrorists also among the Saudi soccer players, and our sons fought with death-defying bravery against these terrorists, so a draw away from home is a fantastic result." This quote received worldwide publicity and damaged not only Gyurcsany's reputation but that of Hungary among Arab states too. The Saudi ambassador left Hungary, whose government was begging him to return to Hungary and had to apologise. In a leaked tape in 2006 Gyurcsany admitted that he and his socialist government "lied in the morning, and lied in the evening" for years which generated worldwide publicity again. Controversial remarks by politicians can also cast the spotlight on a country although this would follow the "there is no such thing as bad publicity" approach, which can be risky.

A country's support of another nation's foreign policy goals and interests may also have implications for public diplomacy. Poland's strong support of the war in Iraq and her pro-American stance in foreign policy had significant bearings on Polish public diplomacy. Poland's willingness to send troops to Iraq must have impressed the Americans and NATO officials but certainly did not achieve the same outcome within European countries. 13 Eastern European head of states supported the US-led war in Iraq in 2003 by signing the "Letter of Eight" and the "Vilnius Statement." The strong support of the war from CEE countries prompted German professor of philosophy, Jürgen Habermas and Jacques Derrida to publish a manifesto invoking the notion of a "core Europe" (including France, Germany, Benelux states and Italy) distinct from those countries that supported the war: both the UK and those Central European countries, which are members of the EU. They argued that "only the core European nations are ready to endow the EU with certain qualities of a state" and they should be the "locomotive" of the Union.[47] Fawn[48] attributed Central European states' support of the Iraq War to American soft power; however, it could also be interpreted as an impression management exercise to impress the US government and to earn credits. Foreign policy decisions indeed can be subject to impression management: policy-makers can assess the symbolic value of an action or decision as well as the impression it could have and decide to pursue a policy or action or not.

Poland's mediating role in the Orange Revolution in Ukraine went down very well in the European Union. Poland could have built on and relied on an old value: Solidarity, something which the country is still associated with. So far, however, it remains a missed foreign policy opportunity and none of the democratically elected governments have used "Solidarity" to promote Poland's image "as a country that strives for respect of human rights all over the world."[49] In other terms, Solidarity could be a "niche" for Polish foreign policy and public diplomacy.

After the collapse of the Iron Curtain the European Union replaced US influence in the region. The European Union's soft power[50] has served as a "magnet" for CEE countries wanting to join the EU. The co-operation between Central European countries and the pre-enlargement European Union is a good example of *symmetrical public diplomacy*, which aims at creating mutual understanding and is based on dialogue. In symmetrical public diplomacy each party has an equal chance to influence policy outcomes, which are mutually beneficial to all, and each party is willing to alter its policies, positions or behaviour accordingly.

Following EU and NATO accessions some CEE countries have been searching for new directions and priorities in their foreign policy orientations as well as trying to find their place and role in the enlarged European Union. Partnership and co-operation have been central concepts in Central European countries' foreign policy visions and public diplomacy strategies. In 2005, the Estonian Foreign Ministry's defined its new vision as "achieving and ensuring democracy, stability, security, and prosperity in Europe and elsewhere in the world" and becoming a "dependable and credible partner in both the EU and NATO, in other international organisations, and in bilateral relations." Central European countries have accumulated valuable experiences in nation building as well as "know-how" of economic and political transformation that could be beneficial to other nations, which are at an earlier stage of their transition. After becoming EU members Central European countries therefore started to look east again with the aim of promoting democracy in the former Soviet Union countries and in Central Asia, including Afghanistan, Moldova, Ukraine, Belarus, Russia, Georgia.

International conferences and congresses are also important public diplomacy tools, especially if the topic is public diplomacy itself. The Diplomatic Academy of the Croatian Ministry for Foreign Affairs has organised four international conferences on Public Diplomacy and gained important "know-how" about PD theory and practice.[51]

The Estonian Ministry of Foreign Affairs runs a quiz every year on its website with the aim of "introducing Estonia to citizens of other countries."[52] A Pakistani girl who was born in the medical tent of the Estonian rescue team in the earthquake that hit Pakistan in 2005 was named "Estonia." This was widely covered by the local and international media and demonstrated that small countries can also achieve serious results by deeds that speak louder than words.

The majority of Central European countries maintain up-to-date country websites, which often serve as a "one-stop shop" on general information on the specific country and serve as an important public diplomacy tool. The web addresses bear the countries' English names (e.g., http://www.poland.pl, http://www.czech.cz; http://www.slovenia.si) and are operated by the Ministry of Foreign Affairs (Czech website), by the government (Slovenian, Slovakian or the Hungarian website), by the institute responsible for country promotion (Latvian website), by the National Tourist Board (Croatian website) or other institutions.

International Broadcasting

International broadcasting is an integral part of both cultural and public diplomacy. Browne identified the following functions of international broadcasting: an instrument of foreign policy, a mirror of society, a symbolic presence, a converter and sustainer, a coercer and intimidator, an educator, an entertainer and a seller of goods and services.[53] The majority of central European governments fund international broadcasting although these stations rarely broadcast 24/7 in all the major languages and often rely on other than government funds as well. Table 25.4 summarizes the radio and TV stations sponsored fully or partly from the central budget which aim at foreign audiences. The websites of some stations also serve as a news portal providing news about the particular country in several languages.

While many of these media outlets aim at minorities living around the countries, expatriates or diasporas, some of them are involved in "democracy promotion." In March 2004, a Spanish language programme was launched by Radio Prague, intended for listeners mostly in Cuba but in Latin-American countries too with the aim of providing information about the Czech Republic's experience of transition. In 2006, the Polish government set up Radio Racja (Radio Right) to broadcast news into neighbouring Belarus with the aim of weakening the state monopoly over information in Belarus and to promote democracy. TV Belsat is the "brainchild" of Agnieszka Romaszewska-Guzy, a Polish broadcaster and journalist, who was expelled from

Table 25.4. International Broadcasting in Central and Eastern Europe

Country	International broadcasting	Languages	Website address
Bulgaria	Radio Bulgaria	Arabic, English, French, German, Spanish, Russian, Serbian, Greek, Albanian and Turkish	http://www.bnr.bg
Czech Republic	Radio Prague	English, German, Spanish, Russian, French, Czech	http://www.radio.cz/english
Estonia	None		
Hungary	Budapest Radio★	English, German, French, Russian, Spanish, Italian	
	Duna TV	Hungarian	http://www.dunatv.hu
Latvia	None		
Lithuania	None		
Poland	Radio Polonia	Polish, English, German, Russian, Belarusian, Ukrainian, Hebrew	http://www.polskieradio.pl/zagranica
	Radio Racja	Belarusian	http://www.radioracja.pl/
	TV Polonia	Polish with English subtitles	http://www.tvp.pl/tvppolonia
	TV Belarus	Belarusian and Russian	http://www.belstat.eu
Romania	Radio Romania International	Arabic, Chinese, English, French, German, Italian, Serbian, Spanish, Russian and Ukrainian, Romanian	http://www.rri.ro
Slovakia	Radio Slovakia International	Slovak, English, German, Russian, Spanish, French	http://www.slovakradio.sk/inetportal/rsi/index.php
Slovenia	None		

★ These foreign language services were abolished in July 2007 due to lack of resources.

Belarus several times and has been actively involved in setting up and running the station.[54] The television station's aim is to broadcast independent news, cultural and musical programmes in Belarusian four hours daily since there is no Belarusian language broadcasting in the country but only in the Russian language, closely controlled and censored by the Belarus authorities. The station went on air in 2007 on the International Human Rights Day (10 December). The Polish state funds TV Belsat with €4.47 million and Lithuania also contributes to its funding. The station hopes to receive assistance from the US, Czech Republic and the EU as well.

Perception Management

The final pillar of the reputation pantheon is *perception management*, where manipulating perceptions is more important than reality and messages do not necessarily reflect the truth; replacing the factual by the representational is the essence of this dimension. The aim can be to discredit countries or regimes, to create "negative images" of other countries or governments (in some Eastern European countries the process is incorrectly called "black public relations"), to create crisis situations, or "sell" and justify unethical policies or wars internationally.

Fortunately, the number of examples in Central Europe is rather limited. In 2000, Romania employed a German PR agency to downplay the damage of the second biggest disaster in the region after Chernobyl. Cyanide leaked from a gold mine in Romania into the river Tisza in Hungary where tens of thousands of fish and other forms of wildlife were killed, flora and fauna completely destroyed and drinking-water supplies poisoned. The campaign aimed at downplaying the effects of the catastrophe and at discrediting the Hungarian government by stating that it had exaggerated the damage. The Romanian government also banned the shooting of a film about Romanian gypsies as it shed a very negative light on the country before its accession to the EU. The negative publicity about the ban resulted in more harm to the country and its government.

Albania's government commissioned an international consultancy in 2005 to change the country's image as a backward corrupt state and to replace with an investor-friendly image of Albania. With daily electricity cuts and lack of infrastructure, however, a campaign can only be an example of perception management.

Russia provides endless examples of perception management. The Russian government and the Russian president have engaged in several "image" campaigns soon after the government's or Putin's image has suffered. Putin used an international PR agency in preparation for the presidential elections in 2000 when an international media and advocacy campaign was developed to explain policies on the war in Chechnya and his approaches to economic and social reforms to Western opinion leaders. In 2006 the Kremlin decided to engage in another international media campaign in the UK, USA and China to 'correct the negative and outdated stereotypes about Russia' and to give the country's image a makeover ahead of the G8 summit with the help of an American public relations agency[55]. The Western media's portrayal of Russia is still often dominated by stereotypes and prejudices, and largely focuses on negative issues.

Russia's negative image further deteriorated in 2006 with the assassination of Anna Politovskaya, a critic of the president and the government and with the poisoning of the former Russian spy, Alexander Litvinenko. A former KGB agent was named as the prime suspect for the murder and Britain made several unsuccessful attempts to extradite him. As retaliation Russian authorities forced the British Council to close two of its offices in Russia in January 2008: a clear attack on the cultural and public diplomacy front rather than using traditional diplomacy. David Miliband, the British Foreign Secretary's response, was pertinent. He said that Russian actions against the British Council were "a stain on its reputation" while a British diplomat "branded" the attack as "punching a librarian." Any campaigns to improve Russia's image in the West following these events and atrocities could only be classified as perception management.

Russia has very negative (in some cases even hostile) images among many Eastern European countries and has so far failed to address its negative reputation in its former sphere of influence. Moscow has attempted several times to discredit the Baltic states and to put them in a bad light about the role they have played in the Russian-EU relationship. Russia has been reluctant to acknowledge the independence of these states and heavily criticised their accession to NATO and EU and also refused to apologise to the Baltic States for annexing them to the Soviet Union and for the communist repressions. Russia also tried to make the most of the large Russian-speaking minorities[56] often manipulating them to its advantage.

The Estonian government's decision to remove a Soviet war monument from the center of Tallinn to a military cemetery in 2007 provoked rioting in Tallinn by local Russians. As revenge, a massive campaign against Estonia and its government was launched. Russia's deputy prime minister called on Russians to boycott Estonian goods and service as a punishment and encouraged Russians not to go to Estonia for holiday. The Estonian embassy in Moscow came under a blockade, followed by a cyber-attack where Estonian governmental, media, financial and telecommunication web-sites were attacked, defaced or replaced by Russian propaganda materials. Russia also intensified its propaganda machine to portray Estonia in a negative light. This bullying resulted in Russia's poor image further deteriorating in the European Union.

Besides the ad hoc perception management campaigns, the Russian government has recently started to be more consistent and pay more attention to its public diplomacy efforts. In 2005, a monthly English-language magazine *Russia Profile* was launched followed by *Russia Today*, a

24-hour, English-language TV station to provide "first-hand news" about Russia with an annual budget of $30 million. Voice of Russia broadcasts in 33 languages to a worldwide radio audience and there are Russian Cultural Centres in 62 countries. The National Information Centre was set up in January 2008 to provide "open" media information and help the work of foreign journalists based in Moscow. For maintaining stability in Russia and the region, *TIME* magazine chose President Putin as the Person of the Year 2007 which boosted his image.

According to Tsygankov,[57] contrary to the popular image of Russia as an aggressive and imperialistic states, Russian foreign policy is driven by domestic priorities, including economic growth and stability and soft power, as well as addressing security threats rather than Russia being a threat to the West. As a part of its soft power, for example, the government is keen to promote the Russian language as the regional lingua franca. As Tsygankov notes, a serious obstacle to mutual understanding between the West and Russia is the Western nations' attitudes toward non-Western countries, which are not viewed as equal partners.

By definition public diplomacy involves a country's government. Any campaigns and initiatives that address foreign public opinion and originate from the Russian government will not be credible in the West. In this sense Russian and American public diplomacy efforts have much in common: they both try to persuade foreign publics that their government's (foreign) policies and actions are legitimate and justified. Instead of changing their policies, they try to change the perceptions of foreign publics. Both the US and Russian governments are puzzled and surprised why their countries have such negative images worldwide.

Mistakes of Reputation Management

The challenges and experiences of Central European countries' reputation management include valuable "lessons" that can be useful to small and medium-sized states as well as to countries in political and/or economic transition.

- *Lack of co-ordination among the pillars of reputation management* (destination and country branding, public and cultural diplomacy). There is no synergy and collaboration among these functions or one of them is overemphasized over the others.
- *No strategic co-ordination among the institutions and actors involved in country promotion.* This could result in uncoordinated messages and the lack of consistency.
- There is a danger of mixing the subject and the specialisation of reputation management. The failed attempt of Branding America in the Arab world, co-ordinated by Charlotte Beers, the branding expert, well demonstrates what happens when foreign policy becomes the subject of branding. A branding-driven approach to public diplomacy can be risky and counterproductive. This substitution game can result in the loss of credibility. Reality and image should always correspond otherwise the messages are not credible and can only further harm the country's already negative reputation.
- Reputation management is *politicised* and it becomes the victim of domestic politics, especially when there is no agreement among the different political parties about how or by whom the country's reputation should be managed abroad. Many Central European countries' branding initiatives came to a halt with the change of government and lack of continuity has prevented the evolution and development of strong and coherent nation brands.
- This can also lead to the *lack of continuity in and strategic approach to reputation management*. Another barrier to continuity is the high turnover of staff and professionals as many of those who developed or worked in public diplomacy or branding at the beginning have moved on.

- *National reputation management or governmental reputation management?* If there is no consensus among political parties about the need and implementation of country promotion, the opposition can easily discredit any governmental initiatives as propagandist. In August 2006 the Polish government appointed a Plenipotentiary to safeguard and promote the image of Poland abroad. The newly appointed Polish Plenipotentiary was quick to dismiss any charges of propaganda. His appointment followed a satirical article published by a left-wing German newspaper about Polish President Lech Kaczynski. The article described him as a "potato" and criticized him for his scepticism toward Germany. In response, the President demanded an apology from Chancellor Angela Merkel's government, which refused to interfere. The German media has dubbed the dispute "the potato war."
- *Lack of financial and human resources*, which is a common problem in each CEE country but innovative and creative approaches to reputation management can save money.
- *Lack of transparency and lack of evaluation.* National reputation management is often financed from the central budget. That is why it should be clearly explained how the money is spent and the whole project should be transparent. Evaluation during and after any campaigns is also of crucial importance.
- *Short-term effects and thinking rather than long-term.* Some elements of reputation management are more visible and easier to measure (e.g. tourists, foreign students) but reputation building can easily take decades and is a slow process. Public diplomacy campaigns may be short term as well as long term. Governments, especially before national elections, can use results of reputation management as justification for their own success and to impress voters. In this case the government strives for short-term and visible impacts from branding and public diplomacy campaigns.

Conclusion

This chapter has outlined the evolution of reputation management in Central Europe, a transitional region which has accumulated two decades of experience. Destination and country branding, cultural and public diplomacy together with perception management were conceptualized as the specializations of international public relations. In the Central European context public diplomacy is conceptualized as foreign policy's communication dimension which contributes to establishing and maintaining mutually beneficial relationships between a governmental organization and foreign publics. As the foreign policy goals of many European Union countries are converging and foreign policy cooperation is on the increase at the EU level, public diplomacy will have a more crucial role for a member state in communicating with other countries and peoples.

In 1994, a few years into the political and economic transition, Wolffs[58] argued that although the iron curtain is gone, its shadow persists. With the growing professionalization of reputation management, and with the fruitful cooperation among Central European countries, this shadow is slowly fading away.

Notes

1 M. Nelson, *War of the Black Heavens: The Battles of Western Broadcasting in the Cold War* (Syracuse: Syracuse University Press, 1997); Carnes Lord, "The Past and Future of Public Diplomacy," *Orbis* 42, no. 1 (1998): 49–73; Yale Richmond, *Cultural Exchange and the Cold War: Raising the Iron Curtain* (University Park, PA: University of Pennsylvania Press, 2003).
2 The BBC World Service, for example, ceased broadcasting in Bulgarian, Croatian, Czech, Hungarian, Kazakh, Polish, Slovak, and Slovene in 2005/06 due to reprioritization, eliminating decades of

broadcasting in these languages. The British Council is to close its information centers and libraries in Latvia, Lithuania, Estonia, Hungary, Slovenia, and Slovakia in 2008 to reallocate resources to the Middle East.

3 L. Wolff, *Inventing Eastern Europe: The Map of Civilization on the Mind of the Enlightenment* (Stanford, California: Stanford University Press, 1994).

4 Slovenia, Hungary, Lithuania, Slovakia, Poland, the Czech Republic, Estonia, and Latvia became EU members in 2004, followed by Bulgaria and Romania in 2007.

5 D.L. Wilcox, P.H. Ault, W.K. Agee, and G.T. Cameron, *Essentials of Public Relations* (New York: Longman, 2001).

6 A. Cooper, *Niche Diplomacy: Middle Powers After the Cold War* (London: Macmillan, 1997).

7 Slovenia is the first country from Eastern Europe to run the EU for a six-month period from January 2008, followed by the Czech Republic from January 2009.

8 The Czech Republic, Hungary, and Poland joined NATO in 1999, followed by the three Baltic States, Slovakia, Slovenia, Romania, and Bulgaria in 2004.

9 Hungary will introduce English as a compulsory foreign language at secondary schools from 2010. During communism Russian was compulsory in the countries under Soviet influence.

10 http://www.missioneurope.eu.

11 This is applicable to any country and region in transition, not only Eastern Europe.

12 http://www3.lrs.lt/pls/inter2/dokpaieska.showdoc_l?p_id=232603.

13 M. Zaborowski and K. Longhurst, "America's Protégé in the East?: The Emergence of Poland as a Regional Leader," *International Affairs* 79, no. 5 (2003): 1009–1028.

14 See György Szondi, "The role and challenges of country branding in transition countries: The Central and Eastern Europe experience," *Place Branding and Public Diplomacy* 3, no. 1 (2007): 8–20; and G. Szondi, "The Eastern European referendum campaigns on the accession to the European Union—a critical analysis," *Journal of Public Affairs* 7, no. 1 (2007): 55–69.

15 Although the Polish version of the website calls the department "Department of Promotion" and only the English version of the website uses the term "Public Diplomacy."

16 http://www.mfa.gov.pl/Organization,chart,2142.html.

17 http://www.ipr.org.uk/direct/careers.asp?v1=whatis.

18 S.M. Cutlip, A.H. Center, G.N. Broom, *Effective Public Relations*, 9th Edition, (Upper Saddle River, New Jersey: Prentice-Hall International, 2006).

19 K. Nessmann, "Public Relations in Europe: A Comparison with the United States," *Public Relations Review* 21, no. 2 (1995): 151–160.

20 See James E. Grunig, "Public relations and international affairs: Effects, ethics and responsibility," *Journal of International Affairs* 47, no. 1 (1993): 138–161; and S. Yun, "Toward Public Relations Theory-Based Study of Public Diplomacy: Testing the Applicability of the Excellence Study," *Journal of Public Relations Research* 18, no. 4, 287–312.

21 B. Signitzer and C. Wamser, "Public Diplomacy: A Specific Governmental Public Relations Function," in *Public Relations Theory II*, ed. C. Botan and V. Hazleton (Mahwah, New Jersey: Lawrence Erlbaum Associates, 2006).

22 The public relations literature refers to this process as "issues management."

23 György Szondi, "International Context of Public Relations," in *Exploring Public Relations*, ed. R. Tench and L. Yeomans (London: FT/Prentice Hall, 2006), 112–140.

24 Michael Kunczik, *Images of Nations and International Public Relations* (Mahwah, NJ: Lawrence Erlbaum Associates, 1997).

25 An example of this is a conference, devoted to images in International Relations (Chong, A. and Valencic, J. (1999). *The Image, the State and International Relations*. Proceedings from the conference on 24 June 1999 at the London School of Economics and Political Science. EFPU Working Papers No.2001/2.) but branding, image, public relations, advertising, and public diplomacy are used interchangeably without clear conceptualization.

26 James E. Grunig, "Image and substance: From symbolic to behavioral relationships," *Public Relations Review*, 19 (1993): 121–139.

27 György Szondi, "The Pantheon of International Public Relations for Nation States – Country Promotion in Central and Eastern Europe" Paper presented at the 4th Public Relations International Conference 'Introducing Market Economy Instruments and Institutions - the Role of Public Relations in Transition Economies', 16–19th June 2005, Poznan, Poland.

28 See, for example, the *Financial Times'* special country reports on Hungary (December 12, 2005), Bulgaria (July 12, 2006), Croatia (October 30, 2006), Slovenia (December 13, 2006), Poland (20 December 2006), Romania (2 March 2007); or *The Economist's* survey on Poland, May 13, 2006.

29 Wally Olins, *Trading Identities: Why Countries and Companies Are Becoming More Alike* (London: The Foreign Policy Centre, October 1999).

30 G. Szondi, "The role and challenges of country branding in transition countries: The Central and Eastern Europe experience," *Place Branding and Public Diplomacy* 3, no. 1 (2006): 8–20.

31 Ibid.

32 Peter van Ham, "Branding Territory: Inside the Wonderful Worlds of PR and IR Theory," *Millennium* 31, no. 2 (2002): 249–269; Peter van Ham, "War, Lies, and Videotape: Public Diplomacy and the USA's War on Terrorism," *Security Dialogue* 34, no. 4 (2003): 427–444; Simon Anholt, *Brand New Justice: The upside of global branding* (Oxford: Butterworth-Heinemann, 2003); Jan Melissen, "Public diplomacy: in tandem with branding," in *Government Communication: The Dutch Experience.* Government Information Service, Ministry of General Affairs (The Hague: Opmeer Printing, 2005); J. Kahn, "A Brand-New Approach," *Foreign Policy* (November/December 2006:): 90–92.

33 Branding scholars and practitioners often refer to "nation branding" instead of state or country branding, using nation and state as synonyms.

34 van Ham, op. cit.

35 György Szondi, "Country Promotion and Image Management – The Case of Hungary" in *Nation Branding. Concepts, Issues, Practice,* K. Dinnie (Oxford: Butterworth-Heinemann, 2008).

36 J. Michael Sproule, "The new managerial rhetoric and the old criticism," *Quarterly Journal of Speech* 74 (1988): 474.

37 H. Chartrand, "International cultural affairs: A 14 country survey," *Journal of Arts Management, Law & Society* 22, no. 2 (1992): 134–154.

38 J.M. Mitchell, *International Cultural Relations* (London: Allen & Unwin, 1986).

39 http://www.einst.ee.

40 As quoted in *The Economist*, May 14, 2005, 46.

41 G. Malone, "Managing Public Diplomacy," *Washington Quarterly* 8, no. 3 (1985): 199.

42 Ibid.

43 Howard Frederick, *Global Communication and International Relations* (Belmont, CA: Wadsworth Publishing, 1993).

44 C. Kegley and E. Wittkopf, *World Politics: Trend and Transformation* (Boston, New York: Bedford/St. Martin's, 1999).

45 György Szondi, "The Eastern European referendum campaigns on the accession to the European Union—a critical analysis," *Journal of Public Affairs* 7, no. 1 (2007): 55–69.

46 B. Ociepka and M. Ryniejska, "Public Diplomacy and EU Enlargement: the Case of Poland Clingendael," Discussion Paper in Diplomacy 99. The Hague: Clingendael Institute, 2005, http://www.clingendael.nl/publications/2005/20050800_cli_paper_dip_issue99.pdf.

47 J. Habermas and J. Derrida, "February 15, or What Binds Europeans Together: Plea for Common Foreign Policy, Beginning Core Europe," in *Old Europe, New Europe, Core Europe. Transatlantic Relations After the Iraq War,* ed. D. Levy, M. Pensky and J. Torpey (London, New York: Verso, 2005).

48 R. Fawn, "Alliance Behaviour, the Absentee Liberator and the Influence of Soft Power: Post-communist State Positions over the Iraq War in 2003," *Cambridge Review of International Affairs* 19, no. 3 (2006): 465–480.

49 A. Bienczyk-Missala, *Human Rights in Polish Foreign Policy after 1989* (Warszawa: The Polish Institute of International Affairs, 2006).

50 Nye, J. Jr. (2004). *Soft Power. The Means to Success in World Politics.* New York: Public Affairs.

51 http://www.mvpei.hr/MVP.asp?pcpid=1765

52 http://quiz.mfa.ee/default.asp

53 D.R. Browne, *International Radio Broadcasting: The limits of the limitless medium* (New York: Praeger, 1982).

54 Personal interview with Mrs. Agnieszka Romaszewska-Guzy, Wroclaw, Poland, May 24, 2007.

55 Details of the award winning public relations campaign are available at http://www.prweekus.com/Global-Campaign-of-the-Year-2007/article/57918.

56 The Russian minority is made up 29% of the Latvian population, 26% of the Estonian population and 8% of the Lithuanians.

57 Tsygankov, A. (2006) Projecting Confidence, Not Fear: Russia's Post-Imperial Assertiveness *Orbis*, Vol.50. Issue 4. pp. 677–690.

58 Larry Wolff, *Inventing Eastern Europe: The Map of Civilization on the Mind of the Enlightenment* (Stanford, California: Stanford University Press, 1994).

26

Australian Public Diplomacy

Naren Chitty

In some ways Australian public diplomacy is a *terra nullus*. In fields related to international relations, it is the research community within a country that usually shows the greatest interest in mapping out the terrain, staking claim to ontographies, definitions, and research priorities. From a research perspective, except for a few isolated studies, Australian public diplomacy is a somewhat empty field. On the other hand, if practice rather than research is the yardstick, the landscape is bustling with activity. However, research interest may be about to dawn over it, illuminating established practice in Australia. The spurs for similar awakening of interest in the United States have been the difficulty for the US in forming military coalitions with its allies and the ease with which Islamist terrorist networks recruit members, when there is a negative climate of public opinion towards the US in parts of the world.[1] The Australian Senate has joined concerned sister parliamentary bodies in Britain and the United States by inquiring, in 2007, into public diplomacy.[2] In so doing, it has opened up the frontiers of Australian public diplomacy; exploration should follow. Hopefully teams of researchers will now begin to stake their claims. This chapter is a "post Senate Inquiry" discussion of Australian public diplomacy, placing it in front of a holistic backdrop. It discusses a holistic diplomacy before looking at the Australian context of practice. Following this it explores the Senate Committee's report and recommendations and maps out some possible areas for research.

A Holistic Diplomacy

International diplomacy has always served a cybernetic function in society. It facilitates purposive intergovernmental communication through negotiation, representation, and reporting. In addition to projecting their governments' views abroad (representation), diplomats capture, for their governments, views from abroad that are pertinent to national interest (reporting). These views may be of developments abroad or they may be views from abroad of developments at home. While the types of actors and venues have expanded to include extra governmental and extra territorial forms, the cybernetic function of diplomacy continues—if this is identified as the interfacing of the interdepartmental cybernetic system of a nation state with external actors and the international environment. Interactions with other interdepartmental systems through nodes such as ministries of foreign affairs, embassies, departments of trade and commerce and so on, continue to play important roles in the transaction of diplomacy. Venues such as foreign

314

ministries and intergovernmental conferences also continue to loom large in the prosecution of diplomatic objectives.

What has changed are the contexts of diplomacy. These have shifted, seeping out from private to public venues, mediated and otherwise. Today, media reports on and influences public opinion in areas of public interest including foreign policy. New media technology also allows other states, corporations, non-government organizations, rogue organizations, and individuals, to publish news and views at will. Governments have to deal with this new context of diplomacy that is conducted publicly and incessantly. In my view public diplomacy should not merely be a therapeutic response by government to an overseas public's adverse reaction to foreign policy or a government's response to negative portrayal of a nation state overseas. Ideally it should include the growing of foreign policy in a nursery of mutual understanding,[3] under a greenhouse of constructive transparency.

There have been discussions of differences between argumentation, deliberation, and persuasion, strategic communication and rule-guided institutionalism. Persuasion had previously been an important concept in international communication, through Lasswell and Lerner's inquiries into wartime propaganda and the propaganda of modernization, dark and light sides of persuasion.[4] This chiaroscuro continues to influence perceptions and practices of public diplomacy. The strategic aspects of public diplomacy condemn it in the eyes of many as being contrary to dialogical Habermasian ethical communication.[5] Recognizing that propaganda as technique can differ from propaganda as content, there have been proposals that aspects of propaganda theory be married with contemporary communication effects theory.[6] The limitations of effects are implicit in cultural approaches that take account of diasporic textures and multiple patriotisms and the challenges to public diplomacy resulting from diasporization have surfaced at recent policy inquiries.[7] Basic definitions are disputed even when the term is equated with strategic communication, which can mean variously support for military missions, program reform, performance measurability, interagency cooperation, or "a comprehensive communication strategy intended to support national security interests and values;" institutional responsibilities are also viewed as varied from outreach agencies to foreign ministries and militaries.[9] A strategic public diplomacy perspective should inform foreign policy development as well as the management of image and diplomatic events and activities. It should include feedforward and feedback loops (including from domestic publics) into policy formulation as well as public diplomacy strategizing and managing. Modern foreign ministries need public diplomacy strategists and public diplomacy practitioners. Strategy is best served by multi-disciplinary teams drawing on experts in foreign policy, political communication, strategic communication, international public relations, and the specialist subject area under consideration. Practitioners of the new public diplomacy need to have skills associated with new media and information technologies and/or public relations, rather than with diplomatic negotiation.

Despite the changes in context there are foreign ministries and other governmental and non-governmental parties as well as scholars, who argue as to whether public diplomacy should mean diplomacy conducted in public, for publics, by publics, or with publics. Examination of brief self-descriptions of relevant British and US organs provides useful insights. The Public Diplomacy Board of the Foreign and Commonwealth Office (FCO) of Britain views public diplomacy as an external oriented activity and differentiates between itself as the strategy charting, fund allocating and performance evaluating agency and services such as the BBC World Service, British Council, British Satellite News, and i-uk.com as well as various FCO-funded scholarships, projects, and events. The United States government views public diplomacy as consisting primarily of "three categories of activities: (1) international information programs, (2) educational and cultural exchange programs, and (3) international nonmilitary broadcasting." The Under Secretary of State for Public Diplomacy and Public Affairs administers the Bureau for International Information Programs and the Bureau for Educational and

Cultural Affairs, while the Broadcasting Board of Governors manages and oversees international broadcasting.[10]

There are other views that "embrace diplomacy, cultural diplomacy, international broadcasting, political communication, democracy building, and open military information operations."[11] In both instances there is a clear view that public diplomacy needs to be directed externally. This view has developed because of the historical suspicion that public diplomacy is rebranded propaganda. The fact that publicity was anathema to the traditional diplomat provided oxygen to this view in its development.

Conventional closed-door elite-to-elite diplomacy came into its own during a period when realpolitik foregrounded the conduct of international relations. The omnipresence and omniscience of new media and information technologies and the spreading internationally of the values of civil society have contributed to the foregrounding of soft power (noopolitik)[12] and drawn aspects of diplomacy out into the open, as an aspect of public diplomacy. The spread of civil society values may be described in terms of two developments. First a high value has been placed in liberal democracies on a healthy public sphere, where politics can be discussed outside of government without fear of retribution. Second, public opinion polling and the use of poll results as commodities by news organizations and political capital by political organizations have become commonplace. As we observe, the importance that even countries that cannot be described as liberal democracies place on public opinion in liberal democracies, has made image management an issue for them as well.

International public relations, a term that is broader than public diplomacy because it does not begin with a state-centric bias, has squeezed the public into international relations. Grunig's four models of public relations may be applied here as much as in the business sector. His ideal typical models range from (1) the uni-directional communication of press agentry/publicity (anything for attention); (2) public information (accentuate the positive); (3) one-way asymmetrical models (research audiences to improve information acceptance); and his prescribed (4) two-way symmetrical model where "practitioners use research and dialogue to bring about symbiotic changes in the ideas, attitudes, and behaviours of both the organization and its publics."[13] In the two-way symmetrical model there is a dialogue with stakeholders that can result in mutual change, change in both the stakeholder and the communicating organization.[14] If we now return to the term public diplomacy, carrying with us Grunig's logic, we may construct a public diplomacy that sits more comfortably with Habermasian communicative action.[15]

Public diplomacy in the contemporary world consists of multiple approaches for the public sector, in engagement with second sector (businesses), third sector (NGOs), fourth estate/sector (media) organizations, and nationwide participation in participatory development of a foreign policy that has support at home and respect and credibility abroad, while serving national interest. Normatively, I would argue, visibility in foreign policy governance cultures, structures, and programs should be promoted. The greater the commitment to and practice of transparency in diplomacy, including and particularly by leading states, the greater will be the sense of security.

My discussion of the Report on Public Diplomacy by the Australian Senate will be informed by the above definition and propositions. Additionally I base my analysis under four rubrics, viz. instrumentality, structure, participation, and scope. Structure refers here to whether operators are conceptualized as being solely within the first sector, whether the first sector coopts or coordinates operatives from other sectors and the fourth estate, or whether other operatives are viewed as free agents. Scope refers to whether audiences are considered to be exclusively external and foreign (as is officially the case in Britain and the United States) or also includes one's own diaspora and one's domestic audiences. Instrumentality refers to how one conceives of public diplomacy, whether as a tool to spread values or as a value-neutral tool associated with techniques. Finally, participation refers to the drawing of public diplomacy into a wider scheme of governance by listening to audiences and being wedded to the interests of one's citizens in relation to foreign policy issues. Clearly, from the submissions received by the Australian Senate Committee, organizations and individuals from the public and third sectors and the fourth estate/sector felt that they had a stake in Australia's public diplomacy. Submissions, written or oral, were received by the Senate Inquiry from over 30 institutions and individuals.[16] It should be explained that most of Australia's universities are state (as opposed to federal) institutions, though in some ways, as critical spaces in society, they may fit more comfortably into the third sector. Submissions received from the second and third sectors and the fourth estate have not been reviewed in this chapter. The federal level government agency stakeholders who made submissions, and whose submissions have been reviewed, are as follows:

Australian Broadcasting Corporation (ABC)
Australian Agency for International Development (AusAID)
Australia Council of the Arts (ACA)
Australia Film Commission (AFC)
Australian Sports Commission (ASC)
Department of Agriculture, Fisheries and Forestry (DAFF)
Australia Film Commission (AFC)
Australian Sports Commission (ASC)
Department of Agriculture, Fisheries and Forestry (DAFF)
Department of Education, Science and Training (DEST)
Department of Defence (DOD)
Department of Foreign Affairs and Trade (DFAT)
Invest Australia (IA)

As one would expect, DFAT sees itself as carrying "the primary responsibility for implementing Australia's public and cultural diplomacy programs on behalf of the Government to advance our foreign and trade policy objectives."[17] DFAT reports that public diplomacy has been mainstreamed in the organization. Expenditure on public diplomacy was AUD187 million in 2005. Its "Images of Australia" branch (established in 1999) is responsible for overall management of public diplomacy activities, focusing on overseas operations but also including public advocacy on trade, arms control, counter-terrorism, environment, and human rights both at home and abroad. It cooperates with other federal, state, and local government agencies as well as non-government organizations in furthering Australia's public diplomacy.[18]

DFAT undertakes its public diplomacy under three temporal strategies, viz. (1) responding to threats and opportunities in the daily news cycle; (2) planning the shaping of national image over weeks or months; and (3) long-term relationship-building (DFAT 2007). DFAT allocates AUD1 million to the Australian International Cultural Council (AICC) that was established in 1998 by the Minister. AICC includes a senior officials group drawn from DFAT; ACA; Department of Communications, Information Technology and Arts; Austrade, AFC, Tourism Australia as well as state-level representation. DFAT has a raft of methods for monitoring impact of public diplomacy. These are:

1 reports on departmental programs;
2 exit interviews for program participants;
3 press monitoring;
4 annual plans from overseas posts including anecdotal evidence of attitudinal change;
5 reports from bilateral agencies; and
6 modest opinion surveys.

DFAT also undertakes public diplomacy training in Australia and at overseas centers. AusAID and the ASC both are economically telogenic and identify the construction of development partnerships as their broad strategic goal in contributing to Australia's public diplomacy efforts (AusAID 2007; ASA 2007). AusAID identifies "partnerships with key international, regional and Australian stakeholders [that] are critical to quality development cooperation" emphasizing "harmonization and alignment of development cooperation activities between donors and partner countries, and among donors."[19]

ABC has public diplomacy functions identified in the Australian Broadcasting Corporation Act of 1983: It is meant to "(1) encourage awareness of Australia and an international understanding of Australian attitudes on world affairs; and (2) enable Australian citizens living or travelling outside Australia to obtain information about Australian affairs and Australian attitudes on world affairs." According to its report it seeks to fulfill this task through Radio Australia, Australia Network (set up in August 2001) under tender from the Department of Foreign Affairs and Trade. It also engages in interagency public diplomacy with counterpart agencies abroad and broadcasting associations. Notably the report only mentions the web as a feedback mechanism rather than as a platform for delivering ABC news and views to the Australian diaspora and overseas publics.[20] The Institute of Public Affairs criticized ABC, in its submission to the Senate Inquiry, for failing to promote positively common themes in Australian values, with respect to liberal democracy, human rights, and free markets. Unlike the Voice of America in the US, ABC has a role as the major state-owned broadcaster, on the lines of the British Broadcasting Corporation. The ACA promotes cultural diplomacy through its (1) Aboriginal and Torres Strait Islander Arts Board; (2) the Arts Development Division (for dance, literature, music, theatre, visual arts, and inter-arts); (3) Community Partnerships and Market Development Division; and (4) Major Performing Arts Board. The AFC sees itself helping to establish "an international profile through screen culture [that] also delivers tangible economic benefits for Australian through tourism and trade." It engages in public diplomacy through its membership of the Australian International Cultural Council (AICC). DAFF identifies (1) market access and reputation; (2) biosecurity; and (3) emergency preparedness as its three broad public diplomacy objectives, in its brief submission (DAFF 2007). Two of these may be classified as security related.

DEST identifies education and training through Australian Education International (AEI), the DEST International Network with operatives on the ground in the Asia-Pacific, the Americas, Western Europe, and the Middle East; "Study in Australia" which promotes Australia as an educational brand, collaborating with Tourism Australia "to ensure consistency of messages across the two brands;" the 27-country Brisbane Communiqué on education; scholarships that further Australia's foreign policy objectives particularly in the Asia-Pacific region while portraying the non-commercial altruistic and externally oriented sides of Australia; science diplomacy; and International Centres of Excellence. DETYA is a member of the DFAT 20-agency Inter-Departmental Committee on Public Diplomacy.[21] DOD promotes public awareness of overseas defense activities in order "to contribute to national interest by ensuring the nature of such activities is understood by public as well as official audiences," engaging broadly with the region in naval exercises and visits, defense cooperation, infrastructure reconstruction, relationship building in Timor-Leste and the Solomon Islands, and humanitarian assistance.

Senate Committee Recommendations and Research Possibilities

The Senate Committee recognized the range of governmental, non-governmental and private organizations contributing to Australia's public diplomacy efforts. While commending Australian agencies engaged in public diplomacy, the Senate Committee noted that Australia faces "fierce competition" with other countries to have itself heard in a "highly contested international space."[22] There are many players in the orchestra of Australian public diplomacy, performing "Waltzing Matilda" sans score or conductor. The performance is out in the open and there are competing orchestras, from Canada, the UK, the US, and other nations, playing their own national favorites. How does Australia ensure that it is heard above the din?

The Senate Committee reported that "Australia's lack of interest in public diplomacy is evident when compared with the growing body of literature on public diplomacy produced overseas and at recent international conferences and seminars discussing all aspects of public diplomacy."[23] The lack of scholarly interest in the area of public diplomacy is of concern. Whether from critical approaches, supporting dialogic communication and encompassing the domestic public sphere, or administrative perspectives supporting the improvement of strategic communication (from the point of view of effectiveness of expenditure on public diplomacy) or shades of grey in between, research in this area must be of crucial concern to a great liberal democracy such as Australia.

The Senate Committee adopted the "basic concept that public diplomacy is work or activities undertaken to understand, inform and engage individuals and organisations in other countries in order to shape their perceptions in ways that will promote Australia and Australia's policy goals internationally." In this it was not unlike the organs in Britain and the US referred to above. However, it applied "this definition of public diplomacy in both an expanded and contracted sense according to the matters under investigation" using "the expanded understanding of public diplomacy when it is considering: the coherence, consistency and credibility of Australia's public diplomacy messages; the nature of Australia's dialogue and engagement with the international community; and the coordination of public diplomacy activities." Acknowledging that AusAID and Defence are "not primarily concerned with public diplomacy" it views their work as having "an important by-product" that "contributes significantly to Australia's international reputation." The committee showed interest "in exploring how the work of these agencies, as well as cultural and educational institutions and other groups including Australia's diaspora, intersects with Australia's public diplomacy."

The Senate Committee made 18 specific recommendations that I have discussed below. There are two recommendations under "Tracking opinion in target countries." Under recommendation 1, the Senate Committee was keen that Australia's image should be tracked in key countries, that "wide-ranging community consultation" be undertaken domestically regarding Australia's foreign policy; and that organizations be encouraged to participate actively in public diplomacy. Construction of national image may be managed by public diplomacy strategists and communicated through media, but as reception theory and polysemic approaches suggest, received images may be reconstructed by media users. There also are a wide range of national image categories, ranging from political to popular cultural, and there are many technologies of delivery, from modern mass media to postmodern interactive and self-selective technologies. We know that different generational cohorts use different technologies to access different messages for different purposes, purposes ranging from entertainment to education. Recommendation 1, if it is to be pursued effectively, will need to take into account these realities. In seeking to measure the effectiveness of Australian image-building campaigns in the United States, for instance, in my view it is important that qualitative and quantitative studies be undertaken across a range of media, generations, and issues. The stated interest in community consultation on Australia's foreign policy and trade policies is indeed gratifying: In the public hearing of the Senate Inquiry in April 2007, mine was a rather solitary voice that sought to enlarge public diplomacy to involve dialogic communication with the domestic audience. In my view consultation with the Australian public on foreign policy views should be linked with a public education program about key issues. Public information campaigns to be conducted by ABC are envisaged under Recommendation 2. In this connection, there is scope for research on the public's knowledge of important issue areas. Grunig's two-way symmetrical model would be one on which to reflect.

Research by academics on attitudes among policy communities to greater public participation in the foreign policy debate, would also be useful. Organizations, non-government or even non-federal government organizations, that engage in public diplomacy are targeted in Recommendation 2 for encouragement in participating in public diplomacy programs. These agencies are also expedient targets of research. For instance there is scope for studying the public diplomacy efforts of states, cities, municipalities, and boroughs, as well as non-government organizations.

There are three recommendations under "People-to-people links." Recommendations 3 and 4 call for more effective use of educational sojourns and visitors' programs respectively. There is useful research that can be conducted about "before and after" opinions of groups of sojourners and visitors. Recommendation 5 is that Australian students should be given additional incentives to study Asian languages and culture.

There is a declaration under the rubric of "Coordination:" that "Australia needs a whole-of-government approach to its public diplomacy programs." While this may be the way in which a government would describe an operation, what this means in the context of people-to-people links, is a whole-of-society approach. Recommendation 6 calls for the IDC to be designated as the central oversight organ. It calls for the IDC to have more senior representation; broader functions; responsibility for ensuring interdepartmental synergies; responsibility for strategic planning and prioritization; acknowledge the role of local government, non-state stakeholders and the Australian diaspora; some cross-membership with AICC; publish meeting reports; establish a subcommittee to incorporate non-state stakeholders and diasporic communities "into an overarching public diplomacy framework;" establish a subcommittee to ensure "that Australia's public diplomacy stays at the forefront of developments in technology." Comparative research into public diplomacy structures in partner countries and Australia would contribute to the development of an appropriate structure for Australia.

Recommendation 8, under "Local councils and public diplomacy" recommends more effective collaboration between federal and metropolitan levels of government in the area of public diplomacy. Interestingly, there is no mention of the state level. Useful research may be conducted on the various public diplomacy efforts of local and state governments. In Australia, citizenship is conferred by local mayors in ceremonies where the federal government is represented. New citizens often continue to have connections with their old countries. They are members of the Australia-based diaspora of their former countries. Are these ceremonies then to be considered as elements of public diplomacy? How do local governments in Australia and other countries see their roles in public diplomacy?

There are three recommendations under the subheading "Cultural Institutions." Recognizing the role of cultural institutions in cultural diplomacy, Recommendation 9 calls for AICC to address the concerns expressed, that AICC be co-chaired by the Ministers of Foreign Affairs and Arts and Sports; that a cultural and public diplomacy unit be set up in the DOC. The area is rich in research opportunities. The role of major sports events or mediated culture in the construction of image would be matters of great interest.

There are notes and statements of belief but no formal recommendations under "Training for Diplomacy" and "Diplomacy as a mainstream activity." It is noted under the heading that while "all DFAT officers should be skilled in the art of public diplomacy . . . that not all can be trained specialists in the area of communications and public relations." Rejecting the notion of a specialized public diplomacy unit, it envisages a mainstreaming of public diplomacy, drawing on the skills of both specialists and generalists. Indeed under the rubric of diplomacy as a mainstream activity, the committee "recommends an independent survey of overseas posts to assess their capacity to conduct effective public diplomacy programs." There clearly are opportunities here for the involvement of research teams from the academic sector.

There is just one recommendation under "Modern technology." Recommendation 16 calls for DFAT to "explore the application of innovative technologies to enhance the delivery of its public diplomacy programs." There is here an opportunity for research collaboration with universities, particularly with researchers in the areas of intercultural communication, international communication, multimedia, public diplomacy, and public relations.

There is also just one recommendation under "Evaluation." Recommendation 17 prioritizes the institution by DFAT of "specific performance indicators that would allow it to both monitor and assess the effectiveness of its public diplomacy programs." "Evaluation" is juxtaposed with "Funding." The latter rubric lists two recommendations. Recommendation 19 is that DFAT should review the performance of FCIs (Foundation, Council, or Institute) in order to determine if funding levels should be increased. Recommendation 20 is that each FCI should report annually to Parliament. The Committee welcomed the "increased funding of $ 20.4 million over four years to enhance Australia's cultural exports." In addition to annual reports, the attention of the scholarly community through research projects can only serve to provide a better view of the work of FCIs so that they could continue to improve their activities.

While the submissions to the Australian Senate Inquiry into Public Diplomacy were lumpy, the report has recognized the role or possible role of players from various sectors, with the exception perhaps of states. The Second Sector (businesses) is also not afforded much attention. While defining public diplomacy in a fairly traditional external oriented way, it has, in terms of scope, recognized the need for involvement of the domestic public. It has broached the topic of participation of citizens in the discussion on public diplomacy. It has taken a largely strategic view of public diplomacy that is nationalist without being propagandist. Importantly it has placed public diplomacy on the political agenda in Australia. It would be serendipitous if this has contributed to the opening up of the area to the scholarly gaze.

Notes

1 Susan Epstein, U.S. Public Diplomacy: Background and the 911 Commission Recommendations (Washington D.C.: Library of Congress, Congressional Research Service, 2006), http://fpc.state.gov/documents/organization/66505.pdf.

2 Lord Carter of Cole chaired a Public Diplomacy Board that published a Review of Public Diplomacy (in the UK) in 2005.

3 In 1965 John Weir Burton launched a challenge to realpolitik in international relations from a platform of realism by arguing that states need to learn about each other's needs and expectations and mutually adapt to each other through this learning.

4 Harold Lasswell, *Propaganda technique in the World War* (New York: Smith, 1927); Naren Chitty, "Configuring the Future: Framing International Communication within World Politics in the 21st Century," *Journal of International Communication* 10, no. 2 (2004): 42–66.

5 Carl Botan, "Ethics in strategic communication campaigns: the case for a new approach to public relations," *Journal of Business Communication*, 1997.

6 Rebecca Curnalia, "A Retrospective on Early Studies of Propaganda and Suggestions for Reviving the Paradigm," *The Review of Communication* 5, no. 4 (2005): 237–257.

7 Arjun Appadurai, "Patriotism and its futures," In *Internationalizing Cultural Studies: An Anthology*, ed. Ackbar Abbas and John Nguyet Erni (eds). Malden: Blackwell Publishing, 413–415;

8 Naren Chitty, "Public Diplomacy: Developing Road Rules." Submission to the Senate Foreign Affairs, Defence and Trade Committee, Inquiry into the nature and conduct of Australia's public diplomacy, 2007; http://www.aph.gov.au/senate/committee/fadt_ctte/public_diplomacy/submissions/sub15.pdf; Naren Chitty, "Toward an inclusive public diplomacy in the world of fast capital and diasporas," International Conference on Foreign Ministries Adaptation to Change, Bangkok, Thailand, June 14–15, 2007; http://www.diplomacy.edu/Conferences/MFA2007/papers/chitty.pdf.

9 Bruce Gregory, "Public Diplomacy and Strategic Communication: Cultures, Firewalls, and Imported Norms." American Political Science Association Conference on International Communication and Conflict. Washington, D.C.: George Washington University, August 31, 2005, 46.

10 Epstein, 6.

11 Bruce Gregory, *Public Diplomacy and Strategic Communication: Cultures, Firewalls, and Imported Norms.* American Political Science Association Conference on International Communication and Conflict, George Washington University, August 31, 46 pp.

12 Noopolitik was coined by RAND scholars John Arquilla and David Ronfeldt in 1999.

13 James Grunig, "Two-way symmetrical public relations: Past, present and future," in *Handbook of Public Relations*, ed. R.L. Heath and G. Vasquez (Newbury Park, CA: Sage, 2001); Larissa Grunig, James E. Grunig and David M. Dozier, *Excellent Public Relations and Effective Organizations: A study of communication management in three countries* (London: Lawrence Erlbaum Associates, 2002).

14 James Grunig, 2005.

15 Jüergen Habermas, *The Structural Transformation of the Public Sphere* (Cambridge, MA: MIT Press, 1991); Jüergen Habermas, *Between Facts and Norms: Contributions to a Discourse Theory of Law and Democracy* (Cambridge, MA: MIT Press, 1996).

16 This is discussed in Naren Chitty, "Toward an inclusive public diplomacy in the world of fast capitalism and diasporas," Paper for presentation at the International Conference on "Foreign Ministries: Adaptation to a Changing World," June 14–15, 2007, Royal Orchid Sheraton, Bangkok, Thailand; http://www.diplomacy.edu/Conferences/MFA2007/papers/chitty.pdf.

17 DFAT 2007. Submission of the Department of Foreign Affairs and Trade to the Senate Standing Committee Inquiry into the Nature and Conduct of Australia's Public Diplomacy; http://www.aph.gov.au/Senate/committee/fadt_ctte/public_diplomacy/submissions/sub18.pdf.

18 Ibid.

19 AusAID 2007, Supplementary submission to the Senate Committee on Foreign Affairs, Defence and Trade Inquiry into the Nature and Conduct of Australia's Public Diplomacy; http://www.aph.gov.au/Senate/committee/fadt_ctte/public_diplomacy/submissions/sub25.pdf/sub22.pdf.

20 ABC 2007, Submission by Australian Broadcasting Corporation to the Senate Committee on Foreign Affairs, Defence and Trade Inquiry into the Nature and Conduct of Ausatralia's Public Diplomacy. Available at http://www.aph.gov.au/Senate/committee/fadt_ctte/public_diplomacy/submissions/sub22.pdf.

21 DEST 2007, Submission of the Department of Education, Science and Training to the Senate Standing Committee Inquiry into the Nature and Conduct of Australia's Public Diplomacy; http://www.aph.gov.au/Senate/committee/fadt_ctte/public_diplomacy/submissions/sub28.pdf.

22 Parliament of Australia. 2007. Senate. Australia'a Public Diplomacy: Building Our Image. Commonwealth of Australia; http://www.aph.gov.au/SEnate/committee/fadt_ctte/public_diplomacy/report/index.htm.

23 Ibid.

Part 6

Advancing Public Diplomacy Studies

How Globalization Became U.S. Public Diplomacy at the End of the Cold War

Joseph Duffey

In 1993, a few months after the inauguration of President Clinton, I accepted his nomination as Director of the U.S. Information Agency (USIA). It was a time of transition, an unsettling time, for the USIA. The Cold War was over. The months of celebration and the victory lap were behind us. What next? It might be argued that the "Cold War" had "ended" several times: with détente, in the early 1970s, with "coexistence" later. But several experiences of U.S. national humiliation, the Vietnam era, the Iranian revolution in the late 1970s, and the aftermath of the first Iraq war, had whetted the desire for a victory celebration. It did occur to some that what was really being celebrated was the "collapse" of the Russian economy, a "collapse" whose consequences lingered for more than a decade and which may well be a subject of some reconsideration and study in decades to come, given the US role is urging policies that provoked and made the "collapse" more damaging to the Russian economy and national pride than might have been the case with alternative policies.

Cambridge University professor Stefan Halper has written that America has from "the beginning" . . . been an "'imagined community,' defined in non-territorial and non-ethnic terms, regularly re-conceptualizing its 'Exceptionalism.'"[1] The Cold War served as a major reference and defining template for explaining and asserting American Exceptionalism for the half century after World War II.

The conception of what the Cold War meant had emerged and enlarged over the decades. At first the conflict with the Russian nation was defined in terms of resistance to efforts of that government to expand and occupy nations in Eastern Europe. Later the definition of the conflict came to be defined as a campaign against Stalinism, and finally, Communism; and for some, and in much national rhetoric, the campaign expanded over the years to a war against Socialism, government regulation of the economy, the Left, and the so-called "welfare state."

Defined primarily as a war of ideas, the Cold War had given birth to the USIA, and defined much of its principal mission. At its origin and over the years the role of USIA was defined as seeking to explain and support American foreign policy and U.S. national interests through overseas information programs and to promote mutual understanding between the United States and other nations by conducting educational and cultural activities. The Cold War had gathered all those functions under one widely accepted mantra, "winning hearts and minds."

I took up my new responsibilities at USIA with the hope that the agency might play some role in helping to define the "new era," the next set of "big ideas" about how Americans might come to understand and explain themselves to the wider world as we looked to a new century and beyond the Cold War in the new era. A long-standing academic interest in the formation of national "identities," inspired my attraction to this opportunity. I had been taken many years ago with the concept proposed by Robert Hutchins of the University of Chicago that a fundamental dynamic of democratic government was a continuing "national conversation."[2]

My goal was to make this effort the theme of my leadership and management of the USIA. At my swearing-in ceremony in early June of 1993, I invited a representative group of men and women from business, education, journalism and other fields to conduct "A Conversation About America." I began the program with this introduction: ". . . a great conversation is taking place in our country today and I've asked some men and women, whose work and achievements I admire and respect, to join in this conversation and to address the question of how America might present itself to the world in a new time, in a new era." This effort might begin, I suggested, by pausing to consider how we were, as a nation, being in fact perceived abroad. There was in Washington a widespread notion, accelerated at the end of the Cold War, that America was universally admired by peoples overseas, and that, as English was becoming the universal language of commerce and learning, the United States was emerging as the worldwide icon of culture and civilization. It seemed to me, however, on the basis of many encounters abroad, that this view of how our nation was perceived around the world was a bit naïve. The view of America from overseas I suggested to my colleagues, based on the examination of a great deal of focus group data more than mass polling, was perhaps more a case of envy rather than universal admiration.

Given the confusing multiple and often contradicting images of America being projected abroad through our politics, the mass media, Hollywood, a growing diversity and division of attitudes and values, I began to propose a new way to describe the mission of USIA, suggesting that perhaps the mission of USIA in this new post-Cold War era might be more "explaining" America rather than "winning hearts and minds," explaining America to our friends as well as to our would-be adversaries around the world. I began to suggest that, as a nation, and particularly an agency with responsibility for interpreting our nation abroad, it might be wise to pause a bit at the end of the Cold War era, to "listen" before we began to launch our new assertions of who we are as Americans. The *Wall Street Journal* editorialized their disdain for my suggestion that America should "listen" to voices from across the seas rather than assuming too quickly the assertive voice of a new ear. Though by the middle of the first decade of the new century Undersecretary of State Karen Hughes, who carried the responsibility for leading our efforts in public diplomacy, seems to have used the term, "listen," quite often!

Looking back I see now how naïve was my academic, didactic approach to "rethinking and redefining America identity for a new era." But I do not regret the attempt and the efforts that followed to reorganize and conceptualize the agency and to seek to define the challenge of a new era.

Several "big ideas" were prominent in the early post-Cold War era and became contending and complementary narratives for defining the new era. One was the opportunity for a major advance in the processes of international trade and commerce, a new era of freer international trade, greater provision for cross-border investment and flows of capital, a new world economic order, and the role America might play in this development. And, on another level, these dynamics were viewed by some in the sense that there seemed to be here, in addition to the economic benefits, a passage to new and greater "understandings" both of local and of "foreign" sensibilities and cultures.

There was also another "big idea" in contention and within some circles of government and intellectual debate. There emerged at the end of the Cold War what has come to be known as the "neo-conservative" movement. This constellation of perceptions and advocacies was by no means an arena without debate, but a movement within which the primary perception of the defining "new" identity for America is a continuing struggle for resistance to tyranny, on behalf of national security, democratic order and free markets, and the role and responsibilities of the

United States in that arena of international affairs. The major emphasis here is upon military strength and readiness and willingness to act preemptively if necessary in defense of these values and emphasis upon the necessity of remaining the world's only "superpower."

Neither of these themes represented a dramatic new turn in the trajectory of how this country has conceived of its role and mission in human history. These were continuations of the ideas and definitions of national destiny and purpose which marked the years of the Cold War. It was clear to thoughtful observers that these "big ideas" were not necessarily exclusive of each other, yet the issue was one of proportion and balance in terms of how we might come to an understanding and assumption of our national identity and destiny approaching a new century as well as a new era.

The challenge to the nation was perhaps best described as an attempt to assess the proportions of each theme in the quest for both security and credibility, and, as well, the capacity to be guided by thoughtful and deliberate reflection on history and human nature, since the dangers of hubristic, nationalistic blindness are inherent in all notions of national identity.

Already in the later years of the first Bush administration the post-Cold War period had become a time of disquiet and uncertainty, to say nothing of growing discomfort within the bureaucracies of the national government. As the Congress and White House, then and later, in the early Clinton years, welcomed the opportunity to reassess and reduce the annual budget increases in defense and security expenditures and international affairs in general that had skyrocketed in the later years of the Cold War, these agencies became centers of resistance and protest.

It is unfortunate that the government bureaucracy, and the often highly talented men and women in the civil service who serve in these agencies, do their work in structural patterns and conditions that often make the size of annual budget allocations the major way in which effectiveness, the appreciation of the public, and often self-respect, come to be understood. These agencies are condemned to be caught up, often consumed, in unending cycles of appropriation, either seeking to justify and persuade the White House to request increases in annual expenditures (budget for future fiscal years) or appropriation struggles seeking to obtain the increases requested by the Administration in the current budget before Congress.

President Clinton began his first term conscious of the need to reduce the significant deficit in government spending and adjust budget allocations and priorities at the end of a long period of "wartime" justifications for rising allocations. This is never an undertaking by the executive branch of government that does not arouse anxiety and resistance from the departments and offices involved. In addition, the Clinton administration, led by Vice President Gore, sought to reassess some aspects of organization, mission, and priorities of government agencies. I shared the sense that these efforts were necessary and devoted much of my early years at USIA to the effort to reassess priorities and patterns of organization of programs and activities, both to make them more efficient and more relevant to a new era.

But the response from many officers in the Foreign Service (which I observed more closely than that of military leadership and personnel) was often resistance and claims that such directives from the Administration were bad for morale. I remember more than one time when my career colleagues at USIA or State expressed sentiments like that of one officer who said to me one day: "Why is this administration trying to reduce our budgets? Don't they know we won the Cold War?"

The battle for post-war "big ideas" with respect to U.S. foreign policy began in earnest in the later years of the first Bush administration. President Clinton was sensitive to this debate as he began his early months in office in 1993. In the waning months of the administration of President George H.W. Bush, the *Washington Post* published excerpts from a "leaked" classified draft of a policy recommendation document prepared for the Secretary of Defense by senior members of his staff for transmission to the President. The paper was described by the *Post* as a "classified blueprint" intended to help "set the nation's direction for the next century." The document called for increasing military budgets, resisting the efforts to make post-Cold War adjustments in defense spending, and for "concerted efforts to preserve American global military supremacy and to thwart the emergence of a rival superpower in Europe, Asia or the former Soviet Union."[3]

The *Washington Post* reported that the document (later modified in response to sharp reaction from both the public and the White House after the "leak") was drafted under the supervision of Paul Wolfowitz, undersecretary for policy at the Department of Defense. The *Post* described the central strategy of the proposed document as stated in the text as an attempt to "establish and protect a new order" that accounts "sufficiently for the interests of the advanced industrial nations" and would serve to "discourage them from challenging . . . [U.S.] leadership," while at the same time maintaining a military dominance capable of "deterring potential competitors from even aspiring to a larger regional or global role."

While this draft memo expressed the sentiments of some within the military and defense establishments that the post-Cold War reassessments of U.S. Strategy and priorities posed major security threats to the nation, and though it was later modified after the classified draft was leaked to the press and responded to by some senior members of Congress, the ideas and convictions expressed here did not disappear. Five years later in 1997, Wolfowitz and several other senior defense officials in the first Bush administration, repeating many of the sentiments in this paper, published the charter for a new organization, the "Project for a New American Century."[4] Together with a number of men and women who served later in senior positions in State and Defense in the administration of George W. Bush, they set forth what they described as "guiding principles for American foreign policy . . . in support of American global leadership." They describe the shape of a foreign policy that would "boldly and purposefully promote American principles abroad . . . increase[d] defense spending . . . challenge[s] to regimes hostile to our interests and values . . . military strength and moral clarity." The following year, 1998, a number of those who authored the charter for the "Project for a New American Century," signed a letter to President Clinton calling for a "remaking" of the Middle East, beginning with the invasion of Iraq.[5]

In late February of 1993, only a few weeks after his inauguration, President Bill Clinton delivered what was among his first addresses on U.S. foreign policy after assuming the Presidency.[6] The theme he chose for that occasion was how we might define America's role in the world at what Clinton described as the "dawn of a new era for our nation." Clinton began with reference to the positions he had taken during the campaign and transition with respect to how we might "update our definition of national security . . . and . . . foster democracy and human rights around the world." He chose, however, for the theme of this address a "focus on economic leadership . . . at home and abroad as a new global economy unfolds before our eyes."

Clinton's presentation, viewed now nearly a decade and a half later, was prescient and compelling in terms of outlining the United States' opportunities and responsibilities in what he described as a "new world economic order." He defined the widespread hope for a more "prosperous America," a share for all our citizens in what he termed "freedom's bounty," at the end of the Cold War. He spoke of a continuing "amorphous but profound challenge in the way humankind conducts its commerce," as the defining challenge of the new era. Referring to the sweeping changes in international trade and business, he continued, we "cannot let these changes in the global economy carry us passively toward a future of insecurity and instability."

The message of Clinton's presentation in those early months of his presidency was that the emerged and emerging era of transnational investment and international trade could prove to be for America an era of greater prosperity and promise but only if we might adapt with greater investment in education, resources for greater competitiveness, and the restraint and disciplines to reduce and contain deficits in national spending. He defined the significant changes that had occurred, were occurring, in the global economy:

When I was growing up, business was mostly a local affair. Most farms and firms were owned locally, they borrowed locally, they hired locally, they shipped most of their products to neighboring communities or states within the United States. It was the same for the country as a whole. By and large, we had a domestic economy. But now we are woven inextricably into the fabric of a global economy. Imports and exports, which accounted for about one in 10 dollars when I was growing up, now represent one dollar in every five. Nearly three-quarters of the things that we make in America are subject to competition at home or abroad from foreign producers and foreign providers of services. Whether we see it or not, our daily lives are touched everywhere by the flows of commerce that cross national borders as inexorably as the weather.

The message that Clinton brought that morning at American University and on several occasions in the early months of his first administration was a sketch of a new post-Cold War agenda, a move toward wider integration of economic forces on behalf of greater prosperity for both the United States and the community of nations. His message was not a simplistic, evangelistic Free Market message. He spoke of significant adjustments required for the U.S. to welcome and compete in a more open economic order. This country must, he said:

.... welcome the subsidiaries of foreign companies on our soil. We appreciate the jobs they create and the products and services they bring ... Our trade policy will be part of an integrated economic program ... Better-educated and trained workers, a lower deficit, stable, low interest rates, a reformed health care system, world-class technologies, revived cities: These must be the steel of our competitive edge. And there must be a continuing quest by business and labor and, yes, by government for higher and higher and higher levels of productivity.

In the American University address, Clinton laid out goals for pursuing a transformational economic policy; "a prompt and successful completion of the Uruguay Round of GATT talks," the completion of the North American Free Trade Agreement (NAFTA) with Mexico, efforts to expand free trade in Asia through the Asian-Pacific Economic Forum, and concerted efforts on behalf of greater "global economic growth." To this agenda, Clinton added efforts to assist Russia's transition through support of the Yeltsin plan for economic reforms. In this way President Clinton had set forth then a new template, a new set of priorities, for America's role on the world stage, what Anthony Lake described a few months later as the move from "containment to engagement."[7]

In the months that followed I became aware of how significant an effort in presidential leadership was represented by the concepts set forth in the Clinton address that morning. What he was attempting to do was well described in hindsight nearly a decade later by a knowledgeable observer of American policy. Steve Clemons of the New America Foundation noted that Clinton had "tried to modify the calculus of national security by raising the priority of economic interests to a level on par with classical security considerations."[8]

Clemons continued:

Clinton perceived a military establishment intoxicated with its own self importance after its Gulf War victory [and the end of the Cold War] but essentially out of step with the mores of centrist Americans. At his November 1992 Little Rock Economic Summit, Clinton made clear that his foreign policy would be driven by economic concerns—and the need to draw nations together in trade and the mutually beneficial bonds of economic enmeshment.

Clinton's call, at the beginning of his first term in office, for the nation to engage the new opportunities and challenges of a "new world economic order," was indeed an effort, as Clemons put it, to "modify the calculus of national security." And the years of the Clinton administration were marked by the nation's struggle with the meaning of and paths to national security in the

329

"new era." The choices were not put by Clinton as one or the other, or one against the other, but in terms of priorities. But he was clearly seeking to turn away from the struggle to maintain a superpower military dominance for the sake of defense and security as the defining "new idea" of the post-Cold War era. He chose as a primary theme of his administration the path to national security through economic integration and balanced growth.

Clinton's emphasis on these themes, at this early point in his presidency, indicated his awareness that this was a meaningful and critical debate within society and the bureaucracy and an effort to set forth his own sense of priorities. The morning of his address at American University a few weeks after his inauguration ended with a portent of the conflicted and troubling times ahead with respect to the "calculus of national security." As Clinton left the platform at the end of the convocation an aide came up to hand him a message about an event that had occurred in New York as he was speaking to the assembled group that morning. An explosion had occurred at the World Trade Building in lower Manhattan. A truck loaded with explosives had been detonated in the garage of one of the buildings there!

Only a few years into the Clinton administration some astute observers of USIA programs noted that themes of international trade and investment, a new world economic order, were becoming a, perhaps *the* significant focus of USIA's programs.[9] The agency directed many of its ongoing programs to the mission of promoting free-market economies, free trade, and U.S. competitiveness. Following the course Clinton had directed in stating primary goals for his administration, USIA inaugurated and shaped a number of its ongoing programs to support of and advocacy for the North American Free Trade Agreement and programs that urged economic free market reform in the former Soviet Union.

As I shaped and participated in these programs, however, I began to lose my innocence about how a calculated, didactic process of "national conversation" might consider the meaning of and our approach to a "new era" in world history. For it soon became clear to me that waves of new Cold War triumphalism were emerging around the concept of a "new world economic order" as well as that of a dominant military power. There was a growing popular view, expressed widely, that the victory of the Cold War was more a triumph of free markets and diminished government than free spirits. However one may view and debate the long-standing and deeply rooted waves of triumphalistic assumptions at the core of American exceptionalism, it has been clear and is more so today that the perceptions abroad of this facet of our national character and consciousness have been a major obstacle to effective public diplomacy.

Clinton anticipated in his remarks at American University the controversy over globalization that was to erupt in the years following his address. He made major recognition of U.S. interests in terms of greater prosperity at home, but focused as well on the issues of rising inequality and the need to more directly address the issues of underdeveloped regions and societies in terms beyond simply more "free trade." His vision and prescriptions went beyond most of simplistic caricatures of views of Milton Friedman and Adam Smith which flowed freely in the chatter of Wall Street and the growing new conservative think tanks that had emerged in Washington during the 1980s.

The moves toward a Mexico-inclusive NAFTA, an effort begun in the prior Bush administration, were contentious and disappointing, given the line up of lobbying and Congressional forces whose support was mandatory for getting any legislation in this area. Assessing the history of the period just over a decade later, Dean Baker, Senior Economist at the Economic Policy Institute in Washington, wrote: "While the agreement was labeled a 'free trade' agreement, the pact actually had relatively little to do with free trade."[10] Baker writes that the strongest supporters of the treaty were mainly interested in "Mexico as a source of low-cost labor . . . to put in place a set of rules that would make US investments in Mexico more secure . . . [and to] . . . extend US patent and copyright protections into the Mexican market."

I have described the theme of the Clinton address as "globalization." That word, however, was not used even once in his remarks. The word was coming into wider use in the early years of the 1990s but did not explode in everyday language until about the middle of the first Clinton term. In a recent book Nayan Chanda of Yale University gives us some background on that term, "globalization."[11] Chanda describes the process of globalization as initially the growing consciousness around the world, dating from ancient times, of "interconnectedness and interdependence." Chanda observes from a review of literature and news reports that the "much touted word," 'globalization' came to mean over decades "all things to all people." However, in a few years through the decade of the 1990s, the term and the concept became more and more controversial as well. Chanda suggests it was more associated with the "worldwide extension of capitalism," than with cultural awareness and interdependence. And indeed this best describes the goals of the "new world economic order," that was among the themes vying for the new "mission" of the U.S. in the early post-Cold War era.

The concept of "globalization" of the economic order was not, in the early 1990s, a new concept. There had long been comment and speculation on the dynamics of international trade, free movement of capital investment, and changing policies of tariff and taxation and how these developments were shaping the future. In 1998 Daniel Yergin and Joseph Stanislaw, in a widely noted study, *The Commanding Heights*,[12] (later a noted series on public television) reminded us of the fact that the aspirations and achievement of "globalization" have a long history of rise and decline, flourishing and regression over the course of modern history.

President Clinton was seeking the themes and actions associated with what has come to be termed globalization in large measure as a counter to those who described "security measures" almost exclusively in terms of military use of force, coupled with triumphal self-proclaiming hegemonic ambition and posture. But as the "new economic order" and "internationalization" of the economic order proceeded, what came later to be more akin to the controversial "globalization process" took shape.

Chanda charts what can perhaps best be described as a rise of manic concentration on "going global" in the culture and aspirations of corporate culture in the mid-1990s. He suggests that far beyond the early concept of greater international trade, the new surge was characterized by a move away from corporate national identities, intense focus on cross-border ownership and investment, the rise of a "twenty-four-hour trading environment." In short, Chanda describes the emergence in the mid-1990s of a stage beyond the global transformation of the market toward what he labels "Go-Go Globalization."

Chanda writes of the shift in rhetoric and perceptions of the international economic trends during the years of the first Clinton term:

> . . . the *Wall Street Journal*'s normally cautious reporter G. Pascal Zachary waxed ecstatic about a new golden age brought about by globalization: "Economists are saying that the global economy is showing signs of entering an extraordinary period of longterm growth," Globalization in the form of a vast expansion of economic freedom and property rights, coupled with reductions in the scope of government and an explosion in trade and private investment, was said to "have produced a world growth rate . . . nearly double that of the prior two decades." Barring a major war or environmental crisis, Harvard economist Jeffrey Sachs was quoted as saying, "Economic growth will raise the living standards of more people in more parts of the world than at any other time in history." . . . Domingo Cavallo, the architect of Argentina's dramatic economic restructuring . . . was euphoric, "We've entered a golden age that will last for decades." . . . Even United Nations Secretary General Kofi Annan, not usually given to hyperbole about business, thought the world [was] entering "a new golden age."

The mood I sensed, as both officials in the government and from the business and chattering class was, with respect to the new economic trends, something of a parallel to the sentiments about American superiority expressed in Madeleine Albright's startling proclamation about

America with respect to the use of preemptive force in international relations: ". . . we are America; we are the indispensable nation. We stand tall and we see further than other countries." (These remarks were made in interviews on NBC-TV "The Today Show" in February of 1998. To set Albright's startling proclamation in context, we should note her introduction by Matt Lauer on the program, Laurer introduced Albright on this morning in 1998, as "traveling around the United States making the . . . case" for a preemptive "strike" against Iraq.[13]

Clinton was attempting to define a "new" and dominant template for U.S. understanding of the nation's role in the post-Cold War era, leadership in a "new world economic order" in the era of globalization. And the major characteristic of the decade to follow was that 'global free markets' meant a new era for U.S. investment abroad. It was not until the middle of the next decade that shifts in the flow of global capital away from dominance of U.S. capital investment began to become evident.

But, in terms of the search for and human quest and need for the "big idea" the direction Clinton pointed to turned out to be something of a disappointing journey. Yes, the quest for greater engagement in international commerce, promotion of free markets, greater prosperity was a rewarding time for the nation and many other nations in the 1990s in many ways. Yes, federal budget deficits were restrained in the Clinton years. Before the end of the eight years of the Clinton presidency, the phenomena he outlined in the address at American University a few weeks after his first inauguration, a rise of cross-border free trade and investment, had morphed into globalization, a different era yet, and a far more controversial one.

And, though Clinton began his administration with some hope of restraining the long accelerating rise in defense budget appropriations, the fact is that appropriations for defense spending during Clinton's two terms in the presidency were increased by a significant degree over annual increases during the first Bush administration. During the 1990s, the Pentagon actually invested more than $1 trillion in the development of new weapons and information technology.[14] These increases in defense budget allocations, during the Clinton years, resulted from greater emphasis on technological aspects for precision weapons targeting and training for the kind of up front military attacks that were later to characterize operations in Iraq.

> The combination of Joint Defense Attack Munitions (JDAMs) and unmanned aerial drones—both products of that shift—made it possible to find and destroy targets, including mobile targets, more precisely and quickly during Operation Enduring Freedom, the response to the Sept. 11 attacks, and in Operation Iraqi Freedom than in any previous war. As many as 70 percent of all munitions dropped on Iraq were the precision-guided munitions developed and built during the Clinton administration. Funding for the JDAM program began in 1993, Clinton's first year in office. The advanced, GPS-guided Tomahawk cruise missile, which proved far more accurate and reliable than the earlier cruise missiles used in Desert Storm under the first President Bush, was funded in 1999. Unmanned aerial vehicles like the Predator and Global Hawk, which enabled U.S. forces to use combat aircraft in close air support in unprecedented ways, also originated in the Clinton years. Appropriations for military spending during the Clinton years also improved pay and benefits for military service.

Secretary of State Madeleine Albright, with the backing of Senate Foreign Relations Committee Jesse Helms (R-NC) succeeded near the end of President Clinton's second term in office in abolishing USIA as an independent and functional organization and to move the resources into the State Department, an increase in the budget and resources of State. As the new century began there has been a continuing assessment and reassessment of what public diplomacy for the U.S. might mean and how it might be conducted, especially since the jolting events of September 11, 2001. Since then in the society at large, discussions, debates, and struggles over the next "big idea" have become more and more intense. And there has been more attention to, discussion of, and concern for the role and goals of public diplomacy than at perhaps any time in our history.

But in nearly all these debates and searches for 'understanding' in recent years these two concerns, the "big idea," the defining template for understanding American 'identity', and the techniques and strategies for "public diplomacy" seem to be separate spheres, two differing areas of consideration.

I remain convinced that they are very much connected.

Notes

1 Stefan Halper, "Big Ideas, Big Problems," *The National Interest* no. 88 (March/April 2007), 92–97.

2 Robert M. Hutchins, *The Learning Society* (New York: F. A. Praeger, 1968), 326.

3 Barton Gellman, "Keeping the U.S. First; Pentagon Would Preclude a Rival Superpower," *Washington Post*, March 11, 1992.

4 Statement of Principles, Project for the New American Century, June 3, 1997, http://www.newamericancentury.org/statementofprinciples.htm.

5 Letter to President Clinton, January 26, 1998, Project for the New American Century. A partial list of those who signed the letter includes John Bolton, Zalmay Khalilzad, William Kristol, Richard Perle, Donald Rumsfeld, Paul Wolfowitz, James Woolsey, and Robert Zoellick, http://www.newamerican century.org/iraqclintonletter.htm.

6 William Jefferson Clinton, Address at Centennial Celebration, American University, Washington, DC, February 26, 1993 http://www.media.american.edu/speeches/clinton97.htm.

7 Anthony Lake, "From Containment to Enlargement," Address at Johns Hopkins School of Advanced International Studies, Washington, DC, September 21, 1993.

8 Steven Clemons, "American Triumphalism and the Conditions that Led to September 11," *Le Monde Diplomatic*, October 1, 2001.

9 Nancy Snow, "United States Information Agency," *Foreign Policy in Focus* 2, no. 40, Albuquerque, New Mexico: Interhemispheric Resource Center, August, 1997.

10 Dean Baker, *The United States Since 1980* (Oxford: Cambridge University Press, 2007).

11 Nayan Chanda, *Bound Together, How Traders, Preachers, Adventurers, and Warriors Shaped Globalization* (New York and London: Yale University Press, 2007).

12 Daniel Yergin and Joseph Stanislaw, *The Commanding Heights* (New York: Simon and Schuster, 1998).

13 ". . . if we have to use force, it is because we are America; we are the indispensable nation. We stand tall and we see further than other countries." Secretary of State Madeleine K. Albright, Interview on NBC-TV *The Today Show* with Matt Lauer, Columbus, Ohio, (February 19, 1998) (To see Albright's startling proclamation in context, she was defending the use of force in Iraq in an Interview on NBC-TV from Columbus, Ohio in February of 1998. http://secretary.state.gov/www/statements/1998/980219a.html.

14 Steven J. Nider, "Clinton's Military Legacy President Bush owes a major debt of gratitude to his predecessor," Democratic Leadership Committee, *Blueprint* magazine, June 30, 2003.

28

Ethics and Social Issues in Public Diplomacy

Richard Nelson and Foad Izadi

Nations have long reached out to foreign audiences when such efforts advance a particular political or economic goal. Promotion of tourism and business enterprises through international expositions and world fairs are an example. With the rise of mass societies, however, governments also became interested in supplementing their traditional diplomatic efforts with more overt and continuous communications directed at residents in other countries. This outreach became feasible largely because of the growing importance of public opinion on government decision making, and inventive advances beginning with the telegraph in the mid-1800s and continuing through today's modern satellite and internet technologies. This concept and practice is known as "public diplomacy"—a process which is to promote the national interest and the national security through understanding, informing, and influencing foreign publics and broadening dialogue between citizens and institutions and their counterparts abroad.[1]

In most cases, public diplomacy has historically been an instrument of foreign policy to meet wartime needs. This has certainly been the case for the United States, which went heavily into the business of shaping foreign as well as domestic opinion in 1917 through the establishment by order of President Woodrow Wilson of the Committee on Public Information (CPI), headed by former newspaperman George Creel. The title of Creel's 1920 book (*How we advertised America; The first telling of the amazing story of the Committee on Public Information that carried the gospel of Americanism to every corner of the globe*)[2] expresses the philosophy of communication employed by this agency. Or, as one of the CPI's most famous alumni, Edward L. Bernays, admitted in an interview with Bill Moyers, that while during the conflict they practiced propaganda he "hoped it was 'proper-ganda' and not 'improper-ganda.'"[3]

Bernays, who as the nephew of Freud applied the science of psychology to mass audiences, argued for the central importance of public relations to an effective democracy. To shape a democracy requires an enlightened leadership, he asserted, using communication to effect what he later called *The engineering of consent*.[4] As a long-lived influential "public relations counsel" and author/editor of other important books including *Crystallizing public opinion* and *Biography of an idea: Memoirs of public relations counsel*,[5] Bernays also always included a corollary principle: utilizing social science research methods was an essential element in structuring such persuasive campaigns.

One of the clearest expositions of his views occurs in Bernays' *Propaganda* published in 1928.[6] He opens by making the case that "The conscious and intelligent manipulation of the organized habits and opinions of the masses is an important element in democratic society. Those who manipulate this unseen mechanism of society constitute an invisible government which is the true ruling power of our country."[7] The marketplace of ideas was not something to be ignored or derided, but rather influenced for the public good. From his elitist vantage point propaganda was "a perfectly legitimate form of human activity."[8] In fact, to govern a modern state, requires it. He asserted that, "Any society, whether it be social, religious, or political, which is possessed of certain beliefs, and sets out to make them known, either by the spoken or written words, is practicing propaganda."[9] Historically, Bernays further argued that:

> economic power tends to draw after it political power; and the history of the industrial revolution shows how that power passed from the king and the aristocracy to the bourgeoisie. Universal suffrage and universal schooling reinforced this tendency, and at last even the bourgeoisie stood in fear of the common people. For the masses promised to become king. Today, however, a reaction has set in. The minority has discovered a powerful help in influencing majorities. It has been found possible so to mold the mind of the masses that they will throw their newly gained strength in the desired direction. In the present structure of society, this practice is inevitable. Whatever of social importance is done today, whether in politics, finance, manufacture, agriculture, charity, education, or other fields, must be done with the help of propaganda. Propaganda is the executive arm of the invisible government.[10]

Bernays' contemporary, and rival as the "father of public relations" had the unusual name of Ivy Ledbetter Lee. Making his mark as an advisor to the Rockefellers, Lee also worked in the war effort for the Wilson Administration promoting the Red Cross. Lee's biographer makes the similar observation that President Wilson's belief "that the state was a beneficent organ of society capable of harmonizing individual rights with public duties and social development" also influenced Lee's ideas about the social utility of public relations.[11]

Despite these influences, United States' public diplomacy approach during World War I, World War II (with the founding of Voice of America/VOA), and the Cold War proved to be one largely of crisis management.[12] After World War II, many in Congress, especially Senator J. William Fulbright (D-AR), questioned the need for an international broadcasting organization in peacetime. To engage in propaganda, they thought, was to contradict America's democratic principles.[13] It was the increase in Cold War tensions and the belief that the United States was losing the war of ideas to the Soviet Union's more sophisticated propaganda apparatus that convinced Congress of the necessity and legitimacy of the VOA during peace time.[14]

The emergence of the Cold War also institutionalized cultural transfer (i.e., what is called cultural diplomacy or public diplomacy) as an important element of U.S. foreign policy. After 1945, a group of U.S. diplomats and scholars argued that, in the fight against communism, the United States needed to take an aggressive approach to winning the hearts and minds of foreign publics. The controversial *U.S. Information and Educational Exchange Act of 1948* (Public Law 402), popularly referred to as the Smith-Mundt Act, legalized peace time propaganda but forbid its use for domestic purposes.[15] The State Department was to carry information and educational exchange programs with the aim of promoting a better understanding of the United States among foreign publics and increasing mutual understanding between Americans and people of other countries.

In 1950, President Truman launched the Campaign of Truth to combat Communist propaganda. In 1953, Eisenhower supervised the creation of the United States Information Agency (USIA). While the CIA was given responsibility to carry out covert propaganda, the USIA was to mange public communication programs such as international broadcasting and the programs of U.S. information posts in foreign countries.[16] The USIA, nevertheless, did at times engage in covert public diplomacy activities as well.[17]

The USIA mission changed several times as a result of changing administrations. Generally speaking, the one central goal that spawned all administrations was the use of public diplomacy for promoting the acceptance of American foreign policy. U.S. information programs were to convince the people of the world that the objectives and the actions of the United States were in harmony with the aspirations of foreign publics.

To fulfill these objectives, the USIA established a press and publication service and a motion and television service. The USIA was given the responsibility for operating the Voice of America and for U.S. libraries and information centers abroad.[18]

The USIA promoted two broad dichotomized themes: anti-communism and positive themes about the United States. The emphasis was on creating a distinction between us and them. To show the evil nature of communism, the USIA concentrated on communism's ideological contradictions, forced labor camps, absence of freedom, and lack of consumer goods in the Soviet Union and its communist surrogates. On the positive theme of American ideology and the virtues of capitalism, the USIA publicized U.S. economic and technical assistance programs, scientific and technological advances, and the virtues of free trade unions.

A prime feature of American public diplomacy was cultural propaganda, to sell the American way of life, celebrate democratic values and practices, and advocate consumer capitalism.[19] In this, the VOA was one of the prime weapons of influence. U.S. public diplomacy programs were in essence publicizing the idea of the American dream vs. the bleak world of Soviet communism. Hollywood movies, music, and other mass-produced cultural goods were the means to do so. The emergence of transnational cultural industries and media enterprises in the post World War II period set in motion a perpetual one-way flow of cultural products to the Third World. These initiatives capitalized on what Nye calls soft power.[20] Soft power refers to a country's ability to attract on the basis of the appeal of its cultural, social, and political values and ideas.[21]

U.S. public diplomacy did not rely on its VOA broadcasting as the only means to reach the mainstream public of target countries. The USIA also pursued "media control projects." These projects were designed to influence the indigenous news media by planting news, placing programs on local television channels, and using personal contacts to influence the perspective of foreign journalists. Personal contacts were also used to influence influential opinion leaders. In this way, the USIA engaged in covert propaganda by obscuring the source of its messages. In addition to relying on the corroboration of foreign journalists, the USIA relied on private cooperation. Private cooperation involved the use of American nongovernmental organizations, businesses, and ordinary citizens in the publicity campaign to cultivate a positive image for the United States.[22]

In addition to the USIA's mostly overt public diplomacy programs, the CIA's clandestine psychological warfare operations were important to the United States' Cold War public diplomacy strategy. The United States made an attempt to directly target the USSR public and the people of its surrogate countries through CIA operated Radio Free Europe (launched in 1950) and Radio Liberation (launched in 1953 and renamed Radio Liberty in 1964). Their goal was to provide counterpropaganda to anti-U.S. messages in Eastern Europe and the Soviet Union. A number of foundations were purported as the source of these broadcasting stations to disguise the fact that the CIA ran these stations.[23]

In addition to its radio programming, the CIA sponsored numerous covert public diplomacy initiatives, including subsidizing non-communist labor unions, journalists, political parties, politicians, and student groups. In Western Europe, the agency helped produce dozens of magazines, organized numerous international conferences, sponsored the publication of numerous books, etc. These activities were done under the guise of the CIA-sponsored Congress for Cultural Freedom.[24] The CIA also carried out a number of covert operations to manipulate political developments in countries such as Iran, Guatemala, Cuba, Chile, and Iraq.[25] In Iran, in particular, the CIA sponsored a successful coup against the democratically elected government of Mohammad Mosaddeq. CIA-initiated black propaganda was central to the success of the coup.[26]

According to Snow,[27] a distinct historical pattern has emerged in which the U.S. government repeatedly views public diplomacy as appeals made during a national crisis or wartime that are dismantled at conflict's end. Congress abolished Woodrow Wilson's Creel Committee within months of the ending of World War I. Truman's Office of War Information was shut down at the end of World War II, just as the USIA was dissolved following the Cold War. Both the legislative and the executive branches of the U.S. government considered public diplomacy a low priority after the Cold War. The Clinton Administration cut funds for public diplomacy and reduced cultural exchange programs. In 1999, Congress eliminated the USIA and transferred its public diplomacy functions to the Department of State. It was the advent of the 9/11 terrorist attacks that once again brought public diplomacy to the forefront of America's foreign policy.[28]

Tools for Evaluating U.S. Public Diplomacy

How we interact as individuals within a society and without is measured through our behavior. Ethics as a branch of philosophy concerned with human conduct evolved from the Greek word "ethos," which means "way of living." Ethical principles allow us to rationally examine our moral judgments in terms of whether our actions are justified or not.

While there are numerous approaches to ethics, most can be classified in terms of utility (who benefits?, who loses?) and/or responsibility (where does our duty lie?). Those who favor utility tend to believe in situational ethics and differing standards depending on the specific instance. Those stressing duty often act on the belief universal norms do exist, even if they are not universally observed. Within representative governments, ethics emphasizes fairness through the promotion of the general good ("the public interest"), open debate in decision-making (the principle of transparency), and accountability in terms of public service. "In government decision-making, ethical considerations are tightly intertwined with political and managerial ones and all three dimensions are essential to successful governance."[29] Readers may also want to consult another Canadian study by Kernaghan[30] which highlights how implementing an "ethics regime" can be accomplished by government officials committed to principled action.

Despite popular perceptions to the contrary, propaganda and public diplomacy are widely accepted by objective researchers to be at least conceptually neutral (neither good nor bad) forms of communication.[31] Scholars do, howerer, emphasize the importance of studying the phenomenon from an ethical standpoint.[32] Earlier works by the authors of this study point to the social utility and ethical implications of advocacy communication,[33] opportunities to build better international relationships though communication,[34] and concerns about public diplomacy and its influence.[35]

Should Public Diplomacy Have a Commitment to Truth?

Propaganda and information have always been intertwined in the practice of public diplomacy. As long standing assumptions about the present world collapse before our eyes, advocacy communicators are among those few philosophically utilitarian pluralists committed to the notion of proactive involvement and futurist preparation. They are also uniquely positioned within their agencies and organizations to work for harmonization between interests. Just as James Madison foresaw in *Federalist* 10 that many factions helped to check one another and in *Federalist* 51 that the most desirable form of governance involved numerous centers of power responsive to offsetting interests, the world-wide yearning for responsiveness to individual needs has led to mobilizing linkages typified by the proliferation of activist interest groups domestically and internationally.[36]

Certainly, persuasion is a component of such domestic and international efforts. When we purposely use communication to influence others (their values, attitudes, emotions, beliefs, and actions) then we are engaging in persuasion for or against something. Adding media to the mix, so we can extend our influence, makes us propagandists. This is not necessarily a bad thing. Without some level of persuasion, common agreements (or social contracts) about public policies would be impossible. Another reason is that although persuasion and propaganda are often negatively associated with falsehoods or half truths, this is not necessarily the case.[37] "Much persuasion is in fact truthful, subject to review and critique. Ironically, democracies as well as dictatorships need such purposeful communication if society is to exist and progress."[38]

It is evident that all of the persuasive variants in propaganda have been present in U.S. public diplomacy practices, given that its one central mission remains the furthering of American foreign policy initiatives. Views differ, though, as to whether or not public diplomacy is propaganda, largely because the image of *propaganda* evokes unsavory connotations. According to Cull,[39] the term public diplomacy itself is in some ways propaganda. By using more neutral phrasing, Cull argues the U.S. government wanted to avoid the pejoratives associated with propaganda to describe the activities of the USIA and its sponsored international broadcasting.

Nelson defines propaganda as "a systematic form of purposeful persuasion that attempts to influence the emotions, attitudes, opinions, and actions of specified target audiences for ideological, political or commercial purposes through the controlled transmission of one-sided messages (which may or may not be factual) via mass and direct media channels."[40] As such, propaganda is a deliberate attempt at persuasion that only considers the intent and interest of the source of the message, or the propagandist. In other words, it is a manipulative technique to make the audience think, believe, and act in a way that is to the benefit of the propagandist. It is an attempt to reproduce the ideology, or the perspective, of the propagandist in the target audience. It is important to note that while propaganda does not necessarily have to be deceptive and untruthful, propaganda does not have a commitment to truth. Thus, when necessary, a propagandist will use lies as in black propaganda. At other times, it will disguise the source of the message, as in gray propaganda. At other times, the propagandist may only give a selective version of truth, as in white propaganda.

Therefore, propaganda's preoccupation is with efficiency and not truthfulness.[41] Cunningham[42] referred to the same concept as an "instrumentalized" approach to truth. With such a utilitarian ethical approach, credibility rather than truth gains significance when judging the efficacy of public diplomatic discourse.[43] As a result, a public diplomacy discourse that relies on selective truths to fulfill its commitment to the policies it aims to propagate does not fulfill the ethical standard of truthfulness. Similarly, Seib argues that, in public diplomacy messages, "the framing of truth through various mechanisms of emphasis must be done [in such a way as] to avoid distortion."[44]

As Black points out, a main feature of propagandistic messages that hinders an open-minded approach to truth is their "finalistic, or fixed view of people, institutions, and situations divided into broad, all inclusive categories of in-groups (friends) and outgroups (enemies), beliefs and disbeliefs, and situations to be accepted or rejected in toto."[45] We believe that such a mindset is an obstacle to an ethically sound public diplomacy. Such an approach is clearly evident in the mindset that underpins United States' variant of public diplomacy. The two concepts of American exceptionalism and Orientalism fuel the value system of American public diplomacy. While American exceptionalism focuses on the virtues of American experience, Orientalism contrasts these virtues to the evils of the opponent.

American exceptionalism has been one of the justifications for America's aggressive and active public diplomacy, including its use of the mass media.[46] American exceptionalism indicates that the United States' moral superiority, its unique democratic and revolutionary origins, its political system, social organization, cultural and religious heritage, as well as its values serve to legitimize its policies.[47] America, as the city on the hill, is thus positioned on the moral high ground with respect to other countries and powers around the world and therefore has a duty to spread American-style thought, democratic ideals and values, and political systems to the rest of the world.

American exceptionalism is very much the essence of describing public diplomacy in terms of soft power. Fitzpatrick[48] argues that conceptualizing public diplomacy as soft power has ethical shortcomings. American cultural policies (as public diplomacy tools) take on a hegemonic characteristic, what critics have argued result in cultural imperialism.[49] American exceptionalism in turn gives rise to an Orientalist view of other cultures, creating a dual world of "us" versus "them."

Said[50] argues that Orientalism is the ideology that supports Western imperialism. Orientalism is a traditional Western discourse, wherein the Orient is a culture of dehumanized inferiority. He further asserts that Orientalist discourse is intimately connected to the political and economic interests of Western powers in dominating the Middle East. Orientalism, like anti-Semitism, is a historical form of discourse that defames Arabs (similar to the way anti-Semitism defames Jews) and justifies their economic and political persecution and subordination. Orientalism relies on a dichotomous language and large-scale generalizations about distinct cultures of the Orient. In defining Orientalism, Said indicates it is the organizational infrastructure that deals with the Orient. In this sense, public diplomacy is in essence America's apparatus for Orientalism, authorizing and perpetuating a certain view of the Orient. This Western style of thought in turn paves the way for Western domination over the region. Orientalism in essence concerns relations of power. This idea is based on Foucault's notion that knowledge produces and reinvigorates power.[51] Through Orientalism, the West attempts to contain competing worldviews. For example, such notions as development, reform, and democracy are all defined according to the hegemonic cultural order of the West.

McAlister[52] traces the prevalence of varying Orientalist representations of the Middle East from 1945 to 2000 and finds that such demonization was consistently present among elites. Mass-mediated Orientalist representations in film and other venues transferred the same perspective to the public. In his study of *The Failure of American and British Propaganda in the Arab Middle East, 1945–1957*, Vaughan[53] shows how the United States and British propagandists viewed their relations with the Arab world in Orientalist terms. This view was most stark in propagandists' perspective with regard to Arab nationalism and the Arab–Israeli conflict. These presuppositions and prejudices still influence policymakers even today.

Messaging based on American exceptionalism and Orientalism display situational ethics, as is evident in double standards when covering international issues. On the same light, Herman and Chomsky[54] propose that by focusing on an enemy as "other," media narrow their coverage of foreign events based on a dichotomy of client vs. unfriendly states. This dichotomy in turn gives rise to notions of "worthy vs. unworthy victims" and "legitimate vs. meaningless Third World elections."

A Call for Two-way Symmetrical Public Diplomacy

Numerous recent conferences, commissioned reports, research studies, published articles, and government hearings have commented on the sad state of U.S. public diplomacy.[55] These all provide a wellspring of intelligent analysis and practical recommendations.[56] A February 10, 2007 *Asian Tribune* report indicates U.S. Secretary of State Condoleezza Rice is indeed reemphasizing the importance of public diplomacy programs. She stated:

> As we work to expand freedom and prosperity, we must champion these ideals in our public diplomacy, for which we are requesting funding of $359 million. Public diplomacy is a vital

component of our national security strategy. We seek to reach out to the peoples of the world in respect and partnership, to explain our policies, and just as importantly, to express the power of our ideals—freedom and equality, prosperity and justice. That is how we build new partnerships with foreign citizens and counter ideological support for terrorism. Public diplomacy is no longer the job of our experts alone; it is the responsibility of every member of the State Department family, and we are mobilizing the private sector and the American people to help.[57]

If so, the future may be brighter for American public diplomacy. Unfortunately—if history is a guide—most of the advice from experts, including incorporating benchmarks for establishing and measuring ethical performance, will be ignored.

We believe one can take two distinct approaches when discussing the challenges and opportunities the United States faces in the post-9/11 era. The first approach is to view public diplomacy as an image-building activity and propose that tactical, skills-based, or administrative changes will improve the effectiveness of the endeavor. Thus, the challenges are framed in terms of insufficient budget, a lack of coherent strategy, and problems with message content or delivery. Taking this approach, the proposed changes will be administrative as well: raising the budget for foreign public opinion polling, fixing the message or its delivery system, and the like. Of course there are those who find an image-oriented public diplomacy doomed to failure and propose that the only remedy lies in changing U.S. policies.[58]

Another way of looking at the challenges U.S. public diplomacy faces is through an examination of the framework that drives the endeavor. Critics see the dominant framework that continues to drive current public diplomacy initiatives as the main challenge in face of success. They argue that short of major structural changes, public diplomacy lacks ethical legitimacy and will prove ineffective in achieving substantive international support for U.S. foreign policies.[59]

The central problem with public diplomacy is its reliance on one-way models of communication. Dutta-Bergman[60] uses Habermas' theory of communicative action to evaluate the ethics of U.S. public diplomacy practices. He finds that U.S. public diplomacy practices applied one-way communication and emphasized building a positive image of the United States. These efforts typically reflected what Habermas calls "concealed strategic action."[61] Dutta-Bergman also finds that U.S. attempts at influencing the public are often hidden in entertainment-oriented guise. Such lack of transparency shows the propagandistic nature of public diplomacy.

Thus, the main challenge lies in incorporating genuine dialogue.[62] Scholars use different terminology for a public diplomacy approach that incorporates such structural changes. Among these are new public diplomacy,[63] dialogue-based public diplomacy,[64] culture-centered public diplomacy,[65] network-oriented public diplomacy,[66] and multistakeholder diplomacy.[67]

For public diplomacy to move beyond propaganda, Snow[68] is among those who argue it has to incorporate two-way communication. However, she suggests that the U.S. government's approaches to public diplomacy have not yet fostered genuine dialogue. One way public diplomacy can encourage dialogue is by adopting two-way symmetrical public relations rather than concentrating on image management.[69] Public relations scholars stress the importance of nurturing long-term relationships with stakeholders through two-way communication strategies with a symmetrical perspective as a viable framework for ethical public diplomacy. Fitzpatrick "questions the moral appropriateness and acceptability, as well as the practical implications, of public diplomacy philosophies and practices motivated and directed by the self-interested desire to gain power over those to whom public diplomacy efforts are directed."[70] She argues that two-way symmetrical public diplomacy maximizes the realization of the sponsoring nation's self-interest while respecting the rights of its global stakeholders.

Ledingham[71] asserts that relationship management should act as the general theory of public relations. James E. Grunig et al.[72] suggest that the establishment of quality relationships is the basis for excellence in the field, which could be done through reconciling the organization's goals with the expectations of its strategic stakeholders. As Melissen notes, "A lesson that public diplomacy can take on board from the sometimes misunderstood field of PR is that the strength of firm relationships largely determines the receipt and success of individual messages and overall attitudes."[73]

James E. Grunig and Larissa A. Grunig[74] indicate public relations practices are variants of "craft" and "professional" forms of public relations. The craft public relations continuum is marked by the two extremes of propaganda and journalism, both of which are one-way communication models. The two-way communication models are also placed along a continuum, with pure asymmetry at one end and pure symmetry at the other. It is the centrality of two-way communication that distinguishes professional public relations with the practice of public relations as a craft. In essence, a dialogue-centered paradigm of public diplomacy calls for a shift from craft public relations to professional public relations, with an emphasis on symmetrical practices. Grunig and Grunig[75] further contend that the two-way symmetrical extreme is not congruent with pure accommodation, to use Cancel et al.'s[76] terms, or pure coordination, in Murphy's[77] vocabulary. The team of Dozier, Grunig, and Grunig make the case that "Total accommodation of the public's interest would be as asymmetrical as unbridled advocacy of the organization's interests."[78] The two-way symmetrical model, according to Dozier et al.,[79] is in fact equivalent with the mixed motive model proposed by Murphy.[80] We suggest that as public diplomacy approaches the symmetrical end of professional public relations, it strengthens its ethical legitimacy.

Theoretical Underpinnings of Dialogue and Symmetry

The dialogic models of professional public relations are moves beyond the one-way models of communication management, in which the primary goal is to disseminate information about the organization's activities and decisions in order to reduce uncertainty in the environment.[81] The information model of communication management is epitomized by Lasswell's famous formula: "Who says what to whom with what effect."[82] Shannon and Weaver's Sender-Message-Channel-Receiver model of communication is also indicative of the public information approach.[83] The two models of rhetorical dialogue and relationship management are departures from the one-way, sender-centered approach to communication management.

Heath[84] argues that rhetoric is the essence of public relations and referred to this process as "enactment of meanings." He insists, "Rhetoric is a dialogue of opinions, counter opinions, meanings, and counter meanings—the process by which interests are asserted, negotiated, and constrained." Persuasion is central to the rhetorical perspective; however, it "treats persuasion as an interactive, dialogic process whereby points of views are contested in public." Based on this view, persuasion is not equivalent with "linear influence," instead it is based on argument and counterargument.[85]

Grunig and Grunig[86] indicate that such an approach to persuasion is compatible with the two-way symmetrical model of public relations since both parties have a chance to persuade the other. Heath[87] contends that persuasion as rhetorical dialogue would result in zones of meaning whereby organizations and their publics arrive at shared understanding of problems through debate and argumentation. Similarly, Riordan[88] makes the case for public diplomats to adopt a dialogue-based paradigm in which the parties of dialogue arrive at shared meanings. Such a paradigm, he asserts, "recognizes that no one has a monopoly of truth or virtue, that other ideas may be valid and that the outcome may be different from the initial message being promoted."[89] Genuine dialogue, he notes, is the means for achieving credibility with foreign publics.

Grunig says that problems of public relations cannot be solved merely through image management. "Public relations must be concerned both with behavioral and symbolic relationships and not with symbolic relationships alone."[90] He states that these behavioral relationships

341

are based on several key components, several of which were first proposed by Ferguson:[91] "(a) dynamic versus static, (b) open versus closed, (c) the degree to which both organization and public are satisfied with the relationship, (d) distribution of power in the relationship, and (e) the mutuality of understanding, agreement, and consensus."[92] Grunig adds two additional components: "trust and credibility, and the concept of reciprocity."[93] Thus, the problem with the public information and press agentry models lies in their preoccupation with symbolic relationships while ignoring behavioral relationships.

In addition to symbolic relationships (as in mediated messages), public diplomacy should concern actual behavioral relationships.[94] This means that not only should the communication of messages involve dialogue, but also the consequences of such messaging should take into consideration the views of the other party. So, for the United States to engage in two-way symmetrical public diplomacy, it has to consider the feedback it gets from other countries when making its policies. Fortunately, models for ethical communication already exist.[95]

Central to Grunig's relationship management model is the concept of symmetry or balance of interests between an organization and its publics. Grunig's approach to public relations is based on systems theory.[96] Miller defines a system as "a set of interacting units with relationships among them."[97]

Grunig and Huang[98] propose a model of stages and forms of relationships. The two-way symmetrical model is viewed as an open system, in which practitioners get input from the organization's environment to bring about changes in the organization, as well as its environment. In this model, Grunig and Huang identify the symmetrical and asymmetrical public relations practices as relationship maintenance strategies. With a symmetrical worldview, an organization is more likely to use symmetrical relationship maintenance strategies, approaching the pure symmetry end of the continuum (the two-way symmetrical model). In contrast, an organization with an asymmetrical worldview is more likely to use asymmetrical strategies, approaching the asymmetrical extreme of the continuum (the two-way asymmetric model). The two-way symmetrical form of public relations is in essence the same as new public diplomacy.

So American public diplomacy will be propagandistic and unethical unless government officials are willing to listen and change, to engage with foreign publics at the communication level and at the policy level. This is while U.S. cultural diplomacy during the Cold War was viewed as subservient to short-term political objectives. With this means-to-an-end approach to cultural diplomacy, U.S. officials often neglected how a flawed or unpopular policy could undermine the best of public diplomacy programs.[99]

The Necessity of Values-based Leadership

To succeed in bringing about organizational change and better targeting public interests in today's volatile world, public diplomacy leaders must practice the moral art of values-based leadership.[100] James O'Toole,[101] vice president of the Aspen Institute, uses examples from business to point out that being willing to change is not enough—leaders often fail because they do not show respect for others. In fact tough, abusive, authoritarian leaders create resistance to change because they do not understand that it is natural for human beings to reject those imposing willful changes. Establishing and maintaining an organizational culture of integrity is a massive internal communications challenge too often underestimated.

Conversely, says O'Toole, those who succeed at bringing about effective and moral change believe in and act on the inherent dignity of those they lead. They listen to their constituents, respect their opinions, and practice the art of inclusion. Although facing different challenges and utilizing different leadership styles that cut across circumstances and cultures, values-based leadership is exemplified by courage, integrity, authenticity, vision, and passion. Such individuals lead by example rather than by power, and they inspire trust, hope, and action in their followers. Those with decision-making authority who prove successful "are dedicated to institutionalizing continuous change, renewal, innovation, and learning. And the bottom line in what they do is adherence to the moral principle of respect for people."[102]

We believe an image-centered model of public diplomacy that circumvents a systemic analysis of the costs and benefits of American foreign policy and is mostly based on one-way mass communication is ineffective as well as unethical. Being committed to ethics takes leadership at the top and support for those implementing policies, yet numerous studies show that many of those most responsible for decision-making lack true intercultural sophistication and are mostly unfamiliar with global ethics expectations. That alone is a prescription for disaster. So for public diplomacy, communications is more vital and more complicated than ever. The steadying hand of the professional communicator is desperately needed in helping senior officials navigate through critical internal and external management areas.[103] Willingness to self-review and to conduct a performance-based ethics audit to "evaluate policies and procedures for preserving and nurturing ethical behavior" is highly recommended.[104]

Adopting the ethical standards of commitment to truth, two-way symmetrical public diplomacy, and values-based leadership is vital to an effective public diplomacy strategy. These structural changes are not premised on ethical grounds only. Realignments in the post-Cold War political environment, the proliferation of new media, and the resulting possibility for more public participation in international relations have made Cold War public diplomacy strategies obsolete and ineffective.[105] With advances in new media and the globalization of information technology, it is no longer possible for the United States to achieve information dominance.[106] Black propaganda, or deceptive public diplomacy, is not sustainable over the long term, given that opponents have quick access to rebuttal. What might have taken decades to become public knowledge now becomes evident in a matter of years or months. An image-oriented public diplomacy will best work in closed societies. Thus, we believe a major obstacle to U.S. public diplomacy program is its emphasis on image building rather than emphasis on genuine dialogue and symmetrical relationships.[107]

More specifically, there is a rift between what public diplomacy advocates and the foreign policies the United States pursues. This perceived rift is most acute in U.S. relations with the Middle East. A main problem with the United States' approach to public diplomacy is that public diplomacy has limited effect on the policy making process. Public diplomacy should go beyond its advisory role and become part of the decision making process. This is an opportunity for the United States to overcome the gap between its image and policies. Today the U.S. communication tactics rely on a hegemonic model of communication. As a result of these hegemonic practices, differences in policy and message, and emphasis on image building rather than mutual dialogue, the United States' credibility has decreased. With this flawed outlook, public diplomacy initiatives are perceived as hypocritical.

Appendix: The Code of Athens

The Code of Athens, which is the international code of ethics for global public relations practitioners, was adopted by the International Public Relations Association General Assembly, held in Athens, Greece, on May 12, 1965 and modified at Teheran, Iran, on April 17, 1968. The author of this code is Lucien Matrat, Member Emeritus (France) of IPRA.

> CONSIDERING that all Member countries of the United Nations Organisation have agreed to abide by its Charter which reaffirms "its faith in fundamental human rights, in the dignity and worth of the human person" and that having regard to the very nature of the profession, Public Relations

practitioners in these countries should undertake to ascertain and observe the principles set out in this Charter;

CONSIDERING that, apart from "rights," human beings have not only physical or material needs but also intellectual, moral and social needs, and that their rights are of real benefit to them only in-so-far as these needs are essentially met;

CONSIDERING that, in the course of their professional duties and depending on how these duties are performed, Public Relations practitioners can substantially help to meet these intellectual, moral and social needs;

And lastly, CONSIDERING that the use of the techniques enabling them to come simultaneously into contact with millions of people gives Public Relations practitioners a power that has to be restrained by the observance of a strict moral code.

On all these grounds, all members of the International Public Relations Association agree to abide by this International Code of Ethics, and if, in the light of evidence submitted to the Council, a member should be found to have infringed this Code in the course of his/her professional duties, he/she will be deemed to be guilty of serious misconduct calling for an appropriate penalty. Accordingly, each member:

SHALL ENDEAVOUR

1 To contribute to the achievement of the moral and cultural conditions enabling human beings to reach their full stature and enjoy the indefeasible rights to which they are entitled under the "Universal Declaration of Human Rights;"

2 To establish communications patterns and channels which, by fostering the free flow of essential information, will make each member of the group feel that he/she is being kept informed, and also give him/her an awareness of his/her own personal involvement and responsibility, and of his/her solidarity with other members;

3 To conduct himself/herself always and in all circumstances in such a manner as to deserve and secure the confidence of those with whom he/she comes into contact;

4 To bear in mind that, because of the relationship between his/her profession and the public, his/her conduct—even in private—will have an impact on the way in which the profession as a whole is appraised;

SHALL UNDERTAKE

5 To observe, in the course of his/her professional duties, the moral principles and rules of the "Universal Declaration of Human Rights;"

6 To pay due regard to, and uphold, human dignity, and to recognise the right of each individual to judge for himself/herself;

7 To establish the moral, psychological and intellectual conditions for dialogue in the true sense, and to recognise the right of these parties involved to state their case and express their views;

8 To act, in all circumstances, in such a manner as to take account of the respective interests of the parties involved: both the interests of the organisation which he/she serves and the interests of the publics concerned;

9 To carry out his/her undertakings and commitments which shall always be so worded as to avoid any misunderstanding, and to show loyalty and integrity in all circumstances so as to keep the confidence of his/her clients or employers, past or present, and of all the publics that are affected by his/her actions;

SHALL REFRAIN FROM

10 Subordinating the truth to other requirements;

11 Circulating information which is not based on established and ascertainable facts;

12 Taking part in any venture or undertaking which is unethical or dishonest or capable of impairing human dignity and integrity;

13 Using any "manipulative" methods or techniques designed to create subconscious motivations which the individual cannot control of his/her own free will and so cannot be held accountable for the action taken on them.

Notes

1 Edward R. Murrow Center for Public Diplomacy, "What is public diplomacy?" (Medford, MA: Author, The Fletcher School, Tufts University, nd), http://fletcher.tufts.edu/murrow/public-diplomacy.html (accessed March 02, 2007).

2 George Creel, *How we advertised America; the first telling of the amazing story of the Committee on Public Information that carried the gospel of Americanism to every corner of the globe* (New York and London: Harper & Brothers, 1920). See also James R. Mock, and Cedric Larson, *Words that won the war: The story of the Committee on Public Information, 1917–1919* (Princeton, NJ: Princeton University Press, 1939).

3 From an interview of Bernays appearing in Bill D. Moyers, "The image makers," an episode in *A walk through the 20th century with Bill Moyers*, a videotape series produced by the Corporation for Entertainment & Learning (Alexandria, VA: PBS Video, 1984). The best biography of Bernays to date is Larry Tye, *The father of spin: Edward L. Bernays and the birth of public relations* (New York: Henry Holt & Co., 1998).

4 Edward L. Bernays, ed., *The engineering of consent* (Norman: University of Oklahoma Press, 1955).

5 Edward L. Bernays, *Crystallizing public opinion* (New York: Liveright, 1923). Edward L. Bernays, *Biography of an idea: Memoirs of public relations counsel Edward L. Bernays* (New York: Simon and Schuster, 1965).

6 Edward L. Bernays, *Propaganda* (New York: Liveright, 1928).

7 Bernays 1928, 9.

8 Bernays 1928, 11.

9 Bernays 1928, 11.

10 Bernays 1928, 19.

11 Ray Eldon Hiebert, *Courtier to the crowd: The story of Ivy Lee and the development of public relations* (Ames, IA: Iowa State University Press, 1966), 22–3. Other influential contemporaries such as Walter Lippmann held similar elite views on the necessity of molding the masses. See Walter Lippman, *Public opinion* (New York: Harcourt, Brace and Company, 1922); Douglas C. Foyle, "Public opinion and foreign policy: Elite beliefs as a mediating variable," *International Studies Quarterly* 41, 1 (1997), 141–169; and John Zaller, *The nature and origins of mass opinion* (Cambridge, UK: Cambridge University Press, 1992).

12 See James R. Vaughan, *The failure of American and British propaganda in the Arab Middle East, 1945–57: Unconquerable minds* (New York: Palgrave Macmillan, 2005); Nicholas J. Cull, "'Public diplomacy' before Gullion: The evolution of phrase" (2006), http://uscpublicdiplomacy.com/pdfs/gullion.pdf (accessed March 22, 2007); and Jian Wang, "Telling the American story to the world: The purpose of U.S. public diplomacy in historical perspective," *Public Relations Review* 33, 1 (2007): 21–30.

13 Kenneth A. Osgood, "Propaganda," in *Encyclopedia of American foreign policy*, Volume 3, ed. Richard Dean Burns, Alexander DeConde, and Frederick Logevall (New York: Charles Scribner's Sons, 2002), 239–54.

14 See David F. Krugler, *The Voice of America and the domestic propaganda battles, 1945–1953* (Columbia: University of Missouri Press, 2000); Osgood 2002; and Alan L. Heil, Jr., *Voice of America: A history* (New York: Columbia University Press, 2003).

15 *U.S. Information and Educational Exchange Act of 1948* (Public Law 402), popularly referred to as the Smith-Mundt Act, 22 U.S.C. § 1461. Amendments to the Smith-Mundt Act in 1972 and 1998 further clarified the legal obligations of the government's public diplomacy apparatus. In addition, several presidential directives, including Ronald Reagan's NSD-77 in 1983, Bill Clinton's PDD-68 in 1999, and George W. Bush's NSPD-16 in July 2002 (the latter two both remaining classified), established new structures and procedures, as well as placed further legal restrictions, in regards to U.S. public diplomacy and information efforts.

16 Wang 2007.

17 Osgood 2002.

18 Hans N. Tuch, *Communicating with the world* (New York: St. Martin's Press, 1990).

19 Jessica C.E. Gienow-Hecht, "Cultural imperialism," in *Encyclopedia of American foreign policy*, Volume 1, ed. Richard Dean Burns, Alexander DeConde, and Frederick Logevall, (New York: Charles Scribner's Sons, 2002), 397–408; and Osgood 2002.

20 Joseph S. Nye, "The decline of America's soft power," *Foreign Affairs* 83, 3 (2004): 16–20; and Joseph S. Nye, *Soft power: The means to success in world politics* (New York: Public Affairs, 2004).

21 See also Jan Melissen, ed., *The new public diplomacy: Soft power in international relations* (New York: Palgrave Macmillan, 2005); Kathy R. Fitzpatrick, "The ethics of 'soft power': Examining the moral dimensions of U.S. public diplomacy" (paper presented at the annual meeting of the International Studies Association, San Diego, California, March 2006); Kathy R. Fitzpatrick, "Rethinking soft power: Toward a relational approach to U.S. public diplomacy" (paper presented at a forum on "Ethics in Public Diplomacy: Exploring the Moral Dimensions of U.S. International Communication," Association for Education in Journalism and Mass Communication [AEJMC] Annual Convention, San Francisco, California, August 2006); and William A. Rugh, *American encounters with Arabs: The "soft power" of U.S. public diplomacy in the Middle East* (Westport, CT: Greenwood Publishing Group, 2006).

22 Osgood 2002.

23 Krugler 2000.

24 Frances Stonor Saunders, *The cultural cold war: The CIA and the world of arts and letters* (New York: New Press, 2000); and Osgood 2002.

25 P[rabhat] K[usum] Goswami, *CIA: 40 inglorious years, 1947–1987* (Calcutta, India: Firma KLM, 1989); John Jacob Nutter, *The CIA's black ops: Covert action, foreign policy, and democracy* (Amherst, NY: Prometheus Books, 2000); Osgood 2002; Bob Woodward, *Veil: The secret wars of the CIA, 1981–1987* (New York: Simon and Schuster, 2005); and Kristian Gustafson, *Hostile intent: U.S. covert operations in Chile, 1964–1974* (Washington, DC: Potomac Books, 2007).

26 Mark J. Gasiorowski and Malcolm Byrne, eds. *Mohammad Mosaddeq and the 1953 coup in Iran* (Syracuse, NY: Syracuse University Press, 2004).

27 Nancy Snow, "U.S. public diplomacy: Its history, problems, and promise," in *Readings in propaganda and persuasion, new and classic essays*, ed. Garth S. Jowett and Victoria O'Donnell (Thousand Oaks, CA: Sage Publications, 2006), 225–41.

28 Peter van Ham, "War, lies, and videotape: Public diplomacy and the USA's War on Terrorism," *Security Dialogue* 34, 4 (2003): 427–44. He "concludes that although the USA's public diplomacy is an essential (and still underdeveloped and undervalued) component of its overall policy towards the Middle East, it will take more than better communications to address the USA's credibility and image problems in that region."

29 Task Force on Public Service Values and Ethics, *A strong foundation: Report of the Task Force on Public Service Values and Ethics* (Ottawa: Canadian Centre for Management Development, January 2000), 68, http://www.myschool-monecole.gc.ca/Research/publications/pdfs/tait.pdf (accessed August 13, 2007).

30 Kenneth Kernaghan, "The ethics era in Canadian public administration," *Research Paper No. 19* (Ottawa: Canadian Centre for Management Development, 1996).

31 Philip M. Taylor, *Munitions of the mind: A history of propaganda from the ancient world to the present day*, 3rd ed. (Manchester, UK: Manchester University Press, 2003); Garth S. Jowett and Victoria O'Donnell, *Propaganda and persuasion*, 4th ed. (Thousand Oaks, CA: Sage Publications, 2006).

32 See Jay Black, "Semantics and ethics of propaganda," *Journal of Mass Media Ethics* 16, 2/3 (2001): 121–37; Stanley B. Cunningham, *The idea of propaganda: A reconstruction* (Westport, CT: Praeger, 2002); Patrick Lee Plaisance, "The propaganda War on Terrorism: An analysis of the United States' 'Shared Values' public-diplomacy campaign after September 11, 2001," *Journal of Mass Media Ethics* 20, 4 (2005): 250–68; Mohan J. Dutta-Bergman, "U.S. Public diplomacy efforts in the Middle East: A critical cultural approach," *Journal of Communication Inquiry* 30, 2 (2006): 102–24; Fitzpatrick August 2006; and Philip Seib, "The ethics of public diplomacy," in *Ethics in public relations: Responsible advocacy*, ed. Kathy Fitzpatrick and Carolyn Bronstein (Thousands Oaks, CA: Sage Publications, 2006), 155–70.

33 Robert L. Heath and Richard Alan Nelson, *Issues management: Corporate public policymaking in an information society* (Newbury Park, CA: Sage Publications, 1989); Richard Alan Nelson, "Bias versus fairness: The social utility of issues management," *Public Relations Review* 16, 1 (1990): 25–32; Richard Alan Nelson, "Issues communication and advocacy: Contemporary ethical challenges," *Public Relations Review* 20, 3 (1994): 225–31; and Janet A. Bridges and Richard Alan Nelson, "Issues management: A relational approach," in *Public relations as relationship management: A relational approach to the study and practice of public relations*, ed. John A. Ledingham and Stephen D. Bruning (Mahwah, NJ: Lawrence Erlbaum Associates, 2000), 95–116.

34 Richard Alan Nelson, "Public policy implications of the new communication technologies," in *Strategic issues management: How organizations respond to public interests and policies*, ed. Robert L. Heath and Associates (San Francisco and London: Jossey-Bass, 1988), 366–85; Richard Alan Nelson, "Using new technologies in international communication: Building a more public relationship between developing nations and the U.S.," in *Business research yearbook: Global business perspectives*, Volume 2, ed. Abbass F. Alkhafaji (Lanham, MD, New York, and London: University Press of America and the International Academy of Business

Disciplines, 1995b), 814–818; and Richard Alan Nelson, "Dispelling U.S. propaganda images of the Middle East and North Africa," in *Advertising and Marketing Communications in the Middle East*, 2nd edition, ed. Kamal G. Darouni (Zouk Mosbeh, Lebanon: Notre Dame University—Louaize, 2002), 286, 301–313.

35 Richard Alan Nelson, "Public diplomacy: Opportunities for international public relations activism," *PR Update* 2 (March 1995a): 5–7; Richard Alan Nelson, "Using information technologies to communicate internationally: Governments, strategic public diplomacy and the internet," in *International business strategies: Economic development issues*, ed. Abbass F. Alkhafaji and Zakaria El-Sadek (Apollo, PA: Closson Press and the International Academy of Business Disciplines, 1997), 87–95; Foad Izadi, "Post-9/11 U.S. public diplomacy: The case of Iran" (paper presented at the National Communication Association 93rd Annual Conference, Chicago, Illinois, November 2007); and Foad Izadi and Hakimeh Saghaye-Biria, "A discourse analysis of elite American newspaper editorials: The case of Iran's nuclear program," *Journal of Communication Inquiry* 31,2 (2007): 140–65.

36 See John M. Holcomb, "Anticipating public policy: An interest group approach," *Public Affairs Review* 1(1980): 72–82; Douglas J. Bergner, "The maturing of public interest groups," *Public Relations Quarterly* 31,3 (1986): 14–16; Seymour M. Lipset, "The sources of public interest activism," *Public Relations Quarterly* 31,3 (1986): 9–13; Walter J. Stone, *Republic at risk: Self-interest in American politics* (Pacific Grove, CA: Brooks/Cole Publishing, 1990); Margaret E. Keck and Kathryn Sikkink, *Activists beyond borders: Advocacy networks in international politics* (Ithaca, NY: Cornell University Press, 1998); Alexander Hamilton, James Madison and John Jay, *The Federalist papers*, ed. Clinton Rossiter with a new introduction and annotations by Charles R. Resler (New York: Mentor, 1999, originally published in 1787–1788); and Akira Iriye, 2002. *Global community: The role of international organizations in the making of the contemporary world* (Berkeley, CA: University of California Press, 2002).

37 Stanley B. Cunningham, "Sorting out the ethics of propaganda," *Communication Studies* 43 (1992): 233–45; Black 2001.

38 Richard Alan Nelson, "Ethics of persuasion," in *Encyclopedia of Business Ethics and Society*, Volume 2, ed. Robert W. Kolb (Thousand Oaks, CA: Sage Publications, 2008), 810.

39 Nicholas J. Cull, "Public diplomacy," in *Propaganda and mass persuasion: A historical encyclopedia, 1500 to the present*, ed. Nicholas J. Cull, David Culbert and David Welch (Santa Barbara, CA: ABC Clio, 2003), 327–28.

40 Richard Alan Nelson, *A chronology and glossary of propaganda in the United States* (Westport, CT: Greenwood Press), 232.

41 Jacques Ellul, *Propaganda: The formation of men's attitudes* (New York: Knopf, 1965).

42 Cunningham 2002.

43 Plaisance 2005.

44 Seib 2006, 156.

45 Black 2001, 134.

46 Siobhán McEvoy-Levy, *American exceptionalism and US foreign policy: Public diplomacy at the end of the Cold War* (New York: Palgrave, 2001).

47 Ian Tyrrell, "American exceptionalism in an age of international history," *American Historical Review* 96, 4 (1991): 1031–56.

48 Fitzpatrick, August 2006.

49 Tanner Mirrlees, "American soft power, or, American cultural imperialism," in *The new imperialists: Ideologies of empire*, ed. Colin Mooers (Oxford, UK: Oneworld, 2006), 198–228.

50 Edward W. Said, *Orientalism* (New York: Pantheon Books, 1978).

51 Michel Foucault, *Power/Knowledge: Selected interviews & other writings 1972–1977* (New York: Pantheon Books, 1980).

52 Melani McAlister, *Epic encounters: Culture, media, and U.S. interests in the Middle East since 1945*, updated ed., with a post-9/11 chapter (Berkeley: University of California Press, 2005).

53 Vaughan 2005.

54 Edward S. Herman and Noam Chomsky, *Manufacturing consent: The political economy of the mass media* (New York: Pantheon Books, 1988).

55 United States House of Representatives, Committee on International Relations, *The role of public diplomacy in support of the anti-terrorism campaign*, Hearing, October 10, One Hundred Seventh Congress, First Session, Serial No. 107–47 (Washington, DC: Government Printing Office, 2001), http://commdocs.house.gov/committees/intlrel/hfa75634.000/hfa75634_0.HTM (accessed November 27, 2007); Fred A. Coffey, Jr. et al., "Our crippled public diplomacy" (Washington, DC: United States Information Agency Alumni Association, September 1, 2002), http://www.publicdiplomacy.org/crippledpd.htm (accessed November 12, 2007); Peter G. Peterson et al., *Public diplomacy: A strategy for reform. A report of an Independent Task Force on Public Diplomacy sponsored by the Council on Foreign Relations* (New York: Council

on Foreign Relations, July 30, 2002), http://ics.leeds.ac.uk/papers/pmt/exhibits/579/Task-force_final2–19.pdf (accessed October 23, 2007); Edward P. Djerejian, *Changing minds, winning peace: A new strategic direction for U.S. Public diplomacy in the Arab and Muslim world*, report submitted to the Committee on Appropriations, U.S. House of Representatives (Washington, DC: The Advisory Group on Public Diplomacy for the Arab and Muslim World, 2003), http://www.state.gov/documents/organ-ization/24882.pdf (accessed July 15, 2007); Stephen Johnson and Helle Dale, "How to reinvigorate U.S. public diplomacy," *Heritage Foundation Backgrounder* #1645 (Washington, DC: The Heritage Foundation, April 23, 2003), http://www.heritage.org/Research/PublicDiplomacy/bg1645.cfm (accessed Septem-ber 22, 2007); William P. Kiehl, "Can Humpty Dumpty be saved?" *American Diplomacy.org* (November 13, 2003), http://www.publicdiplomacy.org/24.htm (accessed October 11, 2007); Andrew Kohut, "American public diplomacy in the Islamic world," remarks of Andrew Kohut to the Senate Foreign Relations Committee Hearing, February 27 (Washington, DC: Pew Research Center for the People and the Press, 2003), http://people-press.org/commentary/display.php3?AnalysisID=63 (accessed January 3, 2008); Peter G. Peterson, et al., *Finding America's voice: A strategy for reinvigorating U.S. Public diplomacy: Report of an Independent Task Force sponsored by the Council on Foreign Relations* (Washington, DC: Council on Foreign Relations, 2003), http://www.cfr.org/content/publications/attachments/public_diploma-cy.pdf (accessed October 13, 2007); United States Senate, Committee on Foreign Relations, *American public diplomacy and Islam*, Hearing, February 27, One Hundred Eighth Congress, First Session, Serial No. 108–21 (Washington, DC: US Government Printing Office, 2003), http://www.senate.gov/~foreign/hearings/2003/hrg030227a.html (accessed November 3, 2007); Fred A. Coffey, Jr. et al., "Making public diplomacy effective: State Department public diplomacy must be realigned" (Washington, DC: United States Information Agency Alumni Association, November 15, 2004), http://www.publicdiplomacy.org/42.htm (accessed November 13, 2007); Defense Science Board Task Force on Strategic Communication, *Report of the Defense Science Board Task Force on Strategic Communication* (Washington, DC: Office of the Under Secretary of Defense for Acquisition, Technology, and Logistics, September 2004), http://www.acq.osd.mil/dsb/reports/2004–09-Strategic_Communication.pdf (accessed July 19, 2007); Heritage Foundation, "Regaining America's voice overseas: A conference on U.S. public diplomacy, July 10, 2003," *Heritage Lectures*, No. 817 (Washington, DC: Author, January 13, 2004), http://www.heritage.org/Research/GovernmentReform/upload/54407_1.pdf (accessed October 3, 2007); Charles Wolf, Jr. and Brian Rosen, "Public diplomacy: How to think about and improve it," Occasional Paper (Santa Monica, CA: Rand Corporation, 2004), http://www.rand.org/pubs/occasional_papers/2004/RAND_OP134.pdf (accessed December 4, 2007); Susan B. Epstein and Lisa Mages, *Public diplomacy: A review of past recommendations* (Washington, DC: Congressional Research Service, Library of Congress, September 2, 2005), http://digital.library.unt.edu/govdocs/crs/perma-link/meta-crs-7900:1 (accessed November 11, 2007); Andrew Kohut, "How the United States is per-ceived in the Arab and Muslim worlds," remarks of Andrew Kohut to the U.S. House International Relations Committee, Subcommittee on Oversight and Investigations (Washington, DC: Pew Research Center for the People and the Press, November 10, 2005), http://pewglobal.org/commentary/display. php?AnalysisID=1001 (accessed August 12, 2007); Public Diplomacy Council, *A call for action on public diplomacy* (Washington, DC: Author, School of Media and Public Affairs, George Washington University, January 2005), http://pdi.gwu.edu/merlin-cgi/p/downloadFile/d/7536/n/off/other/1/name/ACALLFORACTIONONPUBLICDIPLOMACY01-2005prin (accessed October 21, 2007); United States Advisory Commission on Public Diplomacy, *2005 report* (Washington, DC: Author, 2005), http://www.state.gov/documents/organization/55989.pdf (accessed September 13, 2007); United States House of Representatives, Committee on International Relations, *An around-the-world review of public diplomacy*, Hearing, November 10. One Hundred Ninth Congress, First Session, Serial No. 109–128 (Washington, DC: Government Printing Office, 2005), http://commdocs.house.gov/committees/intl-rel/hfa75634.000/hfa75634_0.HTM (accessed November 29, 2007); Dave Dudas and Chris Hornbarger, *Nature of the public diplomacy challenge: Roundtable final report, February 23–24, 2006* (West Point, NY: Department of Social Sciences, United States Military Academy, 2006), http://www.seniorconference.usma.edu/USMA_Public_Diplomacy_Feb_2006.pdf (accessed October 17, 2007); and McCormick Tribune Foundation, *Understanding the mission of U.S. international broadcasting*, McCormick Tribune Conference Series (Chicago: Author, 2007), http://www.mccormicktribune.org/publications/broadcasting07.pdf (accessed December 4, 2007)

56 See, for example, the recommendations of the United States General Accounting Office, *U.S. public diplomacy: State Department expands efforts but faces significant challenges*, report to the Committee on International Relations, House of Representatives, September (Washington, DC: Author, 2003), http://www.gao.gov/new.items/d03951.pdf (accessed April 14, 2007). This indicates, p. 29: "But the absence of an integrated and commonly understood strategy for State's public diplomacy efforts makes it difficult for State to direct its diverse efforts in a systematic manner to achieve measurable results. The methods

and techniques of private sector public relations campaigns merit consideration in developing and implementing such a strategy. Also, because State is not systematically and comprehensively measuring progress toward its public diplomacy goals, its ability to correct its course of action or to direct resources toward activities that offer a greater likelihood of success is limited. While the difficulty of measuring State's long-term influence on audiences overseas should not be underestimated, private sector public relations firms and other U.S. government agencies provide some reasonable examples of where to begin. Shortfalls in staffing, burdensome administrative and budgeting processes, Foreign Service officers with insufficient foreign language proficiency, and insufficient time for public diplomacy training pose additional challenges for State." See also Bud Goodall, Angela Trethewey and Kelly McDonald. *Strategic ambiguity, communication, and public diplomacy in an uncertain world: Principles and practices.* Report #0604 (Tempe, AZ: Consortium for Strategic Communication, Hugh Downs School of Human Communication, Arizona State University, June 21, 2006), http://www.asu.edu/clas/communication/about/csc/documents/StrategicAmbiguity.pdf (accessed November 12, 2007). They write: "There are two major reasons for failures of communication in public diplomacy: (1) reliance on an outdated one-way model of influence, and (2) an inability to prepare for, or respond to the jihadi media and message strategy that has thus far dominated local cultural interpretations of U.S. diplomatic objectives. These failures can be addressed if the U.S. recognizes the need for a new way of thinking about *ambiguity as strategy* in strategic communication initiatives. Strategic ambiguity recognizes that a powerful vision for change among diverse constituents requires an ability to empower local interpretations of its meaning in order to build relationships to that vision without insisting on a fixed meaning for it or alienating potential allies because of it. Ambiguous but mindful communication practices are required in uncertain times, particularly when dealing with audiences we neither fully understand nor trust. Five principles to guide strategic communication policy are: (1) practice strategic engagement, not global salesmanship; (2) do not repeat the same message in the same channels with the same spokesperson and expect new or different results; (3) do not seek to control a message's meaning in cultures we do not fully understand; (4) understand that message clarity and perception of meaning is a function of relationships, not strictly a function of word usage; and (5) seek 'unified diversity' based on global cooperation instead of 'focused wrongness' based on sheer dominance and power."

57 Daya Gamage, "Strategic alignment of foreign economic assistance with foreign policy goals is US aim, says Sec. of State Condi Rice," *Asian Tribune*, February 10, 2007, http://www.asiantribune.com/index.php?q=node/4484 (accessed July 14, 2007).

58 David M. Edelstein and Ronald R. Krebs, "Washington's troubling obsession with public diplomacy," *Survival* 47, 1 (2005): 89.

59 Getinet Belay, "Ethics in international interaction: Perspectives on diplomacy and negotiation," in *Ethics in intercultural and international communication*, ed. Fred L. Casmir (Mahwah, NJ: Lawrence Erlbaum Associates, 1997), 227–66; Rhonda Zaharna, "The unintended consequences of crisis public diplomacy: American public diplomacy in the Arab world," *Foreign Policy in Focus: Policy Brief* 8, 2 (June 1, 2003), http://www.fpif.org/fpiftxt/1025 (accessed May 27, 2007); and Snow 2006.

60 Dutta-Bergman 2006.

61 Jürgen Habermas, *The theory of communicative action*, 2 volumes (Boston: Beacon Press, 1984–1987).

62 Bruce Gregory, "Discourse norms in public diplomacy: Necessary and artificial fault lines" (paper presented at a forum on "Ethics in Public Diplomacy: Exploring the Moral Dimensions of U.S. International Communication," Association for Education in Journalism and Mass Communication [AEJMC] Annual Convention, San Francisco, California, August 2006).

63 Melissen 2005; and Kathy R. Fitzpatrick, "Advancing the new public diplomacy: A public relations perspective," *The Hague Journal of Diplomacy* 2, 3 (2007): 187–211.

64 Shaun Riordan, "Dialogue-based public diplomacy: A new foreign policy paradigm," in *The new public diplomacy: Soft power in international relations*, ed. Jan Melissen (New York: Palgrave Macmillan, 2005), 180–95.

65 Dutta-Bergman 2006.

66 Zaharna 2003; and Rhonda Zaharna, "The network paradigm of strategic public diplomacy," *Foreign Policy in Focus: Policy Brief* 10, 1 (April 1, 2005), http://www.fpif.org/fpiftxt/970 (accessed May 28, 2007).

67 Brian Hocking, *Multistakeholder diplomacy: Foundations, forms, functions, and frustrations* (Msida, Malta: DiploFoundation, 2005); and Jovan Kurbalija and Valentin Katrandjiev, eds., *Multistakeholder diplomacy: Challenges and opportunities* (Msida, Malta and Geneva, Switzerland: DiploFoundation, 2006), http://textus.diplomacy.edu/textusbin/env/scripts/Pool/GetBin.asp?IDPool=956 (accessed July 14, 2007). See p. vii: "Multistakeholder diplomacy is an innovative diplomatic method aimed at facilitating the equitable participation of all parties concerned in discussions on and debate over particular issue or issues at stake. It is based on the principles of mutual recognition and trust and on shared expertise and

information. The multistakeholder approach to diplomacy thus brings about a synergy between state and non-state actors in their efforts to seek co-operative solutions to the most pressing problems of global development, human resources, and environment, to name but a few. The concept accepts and thrives on the widely appreciated wisdom that state bureaucracies alone cannot solve the enormity of the challenges that mankind faces, no matter how powerful any one state may be. Indeed, to a great extent, diplomacy today is less state-centric and more multistakeholder in substance."

68 Snow 2006.

69 James E. Grunig et al., ed., *Excellence in public relations and communication management* (Hillsdale, NJ: Lawrence Erlbaum Associates, 1992).

70 Fitzpatrick, August 2006, 1.

71 John A. Ledingham, "Explicating relationship management as a general theory of public relations," *Journal of Public Relations Research* 15, 2 2003): 181–98.

72 Grunig et al. 1992.

73 Melissen 2005, 21.

74 James E. Grunig and Larissa A. Grunig, "Models of public relations and communication," in *Excellence in public relations and communication management*, ed. James E. Grunig et al. (Hillsdale, NJ: Lawrence Erlbaum Associates, 1992), 285–325 (p. 312).

75 Grunig and Grunig 1992.

76 Amanda E. Cancel et al., "It depends: A contingency theory of accommodation in public relations," *Journal of Public Relations Research* 9, 1 (1997): 31–63.

77 Priscilla Murphy, "The limits of symmetry: A game theory approach to symmetric and asymmetric public relations," in *Public relations research annual*, Volume 3, ed. James E. Grunig, and Larissa A. Grunig (Hillsdale, NJ: Lawrence Erlbaum Associates, 1989), 115–31.

78 David M. Dozier, James E. Grunig, and Larissa A. Grunig, *Excellent public relations and effective organizations: A study of communication management in three countries* (Mahwah, NJ: Lawrence Erlbaum Associates, 2002), 314.

79 Dozier, Grunig, and Grunig 2002.

80 Murphy 1989.

81 Betteke van Ruler and Dejan B. Vercic, "Reflective communication management, future ways for public relations research," in *Communication yearbook*, Volume 29, ed. Pamela J. Kalbfleisch (Mahwah, NJ: Lawrence Erlbaum Associates, 2005), 239–73.

82 Harold D. Lasswell, "The structure and function of communication in society," in *The communication of ideas: Religion and civilization series*, ed. Lyman Bryson (New York: Harper & Row, 1948), 37–51 (p. 37).

83 Claude E. Shannon and Warren Weaver, *The mathematical theory of communication* (Urbana, IL: University of Illinois Press, 1949).

84 Robert L. Heath, "A rhetorical approach to zones of meaning and organizational prerogatives," *Public Relations Review* 19, 2 (1993): 141–55.

85 Heath 1993, 143–4.

86 Grunig and Grunig 1992.

87 Heath 1993.

88 Riordan 2005.

89 Riordan 2005, 189.

90 James E. Grunig, "Image and substance: From symbolic to behavioral relationships," *Public Relations Review* 19, 2 (1993), 121–139 (p. 123).

91 Ferguson 1984.

92 As cited in Grunig 1993, 135.

93 Grunig 1993, 135.

94 Grunig 1993; Dozier, Grunig, and Grunig 2002; and Seong-Hun Yun, "Toward public relations theory-based study of public diplomacy: Testing the applicability of the Excellence Study," *Journal of Public Relations Research* 18, 4 (2006): 287–312.

95 *The international code of ethics of the International Public Relations Association (IPRA)* (Dorking, Surrey, United Kingdom: International Public Relations Association, 1965 and revised in 1968), http://www.ipra.org/detail.asp?articleid=22 (accessed July 4, 2007). Note: The code adopted by the International Public Relations Association General Assembly, held in Athens, Greece, on May 12, 1965 and modified at Teheran, Iran, on April 17, 1968.

96 See Magda Pieczka, "Paradigms, systems theory and public relations," in *Critical perspectives in public relations*, ed. Jacquie L'Etang and Magda Pieczka (London: International Thomson Business Press, 1996), 124–56; and James E. Grunig, "Two-way symmetrical public relations: Past, present and future," in *The handbook of public relations*, ed. Robert L. Heath (Thousand Oaks, CA: Sage, 2001), 11–30.

97 James G. Miller, *Living systems* (New York: McGraw-Hill, 1978), 16. Also cited in Glen M. Broom, Shawna Casey and James Ritchey, "Concept and theory of organization-public relationships," in *Public relations as relationship management: A relational approach to the study and practice of public relations*, ed. John A. Ledingham and Stephen D. Bruning (Mahwah, NJ: Lawrence Erlbaum Associates, 2000), 3–23 (p. 13).

98 James E. Grunig and Yi-Hui Huang, "From organizational effectiveness to relationship indicators: Antecedents of relationships, public relationships strategies and relationship outcomes," in *Public relations as relationship management: A relational approach to the study and practice of public relations*, ed. John A. Ledingham and Stephen D. Bruning (Mahwah, NJ: Lawrence Erlbaum Associates, 2000), 23–54.

99 Vaughan 2005. For another interesting viewpoint, see also Jami A. Fullerton and Alice G. Kendrick, *Advertising's war on terrorism: The story of the U.S. State Department's shared values initiative* (Spokane, WA: Marquette Books, 2006).

100 Alice Kendrick, "Values and ethics in U.S. public diplomacy" (paper presented at a forum on "Ethics in Public Diplomacy: Exploring the Moral Dimensions of U.S. International Communication," Association for Education in Journalism and Mass Communication [AEJMC] Annual Convention, San Francisco, California, August 2006).

101 James O'Toole, *Leading change: Overcoming the ideology of comfort and the tyranny of custom* (San Francisco: Jossey-Bass Publishers, 1995).

102 O'Toole 1995.

103 Seib 2006 and Fitzpatrick 2007.

104 See Carol W. Lewis and Stuart C. Gilman, *The ethics challenge in public service: A problem solving guide*, 2nd ed. (San Francisco: Jossey-Bass, 2005), 262–65.

105 Wilson Dizard, Jr., *Digital diplomacy: U.S. foreign policy in the information age* (New York: Praeger, 2001); Rosaleen Smyth, "Mapping US public diplomacy in the 21st century," *Australian Journal of International Affairs* 55,3 (2001): 421–44; Wayne Nelles, "American public diplomacy as pseudo-education: A problematic national security and counter-terrorism instrument," *International Politics* 41, 1 (2004): 65–93; Zaharna 2005; and Dean Kruckeberg and Marina Vujnovic, "Public relations, not propaganda, for US public diplomacy in a post-9/11 world: Challenges and opportunities," *Journal of Communication Management* 9, 4 (2005): 296–304.

106 For examples of anti-Americanism in Iraq and the sophistication of the insurgent communication network, see Daniel Kimmage and Kathleen Ridolfo, *Iraqi insurgent media: The war of images and ideas*, an RFE/RL Special Report (Washington, DC: Radio Free Europe/Radio Liberty, June 2007), http://realaudio.rferl.org/online/OLPDFfiles/insurgent.pdf (accessed December 2, 2007).

107 Costas M. Constantinou, "On homo-diplomacy," *Space and Culture* 9, 4 (2006): 351–64.

29

Noopolitik

A New Paradigm for Public Diplomacy

David Ronfeldt and John Arquilla

The next big revolution of the information age should occur in the realm of diplomacy. The United States has been undergoing a revolution in business affairs since the 1960s, and has also undertaken a revolution in military affairs (RMA) since the late 1980s. Now the time is ripe for a counterpart "revolution in diplomatic affairs" (RDA):

- Diplomats will have to rethink what is "information," and see that a new realm is emerging—the noosphere, a global "realm of the mind"—that may have a profound effect on statecraft.
- The information age will continue to undermine the conditions for classic diplomacy based on realpolitik and "hard power," and will instead favor the emergence of a new diplomacy based on what we call *noopolitik* (nü-oh-poh-li-teek) and its preference for "soft power."

Information and the Emergence of the Noosphere

Information has always been important to statecraft. But it is moving from being a subsidiary to becoming an overarching concern—"information" matters more than ever for reasons that did not exist even 20 years ago.

One reason is technological innovation: the growth of a vast new information infrastructure—including not only the Internet, but also cable, cellular, and satellite systems, etc.—in which the balance is shifting from one-to-many broadcast media (e.g., traditional radio and television) to many-to-many interactive media. A huge increase in global interconnectivity is resulting from the ease of entry and access in many nations, and from the growing interests of so many actors in using the new infrastructure for all manner of interactions.

Thus, a second reason is the proliferation of new organizations: Vast new arrays of state and nonstate organizations are emerging that directly concern information and communications issues. The new organizational ecology is richest in the United States, with nongovernmental organizations (NGOs) like the Electronic Frontier Foundation (EFF) and Computer Professionals for Social Responsibility (CPSR) exemplifying the trend. These groups span the political spectrum and have objectives that range from helping people get connected to the Net, to influencing government policies and laws, and advancing particular causes at home or abroad.

This trend is spreading around the world, and it is not only the proliferation of individual NGOs but also their interconnection in transnational networks that is raising their influence. As the strength of networked nonstate actors grows, the nature of world politics promises to become less state-centric.

A third reason is ideational: a spreading recognition that "information" and "power" are increasingly intertwined. Across all political, economic, and military areas, informational "soft power" is becoming more important, compared to traditional, material "hard power." This trend may take decades to unfold; and, in the interim, traditional methods of exercising power may remain at the core of international politics. Yet, the rise of soft power provides another reason for attending to the rise of information strategy—power, security, strategy, and diplomacy are increasingly up for redefinition in the information age.

Growth of Three Information-based Realms

As information and communication have come to matter more, so have the realms or domains defined by them. Three that matter most are: cyberspace, the infosphere, and the noosphere. All are about information, and reflect the kinds of technological, organizational, and ideational developments noted above. But each has a different emphasis—and thus significance. They are discussed below in a progression, from the most technological (cyberspace), to the most ideational (the noosphere). Our point is that diplomats should be thinking in terms of the noosphere as much as the other two.

Cyberspace: This, the most common of the terms, refers to the global system of internetted computers, communications infrastructures, on-line conferencing entities, databases, and information utilities generally known as "the Net." This mostly means the Internet; but the term may also be used to refer to the electronic environments and critical infrastructures of a corporation, military, government, or other organization. "Strategic information warfare" is largely about assuring "cyberspace security and safety" at home, and developing a capacity to exploit vulnerabilities in systems abroad.

Cyberspace is the fastest growing, newest domain of power and property in the world. The Internet now embraces some 20 million computer hosts, nearly a hundred million users (expected to exceed a billion by the year 2000), and billions if not trillions of dollars worth of activities. Further developing this realm, nationally and globally, is one of the great undertakings of our time.

The term has a more technological bent than infosphere or noosphere. Yet, there has always been a tendency to treat cyberspace as more than technology, from the moment the term was proposed by cyberpunk writer William Gibson, through recent notions of cyberspace as a realm for building "virtual communities," creating a "global matrix of minds," and strengthening people's spiritual bonds around the world. Such views implicitly portend an overlap of cyberspace with the noosphere.

Infosphere: Knowing the limitations of the cyberspace concept, some analysts prefer the term infosphere. Sometimes the two terms are used interchangeably; but when viewed distinctly, the infosphere is far larger than cyberspace—it encompasses the latter, plus information systems that may not be part of "the Net." In the civilian world, this often includes broadcast, print, and other media (the mediasphere), as well as institutions, like libraries, parts of which are not yet electronic. In the military world, the infosphere may include command, control, computer, communications, intelligence, surveillance, and reconnaissance (C4ISR) systems—the electronic systems said to comprise the "military information environment" of a battlespace.

According to Jeffrey Cooper, the infosphere is emerging, like cyberspace, as a "truly global information infrastructure and environment" in which traditional notions of space and time no longer prevail. The term has merit because it focuses on "information environments," rather than computerized infrastructures. The term is also favored because it "carries resonances of bio-sphere"—meaning the infosphere is "a distinct domain built on information, but one intimately related to the rest of a set of nested globes in which we exist simultaneously." This implicitly entertains a view of the world that partakes of the next concept.

Noosphere: The most abstract—and so far, least favored—of the terms is the noosphere. This term, from the Greek word noos for "the mind," was coined by French theologian and scientist Pierre Teilhard de Chardin in 1925, and spread in posthumous publications in the 1950s and 1960s. In his view, the world first evolved a geosphere, and next a biosphere. Now that people are communing on global scales, the world is giving rise to a noosphere—what he variously describes as a globe-circling realm of "the mind," a "thinking circuit," a "stupendous thinking machine," a "thinking envelope" full of fibers and networks, and a planetary "consciousness." In the words of Julian Huxley, the noosphere is a "web of living thought."

According to Teilhard, forces of the mind have been creating the noosphere for ages. Before long, a synthesis of its pieces will occur in which peoples from different nations, races, and cultures develop minds that are planetary in scope, without losing their personal identities. Fully realized, the noosphere will raise mankind to a high, new evolutionary plane, one driven by a collective devotion to moral and juridical principles. However, the transition may not be smooth; a global tremor and possibly an apocalypse may characterize the final fusion of the noosphere.

The noosphere concept thus encompasses cyberspace and the infosphere. It also relates to an organizational theme that has constantly figured in our own work about the information revolution: the rise of network forms of organization that strengthen civil-society actors. Few state or market actors, by themselves, seem likely to have much interest in fostering the construction of a global noosphere, except in limited areas having to do with international law, or political and economic ideology. The impetus for creating a global noosphere is more likely to emanate from activist NGOs, other civil-society actors (e.g., churches, schools), and individuals dedicated to freedom of information and communications and to the spread of ethical values and norms. We believe it is time for state actors to begin moving in this direction, too, particularly since power in the information age will stem, more than ever before, from the ability of state and market actors to work conjointly with civil-society actors.

Comparisons Lead to a Preference for the Noosphere Concept

As the three realms grow, cyberspace will remain the smallest, nested inside the other two. The infosphere is the next largest, and the noosphere encompasses all three (see Figure 29.1). As one realm grows, so should the others.

In being the most ideational realm, the noosphere has a comparative strength. Cyberspace, the infosphere, and the noosphere are all based on "information" in all its guises, from lowly bits of data to the highest forms of knowledge and wisdom. Thus these realms all amount to information-processing systems. Yet, in being more about ideas than technologies, the noosphere, more than the other realms, also concerns what we call "information structuring." The noosphere, like the mind, is an information-processing and an information-structuring system—and this is an important distinction. The processing view focuses on the transmission of messages as the inputs and outputs of a system. In contrast, the structural view illuminates the goals, values, and practices that an organization or system may embody—what matters to its members from the standpoint of identity, meaning, and purpose, apart from whether any information is really being processed at the time. While the processing view tends to illuminate technology as a critical factor, the structural view is more likely to uphold human and ideational capital.

We believe that strategists should begin attending as much to the dynamics of information structuring as to information processing. Grand strategists rarely ignore the role of values and practices. But this role tends to be downplayed in rhetoric about the information revolution.

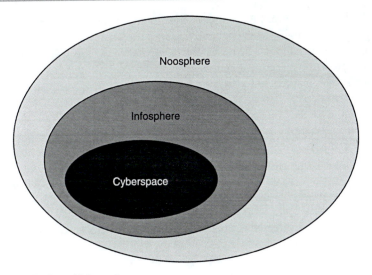

Figure 29.1. Three Realms of Information

New concepts can provide a corrective. Adoption of the noosphere concept could help strategists focus on the significance of information structuring, including with regard to the illumination of value-laden conflicts.

The noosphere presents information in terms of an expanding realm where the emphasis is on the ideational and organizational dimensions, without ignoring the technological one. It inclines the analyst and the strategist to think in terms of the roles of ideas, values, and norms, rather than in terms of Internet hosts, Web sites, and baud rates—that is, in terms of structural information rather than in terms of information processing. More to our point, preferring the noosphere concept sets the stage for our second major point: The time is ripening to develop a new approach to diplomacy and strategy, one we call noopolitik.

The Emergence of Noopolitik

By noopolitik we mean an approach to statecraft, to be undertaken as much by nonstate as by state actors, that emphasizes the role of informational soft power in expressing ideas, values, norms, and ethics through all manner of media. This makes it distinct from realpolitik, which stresses the hard, material dimensions of power and treats states as the determinants of world order. Noopolitik makes sense because knowledge is fast becoming an ever stronger source of power and strategy, in ways that classic realpolitik and internationalism cannot absorb.

In the coming years, diplomats and strategists will be drawn to both realpolitik and noopolitik. As noopolitik takes shape and gains adherents, it will serve sometimes as a supplement and complement to realpolitik, and sometimes as a contrasting, rival paradigm for policy and strategy. As time passes and the global noosphere swells, noopolitik may provide a more relevant paradigm than realpolitik. Noopolitik has much in common with liberal internationalism, but we anticipate that the latter is a transitional paradigm that can and will be folded into noopolitik.

Growing Strength of Global Civil Society

No doubt, states will remain paramount actors in the international system. The information revolution will lead to changes in the nature of the state, but not to its "withering away." What

355

will happen is a transformation. At the same time, nonstate actors will continue to grow in strength and influence. This has been the trend for several decades with business corporations and international regulatory regimes. The next trend to expect is a gradual worldwide strengthening of transnational NGOs that represent civil society. As this occurs, there will be a rebalancing of relations among state, market, and civil-society actors around the world—in ways that favor noopolitik over realpolitik.

Noopolitik upholds the importance of nonstate actors, especially from civil society, and requires that they play strong roles. Why? NGOs (not to mention individuals) often serve as sources of ethical impulses (which is rarely the case with market actors), as agents for disseminating ideas rapidly, and as nodes in networked apparatuses of "sensory organizations" that can assist with conflict anticipation, prevention, and resolution. Indeed, because of the information revolution, advanced societies are on the threshold of developing a vast sensory apparatus for watching what is happening around the world. This apparatus is not new, because it consists partly of established government intelligence agencies, corporate market-research departments, news media, and opinion-polling firms. What is new is the looming scope and scale of this sensory apparatus, as it increasingly includes networks of NGOs and individual activists who monitor and report on what they see in all sorts of issue areas, using open forums, specialized Internet mailing lists, Web postings, and fax machine ladders as tools for rapid dissemination. For example, using these tools to provide early warning about crisis is a burgeoning area of attention and development among disaster-relief and humanitarian organizations.

Against this background, the states that emerge strongest in information-age terms—even if by traditional measures they may appear to be smaller, less powerful states—are likely to be the states that learn to work conjointly with the new generation of nonstate actors. Strength may thus emanate less from the "state" *per se* than from the "system" as a whole. And this may mean placing a premium on state-society coordination, including the toleration of "citizen diplomacy" and the creation of "deep coalitions" between state and civil-society actors. In that sense, it might be said that the information revolution is impelling a shift from a state-centric to a network-centric world (which would parallel a potential shift in the military world from traditional "platform-centric" to emerging "network-centric" approaches to warfare).

This is quite acceptable to noopolitik. While realpolitik remains steadfastly imbued with notions of control, noopolitik is less about control than "decontrol"—perhaps deliberate, regulated decontrol—so that state actors can better adapt to the emergence of independent nonstate actors and learn to work with them through new mechanisms for communication and coordination. Realpolitik would lean toward an essentially mercantilist approach to information as it once did toward commerce; noopolitik is not mercantilist by nature.

Proponents of realpolitik would probably prefer to stick with treating information as an adjunct of the standard political, military, and economic elements of diplomacy and grand strategy; the very idea of intangible information as a basis for a distinct dimension of statecraft seems antithetical to realpolitik. Realpolitik allows for information strategy as a tool of propaganda, deception, and manipulation, but seems averse to accepting "knowledge projection" as amounting to a true tool of statecraft. However, for noopolitik to take hold, information will have to become a distinct dimension of grand strategy. The rise of soft power is essential for the emergence of the second path, and thus of noopolitik.

Without the emergence—and deliberate construction—of a massive, well-recognized noosphere, there will be little hope of sustaining the notion that the world is moving to a new system in which "power" is understood mainly in terms of knowledge, and that diplomats and other actors should focus on the "balance of knowledge," as distinct from the "balance of power."

What would a full-fledged noosphere encompass? What ideas, values, and norms—what principles, practices, and rules—should it embody? We presume that these would include much that America stands for: openness, freedom, democracy, the rule of law, humane behavior, respect for human rights, a preference for peaceful conflict resolution, etc. The growth of the noosphere will depend not only on increased flows of ideas and ideals, but also on growth in the stocks of ideas and ideals to which people subscribe. In addition, a noosphere may have to have complex organizational and technological bases to support its ideational essence.

Mutual Relationship between Realpolitik and Noopolitik

Realpolitik, no matter how modified, cannot be transformed into noopolitik. The two stand in contradiction. This is largely because of the uncompromisingly state-centric nature of realpolitik. It is also because, for an actor to shift the emphasis of its statecraft from realpolitik to noopolitik, there must be a shift from power-maximizing politics to power-sharing politics. Nonetheless, the contradiction is not absolute; it can, in theory and practice, be made a compatible contradiction (rather like yin and yang). Indeed, true realpolitik depends on the players sharing and responding to some core behavioral values—a bit of noopolitik may thus lie at the heart of realpolitik. Likewise, true noopolitik may work best if it accords with power politics—however, this perspective should be less about might makes right, than about right makes might. Understanding this may help in persevering through the transitional period in which realpolitik and noopolitik are likely to coexist. The point we draw for noopolitik, however, is that this kind of world requires governments to learn to work conjointly with civil-society NGOs that are engaged in building transnational networks and coalitions.

The Advance of Noopolitik

In sum, noopolitik is an approach to diplomacy and strategy for the information age that emphasizes the shaping and sharing of ideas, values, norms, laws, and ethics through soft power. Noopolitik is guided more by a conviction that right makes for might, than the obverse. Both state and nonstate actors may be guided by noopolitik; but rather than being state-centric, its strength may well stem from enabling state and nonstate actors to work conjointly. The driving motivation of noopolitik cannot be national interests defined in statist terms. National interests will still play a role, but should be defined more in society-wide than state-centric terms and be fused with broader, even global, interests in enhancing the transnationally networked "fabric" in which the players are embedded. While realpolitik tends to empower states, noopolitik will likely empower networks of state and nonstate actors. Realpolitik pits one state against another, but noopolitik encourages states to cooperate in coalitions and other mutual frameworks. In all these respects, noopolitik contrasts with realpolitik. Table 29.1 summarizes some of the contrasts discussed in this paper.

Kissinger may be said to epitomize the *ZEITGEIST* and practice of realpolitik. Who may stand for the *ZEITGEIST* of noopolitik? One name that comes to mind is George Kennan. His original notion of containment was not essentially military. Rather, it was centered on the idea of creating a community of interests, based on shared ideals, that would secure the free world, while dissuading the Soviet Union from aggression, and eventually persuading it to change. This seems an early expression of noopolitik, geared to a state-centric system. Today, leaders like Nelson Mandela and George Soros, not to mention a host of less renowned individuals who have played leading roles in civil-society activist movements, reflect the emergence of noopolitik.

Some of the best exemplars of its emergence involve "social netwars" waged by civil-society activists. (Netwar is an information-age entry on the spectrum of conflict that is defined by the use of network forms of organization, doctrine, and strategy, made possible by the information revolution.) While all-out military wars, such as World Wars I and II, represent the conflictual heights (and failures?) of realpolitik, nonmilitary netwars may prove the archetypal conflicts of noopolitik. The Nobel prize-winning campaign to ban land mines; NGO-led opposition to the

357

Table 29.1. Contrast Between Realpolitik and Noopolitik

Realpolitik	Noopolitik
States as the unit of analysis	Nodes, nonstate actors
Primacy of hard power (resources, etc.)	Primacy of soft power
Power politics as zero-sum game	Win-win, lose-lose possible
System is anarchic, highly conflictual	Harmony of interests, cooperation
Alliance conditional (oriented to threat)	Ally webs vital to security
Primacy of national self-interest	Primacy of shared interests
Politics as unending quest for advantage	Explicitly seeking a telos
Ethos is amoral, if not immoral	Ethics crucially important
Behavior driven by threat and power	Common goals drive actors
Very guarded about information flows	Propensity for info-sharing
Balance of power as the "steady-state"	Balance of responsibilities
Power embedded in nation-states	Power in "global fabric"

Multilateral Agreement on Investment (MAI); the Greenpeace-led campaign against French nuclear testing in the South Pacific; the swarming of transnational NGOs in defense of the Zapatista insurgents in Mexico; and recent information-age efforts by Burmese and Chinese dissidents, with support from U.S.-based NGOs, to press for human rights and political reforms in these countries all exemplify how transnational civil-society networks, in some cases with strong support from states, can practice noopolitik, with varying degrees of success, to change the policies of states that persist in emphasizing the traditional politics of power.

These cases substantiate that the practice of noopolitik is already emerging, and that traditional ideas about "peace through strength" may give way to new ideas of "peace through knowledge." These cases also show that ideas themselves, particularly ones with deep ethical appeal, may be fused with new communications technologies and organizational designs to create a new model of power and diplomacy that governments will increasingly encounter and have to heed. Activist NGOs, perhaps because they lack the resources for realpolitik, appear to be ahead of states in having the motivation and ability to apply noopolitik and to seek the construction of a global noosphere.

Yet what if states, or other actors, regard noopolitik as attractive, without caring about the emergence and construction of the noosphere? In the hands of a democratic leader, noopolitik might then amount to little more than airy, idealistic rhetoric with little or no structural basis; while, in the hands of a dictator or a demagogue, it could be reduced to manipulative propaganda and perception-management campaigns. Or narrow versions of noopolitik might be attempted for private gain: In the commercial worlds of advertising and public relations, this already occurs when companies develop media blitzes and plant testimonials to "spin" public opinion. These are among the risks that may have to be faced.

The Way Ahead

If an American RDA gets underway, diplomats will find themselves having to focus on how best to develop the noosphere and conduct noopolitik. Much as the rise of realpolitik depended on the development and exploitation of the geosphere (whose natural resources enhance state power), so will the rise of noopolitik depend on the development and exploitation of the noosphere. The two go hand in hand. To pursue this, measures will have to be identified that, in addition to fostering the rise of a noosphere, are geared to facilitating the effectiveness of soft power, the deepening of global interconnections, the strengthening of transnational civil-society actors, and the creation of conditions for governments to be better able to act conjointly (in terms of cooperative advantages), especially with nonstate actors.

In our 1999 writing, we note some measures for U.S. policy and strategy that could assist with the development of the noosphere and noopolitik. All are taken from ongoing discussions about issues raised by the advance of the information revolution—and diplomats would be well advised to take an interest in them. These measures include the following:

- Supporting the expansion of cyberspace connectivity around the world, including where this runs counter to the preferences of authoritarian regimes.
- Promoting freedom of information and communications as a worldwide right.
- Developing multitiered information-sharing systems, not only to ensure cyberspace safety and security, but also to create shared infospheres for openly addressing other issues.
- Creating "special media forces" that could be dispatched into conflict zones to help settle disputes through the discovery and dissemination of accurate information.
- Opening diplomacy to greater coordination between state and nonstate actors, especially NGOs.

These are just some preliminary ideas. Ultimately, there will be much more to developing the noosphere and noopolitik than just asserting, sharing, and instituting the particular values, norms, ethics, laws, and other ingredients of soft power that an actor wants to uphold. Specific policies, strategies, and mechanisms will have to be elaborated that make noopolitik significantly different from and more effective than realpolitik in dealing with issues that may range from "democratic enlargement," to the pressuring of regimes like those in Iraq, North Korea, and the Balkans, to the resolution of global environmental and human-rights issues. Skillful diplomats and strategists are bound to face choices as to when it is better to emphasize realpolitik or noopolitik, or as to how best to alternate between them or apply hybrids, especially when dealing with a recalcitrant adversary who has been able to resist realpolitik types of pressures.

What may turn out to matter for all parties—the advocates and their audiences and adversaries—is the "story" being told, implicitly or explicitly. Realpolitik is typically about whose military or economy wins. Noopolitik may ultimately be about whose story wins.

Postscript (June 2007)

That was what we wrote about noopolitik and its prospects in 1999, shortly after we introduced the idea a decade ago. Today, it still seems to be an idea for the future. Traditional power politics has continued to provide the primary basis for American foreign policy in the years since 9/11. There may indeed be a worldwide "war of ideas" underway, but it is not being waged in a manner reflective of the noopolitik paradigm—not even in pursuit of a global alliance against the scourge of terrorism. Instead, the military invasions and coercive diplomacy of the past several years imply the persistent primacy of older forms of statecraft.

Our quick review of developments over the last decade leaves us optimistic about the long-term promise of noopolitik, but disconcerted about ongoing trends. For this Postscript, we focus on making the following four points:

- Notions like noopolitik are gaining credibility, but all too slowly.
- Soft power lies behind them all, but that concept needs further clarification.

- Activist NGOs representing global civil society are major practitioners of noopolitik, but the most effective may be the global network of jihadis.
- American public diplomacy would benefit from a course correction.

Spreading Notions: Noopolitik, Cyberpolitik, Netpolitik, Infopolitik

We are not alone in proposing that the information age will affect grand strategy and diplomacy so thoroughly that a new concept will emerge. According to David Rothkopf, "the realpolitik of the new era is *cyberpolitik*, in which the actors are no longer just states, and raw power can be countered or fortified by information power." David Bollier favors *Netpolitik* to name "a new style of diplomacy that seeks to exploit the powerful capabilities of the Internet to shape politics, culture, values, and personal identity." Europeans prefer *infopolitik* as the best term for a new era of public diplomacy based on "proactive international communication" and "the projection of free and unbiased information," according to Philip Fiske de Gouveia.

At the time, we considered and rejected such alternative terms because we wanted the focus to be on the noosphere, not cyberspace or the Internet. And we wanted a term whose connotation would be ideational, not technological, in keeping with the nature of Teilhard de Chardin's original noosphere concept. Moreover, we still think that yet another term with "cyber-" or "info-" or "net-" as the prefix will not stand the test of time. So far, it remains to be seen whether noopolitik (or if you prefer, *noöspolitik*) will fare best over the long run.

In any case, similar trends lie behind all our expositions. Noopolitik—or cyberpolitik, netpolitik, or infopolitik—makes sense because of expansions underway in the fabric of global interconnections, the influence of activist NGOs that represent civil society, the appeal of "cooperative advantages," and the relevance of soft power, all due in part to the new information and communications technologies.

These trends do not spell the obsolescence of realpolitik, but they are at odds with it. To a lesser degree, they are also at odds with tenets of realpolitik's main alternative to date: liberal internationalism. Trying to bridge the gap by calling for a modified realpolitik—for example, an "ethical realpolitik" or "principled realism"—misses the point that a paradigm shift is looming. Besides, realpolitik was never necessarily unethical, any more than noopolitik is inherently a tool only for the ethical.

Soft Power: Still Lacking Operational Clarity

The underlying concept that has indeed taken hold these past ten years is "soft power." So much so, it has perhaps delayed the appeal of terms like noopolitik, even though they too seek the strategic, systematic application of suasive rather than coercive power.

Soft power depends on the articulation of appealing values, ethics, and exemplary achievements. Thus, standard descriptions of soft power are normally upbeat, even moralistic. However, from our noopolitik perspective, the soft-power concept needs further clarification and refinement, particularly in two regards.

First, the concept depends on making a distinction between hard and soft power. Is that distinction mainly about military versus nonmilitary power? If so, then trade and investment are aspects of soft power. Or should the distinction be about material versus immaterial (i.e., ideational) modes of power? Physical trade and investment then pertain to hard power, and the ideas and images behind them to soft power. We think that the latter is the correct view, in keeping with the noosphere concept. Besides, there are aspects of military doctrine—such as what constitutes a "just war" and what may be the best role for cohesive psychological operations—that pertain to soft power and noopolitik.

Second, standard presentations tend to portray soft power as "good" and hard power as "bad," or at least mean-spirited. Thus, soft power is said to be mainly about ethical attraction, and to offer a third way for strategy and diplomacy beyond the usual two: sticks and carrots. But in fact, soft power is not simply about beckoning in a nice way. It can be wielded in a tough, heavy, even dark manner too, for example, through messages to warn, embarrass, denounce, shun, or repel a targeted actor. Moreover, soft power does not necessarily favor good guys; malevolent leaders—say a Hitler or a Bin Laden—may also prove eager and adept at wielding soft power and noopolitik, on behalf of their own professed ideals. In fact, this is perhaps the most serious problem confronting American public diplomacy today.

Challenges from Rival Noospheres and Noopolitiks

Activist NGOs who represent global civil society and depend on soft power have become major practitioners of noopolitik—even if by another name—in areas such as human rights, democracy promotion, and the environment. Their leaders sense that old-fashioned, state-centric power politics is giving ground. And in one new "social netwar" after another around the world since the 1990s, noopolitik is becoming a principal NGO strategy for pressing governments and corporations to adopt beneficent reforms.

Elsewhere, however, a strong partisan effort to build a noosphere and practice noopolitik is coming from Islamic jihadis, notably the terrorists and other extremists associated with Al-Qaeda and its affiliates. They have created a vast, detailed online presence, linked to a real-world presence in particular mosques and other centers of activity, that is tantamount to a globe-spanning realm of the mind. It upholds a set of spiritual values and ethics; it fosters a kindred community of believers (what Moslems call the umma); it is globally distributed and guardedly open; and it instructs adherents how to think and act.

But this jihadi noosphere is angrily, narrowly, even brutally tribal in nature, as is the noopolitik that accompanies it through the projection of images, fatwas, interviews, and stories. These enable the jihadis to foment divisions between "us" and "them," claim sacredness solely for their own ends, demonize and intimidate others, view their every kin (man, woman, child, combatant or noncombatant) as innately guilty, revel in codes of revenge, entice and radicalize recruits, instruct as well as celebrate violence of the darkest kinds, call for territorial and spiritual conquests, and suppress moderates. The language is often religious in tone, but the stakes reduce, above all, to the exaltation of ancient tribal notions of honor, pride, dignity, and respect.

This is not the kind of ecumenical, ethical noosphere that Teilhard envisioned, nor the noopolitik that we have had in mind. Moreover, the jihadis' attempt to employ noopolitik for such dark purposes may ultimately be their Achilles' heel, since the vast majority of the world's Muslims reject their doctrines of violent extremism. Yet, the jihadis' impressive advances in building their version of a noosphere and applying noopolitik heighten the significance of both concepts. This is yet another reason why American strategists and diplomats should take noopolitik seriously—it is being used against us. As Newton Minow has warned:

> In virtually every case, those whose rule is based on an ideology of hate have understood better than we have the power of ideas and the power of communicating ideas.

American Public Diplomacy: Awaiting New Directions

At this strategic moment, when it is advisable for U.S. public diplomacy to head in the direction of noopolitik, conditions are not ripe for doing so. They were favorable when we proposed the concept last decade, but they have turned rather contrary to its promise this decade. It may be a while before propitious conditions re-emerge.

As America's soft power rises and falls, so do the prospects for noopolitik. And right now,

America's soft power is unusually questionable. America has long stood for vital ideals—freedom, equality, opportunity. America has also stood for ethical ways of doing things: competing openly and fairly, working in concert with partners, seeking the common good, respecting others' rights, and resorting to war only after exhausting nonmilitary options. By doing so, America built its legitimacy and credibility as a global power in the 20th century. But lately, due to assorted sorry matters this decade (some but not all involving the war in Iraq), leaders and publics around the world have become increasingly doubtful that America is deeply dedicated to the ideals and practices it professes. U.S. public diplomacy is on the defensive more than ever before. Oddly, China is said to be more effective at soft-power appeals and techniques.

What would reinvigorate the prospects for noopolitik? Renewal of a clear intent to favor nonmilitary strategies, operate in partnerships, and abide by stringent ethical standards would surely help. Yet, whatever other answers should be added, the key may well be revitalization of a deep sense that ideas matter, along with a better grasp of how ideas move people to think and act in strategic ways—more along the lines of the complex efforts made during the Cold War than the simplifications seen this decade. And by this, we mean ideas expressed through actions as well as words, including what the State Department has begun to call "the diplomacy of deeds."

The point to which we keep returning is that noopolitik is ultimately about whose story wins. Al-Qaeda and its affiliates have malign intent, but their measures fit their grand narrative about the need to diminish the shadow cast by American power across the Muslim world. In contrast, the U.S. government and its allies remain less successful at fielding a fitting narrative. American ideals, far from serving as a beacon to others—as in President Reagan's "shining city on a hill" strategy—have been obscured by the controversial invasion and occupation of Iraq and by troubling images of destructive war-making and maltreatment of detainees and noncombatants. These events have undermined the preferred American story about fostering a peaceful, prosperous, civilized, democratic world in which all nations are bound together by shared values, dedicated to extirpating the scourge of transnational terror.

New thinking about information strategy and strategic communication is occurring in official circles. But in too many instances, what has been put into practice seems to emphasize perception management, information operations, and propaganda more than the arts of public diplomacy. If noopolitik is to be developed, this imbalance must be corrected. American public diplomacy is too precious to let it be viewed as an exercise in marketing and manipulation, sound-bites and slogans.

There is an urgent reason to revive the prospects for noopolitik: A worldwide war of ideas is underway, maybe several wars. The most evident one—which extends far beyond Al-Qaeda—has spiritual, religious, ideological, philosophical, and cultural aspects; and much of it is taking place on the Internet. In such a war of ideas, one's information posture matters as much as one's military posture. And at this point, America's information posture does not appear to be well designed.

This poses quite a challenge for information strategy, a concept that calls for knowing the enemy, shaping public consciousness, and crafting persuasive messages for friend and foe alike. It is about getting the contents of those messages right, while finding the best conduits. It is about deploying inviting, meaningful narratives to win the battle of the story. And it is about doing all this in ways that make soft power work better than hard power, so that information-age noopolitik finally begins to outperform traditional realpolitik.

Note

1 The main text of this chapter is adapted from *Emergence of Noopolitik: Toward an American Information Strategy* by Ronfeldt and Arquilla (Copyright 1999 by Rand Corporation; reproduced with permission of Rand Corporation in the format Textbook and Other book via Copyright Clearance Center), which

discusses at greater length our earlier views about the prospects for noopolitik. Here, only the Postscript is new. This paper was prepared by the authors on their own, and represents their views only. An interim, slightly longer, footnoted version was posted online in 2007 at http://www.firstmonday.org. Readers who want greater specificity about our sources, especially the quotations, should consult that version. We thank Nancy Snow for her editorial assistance with condensing the text for this paper. We thank Bruce Berkowitz and Bruce Gregory for offering illuminating comments. We also thank the U.S. Institute for Peace (USIP), notably Sheryl Brown and Margarita Studemeister, for publishing the 1999 version of this paper in USIP's Virtual Diplomacy Initiative series.

References

Anderson, Robert, and Norman Shapiro. 1992. Deployable Local Networks to Reduce Conflict. *The Information Society* 8, no. 3: 26–30.

Arquilla, John. 2006. *The Reagan Imprint: Ideas in American Foreign Policy from the Collapse of Communism to the War on Terror.* Chicago, Ill.: Ivan R. Dee.

Arquilla, John, and Douglas Borer, eds. 2007. *Information Strategy and Warfare: A Guide to Theory and Practice.* London: Routledge.

Arquilla, John, and David Ronfeldt. 1996. *The Advent of Netwar.* Santa Monica, Calif.: RAND. http://www.rand.org/pubs/monograph_reports/MR789/index.html.

Arquilla, John, and David Ronfeldt, eds. 1997. *In Athena's Camp: Preparing for Conflict in the Information Age.* Santa Monica, Calif.: RAND. http://www.rand.org/publications/MR/MR880/index.html.

Arquilla, John, and David Ronfeldt. 1998a. Preparing for Information-Age Conflict, Part I: Conceptual and Organizational Dimensions. *Information, Communication, and Society* 1, no. 1: 1–22.

Arquilla, John, and David Ronfeldt. 1998b. Preparing for Information-Age Conflict, Part II: Doctrinal and Strategic Dimensions. *Information, Communication, and Society* 1, no. 2: 121–143.

Arquilla, John, and David Ronfeldt. 1999. *The Emergence of Noopolitik: Toward an American Information Strategy.* Santa Monica, Calif.: RAND. http://www.rand.org/pubs/monograph_reports/MR1033/index.html.

Arquilla, John, and David Ronfeldt. 2001. *Networks and Netwars: The Future of Terror, Crime, and Militancy.* Santa Monica, Calif.: RAND. http://www.rand.org/pubs/monograph_reports/MR1382/index.html.

Bateson, Gregory. 1972. *Steps to An Ecology of Mind.* New York: Ballantine.

Bollier, David. 2003. *The Rise of Netpolitik: How the Internet Is Changing International Politics and Diplomacy.* Washington, D.C.: The Aspen Institute.

Boulding, Elise. 1988. *Building a Global Civic Culture: Education for an Interdependent World.* New York: Teachers College Press.

Boulding, Elise. 1993. Ethnicity and New Constitutive Orders. In *Global Visions: Beyond the New World Order,* ed. Jeremy Brecher, John Brown Childs, and Jill Cutler, 213–231. Boston, Mass.: South End Press.

Brandenburger, Adam M., and Barry J. Nalebuff. 1997. *Co-opetition.* New York: Currency Doubleday.

Brzezinski, Zbigniew. 1997. *The Grand Chessboard: American Primacy and Its Geostrategic Imperatives.* New York: Basic Books.

Capra, Fritjof. 1996. *The Web of Life: A New Scientific Understanding of Living Systems.* New York: Anchor Books.

Casebeer, William D., and James A. Russell. 2005. Storytelling and Terrorism: Towards a Comprehensive "Counter-Narrative Strategy." *Strategic Insights* IV, no. 3. http://www.ccc.nps.navy.mil/si/2005/Mar/casebeerMar05.asp.

Castells, Manuel. 1996. *The Rise of the Network Society: The Information Age: Economy, Society and Culture, Vol. I.* Malden, Mass.: Blackwell Publishers.

Castells, Manuel. 1997. *The Power of Identity: The Information Age: Economy, Society and Culture, Volume II.* Malden, Mass.: Blackwell Publishers.

Cebrowski, Arthur K., and John J. Garstka. 1998. Network-Centric Warfare: Its Origins and Future. *United States Naval Institute Proceedings,* 28–35.

Clark, Ann Marie, Elisabeth J. Friedman, and Kathryn Hochstetler. 1998. The Sovereign Limits of Global Civil Society: A Comparison of NGO Participation in UN World Conferences on the Environment, Human Rights, and Women. *World Politics* 51, no. 1: 1–35.

Cleaver, Harry. 1998. The Zapatista Effect: The Internet and the Rise of an Alternative Political Fabric. *Journal of International Affairs* 51, no. 2: 621–640.

Cleaver, Harry. 2006. Deep Currents Rising: Some Notes on the Global Challenge to Capitalism. http://www.eco.utexas.edu/facstaff/Cleaver/DeepCurrentsRisingFinal2.htm#_ftnref13.

Cobb, Jennifer. 1998. *Cybergrace: The Search for God in the Digital World*. New York: Crown Publishers.

Cooper, Jeffrey R. 1997. *The Emerging Infosphere: Some Thoughts on Implications of the "Information Revolution."* McLean, Va.: Center for Information Strategy and Policy, Science Applications International Corporation.

Dawkins, Richard. 1989. *The Selfish Gene*. New York: Oxford University Press.

De Caro, Charles. 1996. Softwar. In *Cyberwar: Security, Strategy and Conflict in the Information Age*, ed. Alan Campen, Douglas Dearth, and R. T. Goodden, 203–218. Fairfax, Va.: AFCEA International Press.

Dertouzos, Michael. 1997. *What Will Be: How the New World of Information Will Change Our Lives*. San Francisco, Calif.: HarperCollins.

Devji, Faisal. 2005. *Landscapes of the Jihad: Militancy, Morality, Modernity*. Ithaca, N.Y.: Cornell University Press.

Dyson, Esther. 1997. *Release 2.0: A Design for Living in the Digital Age*. New York: Broadway Books.

Fiske de Gouveia, Philip, with Hester Plumridge. 2005. *European Infopolitik: Developing EU Public Diplomacy Strategy*. London: The Foreign Policy Centre. http://fpc.org.uk/publications/euro-infopolitik.

Frederick, Howard. 1993a. Computer Networks and the Emergence of Global Civil Society. In *Global Networks: Computers and International Communication*, ed. Linda M. Harasim, 283–295. Cambridge, Mass.: The MIT Press.

Frederick, Howard. 1993b. *Global Communication and International Relations*. Belmont, Calif.: Wadsworth Publishing Co.

Gibson, William. 1984. *Neuromancer*. New York: Ace Books.

Golden, James R. 1993. Economics and National Strategy: Convergence, Global Networks, and Cooperative Competition. *The Washington Quarterly* 16, no. 3: 91–113.

Gompert, David. 1998. *Right Makes Might: Freedom and Power in the Information Age*. McNair Paper 59, Washington, D.C.: NDU Press.

Gompert, David C. 2007. *Heads We Win: The Cognitive Side of Counterinsurgency (COIN)*. Santa Monica, Calif.: RAND. http://www.rand.org/pubs/occasional_papers/OP168/.

Gregory, Bruce. 2007. Public Diplomacy as Strategic Communication. In *Countering Terrorism and Insurgency in the 21st Century Vol. 1*, ed. James J.F. Forest, 336–357. Westport, Conn.: Praeger.

Henrikson, Alan K. 2006. *What Can Public Diplomacy Achieve?* Discussion Papers in Diplomacy, Netherlands Institute of International Relations Clingendael. http://www.clingendael.nl/publications/2006/20060900_cdsp_paper_dip_b.pdf.

Jenkins, Brian Michael. 2006. *Unconquerable Nation: Knowing Our Enemy, Strengthening Ourselves*. Santa Monica, Calif.: RAND. http://www.rand.org/pubs/monographs/MG454/.

Kedzie, Christopher R. 1997. *Communication and Democracy: Coincident Revolutions and the Emergent Dictator's Dilemma*. Santa Monica, Calif.: RAND. http://www.rand.org/pubs/rgs_dissertations/RGSD127/.

Kennon, Patrick E. 2000. *Tribe and Empire: An Essay on the Social Contract*. Philadelphia, Penn.: Xlibris.

Keohane, Robert. 1984. *After Hegemony*. Princeton, N.J.: Princeton University Press.

Keohane, Robert O., and Joseph S. Nye, Jr. 1998. Power and Interdependence in the Information Age. *Foreign Affairs* 77, no. 5: 81–94.

Kobrin, Stephen J. 1998. The MAI and the Clash of Globalizations. *Foreign Policy*, no. 112: 97–109.

Kohlmann, Evan F. 2006. The Real Online Terrorist Threat. *Foreign Affairs* 85, no. 5: 115–124.

Kumon, Shumpei, and Izumi Aizu. 1993. Co-Emulation: The Case for a Global Hypernetwork Society. In *Global Networks: Computers and International Communication*, ed. Linda M. Harasim, 311–326. Cambridge, Mass.: MIT Press.

Kurlantzick, Josh. 2007. *Charm Offensive: How China's Soft Power Is Transforming the World*. Princeton, N.J.: Yale University Press.

Manheim, Jarel B. 1994. *Strategic Public Diplomacy and American Foreign Policy: The Evolution of Influence*. London: Oxford University Press.

Maynes, Charles William. 1997. "Principled" Hegemony. *World Policy Journal* XIV, no. 3: 31–36.

McFate, Montgomery. 2005. The Military Utility of Understanding Adversary Culture. *Joint Force Quarterly* no. 38: 42–48. http://www.dtic.mil/doctrine/jel/jfq_pubs/1038.pdf.

McLaughlin, W. Sean. 2003. The use of the Internet for political action by non-state dissident actors in the Middle East. *First Monday* 8, no. 11. http://firstmonday.org/issues/issue8_11/mclaughlin/index.html.

Metzl, Jamie. 1997. Information Intervention. *Foreign Affairs* 76, no. 6: 15–20.

Minow, Newton N. 1003. *The Whisper of America: A Decision Memorandum*. Washington, D.C.: The Foundation for the Defense of Democracies. www.defenddemocracy.org/usr_doc/WhisperofAmerica_2.pdf.

Morgenthau, Hans. 1948. *Politics Among Nations*. New York: Alfred A. Knopf.

Nye, Joseph S. 1990. *Bound to Lead: The Changing Nature of American Power*. New York: Basic Books.

Nye, Joseph S. 2004. *Soft Power: The Means to Success in World Politics*. Cambridge, Mass.: PublicAffairs.

364

Nye, Joseph S. 2006. Think Again: Soft Power. *YaleGlobal Online*, March 1. http://yaleglobal.yale.edu/display.article?id=7059.

Nye, Joseph S., and William A. Owens 1996. America's Information Edge. *Foreign Affairs* 75, no. 2: 20–36.

Packer, George. 2006. Knowing the Enemy. *New Yorker*, December 18.

Price, Richard. 1998. Reversing the Gun Sights: Transnational Civil Society Targets Land Mines. *International Organization* 52, no. 3: 613–644.

Quarterman, John S. 1990. *The Matrix: Computer Networks and Conferencing Systems Worldwide*. Bedford, Mass.: Digital Equipment Corporation.

Quarterman, John S. 1993. The Global Matrix of Minds. In *Global Networks: Computers and International Communication*, ed. Linda M. Harasim, 35–56. Cambridge, Mass.: MIT Press.

Rheingold, Howard. 1993. *The Virtual Community: Homesteading on the Electronic Frontier*. Reading, Mass.: Addison-Wesley.

Rheingold, Howard. 2002. *Smart Mobs: The Next Social Revolution*. Cambridge, Mass.: Perseus.

Ronfeldt, David. 1996. *Tribes, Institutions, Markets, Networks: A Framework About Societal Evolution*. Santa Monica, Calif.: RAND. http://www.rand.org/publications/P/P7967.

Ronfeldt, David. 2005. Al-Qaeda and Its Affiliates: A Global Tribe Waging Segmental Warfare? *First Monday* 10, no. 3. http://www.firstmonday.org/issues/issue10_3/ronfeldt/index.html.

Ronfeldt, David. 2006. *In Search of How Societies Work: Tribes—The First and Forever Form*. Santa Monica, Calif.: RAND. http://www.rand.org/pubs/working_papers/WR433/.

Ronfeldt, David, and John Arquilla. 1999. What If There Is a Revolution in Diplomatic Affairs? *Virtual Diplomacy Series*, no. 4. Washington, D.C.: United States Institute of Peace. http://www.usip.org/virtualdiplomacy/publications/reports/ronarqISA99.html.

Ronfeldt, David, and John Arquilla. 2001. Networks, Netwars, and the Fight for the Future. *First Monday* 6, no. 10. http://www.firstmonday.org/issue6_10/index.html.

Ronfeldt, David, and John Arquilla. 2007. The Promise of Noöpolitik. *First Monday* 12, no. 8. http://www.firstmonday.org/issues/issue12_8/ronfeldt/index.html.

Ronfeldt, David, John Arquilla, Graham Fuller, and Melissa Fuller. 1998. *The Zapatista Social Netwar in Mexico*. Santa Monica, Calif.: RAND. http://www.rand.org/publications/MR/MR994.

Rothkopf, David J. 1998. Cyberpolitik: The Changing Nature of Power in the Information Age. *Journal of International Affairs* 51, no. 2: 325–359.

Sassen, Saskia. 1998. *Globalization and Its Discontents*. New York: The New Press.

Simmons, P. J. 1998. Learning to Live with NGOs. *Foreign Policy*, no. 112: 82–96.

Skolnikoff, Eugene B. 1993. *The Elusive Transformation: Science, Technology, and the Evolution of International Politics*. Princeton, N.J.: Princeton University Press.

Slaughter, Anne-Marie. 1997. The New World Order. *Foreign Affairs* 76, no. 5: 183–197.

Snow, Nancy, and Philip M. Taylor, eds. 2008. *Handbook of Public Diplomacy*. London and New York: Routledge.

Teilhard de Chardin, Pierre. 1964. *The Future of Man*. Translated from the French [1959] by Norman Denny. New York: Harper & Row.

Teilhard de Chardin, Pierre. 1965. *The Phenomenon of Man*. Introduction by Julian Huxley. Translated from the French [1955] by Bernard Wall. New York: Harper & Row.

Toffler, Alvin, and Heidi Toffler. 1993. *War and Anti-War: Survival at the Dawn of the Twenty-first Century*. Boston, Mass.: Little, Brown and Company.

Vlahos, Michael. 2003. *Terror's Mask: Insurgency Within Islam*. Occasional Paper, Joint Warfare Analysis Department, Applied Physics Laboratory. Johns Hopkins University, Baltimore, Md. http://www.jhuapl.edu/areas/warfare/papers/mask.asp.

Weimann, Gabriel 2006. *Terror on the Internet: The New Arena, the New Challenges*. Washington, D.C.: United States Institute of Peace Press.

Wolf, Charles, and Brian Rosen. 2004. *Public Diplomacy: How to Think About It and Improve It*. Santa Monica, Calif.: RAND. http://www.rand.org/pubs/occasional_papers/OP134/.

Wright, Robert. 1989. *Three Scientists and Their Gods: Looking for Meaning in an Age of Information*. New York: Harper & Row.

Select Bibliography

Anholt, Simon (with Jeremy Hildreth). *Brand America: The Mother of All Brands*. London: Cyan, 2004.

Arndt, Richard T. *The First Resort of Kings: American Cultural Diplomacy in the Twentieth Century*. Washington, DC: Potomac Books, 2005.

Arquilla, John, and Douglas Borer, editors. *Information Strategy and Warfare: A Guide to Theory and Practice*. London: Routledge, 2007.

Arquilla, John and David Ronfeldt. *Networks and Netwars*. Santa Monica, CA: Rand Corporation, 2001.

Arquilla, John and David Ronfeldt. *The Emergence of Noopolitik: Toward an American Information Strategy*. Santa Monica: Rand Corporation, 1999.

Belay, Getinet. 1997. "Ethics in international interaction: Perspectives on diplomacy and negotiation." In *Ethics in Intercultural and International Communication*, edited by Fred L. Casmir, 227–66. Mahwah, NJ: Lawrence Erlbaum Associates.

Brown, Robin. "Information Operations, Public Diplomacy & Spin: The United States & the Politics of Perception Management." *Journal of Information Warfare* 1 (2002): 40–50.

Carey, James W. *Communication as Culture: Essays on Media and Society*. New York: Routledge, 1992.

Chitty, Naren. "Toward an Inclusive Public Diplomacy in the World of Fast Capital and Diasporas." Paper presented to the International Conference on Foreign Ministries Adaptation to Change, Bangkok, Thailand, June 14–15, 2007.

Chitty, Naren. "Public Diplomacy: Developing Road Rules." Paper presented to the Senate Foreign Affairs, Defence and Trade Committee Inquiry into the nature and conduct of Australia's public diplomacy, Canberra, Australia, February 7, 2007.

Code of Athens, The. *The International Code of Ethics of the International Public Relations Association (IPRA)*. Dorking, Surrey, United Kingdom: International Public Relations Association, 1965.

Coombs, Philip H. *The Fourth Dimension of Foreign Policy: Educational and Cultural Affairs*. New York: Council on Foreign Relations, 1964.

Cowan, Geoffrey, and Nicholas J. Cull, editors. "Public Diplomacy in a Changing World," *Annals of the American Academy of Political and Social Science* 616(1), March 2008.

Cull, Nicholas J. *The Cold War and the United States Information Agency: American Propaganda and Public Diplomacy, 1945–1989*. Cambridge: Cambridge University Press, 2008.

Cull, Nicholas J. "Public diplomacy." In *Propaganda and Mass Persuasion: A Historical Encyclopedia, 1500 to the Present*, edited by Nicholas J. Cull, David Culbert, and David Welch, 327–8. Santa Barbara, CA: ABC Clio, 2003a.

Cull, Nicholas J. "'The Man Who Invented Truth': The Tenure of Edward R. Murrow as Director of the United States Information Agency during the Kennedy Years," *Cold War History* 10 (2003b): 25–48.

Defense Science Board Task Force on Strategic Communication *Report of the Defense Science Board Task Force on Strategic Communication*, September. Washington, DC: Office of the Under Secretary of Defense for Acquisition, Technology, and Logistics, 2004.

Dinnie, Keith. *Nation Branding: Concepts, Issues, Practice*. Oxford: Butterworth Heinemann, 2008.

Dizard, Wilson. *Digital Diplomacy: U.S. Foreign Policy in the Information Age*. Westport, CT: Praeger, 2001.

Djerejian, Edward P. *Changing Minds, Winning Peace: A New Strategic Direction for U.S. Public Diplomacy in the Arab and Muslim world*. Report submitted to the Committee on Appropriations, U.S. House of Representatives. Washington, D.C.: The Advisory Group on Public Diplomacy for the Arab and Muslim World, October 1, 2003.

Dutta-Bergman, Mohan J. "U.S. Public diplomacy efforts in the Middle East: A critical cultural approach," *Journal of Communication Inquiry* 30 (2006): 102–24.

Epstein, Susan B., and Lisa Mages. *Public Diplomacy: A Review of Past Recommendations*. Washington, DC: Congressional Research Service, Library of Congress, September 2, 2005.

El-Nawawy, Mohammed. "US Public Diplomacy in the Arab World: The News Credibility of Radio Sawa and Television Alhurra," *Global Media and Communication* 2(2) (2006): 183–203.

Fisher, Ali. "Public Diplomacy in the United Kingdom," in *The Future of Public Diplomacy: A European Perspective*. Working Paper. The 2006 Madrid Conference on Public Diplomacy, Real Instituto Elcano, Madrid, Spain, November 2006.

Fisher, Glen H. *Public Diplomacy and the Behavioral Sciences*. Bloomington, IN: Indiana University Press, 1972.

Fitzpatrick, Kathy R. "Advancing the new public diplomacy: A public relations perspective." *The Hague Journal of Diplomacy* 2(3) (2007): 187–211.

Fortner, Robert S. *Public Diplomacy and International Politics: The Symbolic Constructs of Summits and International Radio News*. Westport, CT: Praeger, 1994.

Frankel, Charles. *The Neglected Aspect of Foreign Affairs: American Educational and Cultural Policy Abroad*. Washington, D.C.: Brookings Institution, 1966.

Frederick, Howard H. *Global Communication and International Relations*. Belmont, CA: Wadsworth, 1993.

Fullerton, Jami and Alice Kendrick, *Advertising's War on Terrorism*. Spokane, WA: Marquette Books, 2006.

Gass, Robert H. and John S. Seiter. *Persuasion, Social Influence and Compliance Gaining*. 3rd edn. Boston: Allyn and Bacon, 2007.

Goldstein, Col. Frank L. and Col. Benjamin F. Findley, Jr., editors. *Psychological Operations: Principles and Case Studies*. Maxwell Air Force Base, AL: Air University Press, 1996.

Gregory, Bruce. "Public Diplomacy and Strategic Communication: Cultures, Firewalls, and Imported Norms." Paper presented to the American Political Science Association Conference on International Communication and Conflict. Washington, D.C., George Washington University, August 31, 2005.

Grunig, James. "Two-way symmetrical public relations: Past, present and future." In *Handbook of Public Relations*, ed. R.L. Heath and G. Vasquez. Thousand Oaks, CA: Sage, 2001.

Grunig, James E. "Public relations and international affairs: Effects, ethics and responsibility." *Journal of International Affairs* 47(1) (1993): 137–53.

Grunig, Larissa, James E. Grunig and David M. Dozier. *Excellent Public Relations and Effective Organizations: A Study of Communication Management in Three Countries*. London: Lawrence Erlbaum Associates, 2002.

Hansen, Allen C. *USIA: Public Diplomacy in the Computer Age*. New York: Praeger, 1989.

Heil, Alan L. Jr. *Voice of America: A History*. New York: Columbia University Press, 2003.

Helmus, Todd C. et al. *Enlisting Madison Avenue: The Marketing Approach to Earning Popular Support in Theatres of Operation*. Santa Monica, CA: RAND, 2007.

Hitchcock, David I. *U.S. Public Diplomacy*. Washington, DC: Center for Strategic and International Studies, 1988.

Izadi, Foad. "Post-9/11 U.S. public diplomacy: The case of Iran." Paper presented at the National Communication Association 93rd Annual Conference, Chicago, Illinois, November 2007.

Jowett, Garth S. and Victoria O'Donnell. *Propaganda and Persuasion*. 4th edn. Thousand Oaks, CA: Sage Publications, 2006a.

Jowett, Garth S. and Victoria O'Donnell, editors. *Readings in Propaganda and Persuasion, New and Classic Essays*. Thousand Oaks, CA: Sage Publications, 2006b.

Katzenstein, Peter J. *A World of Regions: Asia and Europe in the American Imperium*. Ithaca, NY: Cornell University Press, 2005.

Kelley, John Robert. "From Monologue to Dialogue?: U.S. Public Diplomacy in the Post-9/11 Era." PhD diss., London School of Economics, 2007.

Kiehl, William P., editor. *A Call for Action on Public Diplomacy*. Washington, DC: The Public Diplomacy Council, 2005.

Kiehl, William P., editor. *America's Dialogue with the World*. 2nd edn. Washington, DC: The Public Diplomacy Council, 2007.

Kim, Y.H. "Public Diplomacy and Cultural Communication: The International Visitor Program." Ph.D. diss., University of Southern California, 1990.

Kruckeberg, Dean, and Marina Vujnovic. "Public relations, not propaganda, for US public diplomacy in a post-9/11 world: Challenges and opportunities," *Journal of Communication Management* 9(4) (2005): 296–304.

Lamb, Christopher. *Review of Psychological Operations: Lessons Learned from Recent Operational Experience.* Washington, D.C.: National Defense University Press, 2005.

Lane, Ann. "Public Diplomacy: Key Challenges and Priorities." Report on Wilton Park Conference WPS06/21 (April 2006).

Leonard, Mark and Andrew Small (with Martin Rose). *British Public Diplomacy in the "Age of Schisms".* London: The Foreign Policy Centre, 2005.

Leonard, Mark and Conrad Smewing. *Public Diplomacy and the Middle East.* London: The Foreign Policy Centre, 2003.

Leonard, Mark (with Catherine Stead and Conrad Smewing). *Public Diplomacy.* London: The Foreign Policy Centre, 2002.

Lord, Carnes. *Losing Hearts and Minds? Public Diplomacy and Strategic Influence in the Age of Terror.* Westport, CT: Praeger, 2006.

Malone, Gifford D. *Political Advocacy and Cultural Communication: Organizing the Nation's Public Diplomacy.* Lanham, MD: University Press of America, 1988.

Manheim, Jarol B. *Strategic Public Diplomacy and American Foreign Policy: The Evolution of Influence.* New York: Oxford University Press, 1994.

Martin, Dick. *Rebuilding Brand America.* New York: American Management Association, 2007.

Matsumoto, David. *The Handbook of Culture and Psychology.* Oxford: Oxford University Press, 2001.

McEvoy-Levy, Siobhan. *American Exceptionalism and US Foreign Policy.* Houndmills, UK: Palgrave, 2001.

Melissen, Jan, editor. *The New Public Diplomacy: Soft Power in International Relations.* London: Palgrave Macmillan, 2005.

Mirrlees, Tanner "American Soft Power or American Cultural Imperialism." In *The New Imperialists: Ideologies of Empire,* ed. Colin Mooers, 198–228. Oxford, UK: Oneworld, 2006.

Mueller, Sherry. "The US Department of State's International Visitor Program: A Conceptual Framework for Evaluation." PhD diss., Fletcher School of Law and Diplomacy, 1977.

Nelson, Richard Alan. "Ethics of persuasion." In *Encyclopedia of Business Ethics and Society,* Volume 2, ed. Robert W. Kolb, 810–13. Thousand Oaks, CA: Sage Publications, 2008.

Nelson, Richard Alan. *A Chronology and Glossary of Propaganda in the United States.* Westport, CT: Greenwood Press, 1996.

Nelson, Richard Alan. "Public diplomacy: Opportunities for international public relations activism." *PR Update* 2 (1995): 5–7.

Ninkovich, Frank. *The Diplomacy of Ideas: US Foreign Policy and Cultural Relations 1938–1950.* Cambridge: Cambridge University Press, 1981.

Nye, Joseph S., Jr. *Soft Power: The Means to Success in International Relations.* New York: Public Affairs Press, 2004.

Nye, Joseph. *The Paradox of American Power: Why the World's Only Superpower Can't Go It Alone.* Oxford: Oxford University Press, 2002.

Parta, R. Eugene. *Discovering the Hidden Listener: An Assessment of Radio Liberty and Western Broadcasting to the U.S.S.R. during the Cold War.* Palo Alto, CA: Hoover Press, 2007.

Pearce, David. *Wary Partners: Diplomats and the Media.* Washington, DC: Congressional Quarterly, Inc., 1995.

Peterson, Peter G. et al. *Finding America's Voice: A Strategy for Reinvigorating U.S. Public Diplomacy.* Report of an Independent Task Force sponsored by the Council on Foreign Relations. New York: Council on Foreign Relations, 2003.

Peterson, Peter G. et al. *Public Diplomacy: A Strategy for Reform.* Report of an Independent Task Force on Public Diplomacy sponsored by the Council on Foreign Relations. New York: Council on Foreign Relations, 2002.

Pratkanis, Anthony, editor. *The Science of Social Influence: Advances and Future Progress.* New York: Psychology Press, 2007.

Pratkanis, Anthony and Elliot Aronson. *Age of Propaganda: The Everyday Use and Abuse of Persuasion.* New York: W.H. Freeman/Owl Book, 2002. Revised edition.

Rawnsley, Gary. *Radio Diplomacy and Propaganda: The BBC and VOA in International Politics, 1956–64.* New York: St. Martin's Press, 1996.

Richmond, Yale. *Practicing Public Diplomacy: A Cold War Odyssey.* Oxford and New York: Berghahn Books, 2008.

Richmond, Yale. *Cultural Exchange and the Cold War: Raising the Iron Curtain.* University Park, PA: University of Pennsylvania Press, 2003.

Richmond, Yale. *US-Soviet Cultural Exchanges 1958–1986: Who Wins?* Boulder, CO: Westview Press, 1987.

Riordan, Shaun. *The New Diplomacy.* Cambridge: Policy Press, 2003.

Rugh, William A. *American Encounters with Arabs: The "Soft Power" of U.S. Public Diplomacy in the Middle East*. Westport: Praeger, 2006.

Rugh, William, editor. *Engaging the Arab and Islamic Worlds Through Public Diplomacy*. Washington, DC: The Public Diplomacy Council, 2004.

Schwartzstein, Stuart J. D., editor. *The Information Revolution and National Security: Dimensions and Directions*. Washington, DC: Center for Strategic and International Studies, 1996.

Scott-Smith, Giles. *Networks of Empire: The U.S. State Department's Foreign Leader Program in the Netherlands, France, and Britain 1950–70*. Brusells: Peter Lang, 2008.

Scott-Smith, Giles. "The Ties That Bind: Dutch-American Relations, US Public Diplomacy, and the Promotion of American Studies since WW II," *The Hague Journal of Diplomacy* 2, 2007.

Scott-Smith, Giles. "Searching for the Successor Generation: Public Diplomacy, the US Embassy's International Visitor Program and the Labour Party in the 1980s," *British Journal of Politics and International Relations* 8, 2006.

Scott-Smith, Giles. "Her Rather Ambitious Washington Program: Margaret Thatcher's International Visitor Program Visit to the United States in 1967," *Contemporary British History* 17, 2003.

Seib, Philip. "The Ethics of Public Diplomacy." In *Ethics in Public Relations: Responsible Advocacy*, ed. Kathy Fitzpatrick and Carolyn Bronstein, 155–70. Thousands Oaks, CA: Sage Publications, 2006.

Signitzer, Benno and Carola Wamser. "Public Diplomacy: A Specific Governmental Public Relations Function." In *Public Relations Theory II*, ed. Carl Botan and Vincent Hazelton. London: Lawrence Erlbaum, 2006.

Simpson, Christopher. *Science of Coercion: Communication Research and Psychological Warfare 1945–1960*. Oxford: Oxford University Press, 1994.

Smyth, Rosaleen. "Mapping US public diplomacy in the 21st century," *Australian Journal of International Affairs* 55, no 3 (2001): 421–44.

Sproule, J. Michael. *Propaganda and Democracy*. Cambridge: Cambridge University Press, 1997.

Snow, Nancy. "International Exchanges and the U.S. Image," *Annals of the American Academy of Political and Social Science* 616(1) (2008): 198–222.

Snow, Nancy. *The Arrogance of American Power*. Lanham, MD: Rowman & Littlefield, 2006.

Snow, Nancy. *Information War*. New York. Seven Stories Press, 2004.

Snow, Nancy. *Propaganda, Inc*. 2nd edn. New York: Seven Stories Press, 2002.

Snow, Nancy. "Fulbright Scholars as Cultural Mediators: An Exploratory Study." PhD diss., School of International Service, American University, 1992.

Szondi, György. "The Role and Challenges of Country Branding in Transition Countries: The Central and Eastern Europe Experience." *Place Branding and Public Diplomacy* 3(1) (2007): 8–20.

Szondi, György. "International Context of Public Relations." In *Exploring Public Relations*, ed Ralph Tench and Liz Yeomans, 112–40. London: FT/Prentice Hall, 2006.

Taylor, Philip M. *Munitions of the Mind*. 3rd edn. Manchester: Manchester University Press, 2003.

Taylor, Philip M. *British Propaganda in the Twentieth Century: Selling Democracy*. Edinburgh: Edinburgh University Press, 1999.

Taylor, Philip M. *War and the Media: Propaganda and Persuasion in the Gulf War*. 2nd edn., Manchester: Manchester University Press, 1997a.

Taylor, Philip M. *Global Communications, International Affairs and the Media since 1945*. London: Routledge, 1997b.

Tuch, Hans N. *Communicating with the World: U.S. Public Diplomacy Overseas*. New York: St. Martin's Press, 1990.

van Ham, Peter. "War, lies, and videotape: Public diplomacy and the USA's War on Terrorism," *Security Dialogue* 34(4) (2003): 427–44.

van Ham, Peter. "Branding Territory: Inside the Wonderful Worlds of PR and IR Theory," *Millennium* 31(2) (2002): 249–69.

Vickers, Rhiannon. "The New Public Diplomacy: Britain and Canada Compared," *British Journal of Politics and International Relations* 6(2) (2004): 182–94.

Vlahos, Michael. "Losing Mythic Authority," *The National Interest*, May/June 2007.

Vlahos, Michael. "Terror's Mask: Insurgency within Islam." Occasional paper of the Joint Warfare Analysis Department of the Applied Physics Laboratory, Johns Hopkins University, May 2002.

Wang, Jian. "Telling the American story to the world: The purpose of U.S. public diplomacy in historical perspective," *Public Relations Review* 33(1) (2007): 21–30.

Yamamoto, Tadashi, Akira Irie, and Maokoto Iokibe, editors. *Philanthropy and Reconciliation: Rebuilding Postwar U.S.–Japan Relations*. Tokyo and New York: Japan Center for International Exchange, 2006.

Yun, Seong-Hun. "Toward public relations theory-based study of public diplomacy: Testing the applicability of the Excellence Study," *Journal of Public Relations Research* 18(4) (2006): 287–312.

Zaharna, R.S. "The Network Paradigm of Strategic Public Diplomacy." *Foreign Policy in Focus* 10 (April 2005).

Zaharna, R.S. "Asymmetry of Cultural Styles and the Unintended Consequences of Crisis Public Diplomacy." In *Intercultural Communication and Diplomacy*, ed. Hannah Slavik, 133–42. Malta: Diplo Foundation, 2004.

Zaharna, R.S. "The Unintended Consequences of Crisis Public Diplomacy: American Public Diplomacy in the Arab World," *Foreign Policy in Focus* 8 (June 2003).

Zaharna, R. S. "Understanding Cultural Preferences of Arab Communication Patterns," *Public Relations Review* 21(3) (1995): 241–55.

Zöllner, Oliver. "A Quest for Dialogue in International Broadcasting: Germany's Public Diplomacy Targeting Arab Audiences," *Global Media and Communication* 2(2) (2006): 160–82.

Index

Abe, Shintaro 277
Abe, Shinzo 270, 277, 287
Abu Ghraib 13, 15, 29, 68, 69, 128, 155, 159–60
Acheson, Dean 129
Advisory Committee on Cultural Diplomacy 57
Afghanistan: US military force 43, 63
Ahmadinejad, Mahmoud 156, 158, 159, 161
Ahmed, Akbar S. 159
Al-Arabiya 158, 241
Albright, Madeleine 331, 332
Albritton, Robert 117
Al-Hurra 88, 91, 158, 241
Al-Jazeera 69, 115, 117, 131, 158, 159, 241
Alliance Française 77, 94
Allison, Graham 113
Allport, Gordon 143, 144
Al Manar 158
Al-Qaeda: beneffectance 127–8; communication 12–15; influence 124, 169; Internet 13, 41; propaganda 13; strategic traps 125
Al Sahab 13
Altbach, Philip 242, 244
Ambassador's Fund for Cultural Preservation 58
Amnesty International 41, 160
Anholt, Simon 90, 301
Annan, Kofi 156
anti-Americanism: Bush administration 42, 47, 154; causes 196–7; definition 45–6; mainstream scholarship 46; phenomena conflated 47; surveys 195–6
Aristotle 157
Armstrong, Matthew C. xiii, 63–71
Arnett, Peter 112

Aronson, Elliot 141
Arquilla, John xiii, 352–65
arts diplomacy 57–9
Asch, Solomon 166
ASEAN 275, 276, 278
Asia-Pacific Economic Cooperation 43
Atlantic-Pacific Exchange Program (APEP) 54
Australia: holistic diplomacy 314–18; public diplomacy 314–22; Senate Committee Recommendations 318–21
Axworthy, Lloyd 96

Baker, Dean 330
Baker, Howard 104
Baker, James 222
Ban Ki Moon 157
Bandaranaike, S.W.R.D. 213
Beers, Charlotte 7, 15, 115, 116, 154, 191, 208, 210, 301
Bergen, Peter 188
Bernays, Edward L. 9, 117, 118, 334–5
Berry, Collin 189
Bhutto, Benazir 79
bin Laden, Osama 14, 91, 111, 119, 124, 125, 127, 141, 158, 205, 209, 361
Black, Jay 338
Blackman, Toni 154
Blair, Tony 14, 16, 22, 161, 228, 270, 200
Bob, Clifford 116
Bollier, David 360
Bono (Paul David Hewson) 41
Borah, William E. 20
Bracken, Paul 92

branding: advertising/brand positioning 114–16; destination/country branding 300–2; nation-branding 90

Brezinski, Zbigniew 39

Briggs, David 214, 220

British Council 92, 94, 254–6, 273, 285, 302, 309, 315

broadcasts: Al-Arabiya 158, 241; Al-Hurra 88, 91, 158; Al-Jazeera 69, 115, 117, 131, 158, 159, 241; Al Manar 158; Al Sahab 13; Central and Eastern European Countries (CEECs) 307–8; China 91, 286; Germany 264–5; international broadcasts 90–1; radio see radio; United Kingdom 253–4, 256; see also media

Brown, Gordon 159

Brown, John xiii, 57–9

Brown, Michael 157

Burdick, William 101

Bureau of Educational and Cultural Affairs (ECA) 9, 243

Burger, Jerry 140

Bush administration: anti-Americanism 42, 47, 154; anti-science 158; persuasion 34; post-Cold War 327, 328; public affairs 229; shock and awe 42; submission 35; unilateralism 48; US power checked 45; war on terror 13, 27, 34

Bush doctrine: perception management 15; preemptive security 5; public diplomacy 22; selling democracy 15, 44; with us/against us 15

Bush, George (41st President) 159, 161, 327

Bush, George W. (43rd President): axis of evil 159; credibility 161; democracy 138; national position 7; public approval 154; USS Abraham Lincoln speech 154, 156; war on terror 13

business: actions 198–9; public diplomacy 195–200; world opinion 197–8

Byoir, Carl 117

campaigns: competitive propaganda 111; GRIT 113, 138, 140; information campaigns 91; relationship building 95; Shared Values Initiative (SVI) 7–8, 16, 66–7, 115–16; social influence see social influence campaigns

Campbell, Alastair 228

Cancel, Amanda E. 341

Carey, James 87

Carr, E.H. 65

Carroll, Wallace 119, 130

Carter, James Earl (39th President) 154, 161, 239

catalytic diplomacy 96

Center for Global Engagement 12–16

Central and Eastern European Countries (CEECs): broadcasts 307–8; challenges 293–5; cultural diplomacy 302–3; European Union (EU) 293–5, 301–2, 304–7, 309, 311; international public relations 296–300; national reputation management 292–313; perception management 308–11; public diplomacy 303–7

Central Intelligence Agency (CIA): alleged conspiracies 13; covert operations 335, 336; radio funding 75; rendition flights 68

Chanda, Nayan 331

Chávez, Hugo Rafael 43, 149, 283

Cheney, Richard Bruce (Dick) 158

China: authoritarianism 44; British relationship building 92, 95; broadcasts 91, 286; Confucius Institutes 94, 285; culture 284–6; economics 41, 283–4; foreign aid 283–4; Peaceful Rise 140; personal touch 288–9; public diplomacy 282–91; soft power 282–91; strategy 286–8; talking-back 282, 283; television 91

Chitty, Naren xiii–xiv, 314–22

Churchill, Winston S. 130, 140

citizen diplomacy: beyond public diplomacy 106; definition 102; exchange programs 102–3; history 101–2; public diplomacy 101–7; public/private sector partnerships 103; The Ugly American 101, 107

Clark, Wesley 124

Clausewitz, Karl von 67, 112, 123, 137

Clemons, Steve 329

Clinton, Hillary Rodham 6

Clinton, William Jefferson (42nd President) 5, 6, 159, 161, 219, 221, 228, 234, 325, 327–32, 337

Coalition Information Centers (CICs) 7, 78–9

Code of Athens 343–5

Cold War: balance of power ix; disinformation 111; end 5, 12, 14, 197, 325–33; Iron Curtain 14, 66, 102, 129, 292, 306, 311; nuclear weapons 77; persuasion 24; public diplomacy 9, 12, 63, 64, 75; total war 66; US Vision 14

College, Sarah Lawrence 245

Committee on Public Information (Creel Commission) 4, 68, 117, 130, 334, 337

communication technologies: democratization of access 40; global publics 8; innovation 40; Internet see Internet; public diplomacy 7

communications: credibility 15–16, 89; information and relational frameworks 86–100; propagandist/transparent styles 75–6; Smith-Mundt Act (1948) 68, 143, 188, 226, 236, 243, 244, 335; strategic communications 12–16; US strategies 7–9

Confucius Institutes 94, 285

Coombs, Philip M. 235

Cooper, Jeffrey 353–4

Council on Foreign Relations 129, 143, 160

Council for international Exchange of Scholars (CIES) 236, 243

Council of Muslims for Understanding and the American People 7
Cox, Samuel S. 19
credibility: aims and goals 155; communications 15–16, 89; culture 157, 161–2; expertise 158; goodwill 159–60; multi-dimensional construct 157–8; public diplomacy 154–65; secondary dimensions 160–1; situational specific 157; social influence campaigns 128–30; tenets 155–62; trustworthiness 158–9
Creel Commission 4, 68, 117, 130, 334, 337
Creel, George 4, 68, 334
Cronkite, Walter 5
Crossman, R.H.S. 119, 128, 142–3
Crumm, Robin K. 231
Cuba: missile crisis (1962) 78
Cull, Nicholas J. xiv, 19–23, 75, 338
cultural diplomacy: American Corners 58; arts diplomacy 57–9; Central and Eastern European Countries (CEECs) 302–3; democratization 54; United Kingdom 253
culture: cat and dog problem 168; China 284–6; complexity 171–2; credibility 157, 161–2; cultural brokers 53–4; cultural differences 52, 168; diplomacy see cultural diplomacy; exchange programs 52–4, 93; individualism/collectivism 87, 91; influence 166–80; Japan 278–9; primacy 167–71; taunting 170
CultureConnect 58
Cummings, Milton 253
Cunningham, Stanley B. 338
Cutler, Walter 104
cyberspace 353
Czechoslovakia: localized public diplomacy 215–16

Dalai Lama 116
Darfur: humanitarian crisis 41
democracy: Citizen Democracy 101, 102; electoral democracies 44; public relations (PR) 118; selling democracy 15, 44
democratization: cultural diplomacy 54; Internet access 40
Deng Xiaoping 288, 289
Denmark: cartoon controversy 78, 159
Derrida, Jacques 306
Deutscher Akademischer Austauschdienst (DAAD) 244, 265–6
Dillon, Wilton 140
diplomacy: catalytic diplomacy 96; citizenship see citizen diplomacy; culture see cultural diplomacy; humanitarian diplomacy 79; open diplomacy 20, 21; public see public diplomacy; standard diplomacy 112

disinformation: Cold War 111; counter-tactic 142; World War II 142–3
Djerejian Report (2003) 4, 6
Doak, Kevin 29
Doha trade negotiations 43
Dozier, David M. 341
Drummond, J. Roscoe 20
Duffey, Joseph xiv, 10, 325–33
Duke, Lynne 190
Dutta-Bergman, Mohan J. 340

economics: China 41, 283–4; Japan 274–5; United States 43–4
Ehrenreich, Barbara 5
Eisenhower, Dwight David (34th President) 64, 66, 69, 101, 113, 215, 335
Epstein, Alex 39, 47
ethical issues: public diplomacy 334–51; social influence 142–4
European Union (EU): Central and Eastern European Countries (CEECs) 293–5, 301–2, 304–7, 309, 311; exchange programs 51; influence 41, 51
exchange programs: Atlantic-Pacific Exchange Program (APEP) 54; citizen diplomacy 102–3; cultural brokers 53–4; cultural differences 52; cultural/educational 93; European Union (EU) 51; Germany 244, 265–6; identity/orientation 54; impact 102–3; international political context 50–1; Japan Exchange and Teaching (JET) Program 77, 276; mission 235–7; opinion leaders 53; political influence 51, 237; propaganda 238–9; public diplomacy 50–6; reinforcing opinions 55; relationship building 93; risk/unpredictability 51–2; uniqueness 52–3; value 233–47; valuing exchanges 242–5

Filene, Edward 9
Finland: localized public diplomacy 216–17, 221–3
Fisher, Ali xiv, 251–61
Fisher, Glen 114, 119, 140
Fitzpatrick, Kathy R. 81, 339, 340
Floyd, Price B. 9, 230
foreign policy: foreign policy decisions (P2P) 6, 9; world opinion 42–5
Foucault, Michel 339
France: Napoleonic era see Napoleonic France
Frankel, Charles 235
Frederick, Howard 304
Freeman, Bryan R. 229
Freeman, John R. 139
Freikorps 133, 135
Friedman, Milton 330
Fukuda, Takeo 275

Fukuyama, Francis 14, 44
Fulbright, J. William 234, 235, 236, 242, 335
Fulbright Program 5, 6, 55, 217, 233–4, 242–5
Fullerton, Jami 115

Gass, Robert H. xiv-xv, 154–65, 172
genocide: conflict resolution 137; Croats 111;
    information control 132; Nazism 158, 262, 302;
    prevention 143, 156; Serbia 131; social influence
    analysis 119–20
Germany: actors 263–6; broadcasts 264–5; cultural
    institutes 77, 94, 265; dialogue of cultures 256–63;
    exchange programs 244, 265–6; Foreign Office
    263–4; Nazi era see Nazism; public diplomacy
    262–9; terminology/concepts 262–3
Gibson, William 353
global publics: communication technologies 8; G2P
    6, 9
Global War on Terrorism (GWOT): all about your
    own 29–30; coalition 25; designed for self-defeat
    30–3; domestic persuasion 34–5; dominance of
    action 35; Hegel's reality distortion field 32–3;
    identity 31; information operations 12; inner life
    27–34; Long War 14, 33; media orchestration 26;
    Obsession 33; preemption 25; shock and awe
    28–9, 43, 65; submission 33–4, 35–6; US defeat
    24; world revision 24–6
globalization: nationalism 43; United States 325–33
Globescan 41, 44
Goebbels, Joseph 68, 111, 127, 130, 133, 139, 144,
    188
Goethe Instituts 77, 94, 265
Goldstein, Joshua 138–9
Goodman, Allan 243
goodwill: credibility 159–60
Goonetileke, H.A.I. 220
Gore, Al 41, 208, 327
Government Accountability Office (GAO) 58
governments: foreign policy decisions (P2P) 6, 9;
    global publics (G2P) 6, 9; government-to-
    government (G2G) 6
grand strategy: ideological conflict 14; information
    14; war 24
Gregory, Bruce 80, 251
GRIT 113, 138, 140
Gros, Antoine Jean 28
Grunig, James E. 10, 92, 118, 297, 316, 340, 341, 342
Grunig, Larissa A. 341
Guantanamo 13, 15, 155
Gullion, Edmund 19, 21, 66, 73, 101, 239
Gyurcsany, Ferenc 306

Habermas, Jürgen 263, 306, 340
Hall, Edward T. 87

Halle, Louis 21
Halper, Stefan 325
Hamilton, Lee 102, 241
Hammarskjöld, Dag 21
Hanemann, Yvonne 220
Hara, Takashi 272
Harrison, Patricia 210
Hashimoto, Ryutaro 278
Hassner, Pierre 42
Hayes, Harold B. 157
hearts and minds ix, 5, 12, 64, 66, 67, 112, 118,
    120, 155, 214, 231, 273, 266, 273, 285, 325, 326,
    335
Hegel's reality distortion field 32–3
Heller, Ken S. xv, 225–32
Helms, Jesse 332
Henrikson, Alan 96
Herman & Chomsky 339
Hertling, Georg von 20
Herz, Martin 115, 130, 133
Heyman, Sam 162
Hitler, Adolf 111, 118, 119, 124, 125, 131, 133, 134,
    144, 166, 361
Ho Chi Minh 161
Hocking, Brian 96, 257
Hofstede, Geertz 87
Holbrooke, Richard 75
Hon, Linda Childers 92
Hu Jintao 161, 282, 284, 286
Huang & Ding 283
Huang & Sheng 289
Hughes, Karen 22, 78, 103, 154–5, 211, 239, 240,
    326
Human Rights Watch 160
humanitarian diplomacy 79
Humphrey, Hubert Horatio 101
Hutchins, Robert 325
Huxley, Julian 354

Ilchyman, Alice 245
imagined communities 63, 67, 325
influence: analysis see social influence analysis;
    campaigns see social influence campaigns; culture
    166–80; European Union (EU) 41, 51; exchange
    programs 51; national interest 112–13; political
    consultants 169; replications 175–6; shock and
    awe 64; social see social influence; universals/
    cultural specifics 172–5; western concentration
    166
information: grand strategy 14; politics and war 67;
    strategy control 124–6; Total Information
    Awareness (TIA) 7
information operations: military 66; war on terror
    12

information and relational communication
  frameworks: challenges 96–7; credibility 89;
  information framework 88–9; initiatives 86–100;
  origins 87–8; propaganda 89–90; relational
  framework 91–6; rituals 87–8
Innis, Harold 87
Institute for Cultural Diplomacy (ICD) 54
Institute of International Education (IIE) 233, 236,
  243, 244
intermediate-range nuclear forces (INF) 76, 77
International Committee of the Red Cross (ICRC)
  79
international conflict: conflict resolution 79; public
  diplomacy 111–53; relevant questions 121–2;
  social influence tactics 138–42
International Visitors Leadership Program (IVLP)
  5, 9, 50–3, 104–5, 160
Internet: growth 40; information flows 227;
  YouTube 13, 40, 41, 67, 226, 229, 257
Iran: nuclear weapons 45
Iran-Contra hearings 21
Iraq: Abu Ghraib 13, 15, 29, 68, 69, 128, 155,
  159–60; Gulf War 189
Iraq War: anti-war sentiment 45, 154; journalism 28;
  key problems 173–4; shock and awe 174; US
  military force 43, 63, 69; US national image 6
Islam: crusade against 12–14, 31, 125; despotic
  regimes 31; Islamofascism 33; militancy 12–16;
  portrayal 31
Islam see also Al-Qaeda
Iyengar, Shanto 130
Izadi, Foad xv, 334–51

Jackson, Andrew (7th President) 221
Japan: ASEAN 275, 276, 278, 287, 294; Center for
  Global Partnership (CGP) 277; culture 278–9;
  emerging economic power 274–5; Exchange and
  Teaching (JET) Program 77, 276; history 272–3;
  Japan Foundation 93, 271–2, 275–80; Middle
  East policy 279–80; Minister of Foreign Affairs
  270–1, 273, 275–7, 280; mushrooming main
  actors 275–7; public diplomacy 270–81; Showa
  era see Showa Japan
Jefferson, Thomas (3rd President) 103
Jervis, Robert 119
Jiang Zemin 288
Joffe, Josef 43
Johnson, Dominic 127
Johnson, Joe 7
Joint Psychological support element (JPSE) 190

Kacynski, Lach 298, 306, 311
Katayama, Tetsu 274
Katzenstein, Peter 46–7

Kean, Thomas 241
Kelley, John Robert xv–xvi, 72–85
Kendrick, Alice 115
Kennan, George 65, 357
Kennedy, Darryl 210
Kennedy, John Fitzgerald (35th President) 7, 21, 66,
  113, 161, 242, 242
Keohane, Robert 46–7
Kernaghan, Kenneth 337
Khrushchev, Nikita Sergeyevich 21, 102, 174
Kiehl, William P. xvi, 212–24
Kilbane, Mark xvi, 187–92
Kim Dae Jung 278
Kim Jong Il 159
Kim, Min-Sun 87
Kinder, Donald 130
King, Anthony 39
King, Steven 162
Kissinger, Henry Alfred 66, 357
Kitayama, Shinobu 87
Klein, Helen 167
Klein, Joe 3
Kluckholm & Murray 171
Kohut, Andrew 42
Koizumi, Jun'ichero 161, 278
Konoe, Ayamaro 272
Korean Overseas Information Service (KIOS) 90
Korean War 142
Kovach, Peter J. xvi, 201–11
Kramer, Rod 138
Kristofferson, Kris 234
kula 140
Kwan, Michelle 154, 191

Lake, Anthony 329
Lasswell, Harold D. 9, 188, 341
leadership: opinion leaders 53; values-based 342–3
leadership visits: Albuquerque Council for
  International Visitors (ACIV) 105; International
  Visitors Council of Los Angeles (IVCLA) 105;
  International Visitors Leadership Program
  (IVLP) 5, 9, 50–3, 104–5, 160; National Council
  of International Visitors (NCIV) 104–5;
  relationship building 93–4
Lederer, Eugene 101
Ledingham, John A. 340
Lee, Ivy Ledbetter 117, 335
Leonard, Mark 74–5, 79, 91
Lerner, Daniel 125
Lewin, Kurt 166
Lincoln Group 9, 25–6, 169, 190, 243
Lindsay, Beverly 236, 238
Lippmann, Walter 9, 21, 79
Litvinenko, Alexander 309

localized public diplomacy: case 212–24; concept 212–13; Czechoslovakia 215–16; Finland 216–17, 221–3; publications 214, 215, 220–1; Sri Lanka 213–15, 220–1; Thailand 217–19
Lord, Carnes 76
Lowi, Ted 245
Luers, William 216
Lungu, Angela Maria 187

McAlister, Melani 339
Macarthur, Douglas 26
Machiavelli, Niccolò 69, 136
Madison, James (4th President) 337
Major, John 161
Malaya 133, 141, 142
Malinowski, Bronislaw 140
Manchurian Incident (1931) 30
Mandela, Nelson 357
Manheim, Jarol B. 76, 79, 116–17
Mao Zedong (Mao Tse Tsung) 69, 161, 285, 288
Marder, Murrey 21
Markóczy, Livia 168
Markus, Hazel Rose 87
Marshall, George Catlett 26
Martin, Dick 199
Masséna, André 29
Mauss, Marcel 140
media: Al-Hurra 88, 91, 241; international broadcasts 90–1; media relations 90; orchestration 26; pay-for-play 169–70; perceptions 157; private media 26; radio see radio; reputation management 298–300
Melissen, Jan 73, 91, 340–1
Mencius 144
Merkel, Angela Dorothea 311
Meyer, Christina 66
Meyers, David 172
Miliband, David 309
military power: information operations 66; psychological operations (PSYOP) 15, 66, 187–92; United States 42–3, 63, 69
Miller, James G. 342
Milosevic, Slobodan 131, 141
Minow, Newton 361
Mishra, R.C. 170
Morales, Evo 43
Morgenthau, Hans 55, 65
Mortenson, Greg 107
Morton, Herwald H. 221
Mosaddeq, Mohammad 336
Moyers, Bill 334
Mueller, Sherry L. xvi–xvii, 101–7
Mundt, Karl E. 243
Murayama, Tomiichi 278

Murrow Center for International Information and Communications 21
Murrow Center for Public Diplomacy 19, 101
Murrow, Edward R. 64, 69, 72, 76, 113, 118, 120, 126, 211, 225, 241
Mussolini, Benito 142

Nanjing Massacre 31
Napoleonic France: battle as political authority 28, 30; existentialism 29, 30; God-hero ideology 32; imperialism 29; inner-direction 29; propaganda 30; public diplomacy failure 27; self-sustaining identity 30
nation-branding 90, 300–2
national reputation see reputation management
Nazism: Allied propaganda 133; defeat 126, 127, 216; Freikorps 133, 135; genocide 158, 262, 302; granfalloons 141; Islamic extremism compared 33; propaganda 68, 81, 111, 113, 124, 130, 142, 267, 273; Saarland 20
Nelson, Richard xvii, 334–51
Nessmann, K. 296
New Deal 138
Nichols, John 239
Nicolson, Harold 21
Ninkovich, Frank 58
Nixon, Richard Milhouse (37th President) 154, 274
non-governmental organizations (NGOs): credibility 160, 161
noopolitik: advance 357–8; cyberspace 353; emergence 355–8; global civil society 355–7; information-based realms 353–4; infosphere 353–4; noosphere 352–5, 361; public diplomacy 352–65; realpolitik 357; way ahead 358–9
Norland, Patricia 221
Norman, Nancy M. 156
North American Free Trade Agreement (NAFTA) 5, 329, 330
North Atlantic Treaty Organization (NATO): Afghanistan 196; expansion 294, 295, 299, 303, 305, 307, 309; information 69; Kosovo 78, 117, 128, 131; nuclear weapons 76; perception 64; public diplomacy 266; Visegrád Group 294
Norway: conflict resolution 79
Nye, Joseph 3, 4, 12, 39, 73–4, 75, 76, 89, 94, 113, 136, 138, 231, 283, 289, 336

Obama, Barack 5–6
Obuchi, Keizo 278
Odom, William 144
Office of Global Communications (OGC) 7, 16
Office of International Information Programs 227
Office of Public Diplomacy 21
Office of Strategic Communication 88

Office of Strategic Influence (OSI) 7, 15, 76, 225, 228

Ogawa, Tadashi xvii, 270–81

Olcott, Henry Steele 214, 220, 221

Olins, Wally 300, 301

open diplomacy 20, 21

Open Society Institute (OSI) 54

Operation Desert Storm 12

opinion: exchange programs 53, 55; power of public opinion 39–49; *see also* world opinion

Orientalism 338–9

Oslo Accords (1993) 79

O'Toole, James 342

Pakistan: relations with US 79

Patton, George 215

Peace Corps 7, 206

perceptions: media 157; perception management 15, 308–11; super-empowerment 63

Persson, Liza M. xvii, 225–32

Peterson, Peter G. 154, 195

Pettigrew, Thomas 170

Pew Charitable Trust 91

Pew Global Attitudes project 41, 196

Pew Research Center 42

Pierce, Franklin (14th President) 19

Pipes, Daniel 33

political warfare 65, 128, 142, 144

Politovskaya, Anna 309

Powell, Colin Luther 15, 104, 155, 158

power: Cold War balance of power ix; definition 3; instability 65; public opinion 39–49; soft *see* soft power

Pratkanis, Anthony xvii–xviii, 111–53

primacy-of-culture: dissenting 168–71; perspective 167–8

Program on International Policy Attitudes (PIPA) 41, 44

propaganda: Al-Qaeda 13; black/white 81, 130, 338; communication styles 75–6; competitive propaganda 111; cyber-propaganda 13; definition 338; exchange programs 238–9; fog of propaganda 137–8; information initiatives 89–90; Napoleonic France 30; Nazism 68, 81, 111, 113, 124, 130, 142, 267, 273; negative connotations ix, 19; own goals 15; psychological operations 28–9, 188–9; Showa Japan 29–30; terrorism 13–14; trust 130

psychological operations (PSYOP): approval and oversight 189; current situation 190–1; definition 187; Gulf War 189; military 15, 66, 187–92; primacy-of-culture 167; propaganda 28–9, 188–9; PSYOP 101 188; strategic communications 14; workings 189–90

psychological warfare: national security 64, 66; plague 21; research 55; underground resistance 65

psychology: influence psychology 166–80; psychological reactance 136–7

public affairs (PA): communications technology 7; field officers (PAOs) 6–7, 217; informing 226; public diplomacy distinguished 225–32; strategic communications 14, 15, 225

public diplomacy: actors 195–247; advancing studies 325–65; advertising/brand positioning 114–16; advocacy/advisory 80; applications 63–107; Australia 314–22; business 195–200; Central and Eastern European Countries (CEECs) 303–7; China 282–91; citizen diplomacy 101–7; communication technologies 7; context 6, 19–59; credibility 154–65; cultural mediator 237–8; dimensions 73–9; evaluation 337; exchanges *see* exchange programs; Germany 262–9; global approaches 251–322; influencing 226; international conflict 111–53; Japan 270–81; localized *see* localized public diplomacy; loss of world authority 24–38; management 111–86; meaning/terminology 19–23, 73–4, 88, 112, 197, 262–3; national interest through influence 112–13; necessary evil 6; new directions 361–2; operationalization 63–71; personal account 201–11; pillars 239–42; propaganda *see* propaganda; public relations (PR) 116–23; reactive/proactive postures 78–9; rethinking 3–11; returning to roots 68–9; situational aspects 72–85; social influence 111–53; spectrum of initiatives 86–100; strategic communications 12–16, 76; sub-traits 79–82; take-offs/landings 69, 72; targets 112; timeframes 76–8; truth commitment 337–9; two-way symmetry 339–41; United Kingdom 251–61; world revision in history 27

Public Diplomacy Strategy Board 22

public opinion: power 39–49; *see also* world opinion

public relations (PR): Code of Athens 343–5; definition 296–300; democracy 118; dialogue and symmetry 341–2; Ed Murrowism 118, 120; effectiveness 116–18; public diplomacy 116–23; theoretical underpinnings 341–2; *see also* relationship building

publications: localized public diplomacy 214, 215, 220–1

Putin, Vladimir Vladimirovich 309

Quester, George 127

Qutb, Seyyed 52, 55

radio: BBC World Service 78, 90, 256; private media 26; Radio Free Europe 14, 75, 124, 129, 133, 216, 336; Radio Liberty 75, 129, 336; Voice of America (VOA) 213–14, 216, 226, 227, 241, 292, 318, 335, 336
Rapid Response Unit (RRU) 78–9
Rawnsley, Gary D. xviii, 282–91
Reagan, Ronald Wilson (40th President) 21, 76, 77, 78, 161, 217
reciprocity: norms 138–40
Reinhard, Keith xviii, 107, 195–200
relationship building: campaigns 95; coalition building 96; cultural/language institutes 94; development aid projects 94–5; exchange programs 93; first tier initiatives 93–4; leadership visits 93–4; non-political networking 95–6; second tier initiatives 94–6; third tier initiatives 96; twinning arrangements 85; UK/China 92, 95
reputation management: destination/country branding 300–2; framework 296–300; institutionalization 295–6; media 298–300; mistakes 310–11; positive image 297–8; positive reputation 298; specializations 299
Reston, James 21
Rhoads, Kelton xviii, 166–80
Rhodes Scholarship 77, 234, 235
Rice, Condoleezza 6, 158, 240, 243, 339
Riordan, Shaun 341
Rockefeller, Nelson 65
Rohatyn, Felix G. 44
Rokeach, Milton 171
Rome: rhetoric/symbolism 32
Ronfeldt, David F. xviii–xix, 352–65
Roosevelt, Franklin Delano (32nd President) 113, 124, 138, 273
Roosevelt, Theodore (26th President) 63, 136
Rosenau, James N. 76
Ross, Christopher 74–5
Rotary International 5
Roth, Kenneth 160
Rothskopf, David 360
Royster, Charles 30
Rucker, Derek 142
Rumsfeld, Donald 66, 158, 190, 225
Rushing, John 230
Rusk, David Dean 104

Saddam Hussein 112, 158
Said, Edward W. 339
Sarraut, Albert 20
Schnabel, Rockwell 217
Schneider, Cynthia 58
Schon, Don 212
Schorr, Lisbeth B. 212

Scobell, Andrew 284
Scott-Smith, Giles xix, 50–6
Seese, Greg 175
Seiter, John S. xix, 154–65
Serbia: battle weariness 168; NATO bombing 117, 131; Serbian martyrdom 111; UN peacekeeping 142; World War I 135
Shadel, Doug 119
Shanghai Cooperation Organization 45
Shannon & Weaver 341
Shared Values Initiative (SVI) 7–8, 16, 66–7, 115–16
Shea, Jamie 69
shock and awe: Bush administration 42; Iraq War 174; strategic influence 64; war on terror 28–9, 43, 65
Shotwell, James 20
Showa Japan: existentialism 29, 30; great power 27; Manchuria 30, 31; oppression 31, 34; propaganda 29–30; Russian defeat (1905) 27, 28; see also Japan
Shultz, George 76
Signitzer & Coombs 9
Sister City International 5
Slany, William 222
Smith, H. Alexander 243
Smith, Peter B. 171
Smith-Mundt Act (1948) 68, 143, 188, 226, 236, 243, 244, 335
Snow, Nancy ix–xi, xix, 3–11, 75, 154, 156, 189, 190, 233–47, 336, 340
social influence: additional tactics 139; Al-Qaeda 124; democratic use 142–4; ethical/legal issues 142–4; fear appeals 140; foot-in-the-door (FITD) 141; granfalooning 141; jigsawing 141; projection 142; public diplomacy 111–53; rumour control 142; tactics 138–42
social influence analysis (SIA): attributes 120; public diplomacy 112, 119–23; reciprocity norm 138–40; science 119; specification 119
social influence campaigns: admitting a flaw 129–30; agenda setting 130–2; attitudinal selectivity 132–3; centers of gravity 123–38; deeds 129; expectations 127–8; fog of propaganda 137–8; general strategy 125; information strategy control 124–6; listening 129; moral beneffectance 126–8; perceived injustice 135–6; plans and objectives 126; psychological reactance 136–7; seeds of hatred 134–6; segmentation 132; self-justification 134; strategic attack 123–6; strategic traps 125; trust and credibility 128–30; wedge 132–3
soft power: advantage 4, 39–40; China 282–91; competitive strategies 111–12; goodwill 160; meaning 3; measurement 4; operational clarity 360–1; United States 3–5, 12, 64

Soros, George 54, 218, 357
Spaak, Henri 20
special planning group (SPG) 77, 78
Sri Lanka: localized public diplomacy 213–15, 220–1
Stanislaw, Joseph 331
Stevenson, Adlai Ewing 78
Strang (Lord) 21
Streit, Clarence 20
Sudan: Chinese influence 45
suicide bombing 13
Sullivan, Harry Stack 171
Sun Tzu 67, 120, 123, 187
Sussex Pledge (1916) 20
Sussman, Leonard R. 236, 245
Sutter & Huang 283
Szalay, Lorand 167
Szondi, György xix-xx, 292–313

Takeshita, Noboru 276
Tanaka, Kakuei 275
Taylor, Ian 284
Taylor, Paul M. ix-xi, 12–16
Tedeschi, James T. 156
Teichler, Ulrich 242, 244
Telhard de Chardin, Pierre 354, 360
terrorism: 9/11 attacks 7–9, 12–14, 25, 154; negotiation 15; propaganda 13–14; war on terror see Global War on Terrorism
Thailand: localized public diplomacy 217–19
Thatcher, Margaret Hilda 14, 67, 161
Thucydides 67
Total Information Awareness (TIA) 7
Trandis, Harry 87
Triesman (Lord) 258
Truman, Harry S. (33rd President) 48, 64, 335, 337
trust: credibility 158–9; propaganda 130; social influence campaigns 128–30
Turner, Marlene 135, 143
Tutweiler, Marguerite 210

ugly Americans 101, 107, 154, 197
Uhlfelder, Steve 244
United Kingdom: broadcasts 253–4, 256; cultural diplomacy 253; cultural exchange 253; Department for Culture, Media and Sport 258; facilitation 252; Foreign and Commonwealth Office 257; listening 252; networks 253; public diplomacy 251–61; Public Diplomacy Board 257; spectrum of activity 251–2; Strategic International Priorities (SPs) 251
United Nations: credibility 156–7
United States: 9/11 attacks 7–9, 12–14, 25, 154; Bush years see Bush administration;

communication strategies 7–9; economic power 43–4; globalization 325–33; international education 6; military power 42–3, 63, 69; national image 3–6; Nixon shocks 274, 275; political power 44–5; soft power 3–5, 12, 64; war on terror see Global War on Terrorism; world opinion 39–48, 195–6; see also anti-Americanism
US Advisory Group on Public Diplomacy for the Arab and Muslim World 4
US Agency for International Development (USAID) 187, 206
US foreign policy: Pakistan 79; world opinion 42–5
US Information Agency (USIA) 5, 12, 21, 66, 76, 78, 113, 213, 226, 239, 325–33, 335–8
US International Communication Agency 239
USC Center on Public Diplomacy 197

Van Hollen, Christopher 215, 220
Vaughan, James R. 339
Verheugen, Günter 305
Vietnam 6, 25, 95, 113, 125, 127, 136, 139, 141, 201, 215, 218, 229, 243, 283, 325
visits see leadership visits
Vlahos, Michael xx, 24–38
Vonnegut, Kurt 141

war: grand strategy 24; Iraq see Iraq War; transformation 26, 28; war on terror see Global War on Terrorism; WWI see World War I; WWII see World War II
Ward & McGinnies 162
Watkins, Beverly 244
Watt, Donald 103
weapons of mass destruction (WMD): Iraq 158; proliferation 42
Wen Jiabao 285, 287
Wendt, Alexander 54
White, Ralph K. 119, 128, 137, 143
Whorf, Benjamin 167
Williams, Jodie 41, 96
Wilson, Donald 78
Wilson, Harold 14
Wolfe, Tom 234, 244
Wolfowitz, Paul 328
Woodrow Wilson, Thomas (28th President) 4, 20, 25–6, 124, 138, 334, 335, 337
Woolf, Stuart 29
Woolsey, James 26, 33
Worden, Simon P. 228
World Affairs Council 5
world opinion: business 197–8; looking forward 47–8; origins/characteristics 40–1; profile 41–2; United States 39–48, 195–6; US foreign policy consequences 42–5; see also Anti-Americanism

world revision: history 27; war on terror 24–6
World Trade Organization (WTO) 282, 289
World War I: bombing 127; Creel Commission 4,
    68, 117, 130, 334, 337; Japan 27, 32; public
    diplomacy 19–20; Serbia 135
World War II: V for Victory 126, 127; advertising
    115; bad news 130; bombing 127; disinformation
    142–3; friendly persuasion 24; genocide 111, 158,
    262, 302; morale 143; people's war 25; social
    influence campaigns 119, 124–8, 130–3;
    transformation 26, 28
Wyne, Ali S. xx, 39–49

Yeltsin, Boris Nikolayevich 329
Yergin, Daniel 331
Young, Louise 30
Yun, Seong-Hun 9, 10

Zafar al-Siqilli, Muhammad 69
Zaharna, R.S. xx, 75, 86–100, 154, 155, 169, 253
Zhao Qizheng 282
Zhu Rongji 288, 289
Zinni, Anthony 174
Zöllner, Oliver xxi, 262–9
Zorthian, Barry 81